T0191653

Communications in Computer and Information Science   **1227**

Commenced Publication in 2007
Founding and Former Series Editors:
Simone Diniz Junqueira Barbosa, Phoebe Chen, Alfredo Cuzzocrea,
Xiaoyong Du, Orhun Kara, Ting Liu, Krishna M. Sivalingam,
Dominik Ślęzak, Takashi Washio, Xiaokang Yang, and Junsong Yuan

Editorial Board Members

More information about this series at http://www.springer.com/series/7899

Jian Shen · Yao-Chung Chang ·
Yu-Sheng Su · Hiroaki Ogata (Eds.)

Cognitive Cities

Second International Conference, IC3 2019
Kyoto, Japan, September 3–6, 2019
Revised Selected Papers

 Springer

Editors
Jian Shen
Nanjing University of Information
Science and Technology
Nanjing, China

Yao-Chung Chang
National Taitung University
Taitung City, Taiwan

Yu-Sheng Su
National Taiwan Ocean University
Keelung, Taiwan

Hiroaki Ogata
Kyoto University
Kyoto, Japan

ISSN 1865-0929   ISSN 1865-0937 (electronic)
Communications in Computer and Information Science
ISBN 978-981-15-6112-2   ISBN 978-981-15-6113-9 (eBook)
https://doi.org/10.1007/978-981-15-6113-9

This Springer imprint is published by the registered company Springer Nature Singapore Pte Ltd.
The registered company address is: 152 Beach Road, #21-01/04 Gateway East, Singapore 189721, Singapore

Preface

This CCIS volume presents selected articles from the Second International Cognitive Cities Conference (IC3 2019), held in Kyoto, Japan, during September 3–6, 2019. IC3 2019 provided an open platform for the exchange of research results and experiences in topics from cognitive cities and other related fields. This conference featured all recent advances in an integral concept that highlights the trends in advanced theory, systems, and applications for cognitive cities. This year, IC3 was hosted by Computer Society ROC, Taiwan; Kyoto University, Japan; and co-organizer IEEE Taipei Section Young Professionals Group.

The main theme of IC3 2019, "The Emergence of Intelligent Electronics on Green Signal Processing and Communications for Better Life", reflected the world's current awareness very well. In the four-day program, 23 sessions were organized, in which 11 workshops took place, hosted by many active and outstanding experts in various up-to-date research topics. The main tracks include multimedia and systems, communication systems, digital leaning, and emerging technologies in cognitive cites.

The conference received 206 submissions for peer review. The reviewing process followed a single-blind procedure using a panel of experts and external reviewers (outside the Program Committee). Each submission had an average of three independent reviews and each reviewer was assigned an average of two submissions. 83 articles were selected to be part of this CCIS volume.

December 2019

Jian Shen
Yao-Chung Chang
Yu-Sheng Su
Hiroaki Ogata

Organization

Honorary General Chairs

Tzung-Pei Hong   National University of Kaohsiung, Taiwan
Stephen J. H. Yang   National Central University, Taiwan

General Chairs

Gwo-Jen Hwang   National Taiwan University of Science
         and Technology, Taiwan
Hiroaki Ogata   Kyoto University, Japan
Yi-Shun Wang   National Changhua University of Education, Taiwan

General Co-chairs

Chin-Feng Lai   National Cheng Kung University, Taiwan
Chih-Hsien Hsia   National Ilan University, Taiwan
Chun-Wei Tsai   National Sun Yat-sen University, Taiwan

Technical Program Committee Chairs

Jian Shen   Nanjing University of Information Science
         and Technology, China
Yao-Chung Chang   National Taitung University, Taiwan
Yu-Sheng Su   National Taiwan Ocean University, Taiwan

Poster Chairs

Whai-En Chen   National Ilan University, Taiwan
Chien-Liang Lin   Ningbo University, China

Workshop Chairs

Sheng-Yi Wu   National Pingtung University, Taiwan
He-Hai Liu   Anhui Normal University, China
Wen-Tao Wu   Anhui Normal University, China
Chiu-Lin Lai   National Taipei University of Education, Taiwan
Min-Chai Hsieh   Tainan University of Technology, Taiwan
Shih-Hsin Ma   Feng Chia University, Taiwan
Ching Hai Lee   Ming Dao University, Taiwan
Jiann-Hwa Lue   Central Taiwan University of Science and Technology,
         Taiwan

Chien Weng Yang	National Taiwan University of Science and Technology, Taiwan
Tsung-Xian Lee	National Taiwan University of Science and Technology, Taiwan
Hao Wang	Shandong Normal University, China
Shyang-Yuh Wang	Chinese Culture University, Taiwan
Chih-Hsien Hsia	National Ilan University, Taiwan
Yung-Yao Chen	National Taipei University of Technology, Taiwan
Yi-Zeng Hsieh	National Taiwan Ocean University, Taiwan
Chin-Chun Su	Xiamen University Tan Kah Kee College, China
Chiuhsiang Joe Lin	National Taiwan University of Science and Technology, Taiwan
Hung-Yue Suen	National Taiwan Normal University, Taiwan
Han-Chou Lin	National Taipei University of Business, Taiwan
Anna Yu-Qing Huang	National Central University, Taiwan

Executive Chairs

Shu-Ming Wang	Chinese Culture University, Taiwan
Hui-Chun Hung	National Central University, Taiwan

Publication Chairs

Ting-Jou Ding	Ming Dao University, Taiwan
Yung-Chia Hsiao	Baise University, China

Website Chairs

Ying Hsun Lai	National Taitung University, Taiwan
Shih-Yeh Chen	National Taitung University, Taiwan

Technical Program Committee

Adel M. Alimi	University of Sfax, Tunisia
Adriana Giret Boggino	Polytechnic University of Valencia, Spain
Ajith Abraham	Machine Intelligence Research Labs, USA
Alex Liu	California State University, Fresno, USA
Amjad Anvari-Moghaddam	Aalborg University, Denmark
Andreas Polze	Hasso-Plattner-Institute at University Potsdam, Germany
Antonio Coronato	ICAR CNR, Italy
Anxi Wang	Nanjing University of Information Science and Technology, China
Bheemarjuna Reddy Tamma	IIT Hyderabad, India
Bin Tang	Wichita State University, USA

Bo Zhou	Liverpool John Moores University, UK
Carlo Alberto Nucci	University of Bologna, Italy
Chang-Wook Han	Dong-Eui University, South Korea
Chelsea Dobbins	Liverpool John Moores University, UK
Chen Wang	Nanjing University of Information Science and Technology, China
Ching-Jung Chen	Chinese Academy of Sciences, China
Chiu Chiang Tan	Temple University, USA
Chunbo Luo	University of Exeter, UK
Damas P. Gruska	Comenius University in Bratislava, Slovakia
Dana Petcu	West University of Timisoara, Romania
Daniele Fontanelli	University of Trento, Italy
Davide Brunelli	University of Trento, Italy
Debiao He	Wuhan University, China
Dengzhi Liu	Nanjing University of Information Science and Technology, China
Ding Wang	Peking University, China
Dola Saha	Albany University, SUNY, USA
Driss Benhaddou	University of Houston, USA
Emanuele Lindo Secco	Liverpool Hope University, UK
Eugene John	University of Texas at San Antonio, USA
Fabio Costa	Federal University of Goias, Brazil
Fan Wu	Xiamen University, China
Feng Li	Indiana University Purdue University Indianapolis (IUPUI), USA
Fengjun Li	University of Kansas, USA
Fushan Wei	Information Engineering University, China
Gang Wei	South China University of Technology, China
Gaurav N. Pradhan	The University of Texas at Dallas, USA
George Mohler	Indiana University Purdue University Indianapolis (IUPUI), USA
Giandomenico Nollo	University of Trento, Italy
Gidlund Mikael	Mid Sweden University, Sweden
Guanlin Chen	University of Massachusetts Lowell, USA
Guglielmo De Angelis	IASI CNR, Italy
Gulnara Zhabelova	Luleå University of Technology, Sweden
Guohui Zhang	University of Hawai'i at Manoa, USA
GyuMyoung Lee	Liverpool John Moores University, UK
Habib M. Ammari	Hofstra University, USA
Habib M. Kammoun	University of Sfax, Tunisia
Hao Wang	Norwegian University of Science and Technology, Norway
Hao Wang	Shandong Normal University, China
Harold Rene Chamorro Vera	KTH Royal Institute of Technology, Sweden
Hong Chen	Southwest Jiaotong University, China

Hongji Yang	Bath Spa University, UK
Hongying Meng	University of Brunel, UK
Houcine Hassan	University Politiecnica de Valencia, Spain
Huawei Huang	University of Aizu, Japan
Hui Chen	Virginia State University, USA
Hui Cheng	Liverpool John Moores University, UK
Hyungbae Park	University of Central Missouri, USA
Ilangko Balasingham	Norwegian University of Science and Technology, Norway
Ireneusz Czarnowski	Gdynia Maritime University, Poland
Jakita Thomas	Auburn University, USA
Jejung Lee	University of Missouri, USA
Jen-Tsai Liu	Chinese Academy of Sciences, China
Jia Yuan Yu	Concordia University, Canada
Jie Liang	Simon Fraser University, Canada
Jing Gao	Dalian University of Technology, China
Jingtao Sun	National Institute of Informatics, Japan
Joanna Siebert	Hong Kong Polytechnic University, Hong Kong
Jons Sanchez	National Technological Institute, Mexico
Jose Barata	Universidade Nova Lisboa, Portugal
José Barbosa	Polytechnic Institute of Bragança, Portugal
Julio Sahuquillo	Universidad Politecnica de Valencia, Spain
Jun Kong	North Dakota State University, USA
Jun Liu	University of Michigan at Dearborn, USA
Jung Hwan Kim	Fannie Mae, USA
Junwei Zhang	Xidian University, China
Kashif Kifayat	Liverpool John Moores University, UK
Kaustubh Dhondg	Glaukes Labs, USA
Kimberly Zarecor	Iowa State University, USA
KyoungGon Kim	Korea University, South Korea
Lei Liu	Shandong University, China
Liangxiu Han	Manchester Metropolitan University, UK
Lotfi ben Othmane	Iowa State University, USA
Lu Liu	University of Derby, UK
Luis Gomes	Universida de Nova Lisboa,, Portugal
Maciej Huk	Wroclaw University of Science and Technology, Poland
Marjorie Zielke	University of Texas at Dallas, USA
Mark Hoffman	Children's Mercy Hospital, USA
Mathias Uslar	OFFIS, Germany
Mianxiong Dong	Muroran Institute of Technology, Japan
Ming Li	California State University, Fresno, USA
Miriam Capretz	Western Ontario University, Canada
Mohamed Sellami	ISEP, France
Muhammad Younas	Oxford Brookes University, UK
Nadine Gaertner	SAP, Germany

Narn-Yih Lee	Southern Taiwan University, Taiwan
Nélio Alessandro Azevedo Cacho	Universidade Federal do Rio Grande do Norte, Brazil
Ning Lu	Northeastern University, China
Novais Paulo	Universidade do Minho, Portugal
Ondrej Krejcar	University of Hradec Kralove, Czech Republic
Pedro Merino Gomez	University of Malaga, Spain
Petr Skobelev	Multi-Agent Technology Ltd., UK
Po Yang	Liverpool John Moores University, UK
Po-Han Wu	National Taipei University of Education, Taiwan
Qi Jiang	Xidian University, China
Qingfeng Cheng	State Key Laboratory of Mathematical Engineering and Advanced Computing, China
Rajendra Boppana	University of Texas at San Antonio, USA
Rasha Osman	University of Khartoum, Sudan
Richard Lomotey	University of Saskatchewan, Canada
Sajal Das	Missouri University of Science and Technology, USA
Sangheon Pack	Korea University, South Korea
Sanjay Madria	Missouri University of Science and Technology, USA
Saraju Mohanty	University of North Texas, USA
Sebastian Rohjans	HAW, Germany
Sejun Song	University of Missouri – Kansas City, USA
Seongsoo Hong	Seoul National University, South Korea
Shancang Li	West England University, UK
Shih-Lun Chen	Chung Yuan Christian University, Taiwan
Soufiene Djahel	Manchester Metropolitan University, UK
Stefan Andrei	Lamar University, USA
Tao Jiang	Huazhong University of Science and Technology, China
Thar Baker Shamsa	Liverpool John Moores University, UK
Tianqi Zhou	Nanjing University of Information Science and Technology, China
Tie Wang	Senior Technical Yahoo!, USA
Tony Luppino	University of Missouri, USA
Ulf Jennehag	Mid Sweden University, Sweden
Wei Lu	Keene State College, USA
Wei Yu	Towson University, USA
Weiyi Zhang	North Dakota State University, USA
Wenbo Shi	Northeastern University at Qinhuangdao, China
Wenying Zheng	Nanjing University of Aeronautics and Astronautics, China
Xiao Chen	Texas State University, USA
Xiaojiang Du	North Dakota State University, USA
Xin Zhang	Cisco Systems Inc., USA
Xinghua Li	Xidian University, China
Xinjun Mao	National University of Defense Technology, China

Xiong Li	Hunan University of Science and Technology, China
Xuedong Liang	University of Oslo, Norway
Xuexian Hu	Information Engineering University, Zhengzhou, China
Xuming Fang	Southwest Jiaotong University, China
Yan Zhang	Simula Research Laboratory, Norway
Yiu-Wing Leung	Hong Kong Baptist University, Hong Kong
Yongjun Renv	Nanjing University of Information Science and Technology, China
Yongning Tang	Illinois State University, USA
Younghee Park	San Jose State University, USA
Yu Bai	California State University, Fullerton, USA
Yu Cao	California State University, Fresno, USA
Yu-Hsuan Lin	National University of Tainan, Taiwan
Yulei Wu	University of Exeter, UK
Yung-Yao Chen	National Taipei University of Technology, Taiwan
Zhi Liu	Waseda University, Japan
Zhibo Pang	BB AB Corporate Research, Sweden
Zhihan Lv	University College London, UK

Additional Reviewers

Yu-Xiang Lo	Cheng-Hung Wang
Peng Tom	Kuay-Keng Yang
Xiang-Long Ku	Sheau-Wen Lin
Wen-Yen Wang	Hua-Shu Hsu
Tosti H. C. Chiang	Chih-Ming Chu
Bin-Shyan Jong	Tzong Sheng Deng
Tzu-Chi Yang	Mei-Rong Alice
Yu-Lin Jeng	Sasithorn Chookaew
Chia-Hung Kao	Zou Di
Chester S. J. Huang	Chih-Hung Chen
Owen H. T. Lu	Shao Chen Chang
Tzu-Chi Yang	Niwat Srisawasdi
Jeff Cheng-Hsu Huang	Chih-Chao Chung
Hua-Shu Hsu	Sung-Wen Yu
Chia-Ching Lin	Yen-Chieh Huang
Kelvin H.-C. Chen	Xi-Bin Lin

Contents

XR and Educational Innovations for Cognitive City

Educational Technology and Strategy in Cognitive City

Artificial Intelligence Theory and Technology Related to Cognitive City

Internet of Things for Cognitive City

Business Application and Management for Cognitive City

Big Data for Cognitive City

Engineering Technology and Applied Science for Cognitive City

Maker, CT and STEAM Education for Cognitive City

Cognitive City for Special Needs

Processing Min Cost Queries on Heterogeneous Neighboring Objects

Yuan-Ko Huang[(⊠)]

Department of Maritime Information and Technology, National Kaohsiung
University of Science and Technology, Kaohsiung, Taiwan
huangyk@nkust.edu.tw

Abstract. In this paper, we present a novel type of location-based queries, named the min cost queries (or MCQ for short). Given the n types of spatial objects, O1, O2, ..., On, where Oi has a cost attribute, and a user-defined distanced. The MCQ finds a set of n objects, {o1, o2, ..., on}, such that the distance between any pair of objects in {o1, o2,..., on} does not exceed d and the total cost of {o1, o2, ..., on} is smallest. To efficiently process the MCQ, we design a R-tree-based index, the R^{c-}tree, to man-age the spatial objects with their locations and costs. Then, we develop a top k-based MCQ algorithm combined with the R^c-tree to retrieve the MCQ result.

Keywords: Location-based queries · Min cost queries · R^c-tree · Top k-based MCQ algorithm

1 Introduction

In recent years, the location-based services aim at efficiently managing a large number of spatial objects, so as to provide various types of location-based queries [1–4]. For example, the range queries and the nearest neighbor queries can be used to find the objects within a query range and the closest object to the query object, respectively. There are many applications related to the location-based services, such as location-aware advertisements, traffic control systems, and geographical information systems. Most of the processing techniques for the location-based queries focus on a single type of objects (e.g., hotel, restaurant, or theatre). However, some users may not be interested in obtaining information of one type of objects. Instead, they want to know information about different types of objects. As a result, in [5], we present the heterogeneous neighboring objects (HNOs for short) and propose the location-based aggregate queries on the HNOs. The HNOs and the location-based aggregate queries are defined as follows.

- Consider the n types of spatial objects, O1, O2, ..., On. If there is a set of objects, {o1, o2,..., on}, where oi belongs to Oi and i = 1 ~ n, and the distance between any pair of objects in this set is less than or equal to a user-defined distance d, then the objects set {o1, o2, ..., on} is a set of HNOs.

© Springer Nature Singapore Pte Ltd. 2020
J. Shen et al. (Eds.): IC3 2019, CCIS 1227, pp. 3–7, 2020.
https://doi.org/10.1007/978-981-15-6113-9_1

– Assume that there are m sets of HNOs. Given a query object q, the location-based aggregate queries retrieve a set of objects {o1, o2, ..., on}, among the m sets of HNOs, such that the average, min, max, or sum distance of {o1, o2, ..., on} to q is minimal.

Figure 1(a) shows an example of processing the location-based aggregate queries on the HNOs, where the use-defined distance is set to 2 and the set of HNOs with the shortest average distance to q will be retrieved. There are three types of objects in the space, hotels h1 to h3, restaurants r1 to r3, and theatres t1 to t3. As d = 2, only the two object sets {h2, r1, t3} and {h3, r2, t2} can be the sets of HNOs. By comparing their average distances to q, the set{h3, r2, t2} is returned as the query result because it has the shorter distance. From the above figure, we know that the result of the location-based aggregate queries is mainly based on the distance of the HNOs (i.e., hotels, restaurants, and theatres) to the query object. However, in many real applications, the users may want to experience the facilities while keeping the total cost as low as possible. In such applications, a set of HNOs with the minimum experiencing cost in total is the best choice. Let us consider the example in Fig. 1(b). As we can see, although the set {h3, r2, t2} is closer to q than the set {h2, r1, t3}, its total cost (i.e., 2200 + 800 + 500 = 3500) is much higher than that of {h2, r1, t3} (i.e., 1600 + 600 + 400 = 2600). As such, the set {h2, r1, t3} is the better choice if the cost is a main concern in determining the query result.

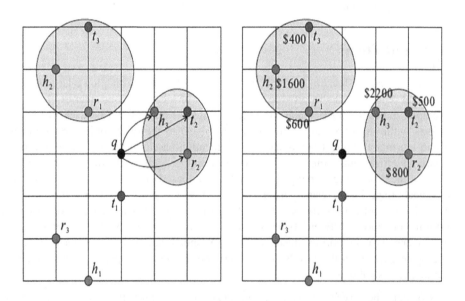

(a) *Location-based aggregate queries*   (b) *Min Cost queries*

Fig. 1. Different types of location-based queries

In this paper, we present a new type of location-based queries on the HNOs, named the min cost queries (MCQ for short), to find the set of HNOs having the smallest total cost. Formally, the MCQ is defined as follows. Consider the n types of spatial objects, O1, O2, ..., On, where Oi has a cost attribute. Based on the user-defined distance d, there are m sets of HNOs. The MCQ retrieves a set of HNOs {o1, o2, ..., on}, among the m sets of HNOs, such that the total cost of {o1, o2, ..., on} is smallest. To efficiently process the MCQ, we first utilize a R-tree-based index, the Rc-tree, to manage the spatial objects with their locations and costs. Then, a top k-based MCQ algorithm is developed to determine a set of objects satisfying the constraint of distance d (i.e., a set of HNOs) and with the lowest total cost.

The remainder of this paper is organized as follows. Section 2 describes the R^c-tree. In Sect. 3, we present the top k-based MCQ algorithm. Finally, we conclude this paper in Sect. 4.

2 Structure of R^c-Tree

The R^c-tree is a height-balanced index structure, where objects are recursively grouped in a bottom-up manner according to objects' locations and costs. Each entry of a leaf node of a Rc-tree has the structure ((o.x, o.y), o.c, o.ptr), where (o.x, o.y) refers to the location of spatial object o, o.c is the cost of object o, and o.ptr is a pointer to the actual object tuple in the database. Each entry of an internal node of the Rc-tree has the structure (MBRE, E.cm, E.ptr), where MBRE is a minimum bounding rectangle enclosing all the objects in the child node E of this internal node, E.cm is the minimum among all costs of the objects enclosed in MBRE, and E.ptr is a pointer to node E.

Let us use the example in Fig. 2 to illustrate the information maintained for the R^c-tree. As shown in Fig. 2(a), eight hotels h1 to h8 in the space are indexed by the Rc-tree. Initially, hotels h1 to h8 are grouped according to their locations and costs into four leaf nodes H4 to H7. Take the leaf node H4 as an example. As hotels h1 and h2 are enclosed by MBRH4, they are the entries of the leaf node H4 and will be stored as ((7, 15), 1800) and ((8, 12), 2000), respectively. Then, the leaf nodes H4 to H7 are recursively grouped into two internal nodes, H2 and H3, that becomes the entries of the root. Because the extent of MBRH2 covers hotels h1 to h4, the node H2 is maintained in the form of (MBRH2, 1500), where 1500 represents the minimal cost among the four hotels. The corresponding structure of the Rc-tree (for the hotels) is shown in Fig. 2(b), and the complete information of the leaf and internal nodes is illustrated in Fig. 2(c).

3 Top k-Based MCQ Algorithm

Given the n types of spatial objects, O1, O2, ..., On, where Oi has a cost at-tribute, and the user-defined distance d, the MCQ is used to find a set of HNOs {o1, o2, ..., on}, such that the total cost of {o1, o2, ..., on} is smallest. To efficiently process the MCQ, we propose the top k-based MCQ algorithm, which consists of the following three steps:

1. For each type of spatial objects, the top-k objects with the smallest cost are retrieved, so as to construct the k^n sets of n objects.
2. For each set of n objects, the distance between any two objects is computed and compared to the distance d.
3. The set of n objects satisfying the constraint of distance d and with the lowest total cost is returned as the MCQ result.

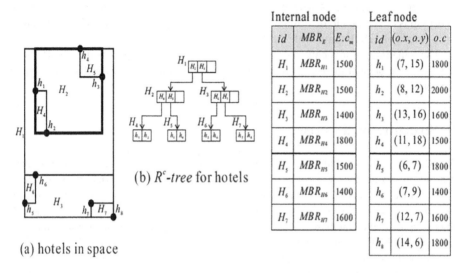

(a) hotels in space

(b) R^c-tree for hotels

(c) information of nodes

Fig. 2. Example of R^c-tree.

To improve the performance of Step 1 (i.e., finding the top-k objects for each object type), we perform a depth-first traversal of the Rc-tree built on each type of objects to filter the non-qualifying objects. The procedure of Step 1 begins with the root node of the Rc-tree and proceeds down the tree. When a MBR MBRE is encountered, the following pruning criterion is used to determine whether MBRE can be pruned or not. If E.cm of the MBR MBRE is greater than the largest value in the costs of the top-k objects considered so far, then all the objects enclosed in MBRE can be pruned, because their costs exceed that of the top-k objects. Consider again Fig. 2, where k is set to 2 (i.e., finding the top-2 objects). Assume that hotels h3 and h4 are the top-2 objects considered so far. For the MBR MBRH4, as its H4.cm is greater than h3.c and h4.c (i.e., 1800 > 1600 and 1800 > 1500), hotels h1 and h2 enclosed in MBRH4 can be filtered using the designed pruning criterion.

For Step 2 (i.e., checking whether a set of n objects satisfies the constraint of distance d), we design the following criterion to determine a set of n objects that must be a set of HNOs, without the need to exhaustively check all pairs of objects for whether their distances exceed the distance d. Let $\{o1, o2, ..., on\}$ be a set of n objects to be considered. Then, $\{o1, o2, ..., on\}$ must be a set of HNOs if

$$(x_r - x_l)^2 + (y_u - y_d)^2 \leq d^2,$$

Where

$$x_r = \max\{o_i.x | i = 1 \sim n\}, x_l = \min\{o_i.x | i = 1 \sim n\},$$
$$y_u = \max\{o_i.y | i = 1 \sim n\}, y_d = \min\{o_i.y | i = 1 \sim n\}.$$

4 Conclusions

4.1 Experimental Design

In this paper, a novel type of location-based queries, the min cost queries (MCQ) is presented to find a set of HNOs with the lowest total cost. In order to process the MCQ efficiently, the Rc-tree is first used to manage the spatial objects with their locations and costs. Then, a top k-based MCQ algorithm, consisting of three steps, is developed. In Step 1, a depth-first traversal of the Rc-tree is employed to find the top-k objects for each type of objects. Step 2 aims at determining the sets of HNOs among the top-k objects obtained from the previous step. Finally, Step 3 retrieves the set of HNOs with the lowest cost in total.

References

1. Benetis, R., Jensen, C.S., Karciauskas, G., Saltenis, S.: Nearest neighbor and reverse nearest neighbor queries for moving objects. VLDB J. **15**(3), 229–249 (2006)
2. Mokbel, M.F., Xiong, X., Aref, W.G.: SINA: scalable incremental processing of continuous queries in spatio-temporal databases. In: Proceedings of the ACM SIGMOD, pp. 623–634 (2004)
3. Sistla, A.P., Wolfson, O., Chamberlain, S., Dao, S.: Modeling and querying moving objects. In: ICDE, pp. 422–432 (1997)
4. Tao, Y., Papadias, D.: Time-parameterized queries in spatio-temporal databases. In: ACM SIGMOD, pp. 334–345 (2002)
5. Huang, Y.-K.: Location-based aggregate queries for heterogeneous neighboring objects. IEEE Access **5**, 4887–4899 (2017)

Intelligent Inspection of the High-Speed Railway Spare Parts Using Three-Dimensional Laser

Shuang Cao[1], Bao Song[2], Fuyang Ke[1(✉)], and Xingwang Zhao[2]

[1] School of Remote Sensing and Geomatics Engineering,
Nanjing University of Information Science and Technology,
Nanjing 210044, China
ke.fuyang@qq.com
[2] School of Geodesy and Geomatics, Anhui University of Science
and Technology, Huainan, China

Abstract. The High-speed railway is regarded as one with the cores and significant elements for cognitive urban mobility and transportation currently. Furthermore, the high-speed railway spare parts called "high-speed rail organs" play an important role in understanding the transportation of city. However, there are few studies on the quality detection of a high-speed rail spare parts in present. The current high-speed rail spare parts detection means are single, the detection efficiency and accuracy are low. To improve the quality detection accuracy and efficiency of high-speed railway spare parts, an intelligent quality detection system is designed for a high-speed railway spare parts using a three-dimensional laser in this paper. The software can complete the task of automatic analysis and processing point cloud data, and make up for the deficiency in poor accuracy and low efficiency of manual detection in the current detection of high-speed rail components. In the system, different algorithm parameters are introduced into different parts to improve the inspection accuracy of components with different characteristics. According to the experimental results, the precision of the detection results of the intelligent detection software can completely meet the requirements of high-speed rail component detection.

Keywords: High-rail spare parts · Three-dimensional laser · High-speed rail component measuring system

1 Introduction

Transportation is a major link connecting cities. Doing a good operation of traffic protection has an important impact on urban safety and development. On June 3, 1998, a high-speed rails accident near the village of Eschede in Germany pulled "Made in Germany" off the altar. The reason is that 101 people died and 105 were injured because of a component problem, which refreshes the data of the world's highest casualty rate of railway accidents. In addition, the public also has taken high-speed rail as one of the symbols of urban modernization. Therefore, how to achieve high-speed rail protection has become the focus on scholars.

© Springer Nature Singapore Pte Ltd. 2020
J. Shen et al. (Eds.): IC3 2019, CCIS 1227, pp. 8–17, 2020.
https://doi.org/10.1007/978-981-15-6113-9_2

Nowadays, there are two main ways of high-speed rail protection, one is rail safety protection, the other is high-speed rail spare parts protection. In terms of track protection, the components of the track itself are related to the safety of the vehicle. The settlement of the base surface will impact the whole track. And the high-speed rail safety is also affected by its traction current and equipment. For high-speed rail spare parts, one is about the research of its materials, another research direction is its quality inspection. However, there are many kinds and quantities of high-speed rail spare parts at present, and the quality inspection of spare parts is strict in the rail transit industry, which results in heavy inspection tasks. Moreover, the current traditional component detection technology is not only laboring intensive and inefficient, but also can not meet the needs of the production cycle. And the detection accuracy is not reliable, which has become a bottleneck in the development of rail transit manufacturing industry. To solve these problems, a three-dimensional laser detection technology is presented in this paper.

In recent years, researchers in many countries have applied three-dimensional (3D) scanning technology to the modeling and quality detection of buildings and industrial components. In 1999, Michelangelo's David statue was measured by a team of 30 people from Stanford University and Washington University using a three-dimensional laser scanning measurement system. In 2002, Purdue University in the United States scanned and measured two Bridges in Indiana and built a complex 3D model of the two bridges [1, 2]. In 2005, Jian Zhengwei of Yan Shan university in China detected body panels and achieved good results based on three-dimensional laser [4]. In 2008, Du Lijie, from Northeastern University in China, applied 3D laser scanning technology in the study of the detection of complex castings. The error accuracy of the detection meets the requirements of castings [5]. In 2009, Yuan Yulei, etc. Information Engineering University in China, used three-dimensional laser scanning technology to measure high-temperature forgings on the production line. At the same time, the cylindrical point cloud data onto high-temperature forgings were fitted according to the detection requirements, and the external diameter size was obtained, which was judged to meet the requirements of manufacturing tolerances [6]. In 2012, Chen Xiuzhong, etc. from Beijing Institute of Architectural Engineering in China, made use of 3D laser scanning technology to assist in the construction survey and port docking with largespan box-type interconnected square network of Tianjin West Railway Station of Beijing-Shanghai High-speed Railway to meet the needs of the project [7]. In 2013, Zong Min of Nanjing University of Information and Technology in China, in the research of complex construction inspection based on 3D laser scanning technology, further inspected the hole positioned error of qualified parts, and perfected the research of 3D laser scanning technology applied to parts inspection [8].

In this paper, an intelligent quality detection system for high-speed rail parts is devised based on high-precision 3D laser scanning technology. It detects components according to their production process, which makes up for the poor accuracy and low efficiency of manual detection in the current detection of high-speed rail components. It realizes the high-precision, high-efficiency and batch detection of high-speed rail components in the processing process, and puts it into production and application.

2 Hardware and Software Theory

The detection platform is composed of data acquisition subsystem and data center subsystem, which cooperate and coordinate with each other. It has three characteristics: high automation, high detection accuracy and personalized service. The overall design of the platform is shown in Fig. 1-a. the overall processing flow of the platform is shown in Fig. 1-b.

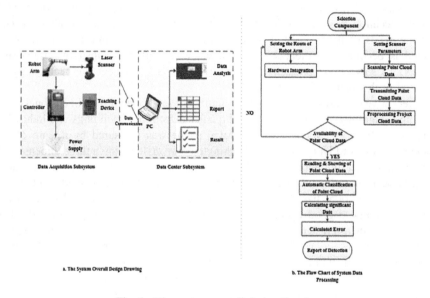

a. The System Overall Design Drawing

b. The Flow Chart of System Data Processing

Fig. 1. The system overall design drawing

2.1 Hardware

The hardware consists of a mechanical arm and a handheld 3D laser scanner. The overall effect is shown in Fig. 2. The component principles and detailed parameters of the data acquisition subsystem are as follows:

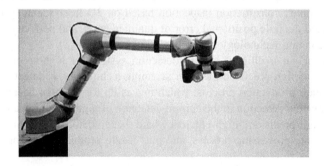

Fig. 2. Data collection schematic diagram

2.1.1 Introduction of Mechanical Arm

The working principle of manipulator is introduced as follows.

(1) according to the size of the working area and the size of the working object, formulate the route trajectory of the mechanical arm, use the teaching device for programming, and define the stretching, lifting, flipping and other actions of the mechanical arm body;

(2) the demonstrator inputs programming information into the control cabinet through communication, and the control cabinet conducts analysis, and transmits the control signal to the robot arm body to realize the control of the movement of the robot arm;

(3) the robot arm body receives the command information of movement and makes all kinds of stretching, lifting and flipping movements within the range of the arm length according to the given trajectory.

The technical parameters of the manipulator are shown in Table 1. Among them, there are two technical parameters of the small manipulator. The arm length can be set to meet the requirements of component detection of different sizes.

Table 1. Mechanical arm specifications and parameters

Working range	703 mm	901 mm
The payload	7 kg	5 kg
Arm load	0.3 kg	0.3 kg
Integrated signal source	Wrist set 10 signal	
Robot installation	Any angle	
Protection level	IP40/IP67	
Range of motion		
Axis 1	+170° to −170°	+170° to −170°,
Axis 2	+135° to −100°,	+130° to −100°,
Axis 3	+70° to −200°,	+70° to −200°,
Axis 4	+270° to −270°,	+270° to −270°,
Axis 5	+130° to −130°,	+130° to −130°,
Axis 6	+360° to −360°,	+360° to −360°,
Voltage	200–600 V, 50–60 Hz	
Power consumption	0.39 kw	0.38 kw
Base size	210*210 mm	
Weight	52 kg	54 kg

2.1.2 Handheld 3D Laser Scanner Components

Principle of hand-held three-dimensional scanner: line laser hand-held three-dimensional scanner, with self-calibration function, using 635 nm red laser flash, equipped with a flash and two industrial cameras, when working, the laser line will be irradiated on the object, two cameras to capture the instantaneous three-dimensional scanning data. Because of the different curvatures of the object surface, the light irradiation on the object will reflect and refract, and these messages will be converted to 3D images of third-party software. In addition, when using a hand-held three-dimensional scanner, it is necessary to paste a reflective corner marker so as to obtain better scanning results.

Table 2 below is the technical parameters of a hand-held three-dimensional laser scanner.

Table 2. Parameters of 3D laser scanner

Weight	0.85 kg	
Size	122 × 77 × 294 mm	
The measurement rate	The 205000 time/s	The 480000 time/s
Scanning area	225 × 250 mm	275 × 250 mm
Light source	3 Crossbeam laser lines	7 Crossbeam laser lines
Laser class	11(Human eye safety)	
Resolution	0.100 mm	0.050 mm
Accuracy	≤ 0.040 mm	0.030 mm
Volume accuracy*	0.020 mm + 0.100 mm/m	0.020 mm + 0.060 mm/m
Volume accuracy (Combined with MAXSHOT 3D)	0.020 mm + 0.025 mm/m	
Datum distance	300 mm	
Depth of field	250 mm	
Component size range (Recommended)	0.1–4 m	
Software	VXelements	
Output format	.dae,.fbx,.ma,.obj,.ply,.stl,.txt,.wrl,.x3d,.x3d,.x3dz,.zpr	
Compatible software	3D System (Geomagic®) Solutions), InnovMetric Software (Polyworks), Dassault Systèmes (CATIA V5 & SolidWorks), PTC (Pro/ENGINEER), Siemens (NX & Solid Edge), Autodesk (Inventor, Alias, 3ds Max, Maya, Softimage)	
Connection standard	1 × USB3.0	
Operation temperature range	0–40 °C	
Operation temperature range (Non-condensing)	10–90%	

2.2 Software

The software of quality inspection system for high-speed railway spare parts designed in this paper includes two parts: point cloud data preprocessing and point cloud data analysis and calculation.

2.2.1 Point Cloud Data Preprocessing

The main function of point cloud data preprocessing is to denoise, simplify and reconstruct the original point cloud data acquired by three-dimensional laser scanner. Among them, the accuracy of scanning points can be set in the software according to the requirements, which is generally set to 0.11 mm. In this software, the pretreatment system adopts the pretreatment process of the software of the three-dimensional laser scanner.

2.2.2 Point Cloud Data Analysis and Calculation

The part is an independent development of a fully intelligent spare parts detection system, which mainly has the functions of parameter detection, parameter evaluation and customized detection report. Among them, the design of parameter detection is a unique innovation of this system. Based on the purpose of measuring precise geometric parameters of high-speed railway spare parts by using three-dimensional point cloud, a new algorithm and idea are proposed in the section. The algorithm flow is roughly divided into three main modules: detection and segmentation of target surface, recognition and grouping of target surface, calculation of geometric parameters, which are introduced as follows.

Module 1: Detection and segmentation of target surface

To measure the geometric parameters of high-speed railway spare parts by using three-dimensional point cloud, the first task is to find out the target surface involved in the measurement of geometric parameters from the three-dimensional point cloud and separate the corresponding points from the original point cloud. Take plane and cylindrical surfaces for example. In order to achieve higher computational efficiency, a curvature-guided "sampling-testing" target surface detection strategy is adopted in the algorithm library. Its core idea is to compare the curvature of each point in the most curvature direction and the curvature in the least curvature direction at the corresponding surface position. If both curvatures are 0, it is a plane point. If the curvature in the most curvature direction of a point is greater than 0, and the curvature in the least curvature direction is 0, it is a cylindrical point. The specific detection and segmentation steps will not be elaborated.

Module 2: Target surface recognition and grouping

The main function of this module is to check the results of module one, which provides data basis for the next geometric parameter calculation. Its specific content is to use the indirect adjustment method to re-fit the segmented target surface point set to determine the precise geometric parameters, and then merge and group the target surfaces according to the precise geometric parameters.

Module 3: Geometric parameter calculation

Geometric parameter measurement methods can be roughly divided into two categories: point cloud-based measurement method and model parameter-based measurement method. There are different measurement methods for different measurement objects. The following is mainly about the measurement methods of several targets:

(1) distance between planes: The measurement method based on point cloud is adopted. Because the surface of high-speed railway spare parts may have processed errors such as surface irregularity, abnormal protrusion or depression, in order to truly reflect such changes in plane distance, a point cloud-based measurement method is adopted, that is, the nearest distance statistics from plane point cloud 1 to plane point cloud 2. The specific calculation method is:

    (a) for each dot p in point cloud 1, find the nearest point q in point cloud 2;

    (b) search the nearest neighbor domain point set near q in point cloud 2, and fit the local plane Sq;

    (c) calculate the vertical distance dq between point p and local plane Sq;

    (d) Statistical DQ values of all points in point cloud 1 to determine maximum, minimum, average and standard deviation.

(2) included Angle between planes: the measurement method based on model parameters is adopted, that is, the included Angle in the normal direction of two plane models is calculated.

(3) cylinder radius: directly take the radius values in the fitting result of the cylinder model.

(4) the distance between the central axes of the cylinder: the measurement method based on model parameters is adopted, that is, the central axis parameters are calculated according to the parameters of the cylinder model, and then the 3D vertical distance between the central axes of the two cylinders is calculated.

(5) the Angle between the central axes of the cylinder: the measurement method based on model parameters is adopted, that is, the central axis parameters are calculated according to the parameters of the cylinder model, and then the 3D spatial Angle between the central axes of the two cylinders is calculated.

3 Experiment and Result Analysis

3.1 Experimental Data

For two typical components (motor damping base, traction rod) to complete the development of detection software, software can achieve component point cloud reading, scaling, rotation, detection, printing report functions.

3.2 Experimental Processing

Step One: Source data import, only motor shock absorbers are shown here. As shown in Fig. 3-a. In the software can zoom in and out of the point cloud image, rotation display.

Step Two: Parts parameter detection.

(1) automatic detection of motor damping base, the result is shown in Fig. 3-b.

(2) automatic detection of traction rod, the result is shown in Fig. 3-c.

Step Three: Display of test results, the result is shown in Fig. 3-d. In addition, after the detection is completed, the measurement result will be sent to the right screen and displayed in the first level interface. Then double-click the result to display the second level interface, and the secondary interface is express in the next Fig. 3-e.

Step Four: Generate the samples' report, as shown in Fig. 3-f.

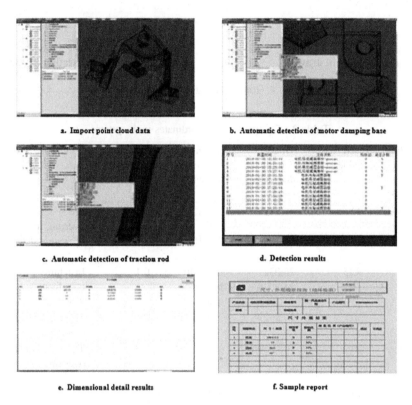

a. Import point cloud data   b. Automatic detection of motor damping base

c. Automatic detection of traction rod   d. Detection results

e. Dimensional detail results   f. Sample report

Fig. 3. Local result of experimental process

3.3 Experimental Results

Taking the original design drawings of the scanned components (shown in Fig. 4-a) and the three-coordinate measurement results (shown in Fig. 4-b) as reference values, the comparison of the detection results of the "shock absorber seat" components is shown in Table 3. The results show that the detection results of the system are better than those of the Three-coordinate Measurement results. Therefore, the detection accuracy of the high-speed railway component detection system based on 3D laser scanning technology meets the production requirements.

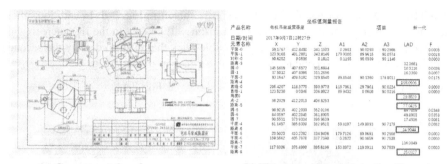

(a) Component drawing	**(b) Three-coordinate Detection Report**

Fig. 4. Reference data of experiment

Table 3. Comparison of coordinates with systems

Detection items	Detection value	Three-coordinate detection results	System detection results	Limit difference	Conclusion
Thickness	77	77.0425	76.842422 (NO) 77.01864 (YES)	0.2	Three-coordinate overrun, instability of system detection
Arc	R25	25.0327 24.9044	Basically, fully qualified	0.1	Instability of three-coordinate detection
Angle	30°	29.8529°	29.974481	0.1	Three-coordinate overrun
Distance	108	108.0606	108.015045	0.3	Three-coordinate overrun

4 Summary and Prospect

In this paper, we design a three-dimensional laser-based intelligent quality detection system for high-speed rail parts, which can make up for the low efficiency of manual detection in the current high-speed rail parts detection, and achieve high-precision, high-efficiency, batch detection of high-speed rail components processing quality. The following results are basically formed:

(1) The algorithm technology route of "feature extraction feature grouping parameter calculation" is formed, and the validity, adaptability and expansibility of the technology route are verified by experiments.

(2) At present, the nominal single-point accuracy of hand-held three-dimensional scanner is ±0.03 mm. The system improves the arithmetic and optimizes the parameters. It can realize the accurate measurement of geometric parameters, and the measurement error is no less than the nominal accuracy of the scanner.

In addition, the degree of automation of the system is relatively weak, and some processes have to resort to other software or steps. Therefore, in order to improve the automation of high-speed railway spare parts rapid detection software, complete scanning automation, point cloud data processing automation and automated detection. The next step is to further to automate the upgrade of hardware and software of the system. Only the automation integration of hardware components can maximize the automation of "fast online" detection.

References

1. Levoy, M., Pulli, K., Curless, B. et al.: The digital Michelangelo project: 3D scanning of large statues. In: Conference on Computer Graphics and Interactive Techniques. ACM Press, Addison-Wesley Publishing Co., pp. 131–144 (2001)
2. Wng, T.: Surface Deformation Monitoring Based on Three-dimensional Scanning Technology. Shan Dong University of Science and Technology, Qingdao (2011)
3. Long, Z.: Slope Deformation Monitoring and Deformation Trend Analysis Based on Three-dimensional Laser Scanning Technology. China Three Gorges University, Yichang (2016)
4. Jian, Z.: Research on the Application of Reverse Engineering in the Modeling Method and Detection of Body Covering Parts. YanShan University, Qinghuangdao (2005)
5. Du, L.: Quality Inspection of Complex Castings Based on Reverse Engineering. Northeastern University, Shenyang (2008)
6. Yuan, Y., Jiang, L., Keshu, Z.: Application of three-dimensional laser scanning technology in the measurement of large high temperature forgings. Surveying Mapp. Bull. 06, 45–47 (2009)
7. Chen, X., Wang, Y., Qiu, D., Lv, Y.: Three-dimensional control survey of steel frame docking at Tianjin west railway station. Surveying Mapp. Bull. 10, 70–72 (2012)
8. Mei, Z.: Detection of complex components based on three-dimensional laser scanning technology. In: Doulliez, P., Jamoulle, E. (eds.) Transportation networks with random arc capacities, RAIRO, vol. 6, no. 3, pp. 45–59. NanJing University of Information and Technology (1972)

Tackling the Challenge of Hands-on Learning from Cognitive Perspective

Yu-Liang Ting[1(✉)] and Yaming Tai[2]

[1] National Taiwan Normal University, Taipei, Taiwan
yting@ntnu.edu.tw
[2] National Taipei University of Education, Taipei, Taiwan

Abstract. Hands-on learning has been advocated by many educators to promote students' motivation and provide concrete learning experience. The end-product of hands-on work is also treated as the main learning goal and adopted to gauge students' performance. However, the industrial automation of robotics and advance of artificial intelligence cast doubt on such education rationale. This study, from the perspective of cognition, addressed the challenge of hands-on learning and summarized contemporary literatures to provide supports for teachers. Students' high-level cognition ability and capability in grasping core concepts and the concepts themselves are claimed to be the undeniable value of learning, especially in higher education. This study hopes to contribute to teachers' better understanding of hands-on learning and adopt such pedagogy accordingly.

Keywords: Hands-on learning · Cognition · Pedagogy · Multiple representations

1 Introduction

Students participating in experience-based learning thought their learning experience was interesting, valuable, meaningful, motivating and fun [1]. However, ideas that are developed without having any prior knowledge of the subject are not necessarily wrong but can be described as preconceptions. When constructing preconceptions and determining the causes of events, people reason using obvious variables rather than considering nonobvious variables and reason linearly rather than systemically [2]. For example, when thinking about pressure and being asked why a balloon partially deflates when driving from the mountains to the coast, students reason using obvious agents, such as a hole in the balloon, rather than reasoning using differentials in air pressure between two regions. Kariotoglou and Psillos [3] noted that the effects of pressure are often not obvious and undetectable. When students are not aware that pressure is a possible option in their causal reasoning, they may turn to concrete, though incorrect, obvious causes to explain pressure-related situations [2].

Experience-based learning refers to constructing knowledge from learners' own experiences, in which learners' participation is at the center of the learning process. Hands-on activities help students analyze their own learning experience through reflection, evaluation, and reconstruction in order to draw ideas from the current

© Springer Nature Singapore Pte Ltd. 2020
J. Shen et al. (Eds.): IC3 2019, CCIS 1227, pp. 18–26, 2020.
https://doi.org/10.1007/978-981-15-6113-9_3

experience considering their prior experience [4]. Experiencing many individual activities does not ensure that students understand the learning concepts that allow them to explain how a similar phenomenon will occur in a wide variety of circumstances.

Dewey [5] cautioned us that "No experience having a meaning is possible without having some element of thought." For example, sticking a finger into flames is not an experience. It is experience only when such movement is connected with pain, which people undergo as a consequence, and its *meaning* is a burn [6]. The results of actions instead of the physical actions are key to meaningful learning [7, 8]. What matters most in an experience for learning is its meaning for the people. People cognitively analyze their experiences and then derive their own personal meaning and understanding of these experiences. The processes of experiencing and reflecting are part of the same augmentative process that constructs meaning [6, 9].

The emphasis on the use of physical artifacts results from a desire to make learning concrete and meaningful but such benefits are not simply because of the physicality but rather how well the artifacts connect ideas to the real world. Therefore, the factor that ensures ideas are concrete is how meaningfully connected to prior experience and knowledge. Furthermore, instead of behavioral activity (e.g., hands-on activity), the type of activity that most effectively promotes meaningful learning is cognitive activity (e.g., selecting, organizing, and integrating knowledge). Instead of depending solely on learning through action, the most genuine approach to learning is learning by thinking [10]. Methods that rely on action should be judged not with respect to the amount of action involved but rather the degree to which these activities promote appropriate cognitive processing.

Kolb et al. [11] suggested that learning from experience is an appropriate method for acquiring knowledge: "*Learning is the process whereby knowledge is created through the transformation of experience.*" His experiential learning cycle illustrates how learners construct and refine their knowledge through experimentation. A related supporting argument is embodied cognition research, which demonstrates that people form metaphorical associations between physical activities and conceptual abstractions [12, 13]. Knowledge acquired through embodied representation may be retained longer in memory as a result of reciprocal encoding of the information [12, 14]. Hence, it should be recognized that after having a concrete experience, individuals should reflect on their observations, form abstract conceptualizations regarding the underlying mechanisms of these observations, and test these newly formed concepts through active experimentation. That is, phenomenological primitives may not be enough for understanding and communicating ideas and explanations about how the world works [15].

2 Examples in Electric Circuit

When students are provided with a battery, bulb, and some wires to prepare a working circuit, they develop thoughts about the circuit that may not be accurate from a scientific perspective. Students may not be aware that the circuit they made encompasses bipolar circuit elements, the circulation of current in a cycle, and the requirement for a closed circuit. Elementary school students typically generate linear representations instead of loop-based representations of circuits [16]. In addition, current flow and polarity are two of the most prevalent misconceptions in students' understanding of simple circuitry [17]. Osborne [16] argued that students must first understand about electric current to conduct the following tasks: (1) use simple circuits to examine conductivity of an electric element; (2) place an ammeter at any position in a series current; (3) understand why a circuit will not work unless it is complete; and (4) understand about series and parallel circuits.

Laboratory activities are essential for familiarizing students with the required basic skills and knowledge. Related physical manipulatives (circuit breadboard and electric elements) are useful for prompting learners to engage in physical movements that are necessary for developing robust understanding and trainings, but physical manipulatives are limited in their ability to display abstract concepts and guide students through a meaningful educational experience. Successful cases may refer to [18], investigating how electrical conductivity and circuits may be learned using digitally augmented exhibit devices within an informal scientific learning experience. Their device featured two metal spheres on a table, with one connected by a wire to a battery and the other connected to a light bulb. When the student grasped the metal spheres, the circuit was completed and the bulb on the table glowed. The lit bulb triggered the projection of an animated flow of electricity on the student's hands, arms, and shoulders, thus showing the complete loop and visualizing the flow of electricity through the completed circuit. If the student released their hold on the spheres, the circuit was broken and the visualization disappeared. The phenomenological primitives enabled students to form theories from their interactions with the device, and understand how the human body functioned as a conductor to form a loop of the completed circuit [18]. Students can then identify all the primary components of a complete circuit, and indicate in a scientific manner about the flow of current from the battery to the bulb.

3   Physical Fidelity Versus Cognitive Fidelity (Concrete Versus Abstract)

Gavish et al. [19] raised the notion of physical fidelity versus cognitive fidelity to contrast the importance of balancing the use of physical and virtual learning artifacts in engineering courses. The physical fidelity claims that the simulator should replicate the real-world task to the greatest degree. In contrast, the cognitive fidelity states that the simulator should engage the trainee in the type of cognitive activities required in the real-world task, without needing to duplicate the physical elements of the task [19]. This study created two figures (Fig. 1 and 2) to illustrate examples in electric circuit.

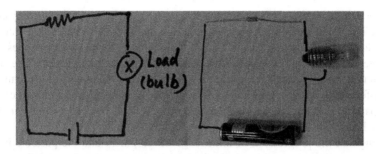

Fig. 1. Abstract (left) and concrete (right) representations of circuit elements (ref: Johnson *et al.* [24])

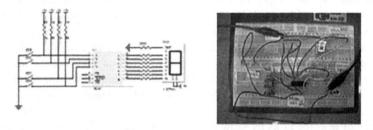

Fig. 2. Abstract electric circuit diagram (left) and concrete circuit connections on breadboard of the seven-segment display

When students are novices in a domain, their early encounters with new concepts and theories to be learned should be tailored to activate and build on their prior knowledge [20]. Novices may easily interpret contextualized representations because these relate to their everyday experiences, for example, the light bulb and battery. Because novices can more readily recognize everyday electrical components, contextualized representations may promote effective organization of incoming information by triggering prior knowledge, thereby increasing learning. These contextualized representations can be used as the foundation to construct a meaningful model of the learning content. Once this meaning is established, then students should find it easier to advance toward thinking about how the electrical principles learned can be used to solve the specific problem [20, 21]. Even if the instructional goal is to develop abstract knowledge in a domain, abstractions can be most effectively grasped by novices through experience with perceptually rich, concrete knowledge representations [20, 22]. Moreover, realistic graphics may promote motivation because they are interesting and evocative [20].

Although concrete representations may have the cognitive advantage of relying less on knowledge conventions and the motivational advantage of being more interesting, they have limited referential flexibility. Specifically, the knowledge contained in realistic representations has limited portability and transfer [20, 23]. Concrete visual representations divert novice students' attention to irrelevant problem information. Realistic visual representations unintentionally focus students' attention on superficial information at the expense of information that is necessary to grasp the learning content [20, 23]. That is, abstract representations may be more effective in leading learners to pay attention to information related to the underlying theories and principles, rather than perceptually salient information that changes from topic to topic [24]. The abstract representation is also conducive to the formation of robust knowledge structures that are transferable across various topics. In contrast, contextualized (authentic) representations may distract learners with perceptually salient, but conceptually irrelevant superficial problem features that change from topic to topic [24].

Throughout the progression of knowledge development and the possible implications for instruction, the notion of physical fidelity versus cognitive fidelity received more support from the work of Bruner [25], who described knowledge in terms of three levels of representation: enactive, iconic and symbolic. These modes of representation implicitly indicate the stages of knowledge development, a sequential graduation progressing from working with hands-on physical materials to reasoning with iconic and ultimately symbolic representations [7]. These literatures addressing the effects of abstract and concrete representations on how a novice learner approach the subject content provide valuable insights into the learning design of hands-on learning, in which versatile representations and physical artifacts should be provided and may co-exist. Varying the combination of physical and virtual learning artifacts along the dynamic cognitive process of learning, teaching could change the nature and lower the complexity of learning tasks by showing the content and tasks in different perspectives and making invisible become observable. An engineering work in a laboratory may be transformed into an authentic one by helping students relate the task to the real world and create meaningful learning experiences for them [26].

4 Hands-on with Multiple Representations for Cognition

Regarding the force and motion of friction and inertia with moving objects, to motivate students to use their experiences as the basis and explore this concept, teaching can begin with street gymnastics, including running up to a building, launching themselves upward with one foot on the wall, then flipping backward to land on their feet [27]. By illustrating the urban phenomenon that students are familiar with and can be genuinely intrigued by, teachers may demand students to provide fully elaborated explanations and construct the related core concepts from this perspective.

Another example is the Gas Laws involving a railroad tanker car that imploded after being steam cleaned [27]. Regarding the relationship between such natural phenomenon and its underlying causal explanation, the explanatory model for this puzzling phenomenon combines the observable (hot steam, rapid implosion after seconds, a not-quite-complete crushing, etc.) and the unobservable (molecules of different types moving at different speeds, collisions with the walls of the tanker, energy being transferred, etc.) to create such types of evidence-grounded scenarios and storyline that contextualized science values. The phenomenon being explained could be approached with first-hand experiences that students engage in, or a puzzling situation for which students will primarily use their intuition or phenomenological primitives to explain it.

This study proposed two examples, illustrating the incurrence of proactively cognitive activity in hands-on work for students in science and engineering education. The first one is about teaching potentiometer in electric circuit. In the textbook, the potentiometer is introduced as a zigzag line symbol that students have never encountered in their earlier life experiences. Students cannot conceptualize the role that potentiometers can play in a circuit. However, the potentiometer exists in some electrical appliances. One suggested teaching method is to display the use of the potentiometer while varying the resistance of a lamp, and then adjusting the lamp's brightness. Students enjoyed interacting with real artifacts and visualizing phenomena augmented with the artifacts in tasks that were achievable for them. The related concepts may then be accessible to students.

The second one is teaching the law of the lever in physics in Fig. 3, showing the three levels of representation in illustrating the law. This may refer to Mayer's multimedia learning theory. However, Mayer focused only on multimedia, without mentioning the senses used during hands-on learning, such as the haptic. As displayed in Fig. 3, a student uses his bare hands to operate the pliers and acquires a sense of force; he can change the holding position of the plier handles to consolidate his haptic experience with the theory of the law of the lever. This is not to be confused with the provision of concrete experience (macro-representation) in Kolb's phase of reflection. The learning design in each phase of Kolb's model should focus on students' learning status, which is not to be confined to the types of instructional representation provided by teachers.

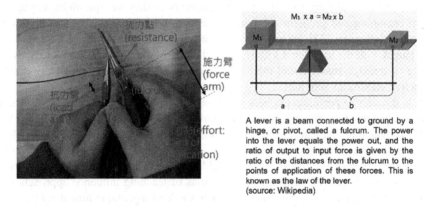

Fig. 3. Hands-on learning of the law of the lever in physics

Finally, in the phase of hands-on learning, it is suggested that the versatile types of representations be fully utilized to help students achieve the learning goal. For example, the technology of augmented reality overlaying symbolic representation on a physical artifact in a hands-on activity helps students focus on and acquire the targeted skills and science information.

5 Discussions and Conclusions

Supporting students in creating evidence-based explanations instead of merely comprehending or reproducing textbook explanations has been associated with increasingly coherent perceptions of theories [28] and the spontaneous use of these theories in related contexts [27, 29]. Students are requested to draw on research, readings, and ideas before selecting an explanatory theory. The students' theories emerge from a chain of reasoning that links hands-on experience, observations and information from various sources that they have had first-hand and concrete experiences with.

The proposed teaching is to base on students' responses to shape further instruction. Students' responses include (1) students' partial understandings, (2) students' alternative understandings, (3) everyday language they use to describe the phenomenon, and (4) everyday experiences they spontaneously use to make sense of the phenomenon [27]. The teaching is to synthesize what students think they currently know and what they want and need to know and offer them initial causal hypotheses about the phenomenon [27]. The teaching is designed to base on the scientific phenomena which students have certain experiences and raise puzzles to make students value and construct the learning content in resolving the puzzles. The teaching also adapts to students' responses to help them construct and value the knowledge. That is, the puzzling questions aim to lay instructional foundation for adaptive instruction.

Students' daily experience and knowledge had to be used as legitimate resources for learning [30, 31]. Instructors who decide to change their teaching must step out of the comfortable role of a lecturer passively disseminating and lecturing content to students and instead learn to actively guide students as they ask questions, engage in logical reasoning and problem solving, and discuss scientific concepts and processes with their classmates [32]. Instructional change is a challenge for many teachers who were taught with the traditional lecture method and thus may not know how to actively engage or manage students and their cognitive process of learning effectively during interactive classroom activities.

It is difficult to persuade teachers to adopt forms of teaching incorporating active student engagement, even though student-centred forms of teaching greatly improve the quality of teaching and learning [33]. In addition, teachers may have an "expert blind spot" and not recognize how different the student's approach is from their own; this blind spot can impede effective instruction [34]. Hence changing teachers' concepts is the first step in improving teaching. Conceptions of teaching influence approaches to teaching which impact upon students' approaches to learning, and in turn affect learning outcomes [33]. Teacher professional placement should engage teachers in a hands-on and student-focused learning practice and that such training allows the participating teachers to experience how the pedagogy and subject content are conveyed coherently.

References

1. Bruguier, L.R., Greathouse Amador, L.M.: New educational environments aimed at developing intercultural understanding while reinforcing the use of english in experience-based learning. Prof. Iss. Teach. Prof. Dev. **14**(2), 195–211 (2012)

2. Hung, W.: Enhancing systems-thinking skills with modelling. Br. J. Educ. Technol. **39**(6), 1099–1120 (2008)
3. Kariotoglou, P., Psillos, D.: Pupils pressure models and their implication for instruction. Res. Sci. Technol. Educ. **11**(1), 95–108 (1993)
4. Andresen, L., Boud, D., Cohen, R.: Experience-based learning. In: Foley, G. (ed.) Understanding Adult Education and Training. Allen & Unwin, Sydney (1995)
5. Dewey, J.: Democracy and education. Teddington: Echo Library. (Original work published 1916) (2007)
6. Ord, J., Leather, M.: The substance beneath the labels of experiential learning: the importance of John Dewey for outdoor educators. J. Outdoor Environ. Educ. **15**(2), 13 (2011)
7. Manches, A., O'Malley, C., Benford, S.: The role of physical representations in solving number problems: a comparison of young children's use of physical and virtual materials. Comput. Educ. **54**(3), 622–640 (2010)
8. Martin, T.: Physically distributed learning with virtual manipulatives for elementary mathematics. In: Robinson, D., Schraw, G. (eds.) Recent Innovations in Educational Technology That Facilitate Student Learning. Information Age Publishing, Charlotte (2007)
9. Greenaway, R.: A view into the future: the value of other ways of learning and development. In: Becker, P., Schirp, J. (eds.) Other Ways of Learning, pp. 347–367. bsj Marburg, Marburg (2008)
10. Mayer, R.: Should there be a three-strikes rule against pure discovery learning? the case for guided methods of instruction. Am. Psychol. **59**, 14–19 (2004)
11. Kolb, D., Boyatzis, R.E., Mainemelis, C.: Experiential learning theory: previous research and new directions. Perspect. Cogn. Learn. Think. Styles **1**(8), 227–247 (2000)
12. Bujak, K.R., Radu, I., Catrambone, R., MacIntyre, B., Zheng, R., Golubski, G.: A psychological perspective on augmented reality in the mathematics classroom. Comput. Educ. **68**, 536–544 (2013)
13. Lakoff, G., Johnson, M.: Metaphors We Live By, p. 256. University of Chicago Press, Chicago (1980)
14. Glenberg, A.M., Brown, M.C., Levin, J.R.: Enhancing comprehension in small reading groups using a manipulation strategy. Contemp. Educ. Psychol. **32**(3), 389–399 (2007)
15. Magnusson, S., Palincsar, A.: Teaching to promote the development of scientific knowledge and reasoning about light at the elementary school level. In: Donovan, M.S., Bransford, J. (eds.) How Students Learn Science in the Classroom, pp. 421–474. National Academies Press, Washington (2005)
16. Osborne, R.: Towards modifying children's ideas about electric current. Res. Sci. Technol. Educ. **1**(1), 73–82 (1983)
17. Litts, B.K., Kafai, Y.B., Lui, D.A., Walker, J.T., Widman, S.A.: Stitching codeable circuits: high school students' learning about circuitry and coding with electronic textiles. J. Sci. Educ. Technol. **26**, 1–14 (2017)
18. Yoon, S.A., Elinich, K., Wang, J., Steinmeier, C., Tucker, S.: Using augmented reality and knowledge-building scaffolds to improve learning in a science museum. Int. J. Comput. Supp. Coll. Learn. **7**(4), 519–541 (2012)
19. Gavish, N., Gutierrez, T., Webel, S., Rodriguez, J., Tecchia, F.: Design guidelines for the development of virtual reality and augmented reality training systems for maintenance and assembly tasks. In: BIO Web of Conferences, vol. 1, p. 00029. EDP Sciences (2011)
20. Moreno, R., Ozogul, G., Reisslein, M.: Teaching with concrete and abstract visual representations: effects on students' problem solving, problem representations, and learning perceptions. J. Educ. Psychol. **103**(1), 32 (2011)

21. Sharp, J., Adams, B.: Children's constructions of knowledge for fraction division after solving realistic problems. J. Educ. Res. **95**, 333–347 (2002)
22. Goldstone, R.L., Sakamoto, Y.: The transfer of abstract principles governing complex adaptive systems. Cogn. Psychol. **46**, 414–466 (2003)
23. Sloutsky, V.M., Kaminski, J.A., Heckler, A.F.: The advantage of simple symbols for learning and transfer. Psychon. Bull. Rev. **12**, 508–513 (2005)
24. Johnson, A.M., Butcher, K.R., Ozogul, G., Reisslein, M.: Introductory circuit analysis learning from abstract and contextualized circuit representations: effects of diagram labels. IEEE Trans. Educ. **57**(3), 160–168 (2014)
25. Bruner, J.: Toward a Theory of Instruction. Harvard University Press, Cambridge (1966)
26. Wu, H.K., Lee, S.W.Y., Chang, H.Y., Liang, J.C.: Current status, opportunities and challenges of augmented reality in education. Comput. Educ. **62**, 41–49 (2013)
27. Windschitl, M., Thompson, J., Braaten, M., Stroupe, D.: Proposing a core set of instructional practices and tools for teachers of science. Sci. Educ. **96**(5), 878–903 (2012)
28. Smith, C., Maclin, D., Houghton, C., Hennessey, M.: Sixth grade students' epistemologies of science: the impact of school science experiences on epistemological development. Cogn. Instruction **18**(3), 349–422 (2000)
29. Brown, A.L., Kane, M.J.: Preschool children can learn to transfer: learning to learn and learning from examples. Cogn. Psychol. **20**, 493–523 (1988)
30. Ting, Y.L., Tai, Y.M.: Using technology in students' daily life to teach science. Int. J. Technol. Eng. Educ. **9**(1), 21–32 (2012)
31. Ting, Y.-L.: Using mainstream game to teach technology through an interest framework. Educ. Technol. Soc. **13**(2), 141–152 (2010)
32. Silverthorn, D.U., Thorn, P.M., Svinicki, M.D.: It's difficult to change the way we teach: lessons from the integrative themes in physiology curriculum module project. Adv. Physiol. Educ. **30**(4), 204–214 (2006)
33. Kember, D.: Promoting student-centred forms of learning across an entire university. High. Educ. **58**(1), 1–13 (2009)
34. Singer, S., Smith, K.A.: Discipline-based education research: understanding and improving learning in undergraduate science and engineering. J. Eng. Educ. **102**(4), 468–471 (2013)

UAV – Virtual Migration Based on Obstacle Avoidance Model

Ci-Fong He[1(✉)], Chin-Feng Lai[1], Shau-Yin Tseng[2],
and Ying Hsun Lai[3]

[1] National Cheng Kung University, No. 1, Daxue Rd., Tainan 70101, Taiwan
quefon@csie.io
[2] ITRI/ICL, 195, Sec. 4, Chung Hsing Rd., Chutung, Hsinchu 31040, Taiwan
[3] National Taitung University, Sec. 2, University Rd., Taitung City,
Taitung County 950, Taiwan

Abstract. In recent years, the obstacles avoidance technology of unmanned aerial vehicles has been developed rapidly. It takes a lot of manpower to control un-manned aerial vehicles, so many researches use reinforcement learning to make unmanned aerial vehicles fly autonomously. In the real environment using rein-for cement learning to train aircraft is an expensive and time-consuming work, because reinforcement learning is a way to learn from mistakes, so there are often bumps in the learning process. In Wu's research, they trained a good model, but the realistic environment and simulation environment differs very big, so we will train this model again and transferred to the real environment, makes unmanned aerial vehicle in the realistic environment can use cheaper and quickly achieve the same task.

Keywords: Unmanned aerial vehicles · Reinforcement learning · Obstacle avoidance

1 Introduction

Quadcopter has been developing for 90 years and is mainly used for military purposes. In recent years, the concept of IOT has appeared [1], and information, communication and network technologies have been integrated. Quadcopter can be used to set all kinds of sensors, and has low cost and high flexibility, thus can be applied to a variety of different tasks, package across target tracking, disaster rescue, crop monitoring.

The tradition methods of uav control are manual operations. There have also been studies using SLAM to make the uav understand the environment and make correspond behaviors [2], and studies using depth image to make decisions [3]. However the method of artificial map building has limitations, and the traditional method is difficult to complete the task in an unknown environment.

Recently, there have been studies using reinforcement learning to train drones to complete tasks in unknown environments [4]. In the process of exploring the environment, unmanned aerial vehicles (uavs) will learn from failures, but this also makes uavs 18 easy to be damaged in training, making the cost expensive. Therefore, in order

© Springer Nature Singapore Pte Ltd. 2020
J. Shen et al. (Eds.): IC3 2019, CCIS 1227, pp. 27–34, 2020.
https://doi.org/10.1007/978-981-15-6113-9_4

to prevent the uav from training in the real environment, we put the model proposed in this article [5] on our system.

Article [5] is put forward the model of training in the virtual environment, and choose the virtual environment for Airsim, Airsim is one to four axis or car or more build simulator, is a virtual engine plug-ins, advantages is that it is not only a cross-platform and open source, the user can use it directly provided by a series of API. The API can be called in c++ or python. In addition, it also provides many different scenarios that allow users to make choices based on their own needs.

In the past, many papers have studied how to construct a virtual environment, which needs to simulate the state of the real world, including physical phenomena such as gravity, magnetic field and wind resistance. Moreover, the four-axis machine module must be provided, which can obtain color image, deep image environment information and body information from the virtual environment, so as to collect data for machine learning training.

Training in virtual environment can greatly reduce the loss of the UAV, and also can increase the speed of training. After the completion of virtual environment training, the virtual quad-axis machine needs to be transferred to the real quad-axis machine. However, there are a lot of differences between the parameters, Settings and body information of the virtual and real quad-axis machine, so how to adapt the parameters of the virtual environment to the real world is a big problem. The aircraft used in this study is pyparrot bebop 2, and the research objective is to transfer the model proposed in this study [5] into the real world, so that the real aircraft can achieve the predetermined tasks. Therefore, the research contribution is as follows:

1. Compare or discuss the differences between virtual and real environments.

2. Shared parameters between the virtual and real quad-axis machine.

3. Transferred the machine learning model trained in the virtual environment to the real quad-axis machine.

2   Related Work

The first purpose of this system is to transfer the results of obstacle avoidance in the virtual environment of aircraft to the real environment, which is the so called integration of virtual and real. In this study [5], a deep reinforcement learning method was proposed for the quadcopter to bypass obstacles in its flight path. In previous studies, the algorithm could only control the forward direction of the aircraft, but in this paper, it completed the two most important functions, the first for navigation and the second for obstacle avoidance. In our system, we referenced his model and successfully transferred him to the real world.

Due to the model of input in [5] is depth image, and our aircraft can't get this image, so we back to virtual environment and change the craft's input to the gray level image and training again.

There are many virtual environment research, Gazebo development platform for the virtual environment [6], which includes a sensor module and the 3 d world, although the Gazebo function is rich, but it is difficult to create large and complex environment.

Hector is mainly composed of ROS and Gazebo and USES Orocos' software-in-loop sensor model [7], but Hector lacks Pixhawk [8] and its reliance on Gazebo limits the richness of its environment. In the virtual world of Drone Racing, the DRL Drone Racing Simulator is a sophisticated free Drone Simulator that provides a realistic physics engine and supports RC controllers, but it does not offer an API for programming, so it cannot be used in machine learning applications. JMavSim is a simple and lightweight quadcopter simulator with high compatibility with the PX4 simulation API and a simple rendering engine, but its environment is also built on a small number of simple objects. Recently, Microsoft launched a virtual environment called Airsim [9], which USES the Unreal engine, which can be used in a variety of environments, such as streets, icebergs and interiors. With support for automotive and quadcopter simulators, Airsim provides apis in multiple programming languages, allowing for more machine learning frame- works to make training easier.

When training a uav in a real world, it is easy to damage the machine, so there are relevant studies to avoid machine collision. In this study[10], a learning algorithm of uncertainty model was proposed to estimate the collision probability and uncertainty environment. In the environment with low confidence, the four-axis chance reduced the flight speed, and this study effectively reduced the dangerous collision in the aircraft training.

And in another research[11], use the kalman filter to estimate its current world co-ordinates for trajectory tracking, and ultrasonic sensor is used to detect related static (dynamic) obstacles, so as to achieve obstacle avoidance function.

3   Approach

First, the quadcopter is placed at the starting point and the target position is defined. Then the system will assist the quadcopter to fly to the target and avoid obstacles in the way. We divide the method into virtual environment and real environment. First, we refer to the [5] model, which has trained the aircraft to complete specific tasks in a virtual environment. In the following paragraphs, we will propose the methods we use to integrate the virtual environment with the real environment, so that the uav can correctly achieve the task in the real environment, and finally compare the results between the virtual environment and the real environment.

3.1   System Architecture

We will unmanned aerial vehicle (uav) take off and fly to the target point, we will remit first unmanned aerial vehicle (uav) of the current screen, but because in the actual environment, and the actual environment of the aircraft is not under the same conditions, we must ensure that enter the CNN Model input should be the same, so you need to picture taken before treatment, we used the Model of the virtual environment is illustrated below transfered to the real environment of architecture diagram.

1.Input image   2.Image pre-processing   3.CNN Model

Fig. 1. The system architecture

3.2   Implementation Method

In order to transfer the results of virtual environment training to the real environment, we use the programmable uav as the real uav, which can control the aircraft by command. On this side we use the pyparrot bebop 2 quadcopter.

Fig. 2. Parrot Bebop 2.

Actually, even if the trained model is used, the model is built according to the virtual environment, and the virtual world cannot completely simulate the real world. Factors influencing the model include wind in all directions, pressure, and many other natural disturbances. Therefore, it is difficult to ensure that the quadcopter will not crash, so we write an exception program. When we find that the quadcopter is ready to crash, we will start the exception program and force the quadcopter to give up subsequent actions and land.

We transfer the model to the real world, according to architecture [5], we accomplished the following two main functions.

1. Uav positioning

In this paper [5], the use of the environment is "airsim", "airsim" has its own coordinate system, let the user know the current location and the target location. In the real environment, we do not have this coordinate system, so we use the GPS positioning system. GPS usually has an error, so when aircraft are landing, we allow it don't have to be precisely stop at the target, but stop at the target can be all around.

2. Model integration between virtual and real world

(1) Input image

Due to the bebop 2 api doesn't support camera shooting, so we use bebop 2 support streaming transmission [12], bebop 2 streaming transmission can be achieved by proper SDP file [13] open in the media to pick up packets, these media include VLC, Mplayer, OpenCV, FFMPEG, and after receiving the streaming, we combine streaming into the general image file, the following is the actual images. In order to ensure that the photos entering the CNN Model are the current images of the aircraft, we will use ffmpeg to obtain 30 photos per second and take the last photo as the input of the CNN Model.

(2) Image pre-processing

In this paper [5], the depth image is used as the input of the network, and the original size of the depth image is 256×144. After adjustment, the image size is 80×80. Finally, model's input was the first depth image of 80*80*4. However, bebop 2 could not obtain the depth image, so we used the method in [5] article to retrain the model in airsim and virtual environment and model's input changed to gray level image as input.

In the first step, we turn image into gray level image, and resize the photo as the input size of model requirements, and finally make the model run successfully.

(3) Collision problem

The method we use is machine learning, which is a way to learn from mistakes. Therefore, even if we use the model completed by training, once bad actions are generated, we still need to feedback and update the model, so as to make the flight mission more and more successful.

Due to the virtual environment and real environment differs very big, it is difficult to determine whether the migration of virtual environment training models to our system will yield good results, and the collision is likely to occur, therefore, we have added the 「Collision avoidance system」 on our original architecture.

Collision avoidance system is a decision system, this system is responsible for deciding whether to execute the action given by the agent. We add a ultrasonic sensor on our UAV, it is used to detect obstacles in front of the UAV. If the output of the agent is to let the flight go forward, but the decision system found obstacles ahead, the UAV will stop moving and get current photo and enter the photo into the model and re-export the model to a new action, until the action is safe.

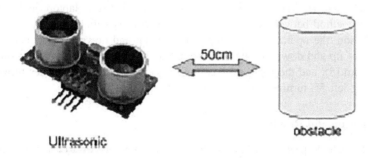

Fig. 3. Ultrasonic sensor detect obstacle.

4 Experiment

4.1 Experimental Design

In our experiments, we did not turn on the exploration function of the model, nor did we continuously update the model. This means that the aircraft will fully perform the actions predicted by the model, and since the model cannot be continuously learned, the probability of aircraft impact is high.

In real life, we use GPS to coordinate our flight system. Our initial point is set as (22.995360, 120.223194) and the target point is set as (22.995649,120.223784).

Due to the common error between GPS and the exact location, which is about one to two meters, we let the aircraft detect the distance from the destination during the flight. When the distance between the aircraft and the destination is less than two meters, the aircraft will land and record the success of the flight. The actual distance between two GPS points is calculated as follows.

This research uses inquiry activities to carry out the game-based library guided learning system combined with a popular science education curriculum. Before curriculum teaching is carried out, the students take a pre-test for prior knowledge structure and learning effectiveness, and then, take the post-test of learning effectiveness after the activity is finished. A total of 63 complete questionnaires are collected. After analysis by the statistical software, the preliminary results can be summarized, as follows:

$$S = 2 \arcsin \sqrt{\operatorname{Sin}^2 \tfrac{a}{2} + \cos(\mathrm{Lat1}) \times \cos(\mathrm{Lat2}) \times \operatorname{Sin}^2 \tfrac{b}{2}} \times 6378.137$$

Fig. 4. The formula for calculating the GPS distance between two points

4.2 Experimental Environment

Our research environment in real world, the scene is set as a flat ground, the obstacle is a large stone, and placed in front of the aircraft. In order to simplify the scene, this obstacle is the only obstacle, and the landing place is also a flat ground.

The equipment configuration includes one Parrot Bebop2 aircraft and one laptop. The obstacle avoidance program is mainly placed in this laptop, and the communication method between the laptop and the aircraft is wifi.

In addition, the operation of Bebop2 includes up and down forward and reverse. The range of up and down and the distance to the first time is calculated according to the algorithm [5], and the flight time is one second. The turning includes turning left 15°, turning left 5°, turning right 5°, and turning right 15°.

4.3 Experimental Results

We had the vehicle perform missions at five-flight intervals, up to a maximum of 30 flights.

We transferred the model in the virtual environment into the real world. However, due to the great difference between the two environments, including air pressure, wind and air creatures in real life, the actual flight could not completely conform to the results in the virtual environment. However, it can be found that we have successfully transferred the model into our system.

In our system architecture, we did not reward, that is to say, we did not let the aircraft learn in the real environment. Therefore, it can be found in the figure below that the number of flights did not increase with the number of successes.

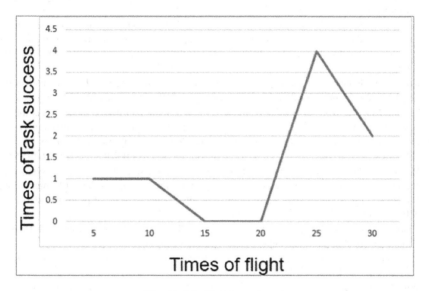

Fig. 5. My flight experiment

5   Conclusion and Future Work

Based on the research method of [5], this study retrains a model in Airsim environment and transfers the model to the real environment.

Considering the cost, we no longer train and update the model in the real environment, but we know that the virtual environment is quite different from the real environment, resulting in the flight effect is not as good as expected. Therefore, we will try to restore and update the model in the future. But in order to prevent the aircraft from collision, we will add a new decision system based on the original model. When the model generates a new action, the system decides whether the action is safe, if not, it forces the landing and gives feedback, and if not, it executes the action.

References

1. Chiang, M., Zhang, T.: Fog and IoT: an overview of research opportunities. IEEE Internet Things J. **3**, 854–864 (2016). https://doi.org/10.1109/JIOT.2016.2584538
2. Bachrach, A., He, R., Roy, N.: Autonomous flight in unknown indoor environments. Int. J. Micro Air Veh. **1**, 217–228 (2010). https://doi.org/10.1260/175682909790291492
3. Bills, C., Chen, J., Saxena, A.: Autonomous MAV flight in indoor environments using single image perspective cues. In: Proceedings of the IEEE International Conference Robot Automation, pp. 5776–5783 (2011). https://doi.org/10.1109/ICRA.2011.5980136
4. Pham, H.X., La, H.M., Feil-Seifer, D., Nguyen, L.V.: Autonomous UAV navigation using reinforcement learning. (2018)
5. Wu, T.C., Tseng, S.Y., Lai, C.F., Ho, C.Y., Lai, Y.H.: Navigating assistance system for quadcopter with deep reinforcement learning. In: Proceedings of the 2018 1st International Cognitive Cities Conference IC3 2018, pp. 16–19 (2018). https://doi.org/10.1109/IC3.2018.00013
6. Koenig, N., Howard, A.: Design and use paradigms for gazebo, an open-source multi-robot simulator, pp. 2149–2154 (2005). https://doi.org/10.1109/iros.2004.1389727
7. Lin, C., Liu, D., Wu, X., He, Z., Wang, W., Li, W.: Setup and performance of a combined hardware-in-loop and software-in-loop test for MMC-HVDC control and protection system. In: 9th International Conference Power Electron Asia Green World with Power Electron. ICPE-ECCE Asia, pp. 1333–1338 (2015). https://doi.org/10.1109/ICPE.2015.7167952
8. Meier, L., Tanskanen, P., Fraundorfer, F., Pollefeys, M.: PIXHAWK: a system for autonomous flight using onboard computer vision. In: Proceedings of the IEEE International Conference on Robotics and Automation, pp. 2992–2997 (2011). https://doi.org/10.1109/ICRA.2011.5980229
9. Shah, S., Dey, D., Lovett, C., Kapoor, A.: AirSim: High-Fidelity Visual and Physical Simulation for Autonomous Vehicles, pp. 621–635 (2017)
10. Kahn, G., Villaflor, A., Pong, V., Abbeel, P., Levine, S.: Uncertainty-Aware Reinforcement Learning for Collision Avoidance. (2017)
11. Wu, Z., Li, J., Zuo, J., Li, S.: Path planning of UAVs based on collision probability and kalman filter. IEEE Access. **6**, 34237–34245 (2018). https://doi.org/10.1109/ACCESS.2018.2817648
12. Lei, X., Jiang, X., Wang, C.: Design and implementation of a real-time video stream analysis system based on FFMPEG. In: Proceedings of the 2013 4th World Congress on Software Engineering WCSE 2013, pp. 212–216 (2013). https://doi.org/10.1109/WCSE.2013.38
13. Lubow, B.C.: Linked references are available on JSTOR for this article : SDP : Generalized software for solving stochastic dynamic optimization problems. **23**, 738–742 (2018)

3D-CNN Based Computer-Aided Diagnosis (CADx) for Lung Nodule Diagnosis

Tzu-Chi Tai[1(✉)], Miao Tian[2], Wei-Ting Cho[1], and Chin-Feng Lai[1]

[1] National Cheng Kung University, No. 1 Daxue Road,
Tainan 70101, Taiwan (R.O.C.)
n96071130@gs.ncku.edu.tw
[2] University of Electronic Science and Technology of China, No. 2006,
Xiyuan Avenue, West High-Tech Zone, Chengdu, Sichuan, China

Abstract. For the lung nodule screening, one of the commonly testing methods is the chest radiograph. However, it is difficult to judge with the naked eye with the initial nodule size is usually less than one centimeter. It is known that skilled pulmonary radiologists have a high degree of accuracy in diagnosis, but there remain problems in disease diagnosis. These problems include the miss rate for diagnosis of small nodules and the diagnosis of change in preexisting interstitial lung disease. The recent studies have found that 68% lung cancer nodules in radiographs can be detected by one reader and 82% by two readers. In order to solve this problem, we proposed a 3D-CNN predicting model to differ malignant nodules from all nodules in computed tomography scan. In the experiment results, the model was able to achieve a training accuracy of 100% and a testing accuracy of 94.52%. It shows the proposed model is able to be used for improving the accuracy of detecting nodules.

Keywords: Lung nodule · Computer-aided diagnosis · 3D-CNN

1 Introduction

According to "Taiwan's Leading Cause of Death in 2016", malignant neoplasms (cancers) was the leading cause of death in Taiwan. Among the leading cause of death, the lung cancer was the major cause. There are three main factors for the highest mortality rate of lung cancer. First of all, the lung cancer is the most common cancer caused by the tobacco hazards, outdoor air pollution, indoor air pollution from cooking and heating, etc. All of these common pollutants around the life are the lung cancer-causing substances. Second, the lung cancer is not easy to detect in the initial lung cancer screening, because the initial symptoms of lung cancer are not obvious in the external symptoms. The recent studies have found that 68% lung cancer nodules in radiographs can be detected by one reader and 82% by two readers [1, 2]. When there are significant symptoms such as hemoptysis and hoarseness, it is usually the late stage of lung cancer. Finally, the nodules will grow with different speeds in various types of lung cancers. It may grow from the early stage to the late stage within one month. This situation will lead people may not be able to treat cancer in time.

© Springer Nature Singapore Pte Ltd. 2020
J. Shen et al. (Eds.): IC3 2019, CCIS 1227, pp. 35–43, 2020.
https://doi.org/10.1007/978-981-15-6113-9_5

In order to solve this problem, the recent study proposed a two-dimensional convolution neural network (2D-CNN) for lung nodule diagnosis [3]. This 2D-CNN is applicable to the recognition of radiographs. The program first performed the suspicious nodules which were round objects in the radiographs. The 2D-CNN determined whether the suspicious image block contains a lung nodule. However, it is difficult to search the suspected nodules correctly in the blurred radiographs. There are also many noises which will interfere with the prediction in the suspicious image block. To address the problem of noises, we proposed a three-dimensional convolution neural network (3D-CNN) which was more accurate than the 2D-CNN. This 3D-CNN is applicable to the recognition of computed tomography (CT) scans.

CT scan makes use of computer-processed combinations of many X-ray measurements taken from different angles to produce tomographic images of specific area of a scanned object, allowing the user to see inside the object without cutting [4]. Digital geometry processing is used to further generate a three-dimensional volume of the inside of the object from a large series of two-dimensional radiographic images taken around a single axis of rotation. Compared with radiographs, we can get more information about lungs from CT scans. There is the contribution in this study. We improved accuracy of the 3D-CNN model for predicting lung nodules.

2 Related Work

The recent studies proposed some methods to preprocess the datasets of lungs, such as radiographs with 2D-CNN [3], computed tomography scan with 2D-CNN [5–9] and computed tomography scan with 3D-CNN [10, 11]. We referenced to their methods which we tried to improve.

2.1 Radiographs

In many models for detecting lung nodules, planar chest radiograph is mostly used for prediction. In [6], they developed an early stage lung cancer diagnosis system named LCDS. LCDS system used convolution filter with Gaussian pulse to smooth the radiographs. The contrast and color of the radiographs were enhanced. Then the nodules in the radiographs were segmented by thresholding. On this basis, a lung nodule identification module was employed to judge whether nodules in the segment or not.

In the radiographs, lungs are covered with ribs. There are a lot of gray lines on the black lungs in the radiograph. In the case of uneven color in the lungs, it will cause serious interference in training. The common method can only find all the lungs, guessing that the white dots are nodules. Therefore, the chance of occurring mistake is relatively high in the preprocessing. Most of these models are trained with 2D-CNN.

2.2   Computed Tomography Scan

Because CT scan is a multi-layer 2D tomogram, we can eliminate the interference caused by the ribs and search accurately where the nodule is located. We also can get more detailed information about the nodules, such as nodule size, nodule length, whether there is hollow inside the nodule, etc. With this information, we can train model with 3D-CNN. Because the amount of data is much more than radiographs, we can get the correct location of the nodules and let the accuracy of prediction be better.

In [7, 10, 12], they demonstrated a computer-aided diagnosis (CADx) system for nodules classification of CT scans. A modified U-Net was used to first detect nodule candidates in the CT scans. The U-Net output were fed into 3D-CNN to ultimately classify the CT scan as positive or negative for lung nodules.

However, after our experiment, we found that the performance of the U-Net was not as good as expected. The candidates selected by the U-Net were often not the nodules. The data used to train the 3D-CNN model was interfered by the non-nodule tissues. So we decided to skip the U-Net and train the 3D-CNN model directly.

3   Method

This study used CT scans for training 3D-CNN model. In 3D-CNN model, we could not use traditional method to segment nodules in datasets. We need the HU filter to eliminate the interference of the other lung tissues.

3.1   Nodule Segmentation

Most studies which use 3D-CNN models will train U-Net to detect the location of the nodules (see Fig. 1) and use another model to predict whether there is a malignant nodule or a benign nodule [10, 12–15]. However, this model is time-consuming and labor-intensive, and the training time is even longer than the nodule predict model. So the benefits are not very good.

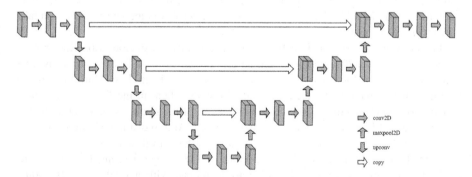

Fig. 1. The architecture of U-Net.

Since the data has the exact location of the nodules, we only need to convert the voxel coordinates of the original data into a card type coordinate. We can get the nodule blocks by simple processing. Therefore, this part which can reduce the noise generated by the wrong place does not need to use U-Net. This process can greatly improve the accuracy of the training model.

3.2   Data Preprocessing

In the CT scans, there are other tissues besides the lungs, such as the trachea, thoracic vertebrae, heart and other human tissues. Therefore, processing the non-lung area into the background can reduce training interference. The value stored in our data is Hounsfield units (HU), also known as X-ray attenuation coefficient or absorption coefficient. The higher the value, the whiter the image, and the lower the value, the darker the image. Different body tissues will affect the value.

Some studies took the range of non-lung tissue from −750 to −300 [8], bet we found that the training was not effective. After the experiment, it was found that the range of non-lung tissue from −1000 to −320 is the best, so we take it to make the screening range.

4   Experiments

4.1   Data Sets

The training and test data used in this study are the lung nodule data sets provided by "LUNA 16" and "Tianchi Alibaba Cloud". In the data sets, we have three types of files, namely "Lung CT Scans", "File Marking Nodule Location", and "File Marking Suspicious Location". The contents of the three files are described blow.

In Lung CT Scans, we can see the slice of the entire lung. The data format is mhd, which is the format of image storage in ITK (Insight Segmentation and Registration Toolkit). ITK is a program proposed by the National Institutes of Health for medical image segmentation and configuration. It hopes to provide medical image storage methods that are as non-destructive, open source, and cross-platform as possible. Therefore, from the mhd file, we can get many nodules from lung slices. Users can take different slices as needed.

In File Marking Nodule Location and File Marking Suspicious Location, record where the nodules and suspicious location are located in the CT scans. There is little difference between the two file. The main difference is in File Marking Nodule Location, which records the location of the nodules. Then, in the File Marking Suspicious Location, in addition to record the location of the nodules, the location that is not a nodule bot looks like a nodule is also recorded. And to distinguish the location is a nodule or not a nodule, which is the problem we have to deal with.

In the two sets of data sets, there are a total of 1486 lung CT scans. Each CT scans may have multiple nodules and suspicious locations, with a total of 2130 nodule locations and 9773 suspicious locations. These data will be used to perform nodule prediction work.

4.2 Experimental Environment

Our experimental environment was built on Ubuntu 16.04, using Python3 to write programs. We use SimpleITK, numpy, tensorflow and other packages to assist in nodule prediction. In a hardware environment, we use an Intel® Xeon® CPU E5-2630 v4 @ 2.20 GHz CPU with nvidia 1080 Ti graphics cards with 16 GB of memory and 11 GB of memory.

4.3 Experiment Procedure

In the introduction, we have mentioned that there have been many researches which studied computer-aided diagnosis. In this study, we will focus on enhancing the accuracy of model prediction. Our experimental procedure is shown below (see Fig. 2) adjusted.

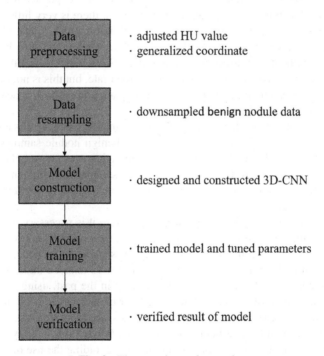

Fig. 2. The experimental procedure.

The flow chart on the left side of the figure is the procedure of the experiment in this study. The right side of the figure are the jobs list that must be completed. The following sections describe several points that are implemented in this study.

4.4 Data Preprocessing

In the data preprocessing section, we will first explain the part of the HU value screening. In many of the aforementioned researches, we know that there are many pieces of information are not related to the lungs in CT scans. Therefore, it is necessary to screen the appropriate HU value to reduce the interference of noise on the model. According to the method proposed in [10], the appropriate HU value range should be from −1000 to −320, and the same scope is adopted in this study. Regarding the generalized part of the coordinate, many research in the past have contributed to the method of mhd processing [16, 17]. This study is also processed according to these methods, we focus on data sets resampling and model design issues.

4.5 Data Resampling

From the section on the introduction of the data sets, we have explained that there are a lot of suspicious locations in these data sets. In contrast, there is very little information on the location of the nodule, which is about 20% of the suspicious data. If you use all the data directly, it will cause skewed classification. The model will have a large amount of data without nodules in the training data. So no matter what the input is, it will predict no nodule. This has more than 99% correct rate, but this is not the result we want. In the past research, there were no specific explanation on how to deal with such problems, so we conducted research on this part.

The main reason for the skewed classification is that the number of samples in the two categories varies greatly. Excessive number of benign nodule samples can cause overtraining of the model, and the chances of predicting various samples as benign nodules are greatly improved. Conversely, too many samples of malignant nodules are also true. When there is a large gap between the sample sizes, it is possible to bias the results to somewhere.

In order to solve the problem of skew classification, it is necessary to find a good ratio between malignant nodules and benign nodules, thereby avoiding overtraining of the model. In the past, when the Internet of Things was not as developed as today, there is a part of machine learning research focuses on how to analyze under skewed data [18–20]. This study took the recommendations made in the past, using all the nodule location data, and randomly taking the same number of suspicious location data of the nodule location data. After many attempts and studies, we found that the optimal ratio between malignant nodules and benign nodules was 0.9467 and 1. Only about 4,000 CT scans are used in each epoch training, in this way avoiding the use of skewed data for training.

Table 1. Setting of model layers.

Layer	Parameters	Activation	Output
Input			$36 \times 36 \times 36 \times 1$
Conv1	$5 \times 5 \times 5$	ReLU	$36 \times 36 \times 36 \times 64$
Maxpooling1	$4 \times 4 \times 4$, stride $2 \times 2 \times 2$		$17 \times 17 \times 17 \times 64$
Conv2	$4 \times 4 \times 4$	ReLU	$17 \times 17 \times 17 \times 28$
Maxpooling2	$2 \times 2 \times 2$, stride $2 \times 2 \times 2$		$8 \times 8 \times 8 \times 128$
Conv3	$3 \times 3 \times 3$	ReLU	$8 \times 8 \times 8 \times 256$
Maxpooling3	$2 \times 2 \times 2$, stride $2 \times 2 \times 2$		$4 \times 4 \times 4 \times 256$
Dense		ReLU	1024
Dense		ReLU	256
Dense		ReLU	32
Dense		Softmax	2

4.6 Model Construction

The nodule prediction of this study was trained using the 3D-CNN model. Table 1 gives the settings of model layers.

4.7 Experiment Result

We randomly selected 80% of the above data sets as the training data set and the remaining 20% as the test data set. We train 100 epochs on this (see Fig. 3). It shows that the model had learned the feature of nodules in the epoch 23.

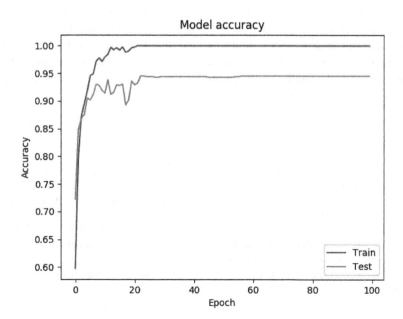

Fig. 3. The model accuracy.

In the final training result, the model was able to achieve a training accuracy of 100% and a testing accuracy of 94.52%. We use the model to predict the original data set, and the overall accuracy is 98.38%. The following Table 2 gives the result of prediction.

Table 2. Result of prediction.

Prediction	Actual status	
	Malignant nodule	Benign nodule
Malignant nodule	2081	19
Benign nodule	49	2231

In order to verify whether our model is overlearning, we retake the suspicious location data which is not in the training data set as a new test data set. And using the same model to directly identify whether it is a nodule, the accuracy of this model is 95.5%. Therefore, we believe that this model successfully learned the characteristics of malignant nodules and benign nodules in this data.

5   Conclusion

This study provided a ratio of nodule prediction model to data sample, and obtained a fairly good identification result in predicting the published lung nodule data. In the future, if we want to apply this model to the real field, we still have to consider two issues.

First at all, because the published lung nodule data is limited, this study can no longer do more testing and tuning of the model. Whether the model can have stable performance still requires more testing. Second, the model proposed in this study is currently only used to predict whether there is a malignant nodule or a benign nodule in a particular block. To apply to a complete lung CT scans, it needs to be preprocessed. This study did not implement this part.

References

1. Heelan, R.T., et al.: Non-small-cell lung cancer: results of the New York screening program. Radiology **151**, 289–293 (1984)
2. Stitik, F.P., Tockman, M.S., Khouri, N.F.: Screening for cancer. In: Chest Radiology, pp. 163–191 (1985)
3. Lo, S.-C., Lou, S.-L., Lin, J.-S., Freedman, M.T., Chien, M.V., Mun, S.K.: Artificial convolution neural network techniques and applications for lung nodule detection. IEEE Trans. Med. Imaging **14**, 711–718 (1995)
4. Brenner, D.J., Hall, E.J.: Computed tomography—an increasing source of radiation exposure. N. Engl. J. Med. **357**, 2277–2284 (2007)

5. VanGinneken, B., Setio, A.A.A., Jacobs, C., Ciompi, F.: Off-the-shelf convolutional neural network features for pulmonary nodule detection in computed tomography scans. In: 2015 IEEE 12th International Symposium on Biomedical Imaging (ISBI), pp. 286–289 (2015)

6. Zhou, Z.-H., Jiang, Y., Yang, Y.-B., Chen, S.-F.: Lung cancer cell identification based on artificial neural network ensembles. Artif. Intell. Med. **24**, 25–36 (2002)

7. Sun, W., Zheng, B., Qian, W.: Computer aided lung cancer diagnosis with deep learning algorithms. In: Medical Imaging 2016: Computer-Aided Diagnosis, p. 97850Z (2016)

8. Ciompi, F., et al.: Towards automatic pulmonary nodule management in lung cancer screening with deep learning. Sci. Rep. **7**, 46479 (2017)

9. Rossetto, A.M., Zhou, W.: Deep learning for categorization of lung cancer CT images. In: Proceedings of the Second IEEE/ACM International Conference on Connected Health: Applications, Systems and Engineering Technologies, pp. 272–273 (2017)

10. Alakwaa, W., Nassef, M., Badr, A.: Lung cancer detection and classification with 3D convolutional neural network (3D-CNN). Lung Cancer **8**(8), 409 (2017)

11. Chen, L., Wu, Y., DSouza, A.M., Abidin, A.Z., Wismüller, A., Xu, C.: MRI tumor segmentation with densely connected 3D CNN. In: Medical Imaging 2018: Image Processing, pp. 105741F (2018)

12. Wang, H.: Deep Convolutional Neural Networks for, pp. 1–9 (2009). https://doi.org/10.1007/978-3-319-44781-0

13. Wang, G., Li, W., Ourselin, S., Vercauteren, T.: Automatic brain tumor segmentation using cascaded anisotropic convolutional neural networks. In: Crimi, A., Bakas, S., Kuijf, H., Menze, B., Reyes, M. (eds.) BrainLes 2017. LNCS, vol. 10670, pp. 178–190. Springer, Cham (2018). https://doi.org/10.1007/978-3-319-75238-9_16

14. Zhao, C., Han, J., Jia, Y., Gou, F.: Lung nodule detection via 3D U-Net and contextual convolutional neural network. In: 2018 International Conference on Networking and Network Applications (NaNA), pp. 356–361 (2018)

15. Shaziya, H., Shyamala, K., Zaheer, R.: Automatic lung segmentation on thoracic CT scans using U-Net convolutional network. In: 2018 International Conference on Communication and Signal Processing (ICCSP), pp. 643–647 (2018)

16. Yaniv, Z., Lowekamp, B.C., Johnson, H.J., Beare, R.: SimpleITK image-analysis notebooks: a collaborative environment for education and reproducible research. J. Digit. Imaging **31**(3), 290–303 (2017). https://doi.org/10.1007/s10278-017-0037-8

17. Kuan, K., et al.: Deep learning for lung cancer detection: tackling the Kaggle data science bowl 2017 challenge. arXiv Preprint arXiv:1705.09435 (2017)

18. Kumar, M.N.A., Sheshadri, H.S.: On the classification of imbalanced datasets. Int. J. Comput. Appl. **44**, 1–7 (2012). https://doi.org/10.5120/6280-8449

19. Alfaro-Cid, E., Sharman, K., Esparcia-Alcázar, A.I.: A genetic programming approach for bankruptcy prediction using a highly unbalanced database. In: Giacobini, M. (ed.) EvoWorkshops 2007. LNCS, vol. 4448, pp. 169–178. Springer, Heidelberg (2007). https://doi.org/10.1007/978-3-540-71805-5_19

20. Maimon, O., Rokach, L. (eds.): Data Mining and Knowledge Discovery Handbook, 2nd edn. Springer, New York (2010). https://doi.org/10.1007/978-0-387-09823-4

The Vision of Design-Driven Innovation in China's Smart Home Industry

Xiaoman Man[1], Zhenya Wang[1], Yaxue Zuo[1(✉)], and Zehan Lin[2]

[1] School of Mechanical Engineering, Shandong University, Jinan 250000, China
928829875@qq.com, 15091313@qq.com, 15209218372@163.com
[2] Germany School of Design, The Hong Kong Polytechnic University,
Hong Kong 999077, China
zehanlin@gmail.com

Abstract. In the last years, "design-driven innovation" has gained popularity-it is now seen as an exciting paradigm for the development of companies, schools, regions, even nations. At the same time, "smart home industry" as an emerging region has been a hot topic for researchers and other stakeholders. But what about the combination of "design-driven innovation" and "smart home industry"? Based on the investigation of related data, cases, and so on, we could find that design-driven innovation of smart home industry is only played by few technology companies. This paper identifies how the design-driven innovation performs in the smart home industry development and clarifies the reasons and benefits of performing design-driven innovation in China's smart home industry by studying the current economics context of China's home automation industry and the examples of design-driven innovation.

Keywords: Design-driven innovation · Smart home · Home automation · Internet of Thing · China · Ecosystem

1 Introduction

In the digital age, with the increasing availability and adoption of Internet, smart device manufacturers, wireless networks, new sensing capabilities and more powerful computing technologies, Internet of Thing (IoT) technology achieves rapid development, especially in smart home products and systems' development. Smart Home, also called Home Automation (HA), has become a new wave of trend influencing the lives of consumers.

The concept of home automation has been developed since the 1990s. The word "smart" has recently become an umbrella term for innovative technology that possesses some degree of artificial intelligence [1]. According to one of the most recent definitions provided by Satpathy, "a home which is smart enough to assist the inhabitants to live independently and comfortably with the help of technology is termed as smart home. Smart home technology based on IoT has changed human life by providing connectivity to everyone regardless of time and place [2, 3]. These systems of smart home provide infrastructure and methods to exchange all types of appliance information and services [4]. In a smart home, all the mechanical and digital devices are

J. Shen et al. (Eds.): IC3 2019, CCIS 1227, pp. 44–53, 2020.
https://doi.org/10.1007/978-981-15-6113-9_6

interconnected to form a network, which can communicate with each other and with the user to create an interactive space" [5]. Alam and Ali [6] define the smart home as an application that is able to automatize or assist the users through different forms such as ambient intelligence, remote home control or home automation systems.

In the smart home industry, innovation is recognized as the driven force of smart home development and value creation. Innovation has been the core task of humans throughout history and it often leads to the scientific breakthrough, technological advances, inspiring ideas that motivate the masses [7].

Verganti [8] identifies 3 approaches to innovation. The first one is technology push innovation, which brings the sources of long-term competitive advantages for organization. Indeed, investigators of innovation have focused mainly on the disruptive effect of novel technologies on the industry [9]. The second one is market pull innovation [10, 11] which focuses more on the existing market and consumer needs. This innovation strategy is widely accepted by most commercial players. The third one is design driven innovation focusing especially on the interplay between radical innovation of meanings and radical innovation of technologies. Instead of the common recognition that meanings and design become relevant only when an industry matures, Roberto Verganti [10] points out that design-driven innovation may overturn industries in the emerging phases of breakthrough technologies. Design-driven innovation focuses on the innovation of product meanings. The product meaning addresses both utilitarian values, as well as more intangible values such as experiential, emotional and socio-cultural values [12]. In other words, design-driven innovation focuses on the purpose a product has to a customer [8, 13].

In the smart home industry, despite of current technology driven innovation dominated by a few big companies and market pull innovation played by most smart home players, there is a lack of research about the design-driven innovation in China's smart home industry. However, the objective of this report is to explore the framework of China's smart home industry and define the position of design-driven innovation in China's current economic context. At the first, this report gives a basic introduction about the topic. Second, it presents cases study of design-driven innovation in smart home. Then it explores the situation of design-driven innovation in China's smart home industry and provides a vision of its development in current economic context.

2   Cases Study of Design-Driven Innovation in Smart Home

2.1   Nest Thermostat Innovation Developing Strategy

The Nest Company was founded by two Apple's former engineers, Tony Fadell and Matt Rogers. Its first product, Nest Thermostat, was launched in October 2011. After the launch of the Nest Thermostat, Nest started to grow in a fast pace, increase its distribution channels to big companies, such as Apple, Amazon and expand into other countries' smart home market. It currently stands as a frontrunner in automated home energy system.

With the mission of redesigning the thermostat product, instead of positioning sustainability as the central value proposition, Nest gives the thermostat a modern technological makeover and a higher meaning. The problem Nest looks to solve is the frustration associated with overly complex home thermostats and it aims to bring simplicity control experience into home automation. Without manually control, the Nest's thermostat can learn people life patterns and preferences over time and then predicts a temperature set point. It integrates information from a range of sensors, and even the weather in your area to make its decision. The thermostat is no longer just a money saving product, but a daily life assistant that helps generating a personalized heating and cooling schedule for homeowners. At the same time, an app of Nest is developed for remote control embedded on computers or mobile phones. With software and platform is built up, the product is surrounded by an ecosystem of service and smart. The product itself also develops smarter with the ability of self-learning, making daily schedule, connecting to a broader home network and managing other electronic smart home appliances. Gradually, a smart house ecosystem based on the energy consumption is built, Nest becomes a regulator as well as the hub of a smart home.

2.2   Amazon Echo Design Driven Innovation

Amazon is an American electronic commerce and cloud computing company which has a strong capability in internet platform building. Alexa is a smart personal assistant developed by Amazon, with nearly 80,000 skills based on its capability of voice interaction.

Before Amazon Echo came out, the development of voice assistant is voice interaction which was mainly based of mobile phone and screen. Different from the main stream's development strategy, Amazon develops the Alexa into a music player to show a different interaction between human and smart home product. While Echo doesn't position itself just as a music player, its aim is to connect with internet-connected appliances or products in the home, and act as a personal assistant in the smart house. What is more, Alexa's capabilities are become broader by adding more functionalities based on different scenarios like ordering foods, calling an Uber taxi, searching weather by just talking to it. The successful launch of Echo makes itself one of the biggest hits in the Amazon's hardware history. It not only helps Amazon avoid the former obstacles from the process of developing technology and hardware, but also points out a new way of product development. Besides the innovation in a new way of interaction, Amazon's Echo also integrates different services on one common platform. Like ordering pizza, calling a taxi or checking the weather by just talking to it. Furthermore, Amazon aims to position the product as the central hub of smart home by controlling other connected home devices.

3   The Design-Driven Innovation in China's Smart Home Industry

When it comes to China, the smart home industry has developed over 20 years. Meanwhile, the China's smart home industry has showed a rapid growth in a few years. The number of the financing cases in smart home sector keeps being higher than that of smart wearable products and smart health care, which indicates that smart home attracts more attention than any other market segments in smart hardware industry. In the organization level, although China smart home high-end market is still occupied by foreign companies, there are more and more domestic players growing up rapidly, such as Haier, Huawei, Xiaomi, 360, JD.COM, etc.

The domestic smart home industry's development is driven by both policy stimulation and the market growing needs. With the unveiled implementation of "*Made in China 2025*" proposed by China's State Council (2015), China's next 10-year national plan to upgrade the mainland's industries was outlined. Moreover, *"The Development Guidance of China Household Electrical Appliance Industry in 13th Five-Year Plan Period"* released by China Household Electrical Appliances Association (CHEAA) stressed home appliances development in the aspect of quality, technology innovation, energy efficiency as well as international competitiveness. These policies show the government's strategy of putting the trend of building smart home product into the process of future household industry's transformation and upgradation. In addition to policy stimulation, there is a huge market need for smart home products. More and more companies and organizations are devoted into the pool, trying to share the benefit brought by the rapid growth of smart home. According to the Smart Home Appliance Market Report, the unit-shipments of several smart-connected home appliance segments are higher than expected in recent years.

3.1   Market Investigation

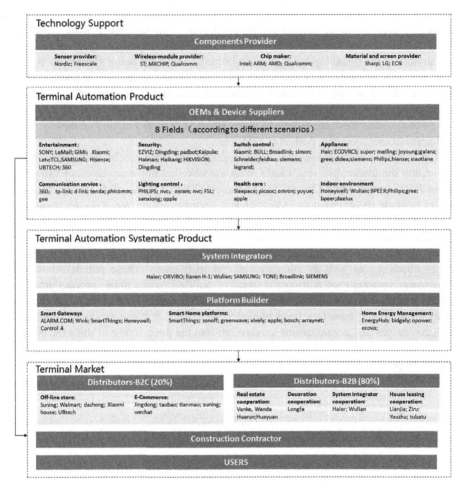

Fig. 1. China's smart home ecosystem map.

In industry chain, the smart home industry mainly includes up-stream's smart module providers, mid-stream's smart device manufactures, down-stream's system integrators, platform builders, distributors, construction contractors and end-users.

Looking into the market distribution, the Fig. 1 shows an unbalanced of development in different chain distributions. The upper stream players are mainly taken up by foreign IoT brands (LG, Nordic, Intel, etc.), having high abilities in hardware development and technology innovation. The mid-stream and down-stream industry show a dynamic development status where is crowded with different patterns of participators, leaded by industry giants such as Haier, Huawei, Xiaomi, etc.

In the relationship between different market distribution segments, the smart modules provider provides key components to mid-stream device suppliers and OEM companies. The quality of up-stream's components decides the performance of terminal automation products. The products produced by OEMs and device suppliers are distributed into two channels. One is sold to terminal market directly, mostly are single products with the basic function of intelligent processing, data collection, remote access, monitoring and remote control. Those products are without a systematic solution and platform, mainly accepted by mass markets. Another distribution for terminal automation products is processed by system integrators and platform builders, which helps those products unify together and build into a systematic smart home product. After that, those products combined with terminal automation systems are sold into the terminal market. Currently, the distribution channel of those terminal automation systematic products is through business to business (B2B) channel which takes up 80% of market shares and mainly focuses on the high-class market.

3.2 Market Competitors Pattern Analysis

In smart home market, US's smart home brands have the biggest influence on the global market. The competitor patterns of US market include six types of organizations: 1. Home Appliance Manufactures; 2. Internet Platform Enterprises; 3. Security Manufacturer; 4. Intelligent Hardware Enterprises; 5. Operators; 6. Public Undertakings.

In China, the market competitor pattern is different from the US market. The Fig. 2 use the concentric circle to indicate different volumes of participators in China's smart home market. The operators and public undertakings appear a slow pace of entering into China's smart home market, resulting in they have the lowest influence in the market among these six types. Therefore, key players in Chinese market are only four types: home appliance manufactures, internet platform enterprises, security manufacturer and intelligent hardware enterprises. Those four types of smart home player in China play a similar role to the US players but have different status within their own markets. And here we will only focus on home appliance manufactures and internet platform enterprises.

With the stimulation of IoT market and government's policy, those home appliance manufacturers are gradually experiencing a transformation in smart home product development. The product transformations are mainly reflecting on the integration of intelligent functions and the promotion of traditional household electrical appliances upgrading. Haier is one of the pioneers who get involved in the smart home appliance industry. As a well-known Chinese home appliance manufacturer, Haier launched the U+ home working as a platform, which allows its home appliances to connect freely without boundaries. Series of smart products are innovated based on the wisdom of life concept, such as smart refrigerator, smart light, and even the whole smart kitchen system. With those diverse smart appliances and well-equipped system, Haier gradually has a greater impact on the global smart home market.

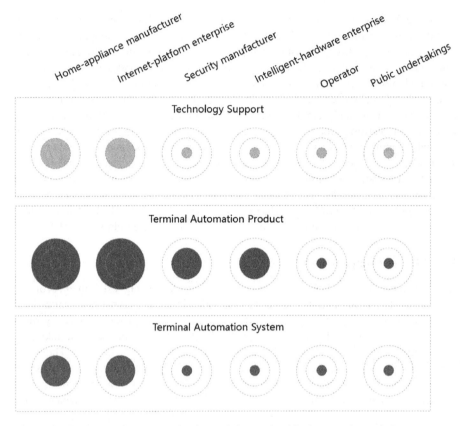

Fig. 2. Type and volume of main participators in china's smart home industry.

Different from home appliance manufacturers, the internet platform enterprises' main mission is to extend the industrial chain layout and build a unified platform for the smart home ecosystem. There are mainly 4 types of player: the first type is the electric business-oriented companies. In the smart home industry, they mainly focus on developing smart control system and extending the coverage of ecosystem, such as JD. COM, Alibaba etc. The second type is user-oriented companies, such as Xiaomi Home, they are using the channel capability to provide industry solutions and products which can satisfy the current market needs. The third type is the content-oriented companies. Internet music companies are good examples of this kind type, they cooperate with hardware manufacturer of products and business lines, with their own platform services and resources, and mainly build the "platform + content + terminal + application" on the basis of music as ecology to bring more users, contents and service resources. The last is ecosystem type, and Huawei Hi Link is included in this group, it plans to build smart home ecology to connect the core of the "people, vehicles, home" through opening its platform to other smart home players and cooperating with other fields of companies.

4 Results and Discussion

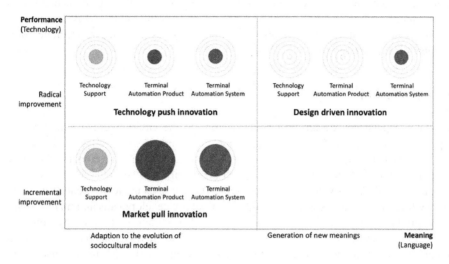

Fig. 3. The participants in different types of innovation.

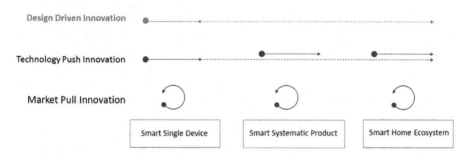

Fig. 4. Impaction of different innovation to smart home development.

There are two figures (Fig. 3 and Fig. 4), presenting the participants in different types of innovation and the impaction of different innovation to smart home development.

In current China's smart home market, smart single products still account for the majority in the markets. It is also a way that has been chosen by most Chinese smart home participants. And these products include TVs, air conditioners, smoke alarms, and so on. But what we can't deny is that smart home pioneers, like Haier, Xiaomi, and JD.COM, are being dedicated to smart system building. Those companies have the large scale of single product manufacturing ability and have been in the process of transferring traditional products like home appliances, security products and entertainment products into smart devices. The main obstacle for China's smart home players in the smart system building stages is the un-unified standard problem, because those smart products and systems are built separately by different companies, they have different rules and standards, then they cannot ensure smooth data exchange. While with more and more smart devices join the smart home system and unify together to share same rules and standards, those intelligent products will have the capability to communicate with each other, even though based on their individual status. In this way, the smart home market will continue its evolution toward machine to machine communication ecosystem [14].

5   Conclusion

This article puts the "design-driven innovation" in the environment of smart home, especially focusing on China's smart home environment. According to the above analysis, we can find a large gap between domestic and foreign developers. Currently the high-end market brand in China's market are mainly applied in luxurious residence project which the mass market cannot achieve. Those brands in the high-end market are mainly foreign developers who own higher technology developments and mature smart home products and systems. The middle-end market is mainly occupied by domestic well-known brands, such as Haier, Bochuang, Anjubao, etc., is relatively mature with integrating smart home system products. The low-end market is still in chaos with different qualities of products, which makes it difficult to form a complete set of system.

And one shortcoming that cannot be ignored of China's smart home industry is the immature market standardization. At present, the China's smart home products in market have been abundant and smart home technologies are also changing with each passing day. However, smart home is a new field without uniform industry standard, and as we can see many weaknesses exist in the products in markets commonly, such as poor compatibility, unstable operation and so on, which requires different manufacturers cooperate actively to establish uniform standards and promote the rapid development of the smart home industry.

In conclusion, smart home industry's development includes different innovation strategies. Some (like some technology-oriented companies) are trying to keep up with larger rivals in an intense technology race. Some (like Haier) are looking into broadly expand the application of the products and system. Design-driven innovation helps in different ways: Creating a distinctive product/systematic solution to break the smart home boundaries. And this kind type of innovation strategy is more suitable for most China's smart home developers in current economic context. For better performing design-driven innovation, companies need to have a clear understanding of their unique capabilities and disadvantages, which would bring different ways of performing design driven innovation.

References

1. Marikyan, D., Papagiannidis, S., Alamanos, E.: A systematic review of the smart home literature: a user perspective. Technol. Forecast. Soc. Chang. **138**, 139–154 (2019)

2. Gaikwad, P.P., Gabhane, J.P., Golait, S.S.: A survey based on Smart Homes system using Internet-of-Things. In: Proceedings of International Conference on Computation of Power, Energy Information and Communication (ICCPEIC), pp. 0330–335. IEEE, New York (2015)

3. Samuel, S.S.I.: A review of connectivity challenges in IoT-Smart Home. In: Proceedings of the 3rd MEC International Conference on Big Data and Smart City (ICBDSC), pp. 364–367. IEEE, Muscat (2016)

4. Kim, J.Y., Lee, H.J., Son, J.Y.: Smart home web of objects-based IoT management model and methods for home data mining. In: Proceedings of 17th Asia-Pacific Network Operations and Management Symposium APNOMS, pp. 327–331. IEEE. Busan (2015)

5. Satpathy, L., Mathew, A.: Technology to aid aging in place-new opportunities and challenges. VDM Verlag (2007)

6. Alam, M.R., Reaz, M.B.I., Ali, M.A.M.: A review of smart homes—past, present, and future. IEEE Trans. Syst. Man Cybern. Part C (Appl. Rev.) **42**(6), 1190–1203 (2012)

7. Lee, S.M., Olson, D.L.: Co-innovation: convergenomics, collaboration, and co-creation for organizational values. Manag. Decis. **50**(5), 817–831 (2012)

8. Verganti, R.: Design, meanings, and radical innovation: a metamodel and a research agenda*. J. Prod. Innov. Manag. **25**(5), 436–456 (2008)

9. Harper, R.: Inside the Smart Home. Springer, London (2006)

10. Verganti, R.: Design driven innovation: changing the rules of competition by radically innovating what things mean. Res.-Technol. Manag. **52**(7), 67–68 (2009)

11. Kortuem, G., Kawsar, F.: Market-based user innovation in the Internet of Things. In: Internet of Things (IOT), pp. 8. IEEE, Tokyo (2010)

12. De Goey, H., Hilletofth, P., Eriksson, L.: Design-driven innovation: making meaning for whom ? Des. J. **20**(sup1), 479–491 (2017)

13. Öberg, Å., Verganti, R.: Meaning - an unexplored path of innovation. Int. J. Innov. Manag. **2**(2), 77–92 (2014)

14. Holler, J., Tsiatsis, V., Mulligan, C.: From Machine-to-Machine to the Internet of Things: Introduction to a New Age of Intelligence. Academic Press, Waltham (2014)

Implementation of Text Classification Model Based on Recurrent Neural Networks

Ming-Shi Wang[(✉)] and Tsung Chieh Wen

Department of Engineering Science, National Cheng Kung University,
Tainan, Taiwan
{mswang, n97021104}@mail.ncku.edu.tw

Abstract. In this report, a deep learning network architecture, which combined with the architecture of convolutional neural network, the architecture of recurrent neural network is proposed and implemented to do the text classification with the pre-trained word vectors. The proposed method set the word vector be as a static lookup table without updating, and the network still can ignore the noise which caused by missing words. The experimental results show that the accuracy of this study is consistent with the accuracy of other studies. It is shown the feasibility of this architecture. And has the following advantages: the accuracy rate of this architecture is higher than that of recurrent neural network only; compared with the convolutional neural network, the accuracy results are more stable; and less epoch is used to get stable results. But the shortcoming of this proposed architecture is that the training time will consumed much time.

Keywords: Deep learning · Text classification · RNN · CNN

1 Introduction

Over the past years, users only can search and get the information from the website, but now the user can become an information provider. Many Internet users began to be willing and keen to share their views out, so there is a lot of text data on the Internet. These contents generated by the user often contains some opinions, evaluation, and other information. These messages can often be converted into valuable information, and be used by individuals or corporate groups. But the amount of text on the Internet is too big to be man-made to collect and analyze. So how to applying machine to help users to collect and analyze these texts is one of the important issue in the field of information capture in recent years.

If it is needed to apply machine automatically to get information from the huge amount of text messages, the first thing is to let the machine can input these texts as that reading by mankind, Natural language processing (NLP) technology is invented for this purpose. And over the last few years, deep learning models have achieved remarkable results in various fields—computer vision [1], speech recognition [2], et al. So nowadays more and more researchers began to use the deep learning model to solve the text classification, machine translation and other natural language processing problems.

© Springer Nature Singapore Pte Ltd. 2020
J. Shen et al. (Eds.): IC3 2019, CCIS 1227, pp. 54–61, 2020.
https://doi.org/10.1007/978-981-15-6113-9_7

In these research reports, the applications of recurrent neural network architecture to do Natural language processing [3, 4] could be beneficial to capture semantics of long texts. The advantage for applying recurrent neural network architecture to this theme is that it can better capture the context information. But the recurrent neural network architecture is a biased model, where later words are more dominant than earlier words. On the other hand, the convolutional neural network architecture is an unbiased model, but it is difficult to determine the window size. However, most of the deep learning architectures that are currently applied to text classification tasks are mostly selected as one of the convolutional neural networks or the recursive neural network as an infrastructure to perform various adjustments.

In 2013, Word2vec was created by a team of researchers led by Tomas Mikolov [5]. It has become the basic part of deep learning model in the field of natural language processing. So we propose a deep learning model, which combined with the architecture of convolutional neural network and the architecture of recurrent neural network. And use to complete the goal of text classification with the pre-trained word vector.

When applying the deep learning model to the natural language processing, the first problem to be faced is how to digitize the text data. The simplest representation is One-hot Representation that each vocabulary is a very long vector that is all zero values, except one dimension is marked as 1, and the dimension of the vector is equal to the number of words in the text data. But One-hot Representation will lead to the curse of dimensionality [6]. Another representation is the Distributed Representation proposed by Geoffrey Hintonin [7]. Use neural networks to converge the vector to a fixed and shorter vector. This representation of a word is called word embedding and is a real-valued vector and let us measure word relatedness by simply using the distance between two embedding vectors. Recent research shows that word embedding greatly alleviates the data sparsity problem [6] and pre-trained word embedding can capture meaningful syntactic and semantic regularities [8]. The model introduced by Kim [9], it is a slight variant of the convolutional neural network architecture. The particular idea in the model is to use multiple filters (with different window sizes) to get multiple features. Use the publicly available word2vec vectors that were trained on 100 billion words from Google News. The results suggest that the pre-trained vectors are good, and can be utilized across datasets. And Fine-tuning the pre-trained vectors for each task gives still further improvements.

The model proposed by [10] is a slight variant of the recurrent neural network architecture. They proposed a bi-directional recurrent neural network to capture the contexts of words. It combines a word with its left side and right side context to present the context of that word. The result shows that the performance of the proposed method can preserve longer contextual information and introduces less noise.

In this study, a deep learning model which combined with the architecture of convolutional neural network and the architecture of recurrent neural network is proposed for text classification.

2 Proposed Model

From the above discuss, we can find the recurrent neural network can keep the information in the vocabulary order and contact the longer distance context information. But the semantic features of the second half of the text have a greater impact on the recurrent neural network. The convolutional neural networks use the max-pooling layer to find the most useful vocabulary from the entire text, it is beneficial to represent the semantic of the entire text. But the performance of a convolutional neural networks is influenced by the window size. So in this study, we propose a deep learning model, which combined with the architecture of convolutional neural network and the architecture of recurrent neural network. Figure 1 shows the network architecture of our model.

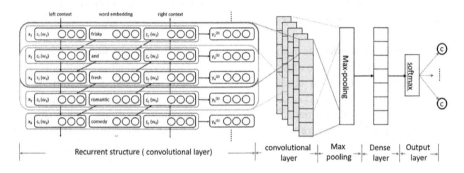

Fig. 1. The architecture of deep learning model for text classification

We define the input of this network is a document D, which is a sequence of words $w_1, w_2, ..., w_n$. $c_l(w_i)$ as the left context of word w_i, and $c_r(w_i)$ as the right context. Both $c_l(w_i)$ and $c_r(w_i)$ are dense vectors with $|c|$ real elements. The left side context $c_l(w_i)$ of word w_i are calculated according to Eq. (1), where $e(w_{i-1})$ is the word embedding of word w_{i-1}, which is a dense vector with $|e|$ real value elements. $c_l(w_{i-1})$ is the left side context of the previous word w_{i-1}. The left side context for the first word in any document uses the same shared parameters $c_l(w_1)$. $W^{(l)}$ and is a matrix that transforms the hidden layer into the next hidden layer. $W^{(sl)}$ is a matrix that is used to combine the semantic of the current word with the next word's left context. ϕ is a non-linear activation function For the right side context $c_r(w_i)$ is calculated in a similar manner, with replace the relative parameters $W^{(l)}$ and $W^{(sl)}$ to $W^{(r)}$ and $W^{(sr)}$, respectively, and as shown in Eq. (2). The right side context of the last word in a document share the parameter $c_r(w_n)$

$$c_l(w_i) = \phi\left(W^{(l)}c_l(w_{i-1}) + W^{(sl)}e(w_{i-1})\right) \tag{1}$$

$$c_r(w_i) = \phi\left(W^{(r)}c_r(w_{i+1}) + W^{(sr)}e(w_{i+1})\right) \tag{2}$$

In this study, the recurrent convolutional neural network proposed by [10], is adopted. The bidirectional Long Short-Term Memory layer (Bi-LSTM) is used to get the left side context, and the right side context of the text to capture the contextual information. If the word embedding of word w_i is $e(w_i)$, then we can combine the word w_i and its left side and right side context vectors to get the representation $x_i^{(2)}$ for word w_i.as shown in Eq. (3). Before send data to the next layer, we do a linear transformation on $x_i^{(2)}$ and apply the *tanh* activation function together, as shown in Eq. (4). We call this layer as Time Distributed-Dense layer. In this manner, we get the representation $y_i^{(2)}$ of word w_i, it represents an implicit semantic and may be better able to disambiguate the meaning of the word w_i.

$$x_i^{(2)} = [c_l(w_i); e(w_i); c_r(w_i)] \tag{3}$$

$$y_i^{(2)} = \tanh\left(W^{(2)}x_i^{(2)} + b^{(2)}\right) \tag{4}$$

In convolutional layer, the kernel is like a window to check words and produce a new feature, as shown in following Eq. 5 and 6, where ϕ is a non-linear function such as the hyperbolic tangent.

$$x_i^{(3)} = \left[y_{i-[win/2]}^{(2)}; \ldots; y_i^{(2)}; \ldots; y_{i+[win/2]}^{(2)}\right] \tag{5}$$

$$y_i^{(3)} = \phi\left(W^{(3)}x_i^{(3)} + b^{(3)}\right) \tag{6}$$

The pooling layer converts texts with various lengths into a fixed-length vector. With the pooling layer, we can capture the information throughout the entiretext. And we want to capture the most important feature—one with the highest value—for each feature map. So we apply a max-pooling layer, and use max-over-time pooling operation over the feature map to find the feature that having most influence as following Eq. 7.

$$y^{(4)} = max\left(y_i^{(3)}\right) \tag{7}$$

Then reassemble the relationship between features in the fully connected network, as shown in Eq. (8).

$$y^{(5)} = \phi\left(W^{(5)}y^{(4)} + b^{(5)}\right) \tag{8}$$

At last, like most of the classification tasks, we use softmax function to convert the output result into probabilities. Using $P(k|D, \theta)$ as shown in Eq. 9, to represent the probability of the document being class k.

$$y^{(6)} = W^{(6)}y^{(5)} + b^{(6)}$$

$$P(k|D, \theta) = \frac{\exp\left(y_i^{(6)}\right)}{\sum_{k=1}^{n} \exp\left(y_k^{(6)}\right)} \tag{9}$$

3   Experimental Environment Settings

The software development environment used for this study is Eclipse IDE, and the computer is equipped with Intel® Core ™ i5-6300HQ 2.8 GHz; 4 core CPU and 8 GB DDR4 memory. The system is designed in Java programming language and create deep learning model by Deeplearning4j. It is the first open-source distributed deep-learning library written for Java.

The word2vec vectors publicly available from https://code.google.com/archive/p/word2vec/ is used in this study. The dimensions of these vectors are 300. Words not present in the set of pre-trained words are initialized randomly. Four datasets are adopted to evaluate the proposed method, that are Movie Review Dataset (MR); Stanford Sentiment Treebank (SST); Question Classification Dataset (TREC); and The 20 news-groups dataset (20News). Table 1 gives the summary of the datasets, where C denotes the classes; Train/Test means the number of train/test set entries, the column max/min/avg means the maximum/minimum/average text length in training dataset, $|V_{rand}|$: Number of words present in the set of randomly initialized word vectors. We preprocess the dataset by use the Stanford Tokenizer to obtain the tokens. Except MR dataset, others have been previously separated into training and testing sets. So we take 90% of all sentences in MR dataset to training, and others for testing. And limited by memory size, we truncate all sentences of all datasets to 256 words, if the length of sentence greater than 256.

Table 1.   Test datasets information

Data	C	Train/Test	max/min/avg	$|V_{rand}|$
20News	4	7876/5244	256/17/189	28727
MR	2	9594/1068	58/1/21	1757
SST	5	8544/2210	51/1/19	433
TREC	6	5452/500	37/2/9	464

We choose one set of hyper-parameters for all dataset. We set the learning rate α as 0.01, The L2 regularization term is set to 0.001, dropout is applied to the output layer with p = 0.5. The size of the word vectors as $|e| = 300$, so we set the size of LSTM layer and Bi-LSTM layer as 300. The size of Time Distributed-Dense layer is 450, and the number of convolutional feature maps is 300. Final we set the size of output layer as 200.

We use DL4j to implement the same architecture as the CNN-static architecture in the literature [9], and call it for CNN-dl4j. And the same way, we implement the same architecture as the RCNN architecture in the literature [10], and call it for RCNN-dl4j, and call our model for RCC.

4   Results and Discussion

Table 2 shows the experimental results that the accuracy of this study is consistent with the accuracy of other studies. It is proved the feasibility of this architecture. From the experiment results, it is found the proposed model is made a slightly better accuracy in SST dataset. But in other dataset, the CNN-dl4j architecture based on convolutional neural network achieves the highest accuracy, then the RCC architecture proposed for this study to obtain the second highest accuracy, and the architecture that get the lowest accuracy is RCNN-dl4j architecture that based on the recurrent neural network.

Table 2. Results comparisons for accuracy (%)

Model	20News	MR	SST	TREC
CNN-dl4j	96.2	79.2	45.8	92.8
RCNN-dl4j	93.2	78.4	45.9	86.4
RCC	94.2	79.0	46.6	90.8

We show the accuracy curve of discussed three structures for training dataset of the MR dataset as in Fig. 2. After observing the chart, it can be found that the proposed architecture uses fewer epochs to starting the converge. The following advantages can be summarized from the experimental results (Fig. 3):

1. The accuracy rate of this architecture is higher than that of recurrent neural network
2. Compared with the convolution neural network, the accuracy results are more stable
3. Use less epoch to get stable results.

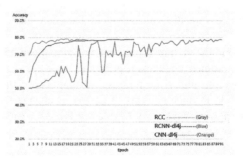

Fig. 2. The accuracy comparison for MR dataset

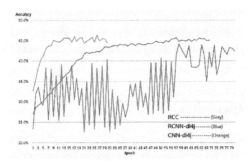

Fig. 3. The accuracy comparison for SST dataset

For comparison the required training time, it is found that the proposed method consumes a lot of time. Table 3 shows the result of training time for each Epoch for each model discussed architecture. The unit of measure is minutes

Table 3. Compare the training time.

Model	20News	SST	MR	TREC
CNN-dl4j	9.2	0.9	1.9	0.6
RCNN-dl4j	11.2	1.8	2.0	0.6
RCC	43.5	5.8	8.7	2.5

5   Conclusions

This aims of this study it to implement a deep learning network which combined with the architectures of both convolutional neural network and recurrent neural network. and evaluate its performance. Through the experiment, it is shown that the proposed method is feasibility. But it is also found the limitations. So, in the future, the following issues can be improved:

1. Pre-train the word vector: we can use the Skip-gram model to pre-train the word embedding. To make sure the vocabulary of dataset is also existed in the word vector table.
2. Add a new channel in the architecture, the new channel can add new word to word vector table and fine-tuned via backpropagation.
3. Modify this architecture under the premise of maintaining the recurrent convolutional neural network. Reduce neurons of LSTM or change the action of the convolution layer and pooling layer. Try to rule out the error caused by random word vector.

References

1. Krizhevsky, A., Sutskever, I., Hinton, G.E.: Image net classification with deep convolutional neural networks. In: Proceedings of the 25th International Conference on Neural Information Processing Systems, Lake Tahoe, Nevada, USA, 3–6 December 2012, pp. 1097–1105 (2012)
2. Graves, A., Mohamed, A.-r., Hinton, G.: Speech recognition with deep recurrent neural networks. In: IEEE International Conference on Acoustics, Speech and Signal Processing (2013). https://doi.org/10.1109/icassp.2013.6638947
3. Lopez, M.M., Kalita, J.: Deep learning applied to NLP (2017). https://arxiv.org/pdf/1703.03091.pdf
4. Brownlee, J.: 7 Applications of deep learning for natural language processing. In: Deep Learning for Natural Language Processing, 20 September 2017. https://machinelearningmastery.com/applications-of-deep-learning-for-natural-language-processing/
5. Mikolov, T., Chen, K., Corrado, G., Dean, J.: Efficient estimation of word representations in vector space. In: Proceedings of the International Conference on Learning Representations (ICLR 2013), Scottsdale, AZ, USA, 2–4 May 2013. https://arxiv.org/pdf/1301.3781.pdf
6. Bengio, Y., Ducharme, R., Vincent, P., Jauvin, C.: A neural probabilistic language model. J. Mach. Learn. Res. **3**, 1137–1155 (2013)
7. Hinton, G.E.: Learning distributed representations of concepts. In: Proceedings of the Eighth Annual Conference of the Cognitive Science Society, Amherst, Massachusetts, USA, 15–17 August 1986, pp. 46–61 (1986)
8. Mikolov, T., Sutskever, I., Chen, K., Corrado, G., Dean, J.: Distributed representations of words and phrases and their compositionality. In: Proceedings of the 26th International Conference on Neural Information Processing Systems, Harrah's Lake Tahoe, Stateline, Nevada, USA, 5–10 December 2013, pp. 3111–3119 (2013)
9. Kim, Y.: Convolutional neural networks for sentence classification. In: Proceedings of the 2014 Conference on Empirical Methods in Natural Language Processing (EMNLP), Doha, Qatar, 25–29 October 2014, pp. 1746–1751 (2014)
10. Lai, S., Xu, L., Liu, K., Zhao, J.: Recurrent convolutional neural networks for text classification. In: Proceedings of the Twenty-Ninth AAAI Conference on Artificial Intelligence, Hyatt Regency in Austin, Texas, USA, 25–30 January 2015, pp. 2267–2273 (2015)

Predictive Maintenance of Water Purification Unit for Smart Factories

Tsung-Yuan Chang[1]([✉]), Wei-Ting Cho[1], Shau-Yin Tseng[2],
Yeni Ouyang[3], and Chin-Feng Lai[1]

[1] National Cheng Kung University, No. 1, Daxue Road, Tainan 70101, Taiwan
`n96071172@gs.ncku.edu.tw`
[2] ITRI/ICL, 195, Sec. 4, Chung Hsing Road, Chutung, Hsinchu 31040, Taiwan
[3] Smart System Institute, Institute for Information Industry, 7F., No. 133, Sec. 4,
Minsheng E. Road, Taipei 105, Taiwan

Abstract. In recent years, the applications of the smart factory are very popular. Predictive maintenance is one of the issues. Some research achieved the goal of predictive maintenance with Artificial Intelligence (AI). Here we focus on the local scrubber (LSR) system, a water purification and recycling system. This paper proposed a machine learning model to solve predictive maintenance problem. The device learns the pattern of input data through the RNN model and classify the different state of device. We can know the current situation of the device and judge whether it is about to be replaced. As far as we know, this is the first predictive task maintenance in the LSR system and has an accuracy of 84% in the datasets of different years. The smart factory will come true while the LSR system can be reduce cost, manpower, time and money with predictive maintenance.

Keywords: Predictive maintenance · Recurrent neural network · Water purification unit

1 Introduction

With the rapid development of machine learning, Internet of Things (IoT) and cloud computing, the smart factory become the mainstream of the industry in the future. In order to make the smart factory come true, it is necessary to connect the various devices of the factory into the network for not only obtaining data from the various devices. When getting the data from the devices, we can visualize and analyze all kinds of data inside the factory. Then we can get the relationship between devices and integrate different devices to the system. This not only improve the quality of factory management and capabilities, but also greatly reduce the management costs, including time, manpower and money.

This paper proposed a machine learning model for predictive maintenance in the local scrubber (LSR) system, a water recovery purification and recycling system. We got the data of LSR system in the past two years from the cooperative company, using the machine learning algorithm as a decision-making method for RO units in the LSR system. With our method, we expect to address predictive maintenance issues in the

© Springer Nature Singapore Pte Ltd. 2020
J. Shen et al. (Eds.): IC3 2019, CCIS 1227, pp. 62–70, 2020.
https://doi.org/10.1007/978-981-15-6113-9_8

smart factory. Comparing to traditional analysis processes, we replace human judgement to machine learning algorithm. We train the Recurrent Neural Network (RNN) model with past two years data. After training, we can feed new data in our model, and it can predict the results based on learning data's pattern. According to the predicted results, engineers decide whether replace the Reverse Osmosis (RO) Unit. Besides our model can also estimate when the components need to be replaced in the future. This information can use to schedule replacement automatically and the other applications in the smart factory.

2 Related Work

2.1 LSR System

The experiments in this paper focus on the local scrubber (LSR) system commonly found in fabs, which is a recycling system that specializes in wastewater generated during the process. We show the procedure of wastewater process in Fig. 1. The wastewater generated in the process contains ammonia and fluorine, and stored in the buffer tank. After being treated layer by layer, the RO unit will filter out the concentrated waste liquid to the HF buffer tank, and then the clean water will be recycled to the LSS Supply tank. The function of the RO unit in the system is to recover clean water and separate waste. Because it needs to continuously filter a large amount of polluted water caused by the process, it is necessary to replace the filter core regularly to avoid problems in the process water quality. This is also our main focus, as discussed in Subsect. 2.3 below on how to combine predictive maintenance and LSR System.

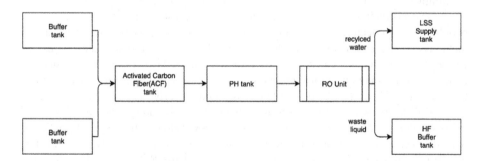

Fig. 1. LSR system flow diagram.

2.2 Predictive Maintenance

Predictive maintenance is a problem that has arisen in recent years. Because once the important equipment in the factory is damaged and cannot be repaired in a short time, it may cause the entire production line to stop. If we have the better predictive maintenance technology, we can improve the productivity of the factory and replace the equipment that is going to be broken soon, creating more profits for the company. This topic is help to the development of smart factories. Many people are also beginning to use different methods to solve predictive maintenance problems in a variety of different applications. For example, predicting the Slitting Machine to identify possible faults and quality defects [1]. Compare the several machine learning methods applied to the predictive maintenance of the water cooling system of the hydropower station [2]. Convolution neural network is used to monitor the operation of the photovoltaic panel, and the abnormal deviation between the predicted and actual power curves can be used to determine the fault panel [3]. Based on a data set of turbofan engines from the NASA database to predict the remaining useful life of the aircraft turbofan engine by machine learning model [4]. The use of a simple classifier based on the fiber-optic sensing network of the railway health monitoring system can promote predictive maintenance of the railway [5]. These examples show the importance of predictive maintenance for our life.

2.3   Predictive Maintenance and LSTM-RNN

The earliest conceptual of recurrent neural network (RNN) was proposed by Elman, J. L. in [6]. The main idea is how to find a specific pattern in the time series. RNN puts timing problems into the neural network, but the simple RNN can't solve the problem of gradient vanishing or exploding [7] with the number of recursions, making it difficult to capture long-term associations. The above problem can be solved by combining Long Short-Term Memory Unit [8]. RNN is one of supervised learning [9]. We need labels and input data for training. Model tries to develop dependences between input data and labels, engineers provide the correct answer, on some question.

Unlike traditional feedforward neural networks, RNN are sequence-based models. It can establish the temporal correlation between previous information and the current environment. That is to say, the decision made by the RNN at time step t − 1 may affect the decision it will make at a later time step t. Because of this characteristic, many people in the application environment for predictive maintenance use the LSTM-RNN method to achieve. For example, applies LSTM to the large-scale data processing engine Spark to predict the current state of the engine [10]. Establish a system to maintain the housing and utility infrastructure to achieve fault detection and estimate the remaining life of the component [11]. Proposed an early fault detection technique for hard disk drives that utilizes LSTM network to predict long-term and short-term interval failures [12]. We use the RO Unit in the LSR system as the target of predictive maintenance, because some of the RO Unit source data is periodic. These characteristics of the RNN are ideal for predicting the state of the RO Unit. We can use the LSTM-RNN network for a series of historical data to predict and monitor device states.

3   Method

3.1   Classification

In the classification, we divide the original data into three types of labels, which are normal, upcoming replacement and during the replacement. However, during the replacement of the RO unit, a large amount of abnormal data will be generated.

Because the pumping unit shut down temporarily, no water comes in. Therefore, in the pre-processing, first we will remove the data of the whole day during the replacement of the RO unit, to avoid affecting the machine for learning. Only keep the normal and upcoming replacement categories for classification. The upcoming replacement is classified as three days before the replacement of the RO unit, and the rest is classified as normal.

3.2 Dataset

The experimental data got from different components' sensor in the LSR system, like RO unit's water input and output values or tank's water quality etc. The 75% data of 7 different RO units in 2017 are used as training data, and the 25% data are used as test data. To compare adaptive in different years, we used the data in the first quarter of 2018 to validate the model. The time interval produces a data every 20 min. After discussing with the engineer, there are 4 weights for training, including conductivity (CIT), pressure differential (PIT), inlet pressure (IP) and influent of the fluoridation (IF). These weights have a cyclical and stable trend.

Before training, in order to prevent different weights from being distributed in different ranges, the data can be characterized, the features must be normalization. We chose to use the MinMaxScaler to scale the distribution of the dataset's range between 0 and 1. Because the weight of the scale is very large, the influence will be huge. After normalization, the feature scale will be controlled within the same range. It can effectively improve the convergence speed of machine learning and avoid the deviation of machine learning results. Its formula is as follows:

$$X' = \frac{x - \min_x}{\max_x - \min_x} \tag{1}$$

$$X'' = X' \times (mx - mi) + mi \tag{2}$$

In the formula (1) max is a series of maximum values; min is a series of minimum values. In the formula (2) Xuu is the final result, and mx, mi are preset values for the specified interval, mx is 1 and mi is 0. The range can be adjusted.

3.3 Data Analysis

In the data analysis, we use Confusion Matrix, a common standard used to judge whether the model is good or bad. The two columns in Table 1 represent the positive or negative of the actual situation, and the two columns represent the positive or negative of the predicted situation.

In addition, when we analyze the accuracy of the model, we will mainly consider two values at the same time. One is the overall accuracy, which is referred to as Acc (accuracy), and the other is the accuracy that should be replaced and predicted to be replaced. It is referred to as TPR (True Positive Rate). The following are the formulas for the two accuracy:

$$Acc = \frac{TP + TN}{Total\ Number} \tag{3}$$

$$TPR = \frac{TP}{TP + FN} \tag{4}$$

The higher the Acc does not necessarily mean the better the precautionary maintenance issue, because the main purpose of predictive maintenance is to be able to replace it correctly when it is predicted that it needs to be replaced. So we must also pay attention to the accuracy of TPR. In such issues, the time points that need to be replaced are lower in the data set, and most of the time is normal. Therefore, the accuracy must to avoid the tendency that all predictions are normal, it leads to the model with a high Acc.

Table 1. Confusion matrix.

Predicted	Actual		
	Actual condition positive	Actual condition negative	Actual condition all
Predicted condition positive	TP (True Positive)	FP (False Positive) Type I error	TP + FP
Predicted condition negative	FN (False Negative) Type II error	TN (True Negative)	FN + TN
Predicted condition all	TP + FN	FP + TN	TP + TN + FP + FN Total number

3.4   Model

Our model construction is using the tensorflow framework. The input size is 1 * 4 and training with Batch Normalization [13], where the Batch size is 1000 * 4. The LSTM unit numbers in the RNN are set to five. The model architecture is one layer of LSTM-RNN, and the activation function uses tanh preset by BasicLSTMCell. The output of each LSTM Cells is followed by one layer of fully connected layer and the activation function uses relu. The optimizer uses AdamOptimizer and the learning rate is 0.001. The loss function uses softmax_cross_entropy. Finally, two classification results are output by the model (Table 2 and Fig. 2).

Table 2. Setting of model layers.

Layer	Parameter	Activation	Output
Input layer			1 * 4
RNN with LSTM layer	num_units = 5	tanh	8 * 16
Dense layer		relu	4 * 2
Output layer			2

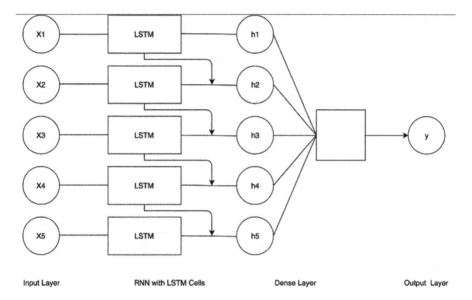

Fig. 2. RNN model architecture.

4   Result

The experiment is divided into two parts, the first is to train our model, and the second is to compare with other machine learning models. In the first experiment, we implement the model of the above design. Under the above data set, from the perspective of Fig. 3, the loss can still continue to decline. But in order to prevent overfitting [14] in training, then generate models that cannot be generalized. We can use the mechanism of early stopping [15] to converge early and solve this problem. In addition, it can be seen from Fig. 4 that due to the disparity between normal and upcoming replacement which are classification of data, the machine tends to predict normal in the early iterations. After about 3500 iterations, the features of the upcoming replacement were learned and the TPR accuracy continued to rise until about 5,000 iterations. From Table 3 both Acc and TPR are higher than 80% in the test data. The results show that this model learns the features of four weights from the LSR System data set. In the second experiment, this model is more adaptive than the common machine learning methods like K-NN and decision tree on the same data set (training and testing data from different years), and it can avoid the problem of overfitting. We compared these three models, and detailed experimental results could refer to Table 4. Although K-NN and decision tree have a good model of training in the 2017 data set, they are not general purpose models in the first quarter of 2018 data set.

Table 3. For this model, the confusion matrix of testing data has an Acc of 84.3% and a TPR of 83.61%.

Predicted	Actual		
	True	False	All
True	301	6980	7281
False	59	37611	37670
All	360	44591	44951

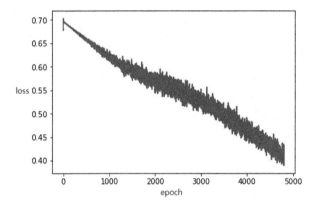

Fig. 3. Loss in training, the X-axis are the number of iterations, and the Y-axis is the loss value.

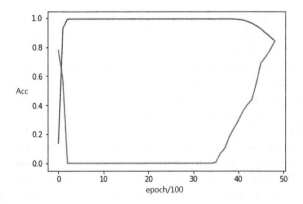

Fig. 4. The blue line is Acc, the orange line is TPR, and the accuracy of the test data set is recorded every 100 epochs. The X-axis is the iteration number unit is 100 times, and the Y-axis is the accuracy rate. (Color figure online)

Table 4. For the same training set, we can compare the different models' accuracy in the first quarter of 2018 dataset in this experiment.

Model	K-NN	Decision tree	LSTM
Acc	0.66	0.52	0.81

5   Conclusion and Discussion

We can get preliminary predictive maintenance results from the above experiments, the results are not bad but still have the enhanced space. We found that there are many problems that need to be overcome. In view of these problems, we visualized the original data set and found that the average inlet pressure of 2017 and 2018's values are very different when the upcoming replacement. This may affect the outcome of the training, so we may consider adjusting or removing some of the standard unstable weights. In addition, some human factors such as replacement time will be delayed by external factors, and there is also the time error that each engineer decides to replace. These reasons may affect the results of the model. If we can get a more accurate label of data set for training, it will help to improve the accuracy.

In the future work, we want to start with the data pre-processing and remove the noise from the original data. In fact, the data set contains some noise, such as the signal is suddenly kept at a low level for a period of time, or pumping interval caused continuous high and low data. We may be based on the knowledge of the system engineers to find a more suitable filter for this data set or better way to remove noise. Then we can also try some more complex model architectures, like adding layers and nodes. Finally, the actual trained model is put into the LSR system, and the devices are monitored in real time. With the prediction information, we want to add scheduling functions in the future, and automatically arrange replacement order and time to achieve the goal of the true smart factory predictive maintenance.

References

1. Kanawaday, A., Sane, A.: Machine learning for predictive maintenance of industrial machines using IoT sensor data. In: 2017 8th IEEE International Conference on Software Engineering and Service Science (ICSESS), pp. 87–90 (2017)
2. Xayyasith, S., Promwungkwa, A., Ngamsanroaj, K.: Application of machine learning for predictive maintenance cooling system in Nam Ngum-1 hydropower plant. In: 2018 16th International Conference on ICT and Knowledge Engineering (ICT&KE), pp. 1–5 (2018)
3. Huuhtanen, T., Jung, A.: Predictive maintenance of photovoltaic panels via deep learning. In: 2018 IEEE Data Science Workshop, DSW 2018 – Proceedings, pp. 66–70 (2018)
4. Mathew, V., Toby, T., Singh, V., Rao, B.M., Kumar, M.G.: Prediction of remaining useful lifetime (RUL) of turbofan engine using machine learning. In: 2017 IEEE International Conference on Circuits and Systems (ICCS), pp. 306–311 (2017)
5. Tam, H., Lee, K., Liu, S., Cho, L., Cheng, K.: Intelligent optical fibre sensing networks facilitate shift to predictive maintenance in railway systems. In: 2018 International Conference on Intelligent Rail Transportation (ICIRT), pp. 1–4 (2018)

6. Elman, J.L.: Finding structure in time. Cogn. Sci. **14**, 179–211 (1990)
7. Bengio, Y., Simard, P., Frasconi, P.: Learning long-term dependencies with gradient descent is difficult. IEEE Trans. Neural Netw. **5**, 157–166 (1994)
8. Hochreiter, S., Schmidhuber, J.: Long short-term memory. Neural Comput. **9**, 1735–1780 (1997)
9. Kotsiantis, S.B.: Supervised machine learning: a review of classification techniques (2007)
10. Aydin, O., Guldamlasioglu, S.: Using LSTM networks to predict engine condition on large scale data processing framework. In: 2017 4th International Conference on Electrical and Electronics Engineering, ICEEE 2017, pp. 281–285 (2017)
11. Kovalev, D., Shanin, I., Stupnikov, S., Zakharov, V.: Data mining methods and techniques for fault detection and predictive maintenance in housing and utility infrastructure. In: Proceedings - 2018 International Conference on Engineering Technologies and Computer Science, EnT 2018, pp. 47–52 (2018)

Cognitive City Theory, Modeling and Simulation

An Efficient Search Economics Based Algorithm for Urban Traffic Light Scheduling

Jian-Ting Liao and Ming-Chao Chiang[✉]

Department of Computer Science and Engineering,
National Sun Yat-sen University, Kaohsiung 80424, Taiwan
mcchiang@cse.nsysu.edu.tw

Abstract. Instead of building more traffic infrastructures, developing a better solution for traffic light scheduling is probably the fastest and most money-saving way for improving the traffic condition or solving the traffic problem. This paper presents a novel metaheuristic algorithm, called search economics for traffic light scheduling (SE-TLS), for urban traffic light scheduling with two goals; namely, maximizing the number of vehicles reaching the destination and minimizing the trip time they take. One of the characteristics of SE-TLS is that it is not easy to get stuck in a local optimum, so it can continue to find better solutions during the convergence process. The traffic simulator, named Simulation of Urban Mobility (SUMO), was used to verify the performance of SE-TLS by applying it to the traffic scenarios of three cities. The experimental results show that SE-TLS outperforms all the other algorithms evaluated in this paper in all cases, thus implying that it provides a better traffic light scheduling for effectively improving the traffic congestion problem.

Keywords: Metaheuristic algorithm · Search economics · Traffic light scheduling

1 Introduction

The boom of automotive industry in the past century has witnessed the explosive increase in the number of vehicles in all the cities around the world. This eventually comes along with many problems, such as traffic congestion, traffic safety, and air pollution. Overall, the traffic condition around the world is getting worse and worse because there are way too many traffic flows. Although the traditional fixed-time traffic light scheduling can be used for controlling the traffic congestion, it is still not efficient enough in handling the load of heavy traffic flow in cities today. Developing a "good solution" for traffic light scheduling is a possible way to mitigate the loading of the traffic, which has attracted the attention of many researchers from different disciplines [2, 12]. These studies also show that vehicular ad hoc networks (VANETs) play a critical role in managing traffic lights. Although VANETs and relevant technologies are good at analyzing real-time data, the hardware equipments for such a real-time system are expensive; therefore, it may not be a suitable traffic control strategy for cities. How to develop a better strategy for traffic light scheduling has then become a promising research topic in recent years. Several recent studies [3–6, 9] considered the traffic light

© Springer Nature Singapore Pte Ltd. 2020
J. Shen et al. (Eds.): IC3 2019, CCIS 1227, pp. 73–83, 2020.
https://doi.org/10.1007/978-981-15-6113-9_9

scheduling as an optimization problem and attempted to use metaheuristic algorithms as a method to solve this problem. For example, [3] used harmony search for urban traffic light scheduling problem to reduce the total traffic delay. Both [4] and [9] used the artificial bee colony algorithm to improve the traffic congestion problem. In [5] and [6], particle swarm optimization was used to make the traffic flow smooth.

The search mechanism of most metaheuristic algorithms may trend to a particular region at later iterations during the convergence process, which may eventually degrade their search ability; thus, there is still plenty of room for the improvement of the metaheuristic algorithms. To solve this problem, in this paper, an efficient metaheuristic algorithms, search economics (SE) [11], for traffic light scheduling problem will be presented to mitigate the traffic congestion problem (SE-TLS). The main contributions of this paper can be summarized as follows: (1) This paper adjusts some mechanisms of the original SE for optimizing traffic light scheduling problem; namely, the way the solutions are encoded, the mutation mechanism in the transition operator, and the way the expected values are calculated. (2) The experimental results show that SE-TLS output-forms all the other algorithms compared in this paper for reducing the traffic congestion for all different cities. (3) The traffic light scheduling obtained by SE-TLS can effectively maximize the number of vehicles reaching their destinations and minimize the total trip time of all vehicles.

The remainder of the paper is organized as follows. Section 2 first defines the traffic light scheduling problem and the objective function of traffic light scheduling problem for this study. Then, a brief review of methods for traffic light scheduling is given. Section 3 provides the concept and details of the SE-TLS, which contain the encoding of solutions of traffic light scheduling problem. Section 4 begins with the simulation environment, followed by the comparisons between SE-TLS and other algorithms for traffic light scheduling problem. Finally, Sect. 5 gives the conclusion and some future work of this research.

2   Related Work

2.1   Traffic Light Scheduling Problem

A good solution for the cycle or phase time of traffic lights [12] will make the traffic better because the fixed-time traffic lights are obviously unable to handle heavy traffic flows in a city. That is why it can be considered as an optimization problem, called the traffic light scheduling problem. Each traffic light scheduling problem has a different objective function, depending on what the study wants to achieve. For example, [13] proposed an intersection economic evaluation model as the objective function, which considers three factors: the cost of exhaust pollutants, the cost of fuel, and the cost of traffic delays. The study described herein is aimed to optimize traffic light scheduling by simultaneously minimizing these three factors.

In this paper, the objective function of traffic light scheduling problem is as defined in [6]. One of the objectives of this problem is to maximize the number of vehicles reaching their destinations. Another objective is to minimize the total trip time of vehicles reaching their destinations. With these two objectives and as far as this study is concerned, the objective function is defined as

$$F(s) = \frac{\sum_{v=0}^{V} j_v(s) + \sum_{v=0}^{V+C} w_v(s) + C(s) \cdot S_t}{V^2(s) + Cr}, \tag{1}$$

where s is the solution (which is a vector), V is the number of vehicles reaching their destinations, C is the number of vehicles not reaching their destinations, j_v is the total trip time of vehicles reaching their destinations, w_v is the total stop and wait time of all the vehicles, S_t is the simulation time. Besides, $C \cdot S_t$ represents the penalty time for vehicles that are unable to reach their destinations after taking all the simulation time. Since the main goal is to maximize the number of vehicles reaching their destinations, V^2 is used to increase its priority in the function. C_r is the balanced number of colors in all the traffic phases. The purpose of C_r is to allow more vehicles to circulate in the states with more green lights and fewer vehicles to pass in the states with more red lights. The ratio of colors in each phase of all the traffic light programs (tlLogic) can be defined as

$$C_r = \sum_{n=0}^{tIL} \sum_{h=0}^{ph} d_{n,h} \cdot \left(\frac{G_{n,h}}{R_{n,h}}\right), \tag{2}$$

where $G_{n,h}$ is the number of green lights in the h-th phase of the n-th tlLogic, $R_{n,h}$ is the number of red lights in the h-th phase of the n-th tlLogic, $d_{n,h}$ is the phase duration in the h-th phase of the n-th tlLogic. To avoid $G_{n,h}$ from being divided by 0, the minimum value of $R_{n,h}$ is 1.

2.2   The Traffic Light Scheduling Methods

Several methods have been presented for solving the traffic light scheduling problem in recent years based on different perspectives. Feng et al. [2] presented a real-time adaptive traffic light control algorithm in which data collected from the connected vehicles are used to minimize the total vehicle delay and the queue length. Their results showed that if the traffic demand is high, minimizing the total vehicle delay is a suitable objective function for reducing the congestion; on the contrary, minimizing the queue length is more suitable. McKenney and White [10] proposed an algorithm that uses sensor devices at intersections to control the traffic signals within a realistic traffic simulation in the city of Ottawa, Ontario. More precisely, the sensor devices are used to detect the incoming and outgoing vehicles to calculate the number of vehicles on the road so as to determine the green light time at intersections. The results showed that adaptive traffic signals will increase the average vehicle speed within the simulation by 6.58% compared to fixed-time traffic signals.

Since it may not be able to develop an integrated solution for traffic light scheduling problem based on only the information of intersections without considering the traffic flow of the overall city, some recent studies have attempted to use metaheuristic algorithms that would also take into account traffic flows of a city in solving the traffic

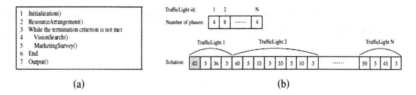

Fig. 1. (a) Outline of the SE-TLS and (b) Encoding of a solution.

light scheduling problem. Gao et al. [4] used an improved artificial bee colony algorithm (ABC) to solve the traffic light scheduling problem in urban areas in which three different local search strategies are used to improve the new solutions generated by ABC. They pointed out that ABC with local search method will provide a better performance than other algorithms. In [8], the enhanced Biham, Middleton, and Levine (EBML) model based on the real urban road networks and the timing scheduling optimization algorithm (TSO) based on the quantum particle swarm optimization were proposed for the traffic light scheduling. Hu et al. in this study used TSO for the traffic light scheduling in EBML model by adjusting the time-span values in a one-dimensional time-span vector. The proposed method gives the best performance in both different time periods and different number of vehicles compared to other algorithms. Garcia-Nieto et al. [6] used the particle swarm optimization (PSO) to solve the traffic light scheduling problem within two simulation maps based on Rivadavia Square, Bahía Blanca and Alameda Avenue, Málaga. The final results showed that PSO has the best performance in two goals: maximizing the number of vehicles that reach their destinations and minimizing the overall trip time.

3   The Proposed Algorithm

3.1   Search Economics for the Traffic Light Scheduling Problem (SE-TLS)

The basic idea of SE can be regarded as the investment for different goods in the market. The concept of SE is to reduce redundant investment in highly invested markets and to invest in least invested markets, as the least invested markets have higher possibilities to get better rewards. In SE, investment represents search and market represents region. The solution space is divided into a certain number of sub-spaces (regions), and the searchers determine the search direction based on the expected value of each region (high expected value represents high potential) rather than the quality of the known solutions. This prevents the searchers from over searching and getting stuck in some regions so that they have more opportunities to find better solutions in other regions.

Figure 1a gives an outline of SE-TLS. Similar to the other SE-based algorithms, the SE-TLS also consists of four operators: Initialization(), ResourceArrangement(), VisionSearch(), and MarketingSurvey(). Here, we first introduce the encoding of SE-TLS, and then discuss the four operators in detail later.

Encoding. Figure 1b shows how solutions of SE-TLS are encoded, by using two vectors the first of which encodes the number of phases while the second of which encodes the duration of phases of all the N traffic lights. Also, all the durations are required to be an integer in the range of 5 to 60 like the encoding way of [6].

Initialization(). The parameters of SE-TLS will be initialized by this operator, and the searchers s_i will be randomly generated in the solution space.

ResourceArrangement(). This operator is responsible for assigning searchers to regions and generating a certain number of samples m_{jk} in each region r_j. In general, s_i will be evenly distributed to all regions because we assume that each region has the same potential at the very beginning of the search in this paper. After the first iteration, s_i will be reassigned to r_j based on the potential. The value of the first element of s_i and m_{jk} will be limited to the segment that matches the characteristics of r_j.

VisionSearch(). This operator is used to generate new candidate samples v^i_{jk} and determine the search directions for searchers; it consists of three sub-operators: Transition(), ExpectedValue(), VisionSelection(). The Transition() operator will exchange information between s_i and m_{jk} to generate v^i_{jk}, by using the crossover operator while the mutation operator will also be used to adjust v^i_{jk}. More precisely, the one-point crossover is used for crossover while the mutation operator regenerate the random values using 2% of the problem size because a small change is less significant in traffic light scheduling problem. Once v^i_{jk} is generated, the value of the first element must be checked to see if it matches the characteristics of the region. If it is not, the value of this element should be regenerated.

The ExpectedValue() operator is used to calculate the expected value of each searcher for each region. The searcher will get the information to distinguish which region has high effect of investment based on the expected value. The expected value e_{ij} is defined as follows:

$$e_{ij} = T_j V^i_j M_j, \tag{3}$$

where T_j denotes the degree of region development, V^i_j the quality of new investments, M_j the best experience of investments in the past. They are defined as follows:

$$T_j = \frac{t^b_j}{t^a_j}, \tag{4}$$

where T_j is the ratio of t^b_j to t^a_j; t^a_j the number of times the j-th region has been invested so far; and t^b_j the number of times the j-th region has not been invested so far. If region j has been searched in this iteration, t^a_j will be increased by one; otherwise, t^a_j will be reset to one, to make T_j a smaller value. On the other hand, t^b_j will be increased by one when region j has not been searched; otherwise, t^b_j will be reset to one. In this case, T_j will be made a larger value. V^i_j in the expected value is used to evaluate the potential of the searcher s_i moving to region r_j which is defined as

$$V_j^i = \frac{\sum_{k=1}^{w} f(v_{jk}^i)}{u}, \tag{5}$$

where f is the objective function, V_j^i is the average of the objective values to show the quality of new candidate samples, w is the number of samples in each region, and u is the number of new candidate samples in each region. To reduce the excess influence of V_j^i on e_{ij}, V_j^i will be normalized to be a value in the range between 0 to 1 here, $V_j^i/\Sigma_{i=0}^{g}\Sigma_{j=0}^{h} V_j^i$. Moreover, g is the total number of searchers, and h is the total number of regions). Since the traffic light scheduling problem is a minimization problem, $1 - (V_j^i/\Sigma_{i=0}^{g}\Sigma_{j=0}^{h} V_j^i)$ is used in this paper where a smaller objective value represents the higher potential. Finally, M_j is used to provide the information to depict the best so far solution in each region, which is defined as

$$M_j = \frac{f(r_j^b)}{\sum_{j=1}^{h} f(m_j)}, \tag{6}$$

where M_j is the ratio of the objective value of the best sample in j-th region to the objective value of all the samples. For the minimization problem, $1 - M_j$ is used in this paper. The VisionSelection() operator will reassign each searcher to a region that has higher potential in terms of the expected value and it will be updated by the best sample in the region. However, it is possible that some searchers may select the same region and are updated by using the same best sample. Moreover, searchers will gradually resemble samples, thus falling into a local optimum at later iterations. To prevent searchers from selecting the same region too early, thus falling into a local optimum, the parameter num player is used to determine how many regions will be selected instead of all the regions.

MarketingSurvey() This operator will update the information of region (t_j^a and t_j^b) and record the best solution found by the searchers.

3.2   The Implementation of SE-TLS to SUMO

A SUMO [1] program can be developed to test the new traffic control strategy, which is basically composed of two xml files, net.xml and rou.xml, though additional file add. xml can be added as needed. The file net.xml is the road networks description of the map, including edges, lanes, junctions, connections, and traffic lights, and it can be imported from different third-party format (e.g., OpenStreetMap (OSM)) besides building your own road networks. The file rou.xml is the detailed description of all the vehicles, including vehicle routes, vehicle types, vehicle status. The file add.xml includes elements of road networks, such as tlLogic, bus stops, and road detector definitions, where tlLogic is used to control the traffic light scheduling.

Figure 2 shows how SE-TLS works seamlessly with SUMO simulator to solve the traffic light scheduling problem. It will first generate n sets of new traffic light durations and encode them into n solutions at the very beginning. For each solution, the second step is to replace the original values in add.xml with new solution. In add.xml, the states of the phases are 'G', 'y', 'r' respectively represent the green light, amber light and red light. Once the file has been modified, the information will be loaded into SUMO simulator. The SUMO simulator outputs the trip information file after the simulation is finished. SE-TLS uses this trip information to calculate the objective value of the solution. When all the solutions have been evaluated, SE-TLS will generate new solutions for the next iteration based on the objective value of all the solutions. This process will be repeated until the termination condition is reached.

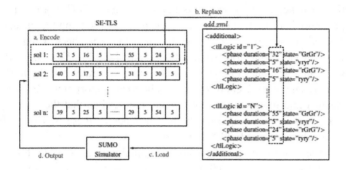

Fig. 2. System flow chart.

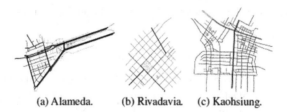

(a) Alameda.   (b) Rivadavia.   (c) Kaohsiung.

Fig. 3. Cities used in the simulations in this study.

4   Simulation Results

4.1   Experimental Setup

Three different road networks for real urban cities are downloaded from the OSM website and used in this paper, as shown in Fig. 3. The simulation time is set to 500 s. In addition, each instance will load two random routes with 500 vehicles generated by the program provided by SUMO named randomTrips.py to verify that SE-TLS is effective in road networks with different characteristics, different numbers of traffic lights and also different traffic conditions. Rivadavia Square, Argentina and Alameda Avenue, Spain are similar to the instances used in [6]. A distinguishing feature of Rivadavia Square is that its road networks look like a chessboard, which has 242 traffic phases; however, Alameda Avenue has the irregular road networks with different road lengths and widths, which has 148 traffic phases. Kaohsiung City, Taiwan, which has 640 traffic phases, is the largest-scale road networks among the three instances, with the above two characteristics: regular and irregular road networks.

In this paper, the SE-TLS is compared with five algorithms described in [6]—namely, particle swarm optimization (PSO), standard particle swarm optimization 2011 (SPSO2011), differential evolution (DE), RANDOM, and SCPG—and genetic algorithm (GA) [7]. The four metaheuristic algorithms have been widely used in various optimization problems, each of which has its own strategy for generating new solutions. RANDOM generates new solutions randomly, and SCPG is a fixed-time traffic light cycle program that SUMO generates for the map after loading the instance into the simulator. The parameters of SE-TLS are set equal to 4 searchers, 4 regions (i.e., the solution space is divided into four segments: [5, 20], [21, 35], [36, 50], and [51, 60], respectively.), 2 samples, and 3 players, and the crossover rates and the mutation rates are set equal to 1. The parameters of other metaheuristic algorithms are summarized in [6]. The crossover and mutation rates of GA are adjusted so that they are the same as SE-TLS for the purpose of comparing the performance of these two algorithms since the transition mechanism of SE-TLS is based on GA.

All the programs are written in C++ and compiled with g++ except for SCPG. The version of SUMO simulator is 0.30.0 for Linux, and the experiments are carried out on a PC with AMD R7 1700 CPU 3.0 GHz and 8 GB RAM running Ubuntu 16.04 LTS. The termination condition is set equal to 30,000 evaluations for all the programs, each of which is carried out for 30 independent runs. The final results of the programs are the best solution so far and the average of the best solution for 30 runs.

Table 1. Route A: objective values of all algorithms.

Instance		SE-TLS	PSO	SPSO2011	DE	GA	RANDOM	SCPG
Aameda	Avg	**0.844**	1.226	0.981	1.255	2.815	1.864	4.105
	Best	**0.630**	1.072	0.782	1.082	1.776	1.555	4.105
Rivadavia	Avg	**0.646**	0.840	0.669	0.865	1.510	1.206	1.717
	Best	**0.551**	0.720	0.606	0.791	1.279	1.076	1.717
Kaohsiung	Avg	**2.820**	4.323	2.917	4.588	6.093	5.345	8.175
	Best	**2.311**	3.679	2.443	4.319	5.467	4.996	8.175

Table 2. Route B: objective values of all algorithms.

Instance		SE-TLS	PSO	SPSO2011	DE	GA	RANDOM	SCPG
Aameda	Avg	**1.021**	1.782	1.153	1.823	4.157	2.674	10.830
	Best	**0.804**	1.282	0.808	1.423	3.325	2.320	10.830
Rivadavia	Avg	**0.793**	1.072	0.863	1.094	1.648	1.402	1.835
	Best	**0.699**	0.970	0.719	1.041	1.473	1.326	1.835
Kaohsiung	Avg	**3.018**	4.583	3.208	4.774	6.181	5.545	3.287
	Best	**2.166**	3.823	2.885	4.324	5.261	5.046	3.287

4.2 Experimental Results

Tables 1 and 2 show the objective values obtained by all the algorithms using the two routes in each of the three instances. The results show that SE-TLS can achieve the best performance in terms of the best value and the average value in all cases. As shown in Fig. 4(a), the feature of SE-TLS is that even if it has the fastest convergence ability, it is unlikely to fall into a local optimum at early iterations. The observations of the convergence process of these algorithms also show that the SE-TLS can find better solutions than other algorithms in the middle stage of the convergence process even though SCPG provides the suitable traffic light scheduling from the beginning. The results given in Fig. 4(b) show that SE-TLS can increase 91.5% of vehicle arrival rate compared to SCPG. More precisely, SE-TLS gets 390 vehicles to their destinations whereas SCPG gets only 151 vehicles to their destinations. Figure 5 shows that the ability of SE-TLS to improve traffic congestion of route B in Alameda, where SCPG is an unimproved situation and SE-TLS is an improved traffic condition. The results in the SUMO simulator show that SE-TLS has the strong ability to improve traffic congestion.

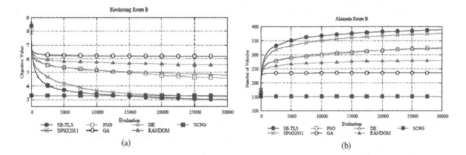

Fig. 4. (a) Kaohsiung route B: convergence of algorithms; (b) Alameda route B: vehicles reach their destinations.

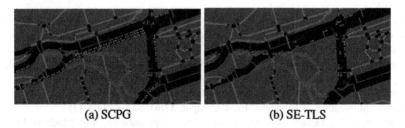

(a) SCPG   (b) SE-TLS

Fig. 5. SE-TLS improves the traffic congestion of route B in Alameda.

5 Conclusions

In this paper, we presented a novel metaheuristic algorithm, named SE-TLS, for the traffic light scheduling problem. SE-TLS uses the expected value of each region to replace the objective value of solutions to generate new solutions and determine the search directions during the convergence process. Since the design of SE-TLS bases not only on the best so far solution but also on the number of investments, it is able to avoid searching only particular regions at early iterations. That is why it is unlikely to fall into a local optimum; therefore, it is able to find better solutions. The experimental results show that SE-TLS gives the best performance in three realistic city instances with two different vehicle routes. SE-TLS allows the maximum number of vehicles to reach their destinations while at the same time reducing their trip times. The testing results of SUMO simulator also show that SE-TLS has a strong ability to solve the traffic congestion at intersections. In the future, we will test the performance of SE-TLS on more city instances with different traffic flows and will try to develop a more effective strategy for traffic control.

Acknowledgement. The authors would like to thank the anonymous reviewers for their valuable comments and suggestions on the paper. This work was supported in part by the Ministry of Science and Technology of Taiwan, R.O.C., under Contracts MOST107-2221-E-110-021 and MOST108-2221-E-110-028.

References

1. Behrisch, M., Bieker, L., Erdmann, J., Krajzewicz, D.: Sumo–simulation of urban mobility: an overview. In: Proceedings of the Third International Conference on Advances in System Simulation (2011)
2. Feng, Y., Head, K.L., Khoshmagham, S., Zamanipour, M.: A real-time adaptive signal control in a connected vehicle environment. Transp. Res. Part C Emerg. Technol. **55**, 460–473 (2015)
3. Gao, K., Zhang, Y., Sadollah, A., Su, R.: Optimizing urban traffic light scheduling problem using harmony search with ensemble of local search. Appl. Soft Comput. **48**, 359–372 (2016)
4. Gao, K., Zhang, Y., Sadollah, A., Su, R.: Improved artificial bee colony algorithm for solving urban traffic light scheduling problem. In: Proceedings of the IEEE Congress on Evolutionary Computation, pp. 395–402 (2017)
5. García-Nieto, J., Alba, E., Olivera, A.C.: Swarm intelligence for traffic light scheduling: application to real urban areas. Eng. Appl. Artif. Intell. **25**(2), 274–283 (2012)
6. Garcia-Nieto, J., Olivera, A.C., Alba, E.: Optimal cycle program of traffic lights with particle swarm optimization. IEEE Trans. Evol. Comput. **17**(6), 823–839 (2013)
7. Goldberg, D.E.: Genetic Algorithms in Search, Optimization, and Machine Learning. Addison Wesley, Reading (1989)
8. Hu, W., Wang, H., Qiu, Z., Nie, C., Yan, L.: A quantum particle swarm optimization driven urban traffic light scheduling model. Neural Comput. Appl. **29**(3), 901–911 (2016). https://doi.org/10.1007/s00521-016-2508-0
9. Jovanović, A., Nikolić, M., Teodorović, D.: Area-wide urban traffic control: a bee colony optimization approach. Transp. Res. Part C Emerg. Technol. **77**, 329–350 (2017)

10. Mckenney, D., White, T.: Distributed and adaptive traffic signal control within a realistic traffic simulation. Eng. Appl. Artif. Intell. **26**(1), 574–583 (2013)
11. Tsai, C.W.: Search economics: a solution space and computing resource aware search method. In: Proceedings of the IEEE International Conference on Systems, Man, and Cybernetics, pp. 2555–2560 (2015)
12. Younes, M.B., Boukerche, A.: Intelligent traffic light controlling algorithms using vehicular networks. IEEE Trans. Veh. Technol. **65**(8), 5887–5899 (2016)
13. Zhou, Z., Cai, M.: Intersection signal control multi-objective optimization based on genetic algorithm. J. Traffic Transp. Eng. (Engl. Ed.) **1**(2), 153–158 (2014)

A Bit Error Rate Optimization Method for WSN Node Energy Consumption

Miao He[1,2(✉)], Shen-shen Cheng[2], Tian-yi Ma[2], and Shi Lv[1]

[1] School of Computer and Software, Nanjing Institute
of Information Technology, Nanjing 210043, Jiangsu, China
hemiao@njcit.cn
[2] School of Energy and Power Engineering, Nanjing University
of Science and Technology, Nanjing 210094, Jiangsu, China

Abstract. In order to reduce the energy consumption of nodes and prolong the lifetime of indoor wireless sensor network nodes, it is necessary to establish an optimal bit error rate model under multiple indoor influencing factors so as to maximize the efficiency of receiving and receiving signals. Based on the researching of relationship between indoor factors such as wall and floor reflection, obstacle shadow fading, channel error rate and energy consumption of node signal transceiver and receiver, the energy consumption model of node single frame transmission is given, it is also proved that there exists an optimal bit error rate to minimize the energy consumption of nodes under the condition of co-channel coding. Finally, the simulation experiments are carried out to further analyze and verify the energy consumption of node. The results show that even if the indoor signal interference factors are complex, the minimum energy consumption of receiving and receiving nodes can be found by optimizing the bit error rate adjustment, which shows that the optimization model has engineering application value.

Keywords: Signal reflection · Path attenuation · Wireless sensor network · Optimal error rate · Node energy consumption

1 Introduction

Wireless sensor networks are widely used because of their flexible network settings and convenient device location changes. Wireless sensor networks are composed of a large number of randomly deployed nodes, which have the characteristics of miniature and low cost. They form a multi-hop self-organizing network through wireless communication to sense some physical phenomena, thus expanding the ability of people to interact with the real world remotely, so they are widely used in indoor scenes.

With the in-depth application of Internet of Things technology in the field of intelligent buildings, there is a need for continuous optimization of wireless sensor networks in indoor environment. Constrained by congenital energy constraints of nodes, how to achieve node energy saving by optimizing the distribution and transmission mode of indoor wireless network nodes is one of the important hot issues in this field.

J. Shen et al. (Eds.): IC3 2019, CCIS 1227, pp. 84–95, 2020.
https://doi.org/10.1007/978-981-15-6113-9_10

Generally speaking, the less energy consumed by the successful communication units between nodes, the longer the lifetime of nodes. Because of the complexity of indoor environment, the transmission success rate and unit power consumption of wireless sensor networks are affected by many factors. Include:

(i)   The influence of transmission path and physical node location. Literature [1–3] focuses on the study of path loss index in wireless networks, and verifies the loss index with self-estimation and its application. Literature [4] analyses the relationship between node location and node energy consumption from the perspective of RSSI attenuation characteristics.

(ii) The influence of indoor obstacles and floors on signal occlusion and reflection. Literature [5] studies the indoor propagation model of multi-room and multi-obstacle wireless networks. The propagation characteristics of wireless signals when encountering wall reflection are studied, and the corresponding path attenuation model is deduced, which takes into account such factors as line-of-sight transmission and wall reflection.

(iii) The influence of signal attenuation on signal attenuation varies with different coding channel communication modes. The influence of signal attenuation on energy consumption is analyzed in literature [6, 7] from Rayleigh and AWGN channel modes respectively. Literature [8] studied the difference of transmission characteristics between the same floor line-of-sight and non-line-of-sight and the change of floor attenuation factor in two typical building environments. Considering the effect of balanced bit error rate on node energy consumption, the dynamic optimal solution of bit error rate under different attenuation modes was derived, and a new indoor path attenuation model was proposed.

(iv) The influence of signal transmission error rate and frame retransmit rate on energy consumption loss is studied in literature [9]. The minimum energy consumption loss model of nodes can be realized by adjusting the error rate and frame retransmit rate under Rayleigh and AWGN channel modes.

On the premise of guaranteeing the transmission quality, the node energy consumption loss model of wireless sensor networks contains the above factors, but only considering one of them, the error of the optimal bit error rate will be large. Therefore, this paper synthetically analyses the influence of distance, occlusion, reflection, coding channel, bit error rate and frame repetition rate on node transmission energy consumption of wireless sensor networks, deduces the complete loss model of wireless sensor networks in the face of complex indoor integrated environment, and then deduces the optimal bit error rate prediction model under indoor integrated impact factors. In general indoor environment, the energy consumption of nodes can be minimized by setting the bit error rate of wireless network.

2 Energy Consumption Model for WSN Node Information Transmission

2.1 Transmission Path Loss Model

Logarithmic-normal model is often used to describe the path attenuation in wireless sensor networks. In the same plane, the average power of the signal received by wireless sensor decreases exponentially with the increase of distance. It is known from reference [3] that the general mode of the attenuation model is as follows:

$$PL = PL(d_0) + 10 \cdot n_p \cdot \log \frac{d}{d_0} \tag{1}$$

Formula (1) The average path attenuation of PL when the distance between nodes is d; $PL(d_0)$ is the path attenuation when the distance between the reference node and the target node is d_0, which can be detected in the actual environment and d is the distance between the nodes; d_0 is the near-ground reference distance, usually set to 1 m; n_p is the path attenuation factor, which varies with the surrounding environment.

Formula (1) reflects the relationship between signal attenuation and distance of nodes under the same indoor plane line-of-sight condition. However, this formula does not take into account the complex indoor space environment, that is, the impact of various obstacles on signal transmission.

In the same indoor plane, when the signal encounters obstacles, part of the signal will be absorbed, part of the signal will be reflected, and part of the signal will penetrate. In consideration of reflection, the above formula is revised as follows:

$$PL = PL(d_0) + 10 \cdot n_p \cdot \log \frac{d}{d_0} + A_w \tag{2}$$

A_w indicates signal attenuation due to wall reflection and absorption.

$$A_b = \sum_{w=1}^{kw} s_{A_w} \tag{3}$$

k_w indicates the total number of walls encountered for signal transmission. s_{A_w} is the attenuation of the signal on the wall of the layer w.

It is known from literature [5] that the attenuation of a simple sinusoidal radio signal when it encounters a wall in propagation can be expressed as:

$$s_{A_w} = \frac{d}{m} \sum_{i=1}^{m} 10 \log \frac{1}{R^2 \left(\frac{\pi}{2} - \theta_i \right)} \tag{4}$$

m is the number of reflected signal; $R \in (0, 1)$ is reflection coefficient; θ_i is phase difference;

Because the signal will propagate between different floors, in the case of cross-floors, the transmission of the signal will also be greatly affected. Considering this factor, the formula (2) is amended as follows:

$$PL = PL(d_0) + 10 \cdot n_p \cdot \log \frac{d}{d_0} + A_w + A_F \qquad (5)$$

A_F Indicates signal attenuation caused by crossing the floor.

$$A_F = \sum_{F=1}^{k_F} s_{A_F} \qquad (6)$$

k_F is the total number of floors encountered for signal transmission; s_{A_F} is the attenuation of the signal on the floor of the f th layer; As walls and floors are similar in physical properties, s_{A_F} calculating formula equals to s_{A_w}.

When a signal passes through a large obstacle, because the size of the obstacle is much larger than the wavelength of the radio wave, it will also cause attenuation to the propagation of the signal. We consider using the lognormal shadow fading model to investigate the effect of the obstacle, and modify formula (5) to:

$$PL = PL(d_0) + 10 \cdot n_p \cdot \log \frac{d}{d_0} + A_w + A_F + A_\sigma \qquad (7)$$

A_σ represents shadow fading, it is a Gaussian random variable with average value 0 and a variance of σ^2, namely $A_\sigma \sim (0, \sigma^2)$, the formula for calculating variance is as follows:

$$\sigma = \sqrt{\frac{1}{n} \sum_{i=1}^{n} [M_e(d_i) - M_d(d_i)]^2} \qquad (8)$$

Where $M_e(d_i)$ is the measured path loss of distance d_i, $M_d(d_i) = K - 10\gamma \log\left(\frac{d}{d_0}\right)$, and K is a constant related to the sensor node transmit module and the average attenuation of the channel.

2.2 Network Energy Consumption Model

Literature [8] gives the E_c expression model of energy consumption of single symbol in physical layer transmission frame of wireless sensor network, as follows:

$$E_c = \frac{P_{Tx}}{\eta} + P_{Tc} + P_{Rc} \times T_c \qquad (9)$$

P_{Tx} is the power of transmitter antenna, η is the amplification efficiency of transmitter antenna, P_{Tc} is the power consumption of transmitter module circuit, P_{Rc} is the power consumption of receiver circuit loop, and communication power consumption in wireless sensor networks mainly includes node loop power consumption and transmission signal power consumption. T_c denotes the time required to complete a symbol, assuming that each symbol takes the same time to complete its transmission.

(1) Initial propagation model

Firstly, all nodes are assumed to be in a free space environment. That is to say, in the case of barrier-free propagation among all nodes, Friis free space model is used to calculate transmission power, because Friis free space equation is:

$$P_R = \frac{P_{Tx} G_T G_R \lambda^2}{(4\pi d)^2} \tag{10}$$

P_R is the power received by the receiver. (10) In formula P_R can be regarded as a function of the distance d between the transmitter and the receiver, d in meters; G_T is the antenna gain of the transmitter, G_R is the antenna gain of the receiver; and Lambda is the wavelength, in meters.

(2) Considering Path Attenuation

On the basis of formula (10), we propose to introduce the transmission path attenuation factors of occlusion, reflection and shadow fading in real environment. Formula (7) PL is known as the average loss of transmission path with respect to d distance. From this, the power of transmitter in indoor space environment can be obtained by sorting out Formula (10):

$$P_{Tx} = \frac{P_R (4\pi d)^2}{G_T G_R \lambda^2 \times PL(d)} \tag{11}$$

(3) Considering frame retransmit attenuation

The error rate will lead to the failure of signal frame receiver verification, which requires frame retransmit to cause additional energy consumption. Assuming that the frame retransmit probability caused by bit error rate p_{ce} is p_{fe}, each frame contains n characters, and assuming that the error probability of each character transmission is equal, there are:

$$p_{fe} = 1 - (1 - p_{ce})^n \tag{12}$$

If the transmission energy consumption of each frame is E_f, the energy consumption of retransmitting the wrong frame until the receiver correctly receives it is E_{f_total}:

$$E_{f\_total} = E_f + E_f \times p_{fe} + \cdots + E_f \times p_{fe}^N \tag{13}$$

N denotes the number of retransmissions of the first error frame, and simplifies the form (9) into the form (13):

$$E_{f\_total} = \frac{1 - p_{fe}^{N+1}}{1 - p_{fe}} \times E_f = \frac{1 - p_{fe}^{N+1}}{1 - p_{fe}} \times E_c \times n$$

$$= \frac{1 - p_{fe}^{N+1}}{1 - p_{fe}} \times (\frac{P_{Tx}}{\eta} + P_{Tc} + P_{Rc}) \times T_c \times n \qquad (14)$$

In this paper, the frame retransmit limit is taken as a reference model for solving energy consumption, that is, $1 - p_{fe}^{N+1} \rightarrow 1$ when $N \rightarrow +\infty$. At the same time, (11) and (12) are substituted into (14) formulas:

$$E_{f\_total} = \frac{nT_c}{(1 - p_{ce})^n} \times \left(\frac{P_R(4\pi d)^2}{G_T G_R \lambda^2 \eta PL(d)} + P_{Tc} + P_{Rc} \right) \qquad (15)$$

(4) Considering Channel Attenuation

Rayleigh attenuation channel is a common statistical model of channel multipath fading in wireless networks. It is generally used in the case of occlusion, reflection, refraction, diffraction and non-direct radiation at the transmitter and receiver. Its use scenarios are similar to those of the complex indoor wireless networks studied in this paper.

We can know the bit error rate p_{bit} and Rayleigh channel average signal-to-noise ratio v is $p_{bit} = \frac{1}{2}\left(1 - \sqrt{\frac{v}{1+v}}\right)$ from reference [10–12], and $p_{ce} = p_{bit}log_2^M$ from reference [13], M is the number of discontinuous signals, where the pulse amplitude modulation (PAM-5) coding is used under the IEEE802.1 standard, $M = 5$, then $p_{ce} = log_2^5\left(1 - \sqrt{\frac{v}{1+v}}\right)$, and the conversion formula is $p_{ce} = log_2^5\left(1 - \sqrt{\frac{v}{1+v}}\right)$, where $x = \left(1 - log_5^2 p_{ce}\right)^2$. It is also known from reference [14] that the relationship between signal-to-noise ratio v and receiving power P_R is $v = \frac{P_R}{2BF\tau^2}$, Where B is the receiving bandwidth of the receiving end, F is the receiver noise figure, and τ^2 is the local average energy spectral density of the receiving signal before receiving, it is obtained:

$$P_R = 2BF\tau^2 \left[\frac{1}{1 - \left(1 - log_5^2 p_{ce}\right)^2} - 1 \right] \qquad (16)$$

Introducing (16) into (15) indoor wireless sensor network, the energy consumption of single frame transmission among nodes considering wall occlusion, floor reflection, shadow fading, path attenuation, frame retransmit, channel attenuation and other factors is all-round:

$$E_{f total} = \frac{n}{(1 - p_{ce})^n} \times \left[\frac{X_1}{1 - \left(1 - log_5^2 p_{ce}\right)^2} + X_2 \right] \qquad (17)$$

where x_1, x_2 are as follow:

$$X_1 = \frac{2BFT_c\tau^2(4\pi)^2}{G_T G_R \lambda^2 \eta} \times \frac{d^2}{\text{PL}(d)},$$
$$X_2 = T_c(P_{Tc} + P_{Rc}) - \frac{2BFT_c\tau^2(4\pi)^2}{G_T G_R \lambda^2 \eta} \times \frac{d^2}{\text{PL}(d)}$$

(18)

2.3   BER Optimization Model

Formula (17) shows that the optimal solution of p_{cerr} is an optimization process under relative constraints. B, F, G_T, G_R, T_c, τ^2, P_{Tc}, P_{Rc} with the fixed physical firmware characteristics of the node, it can be regarded as a constant, λ is physical constant. At the same time, from the analysis of formula (3), (4), (6), it is known that the values of A_W, A_F and A_σ are related to the number of reflected signals m, the total number of shielded signal transmission walls k_w, the total number of signal transmission floors passing through k_F, and the distance d between nodes, respectively. When the location of indoor nodes is fixed, d is constant. Therefore, X_1 and X_2 can be regarded as independent constant terms of p_{ce}.

At the same time, it is known from reference [13] that the Zigbee wireless sensor network standard stipulates that the signal frame length is $22 \leq n \leq 256$, and N is a constant. Obviously, there is E_{f_total} increases positively with p_{ce} in the functional formula $\frac{n}{(1-p_{ce})^n}$, and inversely with p_{ce} in the functional formula $\frac{X_1}{1-\left(1-\log_5^2 p_{ce}\right)^2}$, That is, the physical meaning is: The higher the bit error rate, the higher the frame retransmit probability, which results in more energy consumed by the sender for frame retransmit. However, the increase of the bit error rate is due to the decrease of transmission power each time, and also saves the energy consumption of single frame transmission at the sender. Therefore, according to the influence of different indoor occlusion and attenuation environments, an optimal bit error rate can be found to achieve the optimal compromise of transmission power. In other words, By adjusting the value of p_{ce}, the minimum relative transmission energy can be obtained in different indoor environments.

Finding the First Derivative of p_{ce} for Formula (18) can get the Formula (19):

$$E'_{f_{total}} = \frac{1}{(1-p_{ce})^{n+1}} X$$
$$\left[\frac{n^2 X_1}{\log_5^2\left(2p_{ce}-p_{ce}^2\right)} - \frac{2nX_1(1-p_{ce})^2}{\log_5^2 p_{ce}^2(2-p_{ce})^2} + n^2 X_2 \right]$$

(19)

Formula (18) can be regarded as the relation function of $E'_{f_{total}}(p_{ce})$ with respect to p_{ce}, When $E'_{f_{total}}(p_{ce}) = 0$, the formula (18) has an extreme value, that is, the simplified formula (20):

$$n\phi p_{ce}^4 - 4n\phi p_{ce}^3 + (4\phi n - 2 - n)p_{ce}^2$$
$$+(4+2n)p_{ce} - 2 =$$
$$(p_{ce}^2 - 2p_{ce})^2 - \frac{n+2}{n\phi}(p_{ce}-1)^2 + \frac{1}{\phi} = 0$$

(20)

In the formula above, $\phi = log_5^2 \frac{X_2}{X_1}$ is regarded as a constant. Let the left side of formula (19) be a function of $\varphi(p_{ce})$, we can see that when $p_{ce} = 0$, $\varphi(p_{ce}) < 0$, and when $p_{ce} = 1/n$, $\varphi(p_{ce}) > 0$, then $E'_{f_{total}}(p_{ce}) = 0$ must have solutions in (0, 1/n) interval, so $E_{f_{total}}$ has an extreme value in (0, 1/n) interval.

Further study shows that $\frac{1}{(1-p_{ce})^{n+1}}$ in formula (19) is always greater than zero on (0, 1), order:

$$\Psi(p_{ce}) = \left[\frac{n^2 X_1}{log_5^2(2p_{ce} - p_{ce}^2)} - \frac{2nX_1(1 - p_{ce})^2}{log_5^2 p_{ce}^2(2 - p_{ce})^2} + n^2 X_2 \right],$$

you can get:

$$\Psi'_{(p_{ce})} = 4(p_{ce}^2 - 2p_{ce})(p_{ce} - 1) - \frac{2(n+2)}{n\phi}(p_{ce} - 1) \qquad (21)$$

It can be seen that if $\Psi'_{(p_{ce})}$ is always greater than zero in (0, 1/n) interval, then $\Psi'_{(p_{ce})}$ increases monotonously in (0, 1/n) interval. It can be concluded that $E'_{f_{total}}$ increases monotonously in (0, 1/n) interval. It is proved that when $p_{ce} \in (0, 1/n)$ exists a value can get the minimizes $E_{f_{total}}$, which is the optimal bit error rate.

3   Analysis of Simulation Experiment

According to the optimal bit error rate model of indoor wireless sensor networks analyzed above, the network energy loss is simulated and evaluated. From the analysis model in this paper, we can see that when the indoor node layout is relatively fixed and the physical performance of signal processing modules of sending and receiving nodes is fixed, the energy consumption of successful transmission of a frame signal in wireless sensor networks mainly varies with p_{ce}.

3.1   Simulation Settings

In this simulation experiment, MATLAB is used as the simulation tool, and 2.4 GHz band is used as the carrier frequency of indoor WSN. The sending node broadcasts a fixed size message data to the surrounding area continuously. The hardware characteristics of all nodes are considered to be the same. Referring to the simulation environment of reference [15, 16], the hardware parameters of each node of wireless sensor network in this simulation environment are set as shown in Table 1.

Table 1. Hardware parameter assumptions for simulation environment

Simulation parameters	Value	Company
P_{Tc}	0.0984	W
P_{Rc}	0.1104	W
B	0.01	mHz
F	10	dB
τ^2	−174	dBm/Hz
T_C	5	μs
η	0.35	
G_T	5	dBi
G_R	5	dBi
λ	0.125	m

According to the related factors of path attenuation and distance between nodes, number of walls and floors in formula (7), two common indoor environments are simulated and analyzed in Table 2 in references [3, 15]:

Table 2. Assumption of indoor environmental parameters

Indoor environment	$d(m)$	m	k_F	k_w
Indoor emptiness	1	0	0	0
The same room is sheltered	5	10	2	4

From the analysis in this paper, we know that $p_{ce} \in (0,1)$ exists in the interval of $(0, 1/n)$ so that $E_{f_{total}}$ is the smallest and $22 \leqslant n \leqslant 256$, so the Range of p_{ce} is 0.0001–0.0455 in this simulation.

3.2 Simulation Result

In the open and unshielded indoor environment, the signals between the nodes are arranged along the middle line of the room, the reflection of the wall is weak, and the line of sight transmission occupies the main part. Here, the indoor open situation is regarded as an ideal situation, without considering the impact of path attenuation on energy consumption, the graph of frame character step n under various values shown in Fig. 1 can be obtained.

In the indoor occluded environment, the signals between nodes will be blocked by the occluded objects and can not be received in a straight line. The receiving nodes rely more on the reflected signals from the walls and floors to receive the complete messages. The signal stability is influenced by the environment randomly, which results in the random fluctuation of the energy consumption of single frame transmission at different bit error rates, as shown in Fig. 2.

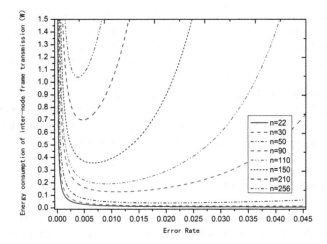

Fig. 1. The relation between bit error rate and single frame

3.3   Simulation Analysis

Because the indoor space does not consider the path attenuation factor caused by wall and floor reflection, the curve in Fig. 1 is smoother, and the curve in Fig. 2 fluctuates greatly. But overall, no matter what value n takes in Fig. 1 and Fig. 2, no matter what value n takes in (22, 256), when the BER is between (0, 1/n), an optimal point can always be found to minimize the total energy consumption of single frame transmission between nodes, only when considering the path attenuation caused by complex indoor environment. The optimal bit error rate point appears randomly in a minimal range, but the general trend of the function is consistent with the research in this paper.

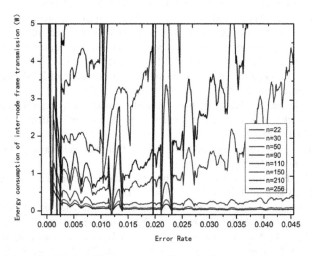

Fig. 2. The relationship between bit error rate and single frame energy consumption in indoor occlusion environment.

Further analysis of Figs. 1 and 2. When the number of characters in each frame is larger, the frame error rate will increase under the same bit error rate, which will lead to the increase of frame retransmit probability, that is, the increase of frame transmission energy between the whole nodes. Therefore, in order to ensure the decrease of frame retransmit rate, a smaller bit error rate must be used. Therefore, the earlier the optimal bit error rate appears on $(0, 1/n)$ when the n value is larger, the smaller it is. At the same time, because the larger the value of n, the higher the number of characters transmitted between nodes and the linear increase of the number of T_c, the greater the minimum energy consumption of single frame transmission between nodes.

4   Conclusion and Future Work

In this paper, considering the path attenuation factors caused by wall, floor signal reflection and obstacle signal shadow fading in indoor complex physical space environment, the influence model of bit error rate on energy consumption of signal transmission between nodes in Rayleigh channel is emphatically analyzed, and the mathematical model derived from physical model is used to further analyze and deduce wireless communication. Based on the mathematical model and related literature, a simulation experiment environment is constructed. According to the simulation results and analysis, it is further verified that under complex indoor conditions, the error rate can be dynamically adjusted according to different channel frame coding modes and different path attenuation. Significantly reduce network energy consumption.

References

1. Hu, Y., Leus, G.: Self-estimation of path-loss exponent in wireless networks and applications. IEEE Trans. Veh. Technol. **64**(11), 5091–5102 (2018)
2. Moshtaghpour, A., Akhaee, M.A., Attarifar, M.: Obstacle mapping in wireless sensor networks via minimum number of measurements. IET Signal Proc. **10**(3), 237–246 (2015)
3. Xu, W., Liu, H.: Path attenuation characteristics of wireless sensor networks in indoor environment. Sens. Microsyst. **35**(12), 11–13+16 (2016)
4. Xie, Q., Lin, J.Y., Lu, Z.G., et al.: The attenuation characteristic of RSSI in wireless sensor networks. Control Instrum. Chem. Ind. **37**(1), 60–62 (2010)
5. Malnar, M., Jevtic, N.: Novel multi-room multi-obstacle indoor propagation model for wireless networks. Wireless Pers. Commun. **102**(1), 583–597 (2018). https://doi.org/10.1007/s11277-018-5859-2
6. Wang, Y., Ge, L.D.: Simulation model of independent multipath Rayleigh fading channels. J. Inf. Eng. Univ. **8**(2), 202–205 (2007)
7. Zhuang, D.S.: Performance analysis of bit error rate for impulse ultra wideband in the AWNG. Mod. Electron. Tech. (17), 68–70+73 (2007)
8. Zhang, C., Wang, R., Fu, S., et al.: Comparative test analysis of RF transmission characteristics in 433MHz/470MH building. Data Commun. (6), 34–37 (2015)
9. Wang, C., Liu, H., Xu, W.: Analysis of physical layer performance of wireless sensor networks under different channels. Comput. Eng. Appl. **52**(12), 112–116 (2016)

10. Panwar, V., Kumar, S.: Bit error rate (BER) analysis of Rayleigh fading channels in mobile communication. Int. J. Mod. Eng. Res. (IJMER) **2**, 796–798 (2012)
11. Fan, C.X.: Communication Principles, 6th edn, pp. 196–213. National Defense Industry Press, Beijing (2006)
12. Wan, Y.G.: Implementation of Digital Signal Processing Based on MATLAB. Science Press, Beijing (2012)
13. IEEE Computer Society: IEEE std 802.15.4-2003. The Institute of Electrical and Electronics Engineers, Inc. (2003)
14. Steyaert, M., de Muer, B., Leroux, P., et al.: Low-voltage low-power CMOS-RF transceiver design. IEEE Trans. Microw. Theory Tech. **50**(1), 281–287 (2002)
15. Cui, S., Goldsmith, A.J., Bahai, A.: Energy-constrained modulation optimization. IEEE Trans. Wireless Commun. **4**(5), 2349–2360 (2005)
16. Cui, S., Goldsmith, A.J., Bahai, A.: Energy-efficiency of MIMO and cooperative MIMO techniques in sensor networks. IEEE J. Sel. Areas Commun. **22**(6), 1089–1098 (2004)

Multi-stage Replica Consistency Algorithm Based on Activity

Gui Liu$^{(\boxtimes)}$, Haijiang Xu, and Shujun Yang

Jiangnan Institute of Computing Technology, Wuxi, Jiangsu, China
lgzhy@163.com

Abstract. A good replica consistency algorithm can complete the overall management of replicas. An effective solution to the problem of replica consistency can significantly improve the performance and scalability of cloud computing environment, and reduce job execution time. This paper proposes an activity-based multi-phase replica consistency algorithm (AMRCA). Firstly, the algorithm divides the replicas into two categories according to their active degree, one is "active" replica and the other is "inactive" replica. For those "active" replicas, we use a strong consistency algorithm, requiring all replicas in the system to be consistent, and any updates must be propagated to all replicas. For those "inactive" replicas, we use the weak consistency algorithm. The advantage of this method is that it avoids the increase of system overhead caused by using strong consistency algorithm for all replicas, and ensures that all replicas with high "activity" in the system are up-to-date and consistent. Secondly, the algorithm divides the process of data updating into several stages, each stage works together to ensure data consistency among all valid replicas, and at the same time, it minimizes the failure interval of replicas in the updating process, thus providing more reliable data access services for upper application.

Keywords: Consistency · OpenStack Swift · Cloud computing

1 Relevant Research

The problem of replica consistency exists widely in the fields of P2P, distributed database, distributed object, cloud computing and so on.

Early research on P2P replicas focused on the establishment strategy and location search of file replicas [1–4], in order to rationally allocate the location of replica resources and ensure the load balance of the network by optimizing resource search. In structured P2P networks (such as Chord, CAN, etc.), the connection of nodes has a regular structure. Data storage and network topology are strictly controlled by specially designed algorithms. Consistency maintenance algorithms can often establish a "replica partition tree" with the help of distributed Hash table (DHT) [5], and obtain the location of each replica to transmit update messages. Although this algorithm can effectively maintain replicas, the DHT algorithm is only suitable for structured P2P networks.

In the field of distributed database, replication technology can be divided into Eager and Lazy technologies. Different replication technologies adopt different replica consistency management mechanisms [6]. Eager replication technology requires that

© Springer Nature Singapore Pte Ltd. 2020
J. Shen et al. (Eds.): IC3 2019, CCIS 1227, pp. 96–104, 2020.
https://doi.org/10.1007/978-981-15-6113-9_11

replicas of all databases be synchronized, and the database can only respond to user requests after all replicas are synchronized. Lazy replication technology allows the synchronization of replicas to take place after the update transaction commits, thus avoiding the cost of replica synchronization, but the implementation of Lazy replication technology is relatively complex.

OpenStack is a cloud computing platform developed by Rackspace and NASA to help service providers and businesses implement cloud infrastructure services similar to Amazon EC2 and S3. OpenStack's Swift module provides object storage services, abandoning strict consistency and adopting the Eventual Consistency model [9–11].

2 Duplicate Consistency in Enterprise Massive Data Environment

Compared with P2P system, distributed database and cloud computing, in order to maintain the consistency among replicas, we need to take full account of the characteristics of the enterprise-level massive data environment studied in this paper: The original data sources of replicas in enterprise-level massive data environment are widely distributed, with large access delay and network failure; the location of replicas is relatively stable, and nodes do not often join or exit; replicas are created and deleted dynamically according to needs at run time; in addition, the total number of replicas in enterprise-level massive data environment is large.

In view of the above characteristics of the enterprise-level massive data environment studied in this paper, the consistency management mechanisms in the fields of P2P system, distributed database system and cloud computing are not applicable to this system. The specific analysis is as follows:

At present, in the field of P2P, there is much redundant information in the replica consistency maintenance algorithm, and the bandwidth is wasted seriously. In addition, some algorithms cann't guarantee the complete consistency of the system, there will be a single point failure problem.

In a distributed database system, the two-stage submission protocol requires that all replica updates be successfully executed before the user's modification operations are completed. If one replica updates unsuccessfully, the user's operations are revoked. In the enterprise-level massive data environment, because of the large number of replicas, the dynamic creation and deletion of replicas according to needs, and the frequent failure of networks and nodes, the implementation efficiency of the two-stage submission protocol will be very low.

The Quorum arbitration mechanism adopted by Swift module in OpenStack, a cloud computing platform, has to wait until all three responses are returned before selecting the best response to return to the client (even Timeout, will wait for Storage Server to return). So once there is a slow node in a cloud computing environment, Swift's overall performance will be greatly affected, resulting in writing speed not going up. Because of the large number of requests and replicas in the enterprise-level massive data environment, if all replicas are returned to the client through all Responses to ensure the consistency of operations later, the implementation efficiency will be very low, which will greatly increase the data response time.

3 Duplicate Consistency Model Architecture

Based on the above analysis, the existing replica consistency management mechanism can't meet the requirements of data storage in enterprise-level massive data environment. Therefore, it is necessary to study a replica consistency management mechanism with high performance.

In this paper, a multi-strategy replica consistency algorithm based on activity is proposed. Firstly, replicas are divided into two categories: active replicas and inactive replicas. In data migration, some copies are not accessed by users, but they belong to the same class because they are related to the accessed files. Such copies have the possibility of being accessed, but not necessarily accessed, and the possibility of being modified may be small, so they may belong to the less active copies. Of course, in practical applications, such copies may be accessed or modified, so they may belong to "active" copies. For those copies that have been duplicated as copies due to frequent visits and may be modified frequently, they may belong to "active" copies. Of course, in practical applications, such copies are less likely to be re-accessed or modified, so they may also become "inactive" copies.

Whether a replica is "active" depends on the size of the replica's "activity". Weak consistency algorithm is used for "inactive" replicas. This algorithm does not guarantee that all replicas are available at any time, and there will be some invalid replicas. Modification messages are first sent to one replica, then asynchronously to other copies, and eventually each replica receives the modification message, thus achieving a consistent state. Weak consistency is the minimum requirement for replication algorithms. Before being updated, these copies always remain in a "broken" failure state, even leading to the final abandonment of the replica.

For those "active" replicas, strong consistency algorithm is used. Strong consistency algorithm requires that all replicas are consistent at any time. Any update must be propagated to all replicas immediately, so that users can get consistent and up-to-date data at any time. The advantage of this method is that it avoids the increase of system overhead caused by using strong consistency algorithm for all replicas, and ensures that all replicas with high "activity" in the system are up-to-date and consistent.

3.1 Design Schema

The design of a replica consistency management strategy involves the following issues: replica propagation mode, user operation update object, dissemination content, subject of propagation trigger and consistency [7].

(1) Replica Dissemination Mode

The dissemination mode of consistency management strategy mainly refers to how to disseminate replica updates, which can be divided into Lazy mode and Eager mode. The difference between them is whether the update operation of the replica requires completion in one transaction, Lazy mode if it does not require completion in the same transaction, or Eager mode.

In the enterprise-level massive data environment, because of the large number of replicas, dynamic and WAN-based environment, the system overhead will increase if all replicas are updated in one transaction. In this paper, Lazy prop-agation mode is used to allow the update operation of the replica to be executed after the end of the user update operation transaction.

(2) Propagation Trigger Subject

The subject of communication trigger refers to who sends out the communication request. According to different propagation trigger subjects, replica consistency management strategies can be divided into Push mode and Pull mode. The "Push" model is similar to the process of rumor transmission in sociology. Rumor-based "Push" algorithm always selects some of its neighbors for further forwarding in each round of transmission. As with the Flooding-based replica consistency maintenance algorithm [8], rumor-based "Push" mode is initiated by the update initialization node to initiate the delivery of update messages, and actively "Push" the update messages to other replica nodes. However, when a node joins and leaves dynamically, the mechanism of "Push" is no longer suitable for the dynamic environment. Therefore, the "Pull" mode, as a complement to the "Push" mode, is also used for consistency maintenance: when a new node joins, the new node requests the latest replica by actively connecting its neighbors, that is, the Pull process.

In order to improve performance, Push and Pull are combined in this paper. After the data update operation is completed, the update result Push is first put on the active replica node, and then the latest replica is obtained by Pull mode when the active replica node requests access to the data item when the replica is not updated.

3.2   Problem Description and Related Definitions

Before discussing the multi-stage replica consistency algorithm based on activity, the following assumptions are given:

Assume 1. The replica nodes cooperate with each other, that is, the replica nodes will participate in the consistency maintenance according to the consistency mainte-nance method.

Assume 2. The size of the update message propagated is the same.

Assume 3. Each replica node has a corresponding IP address.

Assume 4. Any replica node can join or leave the system at random.

Assume 5. The replica nodes are relatively stable, but there will also be failure.

Assume 6. Each replica node can communicate as long as it knows the IP address of other replica nodes.

Assume 7. Each replica node only knows the information of the successor node directly connected to it, and no replica node knows the information of all the replica nodes of a file.

Assume 8. The replica node can determine whether it is a replica node of a file by passing a message.

Then the following definitions are given:

Define 3-1 to define the replica's activity as Act, which can decay over time. Define it as follows:

$$Act = \begin{cases} Act + 1 & \text{when there is a request for access to a replic, record the current access time startime} \\ Act \times e^{-\frac{\ln(t+1)}{k}} & \text{at each scan, } t = \text{current time} - \text{startime} \end{cases}$$

The activity of a replica is reflected in the frequency of users' access to a replica. The more requests to access the replica, the more active the replica is and the more active it is. When there is a request for access to a replica, record the current access time starttime, and Act increases by 1; over time, if no new access request is issued, then the "active" degree of the replica will become smaller and smaller with the passage of time, and its activity will be lower. K is a coefficient used to describe the degree of time attenuation, usually in the range of 1 to 10, in order to make the time attenuation closer to the network environment at that time.

Definition 3-2 Active Replica: If the ACT value of the replica exceeds a given threshold t, it is called active replica.

Definition 3-3 Inactive Replica: If the ACT value of the replica is lower than a given threshold t, it is called inactive replica.

Definition 3-4 Threshold δ: Used to determine whether the replica is active or not. Since the parameter K in Act determines the speed of time attenuation, the greater the value K is, the slower the attenuation will be. The smaller the value K is, the faster the time attenuation will be. Therefore, it is generally related to δ and k: $\delta = \frac{1}{\ln k}$

Definition 3-5 Data Sources: physical files that can be modified stored in data providers.

Definition 3-6 Replicas: Physical copies of data sources stored in data providers in data centers are read-only for upper applications and cannot be modified. There can be multiple copies of a physical file.

Definition 3-6 Replica Catalogue Chain: Record the location information, status information and other related information of each replica when creating a replica. The relevant information of all replicas of the same physical file forms a replica directory chain.

3.2.1   Multi-stage Consistency Maintenance Model Based on Activity

The RCS service of the European Data Grid Project adopts the replica consistency scheme based on distributed lock. Although it can ensure the replica consistency, the bandwidth consumption of the network is relatively large due to the distributed lock mechanism. Gnutella [8] adopts flooding-based replica consistency maintenance algorithm, updates the initialization node to broadcast the message to the neighbor node, and then forwards the message to its next round of neighbor nodes. In this way, the update message is transmitted to all replica algorithms in the network in a similar breadth-first search way, which is simple and can achieve all replicas. Consistency, but the number of messages it transmits is enlarged exponentially, which occupies a large amount of network bandwidth. A replica node receives update messages many times, which is redundant and lack of scalability.

From the above analysis, we can see that there are two core problems to be solved in the replica consistency algorithm: one is the synchronization of all replicas, that is, the need to ensure the consistency of all replicas in the update process; the other is the need to effectively control the large bandwidth consumption in the replica update process of large-scale data.

In this paper, a multi-stage replica consistency algorithm based on Replica Catalogue Chain and "activity" is used to solve this problem. The so-called multi-stage refers to the first stage of disseminating update messages according to the replica directory chain, the second stage determines the target nodes that need to be updated and forms a list that needs to be updated, and the third stage carries out formal data updating; and the adoption of activity can objectively divide the replica into active and inactive nodes, thus reducing the number of replicas that need to be updated. It reduces the consumption of bandwidth.

The idea of the algorithm is as follows: if the data source in the data provider is modified, the consistency service will be started. In the first stage, the replica master node will forward the update message to the replica slave node along the replica directory chain. After each replica in the chain receives the update message from the node, it will decide the next action according to its corresponding replica's "activity" Act. Effective operation or update operation. The second stage is started by the replica slave node. If the replica is an inactive replica, the "invalidation" sign is placed on the replica. If the replica is an active replica, a "need to update" request is sent to the replica master node. After the replica master node receives all replicas' update requests from the node, it forms an update list. In the third stage, the replica master node retrieves the update data from the data source and updates the replicas from the node according to the update list. After all the replica nodes update, all the replicas are switched to the updated version, and then the replica directory chain is reconstructed according to the update list. Active copies are updated immediately, so strong consistency maintenance is achieved; while inactive copies can be deleted directly from nodes without consistency updates, which reduces the cost of replica updates.

4 Performance Analysis and Experimental Results

In order to verify the proposed multi-stage replica consistency algorithm based on activity, a series of simulation experiments have been done. These experiments compare our method with two common replica consistency algorithms (Lazy Con and EagerCon). In order to study the performance and availability of the algorithm, we compare the average response time and network bandwidth consumption of each algorithm under different scales and different update times.

The simulation environment of the experiment is a cloud computing environment consisting of several nodes, each node has a storage unit with a storage capacity of 100T. The network transmission rate between nodes is 1000 Mbps, and the size of each file in the system is 100 GB. There are 600 files distributed evenly on different virtual nodes.

- Effect of Number of Nodes on Average Response Time

As can be seen from Fig. 1, with the enlargement of node size, the average response time of the three replica consistency algorithms will increase, but because LazyCon consistency strategy allows the replica synchronization operation to be

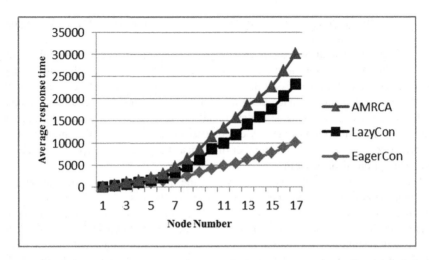

Fig. 1. The influence of the number of nodes on the average response time.

performed after the update transaction submission, thus avoiding the cost of replica synchronization. The average response time of the three replica consistency algorithms is less than EagerCon consistency when the node size is relatively small. Therefore, when the size of nodes is relatively small, the average response time is less than that of EagerCon consistency strategy and AMMA algorithm. However, with the increase of node size, the average response time of LazyCon strategy is more than that of EagerCon strategy and AMRCA strategy because of the access delay of LazyCon strategy when updating data.

- Effect of Update Number on Network Bandwidth Consumption

As can be seen from Fig. 2, when the number of updates is not very large, the network bandwidth consumption of the three algorithms is not significantly different. As the number of replica updates increases, the network bandwidth under the three replica consistency algorithms will gradually increase. However, LazyCon consistency strategy is that replicas are updated only when they are accessed, so it does not need to transmit real-time data when replicas change, thus saving network bandwidth. The EagerCon consistency strategy is to update all replicas in real time when the source file changes, so the network bandwidth is very expensive. The proposed algorithm does not update all replicas synchronously, so the network bandwidth consumption is between the two.

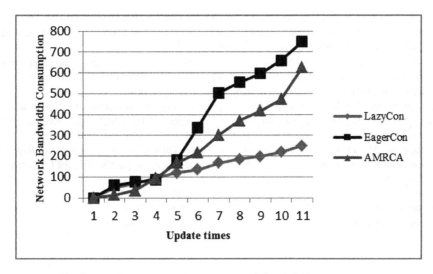

Fig. 2. The impact of updates on network bandwidth consumption.

5 Concluding Remarks

The existence of replicas can save bandwidth, reduce latency, load balance and improve system reliability, improve query performance and data validity. Consistency management of replicas is the key to ensure its correct operation, which directly affects the performance of massive data environment. This multi-stage replica consistency algorithm based on activity takes different consistency measures for different types of replicas. The advantage of this method is that it avoids the system overhead caused by using strong consistency algorithm for all replicas and ensures that all replicas with high activity in the system are up-to-date and consistent. The performance analysis of the algorithm shows that the algorithm is suitable for large-scale nodes, while replica updates are not particularly frequent in massive data environment.

References

1. Ion, S., et al.: Chord: a scalable peer-to-peer lookup protocol for internet applications. IEEE/ACM Trans. Netw. **11**(1), 17–32 (2003)
2. Ranjita, B., Stefan, S., Geoffrey, V.: Replication strategies for highly available peer-to-peer storage systems. Technical report, CS2002-0726, UCSD (2002)
3. Lv, Q., Cao, P., Cohen, E., Li, K., Shenker, S.: Search and replication in unstructured peer-to-peer networks. In: Proceedings of the 16th ACM International Conference on Supercomputing, pp. 84–95 (2002)
4. Wang, Q.B., Dai, Y.F., Tian, J., Zhao, T., Li, X.M.: An infrastructure for attribute addressable P2P network (in Chinese with English abstract). J. Softw. **14**(8), 1481–1488 (2003)

5. Chen, X., Ren, S.S., Wang, H.N., Zhang, X.D.: SCOPE: scalable consistency maintenance in structured P2P systems. In: Proceedings of the IEEE Infocom 2005, pp. 1502–1513. IEEE Computer Society, Washington, D.C. (2005)
6. Wiesmann, M., Pedone, F., Schiper, A., Kemme, B., Alonso, G.: Understanding replication in databases and distributed systems. In: Proceedings of the 20th International Conference on Distributed Computing Systems (ICDCS 2000), p. 464 (2000)
7. Jurk, S., Neiling, M.: Client-side dynamic preprocessing of transactions. In: Kalinichenko, L., Manthey, R., Thalheim, B., Wloka, U. (eds.) ADBIS 2003. LNCS, vol. 2798, pp. 103–117. Springer, Heidelberg (2003). https://doi.org/10.1007/978-3-540-39403-7_10
8. Ripeanu, M.: Peer-to-peer architecture case study: Gnutella network. In: Proceedings of International Conference on Peer-to-Peer Computing Sweden, pp. 99–101. IEEE Computer Press (2001)
9. http://www.kankanews.com/ICkengine/archives/66411.shtml
10. http://www.cnblogs.com/yuxc/archive/2012/06/22/2558312.html
11. http://www.cnblogs.com/yuxc/archive/2012/06/28/2568584.html

Handwritten Text Line Segmentation Method by Writing Pheromone Diffusion and Convergence

Yintong Wang[✉] and Wenjie Xiao

Key Laboratory of Intelligent Information Processing,
Nanjing Xiaozhuang University, Nanjing 211171, People's Republic of China
wyt@njxzc.edu.cn

Abstract. Text line segmentation in offline handwritten documents remains a challenge because the offline handwritten text lines are often inconsistency curved and skewed. More serious is the space between lines is not enough to distinguish them. In this paper, we propose a novel offline handwritten text line segmentation method by writing pheromone diffusion and convergence. According to the principle of gravity, we apply it to the lines location of the offline handwritten texts, the pheromone diffusion and convergence can learn to generate the pheromone matrix for extracting the key locations and fragments of the text line, that is made robust to deal with various offline handwritten documents with curved and multi-skewed text lines. In experiments on a commonly used database with offline handwritten text images, our method can significantly improve upon state-of-the-art text line segmentation methods.

Keywords: Handwritten text · Line segmentation · Pheromone matrix · Diffusion and convergence

1 Introduction

Text line segmentation from offline handwritten text images is one of the major issues in offline handwritten text image analysis. It provides crucial information for the subsequent tasks of text fragments and character segmentation, text string and character recognition. Comparing with the machine-printed document analysis, the complex layout structure and degraded image quality, offline handwritten document image analysis facing with more complex character shapes and irregularity of layout, which due to the variability of individuals writing styles [1–3]. For offline handwritten document images, text line segmentation is not completely solved though greatly efforts have been devoted to them and great advances have been achieved [4–7].

In this paper, we present a handwritten text line segmentation method by writing pheromone diffusion and convergence. The main works of the proposed approach consist of (i) writing pheromone diffusion and convergence mode, (ii) key locations and fragments of text line, and (iii) text line segmentation. The most contribute of the proposed approach is that the pheromone diffusion and convergence can learn to generate the pheromone matrix for extracting the key locations and fragments of the

© Springer Nature Singapore Pte Ltd. 2020
J. Shen et al. (Eds.): IC3 2019, CCIS 1227, pp. 105–113, 2020.
https://doi.org/10.1007/978-981-15-6113-9_12

text line, that is made robust to deal with various offline handwritten document images with curved and multi-skewed text lines.

The rest of this paper is organized as follows. Section 2 reviews briefly previous related work for text line segmentation of offline handwritten document images. In Sect. 3, we explain the proposed methodology for text line segmentation by writing pheromone diffusion and convergence. In Sect. 4, we present the experimental results. Finally, we draw the conclusions and future works in Sect. 5.

2   Related Works

In this section, we review the previous related work for text line segmentation and character segmentation of offline handwritten text images. As far as we know, the following methods either got the best results in the relevant opened offline handwritten document datasets, or are elements of comprehensive systems for specific tasks.

The main approaches of text line segmentation in offline handwritten document images can be practically divided into three categories: global, local, hybrid. The global approach [8–10] more focus on the isolate characters and reference them by their position in the offline handwritten document. That means it estimating the position of the text lines first, then allocating the character strings to the components to likely looking text lines, and dividing the components to multiple independent text lines. Zhang et al. [11] proposes the constrained seam carving method to acquire the global characteristics of the offline handwritten document images. This method calculates the energy map by passing along the connected components, and extracts the represent text line positions by computing the energy map. Quang et al. [12] draw a fully convolutional network to segment text line structure in offline handwritten documents. This method rough estimates of text line by a line map, and then constructs text strings pass through characters in corresponding text line. Sindhushree et al. [3] proposed an global text line segmentation method based on entropy, in which text region with higher entropy compared to that of non-text region in offline handwritten documents, and text line segmentation with the separate text from non-text part.

The local approach exceeds the limits of the global methods, its goal is to find local characters or graphemes first, and then aggregate them to split text lines [13–15]. These approaches in local classification vary from the way to represent and gather the local characters or graphemes. Nguyen and Lee [14] proposed a grouping approach to segment text lines, in which a text string that connects the center points of the characters in this text line is built, each tensor is consisting of a center location of a connected text string, and then compute the curve saliency values and normal vectors to construct the character sequences. Zhang et al. [16–18] proposed text line segmentation method based on Hough transform, which treats the text lines as partitioned character or grapheme blocks of connected components (CCs). Splitting these CCs to small, middle, large sized CCs by their average height value and width value of all CCs, dividing each middle sized CC into equally sized blocks, applying Hough transform to center of these equally sized blocks to extract the corresponding text lines based on the accumulator array, which means each CC is either allocated to the nearest text line or decomposed into multi-parts and then allocated again to the nearest text lines.

The hybrid approach uses a flexible handling to extract text lines, combining the advantages of the local approach and the global approach [6, 19–21]. Guo et al. finds the connected character or grapheme components as symbols, and then the direction of the text lines is computed using a special criterion framework [19]. All the above three approaches have their own advantages and disadvantages, in which global approach do not perform well on abnormal offline handwritten documents, such as adhesion, overlapping and curved text lines. The performance of local approach reliance on some preset parameters or heuristic rules, such as the nearest component distance metric for corresponding text lines. And the hybrid approach is complicated in calculation, and is non-trivial to design a robust combination framework.

3   Handwritten Text Line Segmentation Method

In this section, we introduce the methodology of handwritten text line segmentation method by writing pheromone diffusion and convergence. The objective of the proposed method is to deal with that text line appears in the document have an arbitrary skew angle and characters or graphemes of neighboring text lines may be connected, then made robust to handle various document images with multi-skewed, curved and connected text lines.

3.1   Writing Pheromone Diffusion and Convergence Mode

The character height is important for many parameters estimation in the handwritten text processing, such as character width, line height and line spacing. In this paper, we randomly select multiple positions in the handwritten text, then the nearest neighbor handwriting CCs are obtained from these positions and their heights also are calculated, $\{h_1, h_2, \cdots, h_n\}$. the estimated value of character height (ch) is set as the median value of the height of CCs.

In writing pheromone diffusion and convergence mode, each pixel is treated as a pheromone propagates information around, and then accumulates the information at each points in the handwritten text. The handwritten text image X's pheromone matrix $PM_{n \times m}$, the size of which is $n \times m$, the initial value is 0. In the pheromone diffusion, the writing pixel x_{ij}, ith row and jth column, contains one unit information, whose propagated information to neighboring is inversely to their distance. The farthest information propagation distance of pheromone is set to k, that is to say, x'_{ij} is the farthest point affected by x_{ij}, whose information from later is zero or infinity equals zero. Next, the pheromone information propagation matrix of x_{ij} is $IN_{2k-1,2k-1}$, where $IN_{k,k} = 1$ represents the x_{ij} to its own information is 1 unit, and the information to the pixels in the neighboring k range is

$$IN_{k \pm \delta, k \pm \delta} = fun\_inv(dist_{k \pm \delta, k \pm \delta}), \ 1 \leq \delta < k. \tag{1}$$

The distance between x_{ij} and $x_{i\pm\delta,j\pm\delta}$ is represented as:

$$dist_{k\pm\delta,k\pm\delta} = sqrt((k\pm\delta)\wedge 2 + (k\pm\delta)\wedge 2). \tag{2}$$

In the pheromone convergence, the Information Matrix $PM_{n\times m}$ converge all the writing pheromone of the handwritten text. The ith row and jth column pixel's information PM_{ij} is formula as $PM_{ij} = IN_{ij}^{+}$, where IN_{ij}^{+} represents its k-nearest neighbor pheromone information. Note that, the information quantization of the image X edge pixel needs special processing, for example, the 1th row and 1th column pixel $x_{1,1}$ is affected by the pixel's pheromone in the fourth quadrant of coordinate axis, and the nth row and mth column pixel $x_{n,m}$ is affected by the pixel's pheromone in the second quadrant of coordinate axis.

3.2   Key Locations and Fragments

The pheromone matrix is composed of pheromone diffusion and convergence of each handwriting pixel, the high pheromone value corresponding to the handwriting character pixels in the region, and the low pheromone value is more biased towards non-text line areas. Therefore, the key locations and fragments of text line can be determined by analyzing the peaks and peak regions of the pheromone matrix, and then the text line segmentation of the handwritten text is further realized.

The min-max normalization as a simplest normalization technique, which is suited for the cases where the maximum and minimum bounds of the scores produced by a matcher are known. In pheromone computation case, we can easily shift the minimum and maximum scores of pheromone matrix to zero and one, respectively. The peaks of the pheromone matrix are the positions where the pheromone value in a local region is the highest, and they are also the most representative position of a character belonging to the corresponding text line. In handwritten text, the influence of the writing pixel is one unit by themselves, and gradually affects the pixels with distance of k, form the peak area of characters or the valley area between characters. As shown in the Fig. 1(c), local peak p_{ij} on the pheromone matrix $PM_{n\times m}$, the ith row and jth column position or the central coordinate position of a plurality of adjacent pixels considered to be a character center, that is, a key peaks of the text lines. The formal inequality is as follows:

$$PM_{ij} \geq fun\_nei(p_{ij}). \tag{3}$$

where fun_nei represents the max pheromone function of p_{ij}'s adjacent pixels.

In order to further analyze the directionality of text lines, the pheromone matrix be considered as a surface and slice it at height $\varphi(0 < \varphi < 1)$ to obtain the cross section of the pheromone matrix, these cross sections corresponding to the regions with a higher pheromone value, as shown in Fig. 1(d). If there is a unique long axis in the cross section (the height is less than $3/2 * ch$ and the length is greater than $2 * ch$), then the long axis is a fragment of text line. Otherwise, if there are multiple long axes in the cross section, then multiple text lines in this cross section, the appearance of skew and slant in the text lines.

3.3 Text Line Segmentation

The text line segmentation stage consists of three-step process. First, normal text line segmentation, the key peaks are mapped to the corresponding fragments of text lines, and using the least squares polynomial fitting function to achieve the text line. Second, abnormal text line segmentation, referring to the nearest text line, and gradually obtaining the key peaks cluster and fitting of each text line. Finally, text lines post-processing, there are some scattered key peaks and unconnected lines, merge it into the corresponding text line or as a single text line.

The least squares polynomial fitting technique as a simplest and most common form of linear/non-linear regression, it provides a solution to the case of finding the optimum fitting straight/curve line through a given point set. In the text line segmentation, its math procedure for extracting the optimum fitting text line to a given set of key peaks and fragments of text line by minimizing the sum of the squares of the offsets of the point set from the text line, which benefit is outlying key peaks and

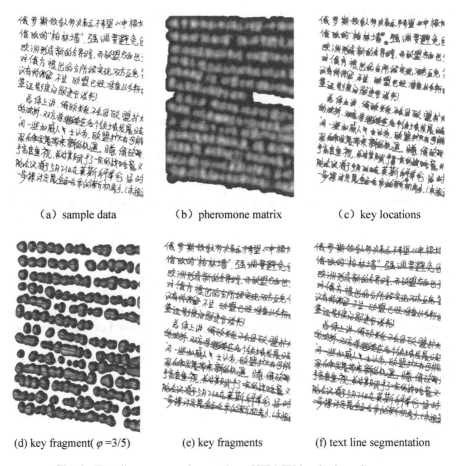

  （a）sample data   （b）pheromone matrix   （c）key locations

(d) key fragment(φ =3/5)   (e) key fragments   (f) text line segmentation

Fig. 1. Text line segmentation result on HIT-MW handwritten document

fragments have minimum effect on the text line's fitting. Let $f(x,p)$ be a known function of x, parametrized in p consisting of a minimal number of coefficients. As we all known, the function is uniquely determined once the parameter set p is known. In text line segmentation, Curve text lines' fitting is to compute the optimal parameter set p by minimizing the sum of squared differences between the real value and the expected value, they are measured values y_i' of f and the values determined from the model $f(x_i',p)$ for measured values x_i' of x, respectively. That is, given n measurement pairs (x_i',y_i'), finding out p to minimize [22]:

$$s(p) = \sum_{i=1}^{n} \left(y_i' - f(x_i',p)\right)^2.$$ (4)

4   Experimental Results

To evaluate the effectiveness of our method, we took into a commonly used database of offline handwritten Chinese documents and compared with some state-of-the-art text line segmentation methods.

4.1   Database Preparation

A commonly used database of offline handwritten Chinese document images, HIT-MW [23], is collected by Harbin Institute of Technology. The document images database consists 853 document images written by more than 780 writers. By analyzing the document images, we know that 8,677 text lines and each line has 21.51 characters on average in this database. Each handwritten document image is scanned at a resolution of 300 dots per inch, so a typical document image size is approximately equal to $1700 * 1500$ pixels, and each document image contains 530 connected components on average.

4.2   Performance of Text Line Segmentation

For evaluating the performance of our method, the matching score table is introduced to describe the degree of matching between the text line segmentation region and the ground truth. When matching score is equal or above 95%, the text line segmentation region is deemed as a one-to-one match to the ground truth region. Let M is the number of text line segmentation region, N is the number of ground truth region, and $o2o$ is the number of one-to-one match pairs, then the detection rate (DR) and recognition accuracy (RA) are defined as follows:

$$DR = \frac{o2o}{N}.$$ (5)

$$RA = \frac{o2o}{M}.$$ (6)

Combining *DR* and *RA*, *F*−*M*easure is the evaluation metric:

$$F-Measure = \frac{2 \times DR \times RA}{DR + RA}.$$
(7)

Offline handwritten Chinese text line segmentation contest is shown in Table 1. Our proposed method generates good results compared to the other state-of-the-art methods, the detection rate is 98.36%, recognition accuracy is 98.20%, and *F*−*M*easure is 98.28%. However, there are still some errors in complex layout structure cases due to the imperfect separation of characters or graphemes in the text line segmentation process.

Table 1. Comparative experimental results

	DR (%)	RA (%)	F-Measure (%)
X-Y projection [8]	45.67	46.13	45.90
Stroke skew correction [9]	55.34	55.12	55.20
Piece-wise projection [4]	92.07	92.51	92.29
MST clustering [5]	95.35	94.96	95.15
CUBS [15]	97.56	96.81	97.18
INMC [10]	98.38	98.24	98.31
NUS [13]	98.24	98.19	98.21
Proposed method	98.36	98.20	98.28

5   Conclusion and Future Work

In this paper, we have proposed a text line segmentation method by writing pheromone diffusion and convergence for the processing of handwritten document images. The main works of the proposed approach consist of (i) writing pheromone diffusion and convergence mode, (ii) key locations and fragments of text line, and (iii) text line segmentation. From experimental results it is shown that our proposed method outperforms state-of-the-art text line segmentation methods in offline handwritten document images. However, there are still some works for improving the segmentation of complex layout structure. Besides that, we also consider the application of writing pheromone diffusion and convergence mode for word segmentation in the future research.

Acknowledgement. This work is sponsored by the National Natural Science Fund of China (61976118, 61806098), Jiangsu Province Natural Science Foundation (BK20180142), Jiangsu Province Natural Science Foundation for Colleges and Universities (17KJB520020, 18KJB520029).

References

1. Ryu, J., Koo, H.I., Cho, N.I.: Language-independent text-line extraction algorithm for handwritten documents. IEEE Signal Process. Lett. **21**(9), 1115–1119 (2014)
2. Renton, G., Soullard, Y., Chatelain, C., Adam, S., Kermorvant, C., Paquet, T.: Fully convolutional network with dilated convolutions for handwritten text line segmentation. Int. J. Doc. Anal. Recogn. (IJDAR) **21**(3), 177–186 (2018). https://doi.org/10.1007/s10032-018-0304-3
3. Sindhushree, G.S., Amarnath, R., Nagabhushan, P.: Entropy-based approach for enabling text line segmentation in handwritten documents. In: Nagabhushan, P., Guru, D.S., Shekar, B.H., Kumar, Y.H.S. (eds.) Data Analytics and Learning. LNNS, vol. 43, pp. 169–184. Springer, Singapore (2019). https://doi.org/10.1007/978-981-13-2514-4_15
4. Arivazhagan, M., Srinivasan, H., Srihari, S.: A statistical approach to line segmentation in handwritten documents. In: International Society for Optics and Photonics in Document Recognition and Retrieval, vol. 65000, pp. 1–11 (2007)
5. Yin, F., Liu, C.-L.: Handwritten Chinese text line segmentation by clustering with distance metric learning. Pattern Recogn. **42**(12), 3146–3157 (2009)
6. Deshmukh, M.S., Patil, M.P., Kolhe, S.R.: A hybrid text line segmentation approach for the ancient handwritten unconstrained freestyle modi script documents. Imaging Sci. J. **66**(7), 433–442 (2018)
7. Pak, I., Teh, P.L.: Text segmentation techniques: a critical review. In: Zelinka, I., Vasant, P., Duy, V.H., Dao, T.T. (eds.) Innovative Computing, Optimization and Its Applications. SCI, vol. 741, pp. 167–181. Springer, Cham (2018). https://doi.org/10.1007/978-3-319-66984-7_10
8. Nagy, G., Seth, S., Viswanathan, M.: A prototype document image analysis system for technical journals. Computer **25**(7), 10–22 (1992)
9. Su, T.-H., Zhang, T.-W., Huang, H.-J., Zhou, Y.: Skew detection for Chinese handwriting by horizontal stroke histogram. In: Ninth International Conference on Document Analysis and Recognition, vol. 2, pp. 899–903. IEEE (2007)
10. Koo, H.I., Cho, N.I.: Text-line extraction in handwritten Chinese documents based on an energy minimization framework. IEEE Trans. Image Process. **21**(3), 1169–1175 (2012)
11. Zhang, X., Tan, C.L.: Text line segmentation for handwritten documents using constrained seam carving. In: International Conference on Frontiers in Handwriting Recognition, pp. 98–103. IEEE (2014)
12. Vo, Q.N., Kim, S.H., Yang, H.J., Lee, G.S.: Text line segmentation using a fully convolutional network in handwritten document images. IET Image Proc. **12**(3), 438–446 (2017)
13. Shi, Z., Setlur, S., Govindaraju, V.: Text extraction from gray scale historical document images using adaptive local connectivity map. In: Eighth International Conference on Document Analysis and Recognition, pp. 794–798. IEEE (2005)
14. Nguyen, T.D., Lee, G.: Text line segmentation in handwritten document images using tensor voting. Trans. Fund. Electron. Commun. Comput. Sci. **94**(11), 2434–2441 (2011)
15. Shi, Z., Setlur, S., Govindaraju, V.: A steerable directional local profile technique for extraction of handwritten Arabic text lines. In: International Conference on Document Analysis and Recognition, pp. 176–180. IEEE (2009)
16. Zezhong, X., Shin, B.-S., Klette, R.: Closed form line-segment extraction using the hough transform. Pattern Recogn. **48**(12), 4012–4023 (2015)
17. Boukharouba, A.: A new algorithm for skew correction and baseline detection based on the randomized hough transform. J. King Saud Univ. Comput. Inf. Sci. **29**(1), 29–38 (2017)

18. Zhang, L., Weidong, Yu.: Orientation image analysis of electrospun submicro-fibers based on hough transform and regionprops function. Text. Res. J. **87**(18), 2263–2274 (2017)
19. Guo, Y., Sun, Y., Bauer, P., Allebach, J.P., Bouman, C.A.: Text line detection based on cost optimized local text line direction estimation. In: The International Society for Optical Engineering, vol. 9395, pp. 1–7 (2015)
20. Adiguzel, H., Sahin, E., Duygulu, P.: A hybrid for line segmentation in handwritten documents. In: International Conference on Frontiers in Handwriting Recognition, pp. 503–508 (2012)
21. Ali, A.A.A., Suresha, M.: Efficient algorithms for text lines and words segmentation for recognition of Arabic handwritten script. In: Shetty, N.R., Patnaik, L.M., Nagaraj, H.C., Hamsavath, P.N., Nalini, N. (eds.) Emerging Research in Computing, Information, Communication and Applications. AISC, vol. 882, pp. 387–401. Springer, Singapore (2019). https://doi.org/10.1007/978-981-13-5953-8_32
22. Motulsky, H., Christopoulos, A.: Fitting Models to Biological Data Using Linear and Nonlinear Regression: A Practical Guide to Curve Fitting. Oxford University Press, Oxford (2004)
23. Su, T.: Chinese Handwriting Recognition: An Algorithmic Perspective. Springer, Heidelberg (2013). https://doi.org/10.1007/978-3-642-31812-2

An Effective Scheduling Algorithm for Wireless Sensor Network with Adjustable Sensing Range

Po-Hsun Chen[1], Tai-Lin Chiu[1], Chun-Hung Fan[1], Huan Chen[1], and Chun-Wei Tsai[2(✉)]

[1] Computer Science and Engineering, National Chung Hsing University, Taichung City, Taiwan
[2] Computer Science and Engineering, National Sun Yat-sen University, Kaohsiung City, Taiwan
cwtsai@mail.cse.nsysu.edu.tw

Abstract. Due to limited energy on sensor nodes, how to achieve a longer lifetime for the WSN has become an essential issue in recent years. Among them, an effective scheduling algorithm can also be regarded as an essential strategy to prolong the lifetime of the entire WSN. Different to most recent studies which only take into account the fixed sensing range of wireless sensors, this study proposed a novel scheme that is designed based on an effective scheduling and a dynamic power control method. The scheduling algorithm can determine which sensors should be turned on, while the power control scheme may dynamically adjust the power levels (sensing range) to enhance the performance of WSN. The salient feature of the proposed algorithm resides in that the proposed search economics based metaheuristic algorithm will divide the solution space into a set of subspaces to search and it will calculate the number of searches for each subspace based on their potential to allocate the computation resource during the convergence process. The simulation results showed that the proposed method is able to significantly extend the lifetime of WSN under the constraint of full-coverage compared with other search algorithms mentioned in this paper.

Keywords: Wireless sensor network · Scheduling algorithm · Meta-heuristic algorithm

1 Introduction

The possibilities of internet of things (IoT) can be found in several recent studies [3, 4] because they showed that IoT technology may promote the development of smart home, smart city, health care, and so forth. That is why IoT and its relevant technologies play an important role in both academia and industries [2] today. Since most IoT applications use various sensors to monitor different targets and collect data from the environment, how to deploy the WSN effectively while prolonging the WSN lifetime has become a critical research issue in recent years. In general, an intuitive way for constructing the WSN is to deploy wireless sensors in environment randomly.

© Springer Nature Singapore Pte Ltd. 2020
J. Shen et al. (Eds.): IC3 2019, CCIS 1227, pp. 114–123, 2020.
https://doi.org/10.1007/978-981-15-6113-9_13

However, maintaining the functionality of IoT systems while enabling the WSN to operate longer is a challenging task. WSN lifetime has become the major measurement to evaluate the performance of WSN. The lifetime of most wireless sensors should be as long as possible. To prolong the WSN lifetime, researchers suggest to reduce the redundant data transmissions or to shorten the transmission range between sensors appropriately [7]. On the other hand, to monitor the environment completely, the wireless sensors of WSN should cover all the targets or as more as possible. Its performance will typically be strongly impacted by the initial deployment of wireless sensors. Once sensors are deployed, how to develop an effective scheduling algorithm for WSN is another difficult research issue because the scheduling problem of WSN has been regarded as a NP-hard problem [17] and it is difficult to find the optimum solution within a reasonable time by using the traditional rule-based search algorithms. As such, some recent studies [11] further considered this optimization problem with the factors of coverage, lifetime, and connectivity at the same time to find a "good scheduling solution" of a multi-objective problem. An effective scheduling strategy can significantly improve the performance and prolong the lifetime of WSN, some studies [16] attempted to use the metaheuristic algorithms to solve such scheduling problems. Metaheuristic algorithms can solve the scheduling problems by providing a more efficient and effective way because they use strategic guessing to replace the deterministic check of rule-based algorithm to solve such complex optimization problems. In this paper, we will first define the scheduling and sensing range adjusting problem of WSN under several constraints such as coverage, residual energy, and energy consumption, and then present an effective scheduling algorithm based on a novel metaheuristic algorithm, search economics (SE) [14], to improve the performance of WSN. The rest of paper is organized as follows. Section 2 will first define the scheduling problem of WSN and then give a brief discussion of deployment strategies for WSN. After then, Sect. 3 introduces the basic idea and operation details of the proposed algorithm. Section 4 shows the parameter settings of the proposed algorithm and other metaheuristic algorithms compared in this paper. The simulation results of the proposed algorithm and other algorithms are also discussed in this section. Finally, Sect. 5 gives a brief summary of our proposed algorithm, results and future works.

2 Related Work

2.1 The Definition of WSN Deployment Problem

In this research, we define the WSN scheduling problem under the constraint of full-coverage, and all the sensor nodes have 5 breath-rate (power levels), from level 1 to level 5. It means that each sensor node has five sensing ranges that we can adjust for each sensor node. The setting of energy consumption is based on [1]. For a wider sensing range, a sensor node consumes more energy. The initial energy θ of a sensor is set to 2000 nano-joule (nJ), and the sensing ranges of a sensor node will be set from 9 nJ/round to 225 nJ/round respectively. Level 1 denotes an active sensor node with the smallest sensor range of 3 m, and level 5 denotes an active sensor node with the largest sensing range of 15 m. The packet size of each target is set to 40 bits, and the data aggregation energy is set to 5 nJ/bit.

ϕ Objective value.
θ Initial energy of each sensor node.
η Set of targets.
τ Energy consumption of one covered target.
c Set of targets which are covered by sensors.
R_t Residual total energy of all sensor nodes.
E_t Total initial energy.
S_r Energy consumption of sensor range r.
T_n Number of target covered by sensor node n.
C_n Energy consumption of nose n.
R_n Residual energy of sensor node n.
C Coverage rate of targets.
R_m Minimum energy among all active sensor nodes.

The initial energy of each sensor node is set to the same energy, denoted as θ. The total initial energy Et is defined as the sum of initial energies of all sensor nodes, which can be defined as

$$E_t = \sum_{i=0}^{n} \theta. \tag{1}$$

The energy consumption of the active sensor node n in each iteration is defined as

$$R_n(t) = R_n(t-1) - C_n(t), \tag{2}$$

where t denotes the t-th iteration.

The energy consumption of each node is defined as the sum of the energy consumption with sensing range r and the energy consumption of those covered targets. For node n, the energy consumption is defined as

$$C_n = S_r + T_n \cdot \tau. \tag{3}$$

The coverage rate is the ratio of the number of covered targets over the total number of targets, which can be expressed as

$$C = \frac{|c|}{|\eta|}. \tag{4}$$

The objective value of the proposed algorithm consists of the following three main factors. (1) First factor is the total residual energy over initial total energy. (2) The second factor is the minimum residual energy among all active node over the initial energy of sensor node. (3) The third factor is the coverage rate. Based on these three factors, the objective function of the WSN scheduling problem then can be defined as

$$\phi = \alpha_1 \cdot \frac{R_t}{E_t} + \alpha_2 \cdot \frac{R_m}{\theta} + \alpha_3 \cdot C, \tag{5}$$

where $\alpha 1$, $\alpha 2$ and $\alpha 3$ denote the weightings of the three corresponding factors, and the sum of $\alpha 1$ and $\alpha 2$ is equal to 1, and $\alpha 3$ is set equal to 2 in this paper. The purpose of this paper is to maximize the lifetime of WSN under the constraint of full-coverage. Furthermore, once the sensors can't afford the energy consumption of full-coverage, how to utilize the rest of active sensors to sustain with a better coverage rate is another objective of our scheduling algorithm.

2.2 Algorithms for the WSN Scheduling Problem

Since the scheduling problem of WSN in this study is to determine which sensors should be turned on/off at what power level, it can be regarded as an NP-hard problem [13]. How to develop an effective method to improve the performance of the WSN has been attracted the attentions of many researchers from various disciplines in recent years. They use different intelligent algorithms to find better scheduling strategies to prolong the WSN lifetime. In [12], Senouci et al. presented a fusion-based WSN deployment method by using the Dempster-Shafer theory to define the fusion scheme to further satisfy the user detection requirement in a finite number of sensors. In this research, they also defined the deployment problem of sensor networks as a binary non-linear and non-convex optimization problem and attempted to apply the genetic algorithm (GA) to solve this optimization problem. Since the deployment problem typically needs to take into account more than one factors to make it more complete to reflect the situation of the environment, Khalesian and Delavar in another recent study [6] attempted to find a trade off between the two conflicting objectives for the WSN, the coverage and lifetime in the sensor deployment problem. Under the constraints of certain connectivity, they presented a constrained Pareto-based multi-objective evolutionary approach (CPMEA) to prolong the lifetime of WSN and maintain the full connectivity of sensor nodes. The experimental results show that CPMEA performs better than the non-dominated sorting genetic algorithm-II (NSGA-II) for such optimization problem. Since the metaheuristic algorithm can provide an effective and efficient way to solve the multi-objective deployment problem of WSN [16], some researchers attempted to combine meta-heuristic with other algorithms for such optimization problem in recent years. For example, Ni et al. in [9] presented a dynamic deployment method based on particle swarm optimization (PSO) to solve the WSN deployment problem. The experimental results showed that their proposed method is able to increase the coverage rate and reduce the total energy consumption of mobile nodes. Another example can be found in the study of [10], Raval et al. presented a hybrid algorithm by combining the harmony search and k-means to optimize the deployment problem. In addition to the PSO and harmony search, the genetic algorithm has been widely used for solving WSN deployment problem in recently years. In [1], Elhoseny et al. first pointed out that some deployment algorithms only make sure the targets to be covered by only one sensor, but once that sensor died or ran out of energy, the targets could not be detected anymore. For this reason, they then presented a k-coverage model based on GA to let the targets can be covered by more than one sensor to further prolong the lifetime of WSN. Jha and Eyong in their study [5] used GA to find the optimal model of WSN by considering three states of sensor nodes that are either idle, sleep or active. Another recent study can be found in [8], where the authors used a new metaheuristic algorithm, called the ant-lion optimization (ALO), to solve the deployment problem to further increase the coverage rate of WSN. The simulation results showed that ALO has higher coverage rate than the PSO and GA algorithms. To address the issue that the metaheuristic algorithms may fall into a local optimum at the early iterations, Tsai in study [15] presented a new metaheuristic algorithm called search economics (SE) to solve the WSN deployment problem. The basic idea of SE is to divide the search space into a set of subspaces and to determine the computation resources to the subspaces via their potentials. The results of [15] showed that SE can provide a better deployment strategy to increase the coverage rate than other deployment methods.

3 Proposed Method

3.1 The Basic Idea

To solve the scheduling problem of WSN and thus to prolong the lifetime of sensors, we proposed a novel metaheuristic algorithm based on search economics [14]. The proposed scheme can determine which sensors should be turned on at what power level, while maintaining the full-coverage constraint. Different from most of metaheuristic algorithms, SE will divide the search space into a set of subspaces (i.e., regions). More computation resources will be invested to the subspace that has a higher potential to find better solutions. An expected value is used for each subspace to represent the potential of each region to find out better solutions. Because SE is able to reallocate computation resources to each region based on their expected values, SE can avoid wasting too much time on unnecessary searches. Moreover, SE will increase the expected value for the region that has not been searched for a while. Since the aims of this research is different to our previous work [15], where we apply the SE in solving the WSN deployment problem. In this work, we aims to solve the scheduling and adjustable sensing range problem with the SE algorithm. As such, the essential components of SE should be redesigned, including the encoding of solutions, methods to divide the search space, the mechanism to exchange the information among regions, and the calculation of expected values. They are quite different for the scheduling problems.

Algorithm 1 is the outline of the proposed algorithm. It contains four main operators that are initialization, resource arrangement, vision search, and marketing research. The initialization operator performs the parameter settings of the SE and it will create the initial solutions s at the very beginning. After the initialization operator, the resource arrangement will divide the search space into several subspaces (regions), then searchers s (solutions) will be assigned to the regions. Each region has its own goods (candidate solutions), and m denotes a set of goods in each region. The vision search is similar to most metaheuristic algorithms, including transition, evaluation and determination. The vision search will allocate computation resources based on the expected value of each region. The marketing research will update information of the regions and searchers will invest the best good in the region.

Algorithm 1: Search Economics Algorithm

Search Economics()
{
    s = Initialization()
    m = Resource_Arrangement()
    While the termination is not met
        s = Vision_Search(s, m)
        m = Marketing_Research(s, m)
    End
    Output s
}

Encoding Scheme. As shown in Fig. 1, the encoding of a solution will be represented in a vector with n elements. The value of each element is in the range from −1 to 4. The parameter n denotes that there are n candidate locations in the sensing filed where sensors can be deployed. Each element in a solution represents the status of the candidate location. The status of −1 denotes that there is no sensor deployed, 0 denotes that the sensor is deployed but in the sleeping mode, and consumes no energy. The larger value of a status indicates a wider sensing range of a sensor node, and thus consumes more energy.

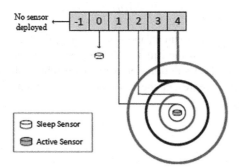

Fig. 1. Example illustrating how a solution is represented.

Resource Arrangement. As for the resource arrangement, the search space will first be divided into m regions r = {r1, ..., rm}. The candidate solutions g = {gi1, ..., gih} for i-th region will be initialized randomly, where h denotes the number of candidate solution in region i. The method of dividing regions is shown in Fig. 2. We first compute the sum of the elements in the candidate solution, and then take the remainder of this sum (mod m) as the region where the solution resides. For example, if m = 4, the region of the candidate solution (0, 4, 3, 0, 2, 1, 2, 1) will be equal to 1. It means that the above candidate solution is in region 1. After the initialization, there will be p searchers s = {si1, ..., sip} assigned to each regions, and each of them will hold a solution in the corresponding region, and each region has its own goods (solutions) a = {ai1, ai2, ..., aik}. After that, the other operator will exchange information between searchers and goods.

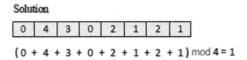

Solution

| 0 | 4 | 3 | 0 | 2 | 1 | 2 | 1 |

$(0 + 4 + 3 + 0 + 2 + 1 + 2 + 1) \bmod 4 = 1$

Fig. 2. Example illustrating how the search space is divided by the proposed algorithm.

Vision Search. The function of vision search is similar to most metaheuristic algorithms, which consists of the transition, evaluation, and determination. The main purpose of the vision search is to allow a searcher to invest the region that has a higher expected value. First, the j-th searcher gij exchanges specific elements with the good ai k during the transition stage.

As shown in Figs. 3 and 4, we adapted a two-point crossover operator and a simple mutation operator in the genetic algorithm. The crossover of goods only occurred in the same region. In the evaluation and determination, the searcher will be reassigned to other regions based on the potentials of the regions. The evaluation metrics for the potential of the regions is called "expected value" [14], which can be defined as

$$\mathbb{E}_{ij} = f_1(\mathcal{M}_j) f_2(\mathcal{V}_j^i) f_3(\rho_j), \tag{6}$$

The Mj represents the investment proportion of the j-th region and searchers. Vji represents the average profit if the i-th searcher is invested in the j-th region. ρj is the comparison value of the best solution compared with other solutions in the region j. Moreover, f1, f2, and f3 represent the normalization functions for Mj, Vji, and ρj, respectively.

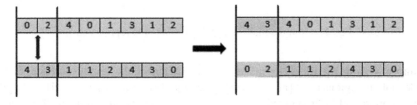

Fig. 3. Example illustrating how a searcher and a good exchanges the information.

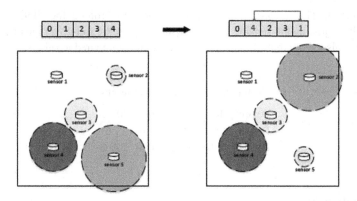

Fig. 4. Example illustrating how a solution perform mutation.

4   Experimental Results

The experimental results are processed by one PC with Intel i5-8400 CPU (2.80 GHz, 9 MB cache, and 6 cores) and 8 GB memory running in Windows 10. The programs are all written in C language. The datasets are simulated according to several studies and based on their simulated environments. As shown in Table 1, the sensors are assumed to be scattered in a sensing filed of 100 * 100 m^2. The number of sensors and targets in each dataset are also listed in Table 1. In order to compare the performance of each algorithm, the number of evaluations will be performed equally for each compared algorithm.

Table 1. The database

Dataset	Sensors	Targets	Evaluations
DS1	500	50	50,000
DS2	600	50	50,000

Three typical metaheuristic algorithms, the hill climbing (HC), genetic algorithm (GA) and simulated annealing (SA) are also implemented in this paper to compare with the proposed algorithm. The parameters settings of the compared algorithms are described as follows. For the GA, the crossover rate and mutation rate are set to be 0.5 and 0.2, respectively. The number of chromosome is set to equal to 50. For the SA, the initial and minimum temperature are set to equal to 100 and 1 respectively, and the cooling rate is set equal to 0.9, the number of neighbors is set equal to 3.

Table 2 shows the comparison results for our proposed scheme with other metaheuristics in this paper. The results of the two datasets show that the proposed SE algorithm has higher potential to search for better solution. The values in the Table 2 represent the lifetime (in rounds) of the WSN for datasets DS1 and DS2. Under the constraint of full-coverage, increasing the number of sensors will also increase the opportunity of coverage for each target. This means that the WSN is able to prolong the lifetime through dynamically adjusting the sensing range to achieve a specific full-coverage rate. Finally, these results also show that SE has the longest lifetime compared to others.

Table 2. The experimental results

Dataset	HC	SA	GA	SE
DS1	10.00	11.33	11.67	12.67
DS2	21.00	12.33	20.67	22.00

5   Conclusions

In this paper, we first define a WSN scheduling problem that determine the deployed sensors to be turned on at an adjustable sensing range. A novel meta-heuristic algorithm based on SE is proposed to solve this scheduling and power control optimization problem. Under the constraints of full-coverage, our method is able to find better solutions than other metaheuristic algorithms compared in this paper. The proposed scheme performs better because it can invest computation resource to higher return regions and avoid wasting the computation resources in the same regions. The simulation results show that the proposed algorithm can significantly prolong the lifetime of WSN. Furthermore, to make the experiment more complete, it is necessary to convey the target's information back to the base station. For our future work, we will develop an algorithm that can consider the connectivity and routing constraints with the scheduling issue solved in this paper for the WSN.

Acknowledgement. This work was supported in part by the Ministry of Science and Technology of Taiwan, R.O.C., under Contracts MOST107-2221-E-110-078, and MOST108-2221-E-005-021-MY3.

References

1. Elhoseny, M., Tharwat, A., Farouk, A., Hassanien, A.E.: K-coverage model based on genetic algorithm to extend WSN lifetime. IEEE Sens. Lett. **1**(4), 1–4 (2017)
2. Fantacci, R., Pecorella, T., Viti, R., Carlini, C.: A network architecture solution for efficient IoT WSN backhauling: challenges and opportunities. IEEE Wirel. Commun. **21**(4), 113–119 (2014)
3. Ghayvat, H., Mukhopadhyay, S., Gui, X., Suryadevara, N.: WSN- and IoT-based smart homes and their extension to smart buildings. Sensors **15**(5), 10350–10379 (2015)
4. Hassanalieragh, M., et al.: Health monitoring and management using Internet-of-Things (IoT) sensing with cloud-based processing: opportunities and challenges. In: Proceedings of the 2015 IEEE International Conference on Services Computing, pp. 285–292 (2015)
5. Jha, S.K., Eyong, E.M.: An energy optimization in wireless sensor networks by using genetic algorithm. Telecommun. Syst. **67**(1), 113–121 (2017). https://doi.org/10.1007/s11235-017-0324-1

6. Khalesian, M., Delavar, M.R.: Wireless sensors deployment optimization using a constrained pareto-based multi-objective evolutionary approach. Eng. Appl. Artif. Intell. **53**, 126–139 (2016)
7. Lazarescu, M.T.: Design of a WSN platform for long-term environmental monitoring for IoT applications. IEEE J. Emerg. Sel. Top. Circ. Syst. **3**(1), 45–54 (2013)
8. Liu, W., Yang, S., Sun, S., Wei, S.: A node deployment optimization method of WSN based on ant-lion optimization algorithm. In: 2018 IEEE 4th International Symposium on Wireless Systems within the International Conferences on Intelligent Data Acquisition and Advanced Computing Systems, pp. 88–92 (2018)
9. Ni, Q., Du, H., Pan, Q., Cao, C., Zhai, Y.: An improved dynamic deployment method for wireless sensor network based on multi-swarm particle swarm optimization. Nat. Comput. **16**(1), 5–13 (2015). https://doi.org/10.1007/s11047-015-9519-0
10. Raval, D., Raval, G., Valiveti, S.: Optimization of clustering process for WSN with hybrid harmony search and k-means algorithm. In: 2016 International Conference on Recent Trends in Information Technology, pp. 1–6 (2016)
11. Sengupta, S., Das, S., Nasir, M., Panigrahi, B.: Multi-objective node deployment in WSNs: in search of an optimal trade-off among coverage, lifetime, energy consumption, and connectivity. Eng. Appl. Artif. Intell. **26**(1), 405–416 (2013)
12. Senouci, M.R., Mellouk, A., Aitsaadi, N., Oukhellou, L.: Fusion-based surveillance WSN deployment using Dempster-Shafer theory. J. Netw. Comput. Appl. **64**, 154–166 (2016)
13. Sirivianos, M., Westhoff, D., Armknecht, F., Girao, J.: Non-manipulable aggregator node election protocols for wireless sensor networks. In: Proceedings of the 2007 5th International Symposium on Modeling and Optimization in Mobile, Ad Hoc and Wireless Networks and Workshops, pp. 1–10 (2007)
14. Tsai, C.: Search economics: a solution space and computing resource aware search method. In: Proceedings of the 2015 IEEE International Conference on Systems, Man, and Cybernetics, pp. 2555–2560 (2015)
15. Tsai, C.W.: An effective WSN deployment algorithm via search economics. Comput. Netw. **101**(4), 178–191 (2016)
16. Tsai, C.W., Tsai, P.W., Pan, J.S., Chao, H.C.: Metaheuristics for the deployment problem of WSN: a review. Microprocess. Microsyst. **39**(8), 1305–1317 (2015)
17. Yao, Y., Cao, Q., Vasilakos, A.V.: EDAL: an energy-efficient, delay-aware, and lifetime-balancing data collection protocol for heterogeneous wireless sensor net-works. IEEE/ACM Trans. Networking **23**(3), 810–823 (2015)

A Study on Improved MRMF Algorithm on Uncertain Graph

Kejie Wen[1(✉)], Juan Yang[1], Wei Liu[2], Yanchun Yang[2], and Baili Zhang[3]

[1] School of Computer Science and Engineering, Southeast University, Nanjing 211189, China
wkj913106903@qq.com
[2] Key Laboratory of Computer Network and Information Integration of Ministry of Education, Southeast University, Nanjing 211189, China
[3] Research Center for Judicial Big Data, Supreme Count of China, Nanjing 211189, China

Abstract. With the increased size and density of graph, the performance of the space decomposition-based algorithm (SDBA) decreases rapidly in terms of the most reliable maximum flow problem (MRMF). To solve this problem, the double filter space decomposition-based algorithm (DF-SDBA) is proposed by applying the probability filter and the cut-set filter. First, among the intervals to be processed in the process of space decomposition, DF-SDBA algorithm uses the probability constraint to filter out the intervals which own smaller probability of the lower boundary distribution than the current maximum flow, reducing the number of iterations effectively. Then the cut-set constraint is applied to unspecified intervals. According to the rule that all the edges in the cut-sets must exist in the upper bound of each interval, the unspecified intervals are filtered out, cutting down the number of partition intervals once again. The experimental results reveal that compared with the SDBA algorithm, the DF-SDBA algorithm can reduce the number of the intervals needed to be divided can obtain better performance.

Keywords: Uncertain graph · Maximum flow · Flow reliability · Minimum cut

1 Introduction

Uncertainty is an inherent feature of network system. Researchers have made a thorough study in recent years and proposed a myriad of issues and solutions [1–8]. Path coverage and heuristic greedy algorithm are adopted to overcome the problem of mining the most reliable subgraph in uncertain graphs based on uncertain graphs in the papers [1, 2]. To solve the problems of mining model construction, reducing time complexity of subgraph isomorphism and mining K-maximal frequent pattern, Zou [3] and Zhang et al. [4] proposed an efficient algorithm. Yuan et al. [5] survey the subgraph similarity query with the idea of filtering validation. For the k-nearest neighbor in uncertain graphs, Zhang et al. [6] establish an efficient neighbor graph index based on the reliable expected distance. Zhang et al. [7] propose a k-NN query to solve uncertain

© Springer Nature Singapore Pte Ltd. 2020
J. Shen et al. (Eds.): IC3 2019, CCIS 1227, pp. 124–133, 2020.
https://doi.org/10.1007/978-981-15-6113-9_14

graphs based on SimRank metric method. The shortest path problem in uncertain graph is expanded in the literature [8] and solutions and algorithms are given.

The maximum flow problem of uncertain graphs is the natural extension of the traditional maximum flow problem in the uncertain graph, which is used to measure the load capacity of the network. It makes many significant issues occur, among which the reliability of the stochastic flow network and the most reliable maximum flow are two interrelated and different issues. Stochastic flow network reliability studies how to evaluate the reliability of the maximum flow or rated flow in networks. Many different algorithms [9–12] have been proposed in recent years. The most reliable maximum flow problem proposed by Cai et al. [12] mainly concerns the relationship between maximum flow and the multiple maximum flow distributions. Among multiple maximum flow distributions, there exists the distribution with the highest reliability. As the preferred scheme of stream transmission, it guarantees reliable transmission, solving practical problems such as the construction of reliability network and the choice of reliable transmission path effectively. SDBA [12] is an effective algorithm available to solve the most reliable maximum flow. It adopts state space partition to obtain all closed intervals satisfying a maximum flow, and then finds out possible subgraphs with the highest probability in lower bounds, that is, the most reliable maximum flow distribution can be obtained. However, with the increased size of graph, the increased vertices make the sub-dimension space larger, affecting the performance of SDBA significantly, and the rise of density causes a sharp increase in the number of intervals to be divided. Therefore, the time cost of the algorithm increases rapidly, affecting availability of the algorithm considerably.

To solve this problem, this paper proposes a state space partition algorithm DF-SDBA based on probability and cut-set double filtering. Probability constraint is first adopted in DF-SDBA algorithm in the process of state space division, and the unspecified intervals which the probability of the lower boundary distribution in the interval is less than the current most reliable maximum flow distribution are filtered out, reducing the number of iterations of the algorithm effectively. Then, the cut-set are used to divide the intervals. It computes the maximum flow in the upper bound of the unspecified interval. Meanwhile minimum cut set can be obtained. All the edges in the cut-sets must exist in the upper bound of each interval, so the number of partition intervals can be reduced once again after filtering the subintervals further, thus effectively improving the efficiency of the algorithm.

2   DF-SDBA Algorithm

2.1   The Thought of DF-SDBA Algorithm

Similar to the issue of stochastic flow networks reliability, the state space partition method is also the basic algorithm to solve the most reliable maximum stream problem. It uses a series of rules to partition the subgraph spaces contained by the uncertain graphs, so as to get the intervals satisfying the maximum stream, the intervals that does not satisfy the maximum flow and the intervals to be divided. The intervals satisfying the maximum stream are added to candidate. The intervals that do not satisfy the maximum flow can be abandoned, and the intervals to be divided need to be further partitioned until there exits no interval to be divided. Finally, the probability of the possible subgraphs corresponding to the lower bounds of all intervals in the candidate set is calculated, the lower bound subgraph which has the largest probability is found, and the most reliable maximum flow is obtained.

The above process is also the basic thought of SDBA, which is similar to the classical algorithm of random flow network reliability. The main difference between them is that only in the final stage, which is the candidate sets are treated differently. The stochastic flow network reliability problem is to add the probabilities corresponding to all intervals in the candidate sets, but the SDBA needs to select the closed interval with the largest probability. The above difference is also the entry point of the improved algorithm proposed in this paper. The stochastic flow network reliability problem needs to find the probability sum of all possible subgraphs corresponding to the closed interval satisfying the maximum flow, and the most reliable maximum flow problem only needs to find the largest one of the possible subgraph probabilities corresponding to the lower bound of the interval in all the intervals that satisfy the maximum flow. Therefore, various filtering methods can be used to filter out the intervals that do not meet the requirements and reduce the number of intervals to be divided as much as possible. Consequently, this paper proposes an improved algorithm DF-SDBA for state space partitioning based on the probability and cut set double filtering. The specific algorithm is as follows:

(1) Run the maximum flow algorithm on the maximum subgraph MSG(G) of the uncertain graph G, and the maximum flow value F_{max} from the source point s to the end-point t is obtained.

(2) According to the maximum flow state vector from (1), subgraph space Ω of the uncertainty diagram G is divided, and intervals satisfying the maximum flow, the intervals that do not satisfy the maximum flow and the intervals to be divided are obtained. We can do the following treatments separately:

- For each untreated interval, if the probability corresponding to the lower bound of the interval is less than the most reliable probability of maximum current distribution, it is abandoned directly.
- For the interval satisfying the maximum flow, if the probability is greater than current probability of the most reliable maximum flow distribution, then the most reliable maximum flow distribution is updated.
- For the intervals to be divided, it is necessary to be further divided, so as to obtain a number of sub-intervals, it is necessary to ensure that the all the edges of the minimal cut-set exist in the upper bound vector, otherwise the sub-interval does not meet the maximum flow, and it can also be abandoned directly.

(3) The maximum flow algorithm runs on the subgraph corresponding probability maximum interval lower bound, and the most reliable maximum flow distribution is obtained.

2.2   Filtering Rules

Rule 1 (Probability filtering rules). For any interval, if the probability of the lower bound of the interval is less than the probability of the current most reliable and maximum flow distribution, the maximum flow distribution of higher reliability is impossible to exist.

According to the previous analysis, different from the reliability problem of random flow network, reliability of random flow network needs to find out all the intervals that satisfy the maximum flow and accumulate their probability values. And the most reliable and maximum flow problem only needs to find the interval with the maximum probability value. This provides a basis for probability screening.

In the process of setting algorithm, the current highest reliability of the maximum flow distribution of the probability value is $P(V_m)$, V_m is the corresponding distribution. According to the calculation rules of the probability of flow distribution, in any interval, the distribution of its lower bound vectors has the maximum local probability value, and there is no other maximum flow distribution with higher probability in the interval range. Therefore, during the execution of the algorithm, first, we compare the probability of the lower bound vector with $P(V_m)$. If it is lower than this value, it is impossible to have the most reliable and maximum flow in the global sense in this interval. So we can omit it.

Rule 2 (Cut set filtering rules). If the minimum cut set corresponding to the subgraph of the upper bound of the interval to be divided is C, then all the qualified sub-interval upper bound vectors contain the edges of the minimum cut set C.

According to the Ford-Fulkerson method [14], the maximum flow value F_{max} that can be transmitted from the source point s to the end t equals the sum of the flows of the edges in the minimum cut set. If reducing the flow of the edges in the minimum cut-set, the maximum flow is reduced accordingly. Therefore, among the sub-intervals of the partition to be divided, the edges of the minimum cut set must be all in a possible subgraph corresponding to the upper bound of the lattice interval. It is possible that there may be an instance of the maximum flow in the interval. Otherwise, if at least one edge does not exist in the upper boundary of the subinterval, the flow value of a cut set which is less than F_{max} must exist in the upper bound subgraph of the interval. According to the maximum flow minimum cut theorem, the maximum flow is less than F_{max}, the sub-interval is an interval that does not satisfy the maximum flow, and is directly discarded.

The specific steps for filtering rules are as follows:

(1) Interval division. Let $C = [l^C, u^C]$ be an interval to be divided, $l^C = \{l_1, l_2, \ldots, l_{|E|}\}$ is the 0-1 vector corresponding to the lower bound vector of the subgraph interval C, $u^C = \{u_1, u_2, \ldots, u_{|E|}\}$ is the 0-1 vector corresponding to the upper bound vector of the subgraph interval C, $V = \{v_1, v_2, \ldots, v_{|E|}\}$ is a maximum flow of u^C in the upper bound of the interval, map it to 0-1 vector $f = \{f_1, f_2, \ldots, f_{|E|}\}$, $I^C = \{i | i \in 1, 2, \ldots, |E|\} \&\& f_i > l_i\} = \{i_1, i_2, \ldots, i_q\}$, then you can get $q + 1$ disjoint sub-intervals [13].

(2) Probabilistic filtering. During the calculation of the algorithm, assume that the most reliable maximum flow distribution which is currently obtained is V_m, and its probability value is $P(V_m)$. For interval to be divided $C = [l^C, u^C]$, first calculate the probability value $P(l^C)$ corresponding to the lower bound of the interval, if $P(l^C) < P(V_m)$, there must exist no maximum flow distribution with a probability value greater than P in interval C. This section is directly discarded.

(3) Cut set filtering. While obtaining the maximum flow vector V, we can obtain a minimum cut set $C = \{C_1, C_2, \ldots, C_{|E|}\}$, its corresponding 0-1 vector is $T = \{t_1, t_2, \ldots, t_{|E|}\}$. According to the rule of cut set filtering, we can get $I^{C'} = \{i | i \in 1, 2, \ldots, |E|\} \,\&\&\, f_i > l_i\} = \{i_1, i_2, \ldots, i_{q'}\}$, C can be divided into $q' + 1$ intersecting intersections, and $q' < q$.

2.3   The Implementation of the Algorithm

According to the basic description of the above algorithm, the DF-SDBA algorithm specific pseudo code is as follows.

Algorithm 1   DF-SDBA algorithm

Input: uncertainty graph G, source point s endpoint t.

Output: $s - t$ most reliable maximum flow value F_{max}, the most reliable maximum flow distribution V_m and its probability value R.

Init $R = 0, V_m = \{0\}$, stack S;

F_{max}=getMaxFlow(MSG(G), s, t);

S. push ({ ($0,0,\ldots,0_{|E|}$), ($1,1,\ldots 1_{|E|}$), Φ, I=0, j=0 });

WHILE S is not empty

  Get the first collection $C=[l^c, u^c]$ from the top of S ;

  IF i < I ; THEN i++;ELSE S.pop();

  IF $P(l^c) < R$, according to rule 1,this collection needs to discard, then go to while again;

  ELSE compute $F(u^c)$ and $F(l^c)$ of collection C;

    IF $F(u^c) < F_{max}$, discard this collection;

    ELSE IF $F(l^c) \geq F_{max}$,calculate $P(l^c)$,IF $P(l^c) > R$, replace R and V_m;

    ELSE, compute max-flow $f = (f1, f2, \ldots, f_{|E|})$ and min-cut c = $(c_1, c_2, \ldots, c_{|E|})$, then computer $I^{c'}$ based on rule 2 to divide C into $C_1, C_2, \ldots, C_0$;

S.push({ $l^c, u^c, (f1, f2, \ldots, f_{|E|}), I', |I'|, j=1$}) && calculate the possibility of C_0, IF P$(C_0) > R$, replace R and V_m.

  Return (R, V_m)

Suppose the iterative times of spatial partition by DF-SDBA algorithm are k', and the Dinic algorithm is applied to calculate the maximum flow, the time complexity of DF-SDBA algorithm is $O(k'|A||V|^2)$. Compared with the time complexity $O(k|A||V|^2)$ time algorithm in document [13], the k' of the DF-SDBA algorithm is much smaller than k of the SDBA algorithm. This is because the SDBA algorithm needs to be processed one by one for a series of subgroups produced after each interval partition, especially those intervals to be divided need to be further divided. This produces a series of sub intervals, recursive process these subgroups until there are no intervals to be divided, and the iteration ends. Before the further division of the interval, the DF-SDBA algorithm has removed a large number of intervals by using the probability and cut-set filter rules. Those intervals to be divided which are screened out are more conducive to reducing the number of iterations, because if you continue to divide these intervals, there will be more subareas. Sifting off an interval to be divided often reduces the treatments of a series of subareas. As the current maximum probability increases gradually, the efficiency of probability filtering becomes higher and higher, which makes the algorithm converges rapidly. Subsequent experiments verify this effect very well, especially with the increase of the density of the graphs, filtering rule is more obvious for the reduction of iterations. When the density is greater than 0.45, there are 2 orders of magnitude or more of performance improvement.

2.4   Proof of Correctness of the Algorithm

Theorem 1: Assume that all subgraphs that can pass the maximum flow F_{max} in the uncertain graph G are filtered by space probabilities and cut-set filters, all subgraphs are divided into r disjoint closed intervals $C_1, C_2, \ldots, C_r$, $C_i = [\alpha_i + \beta_i]$, $\alpha_i = (\alpha_{i1}, \ldots, \alpha_{i|E|})$ is the subgraph corresponding to the lower bound. The most reliable maximum flow of a S-T of the indefinite graph G must exist in the R lower subgraph.

Prove: It is important to prove that probability filtering and cut set filtering do not lose the most reliable and maximum flow distribution.

1) We will prove that probability filtering is correct. In the interval division process, the probability value of state interval's lower bound distribution should be calculated first. If it is less than the current probability value of the most reliable maximum flow distribution, the interval is directly discarded because sum of probability value of potential subgraph fulfilling maximum flow is smaller than current most reliable maximum flow distribution. Assume that the status space $C_j = [l^{C_j}, u^{C_j}]$ is a status space, the most reliable maximum flow distribution at present is V_m, its probability value is $P(V_m)$. $P(l^{C_j}) < P(V_m)$, there must be no maximum flow distribution with reliability greater than $P(V_m)$ in C_j. We can prove it by using reduction to absurdity. If there is any, there is at least one maximum flow distribution f whose reliability is bigger than $P(V_m)$ in the state interval C_j, we will conclude that $P(f) \leq P(l^{C_j}) \,\&\&\, P(f) > P(V_m)$. Because $P(l^{C_j}) < P(V_m)$, $P(f) < P(V_m)$ is in contradiction with $P(f) > P(V_m)$, in other words, the most reliable maximum flow distribution can be concluded by using the DF-SDBA algorithm with probability filtering.

2) We will prove that cut set filtering is correct. The uncertainty interval $C_j = [l^{C_j}, u^{C_j}]$ is further divided. First, a maximum flow distribution $f = \{f_1, f_2, \ldots, f_{|E|}\}$ and a minimum cut set $c = \{c_1, c_2, \ldots, c_{|E|}\}$ in the upper bound subgraph u^{C_j} should be found, thus the $I^C = \{i | i \in \{1, 2, \ldots, |E|\} \,\&\&\, f_i > l_{C_j}\} = \{i_1, i_2, \ldots, i_q\}$ in the SDBA algorithm is obtained, and get $q + 1$ disjoint subsets. The DF-SDBA

algorithm uses the idea of cut set filtering, the number of elements in I^C is reduced, and new $I^{C'} = \{i | i \in \{1, 2, \ldots, |E|\} \,\&\&\, f_i > l_C \,\&\&\, f_i > c_i\} = \{i_1, i_2, \ldots, i_{q'}\}$ will be obtained. The existence of the edges of the minimum cut set in the upper boundary of the subinterval should be guaranteed, otherwise, it does not meet the maximum flow. We can prove it by using reduction to absurdity. If interval $C_{j'} = [l^{C_{j'}}, u^{C_{j'}}]$ is a sub interval produced in the C_j division process, and at least one of the edges in cut set c does not exist in $u^{C_{j'}}$. According to the maximum flow minimum cut theorem, the maximum flow value on the interval $C_{j'}$ is obtained on its interval upper boundary subgraph $u^{C_{j'}}$. There is a cutset on this submap, the traffic value of which is less than F_{max}, conflicting with assumptions.

Theorem 1 shows that the algorithm DF-SDBA will not leak out, ensuring that the most reliable and maximum flow distribution of the $s - t$ of the uncertain graph G can be obtained. It proves the correctness of the algorithm theoretically.

3 Experiment

In order to verify the performance of the proposed algorithm, we conducted a series of experiments. The experimental platform is a PC of Intel Core (CPU i3-2120, 3.3 GHz, memory 4 GB, 64 bits Windows 7 operating systems), the algorithm is implemented by using Visual C++. The data set in document [13] is used in the experiment.

1) Using NETGEN generator [15] produces six groups of directed graphs that includes V_6A_{10}, V_8A_{14}, $V_{10}A_{18}$, $V_{12}A_{22}$, $V_{14}A_{26}$, $V_{16}A_{34}$ (V_nA_m is a graph of n vertices and m edges), The capacity and corresponding probability of a graph should be evenly distributed. We choose the vertices with the largest number of simple paths between any 2 points as the starting point and the endpoint, which ensure that there are as many paths as possible from s to t.

2) The number of vertices of a graph is fixed (The number of points in the experiment is $|A| = 16$). Directed graph with different density is generated. (density d in the experiment take 0.25, 0.30, 0.35, 0.40, 0.45, respectively, the relation among edges $|V|$, Vertex number $|A|$, density is $d = \frac{2|A|}{|V|} * (|V| - 1)$).

3) Experiment uses the Chinese Taiwan power transmission network (TEPN) as the actual data set in document [10]. During the experiment, 58 elements were randomly acquired from 100 elements in document [10] using 10 different random number seeds, forming 1–58 edges in the TEPN network. Since each component has multiple capacity states, its maximum capacity status and probability value are taken as the edge status information. Its source point s is the Third Nuclear Power Plant in Pingdong County, and the Meeting Point t is Taipei City.

Experiment 1: The scale of the graph affects the algorithm.
As it shown in the Fig. 1(a), with the increase of the number of edges, the running time of two algorithms increases, but the rate of growth differs a lot. SDBA algorithm needs to deal with more subintervals, causing the cost of time increasing sharply with the

network regulation modulus increased. DF-SDBA algorithm reduce the number of intervals divided efficiently, and the performance of algorithm is significantly raised, the increasing speed of the expenditure of time is much slower with the network regulation modulus increased. In the Fig. 1(b), with the increase of the number of edges, memory consumption needed by two algorithms shows a trend of upward trend. However, DF-SDBA algorithm needs to consume a bit more memory, because it needs to store more information including probability values and cut set, etc. Generally, based on the method of conversion from space to time, the DF-SDBA algorithm obtains a very good performance of time, Particularly, as the network scale increases, the time performance of the algorithm becomes more outstanding.

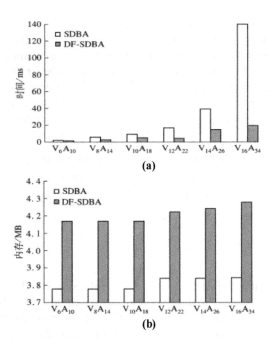

Fig. 1 (a) Relationship between time cost and number of edges. (b) The relationship between memory cost and the number of edges

Experiment 2: The influence of the density of the graph on the algorithm.
It can be seen from Fig. 2, as the density of the graph increasing, the time cost of 2 algorithms is also increasing. The higher the density of graph is, the more the state space is, and the more the number of distributions satisfying the maximum flow, the more iterations the algorithm needs. It causes the algorithm run time t' to become longer. With the increase of density, the time cost of DF-SDBA algorithm is obviously smaller than that of SDBA algorithm. Because DF-SDBA algorithm can filter out the intervals of small probability value and intervals that does not meet the maximum flow effectively, avoiding unnecessary division, reducing number of iteration and improving the performance of the algorithm.

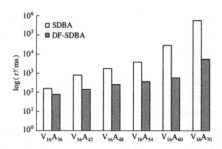

Fig. 2. Performance of two algorithms under different density

Experiment 3: Comparison of TEPN experiment.

Table 1 is the result of the SDBA and DF-SDBA algorithms running on the TEPN dataset, average time is that of the algorithm running on 10 uncertain graphs. As can be seen from Table 1, the DF-SDBA algorithm is significantly better than SDBA, But for graphs of relatively higher density, TEPN dataset performance improved less. Because TEPN is sparse graph, and there are fewer edges in the cut set, the effects of cut set filtering is not obvious, resulting in less performance improvement.

Table 1. TEPN experiment comparison. ms

Algorithm	SDBA	DF-SDBA
Average time	83.75596	38.75596

4   Conclusion

The improved algorithm DF-SDBA of state space division based on probability and cut-set filtering is proposed in this paper, it is applied to solve the most reliable maximum flow problems. The DF-SDBA algorithm filters intervals whose probability of the lower bound distribution is smaller than that of interval of current most reliable maximum flow with probability filtering. And it removes intervals unsatisfying with maximum flow with cut-set filtering. As a result, the number of divided intervals and iterations of algorithm are decreased. The experimental results show that DF-SDBA algorithm can reduce the number of intervals being handled effectively, which speeds up algorithm convergence. Its performance is obviously better than SDBA.

The main work of next step in this paper is to further improve algorithm's performance with multicomputer parallel and study the issue of dynamic network topological changes that may occur in practical applications.

Acknowledgments. This work was partly supported by the National Key R&D Program of China (2018YFC0830200, the Fundamental Research Funds for the Central Universities (2242018S30021 and 2242017S30023) and Open Research Fund from Key Laboratory of Computer Network and Information Integration In Southeast University, Ministry of Education, China.

References

1. Hintanen, P., Toivonen, H., Sevon, P.: Fast discovery of reliable subnetworks. In: Proceedings of the 11th International Conference on Advances in Social Networks Analysis and Mining (ASONAM), Odense, Denmark, pp. 104–111 (2010)
2. Hintsanen, P.: The most reliable subgraph problem. In: Kok, J.N., Koronacki, J., Lopez de Mantaras, R., Matwin, S., Mladenič, D., Skowron, A. (eds.) PKDD 2007. LNCS (LNAI), vol. 4702, pp. 471–478. Springer, Heidelberg (2007). https://doi.org/10.1007/978-3-540-74976-9_48
3. Zou, Z.N., Li, J.Z., Gao, H., Zhang, S.: Mining frequent subgraph patterns from uncertain graphs. J. Softw. **20**(11), 2965–2976 (2009). (in Chinese)
4. Zhang, S., Gao, H., Li, J.Z., Zou, Z.N.: Efficient query processing on uncertain graph database. Chin. J. Comput. **32**(10), 2066–2079 (2009). (in Chinese)
5. Yuan, Y., Wang, G.R., Chen, L., Wang H.X.: Efficient subgraph similarity search on large probabilistic graph databases. In: Proceedings of the 38th International Conference on Very Large Database (VLDB), Istanbul, Turkey, pp. 800–811 (2012)
6. Zhang, H.J., Jiang, S.X., Zou, Z.N.: An efficient algorithm for top-k proximity query on uncertain graphs. Chin. J. Comput. **34**(10), 1855–1896 (2011). (in Chinese)
7. Zhang, Y.L., Li, C.P., Chen, H., et al.: An efficient algorithm for top-k proximity query on uncertain graphs. J. Comput. Res. Dev. **48**(10), 1850–1858 (2011). (in Chinese)
8. Rasteiro, D.D.M.L., Anjo, A.J.B.: Optimal paths in probabilistic networks in uncertain graph. J. Comput. Res. Dev. **48**(10), 1850–1858 (2011). (in Chinese)
9. Jane, C.C., Laih, Y.W.: A practical algorithm for computing multi-state two-terminal reliability. IEEE Trans. Reliab. **57**, 295–302 (2008)
10. Jane, C.C., Laih, Y.W.: Computing multi-state two-terminal reliability through critical arc states that interrupt demand. IEEE Trans. Reliab. **59**, 338–345 (2010)
11. Ramirez-Marquez, J.E., Coit, D.W.: A monte-carlo simulation approach for approximating multi-state two terminals reliability. Reliabil. Eng. Syst. Safe. **87**, 253–264 (2005)
12. Rocco, C.M., Muselli, S.M.: Approximate multi-state reliability expressions using a new machine learning technique. Reliabil. Eng. Syst. Safe. **89**(3), 261–270 (2005)
13. Cai, W., Zhang, B.L., Lv, J.H.: Algorithms of the most reliable maximum flow on uncertain graph. Chin. J. Comput. **35**(11), 2371–2380 (2012). (in Chinese)
14. Ford, L.R., Fulkerson, D.R.: Flows in Networks. Princeton University Press, Princeton (1962)
15. Klingman, D., Napier, A., Stutz, J.: NETGEN: a program for generating large scale capacitated assignment, transportation and minimum cost flow network problems. Manage. Sci. **20**(5), 814–821 (1974)
16. Liu, Z., Wang, C.K., Wang, J.M.: Aggregate nearest neighbor queries in uncertain graphs. World Wide Web **17**(1), 161–188 (2014)
17. Zou, Z.N., Li, F.M., Li, J.Z., Li, Y.S.: Scalable processing of massive uncertain graph data: a simultaneous processing approach. In: 2017 IEEE 33rd International Conference on Data Engineering (ICDE), pp. 183–186 (2017)
18. Schulz, C., Nocaj, A., Goertler, J., Deussen, O., Brandes, U., Weiskopf, D.: Probabilistic graph layout for uncertain network visualization. IEEE Trans. Visual Comput. Graphics **23**(1), 531–540 (2017)
19. Chen, Y.F., Zhao, X., Lin, X.M., Wang, Y., Guo, D.K.: Efficient mining of frequent patterns on uncertain graphs. IEEE Trans. Knowl. Data Eng. **31**(2), 287–300 (2019)
20. Bhatia, V., Rani, R.: Ap-FSM: a parallel algorithm for approximate frequent subgraph mining using Pregel. Expert Syst. Appl. **106**, 217–232 (2018)
21. Moussaoui, M., Zaghdoud, M., Akaichi, J.: A new framework of frequent uncertain subgraph mining. Procedia Comput. Sci. **126**, 413 (2018)

News Headline Corpus Construction and High Frequency Word Extraction

Jianhui Ling[1(✉)], Qihang Zhang[2], Keke Ling[2], and Baili Zhang[1,3]

[1] School of Foreign Languages, Southeast University,
Nanjing 211189, China
220184198@seu.edu.cn
[2] School of Computer Science and Engineering, Southeast University,
Nanjing 211189, China
[3] Research Center for Judicial Big Data, Supreme Count of China,
Nanjing 211189, China

Abstract. It is a fascinating research topic to use the high-frequency words in the news headlines to compare the cultural values of China and the United States. However, the amount of information on various types of news websites is huge on the Internet. If no adopting any intelligent tools it is difficult to obtain information that meets certain conditions (such as specific content for a specific time period) and conduct specialized research. Therefore, this paper proposes a complete solution. First it designs a targeted crawler tool for news headline crawling. The tool can be flexibly set according to the user's needs, and is targeted to specific content such as specific headlines or Web content that meets certain conditions, with the advantages of fast crawling speed, low computing and network resource overhead. Then, by using the crawler tool to achieve a quick crawling of the news headlines of the Xinhuanet (Chinese) and VOA (English) websites for a specific time period, a news headline corpus is constructed for comparison research. Based on the improved TF-IDF algorithm, high-frequency word is extracted in the headline corpus, which provides good data preparation for the study of Sino-US cultural value orientation differences.

Keywords: Crawler tool · TF-IDF algorithm · High-frequency word extraction

1 Introduction

In the news industry, the headline and content of news are considered important data. The headline, as a refinement of the entire news content, is more suitable as an analytical data than a lengthy article. Xin (2012) believes that "the important function of the headline is to reveal the main content of the news to the reader in the most concise language, so that the reader can get as much information as possible in the shortest time." Xin (2012) also mentions that "the headline of the news is an important part of the news, and the differences in values due to cultural differences are reflected in the headlines of the Chinese and English news. "Therefore, news headlines can be used as a data basis for analyzing the differences between Chinese and American cultures and

© Springer Nature Singapore Pte Ltd. 2020
J. Shen et al. (Eds.): IC3 2019, CCIS 1227, pp. 134–143, 2020.
https://doi.org/10.1007/978-981-15-6113-9_15

values. Similarly, news as real-time information, news headlines can also be used as a data base for current affairs hotspot assessment and analysis.

Ling et al. (2015) demonstrate the feasibility of conducting this research under the guidance of cultural value theory, corpus theory and high-frequency word theory. They (2016) believe that, "High-frequency words in news headlines can reflect cultural values more directly and intensively." Moreover, Ling et al. (2017) compare the similarities and differences and changes between Chinese and American cultural values through the study of Xinhuanet and VOA news headline corpus and high frequency words from January 1, 2011 to May 30, 2014. However, five years have passed. From June 1, 2014 to December 31, 2017, whether the cultural values of China and the United States have changed has not been studied. Therefore, it is necessary to use the high-frequency word quantitative analysis method to re-examine the similarities and differences between the current Chinese and American cultural value orientations reflected in the headlines of Chinese and American news.

However, if no adopting any intelligent tools it is difficult to obtain information that meets certain conditions. Therefore, this paper proposes a complete solution. First it designs a targeted crawler tool for news headline crawling. Then, by using the crawler tool to achieve a quick crawling of the news headlines of the Xinhuanet (Chinese) and VOA (English) websites for a specific time period. Based on the improved TF-IDF algorithm, high-frequency word is extracted in the headline corpus to study Sino-US cultural value orientation differences.

2   News Headline Corpus Construction

2.1   Implementation Principle Analysis

Targeted crawling can be used to achieve targeted crawling of specific URLs to obtain static data for the corresponding website. Through analysis of the source code of the website, it is found that most news sites do not use javascript-based dynamic loading technology. In other words, we can use crawler technology to crawl the news data (including the headline and body) of a specific news website.

After resolving the issue of directed crawling of headlines, we also need to consider how to get all the news headlines for a specific time period. By analyzing Xinhuanet (Chinese) and VOA English websites, it is found that both websites have a special URL for querying news headlines on a specific date or for a certain period of time. We can regard this special URL as an open public API. Through this API the acquisition of news headlines within a specified time period can be achieved.

In the implementation of the news headline corpus crawling, we adopted the technical route of the "Requests library+BeautifulSoup library" based on the Python language. To put it simply, the Request library is used to obtain the HTML page source code of a specific URL, and then the BeautifulSoup library is used to parse the HTML tag tree and obtain the news headline content in the corresponding tag. The implementation steps are detailed in the specific implementation process chapter of this article.

2.2   Technical Difficulties Analysis

First, the API for each news site to get news headlines for a specific time period is different, and most news sites do not provide such APIs because news sites need to ensure the performance of their own servers. In order to guarantee server performance, many news sites limit crawling rules in Robots.txt files, and even some sites have anti-crawling tools on the server side to prevent multiple consecutive repetitive accesses from the same IP address.

Second, news in a specific time period cannot be obtained, but only news of the specified date (such as VOA news website) can be reached. If we want to extract the news headlines in the specified segment, we need to automatically add the date in the API to get the news headline URL for each day in the specific time period, and then get all the news headlines in a specific time period.

Third, when the required page is obtained, there may be a large amount of redundant information on the obtained page. How to automatically extract news headlines on a page instead of redundant information such as news text or advertisements is a problem.

Fourth, the obtained news headlines may be repetitive, thus, how to find and remove duplicates is also a difficulty.

In the program designed by the author, the above problems are solved, and a news headline crawling program based on the Python language Xinhuanet (Chinese) and VOA (English) is implemented. In the experiment, we successfully obtained all the Xinhuanet news Chinese headlines and VOA (English) news headlines from June 1, 2014 to December 31, 2017, and calculated the word frequency in the corpus to complete the extraction of high frequency words in the corpus.

2.3   Corpus Construction Process

Building a VOA News Headline Corpus. As mentioned above, the technical route taken to capture the news headline of the VOA website during the specified time period is "Requests+BeautifulSoup". The Python "Request" library allows us to get HTML pages for a particular site via HTTP get requests and allows us to parse the content in the page via json or HTML. The "BeautifulSoup" library can parse and traverse the HTML tag tree, which is convenient for us to extract the headline of the article from the original HTML page.

The URL module will automatically generate all URLs containing all news headlines. After generating all the URLs, each URL is passed to the Request module, which will get the HTML page corresponding to each URL. After obtaining the corresponding HTML page, the HTML page is submitted to the BeautifulSoup module for parsing, and the part representing the news headline in the HTML page is located, thereby extracting the news headline. Finally it is saved to a local file. The details of the program implementation are demonstrated next (Fig. 1).

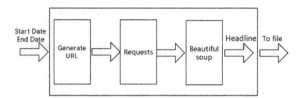

Fig. 1. Xinhua news headline extraction workflow.

First we analyze the Generate URL module. It is found that in the browser, enter 'https://www.voanews.com/z/599/YYYY/MM/DD' (where YYYY/MM/DD indicates a specific date format) to get some news headlines for the VOA news specified time, and all or part of the news headlines remaining can be obtained after clicking the "Load More" button on this page. At the same time, clicking more URLs at a time is 'https://www.voanews.com/z/599/YYYY/MM/DD?p=1'. By analogy, multiple URLs can be obtained after clicking the "Load More" button. There is a problem here that how many times "load more" button should be clicked to get the full news headline for the current date. The solution we have given is to uniformly grab the page after clicking "Load More" three times, and at the end unify the duplicate news headlines. It is found that the removal of duplicates through Python's list data structure is extremely efficient.

In the difficult analysis section, a question is asked on how to automatically add dates to the VOA News website URL to get the news headlines for each day in a specific time period. In fact, this problem can be solved by writing an algorithm. Because the number of days per month except February is fixed, it only needs to judge the number of days in February of each year to automatically get the date of the next day through the algorithm. But in the principle of "not repeating the wheel" (Chinese saying), the "arrow" library in Python is used to solve this problem. The "arrow" library enables date formatted input and output and automatic date addition. The formatted output of the date is required for us to populate the URL, and automatically adding the date is also necessary to automatically get the VOA news headline URL. So here the "arrow" library is applied to implement the formatted output of the date and the ability to automatically add dates. Next a function to automatically generate a URL based on the start date and time span as an argument is given:

Algorithm 1. automatically generate a URL
Input: **date_start, days**
Output: **url_list**
1) url_list = []
2) t = arrow.get(date_start, 'YYYY/MM/DD')
3) root_url = 'https://www.voanews.com/z/599/'
4) for i in range(days + 1):
5)   temp_date = t.shift(days=+i)
6)   str_data=temp_date.format('YYYY/MM/DD')
7)   temp_url = root_url + str_data
8)   url_list.append(temp_url)
9) return url_list

After obtaining the URL list containing all the news headlines in the specified date range, the HTML pages of the corresponding URLs are obtained one by one through the parsing of the "Requests" library and submitted to the "BeautifulSoup" library for parsing.

In the difficult analysis section there is a question on how to automatically extract the news headlines on the page instead of other text or advertising information. Here the functions provided by BeautifulSoup to navigate (traverse) and search the HTML tag tree to get news headlines are used. There are two ways to get news headlines in the HTML tag tree. The first is to use the traversal of the tag tree to navigate to the HTML tag that contains the news headline. The structure of the HTML tag tree is shown in the following figure. After obtaining the BeautifulSoup object through the BeautifulSoup library, the tag tree traversal is used to locate the tag where the news headline is located. The benefit of this approach is a short execution time, but the coding is complex. Another way is to directly use the search function provided by the BeautifulSoup library, call the findAll() function, and specify some attribute values of the tag in the parameter to retrieve the label containing the news headline and extract it. The advantage of using the tag search method is that the coding is simple and suitable for tag retrieval of complex HTML pages, but the disadvantage is that the search speed is obviously slower than the tag tree traversal (Fig. 2).

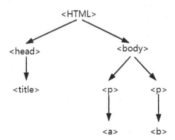

Fig. 2. HTML label tree

The second tag tree described above instead of the faster crawling of the tag tree traversal is adopted. The main reason is that during the experiment it is found that if the first tag tree traversal Take the news headline is taken, in the crawling process with a long time span, there may be a difference in the format of the HTML page label tree corresponding to a few URLs and the rest of the label tree, which may cause errors in crawling the headline error or null pointer. In order to avoid the crawl failure caused by the non-standard page label tree format, the second method of tag tree search or the combination of tag tree traversal and search is adopted to perform VOA news headline crawling.

Building Xinhuanet News Headline Corpus. The process of crawling the Xinhua.com (Chinese) news headline corpus is consistent with the general process of crawling the VOA (English) news headline corpus. The difference is mainly in two aspects. First, the

URL for obtaining the headline of the specified time period is different. Second, after the end of the crawling headline, Chinese word segmentation is needed to support the statistics of the word frequency. Next, we will introduce the above differences.

First, compared with the VOA (English) website, the URL of the Xinhuanet is more like a WEB API on the URL that contains all the news headlines within the specified time period. The parameters required to generate the web page are given by some key-value pairs. We can adjust the web page information displayed by each URL according to the parameters. First the URLs of all the news headlines are obtained in the specified time period. Observing the returned webpages, we can continue to click the next page at the end of the webpage to get more headlines in the specified time period. And the "pn=?" (? is a placeholder) key-value pair in the URL can specify the number of pages returned to the web page. In this way, we can first get the URL of the first page and get the HTML tag tree, and find the total number of news headlines in the specified time period in the tag tree. Then the Pn property can be updated to get the next URL according to the WEB API. Similar to getting a VOA (English) news headline, the function of the BeautifulSoup library is adopted to search the tag tree to get the news headline of the corresponding tag. Finally, the WEB API for Xinhuanet (Chinese) to grab the news headline is given: 'http://info.xinhua-news.com/cn/qui_adv.do?fenlei Search=fenleiSearch&cid=35&dm=0&cdt=&custom_condition_flag=&ct=&root_ap_ Id_t=35&root_ap_t=35&ap_Id_t=35&_t=35&areasDetailId=&areasDetail=&areasCol umnId=&areasColumn=&_SecSearchWord=&_SecAjaxSW=&like_search=&quank u_alldb=&swviewback=&search_out=gailan&DateInputType=0&dc1=date1&dc2=da te2&start_year=&start_month=&start_day=&end_year=&end_month=&end_day=&se lectDate_hide=0&selectDate=%E5%85%A8%E9%83%A8&caption=&isOnloadComp lete=&idKeywords=0&pagecount=210&sort=-DOC_WRITEDATE&wordcookie=& dt=0&trsSID=&Submit=%E6%A3%80%E7%B4%A2&pn=?'. Which, "dc1", "dc2", respectively, indicate the start and end dates, and "pagecount" indicates the number of each page delivers news headlines.

After corpus is successfully achieved, it is necessary to separate the words in Chinese word corpus to support word frequency statistics. The "jieba" library in Python is used to separate Chinese words.

3 Corpus Analysis of Chinese and English News Headlines

Through running the program, we obtain all the Xinhuanet news Chinese headlines and VOA (English) news headlines from June 1, 2014 to December 31, 2017, which are stored in the Windows text documents. The Xinhuanet (Chinese) news headline corpus is 17305517 words, and the VOA (English) news headline corpus is 199346 words. It is a large-scale data for unstructured plain text data. According to the storage characteristics of the crawled corpus, in the next chapter, we will introduce how to perform high frequency word extraction calculation for Chinese and English Corpus.

4 High Frequency Word Extraction Algorithm

- **Step 0:**

(1) For the Chinese corpus, Chinese words are first segmented, the jieba library of Python is used to segment the Chinese news headline text in the corpus, and the word segmentation results are stored in the Python array.

Algorithm 2. Segment Chinese words

Input: path

Output: words

1) import jieba
2) ...
3) text = open(path, "r").read() # "path" is the Chinese news headline corpus path
4) words = jieba.lcut(text)

---

(2) For the English corpus, remove some meaningless special symbols and prepositions, conjunctions, etc., and save the results in a Python array.

Algorithm 3. Remove useless English words

Input: path

Output: words

1) text = open(path, "r").read() # "path" is the English news headline corpus path
2) text = text.lower()
3) stop_words = {' a ', ' an ', ' the ', ' on ', ' of ', ' off ', ' in ', ' for ', ' at ', ' by ', ' to ', ' as ','us ', ' and ', ' over ', ' with ', ' i ', ' we ', ' after ', ' from ', ' is ', ' are ', ' against ',' not ', 'about ', ' more ', ' will ', ' could ', ' no ', ' up ', ' but ', ' into '}
4) for ch in '!"#$%&()*+,-./:;<=>?@[\\]^_'{|}~':
5)   text = text.replace(ch, ' ')
6) for sw in stop_words:
7)   text = text.replace(sw, '')
8) words = text.split()

- **Step 1:**

  The corpus of the pre-processed step 0 is counted for the number of lexical occurrences. The code is given next.

Algorithm 4. Counting occurrences
Input: words
Output: counts
1) for word in words:
2)   counts[word] = counts.get(word, 0) + 1

Finally what is stored in the counts dictionary is the number of occurrences of the corresponding vocabulary. Now the number of occurrences of each vocabulary in the corpus can be obtained.

- **Step 2:**

  Next we can sort the number of occurrences of the words stored in the dictionary (high to low) and save them to a local file.

  After obtaining the number of occurrences of the vocabulary, the TF-IDF formula can be used to evaluate the importance of each vocabulary for one of the documents in the corpus. First the formula is given:

$$\text{TF}_{ij} = n_{ij} / \sum_{k} n_{kj} \tag{1}$$

$$IDF_i = \log(|D| / |\{j : t_i \in d_j\}|) \tag{2}$$

$$freq_{ij} = TF_{ij} \times IDF_i \tag{3}$$

In this formula, n_{ij} is the number of times the word i appears in the document j, and n_{kj} represents the number of times all words appear in the document j. $|D|$ represents the total number of documents, $|\{j : t_i \in d_j\}|$ is the number of files containing the word i. n_{ij} has been calculated through the program.

In the case of good network conditions, we can use the program to get the Xinhuanet news headline corpus and the VOA news headline corpus containing all the news headlines one time (all crawling headlines are saved in a txt document). At this point, the word frequency of all words can be obtained according to formula (1).

However, in actual situations, if the news headline is crawled for a longer interval, the program runtime will increase. There may be network fluctuations or some unexpected conditions during the running of the program. In order to avoid errors such as connection timeouts, this requires the designers to split the specified time period into multiple smaller time periods and obtain a corpus containing multiple txt file documents in batches (which can be implemented by multi-threaded concurrent programming). In this case, lexical importance metrics can be performed on each document in the corpus according to TF-IDF formulas (1) (2) (3). Each document in the corpus extracts vocabulary word frequency statistics based on the vocabulary importance of the first 60% to 80% of the vocabulary, so as to reduce redundancy calculations. The proportion of words in which each document is extracted according to the importance of vocabulary can be adjusted according to experience. Based on the TF-IDF principle and experimental results, we can find that this implementation method is obviously helpful for keyword extraction of fact news headlines.

5   Conclusion

This paper first discusses the implementation and technical route of obtaining a specific corpus through the program. Next, it analyzes the technical difficulties and challenges that it may encounter when implementing the automatic crawling of the news headline program. The difficulty of these technologies has been solved and implemented in the corpus construction process. Then the running program gets all the Xinhuanet news Chinese headlines and VOA (English) news headlines from June 1, 2014 to December 31, 2017.

The work described in the text provides strong data support for the study of Sino-US cultural and value differences, current affairs hotspot assessment, etc. moreover, it also provides a basis for the subsequent research.

Acknowledgement. This work was partly supported by the National Key R&D Program of China (2018YFC0830200), the Fundamental Research Funds for the Central Universities (2242018S30021 and 2242017S30023) and Open Research Fund from Key Laboratory of Computer Network and Information Integration In Southeast University, Ministry of Education, China.

References

Nemeslaki, A., Pocsarovszky, K.: Supporting e-business research with web crawler methodology. Soc. Econ. **34**(1), 13–28 (2012)

Hu, H., Ge, Y., Hou, D.: Using web crawler technology for geo-events analysis: a case study of the Huangyan Island incident. Sustainability **6**(4), 1896–1912 (2014)

Stevanovic, D., Vlajic, A.N.: Feature evaluation for web crawler detection with data mining techniques. Expert Syst. Appl. **39**(10), 8707–8717 (2012)

Minhas, G., Kumar, M.: LSI based relevance computation for topical web crawler (Report). J. Emerg. Technol. Web Intell. **5**(4), 401 (2013)

Chen, X., Li, W., Zhao, T., Piao, X.: Design of the distributed web crawler. Adv. Mater. Res. **204**, 1454–1458 (2011)

Ahmadi-Abkenari, F., Selamat, A.: An architecture for a focused trend parallel web crawler with the application of clickstream analysis. Inf. Sci. **184**(1), 266 (2012)

Wan, F., Xie, X.: Mining techniques of XSS vulnerabilities based on web crawler. Appl. Mech. Mater. **556**, 6290–6293 (2014). (Mechatronics Engineering, Computing and Information Technology)

Chen, M., Yang, X.: Research on model of network information extraction based on improved topic-focused web crawler key technology. Tehnicki Vjesnik – Tech. Gazette **23**(4), 1025–1035 (2016)

Tsai, C., Ku, T., Chien, W.: Object architected design and efficient dynamic adjustment mechanism of distributed web crawlers. Int. J. Interdisc. Telecommun. Network. (IJITN) **7**(1), 57–71 (2015)

Soontornpipit, P.: Monitoring and indexing system for illegal tobacco sales on website in Thailand by using web crawler technique. Appl. Mech. Mater. **781**, 129–132 (2015). (Advanced Engineering Research)

Ranjan, S., Bhatia, K.: Design of a least cost (LC) vertical search engine based on domain specific hidden web crawler. Int. J. Inf. Retrieval Res. (IJIRR) **7**(2), 19–33 (2017)

Grefenstette, G., Muchemi, L.: Determining the characteristic vocabulary for a specialized dictionary using Word2vec and a directed crawler. arXiv:1605.09564, 31 May 2016

Hew, K., Chen, Q., Tang, Y.: Understanding student engagement in large-scale open online courses: a machine learning facilitated analysis of student's reflections in 18 highly rated MOOCs. Int. Rev. Res. Open Distance Learn. **19**(3), 69–93 (2018)

Hamborg, F., Donnay, K., Gipp, B.: Automated identification of media bias in news articles: an interdisciplinary literature review. Int. J. Digit. Libr., 1–25(2018)

Jianhui, L., Liling, S.: A theoretical summary and approach to the comparison of sino-american cultural value orientation - a study of high-frequency words based on the Sino-US news headline corpus. Jiangsu Foreign Lang. Teach. Res. **1**, 47–51 (2015)

Ling, J., Lei, X., Jing, J.: The automatic construction of Chinese and American news headline corpus and the study of high frequency word extraction algorithm. Jiangsu Foreign Lang. Teach. Res. **1**, 60–63 (2016)

Ling, J., Hu, Y., Jing, J.: A report on the comparison of Chinese and American cultural value orientations—based on the high-frequency word research of Chinese and American news headlines corpus. Jiangsu Foreign Lang. Teach. Res. **4**, 55–59 (2017)

Xin, Y.: Cultural differences between Chinese and English news headlines. News Enthusiasts **4**, 47–48 (2012)

Likarish, P., Jung, E.: A targeted web crawling for building malicious Javascript collection. In: ACM First International Workshop on Data-Intensive Software Management & Mining (2009)

The Ionospheric TEC Response to Three Different Intensities Tropical Cyclones Landing in Guangdong Province

Xiaoman Qi[1,2] and Fuyang Ke[2(✉)]

[1] School of Geographical Sciences, Nanjing University of Information Science and Technology, Nanjing, China
[2] School of Remote Sensing and Geomatics Engineering, Nanjing University of Information Science and Technology, Nanjing, China
ke.fuyang@qq.com

Abstract. Using GPS-TEC (Total Electron Content) Sequences processed by a second-order operator and ROTI (Standard deviation of TEC change rate), the effects of tropical cyclones with different intensities landing in Guangdong Province on ionospheric TEC are analyzed. The analysis shows that during the tropical depression ROKE, typhoon PAKHAR and violent typhoon MAN-GKHUT landing in Guangdong Province, ROTI values are less than 0.5 $TEC.min^{-1}$, and no obvious ionospheric disturbances are detected. It can be interpreted by the effect of terrain and severe convective weather on acoustic gravity waves. Severe convective weather and the dramatic undulating terrain provide favorable conditions for the development of acoustic gravity waves. However, the central and southern of Guangdong Province has relatively flat terrain, which cannot meet ideal conditions for the development of acoustic gravity waves.

Keywords: Global navigation satellite system · Ionospheric disturbance · Tropical cyclone · Terrain

1 Introduction

Numerous studies have shown that the ionosphere and tropical cyclones (TCs) are interrelated. Shen found that typhoon had a definite influence on ionospheric foF2 (critical frequency of F2 Layer), which varied along with the distance of typhoon by analyzed the ionospheric response before and after typhoon approaching Hainan Island [1]. Huang's research shown that the high frequency Doppler array can detect the sound and gravity waves caused by typhoons, but its detection ability is not high [2]. Xiao analyzed 24 typhoons using the data of the high frequency Doppler station. Among them, ionospheric disturbances were detected during 22 typhoons [3]. It may be related to the relative position of wave source and response point. The total electron content (TEC) observations can provide ionospheric information in offshore and terrestrial typhoon areas continuously and effectively. Using GPS-TEC data, Mao found that the influence of typhoon Matsa on ionospheric TEC was completely distinguishable, and the changes of TEC and foF2 during Matsa are consistent [4]. Lin indicated

© Springer Nature Singapore Pte Ltd. 2020
J. Shen et al. (Eds.): IC3 2019, CCIS 1227, pp. 144–153, 2020.
https://doi.org/10.1007/978-981-15-6113-9_16

that the ionospheric anomalies during typhoon are caused by vertical acoustic gravity waves, and the ionospheric TEC anomalies can be detected directly over typhoon Nakri by using the method of nonlinear principal component analysis [5]. Using high frequency Doppler array, Wan have observed the ionospheric disturbances in China for many years and found the sources of the ionospheric disturbances in central China. Some of them have to do with the topographic uplift of the Qinghai-Tibet Plateau [6]. In addition, Kong's research shows that the terrain conditions in the mountainous areas of central Taiwan provide an ideal place for the development of acoustic gravity waves [7]. Polyakova's research conclude that the obvious TEC disturbances can be observed when a tropical cyclone reached typhoon stage [8].

In Polyakova's research, when the Tropical Cyclones (TCs) were still in the Pacific Ocean, the TEC data of GPS stations in the Pacific Ocean were used for analysis, but no further analysis has been made after TCs landed. In this work, three TCs with different intensity landed in the coastal area of South-Central Guangdong Province are selected to further study whether the ionospheric response to TCs is related to the intensity of cyclone. The effects of TCs with different intensities on the ionospheric TEC in the landing area are analyzed by using the second-order operator-processed GPS-TEC sequence and the standard deviation ROTI (Standard deviation of TEC change rate) of TEC variation rate.

2 Data and Methodology

2.1 Data

ROKE, PAKHAR and MANGKHUT landing in the south-central coastal area of Guangdong Province are selected as the research objects. ROKE was generated at 0:00 UTC (Coordinated Universal Time) on DOY203 (203th Day Of Year), 2017. It landed in the northeastern coast of Hong Kong at 1:50 UTC on DOY204 (July 23, 2017) with 20 m/s wind speed. It landed as a tropical storm, and dissipated at 6:00 UTC on DOY204. PAKHAR was born in the Western Pacific Ocean at 6:00 on DOY236, 2017. It landed in the southern coast of Taishan, Guangdong Province at 1:00 UTC on DOY239 (August 27, 2017) with 33 m/s wind speed. It landed as a typhoon, and dissipated at 12:00 UTC on DOY239.MANGKHUT was born in the Western Pacific Ocean at 12:00 UTC on DOY250, 2018. It landed in the coast of Jiangmen, Guangdong Province at 9:00 UTC on 259 (September 16, 2018) with 45 m/s wind speed. It landed as a violent typhoon, and dissipated at 17:00 UTC on DOY260. The traces of ROKE, PAKHAR and MANGKHUT are shown in Fig. 1. Guangdong Province is dominated by hills, while the central and southern coastal areas are mostly low hills, platforms or plains. DEM map of Guangdong province is shown in Fig. 1.

(a) (b)

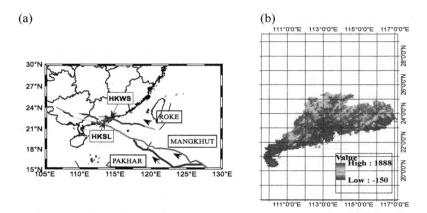

Fig. 1. (a) ROKE, PAKHAR and MANGKHUT traces (HKWS and HKSL are GNSS stations; Black arrow indicates the direction; Red, Magenta, Orange, Yellow, Blue and Green lines respectively represent the six tropical cyclone grades from super typhoon to tropical depression); (b) DEM map of Guangdong Province (Color figure online)

In this study, the possibility of ionospheric disturbance caused by solar, geomagnetic and seismic anomalies is first ruled out. Tropical cyclones in quiet period are selected as the research object. The geomagnetism and solar activity intensity during TCs are analyzed by Dst, Kp and F10.7 index provided by World Data Center and NOAA administration National Environmental Information Center. Generally, F10.7 < 100 sfu represent low-level solar activity [9]. Dst > −30 nT indicates quiet geomagnetic activity [4]. Kp < 4 represents low-level geomagnetic activity [10]. Figure 2 shows that the F10.7 values during the three tropical cyclones were less than 95 sfu. In Fig. 2, the red dotted line frames refer to the time period in which the study area is located within the radius of the TCs 500 km. Except PAKHAR having a small geomagnetic storm of about 2 h after its dissipation, −50 nT < Dst < −30 nT, Dst index values were more than −30 nT two days before and after ROKE and MANGKHUT landed. Except RKOE, Kp < 4 during the two days before and after TCs landfall. Influenced by the high-speed flow in the coronal hole, the solar wind speed rose to about 780 km/s on DOY202, and the geomagnetism was at the level of small magnetic storms within 6 h on DOY203 during ROKE. In addition, previous studies have shown that ionospheric disturbances may also occur when M > 5.0 earthquake occurs [11]. No M > 5.0 earthquake occurred during all the study period.

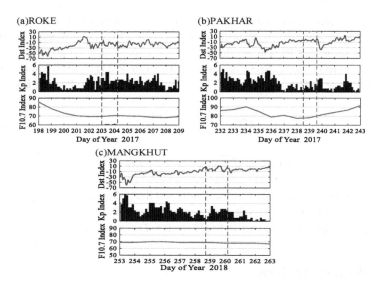

Fig. 2. Dst, Kp and F10.7 indexes during ROKE, PAKHAR and MANGKHUT (Color figure online)

TEC data provided by Ionospheric Research Laboratory and obtained by Reg-Est (Regularized Estimation) are used to analyze whether ionospheric disturbances occur during typhoons. Reg-Est uses all GPS satellites data with elevation of more than 10°, and combines them based on the weighted function of satellite position, and calculates them with least square method. Reg-Est can produce reliable TEC values for calm and disturbed days, and TEC with a time resolution of 30 s is calculated for a single site.

2.2 Methodology

Processing TEC sequence by second-order operator is an effective method for ionospheric disturbance detection [7]. The second-order operator method is not affected by other days with ionospheric disturbances. The principle is to predict the current epoch's normal ionospheric changes using the prior two epoch's TEC variation [7]. For the following TEC sequence,

$$TEC_1, \ldots, TEC_{i-1}, TEC_i, TEC_{i+1}, \ldots, TEC_n \tag{1}$$

The ionospheric disturbance at the *ith* epoch can be determined using the test value given by Eq. (2) and Eq. (3) [7]

$$TEC_{est} = TEC_{i-1} - TEC_{i-2} \tag{2}$$

$$TEC_{test} = TEC_i - (TEC_i + TEC_{est}) \tag{3}$$

Aarons researched the characteristics of irregular structures of ionosphere in the equatorial region using ROT (Rate of Change of the TEC) [12]. A large number of observations show that ROT often fluctuates near a very small value. Pi presented an index based on ROT, and defined the standard deviation ROTI of ROT within 5 min as TEC time change rate index [13]. ROTI is calculated from the following Eq.:

$$\text{ROT} = \frac{TEC_k^i - TEC_{k-1}^i}{t_k - t_{k-1}} \tag{4}$$

$$\text{ROTI} = \sqrt{<ROT^2> - <ROT>^2} \tag{5}$$

In Eq. (4), i is the number of observation satellite, K is epoch, t is GPS time. In Eq. (5), $<...>$ represents averaging the values. The criterion for judging the existence of irregular ionospheric structures is ROTI $\geq$ 0.5 $TEC.min^{-1}$ [14].

3 Results and Analysis

Figure 3 shows the ΔTEC sequences of HKSL and HKWS stations during ROKE, PAKHAR and MANGKHUT landing. ROKE and PAKHAR have no obvious TEC fluctuations at the time of landing. TEC has a weak fluctuation after MANGKHUT landing, but there are weak TEC fluctuations at the same time in two days before and after landing of MANGKHUT. When typhoon Dujuan landed in Taiwan, Kong detected TEC fluctuations ranged from 2–3 $TECU$ by using the second-order operator method [7]. The maximum values of TEC of ROKE, PAKHAR and MANGKHUT are about 0.2 $TECU$, and the fluctuations of TEC are particularly weak. Compared with ROKE, PAKHAR and MANGKHUT, the TEC fluctuations during ROKE is weaker than that of PAKHAR and MANGKHUT. When ROKE, PAKHAR and MANGKHUT landed, they were tropical depression, typhoon and violent typhoon, respectively. Different intensity of landing TCs has different effects on TEC, and violent tropical cyclones have great effects on TEC. However, no significant ionospheric TEC disturbances detected for ROKE, PAKHAR and MANGKHUT landing in the central and southern coastal areas of Guangdong Province.

The TEC data of several GPS satellites closest to TCs landing are selected for ROTI analysis. Figure 4, 5, 6 show the ROTI sequences of HKWS station during the landing of ROKE,PAKHAR and MANGKHUT, and the trajectories of IPP (Ionospheric Pierce Point) on the day of TC landing. PRNi represents the number of GPS satellites. Figure 4 shows that the maximum ROTI of PRN7 on July 21 is 0.8 $TEC.min^{-1}$, and there are irregular structures in the ionosphere. Combined with Fig. 2, it was found that the solar wind speed rises to about 780 km/s on the July 21, which had an impact on ionosphere. The maximum ROTI of PRN7 on July 22 is 0.8 $TEC.min^{-1}$. Combined with Table 1, it was found that no IPP in the research area when the maximum appeared. At other times, ROTI values are less than 0.5 $TEC.min^{-1}$. No irregular structure is detected in ionosphere over Guangdong Province during ROKE landing.

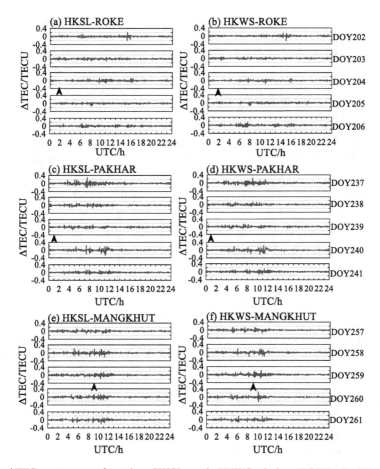

Fig. 3. ΔTEC sequence of station HKSL and HKWS during ROKE, PAKHAR and MANGKHUT (Black arrow represents the landing time)

Table 1, Fig. 5 and Fig. 6 demonstrate that ROTI values are less than 0.5 $TEC.min^{-1}$ during PAKHAR and MANGKHUT landing, and no irregular structures are detected in ionosphere. Polyakova's research conclude that the obvious TEC disturbances can be observed when a tropical cyclone reached typhoon stage [8]. But when PAKHAR and MANGKHUT landed, they were typhoon and violent typhoon respectively, and no obvious ionospheric disturbance was detected.

Kong detected obvious ionospheric disturbances on the day of typhoon Dujuan landed in Taiwan using TEC sequences [9]. During typhoon Matmo landfall in Taiwan Province and typhoon Rammasum landfall in Hainan Province, Song detected ionospheric disturbances using two-dimensional total electron content perturbation maps [16]. Ke detected significant ionospheric disturbances during Sarika landing in Hainan Province using tomography sounding data observed by a Digisonde-4D portable sounder [11]. In the researches of Kong, Song and Ke, TCs are violent typhoons when they landed. Terrain is one of the important factors affecting the generation of acoustic

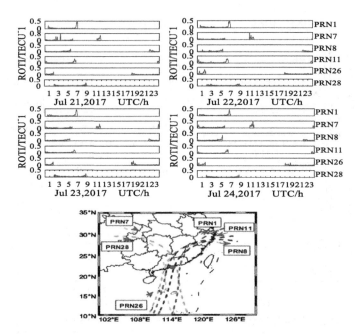

Fig. 4. ROTI sequences during ROKE; Location and orientation of six IPP trajectories (Red arrows indicate direction; Red dot is the location of HKWS station). (Color figure online)

Table 1. The starting and ending times of GPS satellites IPP trajectories over their respective landing area on the day of ROKE, PAKHAR and MANGKHUT landfall

ROKE		PAKHAR		MANGKHUT	
PRN	UTC	PRN	UTC	PRN	UTC
1	00:50–05:59	1	00:00–03:36; 23:54–24:00	6	03:00–06:56
7	00:18–05:22	4	18:08–23:17	10	10:11–15:37
8	0:00–04:07; 22:05–24:00	7	00:00–03:00; 21:53–24:00	13	04:33–09:50
11	00:00–05:32; 23:50–24:00	11	00:00–03:10; 21:28–24:00	15	05:44–12:15
26	18:23–24:00	19	02:00–08:38	19	03:00–06:20
28	02:29–08:19	28	00:05–05:55	24	07:27–12:35

gravity waves [8]. The drag effect of high terrain can provide an ideal condition for the development of acoustic gravity waves [7, 16]. Figure 7 shows that the Central Mountains of Taiwan and the Wu-chih Mountains of Hainan are favorable conditions for the development of acoustic gravity waves during typhoon landfall. However, the central and southern coastal areas of Guangdong Province are mostly low hills, platforms or plains. The terrain is relatively flat, which cannot meet ideal conditions for the

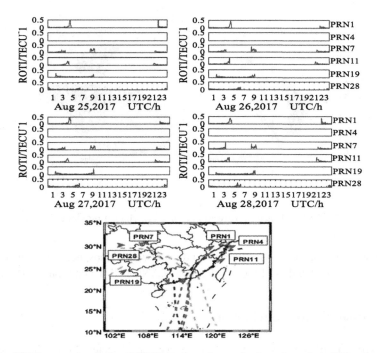

Fig. 5. ROTI sequences during PAKHAR; Location and orientation of six IPP trajectories.

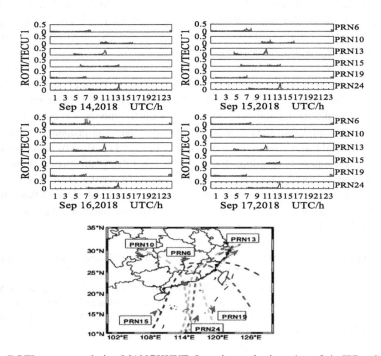

Fig. 6. ROTI sequences during MANGKHUT; Location and orientation of six IPP trajectories.

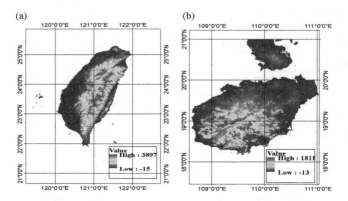

Fig. 7. DEM map of Taiwan province (a), Hainan province (b).

development of acoustic gravity waves. And no obvious ionospheric disturbances are detected during the landfall of violent typhoon MANGKHUT and typhoon PAKHAR.

4   Discussion and Conclusion

In this work, no obvious ionospheric disturbances are detected during the landfall of TCs. Acoustic gravity waves generated during typhoons can propagate to ionospheric altitudes and affect the ionosphere [2, 3]. The drag effect of high terrain can provide an ideal condition for the development of acoustic gravity waves [7, 16]. No ionospheric disturbances are detected in this work can be interpreted by the effect of terrain and severe convective weather on acoustic gravity waves.

When typhoons land in Taiwan and Hainan, the latent heat input from the sea surface is rapidly reduced, at the same time, low pressure brought severe convective weather. Because of the resistance effect of mountains, the steep lapse rate in the air creates ideal conditions for the development of acoustic gravity waves [16]. Affected by the dramatic undulating terrain, acoustic gravity waves can propagate to the ionosphere altitude and disturb the ionosphere electron density [7]. Most of the coastal areas of central and southern Guangdong Province are low hills, platforms or plains. Compared with Taiwan and Hainan, the central and southern coastal areas of Guangdong Province have relatively flat terrain, which cannot provide ideal conditions for the development of acoustic gravity waves during typhoon landfall, and no obvious ionospheric TEC disturbance has been found.

Acknowledgements. This study is supported by the National Natural Science Foundation of China (grant no. 41674036).

We acknowledge the use of data from IONOLAB (Ionospheric Research Laboratory). We are grateful to the US National Oceanic and Atmospheric Administration and World Data Center for Geomagnetism, Kyoto, for solar and geomagnetic activity data support. We acknowledge the use of DEM data from Geospatial Data Cloud.

References

1. Shen, C.: The correlations between the Typhoon and the foF2 of ionosphere. Chin. J. Space Sci. **2**(4), 335–340 (1982)
2. Huang, Y.N., Cheng, K., Chen, S.W.: On the detection of acoustic-gravity waves generated by Typhoon by use of real time HF doppler frequency shift sounding system. Radio Sci. **20**(4), 897–906 (1985)
3. Xiao, S., Zhang, D., Xiao, Z.: Study on the detectability of Typhoon-generated acoustic-gravity waves. Chin. J. Space Sci. **27**(1), 35–40 (2007)
4. Mao, T., Wang, J.S., Yang, G.L., et al.: Effects of typhoon matsa on ionospheric TEC. Chinese Sci. Bull. **54**(24), 3858–3863 (2009)
5. Lin, J.W.: Ionospheric total electron content anomalies due to Typhoon Nakri on 29 May 2008: a nonlinear principal component analysis. Comput. Geosci. **46**(3), 189–195 (2012)
6. Wan, W., Yuan, H., Ning, B., Li, J.: A statistical study for the spacial-temporal scale of ionospheric disturbances in middle China. Chin. J. Space Sci. **15**(4), 301–306 (1995)
7. Kong, J., Yao, Y., Xu, Y.: A clear link connecting the troposphere and ionosphere: ionospheric reponses to the 2015 Typhoon Dujuan. J. Geod. **91**(9), 1087–1097 (2017). https://doi.org/10.1007/s00190-017-1011-4
8. Polyakova, A.S., Perevalova, N.P.: Comparative analysis of TEC disturbances over tropic. Adv. Space Res. **52**(8), 1416–1426 (2013)
9. Wang, H., Xiong, J., Zhao, C.: The mid-term forecast method of solar radiation index. Chin. Astron. Astrophy **39**(2), 198–211 (2015)
10. Ke, F., Wang, J., Tu, M., et al.: Morphological characteristics and coupling mechanism of the ionospheric disturbance caused by Super Typhoon Sarika in 2016. Adv. Space Res. **62**(5), 1137–1145 (2018)
11. Jin, S., Occhipinti, G., Jin, R.: GNSS ionospheric seismology: recent observation evidences and characteristics. Earth Sci. Rev. **147**, 54–64 (2015)
12. Aarons, J., Mendillo, M., Yantosca, R.: GPS phase fiuctuations in the equatorial region during the MISETA 1994 campaign. Geophys. Res. **101**(A12), 26851–26862 (1996)
13. Pi, X., Manucci, A.J., Lindqwister, U.J., et al.: Monitoring of global ionospheric irregularities using the worldwide GPS network. Geophys. Res. Lett. **24**(8), 2283–2286 (1997)
14. Ma, G., Maruyama, T.: A supper bubble detected by dense GPS network at east Asian longitude. Geophys. Res. Lett. **33**(21), 241–255 (2006)
15. Song, Q., Ding, F., Zhang, X., Mao, T.: GPS detection of the ionospheric disturbances over Chinab due to impacts of Typhoons Rammasum and Matmo. Geophy. Res. Space Phys. **122**(1), 1055–1063 (2017)
16. Brooks, H.E., Lee, J.W., Craven, J.P.: The spatial distribution of severe thunder storm and tornado environments from global reanalysis data. Atmos. Res. **67–68**, 73–94 (2003)

Embedded AutoEncoders: A Novel Framework for Face De-identification

Jianqi Liu, Jun Liu, Pan Li$^{(\boxtimes)}$, and Zhengze Kuang

University of Electronic Science and Technology of China, Chengdu, China
jianqi.liu@outlook.com, cnliujun93@gmail.com,
lee79@ieee.org, kuang.zhengze@outlook.com,

Abstract. Recent advances in deep learning and big data have greatly promoted the development of image recognition technology. In the meantime, however, it also makes it more challenging to protect human identify information. In this paper, we propose a novel framework called Embedded Auto-Encoders to address face de-identification problem in deep learning. The structure of our framework contains two parts: a Privacy Removal Network and a Feature Selection Network. The main objective of our framework is to ensure that the Privacy Removal Network is capable of discarding information involving privacy and retaining desired information for certain image recognition applications. In order to achieve this goal, the design of the Privacy Removal Network is crucial. Specifically, we employ two different autoencoders, one of which is embedded within the other. We evaluate the proposed framework through extensive experiments, which show that the Embedded AutoEncoders framework can not only effectively retain data utility, but also protect personal identity information.

Keywords: Deep learning · Autoencoders · Image recognition · Face de-identification · Privacy

1 Introduction

The generation and acquisition of massive images and videos have been facilitated by the rapid development of network communication technology and digital storage. Big data greatly promotes the development of machine learning technology. As part of the field of machine learning, deep learning has played an important role in many applications, especially in computer vision, due to its capability of mining deep hidden features from vast data. In order to train deep learning models to achieve higher prediction accuracy, bulk data is needed. A great many companies and organizations have been collecting data which contains user privacy information from the Internet. However, invasion of privacy is becoming more and more serious. Uploading or sharing photos on social networking sites (such as Twitter, Facebook, Weibo, etc.), probably exposes our privacy to others without our awareness. Moreover, advances in image recognition technology has accelerated the interest in Human Action Recognition. Our images are taken by the cameras of the subway stations and the streets for analysis. It brings benefits for public safety, but arises privacy concerns.

© Springer Nature Singapore Pte Ltd. 2020
J. Shen et al. (Eds.): IC3 2019, CCIS 1227, pp. 154–163, 2020.
https://doi.org/10.1007/978-981-15-6113-9_17

In recent years, a growing number of people start paying attention to their privacy, which is caused by frequent privacy leaks. Meanwhile, considerable researchers and companies have made a lot of effort to protect personal privacy, particularly in face de-identification. Traditional methods, including blurring [1], black-box [2] and pixilation are widely used to conceal personal identity information. Nevertheless, these approaches not only lose some useful information (e.g., age features), but also fail to prevent manners like parrot recognition [3] from recognizing person in the de-identification image. In order to retain the utility attributes as much as possible, K-Same algorithm [3] which is based on the well-known K-Anonymity [4] has been proposed to protect individuals' privacy. It is the main idea to implement K-Same by using Euclidean distances to select k most similar images to generate an average image (the de-identification image). Except for the K-Same, Model-based K-Same (K-Same-M) [5] and K-Same-Select [6] algorithms are also guaranteed to make the recognition rate lower than 1/K. Unfortunately, above methods are not appropriate for addressing privacy protection issues in machine learning, due to the lack of ability to process a large amount of image data.

With the development of deep learning networks, desired features can be automatically extracted from increasingly complex datasets. Compared with traditional multi-layer perceptron (MLP), convolutional neural networks (CNNs) work better for image recognition. From 2012 to 2015, ImageNet Top-5 error rates reduced from 26% to 3.6%. The Residual Neural Network (ResNet) that consists of a very deep network structure, including 152 layers, was introduced by He et al. [7]. This state-of-the-art CNNs got the best results in 2015 ImageNet. Furthermore, it turned out that deep neural network structures are more suitable for tackling complicated image recognition applications. In addition to ResNet, AlexNet [8] and GoogleNet [9] are also impressive networks. Inspired by these state-of-the-art CNNs, many researchers attempt to achieve privacy-preserving through convolutional neural network structure [10, 11]. Recent studies [12, 13] indicate that autoencoder architectures [14] are perfect structures for privacy protection. Autoencoder is the neural network comprised by multilayer structures which can usually be divided into two parts: encoder and decoder. In particular, it has the ability to copy the input features, namely, autoencoder try to make decoder output features to be approximately equal to input.

In many practical application scenarios, it is necessary to protect the privacy of real-time image data, such as removing identity information. In order to approach this problem, we propose a novel framework which is called Embedded AutoEncoders. In theory, our framework can be utilized not only in face de-identification application and person de-identification application (e.g., action recognition), but also in other specific tasks involving image privacy. As far as we know, we are the first to propose the Embedded AutoEncoders architecture composed of two different autoencoders.

The rest of the paper is organized as follows: In Sect. 2, we present the proposed Embedded AutoEncoders framework. The performance of our framework is tested against gender classification task, in Sect. 3. In Sect. 4, we conclude our work.

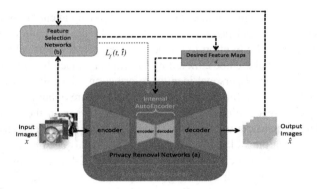

Fig. 1. The structure of Embedded AutoEncoders Framework. This framework consists of two components: (a) the Privacy Removal Network including two convolution autoencoders, (b) the Feature Selection Network.

2 System Design

In this section, we show our framework for protection of identity information. The structure of it is illustrated in Fig. 1. The Privacy Removal Network we designed consists of two autoencoders: an Internal AutoEncoder and an External AutoEncoder. It is worth noting that the architecture of this two autoencoders are different. This part is aiming to remove sensitive information (e.g., identity information) and only to keep the most representative attributes. The main challenge of our framework is to choose appropriate manner to train the Privacy Removal Network. Inspired by the approach used in [13, 15], the Feature Selection Network provide feedback to the Privacy Removal Network, during the training of it. Notice that the data flow represented by the dotted line only exists in the training period. The detailed description of the Embedded AutoEncoders Framework is given in the following subsections.

2.1 Privacy Removal Network

Since the Privacy Removal Network is comprised of two different autoencoders, we first introduce the details of autoencoder.

Autoencoder. Autoencoder is a kind of neural networks. In general, autoencoder is designed to learn a representation for datasets, which can reduce the dimension of input data. As the other tools for feature extraction and generation, the Principal Component Analysis (PCA) is widely used for data dimensionality reduction. Nevertheless, autoencoder has better performance than PCA in some applications, especially for tasks with high-dimensional data [16, 17]. This is due to autoencoder has multilayer and nonlinearity structure. Hidden layers in multilayer structures are very meaningful. The universal approximation theorem [18] has shown that the feedforward neural network with at least one hidden layer and sufficient hidden units can approximate any function. Furthermore, hidden layers have capability to obtain more abstract features at higher layers of representations [19].

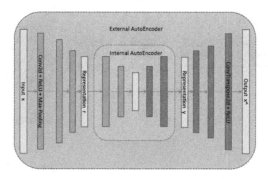

Fig. 2. The input size of the External AutoEncoder is 3 × 224 × 224 and the output size is consistent with the input size. For Internal AutoEncoder, the input size is also the same as the output size which is 512 × 14 × 14.

Embedded AutoEncoders. As depicted in Fig. 2, the Internal AutoEncoder is embedded in the External AutoEncoder. Let x be the input of the External Auto-Encoder, the size of which is 3 × 224 × 224. Let $\hat{x}$ be the output of the External AutoEncoder, the size of $\hat{x}$ is the same as the input. Similarly, let r and y be the input and output of the Internal AutoEncoder. The encoder part of the External AutoEncoder is composed of five convolutional layers. At first, the input image is passed through the external encoder part to get the representation vector r which is a 512 × 14 × 14 dimensional feature map. Next, the representation vector r is fed into the encoder part of the Internal AutoEncoder as an input. Note that the encoder part of the Internal AutoEncoder consists of six convolutional layers, which is different from the structures of the External AutoEncoder. After passing through the decode part with six convolutional layers of the Internal AutoEncoder, the output vector y (representation y) whose size is consistent with the input r is reconstructed. Finally, the output y is processed through the decoder part consisting of five convolutional layers of the External AutoEncoder to obtain the out image ($\hat{x}$) without sensitive information.

The key challenge of training the Embedded AutoEncoders is to train the Internal AutoEncoder. In order to achieve it, we first pre-trained the External AutoEncoder by minimizing the loss function $L_e(x, \hat{x})$. This is to guarantee that the External Auto-Encoder has the capability to reconstruct the original images. After pre-training the External AutoEncode, the Internal AutoEncoder is embedded in the External Auto-Encode and trained on the same datasets. Instead of simply reconstruct the input images by minimizing the loss function $L_i(r, y)$, the Internal AutoEncoder needs to learn how to drop sensitive features but retain desired features in output images. Towards that goal, the Internal AutoEncoder needs to generate y as close as possible to the desired feature maps d coming from the Feature Selection Network. In so doing, the Internal AutoEncoder reserves the most representative features.

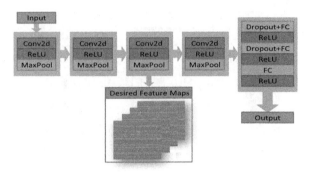

Fig. 3. Architecture of Feature Selection Network consisting of four convolutional layers and three FC layers.

2.2   Feature Selection Network

The Feature Selection Network is to extract desired feature maps that are denoted by a vector $d \in R^{512 \times 14 \times 14}$. As shown in Fig. 3, the Feature Selection Network contains four convolutional layers and three fully connected (FC) layers. The size of the input image x is $3 \times 224 \times 224$ and both of convolutional layers use modules consisting of Convolutional-Relu-Max-pooling. After passing through three FC layers, a vector $\hat{t} \in R^{1 \times k}$ (k is the number of categories of tasks' label) is produced. In fact, the structures of Feature Selection Network are flexible, different networks can be designed for different tasks. In this work, the introduced networks are applied to gender classification task.

There are two main purposes for designing the Feature Selection Network. On the one hand, we pre-trained it by minimizing the loss function $L_f(t, \hat{t})$ (t is the input label) so as to generate desired feature maps well. During training, we use 0.5 probability for FC dropout layers to prevent overfitting. On the other hand, during the training of the Internal AutoEncoder, the input of the Feature Selection Network is replaced with $\hat{x}$ to provide feedback to the Internal AutoEncoder.

2.3   Loss Function

In this section, we clarify the details of loss functions mentioned above. In order to train the Internal AutoEncoder, we first pre-trained the External AutoEncoder and the Feature Selection Network. $L_e(x, \hat{x})$ which is a square error loss function is to ensure that the External AutoEncoder has the capability to reconstruct input images:

$$L_e(x, \hat{x}) = \frac{1}{s} \sum_{i=1}^{s} ||x^{(i)} - \hat{x}^{(i)}||^2$$

The loss function $L_f(t, \hat{t})$ of the Feature Selection Network is a cross entropy function:

$$L_f(t, \hat{t}) = -\frac{1}{s} \sum_{i=1}^{s} t^{(i)} \log(\hat{t}^{(i)})$$

which enables the output of the Feature Selection Network, i.e., d, to preserve desired features.

To train the Internal AutoEncoder, the loss function is

$$L_{sum}(d, y, t, \hat{t}) = L_i(d, y) + \alpha L_f(t, \hat{t})$$

where $L_i(d, y)$ is also a square error loss function, and α is the hyper parameters for multiple losses $L_{sum}(d, y, t, \hat{t})$. Therefore, the Internal AutoEncoder will attempt to only maintain the desired features while discarding other features including those for face identification.

3   Experiments

3.1   Datasets

As shown in Table 1, we use the CelebFaces Attributes (CelebA) Dataset [20] for gender classification. The CelebA Dataset is a large-scale face attributes dataset containing 202599 face images with gender attribute labels. In this work, we divide it into a training set (CelebA-train) and a testing set (CelebA-test). The CelebA-train dataset consists of 162770 images and the CelebA-test dataset has 39829 images. The Embedded AutoEncoders and the Feature Selection Network were trained on the CelebA-train dataset.

Table 1.   The dataset for gender classification.

	Male	Female
CelebA-train	68261	94509
CelebA-test	16173	23656

3.2   Experiment Setup

To validate the proposed the Privacy Removal Network is capable of retaining useful information and protecting individuals' privacy, we trained our framework for gender classification. The purpose of gender classification is to recognize human gender in images. In this work, the Feature Selection Network we introduced in Sect. 2.2 was pre-trained on the CelebA-train dataset and the gender prediction accuracy was 97.9% on the CelebA-test dataset.

After training the Privacy Removal Network with the Feature Selection Network, we obtained the Privacy Removal Network for gender classification (PRN-G). Next, the PRN-G is connected to third party models. To demonstrate the Privacy Removal Network achieves both data utility and flexibility, we select the state-of-the-art AlexNet as the third-party model. It is worth noting that the structure of AlexNet is different from the Feature Selection Network which was used for training the Privacy Removal Network.

3.3   Data Utility

In order to evaluate the performance of our framework for data utility, we first generated the de-identified datasets (D-CelebA) corresponding to the original datasets (CelebA) with the PRN-G. For comparison, two AlexNet networks (AlexNet-O and AlexNet-D) were trained on the CelebA-train and D-CelebA-train, respectively. Finally, we computed the classification accuracy and confusion matrix of above networks on test datasets.

Table 2 shows the gender classification accuracy on test datasets. For AlexNet-O, the gender prediction accuracy was 97.1% on the CelebA-test dataset. AlexNet-D performed better than AlexNet-O and the accuracy was 97.5%. This result indicates that the de-identification images kept all desired information. The confusion matrix is illustrated in Fig. 4, which further verifies that our framework is valid.

Table 2.   Accuracy on test datasets.

	CelebA-test	D-CelebA-test
AlexNet-O	97.1%	–
AlexNet-D	–	97.5%

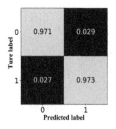 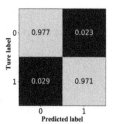

Fig. 4.   The left confusion matrix belongs to AlexNet-O and the right belongs to AlexNet-D. Label '0' represents 'female' and '1' represents 'male'.

Fig. 5. De-identified images for gender classification, which come from the PRN-G. The first and the third rows show the original inputs, the second and the fourth rows are the corresponding de-identified outputs. Note that the de-identified male and female face images have distinctly different characteristics.

3.4 Face De-identification

We verify that the proposed framework can protect identity information on two aspects: visualization and face match accuracy. Visualization has the ability to give us a direct insight about whether our framework can protect personal identity. As shown in Fig. 5, the de-identified images show our framework successfully removed identity information and retained desired features. It is difficult for people to recognize subjects in de-identified images. However, some recognition techniques may infer identity information from de-identified images. Thus, we utilize VGG-face network to further evaluate our framework. The VGG-face network introduced by Parkhi et al. [21] is widely used to evaluate facial similarity. This network contains thirteen convolutional layers and three FC layers and its weight parameters are already publicly available. In this work, we implemented it by PyTorch. We randomly selected 100 images from 100 subjects in CelebA-test and generated the corresponding de-identified images with the PRN-G. For each subject, we paired the original image and de-identified image. Then we computed the face match accuracy for the 100 paired images with VGG-face network. The average face match accuracy of them is only 13%, which confirms that the proposed framework does protect identity information.

4   Conclusion

In this paper, we proposed a novel framework, Embedded AutoEncoders, which aims to protect personal identity information. Our framework consists of two parts: a Privacy Removal Network and a Feature Selection Network. In particular, the trained privacy removal Network can be flexibly applied to third-party models. We validated our framework through gender classification task. The experiments confirm that Embedded AutoEncoders not only protect personal identity information, but also effectively retain data utility.

References

1. Boyle, M., Edwards, C., Greenberg, S.: The effects of filtered video on awareness and privacy. In: Proceedings of the 2000 ACM Conference on Computer Supported Cooperative Work, pp. 1–10, December 2000
2. Ribaric, S., Pavesic, N.: An overview of face de-identification in still images and videos. In: 2015 11th IEEE International Conference and Workshops on Automatic Face and Gesture Recognition (FG), vol. 4, pp. 1–6. IEEE, May 2015
3. Newton, E.M., Sweeney, L., Malin, B.: Preserving privacy by de-identifying face images. IEEE Trans. Knowl. Data Eng. **17**(2), 232–243 (2005)
4. Sweeney, L.: k-anonymity: a model for protecting privacy. Int. J. Uncertainty Fuzziness Knowl.-Based Syst. **10**(05), 557–570 (2002)
5. Gross, R., Sweeney, L., De la Torre, F., Baker, S.: Model-based face de-identification. In: 2006 Conference on Computer Vision and Pattern Recognition Workshop (CVPRW 2006), p. 161. IEEE, June 2006
6. Gross, R., Airoldi, E., Malin, B., Sweeney, L.: Integrating utility into face de-identification. In: Danezis, G., Martin, D. (eds.) PET 2005. LNCS, vol. 3856, pp. 227–242. Springer, Heidelberg (2006). https://doi.org/10.1007/11767831_15
7. He, K., Zhang, X., Ren, S., Sun, J.: Deep residual learning for image recognition. In: Proceedings of the IEEE Conference on Computer Vision and Pattern Recognition, pp. 770–778 (2016)
8. Krizhevsky, A., Sutskever, I., Hinton, G.E.: ImageNet classification with deep convolutional neural networks. In: Advances in Neural Information Processing Systems, pp. 1097–1105 (2012)
9. Szegedy, C., et al.: Going deeper with convolutions. In: Proceedings of the IEEE Conference on Computer Vision and Pattern Recognition, pp. 1–9 (2015)
10. Osia, S.A., et al.: A hybrid deep learning architecture for privacy-preserving mobile analytics. IEEE Internet Things J. **7**, 4505–4518 (2020)
11. Chi, H., Hu, Y.H.: Face de-identification using facial identity preserving features. In: 2015 IEEE Global Conference on Signal and Information Processing (GlobalSIP), pp. 586–590. IEEE, December 2015
12. Malekzadeh, M., Clegg, R.G., Haddadi, H.: Replacement autoencoder: a privacy-preserving algorithm for sensory data analysis. In: 2018 IEEE/ACM Third International Conference on Internet-of-Things Design and Implementation (IoTDI), pp. 165–176. IEEE (2018)
13. Mirjalili, V., Raschka, S., Namboodiri, A., Ross, A.: Semi-adversarial networks: convolutional autoencoders for imparting privacy to face images. In: 2018 International Conference on Biometrics (ICB), pp. 82–89. IEEE, February 2018
14. Vincent, P., Larochelle, H., Bengio, Y., Manzagol, P.A.: Extracting and composing robust features with denoising autoencoders. In: Proceedings of the 25th International Conference on Machine Learning, pp. 1096–1103, July 2008
15. Wu, Y., Yang, F., Ling, H.: Privacy-protective-GAN for face de-identification. arXiv preprint arXiv:1806.08906 (2018)
16. Siwek, K., Osowski, S.: Autoencoder versus PCA in face recognition. In: 2017 18th International Conference on Computational Problems of Electrical Engineering (CPEE), pp. 1–4. IEEE, September 2017
17. Almotiri, J., Elleithy, K., Elleithy, A.: Comparison of autoencoder and Principal Component Analysis followed by neural network for e-learning using handwritten recognition. In: 2017 IEEE Long Island Systems, Applications and Technology Conference (LISAT), pp. 1–5. IEEE, May 2017

18. Hornik, K., Stinchcombe, M., White, H.: Multilayer feedforward networks are universal approximators. Neural Netw. **2**(5), 359–366 (1989)
19. Bengio, Y., Courville, A., Vincent, P.: Representation learning: a review and new perspectives. IEEE Trans. Pattern Anal. Mach. Intell. **35**(8), 1798–1828 (2013)
20. Liu, Z., Luo, P., Wang, X., Tang, X.: Deep learning face attributes in the wild. In: Proceedings of the IEEE International Conference on Computer Vision, pp. 3730–3738 (2015)
21. Parkhi, O.M., Vedaldi, A., Zisserman, A.: Deep face recognition. In: BMVC, vol. 1, no. 3, p. 6 (2015)

XR and Educational Innovations
for Cognitive City

The Experience and Gender Differences Between Handheld and Eye-Controlled Virtual Reality

Wan-Ting Lee and Sheng-Yi Wu[✉]

National Pingtung University, Pingtung, Taiwan
digschool@gmail.com

Abstract. Since the word maker was introduced to Taiwan, it has caused a great wave of education and activities. The maker movement has been rapidly launched in Taiwan. Both government units and the private sector are building maker space, and also refer to foreign makers. Space all the tools, design courses and publicity Maker education. This study is a study of the operation of each of the founding centers. After waves of the maker movement, the two centers of the Maker Center, which can continue to operate, discuss the operational difficulties and business models, and conduct research on the nine aspects of the business model, trying to analyze the key ways in which it operates to make recommendations.

Keywords: Physiological signal · Handheld VR · Eye-controlled VR · VR

1 Research Background, Motivation and Problems

The change of education style, from the old-style duck-feeding education to the prohibition of corporal punishment, and then flipping the classroom and then blowing up the STEM and STEAM education from the United States, the learning environment is changing with the development of information technology, from flat books to 3D rendering. The images allow students to be more integrated.

In response to the application of VR devices, there are currently some user studies related to VR. For example, Peters et al. (2016) use VR to provide insights into the user experience of the welding environment, such as allowing students to simulate the flow of rare metal materials while welding, which can reduce the loss of actual operation, and some welding simulations can make Students train on muscle memory. According to Bohil et al. (2011), VR continues to provide effective treatments for treating phobias because VR can provide virtual sensory illusions in a highly controlled environment. Also because of the change in equipment, it can continue to enhance over time to assist in research and treatment.

In addition, more than 80% of the human cognitive information processing process is obtained by vision, so the process of eye movement is also the most important sensory information source in the cognitive process. Eye tracking can be used to detect the subject's visual trajectory and to understand the subject's internal emotional perception (Williams et al. 2003). In recent years, there have been some studies on VR combined with eye control. For example, Chandon et al. (2006) mentioned the use of

© Springer Nature Singapore Pte Ltd. 2020
J. Shen et al. (Eds.): IC3 2019, CCIS 1227, pp. 167–173, 2020.
https://doi.org/10.1007/978-981-15-6113-9_18

commercial eye tracking data to show the customer's visual attention and brand considerations, and then use visual attention to plan the merchandise. Law et al. (2004) analyze the eye control path of abdominal surgery for novices and experts. It is found that novices rely on tools to complete the operation, but compared with the experts, they are inclined to perform surgery. The gaze of the target is better than the gaze of the operating tool, which in turn leads to the biggest difference between the expert and the novice. Meißner et al. (2017) mentioned that the customer's visual attention can be analyzed during the shopping process, and then the virtual reality and eye tracking are used to provide the shopper with unique shopping behavior. These studies have prompted more manufacturers to invest in VR and eye control device development, and eye control VR also offers people the choice of different control VR helmets.

With the rise of physiological signal research and the maturity of eye-detection detection equipment, researchers can conduct trajectory research on eye control in VR. As new trends emerge, when education and technology can be combined to help students in the disciplines, they can also explore equipment. When the virtual reality is not limited to the game again, when it is extended to education, it is found that less discussion of the user experience on the device is discussed. The related research compares the hand control VR helmet (such as HTC Vive) and the eye control VR helmet (such as FOVE). The lack of information on the experience of users using interactions with interactions is even more lacking. In view of this, manufacturers have designed VR helmets (such as FOVE) that control VR content with eye control signals, which is a brand-new experience for students or the general public. However, with regard to current research trends, there are few related studies comparing the experience differences between users of hand-controlled VR helmets (such as HTC Vive) and eye-controlled VR helmets (such as FOVE). Therefore, this study will use the above two VR helmets, with similar learning content, through questionnaires and interviews, let the students personally experience the interaction of the two VR helmets, and then put forward the advantages and disadvantages of the user experience and suggestions. The research questions are as follows:

1. What are the differences and suggestions between users for the experience and control behavior of hand-operated VR helmets and eye-controlled VR helmets?
2. Are there different gender differences between the experience of hand-controlled VR helmets and eye-controlled VR helmets for users of different genders (male and female)?

2   Research Methods and Steps

2.1   Research Participants, Experimental Procedures and Design

The subjects of the study were college students, and a total of 42 college students were tested. The research design is based on the research purpose, allowing each student to fill in the personal background information and VR experience questionnaire, and then randomize the experience of hand-controlled VR helmet and eye-controlled VR helmet.

After experiencing both, the subject is asked to fill out the QUIS User Interaction Satisfaction Scale and finally interview the experience. Research flow chart contains

1. Experimental description (5 min)
2. Personal background information and VR experience questionnaire (5 min)
3. Hand control VR helmet experience (15 min)
4. Eye-controlled VR helmet experience (15 min)
5. QUIS User Interaction Satisfaction Scale (5 min)
6. Interviews (15 min)

2.2   Research Tools

There are three main research tools in this study. The first is the Quest Customer Experience Satisfaction (Questionnaire for User Interaction Satisfaction), the second is the Hand Control VR Helmet (HTC Vive), and the third is the Eye Control VR Helmet (FOVE 0), which is described below.

2.2.1   QUIS User Interaction Satisfaction Scale

The QUIS User Interaction Satisfaction Scale was designed by the Human-Computer Interaction Lab at the University of Mary Maryland to evaluate the user interface's interactive satisfaction table (Preece et al. 2002), the item contains five aspects of the overall response to the system, the overall response of the screen words and system messages, learning, system functions.

2.2.2   HTC Vive

The head-mounted display is designed to take advantage of the "room size" technology, which turns a room into a three-dimensional space through sensors, allowing users to navigate naturally in the virtual world, moving around, and using motion-tracking handheld controllers to vividly the ability to manipulate objects with sophisticated interactions, communication and immersive environments. In this study, we chose Ocean Rift, a submarine bio-exploration game that explores the wonders of the ocean through a range of habitats and VR experiences and faces the rare species on Earth.

2.2.3   FOVE 0

The VR helmet provides eye tracking and the FOVE 0 uses two 120 Hz infrared cameras in the helmet to track the user's line of sight. FOVE 0 provides an immersive presence and users can experience the depth of field in the game. In this study, the eye-controlled marine life learning system developed by our team will be used as the VR content of our experience. The experience is divided into games, learning, and challenge modes, and the information on marine life is displayed through eye control.

2.3   Analysis Tools

In this study, the quantitative questionnaire part, namely personal background data and VR use experience questionnaire, QUIS user interaction satisfaction scale will use SPSS statistical analysis software for statistical analysis, analysis tools include descriptive statistics, t-test.

3   Research Methods

There were 42 valid samples for this study, 14 for boys (33.3%) and 28 for girls (66.7%).

Secondly, the user is using the QUIS situation of handheld and eye-controlled VR and analyzes through the paired sample t-test. It can be seen from Table 1 that in the overall response and picture presentation of QUIS, system terminology and information, learning operating system and system performance, only the screen presentation is significantly different (T distribution, (t) = −4.120, Significance (2-sided), (p) = .000). From the statistics, the screen display of eye control VR (Mean, (M) = 5.77, Standard deviation, (SD) = 1.18) is significantly larger than that of handheld VR (M = 4.98, SD = 1.09). After the interview, the reason may be that the user is mostly using the eye control VR for the first time. Therefore, it is considered that the eye control VR is simpler than the handheld VR. The handheld VR will not pay attention to the wrong button during the process. While jumping out of different pictures, eye control VR is relatively clear in terms of text reading and organizational structure.

Table 1. Handheld and eye control VR QUIS analysis

	Matched samples difference		T distribution	Degree of freedom	Significance (2-sided)
	Mean	Standard deviation			
Overall response	−.05714	1.11774	−.331	41	.742
Screen presentation	−.78571	1.23592	−4.120	41	.000
System terminology and information	−.17143	.85148	−1.305	41	.199
Learning operating system	0.00000	1.44830	0.000	41	1.000
System performance	−.10714	.86979	−.798	41	.429

Secondly, we explore the use of handheld and eye-controlled VR QUIS for different genders and analyze them through paired sample t-tests. From Table 2, it can be seen that the overall response of QUIS and handheld VR overall response handheld VR screen presentation, handheld VR system terminology and information, handheld VR learning operating system, handheld VR system performance, eye control VR overall response, eye In terms of VR screen rendering, eye control VR system terminology and information, eye control VR learning operating system, and eye control VR system performance, there are six significant differences. Dijon is the terminology and information for handheld VR systems (male t = −2.094, p = 0.043, female t = −2.292, p = 0.028). From the statistics, the terms and information of the handheld VR system for males (M = 4.97, SD = 0.73) were significantly smaller than those of females (M = 5.58, SD = 0.95). Post-interviews show that the reason for this result may be that men often play electric toys more than women, so the system's terminology and information impact are not much different from the game itself. The second is the overall response of the eye control VR (male $t = -3.035$, $p = 0.004$, female $t = -2.838$, $p = 0.01$). From the statistics, the overall response of eye control VR in males (M = 4.89, SD = 1.17) was significantly lower than that in females (M = 5.91, SD = 0.96). Post-interviews show that the reason for this result may be because most women in this study will wear contact lenses, while men wear glasses more. When playing games, because the helmet of FOVE 0 is small, many men are experiencing the process is affected, so the overall response of men is lower than that of women. The third is the eye-controlled VR picture presentation (male $t = -2.157$, $p < 0.037$, female $t = -2.044$, $p = 0.053$). From the statistics, the eye-controlled VR images of males (M = 5.24, SD = 1.25) were significantly smaller than those of females (M = 6.04, SD = 1.07). Post-interviews show that the reason for this result may be that women will seriously look at the marine life information introduced by the game when they are playing games. Men will pay more attention to finding the creatures in the bio-illustration. When filling out the questionnaire afterwards, women will remember the sights in the game, while men will pay more attention to the feeling of moving in the game. The fourth is the terminology and information of the eye control VR system (male $t = -2.727$, $p = 0.009$, female $t = -2.602$, $p = 0.016$). From the statistics, the terminology and information of the eye control VR system for males (M = 4.97, SD = 1.06) was significantly smaller than that of females (M = 5.84, SD = 0.92). Post-interviews show that the reason for this result may be because men pay more attention to the pictures in the process of moving, pay less attention to the information provided in the system and related terms, and women will leave the introduction page after reading the biological information, so when answering the questionnaire, the system terminology and information are more certain than men. The fifth is the eye-controlled VR learning operating system (male $t = -2.406$, $p = 0.021$, female $t = -2.148$, $p = 0.044$). From the statistics, the eye-controlled VR learning operating system for males (M = 5.00, SD = 1.56) was significantly smaller than that of females (M = 6.00, SD = 1.11). Post-interviews show that the reason for this result may be because before the game starts, women will listen carefully to the precautions. Men will be more impetuous and ready to start the game, so when they start the game, women experience more than men. Ask less questions. The sixth is the performance of the eye control VR system (male $t = -2.915$, $p = 0.006$, female $t = -2.666$, $p = 0.014$). From the statistics, the performance of the eye-controlled VR system of males (M = 5.02, SD = 1.18) was significantly lower than that of females (M = 5.97, SD = 0.90). Post-interviews show that the reason for this result may be that women are less likely to play games than men, and men are more likely to play games such as shootouts or action games, so women are less exposed to games in various questions and answers about system performance. Female systems perform better than men.

Table 2. QUIS analysis of hand-controlled VR helmets and eye-controlled VR helmets for users of different genders

Group statistic					Independent samples				
	Gender	Number	Mean	Standard deviation	Levene test with equal variance		Average t-test		
					F verification	Significance	T distribution	Degree of freedom	Significance (2-sided)
Handheld VR overall response	Male	14	5.2143	1.17267	0.721	0.401	−1.297	40	0.202
	Female	28	5.6643	1.00082			−1.229	22.741	0.232
Handheld VR screen rendering	Male	14	4.9286	1.03096	0.276	0.602	−0.232	40	0.818
	Female	28	5.0119	1.13123			−0.239	28.406	0.813
Handheld VR system terminology and information	Male	14	4.9714	0.72688	0.98	0.328	−2.094	40	0.043
	Female	28	5.5786	0.95272			−2.292	33.149	0.028
Handheld VR learning operating system	Male	14	5.5	1.07417	0.413	0.524	−0.641	40	0.525
	Female	28	5.75	1.2435			−0.674	29.813	0.506
Handheld VR system performance	Male	14	5.2143	0.97002	0.079	0.78	−1.628	40	0.111
	Female	28	5.7143	0.92224			−1.601	24.952	0.122
Eye control VR overall response	Male	14	4.8857	1.17333	0.547	0.464	−3.035	40	0.004
	Female	28	5.9143	0.96214			−2.838	22.013	0.01
Eye control VR screen rendering	Male	14	5.2381	1.25015	0.649	0.425	−2.157	40	0.037
	Female	28	6.0357	1.06705			−2.044	22.743	0.053
Eye control VR system terminology and information	Male	14	4.9714	1.05789	0.024	0.879	−2.727	40	0.009
	Female	28	5.8357	0.92224			−2.602	23.148	0.016
Eye control VR learning operating system	Male	14	5	1.55662	3.877	0.056	−2.406	40	0.021
	Female	28	6	1.10554			−2.148	19.778	0.044
Eye control VR system performance	Male	14	5.0179	1.17859	1.883	0.178	−2.915	40	0.006
	Female	28	5.9732	0.90354			−2.666	20.894	0.014

4   Conclusions and Recommendations

This study explores the different genders and experience of handheld and eye-controlled virtual reality devices. By using HTC Vive and FOVE 0 devices, users can experience different helmets, and the experience is completed through questionnaires and interviews.

Questionnaires and interviews can summarize several findings. Different users have different influences on different experience. In the questionnaire presented on the screen, it is found that users who have no experience are significantly different from experienced users. In the emergency interviews of different gender questionnaires, it is found that men are more likely to contact video games, men and women wear contact lenses, males and females have different focus on the game, and the focus on the description before the experience will affect the user's response to the questionnaire.

For handheld VR device users, it is recommended that the device will affect the proper use of the site due to the wide range of activities, such as the part with extended control of the hand, which may be hit by others because it is not noticed during operation. Someone must be assisted by others. For the eye-controlled VR device users, the delay is serious, and the object is too small to be judged. It is recommended to narrow the distance between the body and the tracker. The eye movement judgment will become close to other objects and objects even if they are biased. If the distance is too far, it cannot be judged, and the design of the helmet can be larger.

Since this is a handheld and eye-controlled interactive virtual reality, the same software should be used in the experiment to make the user experience the difference between the two devices. For the eye-controlled interactive virtual reality helmet, the helmet should be fine-tuned for a wide range of users, so that the user is no longer limited to the small helmet, which causes the user with glasses to be inconvenient in tracking. For subsequent studies, it is recommended that the sex ratio and the number collection can adopt more samples.

References

Bohil, C.J., Alicea, B., Biocca, F.A.: Virtual reality in neuroscience research and therapy. Nat. Rev. Neurosci. **12**(12), 752 (2011)

Burdea, G., Coiffet, P.: Virtual Reality Technology. Wiley, New York (1994)

Chandon, P., Hutchinson, J., Bradlow, E., Young, S.H.: Measuring the value of point-of-purchase marketing with commercial eye-tracking data. INSEAD Business School Research Paper (2007/22) (2006)

Law, B., Atkins, M.S., Kirkpatrick, A.E., Lomax, A.J.: Eye gaze patterns differentiate novice and experts in a virtual laparoscopic surgery training environment. In: Proceedings of the 2004 Symposium on Eye Tracking Research & Applications, pp. 41–48. ACM, March 2004

Meißner, M., Pfeiffer, J., Pfeiffer, T., Oppewal, H.: Combining virtual reality and mobile eye tracking to provide a naturalistic experimental environment for shopper research. J. Bus. Res. (2017). https://www.sciencedirect.com/science/article/pii/S0148296317303478

Peters, C., Postlethwaite, D., Wallace, M.W.: U.S. Patent No. 9,318,026. U.S. Patent and Trademark Office, Washington, DC (2016)

Preece, J., Rogers, Y., Sharp, H.: Interaction Design: Beyond Human-Computer Interaction. Wiley, New York (2002)

Williams, L.M., Loughland, C.M., Green, M.J., Harris, A.W.F., Gordon, E.: Emotion perception in schizophrenia: an eye movement study comparing the effectiveness of risperidone vs. haloperidol. Psychiatry Res. **120**(1), 13–27 (2003)

A Virtual Reality Game-Based Library Navigation Learning System for Improving Learning Achievement in Popular Science Education

Shih-Yeh Chen[1] and Yu-Shan Lin[2(✉)]

[1] Department of Computer Science and Information Engineering,
National Taitung University, Taitung, Taiwan
sychen@nttu.edu.tw
[2] Department of Information Science and Management Systems,
National Taitung University, Taitung, Taiwan
ysl@nttu.edu.tw

Abstract. With the popularity of mobile devices in recent years, game-based learning has become a popular way of learning. However, most of them simplify the game-based learning system to repetitive and monotonous questions and score awards, making it deviate from the original purpose of game-based education: let students be immersed in game-based learning, and then, enhance the motivation and effectiveness of learning. Therefore, this study develops a set of virtual reality game-based library guide learning system, which combines popular science education with real-life situations and integrates popular science knowledge to make game events, so that learning is no longer limited to classroom space, but can be explored in the library of virtual reality. This system is applied to general courses in university to achieve the effect of promoting popular science education and a library document guide. The experimental results show that this method can be used to promote popular science education and a library document guide. This method can solve the shortcomings of traditional digital learning and library guides, which cannot attract students' devotion, and thus, improve learning effectiveness.

Keywords: Virtual reality · Popular science education · Digital Game-Based Learning

1 Introduction

In recent years, "UNESCO" and other vital institutions have been promoting lifelong learning. Taiwan's 12-year national education is also moving in this direction, and education reform is centered on literacy [1]. Literacy education emphasizes that learning must be close to the real living environment and shall not be only for loose knowledge or specific abilities [2, 3]. Learning science is to solve problems in life; however, problems in life cannot be divided into subjects, thus, future education policy should pay more attention to core concepts and cross-disciplinary learning [4, 5].

© Springer Nature Singapore Pte Ltd. 2020
J. Shen et al. (Eds.): IC3 2019, CCIS 1227, pp. 174–182, 2020.
https://doi.org/10.1007/978-981-15-6113-9_19

Game-based learning has become a popular way of learning due to the popularity of digital devices. However, most of the digital game textbooks on the market are interactive games with education as the main axis, which emphasize the function of education but lose the original purpose of game-based education. The games are simplified into repetitive and monotonous question-answering and cheap score awards, which deviates from the core spirit of games and cannot achieve the expected learning effectiveness [6]. However, as campus life is a process of education, this system links to campus life and popular science knowledge through mobile digital games to break the barrier of disciplines.

Through this system, learning can become more attractive, players can better understand campus life, freshmen can adapt to the campus more quickly, and older students can have a sense of resonance and identity. It can also integrate popular science knowledge into the campus's daily events; while playing the game, the players can enjoy the feeling of learning with a smile, while subtly learning the relevant cross-disciplinary popular science knowledge [7].

2   Literature Review

2.1   Virtual Reality

Through the drawing function of a computer, virtual reality (VR) displays scenes of real environments on a screen. As the scenes depicted have in-depth information of the scene and can be viewed and interacted with through VR devices, it makes people feel like they are in the actual scenes [8]. As early as 1935, Stanley G. Weinbaum put forward the concept of virtual reality in his novel Pygmalion's Spectacles. In 1962, Morton Heilig realized the concept of virtual reality [9, 10]. It can be seen that virtual reality is not a new technology, but because of the high drawing ability requirements of virtual reality, virtual reality was only a display system in large research centers in the past era of backward computer operation. However, with the gradual maturity of information software and hardware, the mobile devices that have been emerging in recent years make the application field of virtual reality expand from indoor to outdoor, and to almost all fields that apply information technology, such as medical treatment, nursing, education, sightseeing, culture, military, architecture, design, engineering, scenic spot guide, industry, entertainment, etc. [11].

2.2   Popular Science Education

Popular science education generally refers to the use of various media to promote science and technology and disseminate scientific concepts to the general public in a simple but profound approach; therefore, it is also called public science [12]. Unlike traditional scientific papers that only discuss research results in specific professional fields, popular science converts scientific knowledge generally regarded as abstruse by the public into a simple, easy-to-understand, or entertaining mode, making it easy to absorb and internalize. Through the characteristics of the media, popular science can be matched with current events, thus, broadening the content coverage [13, 14]. Nowadays, popular science education is closely related to our daily life and can influence a wide range of aspects, including culture, politics, economy, and education. While the introduction of new things can bring new experiences, they may also be accompanied by dangers; for example, the colorful corn powder used to create an atmosphere is flammable powder, which may cause public safety concerns if it contacts burning conditions [15]. Promoting people's knowledge through the dissemination of popular science education can better guarantee people's life safety.

With the rise of social networks, the channels for disseminating knowledge become more diverse. The information received by the public about popular science education may be written by scholars in non-professional fields, who have limited knowledge about related topics, which may lead to misjudgments between knowledge and rumors by people other than experts. Moreover, according to a survey of popular science education, as conducted by Taiwan's news media, men are more interested in popular science education, as compared with women. In particular, senior high school students are more interested in science, as compared with college students and middle school students [16].

2.3 Digital Game-Based Learning

Digital Game-Based Learning (DGBL) generally refers to the learning environment constructed by integrating learning content and game elements through programming language, which take digital games as the learning platform. It is both educational and game-oriented and allows learners to get a sense of achievement through solving problems in the game, thus, achieving the purpose of learning while having fun. As learners often feel quite happy and interested in the process of learning, it is also called pleasant learning. This learning method has great potential for improving learning effectiveness [17].

Digital games include entertainment and gameplay functions, as well as other characteristics, such as rules, goal-orientation, and human-computer interaction, meaning they allow learners to master their learning process and progress through competition and challenge, while providing repeated practice and real-time feedback, thus, bringing great benefit to learners' learning interest and motivation [18]. Digital game-based learning can arouse learners' intrinsic motivation and interest in learning through simulating real-life situations, as they can directly apply the knowledge taught by teachers to solve the problems that may occur in real life. Therefore, compared with traditional educational media and tools, learning by playing games, practicing, and getting feedback from games can make learners have a profound understanding of what they have learned [19]. Statistics show that research on game-based learning has been on the rise year by year, and has been widely used in different teaching fields [20].

3   System Architecture

To adapt to the users' life experience, the design of this system takes campus life as the story setting, uses a game development engine that is popular in the industry, Unity 3D, as the main axis of game development, uses the free plug-in Fungus, as provided by the Asset Store, as the event triggering system, and uses Google VR as the development tool of the virtual reality exploration system. The purpose of this system is to allow every user of this system to fully experience virtual reality without being limited to specific headwear tools, as Fig. 1.

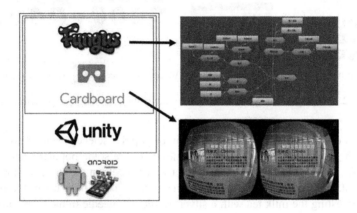

Fig. 1. A virtual reality game-based library navigation learning system structure.

3.1   System Characteristics

This system combines digital game-based learning, popular science education, and virtual reality experience technology, through which, students can achieve cross-domain learning. It also adopts a flow-based framework for each functional module, meaning that, although this work is now based on their own experience as a game script, in the future, different regions or schools can dynamically integrate plots with local characteristics. Its works also allow students to have a better understanding of campus life while helping freshmen to integrate into campus life more quickly and brings the older students a sense of resonance and identity. Through the use of this work, we can also have a more in-depth understanding of cross-domain industrial application technology.

In the design of a game-based library guide learning system, this system is a knight-errant-style business development game. The real campus scenes render the game scenes in ink and wash, and the conditions are four years and eight semesters Fig. 2. Players must find a balance among the attributes in a limited time, which is consistent with real-life experience. When learning events are triggered, users must go to the library to find the relevant knowledge according to the library guides. The National Taitung University Library is a beautiful landmark surrounded by mountains and seas, with the interior design echoing its architectural concepts. It takes landscape images as its construction concept, including clouds, peaks, flowing water, and the earth. While students may have visited it, they do not know the beauty of its images.

| Start the game | Campus tour | Weekday in the classroom | Holiday in dormitory |

Fig. 2. Display of the game-based library navigation learning system interface.

In terms of content design, the integration of popular science events into the game is another highlight in the game. In the game, there are some popular science events close to life, such as testing for poison with a silver needle in the student dining room. In this event, the students feel a stomachache after drinking milk tea in the breakfast shop. After testing the milk tea with a silver needle, the needle immediately turns grey and black because the food contains sulfur, which has a chemical reaction with the silver to form silver sulfide. As the game progresses, the corresponding popular chemistry events will be triggered. To solve these problems, the players must go to the library following the guidance of the system and explore the relevant knowledge through the virtual reality exploration system. Therefore, a 360-degree camera is used to take the view and connect the images of various regions in series, which are matched with the relevant introduction texts. The players can wear a simple cardboard to enjoy the treasure house of knowledge, as shown in Fig. 3.

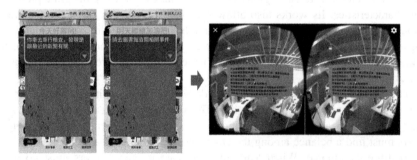

Fig. 3. Exploring virtual reality events in the library.

3.2 Experimental Design

As shown in Fig. 4, this study adopts a quasi-experimental research method. The research subjects are first-year students of the Humanities College of a Taiwanese university, including 31 males and 32 Females, for a total of 63 students. Before the experiment, a pre-test was conducted to understand the subjects' knowledge level of popular science and their familiarity with libraries. While teaching the general education curriculum, the teacher will explain the operation of the game system, integrate the game-based library guided learning system with popular science education into the curriculum teaching, and use virtual reality technology to guide students to explore knowledge in the virtual world. After the course is over, a learning achievement test is conducted through a post-test. Finally, analysis software SPSS is used for analysis, which is supplemented by qualitative interviews with the expectation of understanding the changes in learning effect.

Fig. 4. Experimental process

4   Results and Discussion

This research uses inquiry activities to carry out the game-based library guided learning system combined with a popular science education curriculum. Before curriculum teaching is carried out, the students take a pre-test for prior knowledge structure and learning effectiveness, and then, take the post-test of learning effectiveness after the activity is finished. A total of 63 complete questionnaires are collected. After analysis by the statistical software, the preliminary results can be summarized, as follows:

1) Do science popularization activities make students of different genders have different prior knowledge and familiarity with libraries? This paper uses independent sample t-tests to examine the differences in the structure of the prior knowledge mastered by students of different genders before the science popularization activities (Table 1). The results show that, before the activities, the effect sizes of both prior knowledge and familiarity with library resources of male and female students participating in the activities were less than 0.2, indicating no significant difference.

Table 1. T-test of gender in the prior popular science knowledge and familiarity with libraries.

	Mean (Std. Deviation)		df	t	p	(d)
	Men ($N = 31$)	Women ($N = 32$)				
Popular science knowledge	4.48(1.73)	4.63(1.52)	61	−.34	.73	0.09
Library resource familiarity	4.65(1.62)	4.94(1.54)	61	−.73	.47	0.19

2) Tests on learning effectiveness are conducted both before and after the course. Dependent sample t testing is used to examine the changes in the students' scores in the Learning Effectiveness Questionnaire (Table 2), which are conducted before and after the implementation of the exploration course. The analysis results show $p < .05$, indicating a significant difference in the average scores obtained by the students in the first grade of the Humanities College before and after their participation in the exploration course, meaning the post-test score (M = 60.30 SD = 17.29) is higher than the pre-test score (M = 51.36, SD = 11.40), with the effect size of d = 0.61, which is a medium effect (d $\geq$ 0.5). On the other hand, regarding the part of familiarity with library resources, the post-test score (M = 68.14 SD = 13.63) is higher than the pre-test score (M = 45.70, SD = 15.31), and the effect size is d = 1.55, which is a high effect (d $\geq$ 0.8). It can be seen that learners can improve their familiarity through the exploratory process.

Table 2. T-test of difference between pre-test and post-test (N = 63)

	Mean (Std. Deviation)		df	t	p	(d)
	Post-test	Pre-test				
Learning outcomes	60.30(17.29)	51.36(11.40)	62	3.49	.001	0.61
Library resource familiarity	68.14(13.63)	45.70(15.31)	62	10.62	.000	1.55

3) This research and analysis are conducted by qualitative questionnaires. After the implementation of the game-based library guided learning system combined with a popular science education curriculum, students mostly have positive feedback on the promotion of their popular science knowledge. In particular, there are apparent resonances for the emergence of campus scenes and current affairs issues, which shows that the integration of virtual reality technology into the curriculum is directly or indirectly helpful to students. The content analysis of qualitative questionnaires is summarized, as follows:

S1: Breakthrough traditional teaching sites with virtual reality technology and provide multi-dimensional feedback (visual, audio, somatosensory), which is very interesting.
S2: Break down misconceptions through current issues, which makes people want to explore other events.
S3: Explore necessary knowledge in a guided library with familiar scenes of the real world, which makes people feel like they are actually in the library.
S4: What you see is what you get. Learning is also possible in the virtual world.
S5: Turn sophisticated knowledge into visual presentations, which makes people less likely to reject popular science courses and allows them to become more familiar with libraries.

In summary, most students have positive feedback on the integration of virtual reality into the campus environment, meaning learning scenes that portray popular science courses, which can help students avoid the insecurity and adaptation period brought by unfamiliar environments, and allow them to learn to explore the corresponding popular science knowledge in the right manner.

5 Conclusion

The popularity of mobile devices and networks now enables students to learn in ways different from the past. The integration of popular science education and games frees learning from the limitation of classroom space. Through this game learning system, students can improve their learning effectiveness and campus identity, while interacting with the real world. Students can also learn campus information and discuss it with their peers through this system. To explore the improvements in the understanding of campus life and popular science knowledge, future research can also compare the learning effects of students from different colleges.

Acknowledgment. The authors would like to thank the Ministry of Science and Technology of the Republic of China, Taiwan for supporting this research under Contract MOST 107-2511-H-143-004 and MOST 106-2511-S-143-002-MY2.

References

1. Meihua, Q., Karen, R.C.: Game-based learning and 21st century skills: a review of recent research. Comput. Hum. Behav. **63**, 50–58 (2016)
2. Juho, H.: Challenging games help students learn: an empirical study on engagement, flow and immersion in game-based learning. Comput. Hum. Behav. **54**, 170–179 (2016)
3. Yoori, H., Jung-Yoon, Y., Se-Hoon, J.: What components should be included in advertising literacy education? Effect of component types and the moderating role of age. J. Advert. **47**(4), 347–361 (2019)
4. Grant, M.M.: Getting a grip on project-based learning: theory, cases and recommendations. Meridian Middle Sch. Comput. Technol. J. **5**(1), 83 (2002)
5. Chang, C.Y.: Taiwan's science education research. Newslett. East-Asian Assoc. Sci. Educ. **5**(2), 1 (2012)
6. Köse, U.: A web based system for project-based learning activities in "web design and programming" course. Procedia-Soc. Behav. Sci. **2**(2), 1174–1184 (2010)
7. Krishnamoorthy, V., Appasamy, B., Scaffidi, C.: Using intelligent tutors to teach students how APIs are used for software engineering in practice. IEEE Trans. Educ. **5**(3), 355–363 (2013)
8. Heim, M.: The Metaphysics of Virtual Reality. Oxford University Press, Oxford (1993)
9. Burdea, G.C.: Virtual Reality Systems and Applications (1993). http://doi.org/10.1007/978-3-642-22024-1
10. Pan, Z., Cheok, A.D., Yang, H., Zhu, J., Shi, J.: Virtual reality and mixed reality for virtual learning environments. Comput. Graph. **30**(1), 20–28 (2006)
11. Gavish, N., et al.: Evaluating virtual reality and augmented reality training for industrial maintenance and assembly tasks. Interact. Learn. Environ. **23**, 778–798 (2015)
12. Parkinson, J., Adendorff, R.: The use of popular science articles in teaching scientific literacy. Engl. Specif. Purp. **23**(4), 379–396 (2009)

13. Chao, Y.C., Hsiung, C.T., Yu, H.P.: Content analysis of nanotechnology experimental teaching materials in primary and secondary schools in Taiwan. J. Res. Educ. Sci. **56**(4), 1–42 (2011)
14. Lin, S.-Y., Wu, M.-T., Cho, Y.-I., Chen, H.-H.: The effectiveness of a popular science promotion program on nanotechnology for elementary school students in I-Lan City. Res. Sci. Technol. Educ. **33**(1), 22–37 (2015)
15. Lundy, B.: Engaging the experts: popular science education and breast cancer activism. Crit. Public Health **13**(3), 191–206 (2010)
16. Guo, C.-J., Chiu, M.-H.: Research projects on science education funded by the national science council in Taiwan from 1982 to 2012: a historical review. In: Chiu, M.-H. (ed.) Science Education Research and Practices in Taiwan, pp. 11–41. Springer, Singapore (2016). https://doi.org/10.1007/978-981-287-472-6_2
17. Huang, W.H., Huang, W.Y., Tschopp, J.: Sustaining iterative game playing processes in DGBL: the relationship between motivational processing and outcome processing. Comput. Educ. **55**(2), 789–797 (2010)
18. Prensky, M.: Digital Game-Based Learning. McGraw-Hill, New York (2007)
19. Hogle, J.G.: Considering games as cognitive tools: in search of effective "Edutainment". University of Georgia Department of Instructional Technology (1996)
20. Hwang, G.J., Wu, P.H.: Advancements and trends in digital game-based learning research: a review of publications in selected journals from 2001 to 2010. Br. J. Edu. Technol. **43**(1), E6–E10 (2012)

Preliminary Study on the Application of Virtual Reality Social Skills Course to Improve the Abilities of Social Skills for Elementary and Junior High School Students with High Functional Autism

Chia-Chi Yeh[(✉)] and Ying-Ru Meng

Tsinghua University, No. 521 Nanda Road,
East District, Hsinchu City 300, Taiwan
patma320@gmail.com

Abstract. Teaching exceptional students through assistive technology is very important for the cognitive city. Due to the gradual progress of medical treatment and the educational diagnosis, the number of confirmed cases of students with Autism is rising in Taiwan. These students not only demonstrated serious deficits in social skills but also a tremendous lack of understanding of abstract and cognitive concepts. Based on the viewpoints above, the main topic of this research is using "Art Tour with Classmates" as the topic of a story to pair with the main ideas of teaching in Social Skills Curriculum Outline for Disabilities-Related Special Needs Areas in 12-year National Educational Curriculum to develop four virtual reality teaching systems. This study was conducted upon a group of ten autistic students from primary and middle school.

This study aims to understand the effectiveness of virtual reality teaching methods for students' social skills. After eight weeks of teaching, we used One-way ANOVA to analyze and explain the results of the overall teaching data. It was found that the students' performance in overall social skills has significantly improved and they made the most progress in "The completeness of sentence-structure". Thus we effectively improved the integrity of students' content after the experimental teaching of virtual reality social skills. Finally, through the experimental teaching of virtual reality social skills, students will soon accommodate themselves to the new surroundings and be willing to try their activities.

Keywords: Virtual reality · High functional autism · Social skills

1 Introduction

1.1 The Ability of Autistic Students to Learn Social Skills is Very Weak

Through DSM-5 (The Diagnostic and Statistical Manual of Mental Disorders), we understand that the main obstacles for autistic people include: barriers in social and emotional interactions, non-verbal communication behavioral deficits in social

© Springer Nature Singapore Pte Ltd. 2020
J. Shen et al. (Eds.): IC3 2019, CCIS 1227, pp. 183–193, 2020.
https://doi.org/10.1007/978-981-15-6113-9_20

interaction, development, and maintenance of interpersonal relationships, repetitive biased execution or interests and activities, the main characteristics of autism are related to interpersonal interaction and social skills. According to Dr. Wu from Taiwan, based on early and domestic reports of adolescents and adults with autism, 90% of people have difficulties in social interaction, 69% have behavioral problems, and 65–70% have communication problems [17], showing that even in adulthood, social interaction is still the most difficulty.

Social skills can improve the relationship between individuals and others. Through the training of the project, it helps to learn and judge the social situation, so that it can adapt to development. Scholars indicated that social skills can be obtained through learning [12]. Scholar have pointed out that if adolescents have obstacles to interpersonal and social adaptation and are unable to interact properly with others, they may feel lonely and powerless, easy to learn from school and develop physical and mental adaptation. To enable autistic patients to improve their social skills, it is necessary to enhance their social interaction and effective communication and to make it easier for autistic students to understand and learn through visual aids such as visual images, sound and light images [4].

According to the Ministry of Education's announcement data from the Special Education Network, the number of students with autism in Taiwan has increased in recent years [15].

1.2   By Teaching Through the Virtual Reality System, Students Can Get More Advantages in Learning Social Skills

In recent years, many studies have allowed students with autism to learn social skills and communication through virtual reality because virtual environments have many benefits for children with special needs. Research confirms the effectiveness of immersive virtual reality as a training tool. The skills learned from the virtual world can be applied to real life [9]. Studies point out, confirmed that the characteristics of computer are helpful for patients with autism, including reproducibility of work, visual images with sound effects, etc. [6, 7] Alan, Craig, Sherman and Will [1] listed out the advantages of virtual reality in training autistic students social skills, including the following seven items, 1) Controllable Input Stimuli. 2) Modification for Generalization. 3) Safer Learning Situation. 4) A Primarily Visual/Auditory World. 5) Individualized Treatment. 6) Preferred Computer Interactions. 7) Trackers.

1.3   Literature Reviews of Virtual Reality Teaching Applications

Many documents used this technology in special education. Parsons, Mitchell and Leonard [13] used a VR café with 12 adolescents with ASD between the ages of 13–18 to teach social awareness and then conducted a follow-up study with six adolescents between the ages of 14–15. Parsons, Leonard and Mitchell [14] through the VR cafe and bus scene, let two well-characterized autistic adolescents practice in virtual reality, including responding to emergencies, answering questions properly, and complying with social norms. Lorenzo, Lledó, Pomares, and Roig [8] have established an Emotional Script (ES) as a social script or behavior guideline in which they introduced ten social situations. These social situations are designed based on real situations where the students have shown difficulties. Didehbani, Allen, Kandalaft, Krawczyk and Chapman [3] conducted a research through thirty children between the ages of 7–16 diagnosed with ASD by completing 10; one-hour sessions across five weeks. These preliminary findings suggest that the use of a virtual reality platform offers an effective treatment option for improving social impairments commonly found in ASD. Matsentidou, Poullis [11]; Tzanavari, Charalambous-Darden, Herakleous, Poullis [16] hopes to create a safe road space for children, so they presented the scene of a road in virtual reality, letting children learn to cross the road. Lal, Evren, Andrew [9] created a working environment in virtual reality, a personal vocational training for ten high-functioning autistic patients and five typical autistic patients. DiGennaro Reed, Hyman, and Hirst [2] composed 40 articles on virtual reality technology applications to improve social skills for autistic patients. The findings can be divided into "social skills training format," "training technology application," and "experimental setting location," of which consisted of nine categories, eight types, and six areas. Horace et al. [5] trained 94 children between the ages of 6 and 12 by simulating six virtual scenes and related events, teaching emotional expression and control, and their interaction and emotional communication with others. It was found that after 28 weeks, children showed significant improvement and progress in emotional and human interaction.

After the literature discussion, many studies on social skills exercises for autistic students are based on multiple-choice questions in virtual reality teaching which lets the students choose the options they think are right, followed up with a few open-ended questions to determine the level of social skills. In addition to the lack of comprehensive observation and discussion, it is difficult to classify the learnt social skills in the real environment and actual interaction with people. In the scenarios of reality, many studies are the development of a single location, a single event, the lack of a holistic concatenation, and the extension of context and topic collocation. This situation makes the process of social interaction difficult for autistic students, leading them to imagine and generate an incorrect link. Therefore, in addition to allowing students to interact with avatars through open question and answer, this study also uses the theme of "Art Tour with Classmates" to develop as a whole, including pre-departure discussions with students (located in the classroom), participation with classmates (located in the cultural relics exhibition area), dining with classmates (the location is the restaurant), and bidding farewell to the students (located in the park), so that students can have complete formation and experience in social interaction exercises.

2 Method

2.1 Research Subject

The subjects of this study were sought through the Hsinchu autism association monthly magazine in January 2019. Parents signed up for their children during the announcement period. A total of 14 students signed up to participate. In the end, after the actual interview and implementation of the virtual reality test, one subject could not adapt to wearing head-mounted display and three subjects did not meet the standard scores specified in the study. Therefore, this study eventually collected ten highly functional autistic students who volunteered to participate. The study included students from grade 1 to 8, with an Intelligence Quotient score ranging from 70 to 105 points.

The study originally expected students who participated in the program to have an Intelligence Quotient score of 100, but because of the insufficient number of participants, to increase the number of samples, two students with an Intelligence Quotient score of 103 and 105 were included in the study. For the basic information of the subjects, please refer to Table 1.

Table 1. Subject basic information.

ID	Gender	Age (years)	Grade	Estimated IQ (standard score)
1	Males	10	4	75
2	Males	10	4	78
3	Males	12	6	85
4	Males	12	6	89
5	Males	13	7	98
6	Males	11	5	105
7	Males	7	1	79
8	Males	14	8	70
9	Females	8	3	74
10	Males	10	4	103

2.2 Teaching Location

The teaching took place in the special education counseling room on the 5th floor of the administrative building at National Tsing Hua University's Nanda Campus. The space plan includes a table, two chairs, a desktop computer (including the host, screen, mouse), a set of head-mounted stereo display HTC VIVE, a set of the controller, a pair of base stations, a headset microphone, two digital videos and a code table. Field personnel includes a researcher, a camera operator, and a subject.

2.3 Teaching Time

The teaching time of this study was from January to April 2019, which lasted for three and a half months. Each student has completed eight courses (see Table 2).

Table 2. Time slot-measurement schedule.

Time	09:00–10:00	10:00–11:00	11:00–12:00	13:00–14:00	14:00–15:00	15:00–16:00	16:00–17:00
Saturday	O	O	O	×	O	O	O
Sunday	◎	◎	◎	O	O	O	O

O Arrange for one person to test formally.
◎ Arrange for one person to make-up the session.
× Do not arrange classes.

2.4 Research Tools: Develop Social Skills Performance Evaluation Sheet

This study uses the "Social Skills Performance Evaluation Sheet" (self-made sheet) to reflect the real situation at the time of the test and let the case fully demonstrate the ability at that time, the self-made social skills performance score sheet of this study is based on the familiar interpersonal communication 7/38/55 rule. The concept is proposed by Albert Mehrabian, a professor of psychology at the University of California, Los Angeles. "Total Liking = 7% Verbal Liking + 38% Vocal Liking + 55% Facial Liking.", which means that when you need to convey a message that is "good intentions, but the content may cause negative emotions to the listener," you can use "sincere and positive attitudes" (reactive in tone, expression, and physical) to express favorable results for the listener. Refer to Fig. 1.

Elements of Personal Communication
- 7% spoken words
- 38% voice, tone
- 55% body language

Fig. 1. Interpersonal communication concept proposed by Albert Mehrabian. Take from http://wfhstudy.blogspot.tw/2013/01/blog-post_29.html

The main scoring project in this study contains "Answer Speed," "Conversation and Expression," "The completeness of sentence-structure," and "Conversation etiquette." The scoring method for each item is as follows.

Answer Speed: The time needed for thinking and answering after the students hear the questions raised by the avatars. The time calculation starts from the time the avatar asks the question. The time calculation starts from the time the avatar asks the question and ends upon the subject articulating the first word of his/her response. Five points in 0–3 s, four points in 3–5 s (more than 3 s, including 5 s), three points in 5–8 s (more than 5 s, including 8 s), and two points for more than 8 s. For those who didn't answer the questions get one point. The faster students answer, the higher their score.

Conversation and Expression: This project includes volume control, the appropriateness of the tone, the manner of speaking, speaking speed, the expression of body language, etc.

The Completeness of Sentence-Structure: This project considers whether each sentence answered by the student contains a subject, a verb, an adjective, a noun, an adverb, or even an active invitation or courage to ask a question through a complete sentence. The basic score of this project is 3 points. If the structure of the sentence answered by the subject is more complete, he/she can get a higher score.

Conversation Etiquette: There are five items in this section, including the participants' attention during the dialogue process (eye focus/behavioral performance), whether the conversion process has been interrupted or given an irrelevant answer, meaningless vocabulary or soliloquizing in the conversation, reiteration of the answer, etc. If all five of the above projects have been performed well, the subject gets five points. Poor performances in one of the items results in four points, three points for poor performances in two items, two points for poor performances in three items and one point for poor performances in four or more items. If no response was made to any of the items, the subject also gets one point for this project.

The Likert Scale scored all items in this study. This assessment form is filled in by the researcher (also the examiner). Since teaching style and personal teaching methods could easily affect the accuracy of the research process and results, all teaching was performed by one researcher. The researcher observed each student's performance in eight lessons and rated them on the same criteria.

2.5   Process

In this study, the development of the system scene was carried out according to the predetermined "Art Tour with Classmate." Four scenarios were developed according to the original goal, including the 1st situation - Classroom: Pre-departure discussion with the class before the tour, 2nd situation - Exhibition: Arriving at the venue with the students to see the exhibition (including ticket booths, lighting exhibitions and cultural relics exhibitions), 3rd situation - Restaurants: dining with the students in the restaurant (including Western restaurants and fast food restaurants), 4th situation - Park: Say goodbye to classmates and end the journey.

This experiment is guided by a simple picture book and relative activities to enter virtual reality teaching. The general process includes 5 min for the course content, 10 min for the picture book, and 10 min for the formal activity before the virtual reality situation. The virtual reality teaching lasts 10 min, and the classroom test takes 5 min. This article will illustrate the trigger mode and execution screen (see Table 3).

Table 3. The situation pictures execution and level task.

Level task	Triggered way
Enter the teaching homepage (The numbers in the right column of the screen can be adjusted according to the height of the subject)	The researcher (the Examiner) selects the level with a computer mouse
Classroom This screen task must discuss the content of the itinerary with the classmates	The student answers the question, and the researcher (examiner) selects the corresponding answer item with a computer keyboard. For different answers from the students, the keyboard keys can be used to reply to different options. The numeric keys 1–0 and the English letters a–z respectively represent the sentence response content
Ticket window Students must assist their classmates in buying tickets correctly	The student answers the question, and the researcher (examiner) selects the corresponding answer item with a computer keyboard. Also, to allow students to practice ticket purchases, this scenario allows students to operate the HTC VIVE controllers for payment and ticketing
Lighting exhibition The task must be accompanied by classmates watching the exhibition and expressing their feeling of viewing	The student answers the question, and the researcher (examiner) selects the corresponding answer item with a computer keyboard
Park This task is to say goodbye to classmates and describe today's visit to the exhibition and dining experience. In the end, the student is going to invite the classmate to come out again next time	The student answers the question, and the researcher (examiner) selects the corresponding answer item with a computer keyboard

3   Results and Discussion

3.1   Descriptive Statistics

Live performance in virtual reality social skills course. This study scores through Social skills performance evaluation sheet. The sheet contains four items, including "Answer Speed," "Conversation and Expression," "The completeness of sentence-structure," and "Conversation etiquette."

In Table 4, we listed out the scores obtained in all four projects. Answer Speed: All subjects had their worst performance in the first course, averaging only 3.886 points. The last time was the best, with an average of 4.816. Conversation and Expression: The worst performance is from the first class, only 2.921 points. The best performance is from the eighth course, with a score of 3.665. The completeness of sentence-structure: The lowest appeared in the first class, with an average of only 2.874 points, while the highest appeared in the eighth class, which is 3.421 points. Conversation etiquette: The most unsatisfactory performance is still from the first class, which is 4.166 points. The best performance is from the seventh and eighth class. Both classes received 4.665 points.

It can be seen that the general performance in the first course has the lowest score. As the middle course progresses, the score began to change. After almost eight classes, students have improved their social skills.

Table 4. Descriptive statistics - social performance scores from the 1st to 8th courses

Item	Answer speed			Conversation and expression			The completeness of sentence-structure			Conversation etiquette		
Number of classes	AVG	SD	N	AVG	SD	N	AVG	SD	N	AVG	SD	N
1st time	3.886	1.172	10	2.921	.908	10	2.874	.713	10	4.166	1.024	10
2nd time	4.507	.444	10	3.346	.424	10	3.142	.489	10	4.456	.554	10
3rd time	4.589	.452	10	3.485	.431	10	3.282	.434	10	4.258	.457	10
4th time	4.551	.510	10	3.342	.686	10	3.227	.506	10	4.265	.607	10
5th time	4.612	.538	10	3.447	.388	10	3.206	.499	10	4.340	.569	10
6th time	4.629	.328	10	3.544	.419	10	3.345	.449	10	4.481	.497	10
7th time	4.749	.273	10	3.626	.319	10	3.400	.394	10	4.655	.313	10
8th time	4.816	.138	10	3.665	.656	10	3.421	.330	10	4.655	.284	10

3.2   One-Way ANOVA

Due to repeated teaching and recording of each student's grades, all subjects were observed from the first to eighth performances by repeated measures. This study used One-way ANOVA to analyze students' social skills. According to the data results, the P-Value of the Mauchly Spherical Test on the first three items is significant, including "conversation response speed," "conversation expression effect," and "statement integrity." "Talking etiquette" is the only item with a less significant P-Value.

Therefore, the first three items must be based on the P value of the Greenhouse-Geisser and Huynh-Feldt columns. The only ceremonial scores are judged according to the assumed value of the spherical column. The results showed that the virtual reality social skills course demonstrated significant results for "Answer Speed," "Conversation and Expression," "The completeness of sentence-structure" and "Conversation etiquette" ($P < 0.05$). For details, see Table 5.

According to the research results, we can summarize three conclusions.

1. Students' performance in overall social skills has significantly improved after the experimental teaching of virtual reality social skills.
2. Through the experimental teaching of virtual reality social skills, students achieved the greatest progress in "The completeness of sentence-structure" and effectively improved the integrity of their content.
3. Through the experimental teaching of virtual reality social skills, students will soon accommodate themselves to the new surroundings and willing to try their activities.

Table 5. Tests of within-subjects effects

	Source	Type III SS	DF	MS	F	P	Partial eta squared	Non-centrality Parameter	Observable[a]
Answer speed	Sphericity Assumed	5.644	7	.806	4.690	.000**	.343	32.827	.990
	Greenhouse-Geisser		1.834	3.078		.027*		8.599	.682
	Huynh-Feldt		2.280	2.476		.018*		10.690	.757
	Lower-bound		1.000	5.644		.059*		4.690	.489
Conversation and expression	Sphericity Assumed	3.829	7	.547	3.650	.002**	.289	25.553	.960
	Greenhouse-Geisser		2.585	1.481		.032*		9.435	.684
	Huynh-Feldt		3.717	1.030		.016*		13.570	.808
	Lower-bound		1.000	3.829		.088		3.650	.400
The completeness of sentence-structure	Sphericity Assumed	2.157	7	.308	8.198	.000**	.477	57.385	1.000
	Greenhouse-Geisser		2.231	.967		.002**		18.286	.945
	Huynh-Feldt		3.000	.719		.000**		24.591	.982
	Lower-bound		1.000	2.157		.019*		8.198	.722
Conversation etiquette	Sphericity Assumed	2.356	7	.337	2.761	.014*	.235	19.324	.881
	Greenhouse-Geisser		2.660	.886		.070		7.344	.561
	Huynh-Feldt		3.880	.607		.044*		10.712	.690
	Lower-bound		1.000	2.356		.131		2.761	.318

[a]$\alpha = .05$

4 Conclusion

This study was conducted through elementary school and junior high school students, and there were only ten subjects. It is recommended that scholars who conduct relevant research in the future can expand the age range and number of people. Gender is also recommended by Mesa-Gresa, Gil-Gomez, Lozano-Quilis, Gil-Gomez [10]. In 2018, the gender ratio trend for global autistic patients was 3 (male): 1 (female). The number of samples in this study is small, so the range of results that can be explained is limited. It is recommended that the teaching of a larger sample base be considered in the future. Finally, the expressions of language and social skills in different countries are slightly different. In the future, if countries can begin to use virtual reality courses as the focus of social skills teaching, we will be able to develop a set of quantitative criteria for calculating the actual effectiveness of measuring social skills and will provide more benefits and assistance to the community and autistic students.

Acknowledgement. This research was supported by the Ministry of Science and Technology (MOST) (MOST 107-2511-H-007-010-MY2). The name of the project is "A study related to the effectiveness of constructing and applying Virtual Reality Teaching System to the social skill training for students with autism."

References

1. Craig, A.B., Sherman, W.R., Will, J.D.: Developing Virtual Reality Applications: Foundations of Effective Design. Morgan Kaufmann Books – Elsevier, Burlington (2009)
2. DiGennaro Reed, F.D., Hyman, S.R., Hirst, J.M.: Applications of technology to teach social skills to children with autism. Res. Autism Spectr. Disord. **5**(3), 1003–1010 (2011)
3. Didehbani, N., Allen, T., Kandalaft, M., Krawczyk, D., Chapman, S.: Virtual reality social cognition training for children with high functioning autism. Comput. Hum. Behav. **62**, 703–711 (2016)
4. Falk-Ross, F., Iverson, M., Gilbert, C.: Teaching and learning approaches for children with asperger's syndrome: literacy implications and applications. Teach. Except. Child. **36**(4), 48–55 (2004)
5. Ip, H.H.S., et al.: Enhance emotional and social adaptation skills for children with autism spectrum disorder: a virtual reality enabled approach. Comput. Educ. **117**, 1–15 (2018)
6. Kientz, J.A., Hayes, G.R., Abowd, G.D., Grinter, R.E.: From the war room to the living room: decision support for home-based therapy teams. In: Proceedings of the CSCW 2006 Proceedings of the 2006 20th Anniversary Conference on Computer Supported Cooperative Work, pp. 209–218. ACM Press (2006)
7. Kientz, J.A., Arriaga, R.I., Chetty, M., Hayes, G.R., Richardson, J.: Grow and know: understanding record-keeping needs for tracking the development of young children. In: Proceedings of the CHI 2007, pp. 1351–1360. ACM Press (2007)
8. Lorenzo, G., Lledó, A., Pomares, J., Roig, R.: Design and application of an immersive virtual system to enhance emotional skills for children with autism spectrum disorders. Comput. Educ. **98**(1), 192–205 (2016)
9. Lal, B., Evren, B., Andrew, R.: Vocational training with immersive virtual reality for individuals with autism: towards better design practices. In: 2016 IEEE 2nd Workshop on Everyday Virtual Reality (WEVR), pp. 21–25 (2016)

10. Mesa-Gresa, P., Gil-Gomez, H., Lozano-Quilis, J.A., Gil-Gomez, J.A.: Effectiveness of virtual reality for children and adolescents with autism spectrum disorder: an evidence-based systematic review. J. Sens. **98**(1), 63–77 (2018)
11. Matsentidou, S., Poullis, C.: Immersive visualizations in a VR cave environment for the training and enhancement of social skills for children with autism. In: 9th International Conference on Computer Vision Theory and Applications, pp. 230–236. Springer, New York (2014)
12. Merrell, K.W., Gimpel, G.A.: Social Skills of Children and Adolescents: Conceptualization, Assessment, Treatment. Lawrence Erlbaum Associates Publishers, Mahwah (1998)
13. Parsons, S., Mitchell, P., Leonard, A.: The use and understanding of virtual environments by adolescents with autistic spectrum disorders. J. Autism Dev. Disord. **34**(4), 449–466 (2004)
14. Parsons, S., Leonard, A., Mitchell, P.: Virtual environments for social skills training: comments from two adolescents with autistic spectrum disorder. Comput. Educ. **47**, 186–206 (2006)
15. Special Education Information Network, special education statistics inquiry. Date of declaration 2016. Accessed 21 Nov 2016, Accessed 21 Jan 2019
16. Tzanavari, A., Charalambous-Darden, N., Herakleous, K., Poullis, C.: Effectiveness of an immersive virtual environment (CAVE) for teaching pedestrian crossing to children with PDD-NOS. In: 15th IEEE International Conference on Advanced Learning Technologies (ICALT 2015), pp. 423–427 (2015)
17. Wu, Y.Y.: Autistic Spectrum Disorder, ASD. Taiwanese Society of Child and Adolescent Psychiatry. Health Education. Date of declaration 2016. http://www.tscap.org.tw/TW/NewsColumn/ugC_News_Detail.asp?hidNewsCatID=7&hidNewsID=129. Accessed 24 Dec 2018

Educational Technology and Strategy in Cognitive City

The Application Status and Reflection of Learning Tools Centered on Learning Activities—Based on the Ranking Analysis of Top100 Learning Tools in 2018

Jie Sheng[1] and He-Hai Liu[1,2(✉)]

[1] College of Education Science, Anhui Normal University, Wuhu, Anhui, China
358383418@qq.com
[2] University of Electronic Science and Technology of China, Chengdu, China

Abstract. The advent of the Internet era has promoted the continuous reform and development of college education. In order to adapt to the demand of information technology for teaching, the application of digital learning tools is increasing day by day, but it is still in the exploration stage and faces many opportunities and challenges. Through the analysis of Top Tools for learning ranking in 2018, this paper sorts out the development status and evolution trend of learning tool application, and summarizes, classifies and reflects on the application methods of learning tools in literature research, and finally builds learning tools in learning activities. Application model.

Keywords: Learning activities · Learning tools · Top tools for learning

1 Introduction

Since the "Twelfth Five-Year Plan", education information has adhered to the core concept of promoting the deep integration of information technology and education and teaching [1]. The school teaching environment, resources and models, which are based on the "three links and two platforms", have made breakthroughs. Progress, learning activities are the sum of the teacher-student operations that are carried out to promote more effective learning and accomplish specific learning objectives. More and more learning links occur in the network information environment, and the role of digital learning tools can not be ignored. However, behind the increasing use of learning tools, it also maps many defects and negative influences. The rapid development of educational information makes it extremely urgent to solve the problem of using learning tools in learning activities.

© Springer Nature Singapore Pte Ltd. 2020
J. Shen et al. (Eds.): IC3 2019, CCIS 1227, pp. 197–203, 2020.
https://doi.org/10.1007/978-981-15-6113-9_21

2   The Application of Learning Tools Evolves

2.1   Ranking of Top100 Learning Tools in 2018

The learning tool is a general term for appliances that enable students to intuitively and visually understand the various types of instruments used in teaching content [2]. Since 2007, a statistical result selected by C4LPT every year - Top 100 learning tools, according to tools the functional features are categorized to recommend excellent learning tools for learners. The author selected the 2018 TOP10 learning tool rankings for analysis as shown in Fig. 1.

Rank	category	category	Variety
1.YouTube	Video sharing platform	Web resources	same
2.Presentation	Demo software	Presentation tool	Rise 1
3.Google search	Web search engine	Web search engine	Fall 1
4.Twitter	Public social network	Social network	Rise 1
5.LinkedIn	Professional social network	Social network	Rise 2
6.posse Dpetive	Cloud-based office suites	Office suite	Fall 2
7.Word	Word processing software	Document tool	Fall 1
8.Word press	Blog and website software	Blog and web tools	Rise 1
9.Slack	Teamwork tool	Collaboration platform	Rise 3
10.zoom	Video conferencing tool	Information,conference tools	Rise 18

Fig. 1.   Top tools for learning 2018.

As can be seen from the above table, YouTube, the world's largest video sharing site, was dominated by 2018 and is popular among users of different ages. YouTube, presentations, Twitter, etc. have a higher ranking than last year. Zoom is ranked in the top ten list with 18 rising trends. The basic document office tools are showing a downward trend. Observing the scope of the change tools, the social and collaborative network resource platform has a greater advantage in 2018.

2.2 Trends in the Use of Learning Tools

From the top ten types of learning tools and rankings, it can be concluded that the application of learning tools has the following trends:

The structured evolution of learning tools [3]. Modern learning tools began to support the use of Internet technology to create a variety of data, away from physical limitations, change The object of teaching and learning has produced structural changes that can fully exploit the explicitness of knowledge.

The open evolution of learning tools. Network technology has produced a large number of social tools, breaking through the limitations of time and place, meeting the individual needs of learners, establishing an open and collaborative learning space, and achieving knowledge accessibility.

The social evolution of learning tools. The support of mobile technology allows users to communicate through the network, create a social platform, and social interaction learning activities pay more attention to learning interaction and collaboration.

3 The Application Status of Learning Tools Centered on Learning Activities

The trend of TOP10 learning tools in 2018 confirms that its emergence and evolution occupy a high degree of recognition in contemporary education. The advancement of information technology has continually promoted the development of teaching tools, and its related application research has also increased.

3.1 Theory-Based Application

Marxist philosophy emphasizes guiding practice with correct understanding and theory [4]. Research practice needs to support, select, learn or construct learning tools based on the support of disciplinary theory, and build a new type of instrumentalist. Teaching mode, from the perspective of keywords, there are not many literature based on theory, but the articles using teaching tools for teaching research will have certain theoretical support.

Wang Haying of Nanjing Normal University used the digital Brooms education goal classification theory to guide teachers to design teaching processes and tool prototypes based on classification selection tools, and finally integrate tools into teaching for feasibility testing. The support of the theory gives the designer research inspiration, thus creating, designing or developing a learning tool for the subject, and the theoretical basis combined with the teaching practice can achieve a better teaching effect.

3.2 Application Based on Research Methods

Newton once said: "If I look farther than others, it is because I stand on the shoulders of giants." [5] Use a variety of research methods to sort out and summarize the development and application status of research objects, carry out application and practice, take the essence, and abandon its dross. Tracing back to the source, you can go upstream. Most of these documents will select a tool to practice a learning activity. In the preliminary investigation, the literature review and data review are conducted for the research subjects.

Wang Xin, a Chinese-Chinese Normal University, used the literature review method to summarize the theoretical research status of the development of self-learning and mobile learning APP for primary and secondary school students at home and abroad, define its core concepts and theoretical foundations, and combine interviews and questionnaires to discover the problems and redesign them. A set of learning strategies for case implementation [6]. The scientific method provides reliable data and data for research development, and the educational application of learning tools is also guaranteed.

3.3 Application Based on Experiment

Some documents will choose a learning tool to conduct experimental research in different aspects of learning activities. It includes two categories: self-study application and classroom application. It is divided into three parts: Pre-course, after-school and in-class. It compares the teaching effects before and after use, provides conclusions and choices for practical activities, and effectively teaches learning tools. Accessibility.

For example, in the application of educational APP in college teaching experiments, a certain course is taken as an example for comparative experimental research. The experimental class adopts the teaching mode of educational APP, and uses different latitude questionnaires to analyze the learning effect of students. This kind of teaching method can promote the migration and memory of knowledge, master the learning skills, improve learning satisfaction and have a strong interactive process.

4   The Application of Learning Tools in Learning Activities

There is no lack of doubts, complaints and accusations behind the extensive use of learning tools. Through research, we cannot go deep into the essence, but for its application, it is not difficult to find that there are certain problems. This may also be the application of learning tools. Bottlenecks in Development [7]. According to the research status of the application of learning tools, the following application model is constructed by reflection and summary (Fig. 2).

From the theoretical basis as a support through the application of the model, through the selection, design or development of appropriate learning tools, the design of activities, in the three links of the learning activities before, in the middle, to assist in teaching. The three links of learning activities are the process of introduction, implementation and evaluation, and each process should pay attention to and follow the corresponding rules.

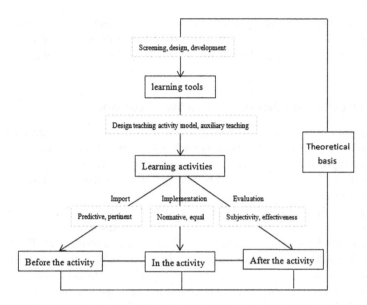

Fig. 2. Application model of learning tools in learning activities

4.1 Pre-visibility and Pertinence Before the Event

Before the learning activities are applied, the learning tools give the learners more rights to choose the learning content, learning time and learning styles published by the teachers to self-prepare the new knowledge, and more activities are not targeted, resulting in the failure of the application.

Teachers need to grasp the students' academic analysis and grasp the students' meta cognitive level, that is, the reserve of knowledge, meta cognitive ability, knowledge processing ability and internal learning requirements, including interest, hobbies, etc. in the fields related to new knowledge. Targeted release of knowledge content that can arouse students' interest in learning. As a pre-class knowledge introduction or a review session of the last class, students have sufficient time and space to prepare and review, which is helpful to stimulate students' learning motivation and learn the atmosphere and promote the further development of learning activities.

4.2 Normative and Equality in Activities

In the network environment, the use of learning tools constructs an open and personalized learning space to visualize students' learning behaviors. However, with the increase of learning autonomy, students' classroom attention is more easily dispersed. Teachers How to develop a normative motivation to stimulate the strategy has become a major difficulty.

The learning process should play the leading role of teachers and the subjectivity of students. Form a system in learning activities and enhance the standardization of application. Teachers can prevent students from using tools to entertain through monitoring. Students can only be in a fixed teaching session. Use the web platform to communicate and collaborate. Teachers should also give guidance and attention to each student fairly, taking into account the commonality of students, but also respect the uniqueness of students, and should not be overly inclined to specific outstanding students.

4.3 Subjectivity and Effectiveness of Activity Feedback

Student learning is a dynamic internal process. Understanding the student's learning starting point and internal conditions helps teachers to predict the feedback of the activity and improve the relevance of the feedback. Timely teaching feedback requires the cooperation of teachers and students, taking learners as the center and giving full play to the effectiveness of feedback.

In order to fully grasp the students' academic situation and timely adjust the teaching content and methods, teachers can conduct assessments after the teaching activities through learning tools, homework, online quiz and assessment. The feedback focuses on the differences between people, reflects the subjectivity of students, conducts supervision and communication through the Internet platform, actively answers the students' questions, and gives students more care and encouragement, so that students will eliminate tension and more confidence. So clear your direction.

5 Summary

The gradual and wide application of new technologies in the information age has made the overall information of society more and more intensive, and the revolutionary influence of information technology on education has become increasingly obvious. People's lives are inseparable from the support of information technology [8]. The Development of Contemporary Learning Activities I began to try to use various learning tools to practice. However, on the road of teaching activities, the integration of learning tools will inevitably lead to problems of large and small. As long as the correct methods and timing are grasped, better teaching results will be achieved. Technology to promote the development of education is the transformation of human initiative. In order to survive, people must vigorously develop education. In order to obtain new life, education must rely on technological means to achieve a qualitative leap.

References

1. Ren, Y., Zheng, X., Wu, Y.: Deeply promote the integration and innovation of information technology and education - "education information" 13th five-year plan interpretation of planning (2016). Mod. Distance Educ. Res. **5**, 3–9 (2016)
2. He, J.: Using teaching tools to promote general technology classroom teaching. Times Educ. (24) (2015)
3. Wu, F.: Activity-oriented network curriculum design under the guidance of performance-oriented. China Elector-Educ. Educ. (6) (2008)
4. Guo, G.: Exploration and practical research on the teaching design of junior high school mathematics network course. Shanghai Normal University (2008)

5. Wang, C.: In the use of "teaching materials" to guide junior high school students to improve writing level. Road Success Writ. (Below) (9), 15 (2015)
6. Liu, H.: Application of nana-box in primary school english extracurricular learning. Ningxia University (2017)
7. Liu, H., Rao, H.: Disciplinary construction of educational technology in normal universities in China: current situation and reflection. China Elector-Educ. Educ. (6) (2015)
8. He, Y.: Research on effective teaching design of moral education in secondary vocational schools under the background of information—taking pre-teaching analysis as an example. Contemporary Educ. Pract. Teach. Res. Electron. J. (4) (2017)

Primary Research on Standardization of Real-Time Interactive e-Learning Platform

Hui Zhang[✉]

Anhui University, 111 Jiulong Road, Hefei, Anhui, People's Republic of China
23375516@qq.com

Abstract. In recent years, under the joint promotion of national policies, science and technology and capital, the e-Learning education market has developed rapidly. Among them, real-time interactive e-Learning is gradually recognized by the public for its good interactivity and effective learning scenes. However, real-time interactive e-Learning is still at an early stage of development and lacks standardization and systematization. How to establish and perfect the real-time interactive e-Learning platform standard conforming to the educational law? How to establish a teaching mode suitable for most teachers? This paper expounds the differences between real-time interactive e-learning and other online learning. The characteristics and advantages of the existing real-time interactive e-learning platform are analyzed, and the hardware equipment standards, teaching standards, standardization activities and organization are proposed. As well as standards-based development practices and driving forces for improving existing standards and developing new standards. Optimizing the educational process, cultivating learning habits and improving learning efficiency are the research objectives of this paper.

Keywords: Real-time interactive · E-learning · Platform standardization

1 Introduction

The development and progress of society cannot be separated from the drive of technological innovation. In the field of education, technological innovation not only brings new knowledge content, but more importantly, it constantly creates new forms of knowledge dissemination and communication for education. To realize the modernization and leap-forward development of education, information technology is the most important breakthrough point. Zhu Xi of the Southern Song Dynasty said in Mencius Collection of Annotations: "All things have laws. If teachers do not obey, they cannot teach well. If students do not obey, they cannot learn well." The "law" here is the rule. Teaching activities in any form of education must follow educational rules in order to exist and develop.

© Springer Nature Singapore Pte Ltd. 2020
J. Shen et al. (Eds.): IC3 2019, CCIS 1227, pp. 204–211, 2020.
https://doi.org/10.1007/978-981-15-6113-9_22

2 Current Situation of Education Live Broadcasting

In August 2016, the State Council promulgated the National Science and Technology Innovation Plan of The thirteenth Five-Year Plan, proposing to apply intelligent interaction and other new generation information technology to the development of emerging services such as education and training. In January 2017, the State Council promulgated the "National Education Development The thirteenth Five-Year Plan" and put forward the inclusive action of online education to promote educational equity. Vigorously promote the education information technology, promote the development of "internet and education" new form. In November 2018, the Ministry of Education issued "Guiding Opinions on Perfecting Education Standardization", proposing that online education and digital education standards should be based on educational reform and development practice, in-depth investigation and argumentation, extensive solicitation of opinions, and guarantee the scientific, normative and timeliness of the standards.

Supported by national policies, economic development and technological upgrading, real-time interactive e-Learning has ushered in new opportunities for rapid development. The Internet can help reform the education supply side, reduce the education cost, improve the efficiency of resource allocation, expand the sharing of high-quality resources, and finally build a learning society of "everyone can learn, everywhere can learn, and at the right time can learn".

However, according to a business research report, as of December 2018, the number of live online users had reached 397 million, accounting for 47.9% of the total number of Internet users, while live online education accounted for only 3.3% [1]. At present, the audience of live broadcast education is still very small compared with other live broadcast fields, and there is great room for development. It is very necessary for the current education reform to vigorously develop real-time interactive e-Learning and construct a real-time interactive e-Learning standard conforming to the educational laws.

On December 3, 2018, iiMedia Research, global leading new economic data mining and analysis organization, authoritatively released "2018 China online education industry white paper". As the data of iiMedia Research showed. It is estimated that the scale of online education users in China will reach 296 million in 2020. The outstanding advantages of online education are flexible and convenient, rich in resources, and combined with AI, VR, AR and other technologies to meet the diversified and personalized needs of users, making up for the shortcomings and shortcomings of traditional offline education. 84.9% of online education users recognize the online and offline education model. In the future, the development and application of artificial intelligence technology will promote the popularization of personalized online education.

3 Advantages of Real-Time Interactive E-Learning

Real-time interactive e-Learning refers to the real-time interactive teaching activities between teachers and students simulated face-to-face by using the Internet as a medium and multimedia and other digital means [2]. Basic network equipment, learning terminal equipment, teachers, teaching content, live teaching platform, students, etc. constitute the basic elements of real-time interactive e-Learning.

3.1 Compared with the Traditional Form of Offline Education

Compared with the traditional offline education, real-time interactive e-Learning is not limited by region and time, and can be learned without leaving home, thus saving time. Students can check the video at any time to check the knowledge points and deepen their understanding. Students have great freedom in choosing courses and teachers. In terms of teaching tools, students can not only come into contact with various emerging teaching tools, expand teaching scenes, but also increase the presentation forms of knowledge points, making students' understanding easier and more interesting. Through online teaching, practice, testing, scoring and other means, the learning effect of students can be timely fed back, so that teachers can timely understand the learning situation of students, adjust the learning tasks of students in real time, and better realize personalized learning. Real-time interactive e-Learning can also optimize the allocation of resources, maximize the allocation and utilization of educational resources, and expand the influence of excellent teachers.

3.2 Compared with the Traditional Form of Offline Education

Compared with video recording and other forms of online education, real-time interactive e-Learning can not only release the influence of high-quality content to the maximum extent, but also realize the maximum utilization rate of resources. At the same time, it can also carry out effective communication and interaction between teachers and students, answer questions in time, and restore offline learning mode as much as possible, thus improving students' learning effect to a great extent. On the other hand, real-time interactive e-Learning has a certain urging effect on students, urging them to study and review, and improving the completion rate of learning content. Therefore, real-time interactive e-Learning is mainly through real-time interaction, answering questions and urging to improve the learning effect and completion rate and realize the teaching value [3] (see Fig. 1).

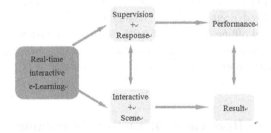

Fig. 1. Advantages of real-time interactive e-Learning

With the improvement of broadband speed, the popularization of mobile networks, the penetration of smart device and other technology upgrades, it provides a solid foundation for real-time interactive e-Learning. Voice recognition, online evaluation and other technologies not only realize the links of teaching, learning, testing and evaluation, but also meet the needs of interaction between teachers and students, answering questions and other requirements, and improve the completion rate of learning. Virtual reality and other Wearable smart devices have been applied to education, expanding learning scenes and enriching learning methods. The development of cloud services and big data analysis technology can realize accurate teaching and provide integrated learning solutions, which is of great significance to the upgrading of education.

3.3   Features of Existing Real-Time Interactive e-Learning Platform

At present, there are five common real-time interactive e-Learning platform: language category (e.g. iTutorGroup, VIPKid), K12 counseling category (e.g. 101 XueCoo), vocational training category (e.g. Wheat College), interest category (e.g. Blue Pencil), comprehensive category (e.g. CCtalk, Tencent Class). Analysis of mainstream platforms has found the following characteristics (see Table 1):

Table 1. Features of mainstream real-time interactive e-Learning platform

Name	Content	Features	Advantage
VIPKid	Online English Learning	Match teachers and learners accurately and create customized courses for learners	Unique dynamic curriculum and learning management system
101 XueCoo	K12 One-on-one tutoring	The combination of education modes in O2O has formed a closed loop in the process of teaching service	Learning path management and parents' real-time participation
Wheat College	Training in IT occupation	Video tasks, time-limited answers, actual combat projects and live courses are combined	Unique intelligent learning process management system
Blue Pencil	Online learning of professional painting art	Full-time service is provided by course consultants, class teachers and tutors, etc	Self-built development, teaching and operation team
Tencent Class	Comprehensive Online e-Learning platform	Community-based learning, exchange of students within the group, and interaction between teachers and students	Live+Learning Group +Material Download +After-class Discussion

4 Standard Setting for Real-Time Interactive e-Learning

In essence, interactive e-Learning also requires a platform to integrate resources such as users, content and tools. Education is very special, with characteristics of long time and many categories. Only by combining the two concepts of Internet and education can we design a platform system that conforms to the laws of education. Through designing a real-time interactive network learning system, enriching teaching courses and teaching tools, exploring and formulating common standards, it runs through all links of real-time interactive teaching and forms an education closed loop of teaching-learning-practice-testing-evaluation. In this way, the educational effect brought by real-time interactive online learning can truly stand out.

4.1 Facilities and Equipment Standards for Real-Time Interactive e-Learning

A complete interactive learning system consists of several links, including information collection, pre-processing, encoding, transmission, decoding and rendering. The teacher side provides the signal source through hardware equipment, and the hardware equipment and the cloud server side jointly complete the pre-processing and coding of information. Information is transcoded in the cloud server to adapt to different formats and support different protocols. Then it is distributed to the students through the content distribution network, and the decoding and presentation of information are completed on the students' equipment. At the same time, it adapts to different playing modes and realizes the effects of audio and video synchronization. In the learning process, the interaction between teachers and students is mainly in the form of text interaction. In the process of live video broadcasting, the cloud server accompanies the corresponding recording function and stores the recorded video in the cloud for students to order and learn anytime and anywhere (see Fig. 2).

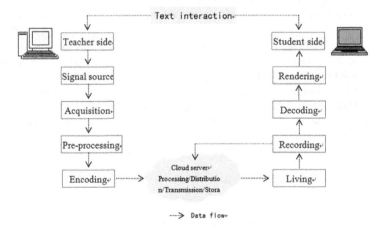

Fig. 2. Real-time interactive e-Learning organizational structure

4.2 Teachers' Application Ability Standards Under Real-Time Interactive e-Learning

Real-time interactive e-Learning puts forward new requirements for teachers: personal characteristics, interactive awareness, refined content and rhythm.

At present, many online and offline education enterprises are transforming or distributing real-time interactive online learning, which is accompanied by the change of offline teachers to online teaching life. The real-time interactive teaching also puts forward new requirements for teachers. First, teachers should learn to package themselves, cultivate their marketing ability, and have their own characteristics and charm in class to attract new traffic and increase user stickiness. Second, real-time interactive teaching has high requirements on teachers' knowledge reserve, which requires teachers to be able to learn knowledge points by quote copiously from many sources and draw inferences from other examples, so as to enhance students' interest in learning and carry out benign expansion. Thirdly, teachers should have the awareness of remote learners and ensure the interaction between teachers and students, students and students at all times to increase their immersion in learning. Fourth, it is necessary to cultivate students' perception of learning effect and adjust the teaching rhythm according to students' feedback.

4.3 Software and Data Standards Under Real-Time Interactive e-Learning

Personalized education requires that we can provide more targeted and accurate services on the premise of providing enough choices for students, so that students can learn efficiently according to their own preferences. The prerequisite for accurate matching of students is to have a sufficient understanding of students and their learning habits. This requires enterprises to establish more knowledge structure dimensions, record more learning paths for students, and then use intelligent algorithms and other methods to analyze the data into standardized, modular and even structured data. In this way, the teacher's analysis of the students will be more accurate, thus proposing more effective service. Entering the era of big data, data has become an asset for all enterprises to compete for, and data may also become a new competition barrier for enterprises. However, how to analyze data should be paid attention to by all parties. In the future, the ability to analyze data will become a new competitive advantage for enterprises or teachers. Teachers should not only improve their teaching ability, but also improve their data analysis ability and teaching sensitivity. The role of teachers will be changed into diagnostic teaching.

With the online learning habits of students, many dimensions of students' learning behaviors, learning methods and knowledge mastery degree will be recorded to form a data repository. Through the analysis of students' big data, we can match the fit between students and teachers' personalities, teaching and learning preferences and find the most suitable teachers for students [4]. Analyzing students' learning habits and knowledge can help them to make appropriate teaching plans, plan the best learning path, and recommend appropriate learning contents for students [5]. This can not only reduce students' repetitive work and improve students' learning efficiency, but also expand the breadth and depth of knowledge. The analysis of big data can accurately locate the demand, and then put forward more targeted, more comprehensive and more innovative service and usage scenarios, so that personalized education is no longer limited to traditional one-to-one teaching. In the future, personalized education will be extensive. Teachers can teach more students in accordance with their aptitude, which is also the demand of parents and society for personalized education.

4.4   The Impact of Emerging Technologies on Standards

At present, the main participants in China's online education industry are: teaching content producers, learning tool developers, technical equipment providers and learning platform providers. Under the network environment set up by network operators, the producers of teaching content provide the developed learning content to various education and training institutions and their platforms. Each training institution uses advanced online education technology and learning tools to impart knowledge to users, and finally forms the ecological environment of the entire online education industry.

Emerging technologies such as augmented reality (AR) and virtual reality (VR) enhance immersion and further optimize teaching scenarios [6].

VR/AR technology has the potential to become a standard tool in the education market in the future. It will become a necessity to display content with more abundant means. For disciplines with strong practical operation or high requirement of scene, VR/AR is used to simulate or create teaching scenes, which make teaching scenes more immersive and interactive. It can not only change the way students perceive knowledge, but also make their understanding of knowledge more intuitive and improve their learning efficiency.

5   Conclusions

The complexity of education makes it resistant to new things. The infrastructure of real-time interactive e-Learning and other underlying technologies are gradually improved, application layer technologies and interactive means are continuously upgraded, and mainstream consumer groups are constantly changing. Real-time interactive e-Learning has been continuously injected with new vitality and improved with new standards. The construction of platform standardization will push online e-Learning to change and will surely open a new era of education.

References

1. CNNIC: 43nd Statistical Report on Internet Development in China, no. 06, pp. 89–101 (2016). http://cnnic.cn/hlwfzyj/hlwxzbg/hlwtjbg/201902/t20190228_70645.htm
2. Jin, X.: Research on the sustainable development mode of China's webcast platform. Sci. Technol. Commun. (06), 89–101 (2016)
3. Wang, G., Bai, C., Lu, H.: An empirical analysis of teaching presence of online distance education courses. China Audio-Visual Educ. (09), 42–47 (2012)

4. Yu, S.: From knowledge transfer to cognitive construction and then to situational cognition-development and prospect of three generations of mobile learning. China Audio-Visual Educ. (06), 7–18 (2007)
5. Pan, J., Lei, Y., Cheng, L., Shi, H.: Review on ubiquitous learning theory. Distance Educ. J. **5**(2), 93–98 (2010)
6. Wei, X.: From e-learning to u-learning. China Educ. Informatiz. (12), 8–10 (2007)

Research on the Integration Mode of Digital Broome Education APP and Classroom Teaching

Yan-Yan Sun[1] and He-Hai Liu[2(✉)]

[1] College of Education Science, Anhui Normal University, Wuhu, Anhui, China
[2] College of Education Science, Anhui Normal University, Wuhu, China
358383418@qq.com

Abstract. In the information age, new knowledge and new things are emerging in large numbers, anywhere, and constantly affecting and changing people's learning. Due to the advancement of technology, there are many digital information learning tools, and their quality is also uneven. Based on digital bloom, several information tools suitable for different Bloom cognitive goals should be selected for teaching. The perfect combination of educational APP and classroom teaching aims to improve students' interest in learning and improve the quality and efficiency of teaching.

Keywords: Education APP · Classroom teaching · Digital bloom

1 Introduction

The APP in the education app is currently referred to as the application software downloaded from the tablet or mobile device [1]. With the widespread use of mobile devices such as mobile phones and ipads, and the support of learning activities, the application of APP in teaching and learning has become a new learning method.

1.1 Characteristics of Educational APP

Intelligence, Education APP has the functions of online teaching, questioning and answering. It can also be evaluated and evaluated according to the learner's learning situation, and ensures the smoothness of teaching information transmission. Mobility, which breaks the limits of time and space, allows learners to learn on any device [2]. Socially, students can create a virtual learning community where students can discuss, communicate and share knowledge with friends. Interesting, designing the teaching of teaching in teaching, increasing the interest of teaching and the participation of students.

1.2 The Advantages of Education APP

Educational APP can effectively stimulate students' inner learning motivation and encourage students to actively discover and explore knowledge. Students can do fragmented learning, arrange their own learning plans and set learning goals, arrange

J. Shen et al. (Eds.): IC3 2019, CCIS 1227, pp. 212–216, 2020.
https://doi.org/10.1007/978-981-15-6113-9_23

their progress according to their own abilities, and choose their own APP for personalized learning. Teachers can set up test questions to develop learners' abilities, such as critical thinking, thinking skills, communication skills, and problem-solving skills. Fragmented and efficient personalized learning in the learning process of intelligent mobile terminal devices and educational APP applications can cultivate students' high-level thinking ability. Promote teacher-student exchanges, the interaction between teachers and students is not limited by time and space, and can feedback each other in a timely and effective manner. Teachers can obtain and analyze student information in the first time, which helps teachers master the students' academic situation and adjust the teaching content and methods in time.

1.3 Digital Bloom's Digital Learning Tools Classification

The Bloom Education Goal Taxonomy has always been a guiding principle in the field of education and technology. In 2001, L.W. Anderson and D.R. Kraswall revised the educational objectives of Bloom's cognitive domain into six levels of "memory, understanding, application, analysis, evaluation, and creation" [3]. "Digital Bloom" was proposed by American scholar Michael Fisher and his team in 2009. They selected 25 information learning tools for Bloom's cognitive target classification [4]. Digital Bloom's proposal is to try to match the revised educational goal classification with digital learning tools. Subsequently, Chen Dan and Zhu Zhiting constructed the Chinese version of "Digital Bloom", and more and more digital Bloom models emerged, thus constructing a digital Bloom-based example as shown in Fig. 1. Nowadays, there are many kinds of digital learning tools, and the quality is not uniform. How teachers in

Target level	Description and behavior	Educational Apps
Memorize	Recognize, list, describe, confirm, point out, find, list points, add bookmarks, etc.	Baidu, 360 browser, Baidu network disk, scallop words, notes
Understanding	Elaboration, summarization, classification, comparison, interpretation, examples, etc.	Weibo, QQ mailbox, Tencent QQ, WeChat, English fluent
Application	Implementing, implementing, using, executing, uploading, sharing, editing, etc.	Pr, Au, Ps, office, Baidu, WPS, Netease cloud reading
Analysis	Contrast, organize, discover, integrate, understand the level of structure, and more.	Xmind, Youku, Douban, Gaode Map, Tudou
Evaluation	Check, hypothesize, criticize, test, comment, identify information, and more.	Youku, Vibrato, Fast Hand, Sina Weibo, WeChat, QQ
Create	Design, construction, planning, creation, programming, animation, and more.	Sina blog, Youku, vibrato, fast, PS, Flash, 3DMAX, C++ programming

Fig. 1. Example of a digital Broome target classification

different disciplines choose the information tools suitable for classroom teaching and integrate with classroom teaching has become a problem for the majority of educators.

2 The Integration of Educational APP and Classroom Teaching

The so-called classroom teaching refers to a bilateral activity process in which a goal-oriented, planned, organized, and step-by-step teacher's teaching is combined with student's learning. The classroom teaching can be divided into three parts, namely, before class, during class, After class, due to the wide application of mobile terminals and mobile phones, the APPs can be classified according to the classification of digital Bloom, and the functions of APP and the different effects of APP on students' learning can be fully grasped. And combined with the digital Bloom classification to select educational APP applications, which can promote teaching quality and teaching efficiency, and help teachers' teaching and student learning. Based on this, a pattern diagram of the integration of the educational APP and the classroom teaching as shown in Fig. 2 is constructed.

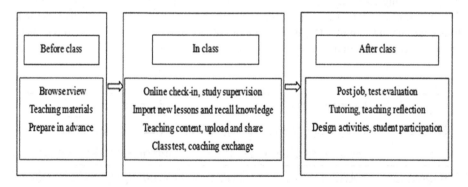

Fig. 2. Pattern of integration of educational APP and classroom teaching

2.1 Before Class: Based on Skills to Help Students Learn Knowledge

Before the class, the teacher organizes the teaching. The students need to remember some basic knowledge. The students can use the resources published in these apps to prepare for the online collection of the content of the next course. Keeping in communication, teachers and students can choose some educational apps that are identifiable.

For example, in the English subject, students can prepare in advance, read and memorize words and articles, practice their English pronunciation, and recite them, thus reducing the burden of learning in the class. According to this, you can choose a language similar to English fluent and English. This is an effective English learning application. It is an effective English learning application. The course content is wide-ranging and the learning materials are rich. It helps students' memory of English words. In the process of oral conversation, you can also score points in time, correct pronunciation, improve students' pronunciation standards, and daily oral conversations, so that students can improve students' vocabulary in a situation where the vocabulary is insufficient and the grammar is not proficient. Speaking, words, grammar, listening, reading and other abilities. It increases the variety of students' learning methods, and students can choose to learn and consolidate according to their own learning style. Students can also be reminded to review regularly, and daily punches to encourage students to insist on memorizing and making the words so boring and interesting are very interesting.

2.2   In Class: Provide Information for Students to Help Learn and Master Knowledge

In the class, you can complete the convenient online check-in function, which helps the teacher to keep abreast of the students' attendance and the students' learning. During the teaching activities, the teachers can send the teaching pictures, videos or documents to the public platform at any time. And monitor the student's learning behavior in real time, and provide guidance and evaluation based on the real-time feedback of the test students.

For example, teachers can choose educational programs such as blue ink cloud class and rain class. In the class, teachers can create their own classes. Teachers can send teaching resources at any time, and track and evaluate each student's learning progress. Teachers can set the fill-in-the-blank questions according to the content of the class, and satisfy each person as much as possible. The student's learning needs can also be face-to-face with the students according to the function of the voice live lecture, or even remote communication. After the end of the answer, the students can also know the answer analysis and timely feedback and Gong. On any mobile device, the teachers are You can easily manage your classes, manage students, share resources, send notifications, correct assignments, organize discussion and answer questions, and engage in teaching interactions.

2.3   After Class: Enable Students to Have the Ability to Transfer Knowledge and Innovate

After the class, the learner becomes the complete controller of the study. Submitting the assignments on the educational APP to obtain the test results in a timely manner, conducting self-evaluation, group evaluation and evaluation, and gaining certain knowledge transfer ability, can also cultivate students' innovative ability. These functions facilitate the modern teaching process, the use of mobile terminals makes the knowledge visible, and the contemporary information students have a strong interest in learning. Based on this, you can choose some educational apps that can assess students' knowledge and develop their innovative ability.

For example, QQ is a popular app among students. Because of its powerful interactive function, QQ can provide one-on-one personalized tutoring and offline individualized tutoring with QQ, and QQ group can publish and submit. Homework, excellent homework can be shared and displayed, and teachers and students can also communicate and communicate with each other. Students can also evaluate each other and take short videos on the course to innovate in thinking.

3   Reflection and Summary

In the era when the Internet and mobile learning are becoming more and more popular, the use of educational APP for learning can achieve networked learning of fragmented learning and personalized learning. In different teaching activities, it can be selected according to different teaching contents and teaching purposes. Appropriate educational apps, and even some educational apps can be either level of understanding or level of evaluation, and can be used interchangeably. This is an effect that traditional learning activities cannot achieve.

But things are two-sided. The implementation of the education APP teaching may improve some of the conscious students, but the students who lack individual self-control ability will be attracted by other things, and the learning effect will be unsatisfactory. In the network environment, the degree of freedom of learners is greatly increased, the attention of students in the classroom is easy to disperse, and how teachers develop effective motivation-inducing strategies to stimulate students' motivation for learning becomes a difficult point. APP teaching has higher requirements for teachers. Teachers fneed to have strong control, perfect knowledge system and rich teaching experience, and choose appropriate subjects according to the characteristics of APP courses for educational practice. Researchers are lacking in analyzing learners and learning needs when designing APP, and APP teaching tends to ignore students' emotions.

The key to integrating educational APP with classroom teaching lies in the guidance of teachers, support in various fields (theory, software, hardware) and self-management of students. The purpose of educational technology applied to classroom teaching is to better promote the development of students and cultivate students' high-level thinking ability [5]. Under the guidance of basic theory, we must pay attention to classroom practice and constantly improve it.

References

1. Xie, Y.: Application of educational APP based on mobile learning in junior middle school Chinese teaching [D] (2018)
2. Liu, S.: Design and application of mobile learning based on WeChat public platform [D]. Shandong Normal University (2017)
3. Hu, X., Dong, H.: The construction of English digital bloom based on bloom's cognitive goals. China Educ. Inf. (18), 8–11 (2017)
4. Sun, Z., Song, J., Shi, C.: Construction and application of mobile version "Digital Bloom". Inf. Technol. Educ. Prim. Secondary Sch. 4, 55–58 (2014)
5. Xiao, L., Li, H., Wang, S.: Research on the development and application of learning resources to promote the development of higher-order thinking ability——taking primary school science as an example. Educ. Inf. Technol. (6), 11–16 + 57 (2015)

Research on the Learning Status and Countermeasures of Online Course for College Students

Kai-Li Wang[✉]

Anhui Normal University,
No. 1 East Beijing Road, Jinghu District, Wuhu, Anhui, China
506403001@qq.com

Abstract. In recent years, with the development of Internet technology, online learning is gradually rising and popularizing. Many colleges and universities in China have opened online courses, and the traditional learning mode of college students has changed a lot. Online courses are favored by the majority of users due to their rich resources, diversified learning forms and flexible and convenient features. This paper conducts an investigation on the application status of online courses in college students' learning, aiming at discussing the learning situation, learning effect and learning demand of college students' using online courses, and then gives corresponding countermeasures to promote the further promotion and construction of online courses in college students' learning.

Keywords: Online courses · Higher education · Learning status survey

1 Introduction

1.1 The Ability of Autistic Students to Learn Social Skills Is Very Weak

In 1998, China's ministry of education officially took Tsinghua university, Hunan university, Zhejiang university and Beijing university of posts and telecommunications as the first batch of pilot universities for network distance education, and started the network education in a real sense. In 2003, the ministry of education officially launched the national network curriculum construction project. By the end of 2010, more than 3,700 national-level high-quality courses have been built, covering nearly 1,000 colleges and universities in 31 provinces, autonomous regions and municipalities directly under the central government, and promoting nearly 10,000 provincial-level high-quality courses and university-level high-quality courses [1]. In 2011, the ministry of education officially approved 68 colleges and universities in China to conduct online education, which gradually expanded the number of college online education recipients in China. With the advent of the "first year of MOOC" in 2012, the scale of China's Internet education market has been on the rise and the growth rate is extremely fast. The country's great investment in the construction of education informatization makes most universities in China carry out online teaching one after another. Online courses in Chinese universities are also becoming mature in their development. The rich online teaching environment and resources have brought new teaching services and experiences to teachers and students.

© Springer Nature Singapore Pte Ltd. 2020
J. Shen et al. (Eds.): IC3 2019, CCIS 1227, pp. 217–226, 2020.
https://doi.org/10.1007/978-981-15-6113-9_24

At the same time, whether the network curriculum and university teaching effective integration? How about the construction of online courses and their learning experience? What problems do college students have in learning online courses? Through literature analysis, the author preliminarily sorted out some problems in the application of online courses in colleges and universities:

1. Compared with the traditional face-to-face classroom teaching mode, online courses are still marginalized in the teaching system of colleges and universities, and lack of curriculum system and attention [2].
2. College students' participation in online courses is not high, their continuous learning intention is not strong, and the completion rate of courses is low.
3. The existing online courses cannot meet the needs of online learners in terms of quality and quantity, and most of them lack corresponding learning guidance and follow-up services.

In order to further understand the current situation of college students using the network course, on the basis of summarizing the relevant research results of this research, the design of the network course in the college students' learning situation questionnaire, a survey of college students' cognitive situation of network course, usage, learning evaluation and demand situation, and provide advice and reference for the construction of network curriculum.

2 Questionnaire Design and Implementation

The questionnaire used in this survey is composed of 31 questions from five dimensions, including basic information of college students, cognition of online courses, use of online courses, learning evaluation of online courses and learning needs of online courses. 3 questions in the questionnaire involve the basic information of the respondents, 3 questions involve the cognition, 10 questions involve the usage, 8 questions involve the learning evaluation, and 7 questions involve the learning needs of online courses. The design problems of each part are as follows (Table 1):

Table 1. The composition of the questionnaire

Dimension of the questionnaire	Questions
Basic information (3 questions)	Gender, grade, major
Cognition (3 questions)	Whether to know, which way, whether it is important.
Usage (13 questions)	Purpose of watching, influencing factors, consideration factors, fields of interest, influencing factors, terminal use, online time, viewing time, viewing frequency, each viewing time, learning habits, persistence, learning disabilities
Learning evaluation (7 questions)	Interest, teaching performance, teaching level, Does it help, learning gain, deficiency, score
Learning needs (8 questions)	Teaching method preference, course duration, the necessity of providing after-class follow-up, whether teachers are expected to provide timely guidance, whether learning partners are expected to discuss, reasons for willingness to pay, learning help, Whether want it to be included in the curriculum

In this survey, students from Anhui normal university were selected as the main subjects. The questionnaire was distributed online through the Wenjuanxing platform (wjx.cn) by means of random sampling. 152 questionnaires were distributed, 152 were collected and 152 were valid.

3   Survey Results and Analysis

3.1   Basic Information of Respondents

Among the 152 questionnaires collected, 63 were male, accounting for 41% of the total number. The number of female students was 89, accounting for 59% of the total number. Subject distribution: 74 people in liberal arts, accounting for 48.6%; Engineering 46 people, accounting for 30.4%; Science 32 people, accounting for 21%. The distribution of grade Numbers is shown in the Table 2 below:

Table 2. The number distribution of each grade

Grade	Freshman	Sophomore	Junior	Senior	Graduate student
Number of people	21	33	29	42	27
proportion	13.9%	21.7%	19%	27.6%	17.8%

3.2   College Students' Cognition of Online Courses

The vast majority of respondents know about online courses. Among the respondents, 138 students said they knew online courses, accounting for 90.79%. The remaining 14 did not know, accounting for 9.21%.

The main channel for college students to learn about online courses is the school and their own online search. In this survey, the main channels for college students to know about online courses are school, online search by themselves and recommendation by others, accounting for 69.74%, 59.87% and 34.87%, respectively. Other channels account for a relatively small proportion, which shows that online courses are not highly publicized among college students (Fig. 1).

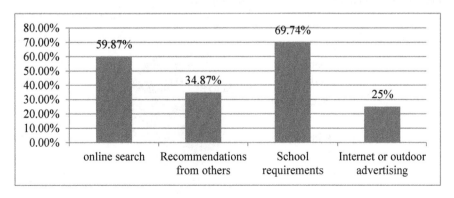

Fig. 1. The cognitive channel of network course

College students can generally accept online learning and have a positive attitude towards online courses. According to the survey data, 78.95% of the students are interested in online courses, and 92.11% agree that online courses are of great importance to one's growth and development.

3.3   College Students' Learning Situation of Online Courses

College students use the Internet for a long time and most of them have learned online courses, but their learning enthusiasm still needs to be improved. According to the survey, college students use the Internet for a long time, with an average of more than 3 h per day accounting for 40%. However, only 23% of them can learn online courses every day. The rate of 2–3 times per week was 30.92%, 57% of college students take online courses once or twice a week, and 13.16% do so less than once or twice a week. Students who took online courses for 30 min to 1 h on average were the most, accounting for 49.34%. Those under 30 min accounted for 24.34%. Those who watched 1 to 3 h and those who watched more than 3 h accounted for 23.03% and 3.29%, respectively (Fig. 2).

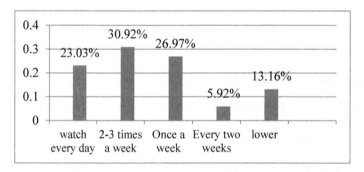

Fig. 2. Frequency of college students' learning network courses

Both PC and mobile phone are important learning devices. Among the respondents, 34.21% mainly use mobile devices to learn online courses, 34.87% mainly use PC to learn, and the remaining 30.92% use both (Fig. 3).

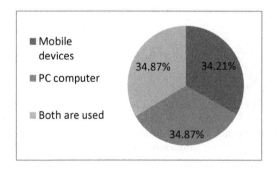

Fig. 3. Major equipment for learning web-based courses

The types and purposes of online courses for college students. In terms of learning types of online courses, interest, hobby and professional skill improvement fields account for a large proportion, which are 64.47% and 58.55% respectively. Other fields (language learning entrance examination, extracurricular guidance) account for an average proportion. 73.68% of students learn online courses to complete learning tasks, elective credits; 67.76% is to pursue their own development, improve professional quality and skills; Still have a plenty of for the sake of individual interest hobby, take an examination of qualification (skill) certificate and the complement that serve as classroom study, occupy 48.68%, 43.42% and 43.42% respectively.

Factors to consider when choosing an online course. The survey shows that 84.84% of college students will consider the course content itself when choosing online courses, followed by the lecturing charm of the lecturers and the popularity of the lecturers or institutions, accounting for 55.26% and 51.97% respectively. Secondly, whether the courses are free or not and the length of the courses account for 50% and 36.84% respectively. It can be seen that the most important thing for college students to choose online courses is the content itself, and the quality of online courses should be strictly controlled. Secondly, the teachers who teach are also very important. Teachers' popularity and teaching style will also affect students' learning enthusiasm (Fig. 4).

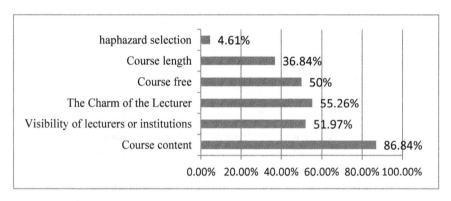

Fig. 4. Factors to consider when choosing an online course

Independent learning ability needs to be improved. Among the surveyed students, 49.34% said they could study independently without the supervision of others, but 38.82% said they could study independently under the pressure of exams and employment, and 8.55% said they could study under the supervision of teachers.

Obstacles in learning online courses. According to the data, most students (51.97%) think that the biggest problem is lack of corresponding textbooks and sometimes can't keep up with the progress; 44.08% think that there is no interaction in the learning process and the learning atmosphere is not good; 42.11% of the students accept knowledge diffusely and their learning efficiency is not high; they are easily bored and difficult to insist on, accounting for 40.79% and 38.16% express doubts can't be solved in time and lack of guidance.

3.4   College Students' Evaluation of Online Courses

The biggest gain from learning online courses is to acquire knowledge and broaden horizon. Survey data shows that more than 80% of students believe that online courses are helpful for their learning, among which the biggest gains are the acquisition of knowledge, the broadening of horizons, the improvement of relevant skills and the acquisition of certificates, accounting for 67.76%, 38.16% and 34.21%, respectively. Secondly, it improves the learning interest and autonomous learning ability.

Evaluation of learning experience and teaching level of online courses. In the recovered questionnaires, only 6.58% of the respondents gave a score of more than 90, 26.97% gave a score of 80–90, and the largest number of respondents gave a score of 70–80, accounting for about 60%. Those who gave a score of less than 70 accounted for 7.24%. For the evaluation of the teaching level of online courses, only 23.03% think that the teaching level of online courses is better than that of physical courses, 28.95% think that the teaching level of online courses is similar to that of physical courses, and 34.87% of students say that the teaching level of online courses is uneven. Thus it can be seen that the overall evaluation of online courses by college students is general, and the teaching level of online courses also has great room for improvement (Fig. 5).

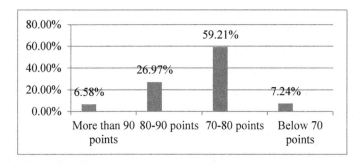

Fig. 5. Learning experience scoring of web-based courses

Shortcomings of online courses. 56.58% of students believe that classroom inter-action is poorer, lack of classroom atmosphere, 51.97% said the online courses lack of binding, learning efficiency is low, 44.74% think that online courses lack of person-alized design, can according to their aptitude, 41.45% thought course of variable quality, resource update is slow, and the inspection is too loose, lack of follow-up study evaluation, teachers' lack of interest, unattractive, early free many high-end course, subsequent tolls, are the problems, accounted for 28.95%, 25% and 21.05% respectively.

3.5   College Students' Learning Needs for Online Courses

Students prefer the combination of classroom teaching and online learning According to the survey data, 73.03% of students prefer the combination of classroom teaching and online course learning. It can be seen from the future learning trend that classroom teaching still occupies a very important position and will not be replaced by online course. However, as a supplement to classroom learning, the role of online course cannot be ignored.

Length preference of online courses. 49.34% of the students think that the time of a lesson should be controlled within 25–40 min. For the evaluation of learning after class, more than 80% of students think that it is necessary to provide course objectives and exercises for online courses, so as to evaluate the learning effect.

Interactive intention of online courses. According to the survey data, for the interaction and communication in learning, 42.76% of students express great hope that teachers can timely communicate and solve the questions raised in learning, 48.03% express hope, and only 1.97% of students express no hope. As for the learning interaction with learning partners, 41.45% of the students are very willing to learn and communicate with them during the learning process, 44.08% are relatively willing, and only 2.63% are unwilling. It can be seen that in learning online courses, students are eager to have the communication and interaction between teachers and students, students and students (Fig. 6).

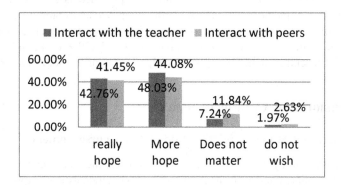

Fig. 6. Interactive intention of online courses

Reasons to pay for online courses. Said 70.39% of students is the teaching content of network curriculum of strong practicability, can help you to solve practical problems, 58.55% thought full rich teaching resources, to meet the diversified demand, 55.26% thought the authority of curriculum resources, strongly professional, trustworthy is paid for, 49.34% said with follow-up service, such as information sharing, interactive q&a, difficult to solve, such as online exercises, refund guarantee service will be more willing to pay. It can be seen that, compared with the cost, learning really attaches more importance to the teaching content, teaching resources, course authority, course service and other factors of online courses.

Willingness to integrate into the curriculum system

According to the data, 25.7% of students strongly want online courses to be included in the school's formal curriculum, while 52.6% of students say they prefer online courses. Only 13.8% and 7.9% said they didn't care and didn't want to. The survey shows that the vast majority of students want online courses to enter the formal curriculum (Fig. 7).

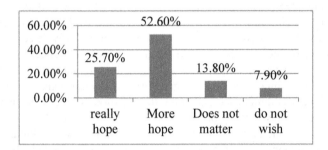

Fig. 7. The willingness to bring online courses into the curriculum system

The aspects of online courses that need to be improved. According to the respondents, curriculum guidance teachers should be provided, accounting for 61.18%; learning evaluation methods should be further improved, accounting for 52.63%; construction of online course teaching resources should be strengthened, and interactive teaching should be strengthened, accounting for 53.29% each; inspection and supervision of teaching should be strengthened, accounting for 48.68%.

4   Conclusion and Countermeasures

4.1   Teachers and Students Jointly Build Online Course Content

According to the survey, when choosing online courses, the most important factor for students is the course content itself. At the same time, students also express that they can insist on completing the study of an online course. The biggest reason is that the course is very useful for their work and study. The existing online courses in colleges and universities are all decided by the schools or teachers, which is difficult to meet the personalized learning needs of students. Student is the main part of the network course, the network curriculum teaching content should be from the perspective of learners, service for learners, at the same time, the teacher is a imparter of knowledge, in the selection of curriculum content with the voice of authority organization, so the teachers and students should participate in the joint network course topic selection and the selection of curriculum content and design in the link. At the early stages of the network course design phase, you can consider more extracurricular expanding teaching contents, through a survey or interview to collect the opinions of the students, select students high expectations for the development of network curriculum, the theme of the teacher is mainly responsible for spending more time on the organization form of the teaching content and its strict quality control.

4.2 Technology Upgrading Establishes the Multiple Interactions Among Teacher-Student-Content

In online learning, the appropriate teaching helps learners to avoid the loneliness and boring feeling, can improve the learning motivation and learning effect, respondents said generally has to deal with a lack of guidance in learning network curriculum, the lack of interaction, the problem such as poor learning environment, at the same time, more than 80% of learners to interact with other learners and teachers, you can see the network curriculum of interactivity is one of the important factors affecting learning experience. With the maturity and educational application of voice recognition, live broadcast interaction, artificial intelligence and other technologies, the teaching interaction of online courses is also constantly innovated. For example, the introduction of automatic oral assessment technology in online courses can realize automatic scoring of learners' oral level, realize man-machine interactive teaching and one-to-one oral guidance, and help users practice oral English anytime and anywhere. In the interaction design of online courses, the interaction between learners and learning content should be emphasized to promote the self-meaning construction of learners in learning. When designing online courses, more diversified interactions should be designed around the interaction between learners and learning content, such as the interaction opportunities between learners and learners, and the interaction opportunities between learners and teachers [3].

4.3 Learning Analysis Enriches Online Course Learning Support Services

Learning analysis technology is an emerging application of educational technology. It is a technical means to realize learning analysis to use complex analytical tools to dig and understand educational data in depth. Network course is a kind of internet-based forms of online learning, learners in the process of online learning will produce rich learning big data, such as the locus of learning, learning time, frequency, social behavior, such as behind the big data may contain the huge potential value can help to improve the teaching quality of network curriculum and optimizing the study effect. By analyzing big data of learners, we can understand their learning characteristics and learning paths, discover their learning preferences and differentiated learning modes, and provide course recommendations and personalized guidance and Suggestions to learners before learning [4]. In the process of learning online courses, through the analysis of learner behavior data, students' learning status can be timely mastered, and learners can be given early warning and certain intervention measures to help them adjust their learning status. In addition, the results of learning analysis can be fed back to students, so that learners can conduct self-reflection, self-assessment, self-diagnosis and self-guidance in their learning process [5]. The multi-aspect detection of learners in network courses by learning analysis technology makes learning optimization possible and also brings integrated personalized learning services for learners of network courses.

4.4   Credit Certification Standardization Promotes the Sustainable Development of Online Courses

A credit is a measure of the degree to which a student has achieved in a subject or course. The credit certification of network courses refers to the recognition of learning quantity and learning achievement of network course learners in colleges and universities and the granting of certain credits. According to the data, nearly 80% of the students surveyed said they wanted to incorporate online courses into their curriculum. Colleges and universities should give online courses "legal" status, bring online course credits into the credit system, and turn them into compulsory courses or elective courses credits of traditional courses. Secondly, the training program and course selection system of the school should be further revised and improved, and online courses should be incorporated into the course selection system and included in the corresponding course selection platform, so that students can select courses according to their own needs [4]. By incorporating online courses into the university curriculum system and standardizing the credit certification system, it is possible to improve students' enthusiasm in learning online courses, effectively push online courses from construction to application, and step out of the current "marginal zone" in university courses, so as to promote the sustainable and healthy development of online courses.

References

1. Opinions of the ministry of education on the implementation of national high-quality open curriculum construction, Department of Higher Education (2011). 8
2. Kang, H.: Based on the distance education quality guarantee system of higher education under the distance learning evaluation research. Shenyang Normal University (2012)
3. Yan, L., Dooley, K.E., Lindner, J.R.: Case study of well deigned web-based course. J. Distance Educ. **29**(01), 90–95 (2011)
4. Jide, W., Bo, L.: Credit recognition of online open course: forms, issues, and suggestions **24**(05), 39–45 (2008)
5. Liang, M.: Reflection on improving the quality of network teaching in colleges and universities. J. Zhengzhou University **47**(01), 42–44 (2014)

Research and Practice of College English Blended Learning Model

Ke Gong[1,2(✉)]

[1] Shandong Jiaotong University, Jinan, China
sdjtgong@foxmail.com
[2] Nanjing Normal University, Nanjing, China

Abstract. This paper explores the blended learning mode of college English through empirical research. This model divides college English teaching into three stages: the first stage is for students to independently conduct web-based self-learning; the second stage is for on-line collaborative learning among learners; the third stage is for teachers to pass classroom teachers through classrooms. Conduct face-to-face teaching for students and interact with teachers and students. The quality of learning at each stage has a corresponding evaluation and monitoring. The study found that the college English mixed learning mode can solve the contradiction between the limited classroom teaching capacity and the students' individualized learning needs, and effectively improve the quality of college English teaching.

Keywords: College English · Classroom learning · Blended learning

1 Introduction

Due to the development of the times, traditional teaching mode has been severely tested, and traditional college English teaching is also facing serious challenges. The first is the challenge of the real environment. Nowadays, college English courses in many universities in China are facing the trend of credit reduction and less class time. A single face-to-face lecture can no longer meet the needs of college students to learn English. At the same time, the "College English Teaching Guide" also puts forward higher requirements for teachers' teaching: "All colleges and universities should make full use of information technology and actively create a diverse teaching and learning environment. Encourage teachers to build and use micro-course, MOOC, and use the internet. The quality education resources will be transformed and expanded, and a hybrid teaching model based on classroom and online courses will be implemented to enable students to develop towards active learning, independent learning and personalized learning." The second is the limitation of traditional teaching methods. In traditional classrooms, there are often problems such as oversized classes, too many students, inaccurate study time, location and progress. Traditional teaching often adopts a "cramming" teaching mode. This way of teaching weakens students' initiative, which constrains students' imagination and divergent thinking, is not conducive to the cultivation of independent learning ability, innovation ability and application ability. The third is the flaw of the network teaching method. Online teaching does have great

© Springer Nature Singapore Pte Ltd. 2020
J. Shen et al. (Eds.): IC3 2019, CCIS 1227, pp. 227–234, 2020.
https://doi.org/10.1007/978-981-15-6113-9_25

advantages. Students can easily and quickly acquire diverse learning resources through the internet, fully realize the individualized learning of students, have greater autonomy in learning, and break through the limitations of time and space. Repeated learning has broken the shortcomings of the traditional classroom only once. However, online teaching also has its own shortcomings, such as over-emphasizing students' independent learning and ignoring the leading role of teachers. Teachers can't monitor the process of student learning, which is not conducive to the completion of teaching objectives, and students are prone to loneliness and the lack of identity in a single network environment. Under this circumstance, the blended teaching combining traditional teaching with online teaching emerges as the times require, combining the advantages of both, avoiding the shortcomings of both, and achieving better teaching results for college English. Teaching reform has played a certain positive role.

2 Literature Review

2.1 The Connotation of Blended Teaching

Blended Learning has long been a reference to a variety of learning methods, such as the combination of traditional learning methods using textbooks and learning methods using multimedia technology, and individual learning methods combined with cooperative learning methods. Wait. Since the 21st century, E-Learning has received extensive attention due to the development of modern information technology. In 2002, Smith and Ellert Masier combined E-learning (digital or networked learning) and traditional learning concepts and created the concept of Blended Learning, a new hybrid learning concept marked by E-Learning, is based on the original foundation. It has been given new content: the combination of the advantages of E-learning and the advantages of traditional learning methods. In the comprehensive domestic research on blended teaching, the blended learning in the new period mainly includes the following three aspects:

2.1.1 Blended Learning Is a Fusion of E-Learning and Traditional Learning Methods

The traditional learning method mainly refers to the teacher's teaching method based on the textbook content system, meticulously explaining the students, and class learning to master the knowledge. This method is conducive to the mastery of knowledge systematically, the communication of teachers and students, and the realization of interpersonal interaction. E-Learning refers to learning and teaching activities through the internet. It makes full use of the learning environment provided by modern information technology with new communication mechanisms and rich resources to realize a new learning style. Nowadays, there are many kinds of network and mobile platforms that can be used for teaching and learning activities. Teachers can use the online teaching platform, micro-course, MOOC, WeChat, QQ, email, and even the self-learning and testing system iTEST which can be downloaded to the mobile client. By arranging learning tasks, sharing learning resources, and supervising and guiding students' learning behaviors, students can also learn independently through these platforms. The rich learning resources on the internet broaden the channels for students to acquire knowledge, break the students' superstitions on books and teachers, and stimulate the enthusiasm and initiative of learning. Students have greater flexibility in their studies and can learn from time to time without being restricted by time and space. At the same time, students' ability to learn independently and solve problems can also be improved. Blended teaching combines the two to complement each other's strengths for optimal teaching results.

2.1.2   Blended Learning "Combines the Advantages of Traditional Learning Methods with the Advantages of E-Learning

Blended learning opposes "teacher-centered theory" and "student-centered theory", and advocates that the leading role of teachers and the subjective status of students should be given equal weight, that is, the combination of "leading" and "subject" is required. The leading role of teachers is not only reflected in the explanation of the content, the organization and management of the classroom teaching, the follow-up evaluation of the students' learning situation, but also the design of the learning environment, such as creating contexts related to the learning theme, providing the necessary information resources and organization. Cooperative learning, enlighten and guide students, and motivate students to learn. Each of these links must be truly inseparable from the leading role of teachers. The teacher-led role is not a denial of the student's subjective status. On the contrary, the two complement each other. The more the teacher's leading role is played, the more fully reflected the student's dominant position.

2.1.3   Blended Learning Requires Diversity of Evaluation Methods

Different teaching modes are used in the blended teaching. Therefore, different evaluation methods should be adopted in the evaluation so that the evaluation results are objective and fair, reflecting the true teaching and learning effects. In summary, the hybrid learning in the new era is a learning model that is marked by E-Learning and flexibly integrates other learning methods and teaching concepts.

2.2   College English Blended Teaching Design

Based on the connotation of blended teaching, this thesis conducts mixed teaching design for college English class and shows how to embody the concept of blended teaching in college English teaching.

Table 1. College English blended teaching content, methods and steps

	Learning content, methods and steps
Self-learning	1. Prepare the text content, master the new words and phrases in the text, get a preliminary understanding of the text topic, find the problem, and mark it well 2. Self-viewing and learning teachers recorded videos and uploaded to the network teaching platform. Combined with the markup problem to check whether it is resolved, the unsolved problem is handed over to the team leader and brought to the classroom 3. Search online for information related to this text (pictures, texts, audio and video), deepen the understanding of the content of the text, and organize the resources investigated to share the results of the group into the online teaching platform 4. "Special Learning" in the self-learning network teaching platform and "resource sharing" provided by students 5. Complete the after-class exercises autonomously, and bring the undefined exercises to the class after checking the answers 6. Log in to the iTEST 3.0 online practice/test system every week to complete the exercises that the teacher posted on the system
Online tutoring	1. The teacher enters the forum online tutoring study during the agreed time period. In addition, Students can also communicate with teachers through QQ, WeChat, and email 2. Open up various learning topics on the network teaching platform 3. Analysis and comment on the completion of the students' practice on the iTEST 3.0 system
Face to face discussion	1. The group takes turns to introduce or explain the content of the unit in report, specific content (language, general idea, structure, cultural or cultural contrast Etc.) is determined by group 2. Students evaluate the above report, teacher comments 3. The teacher asks questions about the text and leads the students to study and discuss together 4. The teams will not answer the questions in the internal self-learning phase of the group The unsolved questions and exercises will be presented to other groups to answer, or will be answered by the teacher 5. Do the presentation as a group, the topic is determined by group 6. Organize classroom activities such as debates and drama performances

According to the above table, the blended classroom has the following advantages compared with the traditional classroom: First, the blended teaching uses MOOC to teach new lessons, which can save valuable time in the classroom, and can also promote the rational distribution and full use of the teacher resources. It is the focus of the text and the difficulty of the text, including text introduction, text understanding, long sentence analysis, vocabulary learning and cultural appreciation. Each knowledge point is followed by several nodes to test the students' mastery of the knowledge points. Students can watch the video on the basis of the pre-study text, which basically gives a general grasp of the text knowledge. At the same time, MOOC videos and all courseware and teaching resources can be used for repeated viewing and learning on the online teaching platform, which greatly enhances the flexibility of students' learning and enables personalized learning, especially for students with poor foundation. Increase opportunities for multiple learning and understanding. Secondly, students use the internet to find more relevant resources on the subject of the text, take the initiative to understand the relevant cultural background and social issues, thereby expanding the learning content, changing "feeding" to "self-sufficiency" and training self-learning ability. In addition, the question and answer session fosters students' habit of thinking independently, and trains students' ability to discover problems, analyze and solve problems. In the classroom, the form of group cooperation is adopted, so that the interaction and communication between teachers and interaction between students are fully realized, and the cooperation spirit, communication ability and leadership ability of students are cultivated and trained. Finally, online tutoring can also be an effective extension of face-to-face teaching. For example, there are still unsolved problems after class. You can use various network means to seek help from teachers. For general problems, teachers can post solutions on the network platform, or concentrate on it in the next face-to-face class. It can be seen that in such a mixed teaching mode, teachers are no longer just the imparters of knowledge, but the instructors, organizers and facilitators of teaching activities. Students can independently construct a personalized knowledge system, and the subject status is fully reflected at the same time, as well as the students' application ability and innovation ability have also been improved accordingly.

3 Empirical Studies

3.1 Experimental Objects and Experimental Design

The research object of this paper is selected from an undergraduate college in Shandong Province. The network construction and multimedia classroom configuration of the school's teaching area and student dormitory area are relatively complete, and it is fully equipped to carry out the conditions of blended learning. The author selected two students from the second year of the school's automotive engineering majors as subjects. From the results of the first-year final exam, the two classes are equivalent in English comprehensive level and English writing level. A random selection method was used to determine one class as the experimental group and the other as the control group with each group of 33 people. In the experimental phase of 52 h, the experimental group used this blended learning mode, while the control group used the traditional face-to-face teaching mode. The two groups had great differences in the teaching environment, teaching methods and modes, but with the same class hours, teachers, teaching materials, learning resources, writing topics, etc.

3.2 Comparison of Experimental Tools

Pre-test and post-test are used, and the test format is a 30-min classroom time-limited composition. The two test essay topics were prepared by the teacher, and ensure that the topic was not used, so that students could write the same topic and affect the validity of the test. The assignment score is based on the CET4 score for the writing topic, but the scores are different (the total score of the two essays is 10 points each). In order to ensure the notarization and reliability of the score, the scores were taken by two teachers who did not undertake the study, and the standards were consistent when scoring.

3.3   Data Collection and Statistical Data from Tests

The pre-test, of the experimental group and the control group before the comparison experiment, and the second test of the experimental group and the control group after the end of the experiment, the post-test. Except for the essay topic, the scores, scoring methods and standards of the two tests were the same. Then use the social science statistical package SPSS 11.0 to make a comparative analysis of the scores of the two writings before and after.

4   Results and Discussion

4.1   Experimental Design

The experimental results are shown in Table 1 and Table 2.

Table 2. Comparison of pretest scores between experimental group and control group

Group	Average score	Standard	Deviation mean	df	p
Pretest experimental group	7.23	0.844	−0.10	64	0.323 8
Control group					

Table 3. Comparison of post results between experimental group and control group

Group	Average score	Standard	Deviation mean	df	p
Post-test experimental group	8.28	0.69	−0.41	64	0.0178
Control group	7.87	0.84			

The above two tables show the changes in English writing scores of the experimental and control groups. It can be seen from Table 1 that before the comparison experiment, the experimental group's practice averaged 7.23, while the control group is 7.33, the writing level of the experimental group is slightly lower than the control group. After one semester of experiments, the average scores of the essays of the experimental group were from the pre-experimental 7.23 raised to the post-experimental 8.28 points; the control group students are 7.33 points increased to 7.87 points, it can be seen that although the two groups of students have made some progress in the writing of college English writing in one semester, the average score of the experimental group students is 1 point lower than the control group before, becomes higher than the control group 0. 41 points. At the same time, the t-test of the difference between the two test results before and after the experiment found that there was no significant difference in the scores of the two groups before the experiment, $p = 0.323\,8 > 0.05$; After the experiment, there were significant differences in the scores of the two compositions in the two groups, $p = 0.017\,8 < 0.05$. The progress made by the experimental group students is even more significant, proving that the blended learning model is successful (Table 3).

4.2 Discussion

Contrastive experiments show that blended learning has obvious advantages over traditional teaching, and it is more conducive to the improvement of students' English proficiency. The main reasons are: First, the complementary platform provides rich writing resources. Blended learning complements traditional classrooms and various teaching resources such as the internet. Students can absorb the deep knowledge of teachers and enjoy the rich knowledge provided by the network. There are also a variety of teaching theories and complementary learning styles for students to absorb knowledge with more opportunities. Second, the facilitation collaboration platform provides plentiful English language training. The combination of classroom and network improves the efficiency of English practice and teacher review. At the same time, stable teacher-student interaction and convenient human-computer interaction can stimulate interest in learning, broaden ideas, internalize knowledge, and practice more efficiently. It should be pointed out that even if the college English class has limited hours, necessary classroom writing teaching cannot be replaced by online writing teaching, and blended teaching should be carried out instead. Therefore, teachers should pay more attention to students' self-learning when applying this model. In particular, they should make full use of the comprehensive evaluation mechanism to supervise and guide students' pre-view, review and extended training to ensure the continuity and effectiveness of their English learning. In addition, preparatory work such as pre-construction software and hardware analysis and teaching resource design before blended teaching is also a necessary condition to ensure the efficient development of blended teaching.

5 Conclusion

Blended learning is a new type of teaching that has been recognized in developed countries in the West and is still in its infancy in China. The collaboration, complementarity, and the new orientation of teacher-led and student-sponsorship are all aimed at improving the efficiency of teaching by making full use of various resources. Therefore, the research and experiment of blended teaching is a useful exploration for the development of teaching in China. This paper applies the blended teaching concept to college English teaching, combines complementary advantages, collaborative learning and effective supervision, and designs a specific teaching mode of blended learning. The experimental results show that the blended teaching model enriches students' English learning resources, realizes the cooperation and complementarity among students, reduces the dependence of students on teachers, and cultivates students' interest in learning and self-study and collaboration. Therefore, today, when the network is developed and the dominant position of teachers is always irreplaceable, the blended teaching mode is of great help to improve college

English teaching. However, this model also has some shortcomings. For example, poor communication caused by network congestion may affect students' discussion of emotions and quality; it takes a long time for discussion group members to work together. In short, the use of hybrid learning for English teaching is still at the stage of exploration, and the sample can be expanded. There is still much room for development in the discussion of the blended English teaching model.

6   Funding

This research is funded by the Shandong Young Teacher Growth Project, Shandong University Research Project (J18RA137); Shandong Provincial Social Science Planning Project Young Scholars Special Project (18CQXJ24); Postgraduate Research & Practice Innovation Program of Jiangsu Province (SJCX17_0307); the Priority Academic Programme Development of Jiangsu Higher Education Institutions (PAPD); Education & Science Research Fund of China Institute of Communications Education (1402-169); Research Fund of Shandong Jiaotong University (JG201521). "13th Five-Year Plan" of Shandong Provincial Education Science in 2019 "Research on the Reform of College English Teaching Evaluation Based on Online Learning Platform" (BYGY201915).

References

1. College English Teaching Guide. http://www.360doc.com/content/17/0203/14/413468_626210661.shtml,2019/03/27
2. Chen, Y., Liu, Z.: Research and practice of college english writing blended learning. Theor. Pract. Contemp. Educ. (06), 83–85 (2013)
3. Yang, Y.: Application of blended teaching mode of opening English in TV university. Guangxi TV University J. (04), 28–32 (2010)
4. Zou, Y.: Blended Teaching Design and Research of English Intensive Reading. Overseas English (10), 94–95 (2017)

Current Situation, Principles and Strategies of Traffic Law Textbooks Writing

Zhi-Wen Zhang[✉]

Shandong Jiaotong University,
NO. 5001, Haitang Road, Changqing District, Jinan, Shandong, China
zzw2366@163.com

Abstract. This paper explores the blended learning mode of college English through empirical research. This model divides college English teaching into three stages: the first stage is for students to independently conduct web-based self-learning; the second stage is for on-line collaborative learning among learners; the third stage is for teachers to pass classroom teachers through classrooms. Conduct face-to-face teaching for students and interact with teachers and students. The quality of learning at each stage has a corresponding evaluation and monitoring. The study found that the college English mixed learning mode can solve the contradiction between the limited classroom teaching capacity and the students' individualized learning needs, and effectively improve the quality of college English teaching.

Keywords: Traffic law · Textbooks writing · Teaching research

1 Introduction

The textbook is the carrier of the curriculum, the basic basis of the teaching activities, the important tool for implementing the goal of quality education, and cultivating innovative talents. It is also the basis and foundation for students to learn knowledge and develop their abilities. It embodies the contemporary educational thoughts and educational concepts. To develop the traffic law, we must first update the existing traffic law textbooks, improve the shortcomings in the current textbooks, integrate the advantages of each textbook, and combine the reality of China's traffic legal system to create a new traffic law textbook.

2 Literature Review

2.1 The Current Situation of Traffic Law Textbooks Writing

The quality of traffic law textbooks directly reflects the teaching level of traffic law in universities, and to a certain extent reflects the school's quality of running schools and the idea of running a school. China's research on the theory of traffic law textbooks is slow, lags behind the study of traffic law teaching. The number of research is small, the research quality is not high. There are insufficient theoretical and methodological

J. Shen et al. (Eds.): IC3 2019, CCIS 1227, pp. 235–240, 2020.
https://doi.org/10.1007/978-981-15-6113-9_26

support for traffic law textbooks in the textbook writing. On one hand, these factors have seriously hindered the development of China's traffic law textbooks. On the other hand, it also restricts the further improvement of the teaching level of China's traffic law.

2.1.1 Imperfect Construction of Traffic Legal System Restrict the Development of Traffic Law Textbooks

The overall lag of China's traffic legal system construction has seriously affected the construction of traffic law textbooks. Most of the textbook content are general concept introductions. The content is relatively boring and single, and students are relatively less accepting in learning. And the imperfect transportation legislation makes the construction of China's traffic law textbooks always in the state of "construction and side-by-side trapping". The practicality and operability of traffic legislation need to be improved, the content is too principled, and some important fields have no corresponding legal system. These factors has led to the inability of edition of traffic law textbooks, which requires constant revision and re-editing.

2.1.2 Traffic Law Content Has Different Opinions and Lacks Unity

The existing traffic law textbooks are the hard work of the authors, and also reflect the different understandings of the authors on the work of traffic law research. The different scholars' different research directions and the different periods of the traffic law have led to the different emphasis and content setting of the textbooks they have compiled. All of the above problems are easy to cause students to have doubts and uncertainties in their study. As students are taught, the knowledge they absorb also affects their views and thinking directions. The concepts and viewpoints that are inconsistent are equivalent to making the students in the study go in different directions. It is impossible to determine the final and clearest meaning of the problem. It also brings inconvenience to the training of traffic law researchers.

2.1.3 Lack of Practicality Is a Major Shortcoming of Current Traffic Law Textbooks

At present, China's traffic law textbooks are taking the "pure theory" route, and can not complete the purpose of textbook construction, which is not conducive to solve practical problems for students. The theory is transformed into practical application, which is lacking in the textbook of traffic law in China. We have repeatedly repeated and focused on the improvement and arrangement of "theory" in the construction of teaching materials, and only pay attention to the construction of "theory", which makes the practicality of the traffic law textbook greatly reduced. With the rapid development of China's traffic legal system construction, the internationalization of China's traffic law, the "theory" of the traffic law textbook has become increasingly mature, which makes the repeated discussion of the "theory" of the traffic law seem meaningless. Traffic law textbooks should absorb the writing experiences of foreign traffic law textbooks and strengthen their practical parts.

2.2   Principles of Traffic Law Textbooks Writing

The traffic law textbook is a highly applied discipline. The purpose of our traffic law discipline is to enhance students' legal awareness and cultivate excellent traffic law research talents. How to apply the knowledge learned to practice, textbooks play a very important role as the carrier and means of subject content. Currently, the speed of transportation legal system construction is fast, theoretical research should be a new stage, and the writing of traffic law textbooks should adhere to the following principles while absorbing theoretical research results.

2.2.1   Scientific Principle

The textbook is an orderly knowledge system that organizes the content of the course in a clever and rigorous manner according to certain teaching purposes. The better the scientific structure of the textbook system, the higher the quality of the textbooks produced. The most basic principle of textbook writing is the principle of science. A non-scientific textbook is equivalent to losing its correctness. The role of the textbook is to guide and transmit the correct scientific knowledge. The textbook that loses its correctness is equivalent to the qualification that has already gone as a textbook.

To make the writing system of textbooks scientific, the relationship between the textbook system of traffic law courses and other curriculum systems must be correctly handled. The content that students study at school includes many courses. Each course is not isolated. It has such links with other courses. Some courses are closely related. Therefore, we must consider the connection with other courses when designing the textbook system of the traffic law course. The second is to correctly handle the relationship between chapters and sections within the textbook system. What kind of content should be included in a comprehensive traffic law textbook, which chapters and sections need to be distinguished; what should be included in each chapter and section, how to connect before and after; which chapters and sections should be the focus, and which chapters and sections should be secondary part of it, etc., should be repeatedly scrutinized and studied carefully. It is necessary to make the whole traffic law textbooks in the chapter structure, with outstanding emphasis, coherent, clear-cut, and rigorous connections.

2.2.2   Systematic Principle

The systemic principle is to form a scientific and integrated textbook writing principle through the scientific and rational organization of the content of the textbook according to the relationship between the contents of the traffic law curriculum arrangement, which makes the teaching material more scientific and rational. The traffic law course is an interdisciplinary subject, that is, the mapping of traffic legal system construction, the way to improve the construction of traffic legal system, the auxiliary means of traffic legislation work, and the integration of knowledge related to transportation and law. Traffic law is a professional knowledge system. It should not be listed and spread as the content of the discipline of traffic law, and it should be integrated into a knowledge system of traffic law with reasonable structure and distinctive characteristics by finding the inner relationship between relevant disciplines and in accordance with the needs of the popularization of traffic law.

2.2.3 Practical Principle

The human thinking ability is gradually improved with the development of human practice. After the human thinking ability is produced, it must be gradually enriched and gradually developed along with the development track of practice, and it is closely linked with practical activities. Human thinking ability and practice are inseparable. The principle of practicality means that people must carry out practical activities in the process of creative thinking. They must proceed from the practice process to sublimation, promote the further development and improvement of thinking ability, and put the test of thinking results or conclusions into practice. The practical principle in the compilation of teaching materials is to pay more attention to the principle of combining theory with practice in the process of writing textbooks. This will help guide students to combine theory with practice and fully use theoretical knowledge to face and solve the problems that arise in reality and gain practical ability to use knowledge.

In the process of writing traffic law textbooks, the practical principles are embodied in the following aspects: First, students are the main body of textbooks, and the beginning of each chapter must state the objectives of this chapter. There must be thinking exercises in each chapter. The setting of details helps students to learn independently, so that learning is more convenient and effective, thus improving students' ability to consciously learn independently, becoming passive and active, improving students' self-conscious learning spirit and allowing students to take the initiative. Let students actively seek knowledge rather than passive acceptance. Second, in addition to theoretical knowledge, there must be specific cases in the setting of textbooks, reflecting the characteristics and hot issues of the traffic law. Case presentation and analysis is an important way for students to apply theoretical knowledge to solve practical problems. It is the link between theoretical knowledge and practicality. The set case should be the specific problem of traffic law in the current society. This is more conducive to the acceptance of students and the cultivation of practical ability.

3 Strategies of Traffic Law Textbooks Writing

With the acceleration of the construction of China's traffic legal system, in order to adapt to the needs of China's traffic legal system development and to train researchers in China's traffic law, the traffic law textbooks writing needs to optimize the structure and strengthen the reform and unification of content. The specific paths for traffic law textbooks writing are as follows.

3.1 Institutionally, Improve China's Legislation and Increase the Selection of Materials for Traffic Law Textbooks

The more extensive and detailed the content of the traffic law textbooks, the more complete and perfect the traffic legal system. At present, although the development speed of China's traffic legal system construction is gradually accelerating, the traffic legislation is not perfect, and it still needs a lot of improvement and development. The narrowness and lack of the scope of traffic legislation makes the construction of traffic law textbooks stagnant. The content selection is mostly a repetitive theory. Without the legal discussion of specific problems, the development of traffic law textbooks is slow and lax, and the practicality is not strong. The wide range of textbooks is of great benefit to students' practical operations and problem solving in the future. Therefore, the traffic law textbook is a means of propaganda of traffic law in China. If you want to develop, you must start from the source and solve the problem that fundamentally restricts the development of the traffic law textbooks. Accelerating the process of China's traffic legal system construction and improving China's traffic legislation are fundamental issues in solving the development of traffic law textbooks.

3.2   Contently, Add Specific Cases and Other Content to Strengthen the Practicality of Traffic Law Textbooks

The traffic law textbooks must be closely integrated with practice while improving and unifying the theoretical foundation. The specific case analysis of the traffic law and the example discussion of social hotspots will help to enhance students' interest in learning and enable students to apply the theoretical knowledge of traffic law to the reality. When students learn the knowledge of traffic law, they no longer simply understand and memorize, but participate in the discussion of traffic law issues as the main body of learning. Students can combine the traffic legal system with today's social hotspots, and use the knowledge of traffic law to learn and master, to explain and solve the traffic law problems in work and life. Traffic law textbook should combine theoretical knowledge with practice, cultivate students' ability to apply traffic law knowledge in society, which could foster outstanding traffic law talents.

3.3   Conceptually, We Should Learn from Foreign Advanced Concepts in Textbooks Writing and Create Chinese-Style Traffic Law Textbooks

China's traffic law has slowly grown up by absorbing foreign advanced traffic law experience. Some developed countries have very mature traffic legislation. The textbooks are mostly related to specific case analysis and problem solving, which is different from the empty "pure theory" in China's traffic law textbook. As a means of propagating the construction of China's traffic law, traffic law textbooks should absorb the excellent and mature experiences and framework of foreign traffic law-related textbooks, combine the situation of China's national conditions and traffic legal system, and combine the research hotspots of China's traffic law to build the framework. At the time of writing, it is necessary to use the theory of socialism with Chinese characteristics as a guide to create an advanced textbook for traffic law with Chinese characteristics.

Funding. Shandong Jiaotong University 2018 Annual School-level Teaching Reform Research Project: Research on the Construction of High-level Teaching Materials for Traffic Law Majors (2018YB51).

References

1. Hu, Y.: On the purpose of writing jurisprudence textbooks. J. East China University Polit. Law (3), 3–16 (2004)
2. Hui, X.: On the legal system—a cultural perspective. J. Polit. Sci. Law (3), 5–16 (2004)
3. Yang, G.: Thoughts on cultural teaching and design of cultural textbooks. World Chinese Teach. (4), 15–20 (1991)
4. Li, S.: Research and thinking on law undergraduate education. Comp. Law Res. **2**, 145–167 (1996)
5. Zhiwen, Z.: Problems and measures in the construction of traffic law textbook from the perspective of legal doctrine. J. Southwest Jiaotong University (Soc. Sci. Ed.) **1**, 22–30 (2019)

An Empirical Study on the Co-application of Dual-Platform for Primary School Writing Courses

Yuan Fang[(✉)]

Anhui Open University, 3 Jiuhuashan Road, Hefei,
Anhui, People's Republic of China
179965198@qq.com

Abstract. Compared with the traditional writing, information technology has played a significant role in creating a free learning environment, providing rich materials, widening channels for writing. However, it was found that there are no suitable writing platforms for the primary school learners. Therefore it is urgent to extend the function of platforms available to suit primary school teaching and learning. To address the gap, this paper, aims at creating a dual-platform, integrating Moodle and E-schoolbag, and exploring the effect of applying the dual-platform on a primary Chinese collaborating writing course in grade five of Baiyunyuan School for one semester, to explore the application model and effect of dual-platform using in writing courses collaboratively. This paper explores the student's change of learning with dual-platform. Interviews, classroom observation and questionnaires are adopted as the main research methods. The results indicated the effectiveness of the approach by enlarging students' vocabulary and promoting students' writing fluency. This paper designs a solution based on dual-platform. The solution, with a certain amount of guidance, can help teachers to improve the present writing class and promote the dual-platform applying in writing courses collaboratively to improve.

Keywords: Dual-Platform · Collaborative application · Writing courses in primary school

1 Introduction

The 1990s has witnessed the thriving of educational informationization. More and more scholars and teachers have begun to notice that the support of information technology has greatly changed the way of learning and teaching, and promoted the modernization of education. To promote a deep integration of information technology and curriculum, and cultivate students' innovative ability through utilizing technology has become a hot topic in curriculum reform of basic education. Writing requires students' comprehensive ability of language [1]. The new curriculum standard emphasizes: "Autonomic, Cooperative and Inquiry", but "Model-Practice-Revision" is still the main mode. With the support of new media technologies, it is particularly important to integrate multiple information technologies and implement innovative composition teaching to improve the writing courses actively [2].

© Springer Nature Singapore Pte Ltd. 2020
J. Shen et al. (Eds.): IC3 2019, CCIS 1227, pp. 241–248, 2020.
https://doi.org/10.1007/978-981-15-6113-9_27

1.1 Dual Platform

Moodle [3] is an open source software package developed by Dr. Martin Dougiamas. It can be used for course management and development, for a dynamic learning community that integrates various teaching resources and activities into the curriculum, including forums, assignments, tests, voting, surveys, wiki collaboration and more provide effective documentation and evaluation tools [4].

In 2001, Palm's Palm Education Pioneer Project found that handheld devices are more suitable for writing activities. iWonderPack2.0, which is a digital learning terminal based on tablet, consists of three subsystems: e-book generation system (generation and editing of electronic digital resources), teaching interactive system (real-time interaction in classroom, synchronous teaching, etc.), electronic book bag management system (implementing account management, digital resource management, etc.).

1.2 Collaborative Application

This study analyzes the design ideas of Moodle and iWonderPack2.0, the positioning of specific educational applications, and summarizes the advantages and disadvantages of the two platforms, as shown in the following Table 1.

Table 1. Comparative analysis of Moodle and e-book bag.

	Moodle	iWonderPack2.0 E-schoolbag
Design thinking	Knowledge-centered	Learner-centered
Educational orientation	Course management system	Digital learning device
Teaching availability	Available	Available
Functional scalability	Weak	Strong
Advantage	Multi-user, forums	Mobile, individual needs
Disadvantage	Single resource, form, limited real-time	Not systematic can't take home

From the above table, Moodle as a course management system has rich functions such as multi-user collaboration and forums, and the E-schoolbag as a digital learning device has the advantages of being movable and satisfying individual needs; the advantages of the E-schoolbag can fill the shortcomings of the Moodle's single resource and limited real-time. The advantages of the Moodle can also fill the shortcomings of the E-schoolbag system that is not systematic and take home. In summary, these two platforms can complement each other. The collaborative application of these two platforms not only can completely break through the limitations of time and space, stimulate students' interest and enthusiasm, but also improve students' comprehensive language use ability, and also facilitate teachers to collect students' writing texts and master the changes in students' writing skills [5].

1.3 Primary School Writing Class

Chinese Curriculum Standards for Compulsory Education (2011 Edition) [6] refers to the writing class of the senior school grades (grades 5–6) as a practice class, and clearly states: "The writing teaching should be close to the students' life, making it easy for students to write and express", "actively and reasonably use the advantages of information technology and network, enrich the writing style and stimulate writing interest actively and reasonably" The primary school writing class of this study refers specifically to the students (Class3, Grade5) of the Nanjing Baiyunyuan Primary School, which participated in the semester of the "Comment on Film" writing class in the "the Project of teaching experiment under the Network and Digital Environment".

2 The Design and Implementation

2.1 The Object of Study

The Object of Study is the students (Class3, Grade5) of the Nanjing Baiyunyuan Primary School. The class has a total of 23 students, 12 boys and 11 girls, including a Greek student. The age of students is generally around 11 years old. It is in the transitional stage from Concrete Operational Stage to Formal Operation Stage. It has certain analytical thinking ability, but it also needs the support of specific.

2.2 The Objectives of Study

This paper, through the collaborative application of Moodle and E-schoolbag in Chinese writing courses, which is in grade five of Baiyunyuan School for one semester, to explore the application model and effect of dual-platform using in writing courses collaboratively.

The instructional design part of the dual-platform collaborative application. Relying on the standard of Chinese essay writing in the upper grades of elementary school, based on the analysis of the fifth-grade elementary school students' learning and the elementary school upper-level Chinese composition class, the Moodle platform and the iWonderPack2.0 e-book package are combined to rationally organize the teaching implementation process from the learning situation. The creation, the provision of learning resources and the realization of the interaction mode are three levels to construct the fifth-grade composition teaching design plan for primary school, and to study the application mode of composition teaching with dual platform synergy.

Experimental research part of dual platform collaborative application. After the one-semester essay teaching, analyze and evaluate the students' writing works, compare the pre-test results of the experimental class, study the students' writing skills change in the dual-platform collaborative composition teaching, and then study the application of the dual-platform collaborative composition teaching.

2.3   The Hypothesis and Variables of Study

This study was designed and implemented under the experimental hypothesis that "the writing skills of primary school students in the composition teaching of Moodle platform and iWonderPack2.0 e-books will be progressively improved". The independent variables of this study are the composition teaching of the Moodle platform and the iWonderPack2.0 e-books. The dependent variable is the language writing skills of the experimental class students. The hypothesis is demonstrated by studying whether the dependent variable under the influence of the independent variable changes and how it occurs in the front and back sides.

Because this study lasted for one semester, during this period, the students were not affected by the external factors such as natural maturity; at the same time, the students' writing skills after the independent variables were taken as the experimental group, and the students' writing skills before the independent variables were used as the comparison. Group, experimental group and control group can form a comparative experiment, no need to set up a control group Finally, considering the configuration of the teachers of Baiyunyuan Primary School, there is no way to set up a control group. Therefore, there is no separate control class in this study.

2.4   The Process of Study

This theme activity includes the following six stages. The six stages are based on learning content and student abilities (Fig. 1).

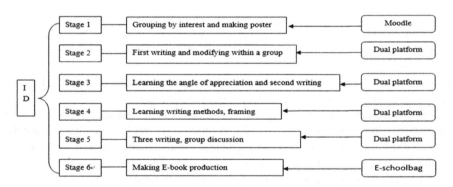

Fig. 1. The framework of instructional design

In the stage 1, with teacher's guidance, the students independently formed a study group and learned how to use the Moodle and E-schoolbag.

In the stage 2, students submitted their first composition in the module of Moodle's homework and public discussion. Teacher evaluated each composition in the module of Moodle's homework. Students commented each other in the module of public discussion. Teachers and students used E-schoolbag to learn modifier such as the symbol of delete and add and exchange. The six teams selected one of the top1 composition in the group and uploaded to the Wiki on the Moodle. Each student in the group used the modifier to modify in turn.

In the stage 3, the teacher selected to play "Life of Pi" according to the composition of the students. The teacher actively guided the students how to comment the film from the shaping of characters, the dialogue between the characters to the soundtrack or the composition of the film. Teachers and students use IRS for discussing. After class, students wrote composition and upload to E-schoolbag, and evaluated each other.

In the stage 4, students collected their favorite movie review articles, uploaded them to Moodle to share with everyone and discussed in the group, found out the methods, made PPT and selected one of a group to intrude their findings. Teachers organized students to summarize the writing methods of film reviews, guided them to determine the topics based their points of interest, and use PPT to make outlines.

In the stage 5, students wrote film reviews based on the outline and evaluated and communicated with Moodle and E-schoolbag.

In the stage 6, students use the editing system of E-schoolbag to attach their own film reviews, music, and videos into an e-book; and introduce e-books to peers in the group and evaluate each other. Teacher organization student to analysis: Can the outline reflect the essay thinking; whether the viewpoint is clear, whether the material can support the viewpoint; whether the statement is smooth, whether there are fluent; whether the picture, music, and video are suitable. At the end of the theme study, the teacher used IRS system to deliver the questions, the parents selected the best e-books of the class.

2.5   The Method of Study

This research originated from the investigation of the status quo of the primary school Chinese composition class, and tried to apply the two teaching platforms to the real classroom. Firstly, the literature analysis method is used to sort out the domestic Chinese composition teaching mode and the characteristics of network-based composition teaching in the past five years. The research results and related experiences of scholars on the Moodle platform and e-bags education application are summarized and summarized. Secondly, through the study of the new curriculum standard to obtain the teaching objectives of the primary school writing class; through the design of questionnaires to investigate students' writing attitudes from the three aspects of cognition, intention and emotion, and interview the teachers, to understand the fifth grade students in the Chinese essay Learner characteristics in the class; through interviews with technicians and managers of Taiwan's Qiqi Digital Technology Co., Ltd., to better understand the system architecture and features of the iWonderPack2.0 e-book package, so that it can be used reasonably in teaching. Thirdly, according to the results of the demand analysis, relying on the standard of Chinese composition in the upper primary school, the teacher and the class teacher discuss the theme of the composition class and construct the teaching design plan. Follow up with the writing class and observe and record the students' performance by taking pictures and videos. Finally, collect and analyze the written texts of students before and after, and summarize the practical application.

There are four main methods of data acquisition: interviews with teachers, students, and technicians, questionnaires for students, participatory classroom observations, and data acquisition of students' writing texts. The needs analysis was conducted through interviews and questionnaires. The data of the teachers and students in the classroom activities were obtained through observation, and the composition text was used as the raw data of the experimental research.

3   The Collect and Analyze

3.1   Completion

The pre-compositions are basically distributed between 90 and 93, which is 71% of the total number of completions, and the score gap is relatively large. The scores of the post-compositions are uniformly distributed, and the number of high scores is higher than that of pre-compositions.

3.2   Output at the Word Level

The maximum number of words in pre-compositions is 720 words, and the minimum is 284 words; while, it is 1264 words and 413 words of post-compositions. The per capita output of pre-compositions was 440 words/person, and 639 of post-compositions.

The pre-compositions are roughly normal distribution with a median of 400–450. There are 9 students between 400 and 450, for 42.8%. The post-compositions showed an upward trend, and the number of words was more than 350 words, of which 7 students were more than 600 words, for 35%.

The minimum type of words pre-compositions is 50, the most is 143, which is concentrated in 80–120 (13 students), and the minimum is 67 and the maximum is 255 of post-compositions. There are 12 people between 80 and 120 of post-compositions. In post-compositions there are 4 students which more than 160 types of words, but there are none in pre-compositions.

3.3   Accuracy at the Word Level

The accuracy of the word level is based on the "Wrongly Written". In the pre-compositions, there were 9 essays with wrongly written, 18 in all, 0.19% of the total number. There are also 9 essays with wrongly written in post-compositions, 0.11% of the total number. The typos that appear in the early and late stages mainly have the following types of errors: confuse the use of "he", "her", "it". There are 9 such errors.2. Confuse the use of "得", "地". There are 2 such errors. Confuse other homophones. There are 21 such errors. Confuse words with similar meanings. This type of error is the least, sharing one.

3.4   Accuracy at the Text Level

The unity at the text level are based on the type of sentences, the number and distribution of central sentences.

The pre-compositions are mainly 6–15 sentences, of which there are no essays more than 16 sentences. The post-compositions are concentrated in 6–20 sentences. In pre-compositions, the type of sentences are 205, the total number of sentences are 227, the meaningful sentences are 90.3% of the total sentences, which are 281,294,95,6.

The topic sentences are 4 mostly in the pre-compositions, most students wrote 2 topic sentences in texts. There are 5 students without topic sentences or only one topic sentence. In the post-compositions, the topic sentences are 5 mostly, most students wrote 1 topic sentences in texts. The topic sentence of pre-compositions is mainly concentrated in 0–2 sentences, and in 1–3 sentences of post-compositions.

4 The Results Visual Communication Knowledge Visual Resource Development and Practice

4.1 The Co-application of Dual-Platform Enlarges Students' Vocabulary

In terms of output, the total output and per capita output of the texts written by late students are larger than those of the previous period. The number of words in the late composition is higher than the minimum threshold (350 words/person) stipulated in the curriculum standard. In the previous period, there were 2 essays that did not meet the number of words specified in the curriculum standard. The number of the highest and lowest words in the late composition is more than that in the previous period, and there are one less in the low-word type (80–120) than in the previous period, and the number of Chinese words (120–160) is flush with the previous period. The number of paragraphs (>160) is two more than the previous period. The highest word frequency of the pre- and post-texts showed a downward trend, and the previous downward trend was steeper than the later period. In terms of accuracy, the total ratio of typos in the previous period will be twice as high as in the later period, and the typos will be more obvious.

From the essays before and after the semester, the students' language skills have been improved. When students face the theme of "movie review", they maintain a certain amount of composition output, indicating that the theme of the film review is close to reality, and students are relished and have the possibility to express themselves. At the same time, the expansion of words is not unrelated to the students learning the words and sentences, but the role of the platform has shown great power.

4.2 The Co-application of Dual-Platform Promotes Students' Writing Fluency

In terms of output, the total number of sentences and meaningful sentences of students' late essays and the proportion of meaningful sentences are increasing. The maximum total number of sentences for student essays has increased from 15 to 20, and the proportion of valid sentences has increased from 90.3% to 95.6%. In the early and late stages, all students expressed the composition in sections according to the needs of the expression.

In terms of accuracy, students have more error punctuation, and the use of punctuation marks required by the course standard is not enough. The change of the error punctuation in the time dimension is not obvious, and different essays in the early and late stages will have different errors.

The fluency of the text is also reflected in the theme of the composition, although there is no obvious change in the number of sentences in the central and late sentences of the students. However, there were more students with no central sentences in the early stage, indicating that the previous essays deviated more from the theme. The distribution of the central sentence in the later period also extends from the end of the previous article to the multiple paragraphs in the middle of the article, indicating that there has been a sense of "reflecting the viewpoint in the full text".

After a more in-depth analysis of the student's writing text, it is found that students widely use expressions such as narrative, argumentation, and lyricism, as well as rhetorical devices such as metaphor, personification, and comparison. They present us with a colorful film world and inner world.

Numerous educational experimental studies have proved to us that the using of technology can help us better achieve teaching goals. The functions of single platform are limited. Therefore, the co-application of different kinds of platforms is a trend. With the understanding of the advantage of platforms and the demand of teaching, teachers can choose and use the platform scientifically and reasonably, and construct an innovative teaching mode, which can improve the overall quality of students and teaching quality.

References

1. Isaacson, S.: Assessing the writing product: qualitative and quantitative measures. Except. Child. **54**(6), 528–534 (1988)
2. Mayer, R.E.: The Promise of Educational Psychology: Learning in the Content Areas. Prentice Hall, Upper Saddle River (1998)
3. Cole, J., Foster, H.: Using Moodle: Teaching with the Popular Open Source Software, 2nd edn. O'Reilly Media, Sebastapol (2005)
4. Ferriter, B.: Learning with Blogs and Wikis. Educ. Leadersh. **2**, 34–38 (2009)
5. Zhang, H.Y., Mu, S., et al.: The comparison of the social interaction function of learning management system—based on the investigation and use experience of blackboard, Moodle and Sakai. Modern Distance Educ. Res. (2) (2013)
6. Department of Education: The Chinese Curriculum Standards of Compulsory Education, Beijing (2011)

On the Cultivation and Path of College Students' Computational Thinking Ability—Taking the Teaching of Basic Computer Applications as an Example

Yanhua Liu[1(✉)] and Qiufeng Ma[2]

[1] Sanya Institute of Technology, Sanya City, Hainan Province, China
350009671@qq.com
[2] Sanya City Vocational College, Sanya City, Hainan Province, China

Abstract. In view of the current situation of College Students' lack of "computational thinking" ability, this paper analyses the factors affecting the cultivation of Computational Thinking ability. Taking the course "Computer Application Foundation" as an example, this paper expounds the links and standards that need to be paid attention to in the cultivation of Computational Thinking ability, as well as some problems that need to be paid attention to in the process of cultivating computational thinking. Through this paper, more scholars have joined the research field of Computational Thinking ability.

Keywords: Computational thinking · Computational thinking consciousness · Basic teaching of computer application

1 Introduction

With the rapid development of computer technology, how to quickly let college students of different majors understand and master the new computer technology and apply it to their own majors is a new subject that every university meets. Improving students' computing thinking ability is an important breakthrough to solve this problem. So far, universities around the world have begun to attach importance to the study of computing thinking. In our higher vocational colleges, the research of computational thinking has been regarded as a core task of quality education. Similarly, various industries are trying to use computational thinking to solve practical problems in their work. How to integrate computational thinking into university teaching in limited time is one of the most effective ways to improve students' Computational Thinking ability, and it is also a problem that every higher vocational college must face. Next, I'll talk about some of my ideas with my own teaching experience. By teaching through the virtual reality system, students can get more advantages in learning social skills.

© Springer Nature Singapore Pte Ltd. 2020
J. Shen et al. (Eds.): IC3 2019, CCIS 1227, pp. 249–255, 2020.
https://doi.org/10.1007/978-981-15-6113-9_28

2 The Connotation of Computational Thinking

To introduce computational thinking into college classroom teaching, we must think deeply about two questions: First, what is computational thinking? What is the difference between the second computational thinking and other thinking? First, answer the first question. As early as March 2006, Professor Jeannette M. Wing, director of the Department of Computer Science of Carnegie Mellon University, first proposed and defined computational thinking. He believed that computational thinking is a series of thoughts covering the breadth of computer science, such as problem solving, system design and human behavior understanding using the basic concepts of computer science. Dimensional activity is a kind of recursive thinking, a kind of parallel processing, a method of using abstraction and decomposition to control complex tasks or design huge and complex systems. Like reading and writing, she should be a basic skill that everyone must possess, not just a scientist. Computational thinking covers three levels of content, namely, consciousness, method and ability. Its fundamental purpose is to solve problems. Dong Rongzhu, a domestic scholar, believes that computational thinking is a series of thinking activities covering the breadth of computer science, such as problem solving, system design, and human behavior understanding by using the ideas and methods of computer science.

For the second question, there are two kinds of thinking in the early period of human beings: theoretical thinking and experimental thinking. Theoretical thinking is characterized by reasoning and deduction, representing mathematics. Experimental thinking is characterized by observing and summarizing natural laws and represents physics. Computational thinking, which is characterized by design and construction, is used to solve many practical engineering problems. At present, it is impossible to raise computational thinking to the same level as theoretical thinking and experimental thinking. This is because computational thinking originates from theoretical thinking and experimental thinking in a certain range, and is the continuation of theoretical thinking and experimental thinking in a certain range. It can solve past rationality. On the unsolved problems of thinking and experimental thinking methods. The goal of Cultivating College Students' computer thinking is to cultivate students' awareness of computational thinking, master Computational Thinking methods, and use computational thinking ability to think, analyze and solve practical problems.

3 The Current Situation and Countermeasure of the Cultivation of College Students' Computing Thinking Ability

3.1 Current Situation of Cultivating College Students' Computational Thinking Ability

Many colleges and universities have different ways of introducing computational thinking into the classroom and using "Computer Application Basis" as the training classroom of computational thinking. Academician Chen Guoliang, chairman of the Higher Education Commission, also gives some teaching suggestions on the implementation of

Computational Thinking in the basic course of computer application in universities. "Guided by the basic problems of computational discipline, based on classical cases, we can understand the basis of applied programming through experiments." This principle, through exercises to strengthen the understanding of basic concepts of disciplines, and strive to improve students' Computational Thinking ability. But we find that the effect is not ideal since the implementation. What is the problem? Mainly for non-computer majors, only one course of Computer Application Foundation is offered in order to gain a deeper understanding of the purpose of mastering Computational Thinking ability. This obviously reflects the lack of understanding of the knowledge points of the course.

3.2   The Countermeasure of Cultivating College Students' Computing Thinking Ability

3.2.1   The Cultivation of Computational Thinking Consciousness Is Integrated into the Whole Knowledge Teaching

We should re-understand and recognize the teaching content, and link the learning of teaching knowledge with the consciousness of thinking. The following is explained in detail through teaching cases, as shown in Fig. 1.

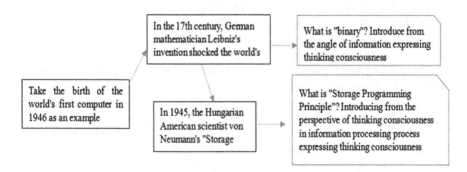

Fig. 1. Teaching thought chart

The world's first computer was born in 1946, so that students think, what are the core elements of computer birth? One is the birth of binary system, the other is the idea of storage program design. Next, let's lead the students to think about why binary system is used. It is very valuable to analyze and teach from the information expression thinking consciousness. Let the students realize that 0 and 1 contain information. They represent the two states of the circuit on and off. Digitalization can easily be expressed as 0 or 1. It is simple to calculate and easy to implement with electronic technology (chip design). They understand this thinking. Conversely, anything can be expressed as information, it can certainly be expressed as 0 or 1. And 1, can be calculated, can be input to the computer to be processed. Then it introduces the "Storage Programming Principle" from the perspective of information processing thinking. The source program is input by input device, compiled or translated, and converted into computer-recognized machine language (0 or 1). Under the control of the controller, the source program is operated by memory and output is displayed by output device. To familiarize students with this kind of thinking is to let students understand that everything processing process has a complete system, which is the result of coordinated work among the various parts of the system.

When teaching information input to computer, we should let students grasp the thinking consciousness of information processing, such as from keyboard input letters to display letters, letters input (information acquisition) electrical signal representation (0/1) encoder coding (character ASCII into a byte) access/ASCII decoder decoding font code display, so that students can clearly be one. The continuous thinking process can be easily extended to Chinese character coding. If further guidance can be given, students can grasp the way of thinking of information processing. Any physical object can identify and display the required information by collecting information, encoding and storing it in accordance with certain rules, and then decoding it with a decoder. Think about whether our modern Internet of Things is also closely related to such thinking? Through the combination of different knowledge points and computer thinking consciousness, it should not be difficult for students to establish Computational Thinking consciousness, which lays a solid foundation for students to further master Computational Thinking ability [4].

3.2.2 The Cultivation of Computational Thinking Consciousness and the Diversification of Teaching Team Members

The object of the teaching of computational thinking consciousness is freshmen of all majors. The source of teaching team should be diversified. Teachers with different professional backgrounds and engaged in computer research and application should be recruited as far as possible, reflecting the differences of computer teaching requirements among different departments and colleges, designing well differentiated teaching cases, and teaching computer in different disciplines. The thinking consciousness involved in using and solving problems cannot be used. For example, students majoring in science use computers more for design and logical judgment. They should allocate more hours when they teach the training of applied thinking meaning of principles, programs and algorithms. For those majoring in culture, they are more concerned with information processing and storage. When they teach, they should spend more time on the arrangement of information and processing of Applied thinking consciousness.

3.2.3 The Design of Teaching Content Is More Enlightening and Interesting

The object of teaching is energetic College students. In the design of teaching content, teachers should be both enlightening and interesting. This is determined by the characteristics of college students themselves. College students are curious about new things and have rich imagination. When designing the teaching content carefully, teachers should choose interesting cases as close to life as possible. For example, when learning WORD typesetting, you can arrange and design a beautiful birthday card production case, so that everyone in the process of making, encourage students to try various typesetting skills, choose the pattern, style, layout they like. In many attempts, designs, explorations and practices, in the face of their constantly improving and gradually shaping works, students will be very interested, learning atmosphere will be very strong. Finally, through the exhibition of works to experience the fun of production, thinking about the importance of computational thinking, it can achieve half the result with twice the effort.

3.2.4 Innovation of Teaching Methods

How to naturally impart computational thinking consciousness to students along with computer knowledge, teaching methods must be flexible. At present, problem-driven, heuristic, thematic discussion and self-construction are commonly used. Through flexible use of these expressions, abstract problems can be instantiated, invisible problems of computational thinking can be "visible" and related problems can be transformed. For example, when teaching the installation of operating system, the new hard disk must be partitioned and formatted. When teaching, the process can be compared to building a house, buying a new hard disk is like buying a land, partitioning a hard disk is like building a house, formatting is like dividing a room number for a well-built house, so the data installed will be placed in one room. With the room number, the next data can be easily read, so that students can understand it more easily.

3.3 The Second Task of the Course "Computer Application Basis" Is to Train Students' Computer Application Ability

At present, the core of the teaching work of Computer Application Basis is to cultivate the students' ability of calculating thinking and computer application. This requires us to renew our educational concept, pay attention to teaching methods and optimize teaching content. The most important thing is teaching design, and bring a large number of daily office cases from different positions into the classroom, such as WORD. Work schedule, posters, resume production, Excel statistical data tables, charts, data perspective tables, as well as PPT production of various speeches, new product introductions, etc., are arranged in the classroom to learn, so that students initially have the computer application ability to edit various types of documents.

4 Discussion on the Way to Cultivate Computational Thinking Ability

4.1 Whether the Ability Level of the Teaching Teachers Meets the Requirements

Professor Zhou Yizhen believes that "the biggest challenge in cultivating computational thinking is that we do not have enough trained K-12 teachers (K-12 American Computer Science Standard)". If the teacher does not have the corresponding ability, the teacher can not "think like a computer scientist", then how to cultivate students' ability in this respect? This requires schools to provide appropriate financial support from both leadership and teachers, formulate effective training plans, and enhance teachers' Computational Thinking ability. After continuous efforts to solve this problem, if the learning effect of teachers is not obvious, we can consider changing jobs.

4.2 Whether the Cultivation of Computational Thinking Ability Is Recognized by Relevant Groups

The cultivation of computational thinking ability has been recognized by many experts and scholars and supported by various universities, but it is still insufficient, because these voices mainly come from the computer field, but few for the non-computer field. Why do we have to "think like a computer scientist" instead of "think like a mathematician, physicist, chemist"? Further details, such as whether the class schedule is reasonable or not, and which semester to open the basic course of computer application. In order to solve these problems, the media should play a guiding role and realize that this is the need of globalization strategy. In an interconnected Internet world, computing thinking ability is one of the basic skills that every modern person needs.

4.3 There Is no Uniform Standard for the Course of Cultivating Computational Thinking Ability

The foundation of computer application is suitable for cultivating students' Computational Thinking consciousness. The cultivation of computational thinking ability includes three levels. For the follow-up courses of computer majors, students will continue to learn computational thinking methods and computational thinking related courses. For non-computer majors, the opinions on how to set up and how to open several doors are not uniform. It is obviously not enough to train in the basic course of computer application. This issue can be discussed by the educational circles in the form of seminars held by colleges and universities to reach consensus.

4.4 Imperfect Evaluation System of Computational Thinking Ability

The cultivation of computational thinking ability is the cultivation of students' changing thinking mode. How to evaluate the cultivation effect of Computational Thinking ability? At present, there is a set of evaluation system abroad, such as formative iteration tools, skills transfer tools, views and attitudes scale [6]. For our country, the cultivation of computational thinking ability is still in the primary stage, and there is little attention paid to the evaluation of computational thinking. The difficulty of the evaluation of computational thinking ability lies in that computational thinking belongs to the cultivation of the ability to change the way of thinking. She is more invisible. How to formulate the evaluation index of computational thinking that we all agree with is an urgent problem we need to study and discuss at present. Without a complete and scientific evaluation system, it is difficult to measure a person's Computational Thinking ability.

5 Conclusion

The cultivation of computational thinking ability is a relatively long-term process. We should constantly improve the theoretical research and practical exploration of computational thinking, constantly strengthen our teachers' training and application ability of computational thinking, and constantly improve the construction of our students' evaluation system of computational thinking. We believe that computational thinking will become one of the most necessary skills for human beings. Here, we call on more scholars to join in the research and promotion of computational thinking, and promote the education of computational thinking ability to a new stage.

References

1. Wing, J.M.: Computational thinking. Commun. ACM (S0001-0782) **49**(3), 33–35 (2006)
2. Dong, R., Gu, T.: Computational thinking and computer methodology. Comput. Sci. (01), 1–4 +42 (2009)
3. Chen, G., Dong, R.: Computing thought and basic education of computer application in universities. Teach. Chinese Universities (1), 7–11, 32 (2011)
4. Cun, X.: Reform of college computer teaching based on the cultivation of computing thinking consciousness. Fujian Comput. (8), 64–65 (2015)
5. Jackon, P.W.H.: A Handbook of Research on Curriculum. Macmillan Publishing Company, New York (1992). 403
6. Fan, W., Yichun, Z., Yi, L.: J. Distance Educ. **2**, 3–17 (2018)

Research on Multimedia Community Teaching Platform into Problem-Based Learning (PBL) - An Empirical Study on the Teaching Mode of Creative Innovation and Entrepreneurship Courses for Technical and Vocational Students

Ming-Hsiu Liu[1], Ta-Feng Tseng[2], Ron Chuen Yeh[1(✉)], and Pansy Chung[1]

[1] MeiHo University, Pingtung, Taiwan
ronchuenyeh@gmail.com
[2] Zhaoqing University, Zhaoqing, Guangdong, China

Abstract. Under the project of technical and vocational reengineering, Teachers' teaching research and teaching practice is an indispensable step, facing the rapid change of industrial environment, Teachers use of the network community and the ability to solve the problem have become the important factors to shorten the learning gap. The purpose of this study is to explore the application of network community and problem-based learning effectiveness and learning attitude and learning satisfaction. This paper aims to understand the teaching outcomes of the network community application and problem-based learning model, and to construct relevant teaching strategies, teaching materials and teaching activities. According to the results, this study found that the integration of Google Hangouts and PBL has obvious effects on the learning of the creativity, innovation and entrepreneurship course. In particular, there are obvious differences in overall academic performance. Secondly, students' learning attitude is also better because of real-time discussion through Google Hangouts. This result reflects that the multimedia teaching method and grouping design strategy can indeed improve the learning effect of students.

Keywords: Problem-based learning · Innovative and create business · Learning outcome

1 Introduction

To improve teaching quality of teachers and promote learning effect of students, the Ministry of Education of Taiwan has adopted proper research methods and assessment tools to review effectiveness through curriculum design, teaching materials, teaching methods, or teaching aids, technological media, etc. In this regard, it has promoted the MOE Teaching Practice Research Program in 2018. Through establishing a continuous peer review and guidance model, such program intends to promote establishment and

© Springer Nature Singapore Pte Ltd. 2020
J. Shen et al. (Eds.): IC3 2019, CCIS 1227, pp. 256–261, 2020.
https://doi.org/10.1007/978-981-15-6113-9_29

dialogue of exclusive communities, set up platforms for publication of results, build professional talent pools, cultivate talent teachers, actively encourage colleges and universities to invest resources through synchronous promotion of different tasks, assist university teachers in improving their teaching ability, prepare complete and excellent lesson plans, and help students improve their knowledge learning and enhance teaching quality through the formal implementation of lesson plans in classrooms.

However, the traditional teaching mode is also responding to the rapid changes of information technology. Instead of adopting traditional mode to satisfy knowledge demands of students or to teach them how to handle relevant affairs, teachers work to enhance planning, communication, team cooperation and problem-solving capacities of students prior to graduation. Therefore, problem-based teaching strategy has become a systematic teaching method in the new century. Specifically, teachers will start from the topics of creativity, innovation and entrepreneurship, integrate courses of cross-disciplinary disciplines, arrange complex and real tasks, design strategies that can enhance learning motivation, develop meta-cognitive strategies, create a peer-to-peer cooperative learning situation, and conduct inquiry learning activities, so that students can acquire knowledge and skills to solve problems. In this way, teachers may improve their teaching quality of vocational education. However, problem-based learning is a student-centered learning. Students will develop research topics, collect and analyze data, solve problems in the process, and finally complete project works for evaluation of learning results [1, 2].

Through the evaluation of project works, teachers can understand the learning process and results of students, and can observe the learning situation of students in the process, give appropriate support and help improve the learning situation. Such learning mode makes use of the Internet to form network problem-based learning. Barrows [1] also proposed that the problem-based learning mode can effectively promote the learning effect. In this study, the problem-based learning strategy uses the grouping design mode to effectively improve students' self-thinking ability through grouping of courses, community analysis and curriculum interaction and design. It is also hoped that the introduction of PBL mechanism can improve the quality of curriculum design, thus strengthening students' learning attitude and effectiveness. Therefore, the purpose of this study is as follows: (1) Develop a community network cooperative learning platform for creativity, innovation and entrepreneurship course to improve learning effect of students and promote curriculum education; (2) Discuss the effectiveness of community network cooperative learning platform on practical teaching in terms of learning attitude, learning satisfaction and learning effectiveness.

2 Literature Review

2.1 Problem-Based Learning Teaching Model

Problem-based learning strategy (PBL) is a teaching method that designs problems and organizes learning process according to the teaching process. Under the teaching strategy, students define problems, make assumptions about the problems, collect data or materials and carry out tests until the best solution to the problems is found and the methods and strategies to solve the problems are formulated. Through PBL, students can cultivate critical thinking, problem-solving ability and cooperative skills [2]. Of course, PBL is also widely used in different teaching situations. For example, Huang, Huang, Wu, Chen, and Chang [8] applied PBL in the information ethics curriculum, and discussed the teaching effects of blogs and micro-blogs respectively. The research results indicate that the teaching strategy of micro-blogs is better for students with low learning achievement, while the teaching effect of blogs is better for overall teaching. Sung, Hwang, and Chen [9] discussed students' learning results. The research compared the learning effect of students before and after using interactive e-books. From the experimental results, it can be seen that teachers' PBL method, together with interactive e-books, achieves better effects in helping students' learning results, and strengthens students' critical thinking and learning motivation. On the cognitive load level, the use of interactive e-books will not increase students' cognitive load in learning.

2.2 Connotation, Function and Implication of Positive Emotion

Garland and Noyes [5] found that positive emotions have complementary effects, making people think and act boldly. On the whole, positive emotions can bring multiple benefits to individual life. Through thinking and action mode expanded by positive emotions, individuals can be more positive, optimistic and energetic. The nature and function of positive emotions are different from those of negative emotions. Even when facing adversity and prosperity, people may how to handle problems and eliminate the effect of negative emotions. In the learning process, the intervention of positive emotions will definitely help to improve students' learning efficiency.

2.3 Related Research on Cognitive Load in Teaching Research

Huang, Huang, Wu, Chen, & Chang [8] explored the cognitive load of learners in English teaching, and believed that learners with higher English listening comprehension have relatively lower cognitive load; learners with low English listening comprehension have relatively high cognitive load. Sung, Hwang & Chen [9] found that under different media forms, the richer the learning media, the higher the cognitive load of learners. Of course, in the mode of operation of the network community, this study mainly used the cooperative function of Google Hangouts' teaching platform to enhance interactive relationship between teams. However, no matter of what technology media is added to the course teaching, the learning constructs of students show certain cognitive load. From the previous literature, it can be known that interactive teaching can reduce the learning load of students and enable them to improve the overall teaching efficiency.

2.4 Learning Attitude and Related Researches

Sung, Hwang, and Chen [9] also held that if teachers can show a positive and positive attitude on the e-learning platform, teachers' enthusiasm can further motivate students in learning. Hence, this study tended to explore whether the integration of creativity, innovation and entrepreneurship course and multimedia interaction of Google

Hangouts has a strong positive teaching influence to motivate and inspire learners and make learners willing to learn on the platform. Thus, the concept of "positive attitude" is also included in this research framework.

3   Research Methodology

This study intends to explore the cognitive load and learning effect of curriculum teaching under the combination of application of network community of creativity, innovation and entrepreneurship course and PBL vocational school students. The focus is to re-use the application of network community media to determine whether the learning effect and satisfaction of students before and after the curriculum study are different. The research framework is as shown in Fig. 1.

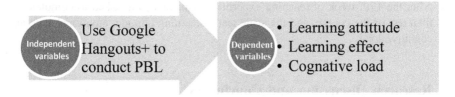

Fig. 1. Research structure

3.1   Research Design and Question Design

The cognitive load scale adopts three benchmarks for measuring students' cognitive load: Intrinsic cognitive load, extraneous cognitive load and Germane cognitive load [7]. The Positive Emotion Scale was prepared in the form of Positive and Negative Affect Scale for Children by Watson & Clark [3] and the Emotion Scale and Emotion Feeling Questionnaire by Kammann & Flett [4].

The operational definition of positive attitude is to form a positive or negative attitude towards people, things and stuff through teaching and learning activities and processes, and to carry out persistent, habitual and consistent internal psychological reactions to certain directions and purposes. After integration, the learning attitude is defined as the attitude of students after using Google Hangouts to assist learning of creativity, innovation and entrepreneurship course, which is divided into three levels: Cognition, emotion and behavior. However, the relevant scale is established based on the scale of Hwang & Chang [6]. All the above scales were designed according to Likert's five-point scale.

In terms of learning effectiveness, based on the scores measured before and after the "skill level" of students, a total of 20 knowledge problems at the skill level of creativity, innovation and entrepreneurship course were designed to improve learning effectiveness, with scores ranging from 0 to 100 as the measurement criteria.

3.2   Experimental Design

The experimental subjects are all students who took the course of creativity, innovation and entrepreneurship in the semester. The number of students taking the course is 80, and the course is mainly discussed in groups of 3–5 students. At the end of the course, a creative project is completed. The whole teaching experiment includes three stages, which are explained as follows:

(1) Pre-test stage and equipment operation training in the first week: The teacher explained the operation of Google Hangouts in the first class and asked students to operate and practice. In the course, students were divided into groups. Later, the teacher would conduct pre-class guidance to explain learning objectives and outline of learning contents, so that students have a basic concept of power saving.
(2) In the third week, students' learning status and overall effect of Google Hangouts-assisted teaching were understood through the test of learning effect analysis, teaching experiment and various scales.
(3) After the 17th week of teaching experiment, students were asked to complete the final test of the course, and the scale test of learning attitude, emotional state and cognitive load.

4   Research Discussion and Conclusion

4.1   Research Discussion

According to the results of this study, it can be found that the overall learning attitude of the creativity, innovation and entrepreneurship course has been significantly improved from the beginning to the end (the average increase is 0.34, $t < 0.05$). Secondly, in terms of learning effect, obvious progress was made in students' learning performance before and after learning, which indicates that students indeed have made progress after the learning of this course. Finally, the post-test results of cognitive load have been obviously increased, the t value in the statistical results is not significant (t-value = 0.76) (Table 1).

Table 1. Results of research and analysis

Variable	Group	Number	Average value	Standard deviation	t
Learning attitude	Pre-test	72	4.04	0.99	2.64*
	Post-test	71	4.38	0.62	
Cognitive load	Pre-test	72	3.79	1.14	0.76
	Post-test	69	4.00	0.97	
Learning outcomes	Pre-test	72	47.82	2.23	3.89*
	Post-test	70	60.87	3.42	

t-value > 1.96, p < 0.05*

4.2 Conclusion

According to the results, this study found that the integration of Google Hangouts and PBL has obvious effects on the learning of the creativity, innovation and entrepreneurship course. In particular, there are obvious differences in overall academic performance. Secondly, students' learning attitude is also better because of real-time discussion through Google Hangouts. This result reflects that the multimedia teaching method and grouping design strategy can indeed improve the learning effect of students, but the actual learning effect in this study is only limited to quantitative analysis. It is also suggested that more qualitative analysis discussions can be added, such as interview method or recorded data in course activities. Researches in the future can focus more on explorations of learning effect of courses featuring multiple thinking such as "creativity, innovation and entrepreneurship".

References

1. Barrows, H.S., Tamblyn, R.M.: Problem-Based Learning: An Approach to Medical Education. Springer, New York (1980)
2. Barrows, H.S.: The essentials of problem-based learning. J. Dent. Educ. **62**(9), 630–633 (1988)
3. Watson, D., Clark, L.A.: Emotions, moods, traits, and temperaments: conceptual distinctions and empirical findings. Nat. Emot. Fundam. Questions, 89–93 (1994)
4. Kammann, R., Flett, R.: Affectometer 2: a scale to measure current level of general happiness. Aust. J. Psychol. **35**(2), 259–265 (1983)
5. Garland, K.J., Noyes, J.M.: Computer attitude scales: How relevant today? Comput. Hum. Behav. **24**(2), 563–575 (2008)
6. Hwang, G.J., Chang, H.F.: A formative assessment-based mobile learning approach to improving the learning attitudes and achievements of students. Comput. Educ. **56**(4), 1023–1031 (2011)
7. Paas, F., Renkl, A., Sweller, J.: Cognitive load theory and instructional design: recent developments. Educ. Psychol. **38**(1), 1–4 (2003)
8. Huang, S.H., Huang, Y.M., Wu, T.T., Chen, H.R., Chang, S.M.: Problem-based learning effectiveness on micro-blog and blog for students: a case study. Interact. Learn. Environ. **24**(6), 1334–1354 (2016)
9. Sung, H.Y., Hwang, G.J., Chen, S.F.: Effects of embedding a problem-posing-based learning guiding strategy into interactive e-books on students' learning performance and higher order thinking tendency. Interact. Learn. Environ. **27**(3), 389–401 (2019)

Evaluation of Classification Algorithms for Predicting Students' Learning Performance Based on BookRoll Reading Logs

Anna Yu-Qing Huang$^{(\boxtimes)}$, Owen Hsin-Tes Lu, and Stephen J.H. Yang

National Central University, Taoyuan City, Taiwan
anna.yuqing@gmail.com

Abstract. To help students' learning, finding at-risk students is an important issue in education. This study has collected students' learning logs in ebook reading environment for 17 blended learning courses in Taiwan. Then, we have construct students' learning performance prediction model based on learning logs by using eight classification methods. To improve prediction performance, we have also propose grading policy rules which include of grading on stringency rule, grading on moderate rule, and grading on leniency rule to define the labels of students' learning performance. According to the prediction performance results, the LR is the suitable classification method for predicting students' learning performance. Besides, the grading on leniency rule has obtained the higher prediction performance. For exploring the influence factors on classification performance, we investigate the relationship between students' online learning actions and students' academic performance by Spearman coefficient analysis the open file (f1), the number of delete marker (f6), the number of next pages (f12), and the number of previous pages (f13) features are the critical factors for affecting the prediction performance of learning logs.

Keywords: Classification · AUC · Spearman correlation

1 Introduction

The mechanism of predicting and classifying students' performance is very important for promoting students' success in learning. Finding at-risk students through predicting students' performance can help teachers give timely interventions to students to improve their success. Following the rapidly growth of Internet, the modern learning environments can provide various learning trace such as online ebook reading, online learning via viewing videos, discussion in forum, online practice. Owing that students' online learning engagement can be captured from learning environment such as number or spent time of viewed content, many scholars have focus on measuring students' engagement in learning environment [1]. Therefore, we aim to extract features from students' tracking logs in learning environment to predict students' academic performance.

With the digital learning environments have rapidly growth up, some researchers have tried to measure students' engagement through tracking logs in learning environment [1]. Besides, some scholars further use the students' tracking logs to predict

© Springer Nature Singapore Pte Ltd. 2020
J. Shen et al. (Eds.): IC3 2019, CCIS 1227, pp. 262–272, 2020.
https://doi.org/10.1007/978-981-15-6113-9_30

students' grade through machine learning methods [2–4]. From previous studies [2–5], machine learning methods such as Naive Bayes (NB), Decision Trees (DT) and Neural Networks (NN), Support Vector Classification (SVC), Logistic Regression (LR) and Random Forest (RF) are the common used classification algorithm to predict students' learning performance. Therefore, this study applied Gaussian Naive Bayes (GaNB), SVC, Linear-SVC, LR, DT, RF, NN, and XGBoost algorithms to construct student classification for academic performance.

The goal of this paper is to build students' academic performance prediction model by using various classification methods for different datasets which were recorded students tracking logs. To improve the prediction performance of classifications, we have also propose grading policy rules which include of grading on stringency rule, grading on moderate rule, and grading on leniency rule to define the labels of students' learning performance. Finally, this study also discuss the factors influence on prediction performance for the six datasets. Therefore, the research questions in this study are proposed as following.

RQ1: Which classification algorithm is the suitable for predicting students' learning performance?

RQ2: Which grading policy rule has the best prediction performance of classification algorithms?

RQ3: Which factors will affect the prediction performance of learning logs?

2 Literature Review

Finding at-risk students in education, classification algorithm is one of the most frequently used methods in machine learning. Classification methods can be generally divided into four types which consisted of statistical classification, NN [6], probabilistic classification, and vector space based classification. LR [7] is a statistical classification for constructing binary classification to deal with linear or nonlinear data. GaNB and NB [8] are statistical classification. The vector space based classification generally includes SVC and Linear-SVC algorithms. SVC is a Support Vector Machine (SVM) for classification [9]. DT [10], RF [11] and XGBoost [12] are tree based classifications.

In general, the area Under the Curve (AUC) of Receiver Operating Characteristic (ROC) is the most used evaluator of classification performance. AUC is the area under the ROC curve. The value of AUC is range from 0 to 1. The value of AUC near to 0.5 indicated that the classification similar to random guess. The classification with higher value of AUC implied the better prediction performance.

The interpretations of the AUC values for different ranges is as follows. The classification is considered as no predictive ability when the AUC value lower than .5. The AUC values from .5 to .7, from .7 to .8, from .8 to .9, and from .9 to 1.0 imply classification with fairly low predictive ability, acceptable or moderate predictive ability, high predictive ability, and outstanding or perfect predictive ability, respectively (Mandrekar 2010; Vanagas 2004).

3 Methodology

3.1 Online Ebook Reading Environment

With online learning environments have gradually introduced into school curriculum, learning materials have also gradually changed from paper textbooks to e-books. For this reason, researchers have development a digital learning material reading system named as BookRoll to provide students with ebooks to learning [13]. For exploring students' ebook reading behaviors, researchers have detailed describe students' ebook reading actions in BookRoll [14]. The BookRoll functionalities include of file, bookmark, marker, memo and page categories. multiple functions. For investigating students' online reading, researchers have proposed some ebook reading features from BookRoll [15]. According to the reading action categories proposed by [15], this study has extracted 15 features showed in Table 1.

Table 1. The constructed 15 features from BookRoll.

Feature ID	Feature name	Feature description
f_1	Open	Number of times students open ebooks
f_2	Close	Number of times students close ebooks
f_3	Add bookmark	Number of times students add bookmarks
f_4	Delete bookmark	Number of times students delete bookmarks
f_5	Add marker	Number of times students add markers
f_6	Delete marker	Number of times students delete markers
f_7	Marker count	Number of markers used by students
f_8	Add memo	Number of times students add memos
f_9	Delete memo	Number of times students delete memos
f_{10}	Change memo	Number of times students change memos
f_{11}	Memo count	Number of memos used by students
f_{12}	Next	Number of times students turn to the next page
f_{13}	Prev	Number of times students turn to the previous page
f_{14}	Jump	Number of times students jump pages
f_{15}	Search	Number of times students search pages

3.2 Students' Learning Performance Prediction Procedure and Description of Students' Learning Logs

The procedure for classifying students' learning performance consist of data preprocessing, classification construction, and classification evaluation steps. Owing that the original range of sample data may have been excessively wide, data preprocessing aims to normalize the features' values of data sample within a smaller range. This study applied z-score to normalize the features' values. The classification construction step focus on constructing students' learning performance classifications by using 8 classification methods which include of GaNB, SVC, linear-SVC, LR, DT, RF, NN, and

XGBoost. In evaluation step, this study applied Area Under the Curve (AUC) of Receiver Operating Characteristic (ROC) to evaluate the prediction performance of these 8 classifications.

To improve classification's performance, we have proposed grading policy rules which include of grading on stringency, grading on moderate, and grading on leniency rules to define the labels of students' learning performance. For the grading on leniency, grading on moderate, and grading on stringency rules, the bottom 20%, 50%, and 80% students in class have been labeled as student with low score, respectively. The symbols of N_L and N_H indicate the number of students with low and high score, respectively. The symbol R represents the ratio of the number of students with low and high score. The higher value of R will cause the dataset with higher degree of imbalance problem.

Table 2. The descriptive statistics of 17 datasets.

	Students: N_H/N_L (R)	Number of logs: Total/Average	Durations	Available features
DS01	15/0(n.a)	4,045/22	12	8
DS02	30/3(10)	5,513/13	12	11
DS03	39/5(7.8)	6,795/19	8	11
DS04	13/4(3.25)	1,937/16	7	10
DS05	32/1(32)	22,018/83	8	15
DS06	128/4(32)	30,684/58	4	15
DS07	53/4(13.3)	40,581/118	6	14
DS08	49/0(n.a)	26,865/78	7	14
DS9	26/14 (1.8)	54,603/91	15	15
DS10	12/1 (12)	3,644/31	9	15
DS11	50/0(n.a)	16,930/21	16	15
DS12	33/0(n.a)	65,443/294	6	15
DS13	37/15(2.5)	50,826/108	9	15
DS14	34/10(3.4)	45,180/114	9	15
DS15	31/6(5.2)	9,248/14	17	15
DS16	26/0(n.a)	28,014/60	18	15
DS17	21/0(n.a)	85,357/225	18	15

Table 2 shows the descriptive statistics for the 17 datasets. The DS01, DS08, DS11, DS12, DS16and DS17 datasets don't have student with score less than sixty. Consequently, these six learning logs can't construct students' learning performance classifications which were labeling student with score less than 60 as at-risk students. For the DS02, DS03, DS05–DS07, and DS10, the proportion of the number of students with low and high score in these 6 learning logs are more than 5 times. This maybe influence the prediction performance of classifications for these 6 learning logs.

4   Results and Discussion

4.1   Prediction Performance Results

For responding RQ1 (Which classification algorithm is the suitable for predicting students' learning performance?), this study aims to collect 18 learning logs and construct students' learning performance classifications by using 8 classification methods which include of GaNB, SVC, linear-SVC, LR, DT, RF, NN, and XGBoost. Table 3 shows the AUC values of 8 classifications for the 17 learning logs. When the students' score less than 60 were considered as at-risk student, the DS01, DS08, DS11, DS12, DS16, and DS17 learning logs can't construct students' learning performance classifications. This is because that the score of all students are more than 60 for these six learning logs according to the descriptive statistics results from Table 2.

Table 3. The AUC values of 8 classifications in 17 datasets.

	GaNB	Linear-SVC	SVC	LR	DT	RF	NN	XGBoost
DS01	n.a	n.a	n.a	n.a	n.a	n.a	n.a	n.a
DS02	.50	.46	.49	.38	.45	.49	.49	.50
DS03	.50	.47	.48	.43	.48	.48	.47	.49
DS04	.47	.43	.45	.43	.45	.45	.41	.48
DS05	.50	n.a	n.a	n.a	.49	.50	.50	.50
DS06	.50	.50	.50	.63	.49	.50	.50	.50
DS07	.50	.49	.50	.60	.50	.50	.50	.50
DS08	n.a	n.a	n.a	n.a	n.a	n.a	n.a	n.a
DS09	.50	.77	.80	.78	.76	.80	.79	.82
DS10	.50	n.a	n.a	n.a	.46	.48	.49	.50
DS11	n.a	n.a	n.a	n.a	n.a	n.a	n.a	n.a
DS12	n.a	n.a	n.a	n.a	n.a	n.a	n.a	n.a
DS13	.50	.57	.53	.74	.62	.62	.55	.59
DS14	.50	.62	.51	.75	.58	.57	.64	.57
DS15	.63	.71	.71	.81	.71	.71	.70	.69
DS16	n.a	n.a	n.a	n.a	n.a	n.a	n.a	n.a
DS17	n.a	n.a	n.a	n.a	n.a	n.a	n.a	n.a

The DS02, DS03, DS04, DS05, and DS10 can be considered as no predictive ability due to the best AUC value of these learning logs are near to .5. The classifications for DS02, DS03, DS05, and DS10 can be considered as no predictive ability as a result of the R values (i.e. the ratios of the high and low score students) described in Table 2 are all large values of 10, 7.8, 32, 8 and 12. Even the R value of DS04 is small, the classification of DS04 also considered as no predictive ability due to the average amount of reading actions for students per week is too small.

The best AUC values of DS06 and DS07 are achieved .63 and .60 by using LR classification, respectively. It means that the prediction performance of DS06 and DS07 are belong to low predictive ability. Although the R values of DS06 and DS07 are 32 and 13.3, respectively, they are all large values. Since the average number of reading actions per week for students is a large number, which is 58 and 118 respectively, the Logistic Regression(LR) classifications for DS06 and DS07 are belong to low predictive ability.

For the DS9, DS13, DS14, and DS15, the best AUC value are .82, .74, .75, and .81, respectively. For the DS13–DS14, the Logistic Regression(LR) classifications can obtain the best AUC values in the used 8 classification methods. The DS09 can obtain the best AUC value by using SVC and RF classification methods. According to the interpretation of AUC range, DS09 and DS15 have high predictive ability, and the DS13 and DS14 have moderate predictive ability. The reason that the DS09, DS13, DS14, and DS15 classifiers can achieve high and medium predictive power is due to the small R values for the four datasets which are 1.8, 2.5, 3.4, and 5.2, respectively.

Among the 17 datasets, the LR classification can achieve the best prediction performance for the DS06–DS07 and DS13–DS15, the DS09 dataset can achieve the best prediction performance through SVC or RF classifications. The other 11 datasets for classifications can be considered as no predictive ability. The answer to RQ1 is that the LR classification is the suitable for predicting students' learning performance.

4.2 Prediction Performance Results for the Four Grading Policies

In general, student's score less than sixty can be considered as at-risk student, and this student can be labeled as negative instance in binary classification. However, the number of students with score less than sixty is small in school education. Then, the performance of classifications will be influenced. To improve classification's performance, this study has propose grading policy rules which include of grading on stringency rule, grading on moderate rule, and grading on leniency rule to define the labels of students' learning performance. For the grading on stringency, grading on moderate, and grading on leniency rules, the bottom 20%, 50%, and 80% students in class have been labeled as at-risk students, respectively.

For responding RQ2 (Which grading policy rule has the best prediction performance of classification algorithms?), Table 4 shows the AUC values from LR classification method of 4 grading policies for 18 datasets. Among the 4 grading policies, the standard, leniency, moderate, and stringency grading polices has constructed 2, 7, 4, and 3 LR classifications with the best AUC values and the AUC values are more than .5. The worst AUC value of LR classification is .29 and is belong to DS10 dataset. For the standard grading policy (i.e. the student with score less than 60 can be, defined as at-risk student) by using LR classification, only the DS06, DS07 and DS15 datasets can obtained the best prediction performance. For the leniency grading policy, the DS04, DS05, DS07, DS09, DS11, DS13, DS14, and DS17 datasets can achieved the best prediction performance of AUC with the range from .66 to .95. For the moderate grading policy, DS01, DS02, DS13 and DS16 can obtained achieved the best prediction performance of AUC with the range from .59 to .83. For the stringency grading policy, DS03, DS08, DS12 can obtained achieved the best prediction performance of AUC with the range from .51 to .72. From the above description, the answer to RQ2 is that the leniency grading policy has the best prediction performance of LR classification.

Table 4. The AUC values of LR with 4 grading policies in 17 datasets.

	Standard	Leniency	Moderate	Stringency
DS01	n.a	0.59	0.69	0.4
DS02	0.38	0.48	0.59	0.4
DS03	0.43	0.54	0.55	0.72
DS04	0.43	0.66	0.63	0.43
DS05	n.a	0.83	0.78	0.53
DS06	0.63	0.55	0.6	0.48
DS07	0.6	0.74	0.61	0.67
DS08	n.a	0.38	0.45	0.59
DS09	0.78	0.83	0.71	0.57
DS10	n.a	n.a	0.29	n.a
DS11	n.a	0.76	0.6	0.53
DS12	0.4	0.41	0.38	0.51
DS13	0.74	0.78	0.83	0.64
DS14	0.75	0.81	0.7	0.66
DS15	0.81	0.75	0.67	0.64
DS16	n.a	0.69	0.75	0.42
DS17	n.a	0.95	0.73	0.74

4.3   Correlation Between Students' Online Reading and Learning Performance

In general, Pearson or Spearman Rank correlation coefficient analysis focus on exploring the correlation between two variables [16]. The Pearson correlation coefficient must support normal distribution and aims to measure the linear relationship for two variables. Spearman's rank focus on measure the correlation trend for ordinary variable. Thus, Spearman's rank correlation coefficient is better when the variables are non-normally distributed and non-linear correlation. For responding RQ3 (Which factors will affect the prediction performance of learning logs?), Table 5 and Table 6 show the values of Spearman's rank correlation coefficient between students' learning performance and online reading features f1–f8 and f9–f15, respectively.

The interpretations of the correlation coefficient values for different ranges is as follows. The value range from .9 to 1.0 (or −.9 to −1.0), .7 to .9 (or −.7 to −.9), .5 to .7 (or −.5 to −.7), .3 to .5 (or −.3 to −.5), .3 to .0 (or −.3 to .0) are indicate very high positive (negative) correlation, high positive (negative) correlation, moderate positive (negative) correlation, low positive (negative) correlation, and negligible correlation [16].

Table 5. The Spearman correlation coefficient between 8 features (f1–f8) and learning performance in 17 datasets

	f_1	f_2	f_3	f_4	f_5	f_6	f_7	f_8
DS01	0.16	0.32	n.a	n.a	0.28	0.09	0.28	n.a
DS02	0.34	.43*	−0.01	0.06	0.13	0.15	0.13	n.a
DS03	0.25	.41**	0.1	0.16	0.11	0.25	0.11	n.a
DS04	0.13	0.25	0.42	0.42	0.27	n.a	0.27	n.a
DS05	.75***	.66***	.60***	.45**	.41*	.38*	.39*	.62***
DS06	.22*	.19*	0.05	0.07	.32***	.22*	.31***	.29***
DS07	.40**	.36**	.41**	0.24	.28*	0.15	.26*	0.06
DS08	−0.12	−0.14	0.11	0.11	.34*	0.21	.34*	−0.17
DS09	.66***	.48**	0.18	0.28	0.19	.33*	0.19	.36*
DS10	−0.08	0.05	0.07	0.08	0	0.21	0	−0.02
DS11	.49***	.43**	.28*	.29*	.43**	.37**	.43**	0.15
DS12	0.22	0.1	0.16	0.03	0.13	0.28	0.16	.34*
DS13	.73***	.63***	.45***	.43**	.60***	.78***	.63***	.42**
DS14	.66***	0.29	0.11	0	.31*	.49***	.33*	.38*
DS15	.65***	.44**	.34*	.37*	.50**	.45**	.51**	.42**
DS16	0.29	.46*	0.13	0.13	−.48*	−.52**	−.52**	−0.06
DS17	.72***	.54*	0.28	0.43	0.24	0.34	0.27	0.36

Table 6. The Spearman correlation coefficient between 7 features (f9–f15) and learning performance in 17 datasets.

	f_9	f_{10}	f_{11}	f_{12}	f_{13}	f_{14}	f_{15}
DS01	n.a	n.a	n.a	0.03	0.31	0.43	n.a
DS02	n.a	n.a	n.a	.37*	0.27	.48**	0.06
DS03	n.a	n.a	n.a	0.2	0.03	0.09	−0.29
DS04	n.a	n.a	n.a	0.29	0.28	0.34	−0.19
DS05	.41*	.65***	.64***	.65***	.53**	.41*	0.072
DS06	.24**	.18*	.27**	.20*	.22*	.25**	0.059
DS07	0.06	n.a	0.06	.38**	.29*	0.05	−0.03
DS08	−0.1	n.a	−0.17	−0.02	−0.03	0.01	0.01
DS09	0.2	.37*	.37*	.63***	.66***	.53***	0.01
DS10	−0.39	0.31	−0.02	0.03	0.17	0.12	0.11
DS11	0.14	0.17	0.15	.47***	.43**	.29*	0.1
DS12	0.21	0.24	0.3	0.04	0.02	−0.1	−0.03
DS13	.39**	.33*	.42**	.76***	.76***	.45***	0.09
DS14	.32*	.41**	.40**	.70***	.68***	.52***	0.28
DS15	0.23	0.28	.39*	.49**	.39*	−0.08	0.12
DS16	−0.12	−0.08	−0.07	0.09	0.04	0.33	0.07
DS17	.61**	.56**	.53*	.68***	.74***	.58**	0.18

Table 7 summary the number of features with negligible, low, moderate, high and very high correlations for learning performance. The negligible rate can be defined as the number of negligible features divide by the number of available features. The prediction performance of classification will obtain lower when the learning log with higher negligible rate. As can be seen from Table 6, the DS01, DS02, DS03, DS04, DS06, DS07, DS08, DS10, DS12 and DS16 learning logs have a negligible feature rate greater than .7. It means that these 10 learning logs maybe obtained lower prediction performance of classifications due to the number of negligible features are too big.

Table 7. The number of features with negligible, low, moderate, high and very high correlations for learning performance.

	Very high	High	Moderate	Low	Negligible	Negligible rate
DS01	0	0	0	0	8	1.0
DS02	0	0	0	3	8	.73
DS03	0	0	0	1	10	.91
DS04	0	0	0	0	10	1.0
DS05	0	1	7	6	1	.07
DS06	0	0	0	2	13	.87
DS07	0	0	0	4	10	.71
DS08	0	0	0	2	12	.86
DS09	0	0	4	5	6	.4
DS10	0	0	0	0	15	1.0
DS11	0	0	0	7	8	.53
DS12	0	0	0	1	14	.93
DS13	0	4	3	7	1	.13
DS14	0	1	3	7	4	.27
DS15	0	0	3	8	4	.27
DS16	0	0	2	2	11	.73
DS17	0	2	6	0	7	.47

From Table 7, there are 6 datasets, including DS05, DS09, DS13, DS14, DS15 and DS17, with low negligible rate of less than .5. Besides, these six datasets have some features with moderate and high correlations of learning performance. Thus, the AUC values of these six datasets can be promoted to more than .8 by applied grading policies which indicates these six LR classifications have high predictive ability.

The f_1 feature in the DS05, DS13, and DS17 datasets are highly correlated with students' learning performance. The f_6 feature in DS13 is highly correlated with students' learning performance. The f_{12} feature in DS14 and DS14 datasets are highly correlated with students' learning performance. The f_{13} feature in DS13 and DS17 datasets are highly correlated with students' learning performance. From above description, the answer to RQ3 is that, the f_1, f_6, f_{12}, and f_{13} features are the critical factors for affecting the prediction performance of learning logs.

5 Conclusion

To investigate the prediction performances of various classifications in education field, this study aims to collect 17 datasets and then construct students' learning performance classification based on students' ebook learning logs. For the comparing 17 datasets, there are 11 datasets for classifications can be considered as no predictive ability, and there are 5 datasets can obtain he best prediction performance through LR classification. Therefore, the LR classification is the suitable for predicting students' learning performance.

For improving the prediction performance of classification, this study has proposed grading policy rules which include of grading on stringency rule, grading on moderate rule, and grading on leniency rule to define the labels of students' learning performance. For the DS04, DS05, DS07, DS09, DS11, DS13, DS14, and DS17 datasets, the leniency grading policy has the best prediction performance of AUC with the range from .66 to .95. Thus, the leniency grading policy has the best prediction performance of LR classification.

In these 17 data sets, we use the Spearman rank correlation coefficient analysis to further explore the critical factors affecting the classification prediction performance. According to the Spearman rank correlation coefficient results, the f1, f6, f12, and f13 features are the critical factors for affecting the prediction performance of learning logs.

References

1. Lu, O.H.T., Huang, A.Y.Q., Yang, S.J.H.: Applying learning analytics for improving students engagement and learning outcomes in a MOOCs enabled collaborative programming course. Inter. Learn. Environ. 25(2), 220–234 (2017)
2. Lu, O.H.T., Huang, A.Y.Q., Huang, J.C.H., Lin, A.J.Q., Ogata, H., Yang, S.J.H.: Applying learning analytics for the early prediction of students' academic performance in blended learning. Educ. Technol. Soc. 21(2), 220–232 (2018)
3. Lu, O.H.T., Huang, A.Y.Q., Yang, S.J.H.: Benchmarking and tuning regression algorithms on predicting students' academic performance. In: 26th International Conference on Computers in Education (2018)
4. Huang, A.Y.Q., Weng, J.X., Huang, J.C.H., Lu, O.H.T., Jong, B.S., Yang, S.J.H.: Prediction of students' academic performance based on tracking logs. In: 26th International Conference on Computers in Education (2018)
5. Asif, R., Merceron, A., Pathan, M.K.: Predicting student academic performance at degree level: a case study. Int. J. Intell. Syst. Appl. 7(1), 49–61 (2014)
6. McCulloch, W.S., Pitts, W.: A logical calculus of the ideas immanent in nervous activity. Bull. Math. Biophys. 5(4), 115–133 (1943)
7. Cox, D.R.: The regression analysis of binary sequences. J. Roy. Stat. Soc. Ser. B (Methodol.) 20(2), 215–242 (1958)
8. John, G.H., Langley, P.: Estimating continuous distributions in Bayesian classifiers. In: Proceedings of the Eleventh conference on Uncertainty in Artificial Intelligence, pp. 338–345. Morgan Kaufmann Publishers Inc., Burlington (1995)
9. Cortes, C., Vapnik, V.: Support-vector networks. Mach. Learn. 20(3), 273–297 (1995)

10. Quinlan, J.R.: Learning Efficient Classification Procedures and their Application to Chess end Games. Machine Learning, pp. 463–482. Springer, Heidelberg (1983)
11. Breiman, L.: Random forests. Mach. Learn. **45**(1), 5–32 (2001)
12. Chen, T., Guestrin, C.: Xgboost: a scalable tree boosting system. In: Proceedings of the 22nd ACM Sigkdd International Conference on Knowledge Discovery and Data Mining, pp. 785–794. ACM 2016
13. Flanagan, B., Ogata, H.: Integration of learning analytics research and production systems while protecting privacy. In: Proceeding of International Conference on Computers in Education (ICCE 2017), pp. 333–338 (2017)
14. Ogata, H., et al.: E-book-based learning analytics in university education. In: Proceedings of International Conference on Computer in Education (ICCE 2015), pp. 401–406 (2015)
15. Yamada, M., Oi, M., Konomi, S.I.: Are learning logs related to procrastination? from the viewpoint of self-regulated learning. In: 14th International Conference on Cognition and Exploratory Learning in the Digital Age, CELDA 2017, pp. 3–10. IADIS Press (2017)
16. Mukaka, M.M.: A guide to appropriate use of correlation coefficient in medical research. Malawi Med. J. **24**(3), 69–71 (2012)

Exploring Augmented Reality Teaching Aids in Children's Emotional Learning

Whei-Jane Wei[1]([⊠]) [iD] and Lai-Chung Lee[2] [iD]

[1] University of Taipei, Taipei, Taiwan
wwj@utaipei.edu.tw
[2] National Taipei University of Technology, Taipei, Taiwan

Abstract. How can a preschool teacher combine tablet with real teaching aids to improve the learning efficiency of children? How can a teacher apply science and technology to record the learning route of children? This research is aimed to develop the teaching aids of points of interests (POI) and MAKAR database in order to record children's learning preference and effectiveness in the learning center of drama. Thirty-seven 4–6 years old were randomly selected. This research used tablet PC to develop nine emotional theaters. Each theater was designed by four POIs for creative thinking including Inquiring, Thinking, Trial and Sharing (ITTS). System would record autonomously the learning process when children manipulated the tablets. When children made decisions, system would autonomously record the decision they made, including the using time and frequency, then updated to database. Findings indicated that children are more interested in MAKAR teaching. MAKAR teaching has extremely significant effect on emotional ability ($p = .000$). The overall reliability analysis showed a 74.7% consistency. The learning records will be used as foundation for future revision and improvement. The result of this research supported that the learning effectiveness by using Unity and Vuforia Augmented Reality (AR) is much better than traditional teaching. MAKAR facilitates children's ability not only emotional learning but also creative problem-solving.

Keywords: Inquiring · Thinking · Trial and sharing (ITTS) · MAKAR database · Vuforia AR

1 Introduction

There are three trends worldwide today such as internet of things (IoT), artificial intelligent (AI), and big data (BD). Teachers must apply IoT, AI, BD in preschool teaching. However, most preschool teachers are not familiar with these technologies. This study attempts to apply the most convenient MAKAR in flip teaching. AR and tablet are explored in the following sections.

1.1 Augmented Reality Application

The shortage of traditional teaching was lack of interaction between parent and children so that learning efficiency was low. Mobile AR system enhanced preschoolers' hands-on ability, imagination and fun [1]. In fact, creativity comprised imagination, flexibility,

© Springer Nature Singapore Pte Ltd. 2020
J. Shen et al. (Eds.): IC3 2019, CCIS 1227, pp. 273–283, 2020.
https://doi.org/10.1007/978-981-15-6113-9_31

uniqueness, elaboration and fluency [2]. Related studies indicated that AR enhanced preschoolers' interest, engagement and creativity [3]. AR also improved preschoolers' second language ability [4], music performance, cognitive and socio-emotional development [5], and mathematics [6]. In mobile age, educational apps have enhanced the quality of parent-child interaction in 36 families with preschool-aged children in the United States. Findings indicated that children took initiative in learning and became more self-reliant and immersive in learning. Moreover, there is not only less negative influence but also more positive impact during the educational apps interactions [7]. Parents who hold a more positive view about digital media encouraged their children under 8 years old to use tablets in playing activities and video watching [8].

1.2   Tablet Learning Impacts on Interest, Emotional Development, Creativity

Tablets as learning tools has been popular in Vietnamese that parents strongly support tablets good for their children in educational achievement. However, scaffolding inquiring is not available for parents and teachers in early childhood education [9]. There is a lack of an individual interactive learning corner for children aged 6–8 years in Thailand [10]. iPads in the early years supported children with 4 and 5 years of age for investigating, reflecting, making meaning, knowledge building, and communicating in Australia [11]. The use of touch-screen tablets enhanced children's knowledge, skills, and attitudes in the early years. Findings indicated that gaming and entertainment apps on the touch-screen tablets dominated rather than the traditional play-based activities in early childhood [12].

2   Research Methods

Therefore, this research was to firstly develop MAKAR database and nine emotional theaters. Each theater individually proposed four ITTS frames for creative thinking, totally 36 interactive games. Secondly, the study intended to establish big data in order to understand children's interest and trigger their learning motivation. Thirdly, this research attempted to explore the factors which will have influence on learning, for instance, increasing learning interest, emotional quotient and the capability of creative solving problems. Research data will be collected by MAKAR database. When children make decisions, system will autonomously record users' messages of manipulation, including the decision they make, using time and frequency. After updating to database to conduct analysis through MAKAR, the learning document of users will be used as foundation for future revision and improvement. This research dedicated to conduct AR application in the kindergarten classroom.

Miffy Multimedia provided a MAKAR editing platform for preschool teachers to develop learning tools. The researcher developed the nine emotional theaters based on *Young Children Emotional Competency Scale (YCECS)* for children aged 4–6 years [13]. Researchers published the YCECS and designed nine emotional theaters with four POIs for scaffolding creative problem solving of ITTS in this study. Children's creativity or emotional was accordingly evaluated [3, 13].

2.1   APP System Frame Development

Child Data Parser Module. This module performs the parsing process for the data returned from Child Database for subsequent actions; such as the text of the question, the name of the scaffolding voice file, the image file name, the video file name, and the AR identification file name, and so on.

Layer Controller Module. This module transforms the different scene layouts according to the instructions sent by the Trigger Event Management module.

Trigger Event Management. This module detects the triggering of all buttons or images to produce the corresponding program action. For example, pressing (clicking) an image triggers the Camera Controller module to perform the scanning operation, and transmits the scanned image to the MAKAR server via the MAKAR SDK to compare whether the same image has AR recognition. The image file, if the comparison is correct, responds to the corresponding AR display content (such as 3D object display), otherwise it will respond to the message "Unrecognized, can't find the corresponding AR content".

MAKAR SDK. This is the SDK tool provided by MAKAR, which is integrated with the system design of this research. It has the relevant links such as link URL, mailbox, community forum, display video and 3D object that can be returned to the corresponding AR identification points (see Fig. 1).

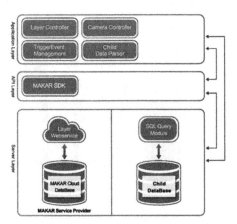

Fig. 1. App architecture

Figure 1 indicates that App design and development is to use the MAKAR platform to interact with the four learning centers (including puzzle center, language center, science center, and play center). When you select the mobile phone's "MAKAR Early Childhood Learning Platform" icon, after loading, enter the home page. Firstly, login basic data when the child scans the POI provided by the project to jump out of the preset content (such as pictures, video, 3D, animation), the system will automatically record the child's answer options, and upload Go to the database built by the project and carry out subsequent analysis. When an experience zone is over, voice prompts will appear and then go to the lower zone to search for treasure. Once all POIs have been scanned, an animation will prompt all treasure hunt activities to end.

2.2 Manipulating Procedure of APP

To construct experimental and reference groups, the researcher developed nine storyboards according to YCECS. For instance, in play center, the researcher designed four POIs of creative thinking teaching and learning through ITTS (see Fig. 2, 3, 4, 5 and 6).

Fig. 2. Traditional teaching (Reference group)

Fig. 3. MAKAR teaching (experimental group)

Fig. 4. MAKAR theater

Fig. 5. One of 4 POIs

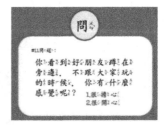

Fig. 6. One of ITTS

3 Results

3.1 Development of MAKAR Database and Nine Emotional Theaters

This research made use of augmented reality edition platform. After understanding teachers' experience evaluation of using MAKAR platform, compiling questionnaire, and applying Structured Equation Model, called SEM, we finally complete factor analysis and establish validity.

3.2 Establishing Big Data in Order to Understand Children's Interest and Trigger Their Learning Motivation

This research explored relative preschool academic research in Taiwan, and found there was no database in the past and didn't apply big data analysis into children's learning need and teachers' teaching adjustment. Big data is the terminology that refers traditional data processing application was not enough to handle their big or complicated data. It can also be identified as numerous unstructured or structured data from lots of different resources. From academic aspect, the appearance of big data promotes new researches of various topics. Due to the progress of recent technology, the convenience of publishing new data and the request towards high transparence from the majority of government around the world, big data becomes more and more prominent among current research. Consequently, this research also applied big data to analyze children's learning need and let teachers adjust their teaching method conveniently.

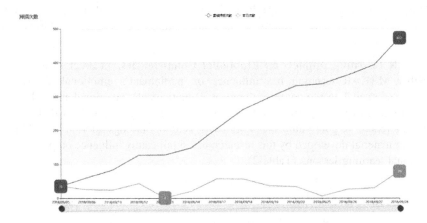

Fig. 7. Scanning frequency analysis by MAKAR (Color figure online)

Figure 7 indicted that the green line graph represents the cumulative number of times the tablet is used up to 9/5. The cumulative number of uses of the tablet to 9/28 is 472. The purple line chart represents the number of times the tablet was used on the 9/28 day.

3.3 Exploring the Factors Which Will Have Influence on Learning

Emotional quotient and the capability of creative solving problems are two dependent variables of this study. This study explores whether experimental treatment of MAKAR enhances children's interest in learning. The learning content includes emotional ability and creative thinking. Learning impacts of MAKAR includes learning interests, emotional ability, and creativity.

MAKAR Learning Impacts on Interest. MAKAR Teaching can cultivate children's learning interest. In order to understand whether MAKAR has impact on children's learning interest, this research conducted average difference test (t-test) towards children's preference level by comparing traditional teaching theater with MAKAR teaching theater. The result is as Table 1.

Table 1. T-test on traditional and MAKAR teaching

Group	Unit	Mean	SD	t	Sig.
Traditional teaching	9	11.8889	3.21887	−3.686	.002
MAKAR teaching	9	17.6667	3.42783	−3.686	.002

Table 1 reveals that the average of these two groups are discrepant (11.8889 and 17.6667). The latter is significantly higher. Children have higher interest towards MAKAR teaching. T-test results a significant difference between traditional and MAKAR teaching.

MAKAR Learning Impacts on Emotional Competencies. In order to understand whether MAKAR teaching has influence on participant's emotional ability, this research adopted T-test to compare the mean of participant's emotional ability between pre-test and post-test experiments. Calculated by paired variant, and divided by standard difference, we got t-value and significance is .000. Findings referred that MAKAR teaching material developed by this research has significantly influence on participant's emotional learning lessons (Table 2).

Table 2. Emotional competencies scores between Pre-test and Post-test

Paired	No.	Mean	SD	t	Sig.
Pre-test	30	36.0000	5.40753	−7.609	.000
Post-test	30	43.9333	1.59597		

The difference between the average scores of the 30 children's emotional ability pretest scores and the post-test emotional ability scores was tested. The results were extremely significant (***p < .000).

Figure 8 indicates that MAKAR teaching in experimental group benefits participants' emotional learning effectiveness. Reliability analysis is used to evaluate the reliable level of whole scale. The reliable evaluation of this research is aimed the questionnaire content of pre-test and post-test database to conduct Cronbach's Alpha test. The reliability is estimated as Table 3.

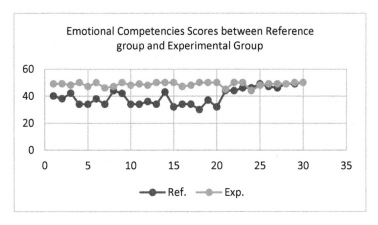

Fig. 8. Emotional competencies scores between reference group and experimental group

Table 3. Reliability analysis

Reliable statistics		
Cronbach's Alpha value	Cronbach's Alpha value that treat standard project as norm	The number of project
.747	.710	30

Table 3 indicates that Cronbach's α is .747. Thirty children have 74.7% consistency towards the whole reliable analysis.

MAKAR Learning Impacts on Creativity. Creativity comprises fluency, flexibility, elaborateness, uniqueness, and imagination [(see Fig. 9). In order to understand whether there is significant difference between traditional teaching and MAKAR teaching towards students' creative ability for solving problems. T-test was applied to compare the mean of participant's creative thinking ability between pre-test and post-test experiments.

Figure 9 indicates that four components of creativity scores distribution in MAKAR teaching. MAKAR is most helpful for the elaborative performance of young children. Secondly, the order is flexibility, fluency, and uniqueness.

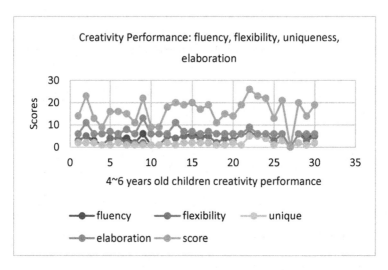

Fig. 9. Creativity performance: fluency, flexibility, uniqueness, elaboration

Table 4 reveals that the average between these two (15.9333 and 16.5333) have difference. Using MAKAR has higher average towards creative ability for solving problems. Calculated by paired variant, and divided by standard difference, we got t-value and significance is .000. Findings referred that MAKAR teaching material developed by this research has significantly influence on participant's creative ability. Results of t-test calculated by paired variant, and divided by standard difference, we got t-value and significance is .000. Findings referred that MAKAR teaching material developed by this research has significantly influence on participant's creative ability.

Table 4. MAKAR teaching impacts on creativity

	No.	Average	Standard deviation	Standard error of average
Paired t-test	15	15.9333	6.25033	1.61383
	15	16.5333	4.76395	1.23005

4 Discussions

The outcome displayed that MAKAR for improving children's emotional capability is p = .000 which means extreme importance. The integral reliability of Cronbach Alpha value is 7.47. The learning outcome of experimental group also reach high significance (p = .002). What's more, this research declared that making use of Vuforia AR can efficiently increase students' learning experience and understanding towards complicated problems. In another research, it also mentions the advantages of AR as below, for example, when participants learnt the concept of computer easily from immediate feedback of AR maze game, they got confidence and interest. AR tool has low cost, intuitive and portable [14]. In this research, it also supports to combine real objects with AR teaching [15]. This will assist participants to understand complicated concept a lot. According to literature [16], the following factors affected children's learning such as child-centered learning, creative thinking inquiring skills. Therefore, this research also conducted detailed record in the database of children's learning development in order to understand if the identity of children will have impact on their learning.

The relative research indicates that complicated virtual 3D can help students to understand the concept since sometimes it's hard to make children understand the content only by vision [17]. Therefore, we assume that using MAKAR to conduct 3D teaching will make children more easily understand the content teacher wants to deliver. Besides, this research displayed that this kind of reading will be more attractive and interesting compared with 2D animation, especially for children. AR interactive teaching method enhances children's learning. In this learning processing, children can choose to learn by themselves or to work with their fellow in a cooperative learning environment; furthermore, to provide students scientific research and curiosity of solving problems. The application of MAKAR revealed that this multimedia and interactive digital learning platform will motivate students' learning. In the process of learning, children will gain practical experience, so it may be impossible for children to forget what they learn. According to the feedback of experiment, most of children prefer this kind of learning, especially the process of practical manipulation. This will make them have chance to try different things. On the other hand, in the aspect of course design, teachers can integrate this interactive learning platform in time, for-mulate learning activity of each course, broaden the breadth of learning contents, diversify learning material, strengthen interactive activity of course, and finally increase the efficiency of whole teaching. The MAKAR research found that there will be better learning efficiency by applying ITTS. Children prefer MAKAR teaching method rather than traditional teaching form. Besides, MAKAR teaching method has higher trigger for learning interests, creativity and emotional expression.

In teaching practice, we found that AR interaction and multimedia contents can attract children to learn quickly. The outcome of this research has positive relation with the theory of ITTS. Multimedia can more easily provoke children's learning interest, compared with traditional teaching. Even for the children who never use MAKAR, they can still gain the positive feedback and use this application by themselves with the help of virtual teachers [18]. Besides, multimedia contents surpass traditional teaching which means multimedia is more attractive for children. Virtual environment integrates with reality will be more attractive for children to motivate their learning interest, and facilitate availability of quick-learning process. The research also found that when virtual environment integrates with reality, it will be more attractive for children to motivate children's learning interest, and facilitate availability of quick-learning pro-cess [19]. Consequently, we assumed that the real nine emotional teaching theaters in interactive platform can motivate children to have more learning interest and be willing to learn. Clicks and mortar can higher children's learning motivation and help them to learn interestingly.

References

1. Hou, S.M., Liu, Y.Y., Tang, Q.B., Guo, X.G.: Mobile augmented reality system for preschool education. In: 2017 International Conference on Virtual Reality and Visualization (ICVRV), pp. 321–323. IEEE, Hong Kong (2017)
2. Antonia, D., Evgenia, R.: Artful thinking and augmented reality in kindergarten: technology contributions to the inclusion of socially underprivileged children in creative activities. In: Proceedings of the 8th International Conference on Software Development and Technologies for Enhancing Accessibility and Fighting Info-exclusion, pp. 187–194. ACM, Greece (2018)
3. Kyung, H.K.: Can we trust creativity tests? a review of the torrance tests of creative thinking (TTCT). Creativity Res. J. 18(1), 3–14. https://doi.org/10.1207/s15326934crj1801_2
4. Lee, L.K., et al.: Improving the experience of teaching and learning kindergarten-level English vocabulary using augmented reality. Int. J. Innov. Learn. **25**(2), 110–125 (2019)
5. Preka, G., Rangoussi, M.: Augmented reality and QR codes for teaching music to preschoolers and kindergarteners: Educational intervention and evaluation. In: Proceedings of the 11th International Conference on Computer Supported Education, pp. 113–123. SciTePress, Greece (2019)
6. Zaranis, N., Alexandraki, F.: Comparing the effectiveness of using tablet computers for teaching division to kindergarten students. In: Tsitouridou, M., A. Diniz, J., Mikropoulos, Tassos A. (eds.) TECH-EDU 2018. CCIS, vol. 993, pp. 280–295. Springer, Cham (2019). https://doi.org/10.1007/978-3-030-20954-4_21
7. Blumberg, F.C., et al.: Digital games as a context for children's cognitive development: Research recommendations and policy considerations. Soc. Policy Rep. **32**(1), 1–33 (2019)
8. Brito, R., Dias, P.: Technologies and children up to 8 years old: what changes in one year? Observatorio (OBS*), 13(2) (2019). https://doi.org/10.15847/obsOBS13220191366
9. Pham, B., Lim, S.S.: Vietnamese pre-schoolers' tablet use and early childhood learning: an ecological investigation. J. Child. Media **13**(3), 241–259 (2019). https://doi.org/10.1080/17482798.2019.1613247
10. Jintapitak, M., Chakpitak, N., Sureepong, P., Chaipravat, O.: Constructionism for language immersion: a case study of Thai education development. Adv. Sci. Lett. **23**(2), 735–738 (2017). https://doi.org/10.1166/asl.2017.7456
11. Yelland, N., Gilbert, C.: Transformative technologies and play in the early years: using tablets for new learning. Global Stud. Child. **8**(2), 152–161 (2018)
12. Oliemat, E., Ihmeideh, F., Alkhawaldeh, M.: The use of touch-screen tablets in early childhood: Children's knowledge, skills, and attitudes towards tablet technology. Child Youth Serv. Rev. **88**, 591–597 (2018)
13. Wei, W.J.: Emotional Competencies Assessment for Young Children. Psychological Publisher, Taipei (2011). http://www.psy.com.tw/ec99/ushop20128/GoodsDescr.asp?category_id=123&parent_id=118&prod_id=87320. Accessed 11 July 2019
14. Yip, J., Wong, S.H., Yick, K.L., Chan, K., Wong, K.H.: Improving quality of teaching and learning in classes by using augmented reality video. Comput. Educ. **128**, 88–101 (2019). https://doi.org/10.1016/j.compedu.2018.09.014
15. Jin, Q., Wang, D., Deng, X., Zheng, N., Chiu, S.: AR-maze: a tangible programming tool for children based on AR technology. In: Proceedings of the 17th ACM Conference on Interaction Design and Children IDC 2018, pp. 611–616. Trondheim, Norway (2018). https://doi.org/10.1145/3202185.3210784

16. Fan, M., Baishya, U., McLaren, E.S., Antle, A.N., Sarker, S., Vincent, A.: Block talks: a tangible and augmented reality toolkit for children to learn sentence construction. In: Extended Abstracts of the 2018 CHI Conference on Human Factors in Computing Systems CHI 2018, Paper No. LBW056. Montreal QC, Canada (2018). https://doi.org/10.1145/3170427.3188576

17. Chang, R.C.: A novel AR-based interactive E-learning platform. Adv. Mater. Res. **403–408**, 1244–1248 (2011). https://doi.org/10.4028/www.scientific.net/AMR.403-408.1244

18. Martínez, H., Hoyo, R.D., Sanagustín, L.M., Hupont, I., Abadía, D.: Augmented Reality Based Intelligent Interactive e-Learning Platform. In: Joaquim, F., Ana, F. (eds.) Proceedings of the 3rd International Conference on Agents and Artificial Intelligence ICAART 2011, vol. 1, pp. 343–348, Rome, Italy (2011). https://doi.org/10.5220/0003181503430348

19. Martínez, H., Abadía, D., Sanagustín, L.M., Hupont, I., Hoyo, R.D.: A novel tutor-guided platform for interactive augmented reality learning. In: Verbraeck, A., Helfert, M., Cordeiro, J., Shishkov, B. (eds.) Proceedings of the 3rd International Conference on Computer Supported Education CSEDU 2011, vol. 1, pp. 88–93. Noordwijkerhout, Netherlands (2011). https://doi.org/10.5220/0003337600880093

A Pilot Study of the Effects of Instructional Design with Learning Analytics on a Computer Simulation-Based Learning Environment

Yuling Hsu[1] and Sheng-Kuei Hsu[2]

[1] Tzu Chi University, Hualien, Taiwan
[2] Zhaoqing University, Zhaoqing, China
skhsu@foxmail.com

Abstract. With this study, we aim to explore the learning analytics framework that was based on the learning theory and combine data mining approaches. It is expected to explore the spontaneous learning behavior and cognitive process of the concept of geometric area during the learning process and present interesting results. This pilot study recruited 160 11-year-old children in Grade 5 of elementary schools in urban and rural areas of Taiwan. The simulation-based environment embedded four instructional designs to support students learning geometric area, which we named the simulation-based assist area concept learning environment (SAACLE). According to the statistical analyses, we found the pilot results showed that the indigenous children seemed to outperform the nonindigenous children in highly directed learning environments; in contrast, the urban children outperformed the indigenous children in learning environments with little direction. Interestingly, such a performance did not exist during the learning processes, and the indigenous and nonindigenous children demonstrated different learning patterns in retention- and transfer-level posttests. Furthermore, we explored the learning analytics framework to analyze the leaning process log file and clarify the learning patterns of children with different sociocultural backgrounds.

Keywords: Educational data mining · Learning analytics · Simulation-based learning

1 Introduction

1.1 Computer Simulation-Based Learning and Learning Analytics

Simulation has been lauded for its ability to embed dynamically linked multiple representations in a manipulative interface to be explored, to provide real-time feedback, characterized as flexible time in one self-study, and to be repeated. Its powerful functions allow students to observe the linkage between variables and develop their own hypotheses, and it also provides a rich environment for eliminating distractions and constraining learning to relevant evidence. According to statistical-based analyses, numerous empirical studies have demonstrated that computer simulation has significant potential as a supplementary tool for effective conceptual change learning based on the

© Springer Nature Singapore Pte Ltd. 2020
J. Shen et al. (Eds.): IC3 2019, CCIS 1227, pp. 284–289, 2020.
https://doi.org/10.1007/978-981-15-6113-9_32

integration of technology and appropriate instructional strategies [3]. Moreover, by way of bringing students to spontaneously engage in the use of the personal construct knowledge of mental ability, simulation-based learning environments had been considered the best aids for supporting discovery-based learning and active learning [11, 18]. However, work focusing on the changes that occurred in the learning processes to drive performance is still quite rare.

Fruitful learning analytics will offer specific feature extraction and data pattern identification to increase our knowledge of learning processes; learning analytics are intended to help administrators, teachers and students improve learning [13, 21]. Past studies of learners' learning processes and performance mostly used statistical analysis methods and expert decision-making models to judge learning outcomes. However, in the field of educational data mining [1, 6, 16, 17, 19], data-driven analysis strategies can be used to explore the variety and richness of learning processes and thus a deeper understanding of learning process behavior.

1.2 Exploring the Learning Science Framework to Analyze Learning Processes

Learners' learning trajectory in a computer-based simulation environment is quite rich, and it is worthwhile to develop a data-driven analysis strategy to further understand learners' learning styles. In order to further explore students' learning behaviors in experimental conditions, we examined the log files generated by the experimental environment (i.e., SAACLE). The log file recorded in SAACLE included artifacts of tactics and strategies in a log of fine-grained, temporally identified data that can advance our study about how learners go about learning [2, 10, 20].

Data-Driven Approach. According to Witten et al., data mining is a program-oriented approach that extracts unknown, useful, and understandable knowledge from a large and heterogeneous source. The basic tools that would be used in this study included the following: (1) *Association analysis* aims to discover the regularity between two or more variables. Generally, the two thresholds of support degree and credibility are used to measure the correlation of association rules. (2) *Clustering* is the classification of data into several categories based on the similarity of certain eigenvalues. Cluster analysis can establish macro concepts and discover patterns of data distribution and the relationships between possible data attributes. (3) *Classification* refers to finding a conceptual description of a category and using this description to construct a classification model. It is often expressed in a regular way or in a decision-tree mode. Classification is the use of a training data set to obtain classification rules or patterns with a certain algorithm and then use this rule or pattern for subsequent classifications or predictions. (4) *Prediction* means to find the law of change and establish a model of historical data identification and then predict future data with this model. (5) *Time-series pattern* refers to a pattern with a high probability of recurrence occurring in a time series search. Like regression analysis, it uses past data to predict future values [21].

However, with purely data-driven analysis, if it lacks the basis of learning theory or fails to clarify the goals of instructional design, it is easy to produce results that are useless for pedagogy and will ultimately erode the effectiveness of learning analytics

[7, 8]. Moreover, most learning systems currently used in the field of educational data mining, such as the e-learning system, usually analyze the unit of learning behavior with page through of the framework in a web page. The unit of computer simulation learning system exploration is a learning action (a student action on the simulation platform, such as selecting a tool or setting a parameter) that is more capable of performing sophisticated learning behavior mining than the former. Thus, for finding a better analytical framework, we have considered not only the data-driven approach but also the theoretical-driven approach.

Theoretical-Driven Approach: CTML and ICAP. According to *Cognitive Theory of Multimedia Learning* (CTML) [14], the theoretical-driven approach was developed from human cognitive architecture and informs guidance design in computer-based simulation learning environments. It proposes that computer-based simulation learning is an active process of meaning-making, and these knowledge constructions occur within the constraints of the limited resources of learners' working memories; knowledge construction needs several types of sequential processes, such as selecting relevant words/images for processing, organizing the selected verbal/visual information into a mental model, and/or integrating verbal/visual representations and learner-relevant prior knowledge systems [14]. In this study, CTML was used to explain cognitive activities such as selecting, organizing and integrating the learning processes and in the learning analytics framework, to provide a theoretical basis for explaining the implicit cognitive activities.

Furthermore, the Interactive, Constructive, Active and Passive framework (ICAP) [4, 5] defines cognitive engagement activities on the basis of students' overt behaviors and proposes that engagement behaviors can be categorized and differentiated into one of four modes: interactive, constructive, active or passive. The ICAP hypothesis predicts that as students become more engaged with the learning materials, from passive to active to constructive to interactive, their learning will increase. For learning in a simulation-based environment, the role of the teacher is often moved to an assistive position. Therefore, the learners' ability to learn independently and their degree and manner of cognitive engagement will become the main factors affecting learning outcomes. Because ICAP focuses on the amount of cognitive engagement that can be detected by smaller grained behavioral activities while students learn, this study incorporates the ICAP into the theoretical basis for investigating the indicators to analyze behavior during the learning process.

2   Method

This pilot study aims to explore the learning science framework to analyze the log file that was generated in a computer-based simulation environment. The environment was set up by the authors' team to assist students in learning concepts involving geometric area; namely, the SAACLE embedded four instructional designs to support students learning geometric area. The participants consisted of 160 11-year-old children (97 boys and 63 girls; 80 nonindigenous and 80 indigenous) who were Grade 5 students recruited from elementary schools in urban and rural areas of Taiwan.

3   Pilot Study Results and Learning Analytics Framework

3.1   Pilot Study Results

According to the statistical analyses, we found there were statistically significant differences in the pretest between the indigenous and nonindigenous group. In addition, the results showed that the indigenous children seemed to outperform the nonindigenous children in highly directed learning environments; in contrast, the urban children outperformed the indigenous children in learning environments with little direction. Interestingly, such a performance did not exist during the learning processes, and the indigenous and nonindigenous children demonstrated different learning patterns in retention- and transfer-level posttests.

3.2   Learning Analytics Framework

After the statistical analyses, we would like to find more clues from educational data mining to strengthen our theoretical deduction and further clarify the learning styles and learning patterns of minority students (indigenous students). Figure 1 shows the learning analytics framework.

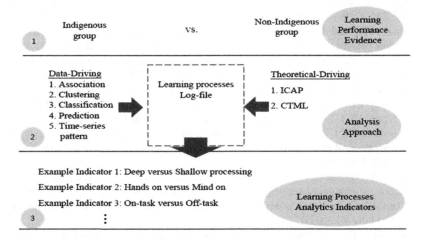

Fig. 1. Framework of learning analytics for learning processes log file

Therefore, for the data analysis of this study, in addition to using the existing analysis strategy (statistical analysis and expert decision-making), we also used a data-based approach to explore learners' learning processes on the geometric area concept in a computer simulation environment. As follow-up, the level of learning behavior interpretation will be compared with the opinions of domain experts. It is expected to mimic the spontaneous learning behavior and cognitive process of the concept of geometric area and present interesting results [9, 12, 15].

References

1. Angeli, C., Howard, S.K., Ma, J., Yang, J., Kirschner, P.A.: Data mining in educational technology classroom research: can it make a contribution? Comput. Educ. **113**, 226–242 (2017)
2. Azevedo, R.: Understanding the complex nature of self-regulatory processes in learning with computer-based learning environments: an introduction. Metacognition Learn. **2**, 57–65 (2007)
3. Chen, Y.L., Pan, P.R., Sung, Y.T., Chang, K.E.: Correcting misconceptions on electronics: effects of a simulation-based learning environment backed by a conceptual change model. Educ. Technol. Soc. **16**(2), 212–227 (2013)
4. Chi, M.T., Wylie, R.: The ICAP framework: linking cognitive engagement to active learning outcomes. Educ. Psychol. **49**(4), 219–243 (2014)
5. Chi, M.T., et al.: Translating the ICAP theory of cognitive engagement into practice. Cogn. Sci. **42**(6), 1777–1832 (2018)
6. De Jong, T., Van Joolingen, W.R.: Scientific discovery learning with computer simulations of conceptual domains. Rev. Educ. Res. **68**(2), 179–201 (1998)
7. Gašević, D., Kovanović, V., Joksimović, S.: Piecing the learning analytics puzzle: a consolidated model of a field of research and practice. Learn. Res. Pract. **3**(1), 63–78 (2017)
8. Gašević, D., Mirriahi, N., Dawson, S., Joksimović, S.: Effects of instructional conditions and experience on the adoption of a learning tool. Comput. Hum. Behav. **67**, 207–220 (2017)
9. Geng, L., Hamilton, H.J.: Interestingness measures for data mining: a survey. ACM Comput. Surv. (CSUR) **38**(3), 9 (2006)
10. Hadwin, A.F., Nesbit, J.C., Jamieson-Noel, D., Code, J., Winne, P.H.: Examining trace data to explore self-regulated learning. Metacognition Learn. **2**, 107–124 (2007)
11. Landriscina, F.: Simulation and Learning: A Model-Centered Approach. Springer, New York (2013). https://doi.org/10.1007/978-1-4614-1954-9
12. Mahzoon, M.J., Maher, M.L., Eltayeby, O., Dou, W., Grace, K.: A framework for interactive exploratory learning analytics. In: Zaphiris, P., Ioannou, A. (eds.) LCT 2018. LNCS, vol. 10925, pp. 319–331. Springer, Cham (2018). https://doi.org/10.1007/978-3-319-91152-6_25
13. Mangaroska, K., Giannakos, M.N.: Learning analytics for learning design: A systematic literature review of analytics-driven design to enhance learning. IEEE Trans. Learn. Technol. **12**(4), 518–531 (2018)
14. Mayer, R.E.: Cognitive theory of multimedia learning. In: Mayer, R.E. (ed.) The Cambridge handbook of multimedia learning, pp. 43–71. Cambridge University, New York (2014)
15. McGarry, K.: A survey of interestingness measures for knowledge discovery. Knowl. Eng. Rev. **20**(1), 39–61 (2005)
16. Papamitsiou, Z., Economides, A.A.: Learning analytics and educational data mining in practice: a systematic literature review of empirical evidence. J. Educ. Technol. Soc. **17**(4), 49–64 (2014)
17. Rodrigues, M.W., Isotani, S., Zarate, L.E.: Educational data mining: a review of evaluation process in the e-learning. Telematics Inform. **35**(6), 1701–1717 (2018)
18. Rutten, N., van Joolingen, W.R., van der Veen, J.T.: The learning effects of computer simulations in science education. Comput. Educ. **58**(1), 136–153 (2012)

19. Slater, S., Joksimović, S., Kovanovic, V., Baker, R.S., Gasevic, D.: Tools for educational data mining: a review. J. Educ. Behav. Stat. **42**(1), 85–106 (2017)
20. Veenman, M.V.J.: The assessment and instruction of self-regulation in computer-based environments: a discussion. Metacognition Learn. **2**, 177–183 (2007)
21. Winne, P.H.: Leveraging big data to help each learner upgrade learning and accelerate learning science. Teachers Coll. Rec. **119**(3), 1–24 (2017)

What Kind of Educational Technical Ability Are Chinese Normal University Students Cultivating? – Based on the Analysis of Educational Technology Teaching Materials

Jin Cai[✉] and Wen-Tao Wu

College of Education Science, Anhui Normal University, Wuhu, Anhui, China
1105215933@qq.com

Abstract. With the advent of the education information 2.0 era and the development of teacher professionalism, more attention has been paid to the development of teachers' educational technical ability. The public course of educational technology in normal colleges and universities is responsible for the pre-service training of students' educational technical ability. This paper analyzes the textbooks used in the public courses of educational technology in ten normal universities, trying to answer the question "what kind of educational technology are normal university students learning?

Keywords: Educational technology · Teaching material construction · Text analysis

1 Background

In recent years, with the release of a series of national documents promoting the development of educational informatization, such as the 13th five-year plan for educational informatization, the cause of educational informatization in China has achieved unprecedented rapid development. New goals are also proposed in the document "key points of work on education informatization and network security in 2019" just released by the general office of the ministry of education: "launch the Internet +teacher education innovation action, and issue the opinions on implementing the 2.0 project of improving the information technology application ability of primary and secondary school teachers nationwide". Therefore, the public courses of educational technology offered by teachers' colleges and universities, which are responsible for the pre-service training of teachers' educational technology ability, are particularly important. No matter in the process of teaching or learning, the importance of textbooks as carriers of knowledge is self-evident. At the same time, the quality of textbook compilation is also one of the key factors affecting the quality of education and teaching ability cultivation.

J. Shen et al. (Eds.): IC3 2019, CCIS 1227, pp. 290–296, 2020.
https://doi.org/10.1007/978-981-15-6113-9_33

2 Source of Textbooks for Public Courses of Educational Technology

As the material carrier of learning content, textbook is the medium for students to acquire knowledge and teachers to impart knowledge. Therefore, we choose to carry on the thorough analysis from this aspect, carries on the comparative research to the teaching material. Has certain representativeness in order to make the sample material, we according to AiRuishen research institute of China alumni association network published in May 2018 of the 2018 Chinese university evaluation report - the Chinese college entrance examination to college guidance (association) of China normal university in 2018 in the ranking AiRuishen research institute of China alumni association network is recognised by the social from all walks of life, has the good credibility of China university of third-party evaluation consultation institutions), selected the top 10 normal school, one of the source of the material basis as a sample. The specific composition of the sample textbook is shown in Table 1.'

Table 1. Selection of teaching materials for public courses of educational technology in ten normal universities.

Number	School	Textbook Title	Edition	Chief editor	Press
1	Beijing normal university	Modern educational technology	Edition 1, 2005	Zheng-chao Li	Beijing normal university press
2	East China normal university	Educational technology	Edition 1, 2011	Wei-jie Wang	Renmin university of China press
3	Northeast normal university	Modern educational technology	Edition 2, 2012	Xiao-hui Chen	Beijing university of posts and telecommunications press
4	Central China normal university	Modern educational technology	Edition 1, 2005	Jiu-ning Yang	Central China normal university press
5	Nanjing normal university	Modern educational technology	Edition 1, 2003	Hong-quan Bai	Higher education press
6	Hunan normal university	Application of modern educational technology	Edition 1, 2013	Shao-dong Peng	Higher education press
7	South China normal University	Application of modern educational technology	Edition 1, 2016	Qing-chao Ke	Higher education press
8	Shanxi normal university	Modern educational technology	Edition 3, 2009	Shan-gang Peng	Shanxi normal university press
9	Capital normal university	Application of modern educational technology	Edition 1, 2015	Lu Wang	Higher education press
10	Fujian normal university	Modern educational technology	Edition 1, 2007	Yu-xing Huang	Fujian education press

3   What Kind of Appearance Does Current Education Technology Learn Public Course Teaching Material to Present

3.1   How Many Different: Analysis of the Chapter Arrangement of the Textbook

Table 2. Sample arrangement of the sample.

Number	Chapter number (module)	Section number	Total words (ten thousand)	Average word count per segment (ten thousand)
1	9	37	40.4	1.09
2	12	42	32.1	0.76
3	7	21	32.9	1.57
4	6	16	38	2.38
5	7	21	41.3	1.97
6	12	56	69	1.23
7	6	24	31	1.29
8	12	49	34.8	0.71
9	12	60	38	0.63
10	8	28	43.7	1.56

Through comparative analysis of Table 2, it can be seen that:

a. The number of chapters (modules) of the ten textbooks is quite different. The maximum number of chapters is 12, and the minimum is 6, with a difference of 6 chapters. The average number of chapters is 9.1, and the standard deviation is 2.51.

b. The number of sections in the ten textbooks varies greatly. The maximum number of sections was 60, and the minimum was 21, with a difference of 39 sections. The average number of sections was 35.4, and the standard deviation was 14.77.

c. The total number of words in the book varies greatly. The maximum number of words was 690,000, and the minimum was 310,000, with a difference of 380,000 words. The average total number of words was 40.12, and the standard deviation was 10.39.

d. The average number of words in a single section varies greatly. The average number of words was the highest (28,800 words) and the lowest (6,300 words), with a difference of 17,500 words. The average number of words in a single section was 1.32 and the standard deviation was 0.54.

3.2   Disorganized: Thematic Analysis of Textbooks

Compared with the chapter and the word arrangement, the subject matter of the textbook is the core module of the textbook. We conducted a classified statistical analysis of the topics of the catalogues of 10 sample textbooks. The 10 textbooks generally cover 38 topics, and the number of topics in each textbook design varies. The specific results are shown in Fig. 1.

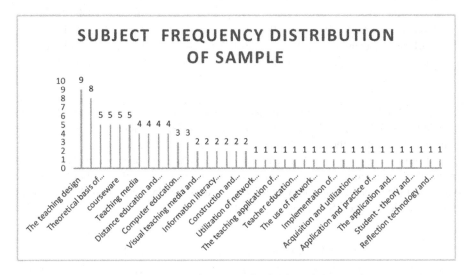

Fig. 1. The subject frequency distribution of the sample.

The specific distribution of the topics covered in the ten sample textbooks is as follows: a. The frequency of the introduction of modern educational technology and instructional design is more than 8, indicating that most of the textbooks cover these two topics; b. modern The four themes of educational technology theory, learning and teaching environment, courseware production, and multimedia technology appear at a frequency of 5, indicating that half of the textbooks cover this topic; c. four of the remaining 32 topics. The frequency of the theme is 4, the theme of the 2 is 3, the frequency of the 6 themes is 2, and the frequency of the remaining topics is 1, and the number of occurrences is small.

In addition, the confusion of the concept of education proposition has always been a question worth exploring. It is a common phenomenon for writers to differ in the expression of concepts from different perspectives and positions, but the accuracy and unity of conceptual expressions should be taken seriously.

3.3 Neglected in Practice: Analysis of Module Settings for Textbooks

The setting of materials and cases in the textbook is conducive to expanding the students' thinking space and helping students to better understand theoretical knowledge. We chose "Introduction to Modern Educational Technology (Educational Technology)", "Theory of Modern Educational Technology", "Learning and Teaching Environment". Form the four topics with high frequency of "teaching design" and "teaching design" are the research objects. The specific analysis results are shown in Table 3.

Table 3. Expanding statistics on materials and case settings.

	1	2	3	4	5	6	7	8	9	10	Total
Generality	0–0	0–0	0–0	/	0–0	0–4	1–5	0–0	1–1	0–0	2–10
Theoretical basis	0–0	0–0	/	/	/	0–4	/	0–0	/	0–0	0–4
Teaching design	0–0	0–0	0–0	3–3	2–3	5–0	2–4	0–0	2–0	/	14–10
Teaching environment	/	/	/	4–4	2–0	4–0	2–4	0–2	/	/	12–10
Total	0–0	0–0	0–0	7–7	4–3	9–8	5–13	0–2	3–1	0–0	23–34

After-school exercises are designed to consolidate the learning of classroom knowledge, and it is a good test of the learning outcomes of students. In the process of statistics, we divided the after-school exercises of 10 sample textbooks into the following four categories: brief discussion, data collection, operational design, and practical investigation. Due to the different module settings of the textbook, here we only select the after-school exercises after the end of the classroom knowledge content as the statistical object. See Table 4 for details.

Table 4. Distribution of exercises in the textbook.

Question types	1	2	3	4	5	6	7	8	9	10	The total number of problem sets	Each mean
Brief discussion	38	51	47	27	17	62	23	48	44	50	407	40.7
data collection	0	3	0	0	2	0	0	2	0	0	7	0.7
Operational design	16	2	2	2	22	10	6	7	4	14	85	8.5
Practice survey	0	0	0	1	0	0	6	10	1	0	18	1.8
Total number of exercises	54	56	49	30	41	72	35	67	49	64	517	51.7
Mean number per chapter	6	4.67	7	5	5.86	6	5.83	5.83	4.08	8	58	5.8

4 Neglect of Practice: Analysis of the Module Setting of Teaching Materials

4.1 The Teaching Material Localization Is not Clear, the Knowledge System Is Different

Due to the unclear training objectives of the public courses of educational technology, the editors have different understandings of the positioning of the textbooks, which leads to the great differences in the knowledge structure system of the current public courses of educational technology. The existence of such problems as wrong positioning and vagueness of teaching materials disconnects the teaching materials from the teaching requirements and results in the dislocation of teaching objectives and teaching contents, which not only affects the transmission of advanced educational concepts, but also easily affects the realization of talent training objectives.

4.2 The Subject Content Is not Unified and the Concept of Proposition Is Confused

There are some problems in most textbooks, such as disunity of subject and content and confusion of propositional concepts.

The disunity of subject and content is firstly reflected in the lack of a unified outline or standard stipulated by the state or an authoritative textbook. Although in recent years, the ministry of education has issued a series of documents to improve the information technology ability of primary and secondary school teachers, there are still some textbooks written by different writers based on different positions and understandings. The confusion of propositional concepts in pedagogy has always been a problem worth exploring. The phenomenon that the concept difference is too large is not only bad for students to master the knowledge ability, but also bad for the application in the future education and teaching.

4.3 The Module Setting Is Unreasonable and the Practice Performance Is Poor

Based on the above analysis of the expansion materials, case Settings and exercises, we can see that the textbooks are generally short of case Settings and reading materials. The writing of exercises after class is mainly based on theoretical defense, and students are short of hands-on practice modules. As a course closely related to information technology, the textbook pays too much attention to the explanation of theoretical knowledge, and most of the textbooks only stay at the level of paper-based text textbooks. At the same time, there is a strange phenomenon that there is only theory in the teaching content and no experimental design. As a bridge between educational theory and educational practice, educational technology is a subject with strong practicality and operability [1]. However, the lack of experimental courses is a common problem in the public courses of educational technology offered by colleges and universities.

5 Possible Recommendations in Textbook Preparation

5.1 Make Clear Teaching Material Fixed Position, Build Reasonable Knowledge System

Teaching material orientation is the primary work of teaching material construction [2]. While pursuing innovation, school textbooks should not violate the basic subject knowledge structure. On the basis of making clear the positioning and compilation intention of textbooks, school textbooks should follow a unified curriculum standard and take this as the benchmark to compile textbooks and build a reasonable knowledge system.

In 2014, the ministry of education of the People's Republic of China studied and formulated the information technology application ability standard for primary and secondary school teachers (trial). Based on this, textbook writers can select valuable knowledge for arrangement and integration, build a reasonable knowledge structure system, and improve the content of textbook knowledge.

5.2　Optimize Integration Modules and Add Adjustment Practice Items

The most important role of the public course of educational technology should be to contribute to the professional development of primary and secondary school teachers. Cases can be constructed based on the actual teaching situation of primary and secondary school education, and the expanded materials can be enriched to not only directly respond to educational problems, but also have practical value, which is conducive to helping students better deal with practical problems in future teaching practice.

Secondly, moderately increase experimental design projects. Compared with theoretical courses, most students are more enthusiastic about experimental courses. We can take this factor into consideration when compiling textbooks, and reasonably arrange the theoretical knowledge learning and experimental design projects in a certain proportion.

5.3　Compile Supporting Materials to Enrich Network Learning Resources

We should develop more online multimedia teaching resources and online learning platforms on the basis of paper textbooks, and combine paper textbooks, multimedia resources and online courses to build a good learning ecosystem, with classroom learning as the main part and after-class learning as the supplement [3].

At the same time, the three-dimensional teaching material construction will be the future teaching material construction key point, will make up the traditional classroom the insufficiency and the printing teaching material will form the good complementary. Teachers can also share some of the latest application results or some excellent courseware in today's educational technology field in multimedia teaching resources, which can provide more effective help for students in learning, and can also improve students' learning initiative and interest.

References

1. He, K.: Education Technology, 2nd edn. Beijing Normal University Press, Beijing (2009)
2. Quan, L.: Thoughts on the positioning of textbooks. Sci. Technol. Publ. **10**, 13–15 (2011)
3. Zhang, J., Peng, Y.: Construction and reflection of three-dimensional textbooks in universities in the post-MOOC era. Educ. Rev. **07**, 142–145 (2018)

The Application Status and Enlightenment of Smart Phones in College Classroom Learning

Gao-Liang Zhang and He-Hai Liu[✉]

College of Education Science, Anhui Normal University, Wuhu, Anhui, China
358383418@qq.com

Abstract. With the continuous advancement of Internet technology, terminal devices represented by mobile phones have begun to deeply integrate into people's lives. Mobile phones affect people's lives, learning and value orientation. According to the latest issue of the "Statistical Report on the Development of China's Internet Network", the number of Chinese netizens reached 802 million. Among them, the number of mobile Internet users has reached 788 million, and the proportion of Internet users accessing the Internet through mobile phones is as high as 98.3%. Young students already account for a very high proportion of the total number of netizens. With the rapid development of the Internet, the rapid update of knowledge has made smartphones an indispensable tool for college students' daily life and learning. This paper uses questionnaires to obtain the current situation of college students using mobile phone learning in daily classroom learning, and through the analysis of the data, it provides some inspiration for better use of mobile phone learning in course learning, and better integrates mobile phone and course teaching. Provide a guiding strategy.

Keywords: Smart phone · Classroom learning

1 The Application Significance of Smart Phones in College Classroom Learning

1.1 Stepping Forward: From the Passive Classroom Instilled in Oral to the Efficient Active Classroom Under the Support of Mobile Technology

Most of the traditional classroom teaching methods are teachers' lectures, the structure is too single, some of the knowledge can not be presented well, and the students can understand the contents of the teaching. Their questions, thoughts, evaluations, etc. on the teaching content cannot be obtained. Timely expression and feedback. There are problems of low teaching efficiency and easy to form indoctrinated teaching, which causes students to lose the subjectivity of the classroom, and is not conducive to the independent learning and individualized development of students. Modern devices such as smart phones enter the classroom, which can bring about the application of new teaching modes such as flipping classrooms and BYOD. In the classroom teaching

© Springer Nature Singapore Pte Ltd. 2020
J. Shen et al. (Eds.): IC3 2019, CCIS 1227, pp. 297–305, 2020.
https://doi.org/10.1007/978-981-15-6113-9_34

process, teachers can make full use of the functions of reading, recording and storage, communication and communication, search and query, innovation and creation of smart phones, so that students are accustomed to frequently use mobile phones to find information and real-time question and answer interactions in the classroom., team exchange discussions, course recordings and video recordings, thus enriching the form and content of classroom teaching, enhancing classroom appeal, enhancing learning interaction, making feedback and interaction easier, allowing students to adapt from classroom teaching to active use of mobile phones and classrooms The content is closely combined to achieve teaching interaction and teaching and learning, fully demonstrating the subjectivity of students and the leadership of teachers.

1.2   Extension: Time and Space Extension of Traditional Classrooms Under Technical Support

The smart phone itself has the characteristics of portability and simplicity. Combined with the expansion of today's mobile Internet bandwidth, the popularity of wireless networks, and the rapid development of social platforms such as Weibo and WeChat, mobile learning and ubiquitous learning are more widely used in the college student community. The characteristics of mobile learning portability, personalization, real-time, and interactivity are also better reflected. After class, students can not only use smart phones to review and consolidate the content of teachers' classroom teaching, but also expand and supplement according to their own situations. At any time, we can use various social media to interact with teachers and classmates, explore learning experiences, gain knowledge, and continuously share and expand knowledge, which constitutes the time and space extension of traditional classrooms.

2   Application Status and Problems Analysis of Smartphones in College Classroom Learning

2.1   Basic Situation of the Sample

grade of the student	Total	The major you are studying is?					
		Literature and history	Science, engineering, agriculture and medicine	Economic management	Education	Art class	other
Number of questions	132	15	33	12	21	11	40
Freshman	20.50%	40%	9.10%	16.70%	9.50%	18.20%	30%
Sophomore	11.40%	6.70%	15.20%	8.30%	0%	9.10%	17.50%
Junior	27.30%	20%	33.30%	25%	9.50%	36.40%	32.50%
Senior	19.70%	33.30%	27.30%	16.70%	14.30%	9.10%	15%
Postgraduate	21.20%	0%	15.20%	33.30%	66.70%	27.30%	5%

Fig. 1. Basic situation of the sample.

In this study, questionnaires were used to conduct random questionnaire surveys for students from Anhui Normal University. A total of 150 questionnaires were issued and 132 valid questionnaires were returned. Among the 132 questionnaires that were collected, the students participating in the questionnaire were involved in various majors. Among them, junior high school students and graduate students accounted for a high proportion, and the proportion of educational graduate students reached 66.7% (Fig. 1).

2.2   Basic Situation of College Students Using Mobile Phones in Class

2.2.1   Basic Situation of Using Mobile Phones in College Students' Classrooms

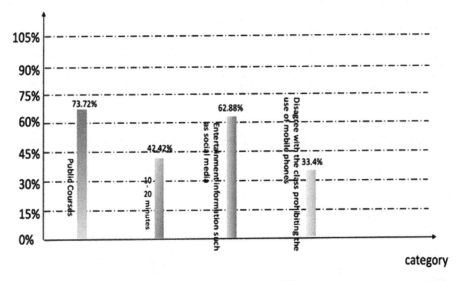

Fig. 2. Basic situation of using mobile phones in college classrooms.

Through the collection and collation of data, we can see the basic situation of college students using mobile phones in classroom learning. Among them, the collection usage rate in public classes reached 73.72%, and the mobile phone usage time of students in one class mostly concentrated in 10–20 min (45 min in one class), which reached 42.42%, using mobile phones in class. 62.88% of students use mobile phones to view entertainment information such as social media, most of which are unrelated to learning. 33.4% of students expressed strong protests about whether mobile phone use should be banned in the classroom. According to the above data, students have a development attitude toward the use of mobile phones in the classroom, but there will be deviations in the daily classroom use process, and most of the students are doing nothing to learn in class (Fig. 2).

2.2.2   College Students' Attitude Towards Introducing Mobile Phones in the Classroom

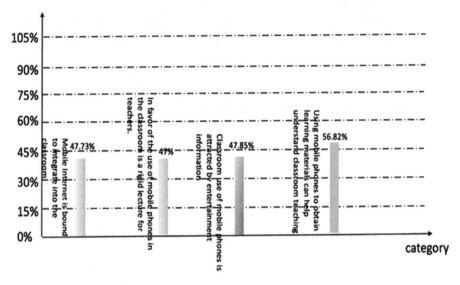

Fig. 3. College students' attitude towards introducing mobile phones in the classroom.

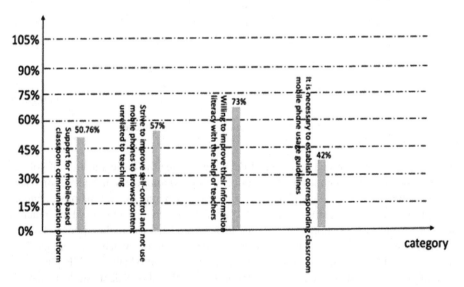

Fig. 4. College students' attitude towards introducing mobile phones in the classroom.

College students' attitude towards the introduction of mobile phones in daily classroom learning, through the collection and analysis of data, it is known that for the state that technology is about to enter the 5G era and classroom teaching is almost at 0G, 47.33% of students believe that mobile Internet will inevitably be integrated. classroom. 47% of the students also believe that the use of mobile phones in classroom learning is caused by the unattractiveness of the teacher's lectures. Similarly, 47.85% of the students believe that the use of mobile phones in the classroom is attracted by entertainment information. 56.82% of students believe that using mobile phones in class learning can help them obtain useful learning materials. For the introduction of mobile phones in classroom learning, 50.76% of students agree to establish a mobile-based classroom communication platform in the daily teaching process, 57% of students strive to improve their self-control, and do not use mobile phones to browse content that is not related to learning. For the information literacy ability of using mobile phones in classroom learning, 73% of students are willing to improve themselves with the help of teachers. 42% of them agree that the corresponding classroom mobile phone usage guidelines should be established (Figs. 3 and 4).

3 Analysis of the Problems Existing in the Application of Smart Phones in College Classroom Teaching

3.1 Students Have Poor Self-control and Weak Learning Ability with Mobile Phones

The use of mobile phones in college students' classrooms is common, showing that the frequency of elective courses is higher than the compulsory courses and the length of use is too long. The general use of mobile phones reflects the relatively weak self-control of students. The deeper reason is that traditional classroom teaching and mobile Internet are gradually losing their minds in capturing the students' attention. Students' psychology is monotonous and realistic. Disregard of the disjointed classroom teaching content. Although most students can recognize the function and value of smartphone-assisted learning, many students are prone to mobile phone addiction in classroom learning, and are attracted by the entertainment function of mobile phones, which reduces the initiative and enthusiasm of learning, affecting the learning and listening effects. learning atmosphere. Most of the students' mobile learning lacks systematic planning, the content of learning is fragmented, and the learning ability of mobile phones is weak, and there is a lack of teacher guidance and supervision [1].

3.2 Students' Low Network Learning Ability and the Solidification of Teachers' Teaching Concepts

Classroom mobile phone behavior reflects the low e-learning ability of college students, the solidification of teaching concepts and models of college teachers, and the lack of communication between teachers and students. According to the survey data, it is shown that the use of mobile phones in the classroom is mostly for entertainment purposes. The college students' own online learning ability or the ability to accept new

Internet learning models is still weak. They have not fully realized that mobile phones are the medium of mobile Internet. They are not only entertainment information, but also richer learning resources, more convenient communication and cooperation, a fragmented, non-linear, decentralized way of thinking. Communication problems between teachers and students are also hindered; the transformation of college class-room paradigm. College students did not communicate with teachers on classroom teaching issues through reasonable channels. Second, they passively chose to use mobile phones in the classroom to express their dissatisfaction with the traditional classroom teaching model.

3.3   The Old Teaching Concept and the Lack of Use Guidelines

Today, the Internet is an open, interactive, interconnected and efficient community, and the traditional teaching philosophy has a wait-and-see attitude towards the various conveniences brought about by technological development. Education technology cannot keep up with the trend of the times, and now our daily life The inability to participate in the Internet is inseparable from the convenience brought by the Internet. The concept of oral indoctrination advocated by the traditional teaching concept runs counter to the idea of the Internet. As a result, the use of mobile Internet technology represented by mobile phones in the classroom is difficult, and the use of guidance and reasonable control is inevitable for the current classroom. Come shock. The students' attention is not concentrated, and they are addicted to the junk entertainment information brought by the mobile phone. The lack of school management mechanisms and imperfections provide a basis and guidelines for mobile devices to be used in the classroom.

4   The Application of Smart Phones in College Classroom Learning

4.1   College Students Need to Correctly Understand the Meaning of the Classroom and Improve Their Self-control

Students are the main body of the classroom, students should change their thinking and correctly understand the meaning of the university classroom. Due to the unclear understanding of the relationship and role of elective courses and compulsory courses, the length of time that students use mobile phones in elective classes far exceeds the compulsory courses. The self-control of students is also an important part of the problem of mobile phone behavior in the classroom [2]. The weak self-control of students can't restrain themselves from attracting information that is not related to teaching by online games, novels, entertainment information, etc., indicating that students lack a clear understanding of the university curriculum and lack the goals of learning and life. If you want to truly use your mobile phone instead of being bound by the information network presented by your mobile phone, you should be clear about your learning goals, develop your own learning methods, and develop your own self-control in the face of information interference and sensation. To correctly understand the meaning and value of learning in different courses.

4.2 College Students Need to Actively Change Their Learning Concepts and Improve Their Online Learning Ability

The lack of college students' online learning ability is a major obstacle to the transformation of university classroom teaching paradigm. In today's society, the requirements for online learning ability and media literacy of talents are getting higher and higher. In the era of mobile Internet, the information or knowledge that students are exposed to on mobile phones and other mobile terminals are characterized by fragmentation and non-linearity. In the face of the messy information, students are likely to be lost in the wave of information. The survey data is also verifying this point. In the course of college classroom teaching, although some students use mobile phones to find information related to classroom teaching in the classroom, the vast majority of students use mobile phones for entertainment purposes.

Therefore, it is imperative to improve the network learning ability of college students. First, establish a correct view of learning, recognize that mobile phones are tools for accessing information and expanding cognition; second, improve information search and screening capabilities. Finally, I will participate in some related courses to improve my digital learning ability, including the ability to search, screen, extract, and internalize academic information, and improve my digital learning ability with the help of teachers [3]. In this case, the smart phone can be well utilized, break the boundaries of the classroom, remove the shackles of the classroom, abandon the reading, and form a new classroom teaching model based on the flipping classroom. Turn learning into a kind of exploration, a kind of cooperation and a kind of fun.

4.3 Colleges and Universities Should Reasonably Formulate Rules and Regulations and Innovate Classroom Teaching Evaluation Mechanism

At present, some colleges and universities in China use a one-size-fits-all ban on the use of mobile phones in the classroom, and some colleges and universities are indifferent. Digital learning mode or mobile learning is a trend in higher education. It will also be integrated into classroom teaching in the future. The old concept of rejecting new things will also be eliminated by the times. So how to use the mobile phone in the classroom has become an unavoidable problem. The evaluation system for teachers' classroom teaching should also be changed. It should not be too arbitrary to criticize the behavior of teachers and students using mobile phones in the classroom. It should be set up to encourage teachers and students to use mobile devices such as mobile phones to promote teachers. The teaching interaction between students forms a multi-evaluation index and evaluation system based on mobile phones. Colleges and universities should also establish corresponding access systems and rules and regulations to provide guidance and constraints for the use of mobile devices represented by mobile phones in classroom teaching and integration with courses.

4.4 Colleges and Universities Should Change the Concept of Classroom Teaching and Form an Ideal Classroom for Everyone to Participate

The enemies in the classroom are not mobile phones, not emerging technologies, but the rigid teaching philosophy of colleges and universities. How to get rid of the solidification of thinking, stepping out of the times is the university should reflect. Only actively participate in the integration of classrooms and mobile terminals, face the challenges of technology, and use technology for me. The construction of future university classrooms in the context of mobile Internet and the improvement of hardware facilities are indispensable conditions. To achieve real-time online interaction between teachers and students, real-time indexing of massive knowledge, high-speed smooth mobile networks, servers and other equipment have high requirements, must be able to carry a large number of users concentrated load, maintain high-speed, smooth operation. In the software facilities, there are some classroom teaching management softwares, but most of them focus on the use of computers, and related classroom teaching management software for portable mobile terminal devices such as smart phones, both in terms of technology and popularity. There is still a lot of room for improvement.

5 Conclusion

The current mobile network is highly developed, and it is only a matter of time before mobile terminals enter the classroom. The development of technology will never stop the nostalgic sentiment of any era. Smartphones are only a representative of Education informatization. and the combination of technology and education is still ongoing. Many foreign universities have introduced personal learning analysis software with their own devices as the carrier, providing each student with learning analysis and developing a personalized learning program [4]. At the same time, the development of VR and AR technology, as well as the emergence of maker space, are likely to subvert traditional university classroom teaching. In the future classroom teaching, the integration of wearable devices equipped with AR technology and emotional computing systems into classroom teaching is not a dream. Future students may be able to use virtual reality technology to learn all kinds of knowledge in a timely manner in any time environment. The development of education can never be separated from the advancement of technology.

References

1. Zheng, H.: Investigation and countermeasures on the current situation of college students using mobile phones in class [D]. 2017
2. Ou, X., Wu, X., Zeng, L.: Investigation and countermeasures of classroom mobile phone usage in college students. University Education (03), 158–162 (2017)

3. Li, Y.: Investigation on the Status Quo of college students' digital learning ability. Zhejiang Normal University (2014)
4. Li, L., Zheng, Y.: The carrier of community maker education in the UnitedStates——development motivation, function and application of community maker space. Open Educ. Res. **21**(05), 41–48 (2015)

The Effectiveness of Giving Students In-Game Cards as Rewards

Cheng-Li Chen[1(✉)], Maiga Chang[1], Hung-Yi Chang[2],
Chun-Hung Lin[3], Kuo-Chen Li[4], Rita Kuo[5], and Hongxue Wang[1]

[1] School of Computing and Information Systems, Athabasca University,
Athabasca, Canada
eric.chenglichen@gmail.com
[2] Department of Information Management,
National Kaohsiung University of Science and Technology, Kaohsiung, Taiwan
[3] Center for Teacher Education, Chung-Yuan Christian University,
Taoyuan City, Taiwan
[4] Department of Information Management, Chung-Yuan Christian University,
Taoyuan City, Taiwan
[5] Department of Computer Science and Engineering,
New Mexico Institute of Mining and Technology, Socorro, USA

Abstract. Reward has become an important role to increase students' motivation in traditional classroom learning. The research team designed an In-game Card as Education Reward (ICER) web-based system which helps teachers give students reward while students have good performance in learning activities such as assignment, presentation, discussion, quiz, and exam. Whenever students complete a learning activity, their teacher can choose different type and rarity in-game cards and deliver the cards to the students by using ICER web-based management system. Students can redeem the reward on ICER website and receive in-game cards in the game. Students can have more fun in the game-play or even show-off the cards that they have to other students. For this reason, students may put more efforts on studying and doing learning activities and may be even actively participated in the discussions in the class for getting better rewards.

Keywords: In-game card · Learning performance · Trading card game ·
Educational game · Educational reward

1 Introduction

In traditional classroom learning, teachers usually award students while they have good performance in different learning activities. Taking a science teacher – Eric as an example, he wants to encourage students to study. He may choose to give pencils as rewards for the top three students who receive highest marks in the midterm exam. What he expects to see is that students will have better performance for the incoming learning activities include final exam if they find themselves can receive rewards for their good performance from this one.

J. Shen et al. (Eds.): IC3 2019, CCIS 1227, pp. 306–315, 2020.
https://doi.org/10.1007/978-981-15-6113-9_35

In the context of distance education and online learning, for instance, all students at Athabasca University are learning online in different time zones across Canada and worldwide, giving students real items as rewards is impractical and unrealistic. In order to make teachers still capable of awarding students just like how they did in traditional classroom learning situations, an educational reward system needs to be designed and developed. The research team developed In-game Card as Educational Reward (ICER) web-based system. Teachers can use similar way to give students rewards as usual. With the ICER web system's help, students' learning performance may be improved.

The next section introduces how educational reward influences students' learning performance. The research team integrated ICER web-based system with a trading card game (TCG) for delivering in-game cards for students as educational rewards. The trading card game was developed by Chen and colleagues [5] and its details can be found in Sect. 2. Section 3 describes the architecture of ICER web-based system. The implementation of ICER web-based system can be seen in Sect. 4 and Sect. 5 explains the evaluation plan the research has for verifying the usability of the ICER web-based system and the effectiveness of the use of in-game cards as rewards. Section 6 summarizes the research and discusses possible future works that we can do later.

2 Related Work

Reward is a feedback that can encourage students to learn more [8]. With appropriate goal settings, rewards can be valuable and more attractive for students [6]. In addition, bringing rewards into learning activities such as a course's assignments can increase the persistence of achieving the goal [10]. Some researchers even believed that rewards positively affect students' learning performance [9]. According to the above studies, we can find out that only when students think the rewards they received are valuable or meaningful, the reward mechanism can be effective in terms of engaging students in learning.

To make rewards more attractive for students, Chen and colleagues develop a trading card game, namely TCG, and want to use the cards in the game as educational rewards. Teachers can give students higher-level or rarer cards if students did exercises well. Once students receive higher-level or rarer cards, they have higher chance to win the duels in the game. On the other hand, when students are not doing exercise well, they probably will not receive cards as rewards or only receive lower-level or common cards for what they have done.

They also conducted an experiment to find out whether or not the use of the trading cards as educational rewards affects students' motivations and academic achievements [4]. There were 172 fifth-grade students, 80 boys and 92 girls, participated in the experiment and were separated into two groups. The 68 control group students only used a web-based vocabulary learning system for learning and practicing their English vocabularies, and the 104 experiment group students used the web-based learning system and received cards as rewards automatically every time after they practiced vocabularies with the system. Their research result showed that students who played the game more, they used the web-based learning system more often. The result suggested that students were study harder in order to receive higher-level or rarer cards.

3   The Integration of ICER Web-Based System and TCG

This research aims to design ICER web-based system which delivers cards of the TCG that Chen and colleagues developed. The system needs to support teachers awarding their students by giving particular cards according to students' performances on different learning activities. With the help of Educational Resource Information Communication API (ERIC API), students' identities won't never be revealed to the TCG and the game won't know anything about the student during the reward redemption process [3].

ICER web-based system and the TCG are two systems that this research aims to integrate together so teachers can choose in-game cards as rewards for the students to redeem according to students' performances of particular learning activities. Whenever a teacher wants to give a student reward, he or she just need to sign on the system and choose type and level of the in-game card. The system will generate an URL for the teacher so that he or she can give out the URL for the student to redeem the reward. Once the student has the URL, he or she needs to authorize ICER web-based system (for once) to access his or her TCG account by entering their credentials at TCG if it is the first time he or she redeem for the reward on TCG.

ICER web-based system has two modules: reward setup module and reward distribution module. Using an example to explain the architecture and workflow of relationship between the ICER system and the TCG. A science teacher, Eric, who teaches Math and he wants to give out his students a three-star avatar card when the student gets A+ for the midterm exam. He needs to setup the reward as the Step 1 in Fig. 1 shows. The reward setup module will check reward database (i.e., Step 2 in Fig. 1) to remind him if the student has been awarded before (i.e., Step 3 in Fig. 1). The reward distribution module will generate an URL and write a record into the reward database as Steps 4 and 5 in Fig. 1 show. Eric then will send the specific URL to the students as Step 6 shows.

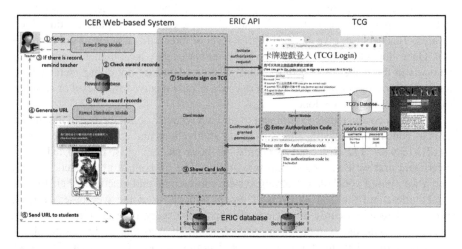

Fig. 1. Architecture of integrating ICER web-based system and TCG with ERIC API.

Assuming a student – Chris who has received the URL, he can copy and past it into any browser like Chrome, Firefox, Safari or IE to redeem the reward. ERIC API will redirect him to the TCG and ask him to sign on the TCG to grant the permission(s) for ICER web-based system to deliver card to the TCG as Step 7 shows. Chris then will be asked to enter the current authorization code to make sure that communication has not been hacked (i.e., Step 8 in Fig. 1). After entering the authorization code, Chris can see what kind of cards has been delivered to his account in the TCG as Step 9 in Fig. 1 shows.

4   The Implementation of ICER

4.1   ICER Web-Based System

When a teacher signs in ICER web-based system, he or she can see the "Give card as educational reward" and "Manage all given rewards" hyperlink on the main page as Fig. 2 shows.

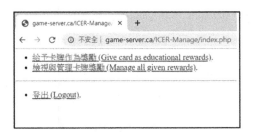

Fig. 2. Main page of ICER web-based system.

Fig. 3. Reward setup module.

After the teacher clicks "Give card as educational rewards", he or she can enter the student's unique ID or username, select the drop-down card type and level. As Fig. 3 shows, the teacher wants to award Chris a three-star avatar card. As Fig. 4 shows once the teacher clicks "Give and Generate URL", he or she can see a URL generated for student to redeem the reward in the TCG. She or he can then send the URL to Chris by any means.

Fig. 4. URL generated for student to redeem the reward on the TCG.

By clicking the link of "Manage all given rewards" shown on the main page, the teacher can also see all of the rewards that he or she has given as well as knows who have redeemed the given rewards and who haven't as Fig. 5 shows. If Chris loses the given URL, the teacher can also retrieve the link here from this page.

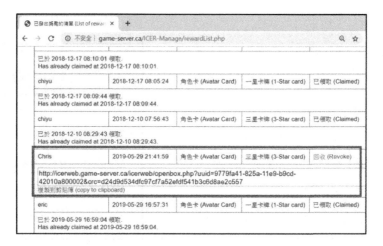

Fig. 5. List of rewards that have been given.

4.2   Reward Redemption on ICER Web-Based System

When a student receives the URL from the teacher, he or she can copy and paste the URL into any browser to start his or her reward redemption. Take Chris as example again. As soon as Chris starts the redemption process as Fig. 6 shows, he needs to enter his unique ID or username and click "Open Now!" button to redeem the reward.

Fig. 6. Reward redemption page.

Fig. 7. Permission granting page at TCG.

After Chris clicks "Open Now!" button, he will be redirected to the TCG Login page as Fig. 7 shows. Since he is on the TCG's website, he would be feel comfortable to grant the permission(s) that allow the ICER web-based system to deliver the reward card to the TCG as well as retrieve his card collection information from the TCG by entering his credentials of TCG.

Figure 8 shows that ICER web-based system delivered the reward card to the TCG via sending requests to the TCG with client side of ERIC API.

Fig. 8. ICER web-based system has delivered an in-game card as reward.

5 Experiment and Discussion

5.1 Experiment Design

To understand whether or not the ICER web-based system can help students improve their learning performance, the research team had recruited two classes from different departments, Department of Information Management (DIM) and Graduate School of Education (GSE), at Chung Yuan Christian University, Taiwan after midterm exam. There were twenty-five students in the DIM class and sixteen students in the GSE course. For the DIM class, the research team only introduced the TCG and the ICER web-based system for them but not gave anyone any in-game card as reward later. On the other hand, the research team not only introduced both of the TCG and the ICER web-based system but also gave them in-game cards as rewards for the learning activities after.

In the beginning both classes of students were asked to fill out a pre-survey questionnaire that includes Computer Game Attitude Scale (CGAS) and Diffusion of Innovation (DoI) parts [2, 7]. After the two classes of students completed their final exams, they were also asked to complete the post-survey questionnaire regarding their perceptions toward the usability of the ICER web-based system [1].

Despite of the students' computer game attitude and diffusion of innovation are collected, this paper mainly focuses on answering three questions: (1) "would the ICER web-based system has impact on their usage of the TCG?" (2) "how they perceived the usability of ICER web-based system?" and (3) "whether or not the ICER web-based system helps students engage into the learning and have better learning performance?"

The research team proposed the following hypotheses and verified them with the data analysis results.

- H1: GSE students play TCG more often than DIM students.
- H2: GSE students give higher System Usability Scale score for the ICER web-based system than DIM students.
- H3: GSE students' improvement from midterm to final exam is higher than DIM students'.

5.2 Evaluation

In order to compare two classes of students, the research team used t-test to verify whether or not the two classes have differences in terms of the times of playing the TCG, the score of System Usability Scale, and the improvement from midterm to final. The t-test results listed in Table 1 show that GSE students has no significance difference on playing the TCG from DIM students. However, the Hedges' g value reach to medium effect size 0.5 which means GSE students' behaviour still different from DIM students – they played the game more. Therefore H1 can be said partially supported.

Table 1. Independent t-test result for TCG login times

	Descriptive statistics			t-test			
	N	Mean	SD	t	df	p	Hedges' g
DIM	25	2.72	1.487	−1.573	39	.124	0.50249
GSE	16	3.81	2.949				

The t-test is also applied on the given SUS scores from both groups and the result is listed in Table 2. The result shows the given SUS scores for the ICER web-based system from both groups are remaining at poor level (i.e., 51 to 68) [1] and there is no significance difference between the two classes. Therefore, H2 is not supported.

Table 2. Independent t-test result for SUS scores

	Descriptive statistics			t-test		
	N	Mean	SD	t	df	p
DIM	25	57.4	7.2701	−.122	39	.903
GSE	16	57.8	14.3142			

In order to compare whether or not GSE students have better performance improvement from midterm exam, the research team applied t-test to compare the two classes of students' improvement (i.e., the difference from midterm to final) and the result is listed in as Table 3. The result shows both classes have positive improvement from midterm to final; however the GSE students' improvement is significantly different from DIM students. Therefore H3 is supported.

Table 3. Independent t-test result for improvement

	Descriptive statistics			t-test		
	N	Mean	SD	t	Df	p
DIM	25	3.2	8.367	−2.967	39	.005**
GSE	16	11.56	9.458			

*: p < 0.05 **: p < 0.01

5.3   Findings and Discussions

Based on the above data analysis results, the research team have concluded the following findings:

- GSE group of students are more likely to play TCG.
  The result is a kind of evidence that shows giving students in-game cards as rewards can stimulate and engage them to play the game. On the other hand, the research team raised a question from the data analysis result and this finding – "why both groups are not playing the TCG as often as the research team expected?" The simplest explanations might be (1) the TCG is not fun or (2) the TCG is difficult to play. However, this finding might also have causal relation with the next finding.
- Both groups of students give low scores on the usability of the ICER web-based system.
  The research team was expecting to see that GSE group will have more positive perception toward the system due to they received in-game cards as rewards and did use the system. The unexpected results show that both groups of students think the usability of the ICER web-based system is low. One possible reason is that the students may feel the process of getting in-game cards with ICER web-based system is different from or more complicated than they usually did in commercial trading card games.
  It is acceptable as in the commercial games players actually purchase and redeem/open cards inside the game so no further permission granted step/process needed; but the extra redemption/open and permission grant steps outside of the game are necessarily from the viewpoint of educational reward as well as the privacy issue and the dependency between games and awarding system.
  Last but not the least, this finding also explains the potential answer for the question, "why both groups are not playing the TCG as often as the research team expected?" Perhaps the difficulty of redeeming the cards makes them have less motivation to play the game.
- Give students reward can improve their learning performance.
  This finding is the research team looks for and proves the effectiveness of adopting the in-game cards as rewards mechanism and the ICER web-based system do get students motivated to learn. Although the finding is what the research team is looking for, the experiment and its data collection still need to improve. First of all, the current two groups of students in the experiment were coming from two different departments or even say different disciplines. In such case, not only the learning subjects and activities as well as their teachers are different but also their gaming experience, backgrounds, and attitude towards gaming might be different and may have influence on the results. Second, the research goal is not only seeing the improvements on the academic achievement but also wants to see the students will work hard on learning activities for getting in-game cards as rewards.

6   Conclusion

The research team developed In-game Card as Educational Reward (ICER) web-based system which is connected to TCG by using ERIC API. The ICER web-based system helps teachers give students reward in very few steps easily. Students can redeem in-game cards quickly after they received a specific URL given by their teacher.

The research team has conducted a pilot to understand whether or not giving students in-game cards as rewards can improve their learning performance. The data analysis results show that giving students in-game cards as rewards with the ICER web-based system can improve their learning performance.

However, from the findings and discussions, the research team also identifies some limitations and correspondent future works may need to be planed and done further. First of all, the research has to at least recruit two classes from the same department or disciplines to get rid of the potential influences. Second, the experiment should be a longer term one that involves many different learning activities and students' performances of each activity should be recorded. In such case, the research team can investigate whether or not the ICER mechanism and system can really get students motivated. Moreover, using ICER system longer may eliminate or educate students the difference between commercial games and educational awarding.

References

1. Brooke, J.: SUS: a quick and dirty usability scale. In: Jordan, P.W., Thomas, B., Weerdmeester, B.A., McClelland, I.L. (eds.) Usability Evaluation in Industry, pp. 189–194. Taylor & Francis, London (1996)
2. Chang, M., Kuo, R., Liu, E.Z.-F.: Revised computer game attitude scale. In: Proceedings of 22nd International Conference on Computers in Education, pp. 598–607. Asia-Pacific Society for Computers in Education, Japan (2014)
3. Chen, C.-L., Chang, M., Chang, H.-Y.: Educational resource information communication API (ERIC API): the case of moodle and online tests system integration. In: The Proceedings of 3rd International Conference on Smart Learning Environments, Tunis, Tunisia, pp. 225–229 (2016)
4. Chen, P., Kuo, R., Chang, M., Heh, J.-S.: The effectiveness of using in-game cards as reward. research and practice in technology enhanced learning (2017, in-press)
5. Chen, P., Kuo, R., Chang, M., Heh, J.-S.: Trading card game. In: The Workshop Proceedings of the 24th International Conference on Computers in Education, Mumbai, India, pp. 6–11 (2016)
6. Ek, K.E., Miltenberger, R.G., Valbuena, D.: Promoting physical activity among school-age children using feedback, goal setting, and rewards. Behav. Anal. Res. Pract. **16**(1), 41–46 (2016)
7. Park, Y., Chen, J.V.: Acceptance and adoption of the innovative use of smartphone. Ind. Manage. Data Syst. **107**(9), 1349–1365 (2007)
8. Tunstall, P., Gipps, C.: T: teacher feedback to young children in formative assessment: a typology. Br. Educ. Res. J. **22**(4), 389–404 (1996)
9. Winefield, A.H., Barnett, J.A., Tiggemann, M.: Learned helplessness and IQ differences. Personality Individ. Differ. **5**(5), 493–500 (1984)
10. Woolley, K., Fishbach, A.: For the fun of it: harnessing immediate rewards to increase persistence in long-term goals. J. Consum. Res. **42**(6), 952–966 (2016)

An Analysis of Student Inquiry Performances in Computer Supported Light-Weighted Collaborative Experiment

Cai Ting Wen[1], Chia Jung Chang[2], Ssu Chi Huang[1],
Ming Hua Chang[1], Shih Hsun Fan Chiang[1], Chen Chung Liu[1(✉)],
Fu Kwun Hwang[3], Hsin Yi Chang[3], and Chih Wei Yang[4]

[1] National Central University, Taoyuan City, Taiwan
ccliu@cl.ncu.edu.tw
[2] Yuan Ze University, Taoyuan City, Taiwan
[3] National Taiwan Normal University, Taipei, Taiwan
[4] National Taichung University of Education, Taichung, Taiwan

Abstract. Collaborative simulations was found more flexible and enhance students' motivation. Although it is an effective way to implement science inquiry in classroom, the orchestration is complex and how the pedagogy influence students' inquiry is still not clear. Therefore, this study address a light-weighted collaborative experiment pedagogy, which consists of computer simulations, teacher's guidance and the whole-class reflection. To investigate the impact of such pedagogy on students' inquiry performance and the science knowledge change, 33 8th grade students participated in this study. Results show that although the students design the experiment properly, their concept improvement is not significant which is not aligned with our expectation. Their inquiry process of the first time participating in light-weighted experiment demonstrated their inadequate ability of analyzing the experiment data, which led to obstacles of constructing knowledge by using computer simulation. Therefore, more de-briefing on data processing while conducting light-weighted experiment is suggested. Besides, whether a series of light-weighted experiment implementation enhance students' performance is valuable to further investigate.

Keywords: Collaborative inquiry · Light-weighted experiment · Collaborative simulation · Computer simulation · Science inquiry

1 Introduction

Hands-on laboratories are broadly implemented where students can engage in science inquiry activity and learn in an active and constructive way [1]. However, inquiry in the laboratory is not only time consuming, but also requires effort of the teachers to set up the environment for inquiry experiments [2]. Moreover, previous studies indicated that hands-on laboratory afford less flexibility in supporting different type of inquiry and lower level of openness than virtual experiment environment [3]. Furthermore, previous studies have demonstrated that students improve more conceptual understanding, motivation, and attitude with virtual computer simulations [1, 4]. Therefore, computer

© Springer Nature Singapore Pte Ltd. 2020
J. Shen et al. (Eds.): IC3 2019, CCIS 1227, pp. 316–322, 2020.
https://doi.org/10.1007/978-981-15-6113-9_36

simulations can support flexible and effective science learning activities in classroom in an economic way. Recently, the computer simulations are increasingly applied with collaborative learning to enhance students' engagement in the science inquiry activities [5]. However, students in the collaborative inquiry without shared focus may had negative impact on the perspective exchange process [3], which might lead to unfavorable learning performance [6]. Therefore, it is worthwhile to understand how different resources can be orchestrated to effectively support collaborative science inquiry in classrooms.

Recently, mobile devices are extensively used for implementing science inquiry activity in classrooms. It was found that such devices can improve students' engagement and interaction during the collaborative learning activity [3]. Therefore, this study aims to investigate the effect and limitation of a light-weighted collaborative experiment pedagogy that can be implemented with computer simulations and mobile devices in regular classrooms. The pedagogy addresses the role of computer simulation, peer collaboration and the teachers' guidance which could be implemented in the classroom with simple tablets or mobile devices. Students could manipulate the computer simulation collaboratively on the tablet under teachers' guidance to experience the knowledge construction process. The approach provides an easy and effective way for teachers to orchestrate the collaborative science inquiry in classrooms. This study analyzed students' reactions when they participated in such a light-weighted collaborative experiment to answer the questions below:

1. How do students perform in the light-weighted collaborative experiment?
2. How does students' science knowledge change after participating in the light-weighted collaborative experiment?

2 Method

2.1 Participants

This study was conducted in a regular classroom in a junior high school. The main purpose of this study is to understand the impact of the light-weighted collaborative experiments to help students learn the concept of heat capacity. The participants of this study were 33 8th grade students, aged from 14–15, who generally only receive lecture-oriented instruction in science classes. The participants did not learn the heat capacity concept before the study. The whole class would be divided into pairs randomly by the teacher in advanced. Each of students were provided with an iPad to complete the experiment task with the team-mate face to face.

2.2 Procedure

The pre and post learning test were implemented for 10 min before and after the intervention. The light weight experiment activity lasted 100 min. In the first 10 min, the teacher introduced the use of the system and the light weight experiment. Then the student pairs participated in the 70-min light-weighted collaborative experiment.

The orchestration of the experiment composed of three critical elements as shown in Fig. 1, which are the collaborative simulations, teachers' guidance and the whole-class reflection.

More specifically, the students used the heat simulation (described later) collaboratively to explore the heat concept while provided with worksheet. Since the students did not experience inquiry process, the teacher guided the students to collaboratively complete the experiment task with a predefined worksheet. More specifically, the worksheet guided students make a hypothesis about a given assertion about the target science phenomenon, design an experiment with the simulation and collected data with the simulation. They were requested to analyze the data and draw a conclusion about the hypothesis. During the light-weighted collaborative experiment, the teacher provided assistance only when the students asked for clarification about the procedure or of the problem on system manipulation, and did not provide further instruction on the scientific concept. After the experiment, the teacher guided the whole class to reflect the scientific concepts learnt from the experiment.

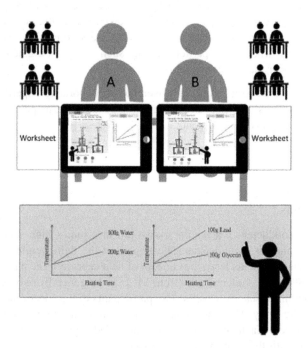

Fig. 1. Light-weighted collaborative experiment pedagogy.

2.3   The Collaborative Simulation

The Collaborative simulation is designed on the CoSci (https://cosci.tw/), which is a web-based simulation design platform [7]. The simulation provides equipment and material with variety of physics features for students to conduct the experiment. The materials include water, lead, glycerin and sand of different mass (100 and 200 g).

To strengthen student participating in the experiment, the collaborative simulations enforced an asymmetric accountability mechanism which required both of the students to complete their mission. In this study, one student had to choose an experiment material, and the other would need to choose another material for a comparative observation, as shown in Fig. 2. Therefore, it is hoped that such a mechanism can facilitate students to closely collaborate with their partner to design, conduct the expediment, and clarify the key factor influences the change of the temperature.

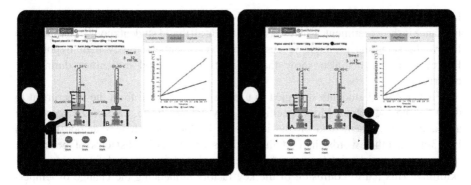

Fig. 2. The collaborative simulation in light-weighted experiment.

2.4 Data Collection and Analysis

The pre- and post-test consist of ten multiple choice questions designed by two experienced science teachers. Five of the questions evaluate students' understanding of concept about the heat, and the other five assess how the students could apply the concept to solve problems. A paired-t test was used to understand the students' learning improvement after the light-weighted collaborative experiment. Besides, the work-sheets students completed were analyzed to better understand students' performance in the experiment.

3 Result

3.1 Pre- and Post-test

Table 1 presents the improvement of students after participating in the light-weighted collaborative experiment. Students performed better after the light-weighted collaborative experiment (M = 5.12, SD = 2.03) than before (M = 4.73, SD = 1.28). However, the difference is not significant. Such a result indicated that students still encountered difficulties to transfer what they learnt from the experiment to solid understanding about the target concept of the experiment.

Table 1. The improvement of learning test.

	Pre		Post		t	p
	M	SD	M	SD		
Concept	2.56	1.35	2.85	1.23	−.99	.33
Application	2.15	1.28	2.27	1.28	−.50	.62
Total	4.73	2.32	5.12	2.03	−.98	.33

3.2 The Evaluation of the Worksheets

Each of the worksheets students completed was analyzed to understand students' performance in the experiment. The results present that all the 33 students could appropriately follow the scientific principle to design the experiments to verify their hypothesis. However, the results also show that students encountered difficulties during the experiment.

First, 16 of 33 students struggled to use the data collected from the experiment to draw the representation. More specifically, they neglected the scale of the coordinate and added experiment data on the inaccurate location, which was demonstrated in Fig. 3(a). In other words, half of the students encountered obstacles of generating representation appropriately to analyze the complex data collected from experiment skillfully. This led to confusion of the key factors influencing the change of temperature. Furthermore, as shown in Fig. 3(b), there were 8 students inadequately plotting the result charts. They connected the first point to the origin (of coordinates), even though it was not shown in the experiment data. These inability in analyzing the data cause difficulties to understand the relationship between the temperature change and the time of heating.

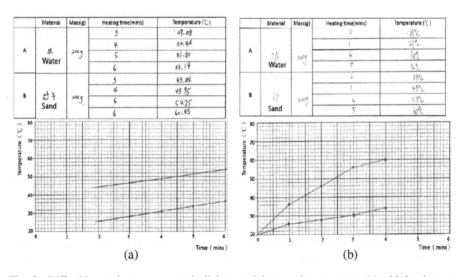

Fig. 3. Difficulties students encounter in lighten-weight experiment system (a) add the data on incorrect location of coordinate (b) Connect the first data to the origin.

4   Conclusion

This study proposed a light-weighted collaborative experiment pedagogy to implement collaborative science inquiry in a regular classroom. The students' worksheets demonstrated that students were able to design the experiment with teammates to test scientific hypothesis. However, the pre- and post-test did not show significant enhancement after they participated in the light-weighted collaborative experiment. This study identified some problems in promoting inquiry ability using simulations in classrooms. More specifically, students showed low data processing ability in dealing with the data obtained through simulations. It was demonstrated that they could not correctly transform the data into different representations such as mathematical charts in order to make sense of the data they obtained. Such a finding aligned with a previous study [8] suggesting the necessity to enhance data processing ability in curriculum.

This paper presents students' first experience in the light-weighted experiment. The result is not as significant as we expected. Several issues need to be addressed to improve students' science inquiry ability through the light-weighted experiment. For example, debriefing for the data processing after or during the experiment may be necessary helpful to enhance students' data processing ability. Secondly, a series of implementation of such a light-weighted experiment may be helpful to increase their ability as they will understand the skill they need in each stage of the inquiry. Gathering the experience in the implementation may gain insight to improve the current curriculum to enhance students' science inquiry ability.

Acknowledgement. This work was supported by Ministry of Science and Technology, Taiwan, under Grants MOST107-2511-H-008-003-MY3, MOST 106-2511-S-008-002-MY3, MOST 106-2511-S-008-012-MY3, MOST 107-2811-H-008-006-

References

1. Rutten, N., Van Joolingen, W.R., Van Der Veen, J.T.: The learning effects of computer simulations in science education. Comput. Educ. **58**, 136–153 (2012)
2. Peffer, M.E., Beckler, M.L., Schunn, C., Renken, M., Revak, A.: Science classroom in-quiry (SCI) simulations: a novel method to scaffold science learning. PLoS ONE **10**, e0120638 (2015)
3. Beach, R., O'Brien, D.: Fostering students' science inquiry through app affordances of multimodality, collaboration, interactivity, and connectivity. Reading Writing Q. **31**, 119–134 (2015)
4. Sullivan, S., Gnesdilow, D., Puntambekar, S., Kim, J.S.: Middle school students' learning of mechanics concepts through engagement in different sequences of physical and virtual experiments. Int. J. Sci. Educ. **39**, 1573–1600 (2017)
5. Sun, D., Looi, C.K., Xie, W.: Learning with collaborative inquiry: a science learning environment for secondary students. Technol. Pedagogy Educ. **26**, 241–263 (2017)
6. Eid, M.I., Al-Jabri, I.M.: Social networking, knowledge sharing, and student learning: the case of university students. Comput. Educ. **99**, 14–27 (2016)

7. Chang, C.J., et al.: An analysis of student collaborative problem solving activities mediated by collaborative simulations. Comput. Educ. **114**, 222–235 (2017)
8. Rau, M.A.: Conditions for the effectiveness of multiple visual representations in enhancing STEM learning. Educ. Psychol. Rev. **29**, 717–761 (2017)

Effects of Incorporating a Topic-Scanning Guiding Mechanism in E-books on EFL Reading Comprehension, Learning Perceptions, and Reading Behaviors

Mei-Rong Alice Chen[1(✉)], Hiroaki Ogata[1], Gwo-Jen Hwang[2],
Yihsuan Diana Lin[3], and Gökhan Akçapınar[1,4]

[1] Kyoto University, Kyoto 606-8501, Japan
ntustalice@gmail.com
[2] National Taiwan University of Science and Technology, Taipei 10607, Taiwan
[3] Chinese Culture University, Taipei 11114, Taiwan
[4] Hacettepe University, Çankaya, Turkey

Abstract. Reading academic textbooks in English has been an uneasy task for non-native English students. In addition, e-books are gradually popular across educational contexts. Previous studies indicated that students generally could not comprehend texts well on screen, so this study proposed a topic-scanning guiding mechanism with e-books to support EFL students reading comprehension from e-books. This paper aims to investigate the effects of an e-book on EFL students' reading comprehension, learning perceptions, and reading behaviors in EFL freshman reading the course, incorporating a topic-scanning guiding mechanism with the e-book. A quasi-experiment with a pretest-posttest design was conducted in a university freshmen English course, 50 students were assigned as the experiential group, and 46 students were in the control group. Findings from this study would further contribute to students' learning perceptions and reading behavior analysis on designing e-book system to improve their reading competence.

Keywords: Reading comprehension · Learning analytics · E-book

1 Introduction

E-books have become one of the popular reading tools (Woody et al. 2010). The use of e-books has some beneficial impacts on supporting readers. Liu and Leveridge (2017) mentioned that reading in e-books can enhance learners' vocabulary. Chen et al. (2013) claimed that e-books showed positive effects on EFL students' reading fluency. However, several researchers indicated that reading academic materials in English has been recognized as a challenging task for English as a foreign language (EFL) learners (Li et al. 2013). In addition, Chou (2012) found that e-books have decreased EFL graduate students' reading comprehension. Therefore, it is substantial to explore a method of e-book instructional scaffolding as it helps EFL students facilitate their reading comprehension. A topic-scanning guiding mechanism in e-books was

© Springer Nature Singapore Pte Ltd. 2020
J. Shen et al. (Eds.): IC3 2019, CCIS 1227, pp. 323–332, 2020.
https://doi.org/10.1007/978-981-15-6113-9_37

developed in this study to foster EFL students' reading. Additionally, the ultimate aims of the research are to assess the effects of the proposed mechanism by collecting and students' reading achievement, learning perceptions, and reading logs of students reading behaviors. The research questions are as follows:

1. Is there a difference in reading comprehension for the topic-scanning guiding mechanism with e-books compared to the conventional reading approach with e-books?
2. Is there a difference in learning perceptions: learning satisfaction, ease of use, and cognitive load for the topic-scanning guiding mechanism with e-books compared to the conventional reading approach with e-books?
3. Is there a difference in the reading behaviors: numbers of highlighting in red and yellow markers, total time and words annotation in e-books for the topic-scanning guiding mechanism with e-books compared to the conventional reading approach with e-books?

2 Literature Review

2.1 E-books on EFL Learners' Reading

Reading e-books is different from reading textbooks (Rockinson-Szapkiw et al. 2013). Lately, technologically advanced e-books and application de-vices are more innovative, so it became suitable for educational use and may continue to adjust the reading familiarity for readers. Adopting e-books can increase intermediate level EFL students' vocabulary ability and attitude (Chen et al. 2013). Nevertheless, reading is an intricate cognitive process since learners need to construct meaning from the context in the reading text during the reading (Hwang et al. 2018). Reading strategies such as underlining, taking notes, or highlighting the text, can support EFL readers comprehend and recall the content. (Cogmen and Saracaloglu 2009). Since the mental reconstruction of text structure and reading comprehension are correlated (Mangen et al. 2013), this study utilized the above reading strategies to facilitate students in reconstructing the text structure. Direct demonstrating and scaffolding of instruction are important in training EFL students to tactically read information from text structure (Meyer and Ray 2017). Accordingly, reading instructors' guidance in setting the reading goals that motivate topic scanning (Duggan and Payne 2009; Just et al. 1987) is often adopted, as the text is first skimmed to extract the gist for reading comprehension. This study, therefore, focused on utilizing the above reading strategies, especially in using the topic-scanning mechanism, to identify main ideas for e-book reading comprehension.

2.2 Topic-Scanning Guiding Mechanism

Previous studies showed that reading strategies, such as scanning and skimming could help readers' reading comprehension (Anderson 2010; White et al. 2015; Yusuf et al. 2017). Scanning is one of the pre-reading strategies that require readers to look at specific keywords through text (Liaw 2017). Brown (2003) specified that scanning is to look for a particular piece or pieces of information in a text. Topic scanning means to browse promptly for the main ideas and specific information related to the main ideas of the texts (Duggan and Payne 2009). Topic scanning is essential to improve a comprehensive understanding of the developments involved in word recognition. White et al. (2015) defined topic scanning is that the texts were browsed only the essential main point. In addition to topic scanning, a concept mapping reading instruction offers students a more structural and organized method to make it easier to understand the texts (Hwang et al. 2018; Liu et al. 2010). Both concept mapping and scanning are two of the practical and constructive reading strategies. Therefore, this study proposes the topic scanning with concept mapping reading strategy instruction as the topic-scanning guiding mechanism.

3 Instructional Design

Learning management platform, Moodle was integrating with the BookRoll and Analysis Tool. The e-book system, BookRoll, is to support students' reading and learning (see Fig. 1). The instructor can simply log in to the Moodle system to manage the course reading materials, conduct questions for students' comprehensions, and provide scaffolding materials; such as concept maps of the text in the BookRoll (Akçapınar et al. 2019), and monitor students' reading and learning in the Analysis Tool (Flanagan et al. 2019; Ogata et al. 2017).

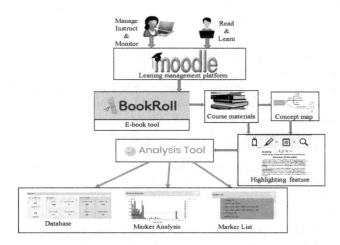

Fig. 1. Structure of the learning management platform with an e-book tool and an analysis tool for supporting students reading.

4   The Research Design

4.1   Participants

The present study examined a convenience sample of 96 undergraduate students. Two classes of one Freshman English course were taken part in the experiment with a quasi-experimental design. The participants were 62 male 34 female first-year college students taking the Freshman English course in the Spring Semester of the 2019 academic year. The two classes were taught by the same experienced EFL instructor to avoid the effect of different instructors on the experimental results. The students 50 (30 male 20 female) in the experimental group read with the topic-scanning guiding approach incorporated into the e-books whereas those 46 (32 male 14 female) students in the control group read with the conventional reading approach. The participants' English proficiency was ranked as the elementary proficiency level based on their TOEIC scores (Qu et al. 2017).

4.2   Procedures

To evaluate the effect of the topic-scanning guiding model with e-books on students' reading comprehension, learning perception, and reading behaviors, quantitative measurements of data collection, and a quasi-experimental design have been utilized. This study was conducted in 8 weeks. The two groups of the participants completed a pretest of reading comprehension one week before the experiment. The instructor went through three chapters: Chapter 9-Innocent until Proven Guilty, Chapter 10-Saving lives with new organs, Chapter 12-Medicine today from the textbook Reading for Today 3: Issues (Smith and Mare 2017) in this experiment for 6 weeks. All the participants spent 2 weeks learning each chapter.

This study was conducted in 8 weeks. The two groups of the participants completed a pretest of reading comprehension in the first week before the experiment. The instructor went through three chapters: Chapter 9-Innocent until Proven Guilty, Chapter 10-Saving lives with new organs, Chapter 12-Medicine today from the textbook Reading for Today 3: Issues (Smith and Mare 2017) in this experiment for 6 weeks. All the participants spent 2 weeks learning each chapter. In the first hour of the class each week, the instructor generally taught and explained new words, or phrases and reading skills such as skimming, scanning, fact-finding, and paraphrasing for both groups. In the second hour of the class, the participants of the experimental group were required to scan and highlight the topic and main idea and answer the questions in the BookRoll according to the instructor's concept map while the participants of the control group were required to read the text materials and answer the questions in the BookRoll. After all the class activities, a post-reading comprehension test, and technology acceptance were conducted. Figure 2 exhibits the procedure of the study.

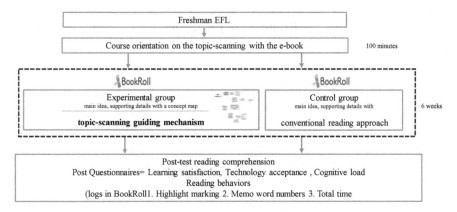

Fig. 2. The experiment process of the data collection.

4.3   Measuring Instruments

In this study, the students' reading comprehension, learning perceptions, and reading behaviors were assessed. To evaluate the participants' reading comprehension, they took pre- and post-reading comprehension tests, which are 30 multiple-choice questions. The reading tests were provided by the textbook Reading for Today 3: Issues (Smith and Mare 2017) and revised by the two experienced instructors. The total score of both tests was 100. The Cronbach's alpha value of the reading comprehension test is 0.86.

The questionnaire of learning satisfaction was adopted based on the questionnaire to measure the level of learning satisfaction developed by Chu et al. (2010). It consists of 12 items. To measure participants' technology acceptance, the questionnaire of the seven items for the ease of use dimension, and the 8 item of the cognitive load was from Hwang et al. (2013). The Cronbach's alpha values of the three were 0.95, 0.93, and 0.93, respectively.

The time spent reading the text and the words highlighted in the assigned tasks were recorded for analysis of participants' reading behaviors on BookRoll from the Analysis Tool (Akçapinar et al. 2019; Hasnine et al. 2019; Ogata et al. 2017).

5   The Research Design

5.1   Analysis of Reading Comprehension

One-way ANCOVA was conducted to eliminate unwanted variance on the dependent variable and increase test sensitivity (Tabachnick & Fidell, 2013), and to evaluate reading comprehension. The results of a one-way ANCOVA on reading comprehension demonstrated the analysis of homogeneity of regression with ($F = 0.197$, $p = 0.659 > 0.05$), indicating that the prior English reading of the two groups was equivalent before the experiment. The experimental group of the pretest scores was 66.80, SD = 17.59 while the control group is 66.52, SD = 16.60 as in Fig. 3, which showed no significant level of difference in the pre-test scores of the two group.

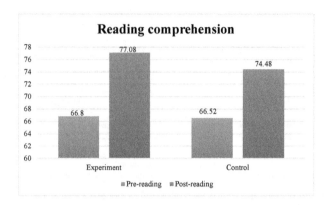

Fig. 3. The result of the reading comprehension for the two groups

There was a difference between the experimental and control groups in reading comprehension and shows the descriptive data and the ANCOVA of the post-test results. The adjusted mean values of the post-test scores were 77.08 (*Std. error* = 1.38) and 74.48 (*Std. error* = 1.28) for the experimental group and the control group, respectively as shown in Fig. 3, The result of the ANCOVA identified a significant difference between the two groups (F = 3.75, p = 0.05, η^2 = 0.039), indicating that the topic-scanning mechanism had significantly positive effects on the reading comprehension of students in the experimental group.

The independent samples t-tests were performed to assess the impact of the learning perceptions, such as learning satisfaction, the technology acceptance-ease of use, and cognitive. It is recognized that learning satisfaction t = 1.72 (p > .05, d = 0.34) had a little higher degree, but with no significant difference, on the experimental group (M = 3.73 SD = 0.86) than on the control group (M = 3.45 SD = 0.78). It is found that the technology acceptance-ease of use t = 0.90 (p > .05, d = 0.18) was with no significant difference on the experimental group (M = 3.75 SD = 0.81) and the control group (M = 3.60 SD = 0.83) as shown in Fig. 4.

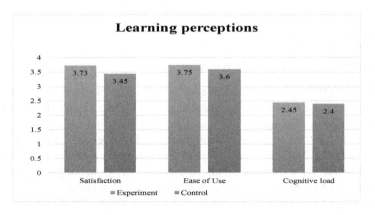

Fig. 4. The results of the three learning perceptions

The results of the cognitive load $t = 0.31$ ($p > .05$, d = 0.06) revealed that there is no statistically significant differences between the experimental group (M = 2.45 SD = 0.87) and the control group (M = 2.40 SD = 0.82).

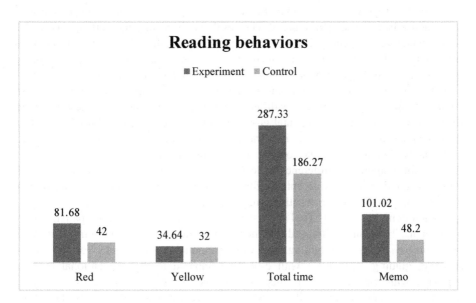

Fig. 5. The reading behaviors and results for the two groups.

The students' reading behaviors were retrieved for explorative data analysis to thoroughly gauge the information concerning the students' reading behavior patterns. The independent-samples t-tests compared between two groups to assess the reading behaviors include the number of red markers highlighted, number of yellow markers highlighted, the total time spent on the eBook system in minutes, and number of memos typed by the students. The results of the t-tests showed significant difference between the two groups (in Fig. 5) in terms of red markers highlighted (t = 2.87, p < .001, *Cohen's d* = 0.62), the total time spend on eBook system in minutes (t = 2.59, p < .05, *Cohen's d* = 0.50), and number of memos typed by the students (t = 2.40, p < .001, *Cohen's d* = 0.50).The experimental group in red markers, the total time, number of memos were M = 81.69, SD = 79.34, M = 287.33, SD = 250.75, and M = 101.02, SD = 138.78 respectively. For the control group they were M = 42.00 SD = 42.96, M = 186. 27 SD = 151.36, and M = 48.20 SD = 57.37. However, it was found that there was no significant difference between the two groups in terms of the number of yellow markers highlighted by the students (t = 2.873, p > .001).

6 Conclusion

This study proposed the topic-scanning guiding mechanism in e-books for supporting EFL students' reading comprehension. An experiment was conducted to examine the effects of the proposed mechanism on the reading comprehension, learning perceptions, and reading behavior of participants. The results showed that the participants in the experimental group gained higher comprehension scores than the control group. This indicated that there is a difference in reading comprehension for the topic-scanning guiding mechanism with e-books compared to the conventional reading approach with e-books. However, we found that the participants in the experimental group and the control group were not significantly different in learning perceptions. The result may be explained that both the experimental group and the control group read used BookRoll system which can be inferred that it did not affect their learning perceptions whether the participants integrated with the topic scanning guiding mechanism or not. Therefore, there is not a significant difference in learning perception: learning satisfaction, cognitive load, and technology acceptance for the topic-scanning guiding mechanism with e-books compared to the conventional reading approach with e-books.

In addition, the Analysis Tool was used for recording reader behavior patterns from participants. The results displayed that there were significant differences in the reading behaviors of words highlighting and words annotation in e-books for the topic-scanning guiding mechanism with e-books compared to the conventional reading approach with e-books. The results of students' reading behaviors (highlighting, reading time, and memo word numbers) provided evidence to support the topic-scanning guiding mechanism in e-books. As Meyer and Ray (2017) indicated that the importance of scaffolding and instructing in training students to tactically read information from text structure should not be overlooked. Providing reading strategies in e-books, such as the topic-scanning guiding mechanism can promote students reading behaviors in e-books.

This study makes distinct contributions to an e-book system development and the conduct of research related to an e-book adoption. First, this study confirms the importance of reading strategies in the adoption for reading comprehension purposes (Ness 2016). While authors have examined perceived satisfactory, ease of use, and cognitive load in research related to e-books, this study finds strong support for behavioral patterns to use eBook readers. The robust impact of reading strategies with an e-book is suitable in future research related to e-book research and readers' reading behavioral patterns. This study demonstrated that, in the context of e-book learning, avail-ability of reading strategy guiding is an essential factor. Future studies should further consider and examine the use of other English learning strategies intended at improving not only the reading but the writing of EFL learners by using e-books.

Acknowledgments. This research was supported by JSPS KAKENHI Grant-in-Aid for Scientific Research (S) Grant Number 16H06304 and NEDO Special Innovation Program on AI and Big Data 18102059-0.

References

Anderson, N.J.: Active Skills for Reading: Book Three. Thomson, Singapore (2010)

Akçapınar, G., Hasnine, M.N., Majumdar, R., Flanagan, B., Ogata, H.: Developing an early-warning system for spotting at-risk students by using eBook interaction logs. Smart Learn. Environ. **6**(4), 1–15 (2019)

Brown, H.D.: Language assessment: Principles and classroom practices. Pearson Education, San Francisco, CA (2003)

Chen, C.N., Chen, S.C., Chen, S.H.E., Wey, S.-C.: The effects of extensive reading via e-books on tertiary level EFL students' reading attitude, reading comprehension, and vocabulary. Turk. Online J. Educ. Technol. **2**(2), 303–312 (2013)

Cogmen, S., Saracaloglu, A.S.: Students' usage of reading strategies in the faculty of education. Procedia Soc. Behav. Sci. **1**, 248–251 (2009)

Chou, I.C.: Understanding on-screen reading behaviors in academic contexts: a case study of five graduate English-as-a-second-language students. Comput. Assist. Lang. Learn. **25**, 411–433 (2012)

Chu, H.C., Hwang, G.J., Tsai, C.C., Tseng, J.C.R.: A two-tier test approach to developing location-aware mobile learning systems for natural science courses. Comput. Educ. **55**(4), 1618–1627 (2010)

Derakhti, F.M., Sharififar, M., Moghimizade, R.P.: The study on the role of reading comprehension strategy instruction on english reading comprehension development among intermediate students. Mod. J. Lang. Teach. Methods **5**(3), 75 (2015)

Duggan, G.B., Payne, S.J.: Text skimming the process and effectiveness of foraging through text under time pressure. J. Exp. Psychol. Appl. **15**, 228–242 (2009)

Flanagan, B., Majumdar, R., Akçapınar, G., Wang, J., Ogata, H.: Knowledge map creation for modeling learning behaviors in digital learning environments. In: Companion Proceedings. of 9th LAK (2019)

Hwang, G.J., Chen, M.R.A., Sung, H.Y., Lin, M.H.: Effects of integrating a concept mapping-based summarization strategy into flipped learning on students' reading performances and perceptions in Chinese courses (2018)

Hwang, G.J., Yang, L.H., Wang, S.Y.: A concept map-embedded educational computer game for improving students' learning performance in natural science courses. Comput. Educ. **69**, 121–130 (2013)

Just, M.A., Carpenter, P.A.: Speed reading. In: Just, M.A., Carpenter, P.A. (eds.) The Psychology of Reading and Language Processing, pp. 425–452. Allyn & Bacon, Newton (1987)

Li, L.-Y., Chen, G.-D., Yang, S.-J.: Construction of cognitive maps to improve e-book reading and navigation. Comput. Educ. **60**(1), 32–39 (2013)

Liaw, M.L.: Reading strategy awareness training to empower online reading. Engl.Teach. J. **38**, 133–150 (2017)

Liu, P.-L., Chen, C.-J., Chang, Y.-J.: Effects of a computer-assisted concept mapping learning strategy on EFL college students' english reading comprehension. Comput. Educ. **54**(2), 436–445 (2010)

Liu, Y.T., Leveridge, A.N.: Enhancing L 2 vocabulary acquisition through implicit reading support cues in e-books. British Journal of Educational Technology **48**(1), 43–56 (2017)

Mangen, A., Walgermo, B.R.: Brønnick, K: Reading linear texts on paper versus computer screen: Effects on reading comprehension. Int. J. Educ. Res. **58**, 61–68 (2013)

Meyer, B.J., Ray, M.N.: Structure strategy interventions: Increasing reading comprehension of expository text. Int. Electron. J. Elementary Educ. **4**(1), 127–152 (2017)

Ness, M.K.: Reading comprehension strategies in secondary content area classrooms: teacher use of and attitudes towards reading comprehension instruction. Reading Horiz. **49**(2), 5 (2016)

Ogata, H., et al.: Learning analytics for e-book-based educational big data in higher education. In: Yasuura, H., Kyung, C.-M., Liu, Y., Lin, Y.-L. (eds.) Smart Sensors at the IoT Frontier, pp. 327–350. Springer, Cham (2017). https://doi.org/10.1007/978-3-319-55345-0_13

Qu, Y., Cid, J., Chan, E., Huo, Y.: Statistical Analyses for the Expanded TOEIC® Speaking Test. ETS Research Memorandum Series (2017)

Rockinson-Szapkiw, A.J., Courduff, J., Carter, K., Bennett, D.J.C.: Electronic versus traditional print textbooks: a comparison study on the influence of university students' learning. Comput. Educ. **63**, 259–266 (2013)

Smith, L.C., Mare, N.N.: Reading for Today 3: Issues, 5th edn. Natl Geographic, Washington DC (2017)

Tabachnick, B. G., Fidell, L.S.: Using multivariate statistics: International edition. Pearson2012 (2013)

White, S.J., Warrington, K.L., McGowan, V.A., Paterson, K.B.: Eye movements during reading and topic scanning: effects of word frequency. J. Exp. Psychol. Hum. Percept. Perform. **41**(1), 233 (2015)

Woody, W.D., Daniel, D.B., Baker, C.A.J.C.: E-books or textbooks: students prefer textbooks. Comput. Educ. **55**(3), 945–948 (2010)

Yusuf, Q., Yusuf, Y.Q., Yusuf, B., Nadya, A.: Skimming and scanning techniques to assist EFL students in understanding English reading texts. Indonesian Res. J. Educ. IRJE **1**(1), 43–57 (2017)

Investigating and Predicting the Usability of an E-Book System for University Students: The Role of Prior Knowledge

Cheng-Huan Chen$^{(\boxtimes)}$, Yi-Xuan Chen , Yun-Hsin Chow ,
and Shin-Hung Pan

Asia University, Taichung, Taiwan
chchen@asia.edu.tw

Abstract. Students' prior knowledge contributes to their e-book reading comprehension and might affect the usability of an e-book system. This study explored the influence of university students' prior knowledge on the usability of an e-book system termed "BookRoll," which was introduced in the context of an information and technology course in this study. One hundred first-year students (36 male and 64 female students) at a university in central Taiwan participated in this study. Students previewed the lecture slides and used e-book functions such as bookmarks, highlights, and memos during seven weekly lessons. Students' prior knowledge in the domain of information and technology and the Usefulness, Satisfaction, and Ease of use (USE) dimensions of the BookRoll system were collected before and after the treatment course, respectively. This study revealed that students' prior domain knowledge had no significant effect on the usability of the e-book system. In general, students' ratings of BookRoll's usability were high. Positive qualitative feedback across categories was given by students with high and low prior knowledge; however, some negative but constructive qualitative feedback was also provided. In addition, a short questionnaire to measure the USE dimensions of an e-book system for undergraduate users was developed and provided.

Keywords: E-book system · Prior knowledge · Usability

1 Introduction

An e-book is an electronic document that can be read on a computer or electronic devices. Most e-book systems support bookmarks, annotations, and queries, which make it more convenient for users to read and study. Developed by Kyoto University, BookRoll is an online e-book system that allows students to view digital materials used in lectures [1, 9]. Students can browse online materials anytime and anywhere from a web browser through their personal device (e.g., a computer, tablet, or smartphone). Main features of BookRoll include bookmarks, highlights, and memo functions by which students can use for reading and learning [2, 10].

Students' prior knowledge is the premise of reading comprehension and should be taken into consideration in e-book reading; reading comprehension needs to be generated by the interaction between the reader who uses his/her prior knowledge and the

© Springer Nature Singapore Pte Ltd. 2020
J. Shen et al. (Eds.): IC3 2019, CCIS 1227, pp. 333–342, 2020.
https://doi.org/10.1007/978-981-15-6113-9_38

reading materials [3]. Hwang et al. [4] found that high knowledge readers' annotation behavior was more than that of low knowledge readers on an annotatable e-book system. With a focus on the possible effects of prior domain knowledge on the use of learning system, Chen [5] also found that high and low prior knowledge learners had different approaches to use the system to learn. In view of the above, it could be expected that students' prior knowledge may affect the system usability, which refers to "the extent to which a product can be used by specified users to achieve specified goals with effectiveness, efficiency and satisfaction in a specified context of user," as defined in ISO 9124-11.

To date, and to the best of our knowledge, limited research has assessed the usability of BookRoll, as well as the relationship between students' prior domain knowledge and their ratings of usability. This study thus set out to understand: (1) the usability of the e-book system BookRoll, and (2) whether the usability changes when students' prior domain knowledge is different.

2   Method

2.1   Participants

This study employed an experimental design, and two intact first-year classes at a university located in central Taiwan were involved in this study. The participants were 100 first-year students, including 36 males and 64 females and ranging in age from 18 to 19 years. All participants had basic computer skills to operate browsers.

2.2   The BookRoll System and Treatment

This study introduced the BookRoll system, which was linked to Moodle (a learning management system required in the courses), to a two-credit compulsory course "Information and Technology." Students could use different BookRoll functions, as shown in Table 1 and Fig. 1, when viewing the course materials on the system. A teacher could summarize the viewing status of course materials through the BookRoll dashboard, as shown in Fig. 2, regarding the number of highlights (i.e., markers) for each slide, page transition status, marker text, comments and the number of comments on each page, students' reading progress, event rate and total numbers in a range of time.

Table 1. BookRoll main functions for students.

Function	Feature
Bookmark	Attaching/removing a bookmark
Highlight	Adding/deleting a marker
Memo	Attaching/removing/editing a memo

Fig. 1. Screenshot of the user interface of BookRoll.

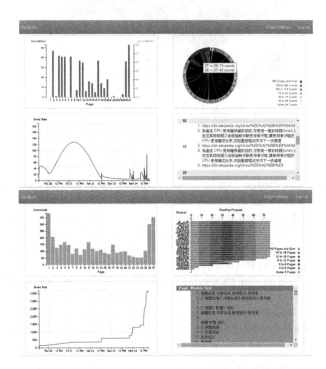

Fig. 2. Screenshot of the BookRoll dashboard.

The treatment course included seven lessons and lasted seven weeks, with one lesson per week. The seven lessons were: free website builders, introduction to computers, word processing software, presentation software, spreadsheet, cloud computing and services, and operating system and system management, respectively. Students were told to preview the lecture slides using BookRoll before the class. Each lesson was conducted in a computer classroom (see Fig. 3) by the same teacher (viz., the first author) at the participants' university. At the beginning of each lesson, the teacher took ten minutes to summarize the previewing status of lecture slides through the dashboard, to let students get an overview and critical information for learning this lesson. The teacher broadcasted his screen for lecturing, and each student watched a computer monitor while listening to a lesson.

Fig. 3. Classroom environment.

2.3   Measures

Prior Domain Knowledge. An information proficiency test was used to evaluate students' prior knowledge in the domain of information and technology. This proficiency test was administered three weeks before the instructional experiment by the participants' university, covering: introduction to computers, web page design, application software, cloud services, and operating systems. This test consisted of 35 multiple-choice questions (each with four choices), and the total score of this test was 70 points. There was no difference in scores between the two participants' classes, $t(90) = -1.38$, $p = .17$. Eight students did not take the proficiency test due to the fact that they are transfer students or were absent for the test. The reliability was established by testing it with another 90 students (aged 18–19) different from the participants, and the Kuder-Richardson reliability index (*KR20*) was .75 for this proficiency test.

Usability. A short questionnaire was created to measure the BookRoll usability for undergraduates. The questionnaire was based on Lund's USE Questionnaire [6], which has been reported as having good reliability and validity in a recent study [7], for measuring usability. USE stands for Usefulness, Satisfaction, Ease of use, and are the three dimensions of this questionnaire. Usefulness contains 3 items; satisfaction contains 2 items; ease of use contains 3 items (see Appendix for the complete questionnaire). These 8 items were rated on a 5-point Likert scale from *strongly disagree* (1 point) to *strongly agree* (5 points). Cronbach's α reliability coefficient for this questionnaire was .94 in this study, and the α coefficients were .91, .92, .86 for the three dimensions of usefulness, satisfaction, and ease of use, respectively, thus indicating good internal consistency and reliability. In addition, two open-ended questions (1. My positive comments or suggestions on the use of BookRoll; 2. My negative comments or suggestions on the use of BookRoll) were conducted with participants to understand their perceptions of using the BookRoll system. These two questions were optional.

2.4 Procedure

The instructional experiment was run over a period of eight weeks, with one class session (50 min) per week, during the fall semester of 2018. The procedure consisted of a practice activity and a treatment activity, as detailed below:

Practice Activity (Week 1). All participants received a practice activity, lasting 15 min. The teacher taught students how to operate the BookRoll system and enabled them to practice the use of the bookmark, highlight, and memo functions.

Treatment Activity (Weeks 2–8). Each student was required to preview the course materials that were uploaded on BookRoll. The treatment course ran over seven weeks, with seven lessons in seven weekly lessons (week 2: free website builders; week 3: introduction to computers; week 4: word processing software; week 5: presentation software; week 6: spreadsheet; week 7: cloud computing and services; and week 8: operating system and system management).

2.5 Data Analysis

This study first used descriptive statistics for the variables of students' prior domain knowledge and their ratings of BookRoll usability. Second, with prior domain knowledge as an independent variable, this study performed a simple regression with the post-experimental measure of usability as a dependent variable. In this study, the threshold for statistical significance (two-tailed) was set at .05. Data analyses were performed using SPSS Statistics 23. In addition to the quantitative data, students' feedback to the open-ended questions was presented as additional data for discussing the results, to provide a more in-depth understanding of students' perceptions for previewing course materials on the BookRoll system.

3 Findings

Four students who are transfer students and four students absent for the information proficiency test were unavailable from the analysis of this study. There were thus 92 students included in the following analysis. Table 2 presents the means and standard deviations of the usability of BookRoll and the proficiency test scores (i.e., students' prior knowledge in the domain of information and technology) for the participants. The scores indicated that BookRoll had good usability ($M = 32.29$). Students were generally satisfied with using BookRoll to preview lecture slides ($M = 7.79$). They also found using BookRoll to be simple ($M = 12.41$) and useful to learn ($M = 12.09$).

Table 2. Descriptive statistics for the prior domain knowledge and usability.

Measure		Maximum score	M	SD
Prior domain knowledge		70	34.85	7.86
Usability	Usefulness	15	12.09	2.25
	Satisfaction	10	7.79	1.67
	Ease of use	15	12.41	2.23
	Total	40	32.29	5.63

This study used Durbin–Watson statistic to detect the presence of autocorrelation in the residuals from the regression analysis. The test statistic was 2.06, which lied between 1.5 and 2.5 [8], indicating this assumption was not violated. Simple regression was then carried out. Table 3 shows the regression summary for the usability of BookRoll, $F(1, 90) = 0.79$, $t = -0.89$, $p = .38$, indicating that the students' prior domain knowledge did not prove to be a predictor.

Table 3. Regression summary for usability.

Variable	Model of usability				
	B	SE	β	t	p
Intercept	34.40	2.64		13.03	< .001
Prior domain knowledge	−0.07	0.07	−.09	−0.89	.38
Adj. R^2		−.002			
F		0.79			

Students' qualitative feedback, which may account for some aspects of the regression result, was partially[1] summarized in Table 4. Table 4 categorizes students' feedback into three groups, including system function, system interface, and course. It can be found that students with high, moderate, or low prior knowledge considered BookRoll simple and easy to use, and found it useful for learning. The finding indicates that low or high prior knowledge students were, in general, satisfied with BookRoll, in the aspects of user-friendly and identification with the system, as well as learning improvement. On the other hand, some negative feedback such as turning page was less irrelevant to the prior knowledge. We could also find that the same negative feedback regarding reading and learning was reflected by low and high prior knowledge students, such as the memo issue. In addition, more moderate and high prior knowledge students suggested more colors (currently it only has red as "important" and yellow as "unclear") to highlight the text; this may be because higher prior knowledge students have good classification ability.

---

[1] The complete qualitative feedback (in Traditional Chinese) generated in the current study is available from the corresponding author on reasonable request.

Table 4. Summary of students' feedback on the use of BookRoll.

	System function	System interface	Course
Pros	Simple and easy to highlight or memo.−1 low, 1 moderate, and 1 high prior knowledge students	The interface is neat/convenient.−1 moderate and 1 high prior knowledge students	It has changed lots of problems that traditional notes may encounter, like missing or moldering.−1 low prior knowledge student
	Attaching a bookmark and/or highlighting is useful.−1 moderate and 1 high prior knowledge students	Simple and easy to use/operate.−3 moderate prior knowledge students	Teachers can better understand the needs of students.−1 low prior knowledge student
			Being able to review at any time.−1 low and 1 high prior knowledge students
			Study the course through the Internet.−1 moderate prior knowledge student
Cons	Users must click the highlight function again to continue using highlighting.−1 low, 3 moderate, and 1 high prior knowledge students	Turning page is slow or often stuck.−1 low and 3 high prior knowledge students	
	There are too few colors with markers.−2 moderate and 2 high prior knowledge students	Difficult to operate with a mobile phone and unable to enlarge the page.−1 low, 1 moderate, and 1 high prior knowledge students	
	Users cannot move the memo icon on the lecture slide and must click it to see the memo content.−1 low and 1 high prior knowledge students	It's a little troublesome to log in.−1 low and 1 moderate prior knowledge students	
		Cannot select text.−1 high prior knowledge student	

4 Conclusion

This study introduced an e-book system, BookRoll, to a university course, and determined whether students' prior domain knowledge predicts the usability of BookRoll. An instructional experiment was carried out. This study found that Book-Roll provided good usability in terms of usefulness, satisfaction, and ease of use for university students, and their prior domain knowledge did not prove to be a predictor for usability. Students' qualitative feedback reflected that high, moderate, and low prior knowledge students had similar opinions on usability issues, although some focus was different in system functions and interface categories.

This study provides empirical evidence contributing to a better understanding of the relationship between students' prior domain knowledge and e-book system usability, as well as the usability of BookRoll for Taiwanese undergraduates and their constructive feedback regarding the use of the system. Additionally, this research provides a short e-book system usability questionnaire for undergraduate students. Although the questionnaire administered in this study demonstrated high reliability in the three dimensions (usefulness, satisfaction, and ease of use), future research could consider adding more items to the satisfaction dimension, as it currently has only two items. Nevertheless, caution should be taken in generalizing the findings to other e-book systems or students in different educational stages. Continuous research and practice are encouraged to introduce the BookRoll system to other subject domains and investigate the effectiveness of the system, as it demonstrated good usability and students' prior domain knowledge would not affect its use to achieve learning objectives and meet student needs.

Acknowledgments. The authors thank Prof. Stephen J.H. Yang for his insightful suggestions and Mr. Jian-Zhi Yu for the assistance in sorting the raw data. The authors also thank the Ogata Laboratory in Kyoto University for authorizing them to use the BookRoll system.

Appendix

Short E-book System Usability Questionnaire

Item	Original item	Dimension
1. It helps me be more effective to learn when using BookRoll. [使用BookRoll對於我的學習是有幫助的。]	It helps me be more effective.	Usefulness
2. It saves me time when I use BookRoll. [使用BookRoll可以節省我的學習時間。]	It saves me time when I use it.	Usefulness
3. BookRoll functions meet my needs. [BookRoll平台的功能符合我的需求。]	It meets my needs.	Usefulness
4. It is easy to learn to use BookRoll functions. [學習BookRoll平台的功能是很簡單的。]	It is easy to learn to use it.	Ease of learning (contributing to Ease of use)
5. It is easy to use BookRoll functions. [BookRoll平台的功能使用起來很容易。]	It is easy to use.	Ease of learning (contributing to Ease of use)
6. BookRoll interface is user friendly. [BookRoll平台的介面是友善的。]	It is user friendly.	Ease of use
7. I would recommend BookRoll to other classmates or friends. [我會推薦BookRoll平台給其他同學或朋友。]	I would recommend it to a friend.	Satisfaction
8. I am satisfied with BookRoll and willing to continue using BookRoll. [我對於使用BookRoll平台教學效果滿意，願意再繼續使用BookRoll平台。]	I am satisfied with it.	Satisfaction

9. My positive comments or suggestions on the use of BookRoll:
[我對使用BookRoll平台的正面（優點）意見或建議：]
10. My negative comments or suggestions on the use of BookRoll:
[我對使用BookRoll平台的負面（缺點）意見或建議：]

References

1. Ogata, H., et al.: Learning analytics for E-book-based educational big data in higher education. In: Yasuura, H., Kyung, C.-M., Liu, Y., Lin, Y.-L. (eds.) Smart Sensors at the IoT Frontier, pp. 327–350. Springer, Cham (2017). https://doi.org/10.1007/978-3-319-55345-0_13
2. Akçapınar, G., Hasnine, M. N., Majumdar, R., Flanagan, B., Ogata, H.: Using learning analytics to detect off-task reading behaviors in class. In: Paper presented in the 9th International Conference on Learning Analytics & Knowledge, Tempe, AZ (2019)
3. Huang, T.-H.: The study of exploring high/vocational school students' reading comprehension on reading e-books. Educ. Technol. Learn. 2(2), 143–164 (2014)

4. Hwang, W.-Y., Liu, Y.-F., Chen, H.-R., Huang, J.-W., Li, J.-Y.: Role of parents and annotation sharing in children's learning behavior and achievement using e-readers. J. Educ. Technol. Soc. **18**(1), 292–307 (2015)

5. Chen, H.-C.: The effects of prior knowledge on the use of English learning systems with scaffolding instruction: limitation and deduction. Unpublished master's thesis, National Central University, Taoyuan, Taiwan (2016)

6. Lund, A.M.: Measuring usability with the USE questionnaire. Usability Interface **8**(2), 3–6 (2001)

7. Gao, M., Kortum, P., Oswald, F.: Psychometric evaluation of the USE (Usefulness, Satisfaction, and Ease of use) Questionnaire for reliability and validity. Proc. Hum. Factors Ergon. Soc. Annu. Meet. **62**(1), 1414–1418 (2018)

8. Ayyangar, L.: Skewness, multicollinearity, heteroskedasticity - you name it, cost data have it! solutions to violations of assumptions of ordinary least squares regression models using SAS. In: Proceedings of SAS Global Forum 2007 (Paper 131-2007). Cary, NC: SAS Institute (2007)

9. Ogata, H., Yin, C., Oi, M., Okubo, F., Shimada, A., Kojima, K., Yamada, M.: e-Book-based learning analytics in university education. In: Ogata, H., Chen, W., Kong, S. C., Qiu, F. (eds.) Proceedings of the 23rd International Conference on Computers in Education, pp. 401–406. Asia-Pacific Society for Computers in Education, Hangzhou, China (2015)

10. Chen, C.-H., Su, C.-Y.: Using the BookRoll e-book system to promote self-regulated learning, self-efficacy and academic achievement for university students. J. Educ. Technol. Soc. **22**(4), 33–46 (2019)

An Experimental Study on the Integration of Mind Mapping into the Teaching of Mathematics Review Class in Primary Schools

Lu Sun[(✉)]

Huangshan University, No. 39, Xihai Road, Tunxi District,
Huangshan City 245041, Anhui, China
slahua@163.com

Abstract. Promoting the development of students' mathematical cognitive structure is one of the important tasks of mathematics teaching. Using mind mapping to carry out the experiment of teaching reform of mathematics review course based on core knowledge. The results show that the teaching of mathematics review course in primary schools with mind mapping can promote pupils to construct a more complete, systematic, hierarchical and concise mathematical cognitive structure, and help students to form mind mapping skills.

Keywords: Mind mapping · Primary school mathematics · Experimental study

1 Problem Posing

The fourth grade as the key transitional period of primary school mathematics learning, the phenomenon of students' mathematics achievement differentiation began to appear initially. Compared with the lower grades, the number of students with learning difficulties in mathematics is gradually increasing, and "most of them have problems such as small knowledge reserves, disordered structure, disordered ways, and difficult to activate" [1]. It can be seen that mathematics cognitive structure is one of the key factors affecting students' mathematics learning. Therefore, "from the cognitive point of view, the fundamental task of mathematics teaching is to shape students' good mathematical cognitive structure [2]".

Revision lesson is one of the important lessons. If you blindly list the knowledge or sea training, it can't achieve the teaching objectives of perfecting and optimizing students' knowledge structure. We need to try our best to "enlarge the role of core knowledge, to further clarify its connotation and extension, presentation, various variants and the relationship between them, and to expand and spread it as the center. In this way, students can grasp core knowledge's vertical and horizontal linkages and hierarchical structure, and form and improve the dynamic cognitive structure with core knowledge as the link point" [3]. How to carry out mathematics review teaching based on this idea? This problem needs to be explored and thought.

© Springer Nature Singapore Pte Ltd. 2020
J. Shen et al. (Eds.): IC3 2019, CCIS 1227, pp. 343–350, 2020.
https://doi.org/10.1007/978-981-15-6113-9_39

Mind mapping is a new method of note taking and teaching. "Simulate the radiation structure of human brain neural network, visualize the cognitive structure and externalize the mental map of the brain with visual pictures [4]." It has the main characteristics of divergence from the central vocabulary to the outside vocabulary. In recent years, it has been widely used in the teaching of biology, physics, chemistry, English and other disciplines, playing an important role in optimizing the way of thinking and clarifying the context of knowledge. The comparison shows that its connotation and characteristics are in good agreement with the teaching idea of mathematics review course based on core knowledge. Therefore, this paper chooses mind mapping as a tool for empirical research to study "how to integrate mind mapping into the teaching of mathematics review in primary schools? Will it promote the formation and improvement of students' cognitive structure?"

2 Experimental Study

2.1 Experimental Purpose

Whether the teaching of math review course in primary school incorporating mind mapping is helpful to the development of students' mathematical cognitive structure?

2.2 Experimental Object

In this study, two parallel classes of the fourth grade of Huangshan Experimental Primary School were selected. Both classes were trained in mind mapping at the beginning of the second semester of the fourth grade. At the end of the first semester, the performance level of the two classes was similar to that of the first three chapters before the second semester. Class 1 of Grade 4 is the control class and Class 3 of Grade 4 is the experimental class. There are 55 students in both classes.

2.3 Experimental Process

In chapter 4–8 of the second semester of the fourth grade, the experimental class was taught with mind map, that is, the teacher guided the students to brainstorm the core concepts in the review class, encouraged the students to draw their own mind map after class to review and collate the concepts and nature of each chapter, and evaluated them on the basis of the exchange of students' works in the control class. However, the traditional review teaching activities should be carried out.

2.4 Test Content

Students are required to integrate the contents of Four Operations and Operational Law and draw independent mind maps.

2.5   Experimental Evaluation Tool

According to the characteristics of mind mapping and the evaluation criteria of students' mind mapping works proposed by Yang Yan-jun [5], and combining with the actual level of primary school students, the evaluation indicators including five dimensions of correctness, completeness, conciseness, structure and aesthetics are formulated. Each dimension was divided into four levels, level 1 to level 4 scored 1, 2, 3 and 4 points respectively.

The dimension of correctness concerns the expression of concepts and the reflection of relationships.

Level 1: It can't correctly express multiple concepts of the theme and can't reflect relations.
Level 2: It can correctly express multiple concepts of the theme, but can't reflect the relationship.
Level 3: Correct expression of multiple concepts of the subject and partial relationship.
Level 4: Correct expression of multiple concepts of the subject and their relationships.

Integrity dimension focuses on reflecting the overall extent of the topic.

Level 1: Can't reflect the relevant content of the subject.
Level 2: Part reflects the relevant content of the theme.
Level 3: It reflects the relevant contents of the theme more completely.
Level 4: Fully reflect the relevant content of the theme.

The conciseness dimension focuses on the extraction of keywords.

Level 1: No key words are refined.
Level 2: Select and refine some key words.
Level 3: Choose refined keywords, but some of them are incorrect.
Level 4: Choose the right keywords instead of long sentences.

The structural dimension focuses on the level of clarity.

Level 1: The structure is not clear and there is no hierarchy.
Level 2: The structure is clear, with only two levels.
Level 3: The structure is clear and has many levels.
Level 4: The structure is clear, has multi-levels and reasonable.

The aesthetic dimension focuses on the use of graphics and colors.

Level 1: Without the use of graphics, layout is not reasonable enough, no use of color to distinguish.
Level 2: The layout is more reasonable, use color to distinguish.
Level 3: The layout is reasonable and beautiful, using color and graphics to distinguish.
Level 4: The layout is reasonable and beautiful, using color and graphics to distinguish, with creative and aesthetic.

2.6   Data Coding and Analysis

The two members of the task group scored and coded the students' works according to the evaluation indexes, and discussed the objection scores. All data were analyzed by SPSS19.0.

3   Research Results

3.1   A Comparative Analysis of the Overall Level of Students' Mind Mapping Works

According to the total score of evaluation index, the overall situation of students' mind mapping works can be divided into four levels. The level of students in the control and experimental classes is shown in Table 1.

Table 1. Statistical table of general level of students' statistical mind map.

Class	Level 1	Level 2	Level 3	Level 4	χ^2	df
Control class	14	25	16	0	33.879	3
Experimental class	1	12	29	13		

Statistical results show that the overall level of mind mapping works of students in experimental class is mainly concentrated in level 3, while that of students in control class is mostly concentrated in level 2. According to the proportion of the two extreme levels, none of the students in the control class reached the level of 4, while 23.5% of the students in the experimental class reached this level. For Level 1, about a quarter of the students in the control class showed this level in their works, while only one student in the experimental class showed this level. It can be seen that the overall level of the experimental class is higher than that of the control class in terms of the proportion of the number of students at all levels. Further chi-square test on the total number of students in the two classes shows that there are significant differences in the overall level between the experimental class and the control class ($\chi^2 = 45.013$, $P = 0.000 < 0.001$).

3.2   Comparative Analysis of Dimensions of Students' Mind Mapping Works

In order to further explore whether the purpose of the experiment is achieved, the students 'mind mapping works are effectively compared and analyzed. Table 2 makes statistics on students' work scores from five dimensions. The data show that the test performance of the students in the experimental class is higher than that of the control class in five dimensions.

The data show that the test performance of the students in the experimental class is higher than that of the control class in five dimensions:

In the dimension of correctness, 81.8% of the students in the experimental class concentrate on Level 3–Level 4. In contrast, 56.2% and 29.2% of the students in the control class were at level 2 and 3. It can be seen that the level of the experimental class students in this dimension is better than that of the control class as a whole. Further Chi-square test results also show that there are significant differences between the two classes in the dimension of correctness (P = 0.000 < 0.001).

For the integrity dimension, more than half of the students in the experimental class and the control class showed level 3. From the proportion of the number of students at all levels, the performance of the experimental class in the dimension of integrity is better than that of the control class. Chi-square test results also confirm this conclusion. There is a very significant difference between the two classes in this dimension, which is less than 0.001 levels.

About the dimension of conciseness, more than 50% of the students in the experimental class and the control class reached the level of Level 3. However, at the highest and lowest levels, 10.9% of the students in the experimental class could choose to extract correct keywords, while none of the students in the control class reached this level. On the contrary, 14.6% of the students showed no awareness of extracting keywords. Compared with the control class, the experimental class has a significant change in the dimension of conciseness (χ^2 = 15.810, P = 0.001 < 0.05).

From the structural dimension, two classes are more evenly distributed in Level 2 and level 3, but the difference is that the proportion of the experimental class in Level 3 is higher than that in level 2, while the control class is the opposite. The results of Chi-square test further show that the structural performance of students in the experimental class is better than that of the control class (χ^2 = 18.701, P = 0.002 < 0.05). Nine students in the experimental class were able to give multiple levels with clear and reasonable structure, while none of the students in the control class reached this level.

As far as aesthetic dimension is concerned, about one-half of the students' works in the experimental class and the control class show the characteristics of Level 2. The difference is that the proportion of people in the experimental class at Level 3 is higher

Table 2. Statistical table of five dimensions of students' mind map.

Dimension	Class	Level 1	Level 2	Level 3	Level 4	χ^2	df
Correctness	Control class	8	31	16	0	45.013	3
	Experimental class	0	10	19	26		
Completeness	Control class	4	22	29	0	31.101	3
	Experimental class	0	5	34	16		
Conciseness	Control class	8	14	33	0	15.810	3
	Experimental class	0	21	28	6		
Structural	Control class	14	23	18	0	18.701	3
	Experimental class	2	21	23	9		
Aesthetics	Control class	14	32	9	0	12.634	2
	Experimental class	3	30	22	0		

than that in the control class. Statistical results show that there are significant differences between the two classes in terms of aesthetics ($\chi^2 = 12.634$, P = 0.002 < 0.05).

4 Research Conclusions

The results of two classes of mind mapping tasks for a given topic can be found as follows:

In terms of correctness, compared with the control class, the experimental class students can more comprehensively express multiple concepts related to the theme, and consciously seek the connection between concepts or knowledge points. The statistical results show that the level of students in the experimental class is significantly higher than that in the control class. It can be seen that introducing mind map into the teaching of mathematics review in primary schools can promote students to connect each knowledge point, form a systematic knowledge structure, improve the efficiency of review and promote the construction of cognitive structure.

For completeness, compared with the control class, the experimental class students can more comprehensively reflect the concepts and knowledge points of related topics. Chi-square test results show that there are also significant differences in this dimension between the two classes. It can be seen that the teaching of mind mapping can make tacit knowledge visualized, facilitate students' understanding and promote the formation of their divergent thinking, grasp more comprehensively multiple knowledge points related to core concepts through drawing, and form a more comprehensive cognitive structure.

For simplicity, the statistical results show that although more than 50% of the students in both classes have reached level 3, there are still significant differences between the two classes. From the perspective of students' works, both classes have a preliminary awareness of extracting keywords in drawing, but unlike the experimental class, the students in the control class mainly concentrate on the first level, while ignoring the extraction of keywords at other levels. Therefore, the self-drawing training of mind mapping can promote students to learn to extract keywords and form a more concise cognitive structure, which will help them find and acquire knowledge in information processing.

For the structural aspect, although both classes are at level 2, from the test results and the analysis of the works, the experimental class students are better than the control class in the number of levels and rationality in drawing. This shows that the integration of mind mapping into teaching can help students form a richer and more reasonable level consciousness to a certain extent.

As for aesthetics, compared with the control class, the students in the experimental class have mastered the skills of mind mapping. That is, they can use color or graphics to distinguish. Statistical results also show that the theoretical training of mind mapping alone can't really improve the students' drawing skills. "Practice - Communication - Evaluation" and other links is the effective forming path. However, compared with the other four dimensions, the effect of this experiment on the aesthetic sense and creativity of the layout of students is still not obvious. Therefore, it is necessary to further consider the teaching and guidance of this aspect in the future experimental teaching process.

To sum up, it can be seen that the review course of primary school mathematics integrated with mind mapping can promote pupils to construct a more complete, systematic, hierarchical and concise mathematical cognitive structure, and contribute to the formation of mind mapping skills. For example, the work of a student in the experimental class of Fig. 1 shows that the student has mastered the basic skills of drawing. On the basis of focusing the core knowledge on the center, he can not only comb and present the knowledge points of addition, subtraction, multiplication and division by four colors in turn, but also better. Grasp the relationship between the four operations and the relationship between the four operations and the operation law, clear hierarchy, concise structure. From the visibility of mind map, students have a holistic grasp of the vertical and horizontal connection and hierarchical structure of the two core knowledge, namely "Four Operations" and "Law of Operations", and have initially formed a cognitive structure with core knowledge as the link point. It can be seen that mind mapping is not only a teaching method, but also a good evaluation tool to understand students' mathematical cognitive structure.

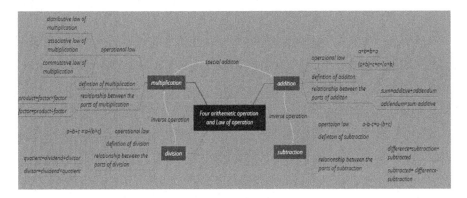

Fig. 1. Level 4 students' works in the experimental class.

Therefore, teachers should be good at using mind mapping as an effective tool to promote the development of students' mathematical cognitive structure by guiding students to read, supplement and draw. At the same time, they should use their thinking visualization function to understand the level of students' mathematical cognitive structure, guide students to recognize their own shortcomings in the process of communication, and design corresponding teaching activities in a targeted way. To help them build a better cognitive structure.

References

1. Zhang, H.L.: Investigation and countermeasure research on factors affecting pupils' mathematics learning difficulties. Contemp. Educ. Forum **10**(6), 59–61 (2011)
2. Wu, F.W., Wang, J.J.: On the influence and role of intellectual participation on the construction of good mathematical cognitive structure. Teach. Manag. **19**(3), 70 (2002)

3. Wei, G.M.: Making cognitive structure grow vigorously—on the reform direction of mathematics review course. People's Educ. **59**(5), 41–44 (2008)
4. Zhao, H.Y.: Perfecting cognitive structure and improving mathematical literacy—brief analysis of the application of mind mapping in mathematics review in primary schools. Prim. Sch. Teach. Ref. **56**(23), 61–62 (2017)
5. Yang, Y.J. http://blog.sina.com.cn/s/blog_5955b2830100y9sx.html. Accessed

Demand Analysis of Learning Support Service in MOOCs Based on Kano Model

Qian Bai[✉]

College of Education Science, Nanjing Normal University,
Nanjing 210097, Jiangsu, China
1658521929@qq.com

Abstract. Based on the analysis of existing research, MOOC learning support service is defined into five dimensions: technical support service, resource support service, personnel support service, emotional support service and evaluation support service. Taking the MOOC learners' demand as the starting point of research, combing the kano model's theoretical connotation and research method, a survey about "MOOC Learners' Demands for Learning Support Service" to some learners on domestic MOOC learning platforms was investigated. The result shown that MOOC learning support service demands under Kano model mainly divided into three parts which included attractive demand, must-be demand and expected demand. Finally, some strategies to construct learning support service system in MOOCs were also put forward.

Keywords: Kano model · MOOCs · Learning support service · Demand analysis

1 Introduction

In the current era of "sharing economy", major MOOCs platforms are like "self-service" stores. MOOCs are featured "self-service" goods displayed in stores, and learners naturally become consumers who choose "goods" randomly in "stores". The development of economy makes more and more similar goods tend to homogenize on performance, the difference of quality and value is smaller and smaller, at this time, the high-quality service of shopkeeper humanization often became capture popular feeling best sharp weapon, "what buy is not a commodity, it is a service" this sentence also got very good verify. In contrast, the "self-service" commodity of MOOCs, the quality of courses is indeed important, but what kind of services course developers and platform builders can provide for learners, and whether these services can meet the demands of learners are also the key points. Consequently, how to provide MOOCs learning support services based on learners' needs is an urgent problem to be solved.

1.1 The Evolution of Learning Support Services' Concept

Learning support services originate from the field of distance education and evolve from the concept of "student support" [1]. Looking through the existing literature, the research on MOOCs learning support service in China is still in the preliminary

© Springer Nature Singapore Pte Ltd. 2020
J. Shen et al. (Eds.): IC3 2019, CCIS 1227, pp. 351–358, 2020.
https://doi.org/10.1007/978-981-15-6113-9_40

exploration stage. Wen-qiang Fan points out that special learning support services should be built on the basis of understanding the characteristics of MOOCs [2]. From the perspective of research content, some researchers found that the current MOOCs lacks effective learning support services. Huihui Zhou studied the design of MOOCs learning support service system by taking MOOCs course of modern educational technology as an example [3]. By analyzing several typical MOOCs platforms, Dong Yang summarized the current construction status of each subsystem of learning support service on the MOOCs platform, and proposed improvement strategies [4]. Starting from the perspective of learners' satisfaction with MOOCs learning support services, Xu Fang constructed a MOOCs learning support service evaluation model based on the learning support service-related model and the characteristics of MOOCs [5].

By summarizing existing studies, the MOOCs learning support services in this study are defined as technical support service (TSS), resource support service (RSS), personnel support service (PSS), emotional support service (ESS1) and evaluation support service (ESS2).

1.2   The Development of Kano Model

Kano model was proposed under the inspiration of Herzberg's two-factor theory [6]. 1974, Herzberg in the study of employee satisfaction, proposed the theory of double factors and the "satisfaction with dissatisfied is completely the opposite" the traditional concept of the single dimension put forward the criticism, pointed out: the opposite of "happy", not "not satisfied", but not "completely satisfied", that is to say, even if will be satisfactory factor, employees also will not necessarily not happy, in the same way, let a person not satisfied factors vanish, the employees are not satisfied. In 1982, Noriaki Kano, a professor at Tokyo Polytechnic University in Japanese set up the famous Kano model [6], as shown in Fig. 1: horizontal axis' satisfaction with the product quality characteristics, the more to the right to say the quality of the product features more able to meet and exceed customer expectations; The vertical axis represents the level of customer satisfaction, and the higher the vertical axis is, the higher the customer satisfaction is.

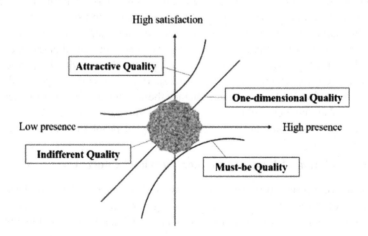

Fig. 1. Kano model

In 1996, Kurt Martzler proposed a more detailed application method of Kano model based on previous studies, which has become a more mainstream application method of Kano model [7]. Firstly, we should design Kano questionnaire: for each requirement, positive and negative questions were set in terms of whether it was satisfied or not. The structure was referred to Likert's five-dimensional scale, and the degree of "I like" to "I don't like" decreased successively. Then, questionnaires were given out and a survey was conducted. According to the survey results, data analysis was conducted on the Kano evaluation form (as shown in Table 1). Where "M" represents the must-be quality, "O" represents the one-dimensional quality, "A" represents the attractive quality, "I" represents the indifferent quality, "R" represents the reverse quality. Finally, the data are classified into demand characteristics by the "maximum frequency method".

Table 1. Kano questionnaire evaluation form

Positive question	Negative question				
	I like	It should be	Doesn't matter	I can stand	I don't like
I like	Q	A	A	A	O
It should be	R	I	I	I	M
Doesn't matter	R	I	I	I	M
I can stand	R	I	I	I	M
I don't like	R	R	R	R	Q

2   Research Setting

As the most popular online open courses at present, both the platform itself and the course team have actively provided many learning support services for learners, intending to attract more learners to join in. However, the provision of learning support services is mostly from the perspective of platform builders and course developers, and rarely from the perspective of learners' needs. Therefore, from the perspective of learners, all learning support services involved in MOOCs are classified according to the Kano model, which can provide references for the future construction of MOOCs learning support services.

2.1   Original Acquisition of Requirement Item

Before using Kano model to analyze the demand of MOOCs learning support service, learners' original demand items should be acquired first. By consulting relevant materials, sorting out the support service functions of major MOOCs platforms, and combining with interviews with some MOOCs learners, the original demand items of each part of MOOCs learning support service are summarized, as shown in Fig. 2.

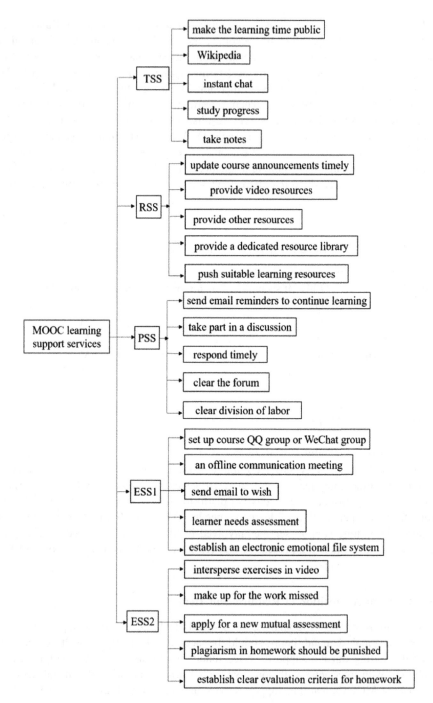

Fig. 2. Collation of requirements for MOOCs learning support services

2.2   Preparation and Distribution of the Questionnaire

After the original demand items are determined, positive and negative questions need to be set for each demand item of the support service to form a "questionnaire on the demand of MOOCs learners for learning support services". Learners' feelings on whether each support service is provided are respectively expressed by "I like", "it should be", "doesn't matter", "I can stand" and "I don't like". In order to make learners clearly distinguish the five feelings, the questionnaire needs to explain the five options, as follows: "I like" means to make you feel satisfied, happy and surprising; "It should be" means what you think is necessary; "Doesn't matter" means you don't particularly care, dispensable; "I can stand" means you don't like it, but you can live with it; "I don't like" means something that makes you feel dissatisfied or even a little annoying.

The questionnaire was compiled by using the online editing tool "questionnaire star", and the respondents were mainly MOOCs learners on some MOOCs learning platforms in China (e.g., MOOCs of Chinese Universities, Xuetang Online, Good Universities Online, etc.). In the process of questionnaire distributed, on the one hand, with some courses, consultation, head of the team will survey questionnaire to normal way of link (https://www.wjx.cn/jq/22573634.aspx) learners to send to you to fill in, such not only can ensure the efficiency of the questionnaire to send, also can to a certain extent, improve letter validity of the questionnaire, to prevent the phenomenon of random fill in; On the other hand, the questionnaire links will be sent to various MOOCs learning groups through WeChat, QQ and other social tools to encourage learners to fill in the form of red packets. The groups are all learners of different educational backgrounds and ages, which can cover the survey subjects in a larger scope. The distribution of questionnaires lasted for nearly a month, and a total of 326 questionnaires were received, among which 312 were valid, with an effective rate of about 96%.

2.3   Data Analysis and Processing of the Questionnaire

Relevant data collected from the questionnaire were analyzed mainly through SPSS 22.0 and questionnaire star online tools, combined with descriptive analysis and "maximum frequency method". The Cronbach's Alpha coefficient and KOM value of the tested questionnaire were 0.928 and 0.756, indicating that the reliability and validity of the questionnaire were good. Classifying each option, count the number of each demand category, and determine the final demand characteristics of each option according to the "maximum frequency method".

According to the demand classification results, the demand categories of MOOCs learning support service based on Kano model mainly include attractive demand, must-be demand, one-dimensional demand and indifferent demand, which are sorted out as shown in Fig. 3. Among them, indifferent demand has little impact on the research itself, which is a dispensable demand. Therefore, it will not be considered in the subsequent analysis.

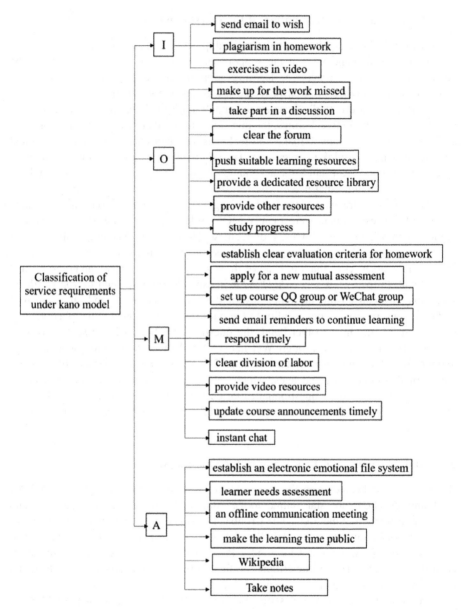

Fig. 3. Classification of service requirements under kano model

3   Advice

Finally, some strategies to construct learning support service system in MOOCs were also put forward which can be concluded as followed.

3.1 For Must-Be Demand

For MOOC learners, the must-be demands are the most basic ones. For example, "video" and "course announcement" in the survey results are essential requirements for resource support, which are the most basic components of MOOCs. It can be said that all MOOCs can provide these requirements for learners. However, how to make the most basic requirements be better and achieve the goal of "no one is better than me" is also the key issue for MOOC platform builders and course builders. The author also pointed out in a 2016 study on "negative motivational factors of MOOCs learners in China" that "video effect in MOOCs" is an important influencing factor for negative motivational factors of learners [8]. For video resources, the fluency and aesthetics should be guaranteed on the premise of quality first. For course announcements, the key issues to be considered by course builders and MOOC platforms are whether to release them timely and regularly, how to let all learners indirectly receive updated course announcements at the first time, and how to attract learners to actively view course announcements.

3.2 For Attractive Demand

To meet the basic needs of learners, MOOC builders should focus on the attractive demands of learning support services, which can effectively improve the core competitiveness of MOOCs and increase the highlights of MOOCs products. In terms of emotional support, the support of "offline meeting" and "learner needs assessment" is mainly provided by the course team itself. Although emotion is very abstract, in the learning process, students' emotion affects the learning effect to a great extent. The phenomenologist Scheler once said: "emotion guides cognition, and emotion determines which objects can enter the scope of cognition and determines the next development direction of cognition" [9]. As for the emotional support in learning support service, more scholars put forward that "emotion, as an irrational factor, should be permeated in cognition and cannot be designed alone" [10]. Therefore, the emotional support in learning support service system should not be an independent existence, but will permeate the process of resources, personnel and evaluation of these supports, and integrate with them, so that students can feel the existence of this support. At present, many courses on the domestic MOOCs platform will hold offline communication activities on a regular basis, changing the "distance" into "face-to-face", which effectively promotes the in-depth communication between learners and enhances the emotional experience of MOOCs learning.

3.3 For One-Dimensional Demand

The quality of one-dimensional demand will directly affect learners' overall satisfaction with support services. According to the survey results, one-dimensional demands include resource support of "courseware", "expanded resource" and "push suitable learning resources", which are important factors to determine learner satisfaction. Courseware and video resources complement each other, a good courseware should have prominent key points and clear learning objectives. In terms of expanding resources, many courses only recommend some textbooks or books related to the courses, while few resources are available for expanding specific knowledge points in the courses. In fact, each course in the teaching process will produce a lot of learning resources, some are carefully prepared by the course builder, some are published in the learning process of the course learning sentiment, course assignments, learning works, and so on, which can be used as curriculum development resources. For active push resources, it is not only the category of resource support that needs to be considered, but also the support of technical support services. With the wide application of big data and learning analysis technology, more and more scholars shift their research perspective from autonomous learning to adaptive learning. At present, domestic MOOCs learning platforms can't fully utilize such technologies to provide personalized learning support services, but many scholars have begun to pay attention to the construction of adaptive learning and its learning support system, which is also a problem that the whole online education needs to focus on.

References

1. Sewart, D.: Continuity of concern for students in a system of learning at a distance. Fem University, Hagen (1978)
2. Fan, W.Q.: Large-scale open online course (MOOC) based on relevance theory and its learning support. J. Distance Educ. (3), 31–36 (2012)
3. Zhou, H.H.: Research on the design of MOOC learning support service system. Shaanxi Normal University (2015)
4. Yang, D.: Study on the status quo and countermeasures of learning support services in MOOCs localization practice. Southwest University (2015)
5. Fang, X., Cui, X.P., Yang, G.X.: Study on the satisfaction of MOOCs learning support services from the perspective of structural equation model. Open Educ. Res. **22**(5) (2016)
6. Wu, J.H.: Research on medical service demand management system based on KANO model – based on data of community service center in Q district. Donghua University (2015)
7. Matzler, K., Hinterhuber, H.H., et al.: How to delight your customers. J. Product Brand Manag. (2), 6–18 (1996)
8. Bai, Q., Zhao, L., Zhang, S.Y.: Learning status and reflection of MOOCs – from the perspective of negative motivation influencing factors of MOOCs learners in China. Mod. Educ. Technol. (12), 65–71 (2016)
9. Li, X.Y., Lei, J.: Composition of teachers' emotional support for students in distance learning – theoretical and empirical research. Audio-Vis. Educ. Res. (5), 57–62 (2012)
10. Hu, L.F., Zhang, S.G.: On emotional support in distance education. Res. Contin. Educ. (6), 86–87 (2011)

Research on Online Learning Platform Based on Cloud Computing and Big Data Technology

Guan-Qun Cai[1(✉)] and Qing-Hua Wang[2]

[1] Office of Educational Administration, Xuan Cheng Vocational
and Technical College, Xuancheng 242000, Anhui, China
64114628@qq.com
[2] Training Center, Xuan Cheng Vocational and Technical College,
Xuancheng 242000, Anhui, China

Abstract. The online learning platform is the key category of online education research, cloud computing and big data technology combined with the form of online learning, points out the new direction of development, had a great change and to enhance the online learning platform of the traditional operation mode and method of data analysis. Aiming at the problems of online learning platform, the use of cloud computing and big data technology, the design and implementation of online learning platform, improve the interaction effect between teachers and learners online.

Keywords: Cloud computing · Big data · Online learning · Hadoop · MapReduce1

1 Introduction

At present, with the development of communication technology and Internet technology, the concept of "online learning" has gradually been accepted, and many studies have been carried out [1]. Luo and others put forward that uses rich online learning activities to stimulate online learners' learning motivation, so as to relieve loneliness in the process of learning [2]. Gianni points out that the depth of interaction in online learning can influence the learning effect of learners [3]. Chen and other demonstrate that the social function of online learning platform can improve the quality of teaching [4]. Zhang Yunchun proposed a new online learning platform model, from low-level to high-level, and gradually analyze the factors affecting online learning effectiveness. Tang Jintao have made a deep discussion on the interaction model and the isomerization data composed of online teachers and students by means of social network. Uses machine language programming and networking to develop an online learning service system to evaluate learners and online resources. Wu Yanwen and other use cloud computing to develop online learning systems.

In summary, online learning is a new learning upsurge of cloud computing development background, reflects the change of learning vector, at the same time, the rapid development of big data but also to reform the traditional learning mode, learning information service relying on big data can provide a broader and deeper. Existing online learning platforms do not take into account unstructured data in the early stages

© Springer Nature Singapore Pte Ltd. 2020
J. Shen et al. (Eds.): IC3 2019, CCIS 1227, pp. 359–366, 2020.
https://doi.org/10.1007/978-981-15-6113-9_41

of design, which greatly limits the development of online learning. Therefore, take the combination of cloud computing and big data technology, can achieve data acquisition, identification, analysis, explore the potential value of information by itself, solve the potential demands and predict the development trend of online learning. This article tries to improve the existing online learning model, equilibrium of online learning efficiency and learning efficiency, based on the deep analysis of the online learning platform, realize the online learning platform based on cloud computing and big data technology.

2 Literatures Reviewing

Cloud computing (Cloud Computing) is a commercial implementation of computer concepts such as Distributed (Computing), parallel processing (Parallel Computing) and Computing (Grid) [5]. The cloud computing advantage fully using the Internet, need to deal with the program is split into many sub modules, and then return to the cluster system composed of multiple servers, will eventually result in the user query,

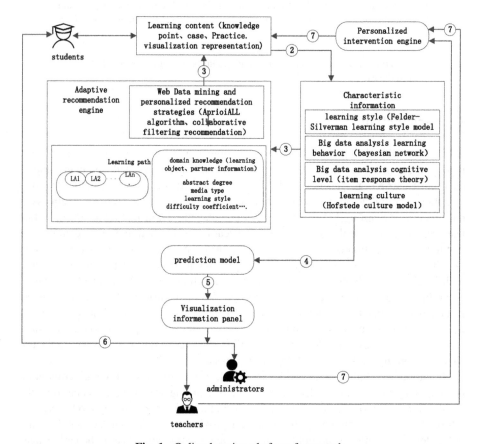

Fig. 1. Online learning platform framework

data feedback through the calculation and analysis methods. Because of the emergence of cloud computing, it has greatly expanded the level of network applications. Big data technology means discovering interesting, useful, and unexpected information from various types of data as Fig. 1 [6].

Cloud computing technology highlights computing power, especially dynamic computing capability; large data is the object of cloud computing technology, while emphasis on static storage function. Big data relies on cloud computing platform for data processing and analysis; cloud computing relies on massive amounts of data as the basis of calculation, so their combination is the trend dictates. Large data through cloud computing can greatly enhance the speed of operation, greatly reducing the computational overhead. In recent years, big data technology and cloud computing have been combined in biomedical fields such as astronomy, climatology and reflect, but relates to education in the field of cloud computing and big data with less.

Online learning platform will adopt a combination of cloud computing and big data technology framework to achieve flexible platform expansion. To build a stable and reliable, advanced and applicable "a cloud multiport" education cloud service system using advanced cloud technology to build high-quality support resource sharing and information management, will do the unified portal platform construction from the top-level design, improve the unified user management. And the integration of large data resources and teaching management system, unified deployment on the cloud platform, and ultimately realize the online learning platform function.

The online learning platform is the gateway and news release center of the information education management department first, so that the majority of students will be informed of the new developments of the Institute and the online education management department for the first time. Online learning business requirements and positioning platform: the middle layer of the platform should be all the teaching and management function set, including but not limited to educational management, online teaching, examination system, performance management, platform monitoring and statistical analysis module. The business of renewal and positioning of the online learning platform: online learning platform at the bottom should be a learning, training, education and teaching resource collection, students can learn through the required learning platform, staff can upload courseware, teaching platform resources, courseware resource type according to their learning needs to be convenient, increasingly rich. Including the teaching curriculum, teaching, teaching micro micro-blog WeChat and other diversified display, so the bottom is the foundation of the whole platform data center.

3 Research Design

Online learning platform integrates a large amount of data, and can not predict the growth of data. Only by using the linear expansion capability of the cloud model, can the online learning platform be satisfied. At present, cloud model mainly adopts Hadoop based distributed processing framework. Hadoop, developed by the Apache foundation, is able to run distributed programs on multiple hardware clusters, characterized by superior performance, high reliability, scalability, and low cost. Hadoop three core technologies are: distributed file system, used to store files in cluster hardware; programming model MapReduce, used to handle a variety of data sets; distributed database HBase. Using the distributed technology of Hadoop, we build an online learning platform, large data system, to achieve the storage, analysis and efficient processing of various types of data, to improve the level of online learning platform. The data acquisition and storage application layer distributed file system, online learning platform data analysis application layer MapReduce model, data source layer, data acquisition and storage of data extraction layer, need to develop suitable underlying docking adapter module, used to study multi class data acquisition platform big data environment in line.

Adhering to the "design of online learning platform to students as the center, technology development with the principle of curriculum for teaching design unit" and "humanity, cloud concept, unity, modular, multi terminal, localization, eventually building into integration, one-stop, unified logic, software system, open and digital the environment, providing strong support for the development of teaching, management and service of different service objects, realize the localization of management, technology facing the new development trend and construction of new demand, online learning platform in the process of construction are as follows:

(1) relying on cloud computing to deepen online learning services. The mode for online students available, convenient, on-demand network access, can be configured into the learning resource pool, learning resources integration learning center network, learning center learning center server, data storage, online learning related software applications and services, these learning resources for students provide.

(2) use the fragmented learning time of learners to improve the learning effect. Online learning should focus on developing content that best suits auditory, fragmentary, and learners' interests in the design of learning content. Rely on large data mining analysis of learner behavior trajectory: to improve the quality of learning, to in-depth analysis of the students' interest and accurate grasp of students learning preferences, the behavior of trace data to students in-depth mining analysis, the best learning resources in the best way to make the most convenient and most students learning use.

Online learning platform users are divided into online teachers and online learners, providing the four types of services corresponding to both. For specific user categories, users can access different user interfaces and experience different services according to their privileges. The interaction of learning resources is realized mainly through the user application window, will directly affect the user experience, so the service layer according to the user's specific requirements can apply for the reconstruction of the application of information resources, to provide users with services of resources. Users do not need to understand the background data integration, all through the data processing layer of learning platform to achieve. Consider online teachers, online learning platforms, and timely release of learners' analysis, especially learning styles, interests, and other content. Record and analyze the learner's behavior on the platform and record of learning, and realize the purpose of tracking all the learning process.

For online learning, set up platform learning, answering, evaluation and interactive combination of learning mode, let the experience of learning style liberalisation, according to their own preferences for instant record; of course studies the implementation of the correspondence of the review and examination, online learning experience multi service; according to the results of data mining algorithms. Tailored learning schedule and learning scheme is reasonable.

4 Evaluated Measurements

It consists of 3 modules, which are data standardization layer, data mining analysis layer and data layer. Among them, the data mining analysis layer is the most important part, as shown as Fig. 2.

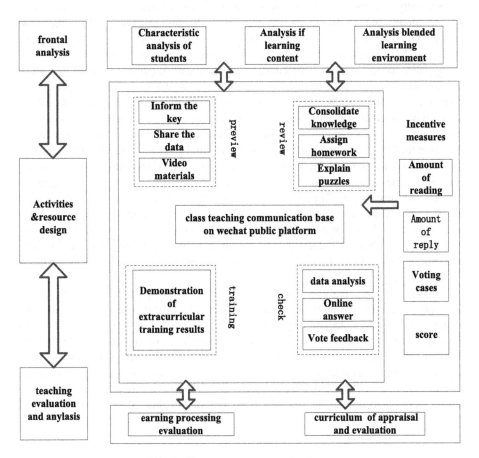

Fig. 2. Data resource processing layer

First, consider the magnitude, speed, and complexity of data growth. The global data is always stored in the "cloud storage" data server, and the data update function is added, which lays the foundation for data sharing, mining and integration. Data mining needs to depend on the standard data file with process information as input, and the data format is fixed. Raw data can not be directly used for mining, so it is necessary to consider the needs of online learning platform to preprocess data and integrate them into standard data format, that is, to adapt to the form of large data algorithms. Offline data refers to the user access and behavior information collected by various server-side and client, stored in the data center, and the user can access it directly. The algorithms of clustering and classification are used to eliminate redundancy, and standard data resources are built to lay the foundation for data stream mining and analysis. For the online mining of dynamic data, we can make use of the advantages of cloud computing, such as less memory, and so on, to realize the rapid mining of association rules, classification and clustering.

Secondly, the data mining is considered. The original data is scattered in various data resources, and the data is read through the application interface (API) of the cloud storage server, and the data preprocessing is carried out by using the MapReduce algorithm. Map (map) by mapping, to achieve a set of key value pairs into a set of key value pairs, specify the parallel Reduce (simplification) function, to ensure that all of the key mapping each member of the group to share the same key, the process of continuous iteration until enough information is simplified. Its essence is to extract huge amounts of data as data bases for data mining and intelligence analysis. Online learning data formats, using MapReduce can reduce the difficulty of data processing; at the same time, parallel processing continues, the final processing results will converge to the online learning platform, so the platform processing ability can be greatly improved. The analysis mining design consists of 4 steps: mapping, sorting, partitioning and simplifying. The steps are independent and cannot be invoked by each other. They can be connected by key value pairs, and the output of the upper step is used as input to the subordinate step. The results of online learning can not be directly regarded as the basis for decision making. It is necessary to combine the learning evaluation system to make decision on the requirements in order to achieve better access and service.

Finally, the data analysis results of the online learning platform is sent in the corresponding user, through the operation of short treatment time, abstract data into visual data, therefore, the online learning platform users can simply view the data directly. Considering the fact that the data resource processing layer has just started and the data has no practical significance, the data processing layer is mainly assigned according to the experience of the online teacher. With the accumulation of user data to a certain extent, the algorithm model built with big data technology can reflect the utility, so the learning plan of different users is different (Fig. 3).

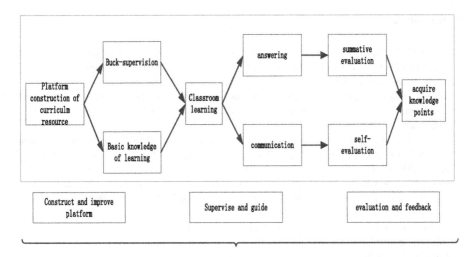

Fig. 3. Platform specific functions

This layer covers 4 parts: storage, network, security, and backup device. The adoption of cloud computing mode can eliminate the phenomenon of "hardware island", and realize integrated management of hardware resources, reduce complexity and energy consumption, and improve the utilization of equipment. By integrating the server and other hardware resources, it is automatically allocated to the application system according to the computing requirements. During peak use period, hardware resources are highly distributed and equipment efficiency is improved. In the use of low peak period, hardware resources are recovered or services are turned off, so as to reduce unnecessary waste. When the hardware device fails, other hardware can replace the fault device and restart the work by backing up the data, and its robustness is reflected.

5   Conclusion and Recommendation

With the combination of cloud computing and big data technology is of great significance to the study of the online learning platform, not only marks the construction method of the online learning platform to mature, but also provides a new idea for analyzing learning behavior. On the one hand, the emergence of the technology makes the learning behavior toward timely, fragmented development; on the other hand, but also facilitate the integration of the mass data of online learning, especially students learning behavior data, which can provide the decision-making basis for online learning and teaching analysis. Online learning platform is sensitive to construction technology because of its characteristics of information service. Therefore, the online learning platform in this paper, using cloud computing and big data technology innovation, to promote the development of online learning level.

References

1. Tzeng, G.H., Chiang, C.H., Li, C.W.: Evaluating intertwined effects in e-learning programs: a novel hybrid MCDM model based on factor analysis and DEMATEL. Expert Syst. Appl. **32**(4), 1028–1044 (2007). https://doi.org/10.1016/j.eswa.2006.02.004
2. Luo, N., Zhang, M., Qi, D.: Effects of different interactions on students' sense of community in e-learning environment. Comput. Educ. **115**, 153–160 (2017). https://doi.org/10.1016/j. compedu.2017.08.006
3. Gianni, F., Mirko, M., Ludovico, B.: A multi-biometric system for continuous student authentication in e-learning platforms. Pattern Recogn. Lett. (2017). https://doi.org/10.1016/j. patrec.2017.03.027
4. Chen, X., Vorvoreanu, M., Madhavan, K.P.C.: Mining social media data for understanding students' learning experiences. IEEE Trans. Learn. Technol. **7**(3), 246–259 (2014). https:// doi.org/10.1109/TLT.2013.2296520
5. Ferrucci, F., Salza, P., Sarro, F.: Using hadoop MapReduce for parallel genetic algorithms: a comparison of the global, grid and island models. Evol. Comput. (2017). https://doi.org/10. 1162/evco_a_00213
6. Kremer, J., Stensbosmidt, K., Gieseke, F., et al.: Big universe, big data: machine learning and image analysis for astronomy. IEEE Intell. Syst. **32**(2), 16–22 (2017). https://doi.org/10.1109/ MIS.2017.40

Integrating Educational Content into Game: An Encapsulation Method

Fan Zou[1]($\boxtimes$) and Yucheng Cao[2]

[1] College of Foundation Education, Sichuan Normal University,
Chengdu, People's Republic of China
zoufan@sicnu.edu.cn
[2] School of Education, University of California-Irvine, Irvine, USA
yuchc10@uci.edu

Abstract. It has been well established that introducing game elements to education may engage young learners in an active learning process while achieving decent learning results. However, few previous educational game design models emphasize the balance between education and entertainment. More importantly, few of them are sustainably compatible with formal education. To meet these goals, we proposed a game design method and developed a sample game to help and improve lower grade-level students' math learning. Empirical study was conducted to evaluate the effectiveness of the proposed method and students' game-based learning performance.

Keywords: Educational game · Game design · Game-based learning · Encapsulation method

1 Introduction

Research has consistently shown that well-designed games are able to provide players with a multi-sensory, experiential, and problem-based learning environment, massive and immediate feedback, a series of self-adaptive tasks with self-assessment, and dynamic social interaction involving diverse communities of players [1–4]. In the past two decades, many theoretically or empirically driven game design models have been created and developed. However, there remain concerns and inconsistent findings regarding modest academic gains through educational games resulted from the improper or disruptive integration of education content into gameplay [5–9]. When reviewing the previous models [10–18], we noticed that the majority were proposed before 2010 while few models were proposed over the last decade. It's also very interesting to know that many models stressed either the entertainment or educational aspect with limited attention to cooperating with formal education (e.g., syllabus or curriculum used in school).

According to Umetsu, Hirashima and Takeuchi [19], there are three ways of integrating educational games into the curriculum: simple simulation method, combination method, and the fusion method. Although the fusion method seems to be a perfect solution to integrate education into game, it is very challenging to create a game in which the educational content is directly tied with the goal of the game without

© Springer Nature Singapore Pte Ltd. 2020
J. Shen et al. (Eds.): IC3 2019, CCIS 1227, pp. 367–372, 2020.
https://doi.org/10.1007/978-981-15-6113-9_42

making the game dull and boring. To circumvent this problem, we proposed a new method of game design, that is, the Encapsulation Method (see Fig. 1).

2   Proposed Method: Encapsulation Method

In this method, there are two goals: educational goal and entertainment goal. The two goals are not parallel, the educational goal is encapsulated into the entertainment goal instead. Hence, players are expected to be immersed in the enjoyable game playing process while acquiring the target knowledge unconsciously. Meanwhile, the educational goal is visible only to the instructors and the designers.

To be more specific, the skills required for learning are the only key to play the game. Therefore, the educational content should be delivered in a way that is rewarding, attractive, and confidence-inspiring. The game is entertaining as the players gaining more scores and winning more awards, which means they acquire more knowledge through accomplishing these tasks.

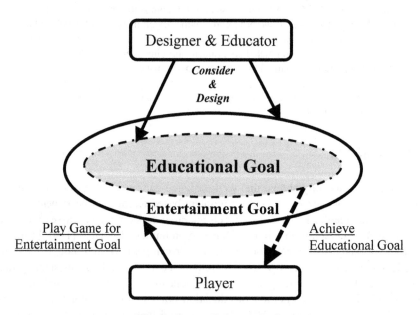

Fig. 1. Encapsulation method.

Based on the Encapsulation Method, the educator and designer first determine the goal of the game, which should be clear, specific and compatible with formal education. To conceal the content knowledge into the game process, it is necessary to subdivide educational content into small "cells" so that players can be guided to tackle the problem piece by piece. Next, the educator and designers should analyze the target audience, determine the game characters and format, and create the story line together. Finally, the designer will program the game and the educators can help find sample students to test the draft version and optimize it.

3 Sample Game and Evaluation

Based on the aforementioned Encapsulation Method and design procedures, we created a formal educational game named Perry's game (see Fig. 2) aiming at meeting the following three goals: 1) be suitable for the K-12 audience; 2) be compatible with classroom teaching; 3) achieve a balance between entertainment and education. In this case, we selected the measurement skills from the K-12 curriculum [20].

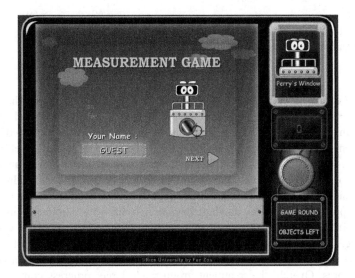

Fig. 2. The interface of Perry's game

3.1 Procedures

To test whether our game has achieved the intended goal of allowing students to master the skill of measuring more quickly and easily in comparison to the conventional classroom teaching, we conducted an experiment in which 283 children at a local elementary school in South Central America were randomly assigned into control and treatment groups. Pre- and post-tests were administered before and after the treatment for evaluation.

3.2 Results

Students' pre- and post-tests scores were imported to Stata software [21] for data analysis (see Table 1).

Table 1. Pre- and post-test mean scores and growth comparison by group

	N	Pre-test	Post-test	t (*df*)	Cohen's d	Hedges's g
Control	145	46.95 (2.66)	57.49 (2.98)	−4.83*** (144)		
Treatment	138	48 (2.58)	75.77 (1.69)	−14.01*** (137)		
Paired t (*df*)		−.28 (281)	−5.27*** (281)			
Effect sizes [95% CI]					−.69 [−.93, −.45]	−.69 [−.93, −.45]

Note. Standard errors in parentheses. *p < .05; **p < .01; ***p < .001.

For the control group, the post-test scores were significantly higher than pre-test scores (t = −4.83, p < .001), and same for the treatment group (t = −14.01, p < .001) indicating that both conventional teaching and game-based learning improved students' measurement skill. Moreover, the two groups were comparable in math level before the treatment (t = −.28, p = .78), but the treatment group obtained significantly higher scores in post-test compared to the control group (t = −5.27, p < .001). In addition, Cohen's d and Hedges's g both indicate that the average math growth of the two groups differ by approximately −.69 standard deviations with 95% confidence intervals of (−.93, −.45), respectively. Moreover, none of the confidence intervals for Cohen's d, Hedges's g, Glass's Delta 1 and Glass's Delta 1 include the null value of zero, suggesting that we can completely rule out the possibility that the treatment had no effect on math scores. Overall, the treatment group made larger progress compared to the control group (see Fig. 3).

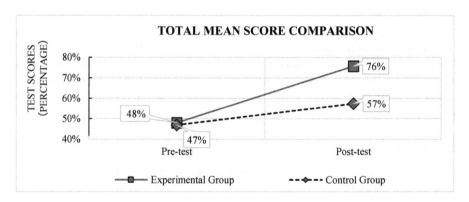

Fig. 3. Total mean score comparison

4 Conclusion

To sum up, the evaluation of the sample game, Perry's game, confirmed the effectiveness of the encapsulation method and our proposed game design procedures. Our feedback from both students and teachers corroborated that students are engaged in game-based learning, and educational game can be integrated into conventional classroom teaching as a supplementary activity. Future research with a larger sample size investigating diverse educational games in different disciplines are warranted.

References

1. Barab, S.A., Gresalfi, M., Ingram-Goble, A.: Transformational play using games to position person, content, and context. Educ. Res. **39**(7), 525–536 (2010)
2. Garris, R., Ahlers, R., Driskell, J.E.: Games, motivation, and learning: a research and practice model. Simul. Gaming **33**(4), 441–467 (2002)
3. McFarlane, A., Sparrowhawk, A., Heald, Y.: Report on the educational use of games (2002). http://www.teem.org.uk/publications/teem_gamesined_full.pdf. Accessed 27 Aug 2007
4. Weiss, D.J., Kingsbury, G.: Application of computerized adaptive testing to educational problems. J. Educ. Meas. **21**, 361–375 (1984)
5. Connolly, T., Boyle, E., MacArthur, E., Hainey, T., Boyle, J.: A systematic literature review of empirical evidence on computer games and serious games. Comput. Educ. **59**, 661–686 (2012). https://doi.org/10.1016/j.compedu.2012.03.004
6. Hays, R.T.: The effectiveness of instructional games: a literature review and discussion. Naval Air Warfare Center Training Systems Division, Orlando, FL (2005)
7. Hickey, D.T., Ingram-Goble, A., Jameson, E.M.: Designing assessments and assessing designs in virtual educational environments. J. Sci. Educ. Technol. **18**(2), 187–208 (2009)
8. Nelson, B.: Exploring the use of individualized, reflective guidance in an educational multi-user virtual environment. J. Sci. Educ. **16**(1), 83–97 (2007). https://doi.org/10.1007/s10956-006-9039-x
9. Randel, J.M., Morris, B.A., Wetzel, C.D., Whitehall, B.V.: The effectiveness of games for educational purposes: a review of recent research. Simul. Gaming **23**(3), 261–276 (1992)
10. Barendregt, W., Bekker, M.M.: Towards a framework for design guidelines for young children's computer games. In: Rauterberg, M. (ed.) ICEC 2004. LNCS, vol. 3166, pp. 365–376. Springer, Heidelberg (2004). https://doi.org/10.1007/978-3-540-28643-1_47
11. Andre, T.S., Hartson, H.R., Belz, S.M., McCreary, F.A.: The user action framework: a reliable foundation for usability engineering support tools. Int. J. Hum. Comput. Stud. **54**(1), 107–136 (2001)
12. Said, N.S.: An engaging multimedia design model. In: Proceedings of the 2004 Conference on Interaction Design and Children: Building a Community, pp. 169–172. ACM, June 2004
13. Kiili, K.: Digital game-based learning: towards an experiential gaming model. Internet High. Educ. **8**(1), 13–24 (2005)
14. Tan, P.H., Ling, S.W., Ting, C.Y.: Adaptive digital game-based learning framework. In: Proceedings of the 2nd International Conference on Digital Interactive Media in Entertainment and Arts, pp. 142–146. ACM, September 2007
15. Amory, A.: Game object model version II: a theoretical framework for educational game development. Educ. Tech. Res. Dev. **55**(1), 51–77 (2007)

16. Fu, F.-L., Yu, S.-C.: Three layered thinking model for designing web-based educational games. In: Li, F., Zhao, J., Shih, T.K., Lau, R., Li, Q., McLeod, D. (eds.) ICWL 2008. LNCS, vol. 5145, pp. 265–274. Springer, Heidelberg (2008). https://doi.org/10.1007/978-3-540-85033-5_26

17. Ibrahim, R., Jaafar, A.: Educational games (EG) design framework: combination of game design, pedagogy and content modeling. In: 2009 International Conference on Electrical Engineering and Informatics, vol. 1, pp. 293–298. IEEE, August 2009

18. Song, M., Zhang, S.: EFM: a model for educational game design. In: Pan, Z., Zhang, X., El Rhalibi, A., Woo, W., Li, Y. (eds.) Edutainment 2008. LNCS, vol. 5093, pp. 509–517. Springer, Heidelberg (2008). https://doi.org/10.1007/978-3-540-69736-7_54

19. Umetsu, T., Hirashima, T., Takeuchi, A.: Fusion method for designing computer-based learning game. In: 2002 Proceedings of the International Conference on Computers in Education, pp. 124–128. IEEE, December 2002

20. Texas Education Agency. TAC Chapter 111, Texas Essential Knowledge and Skills for Mathematics Subchapter an Elementary School (2012). http://ritter.tea.state.tx.us/rules/tac/chapter111/ch111a.pdf

21. StataCorp. Stata Statistical Software: Release 14. StataCorp LP, College Station, TX (2015)

Safety, Security and Privacy in Cognitive City

Survey of Attribute-Based Encryption in Cloud Environment

Yong Lu$^{(\boxtimes)}$, Yan Wang, Xiaoyu Dai, Jinghua Li, Jie Li,
and Manyu Chen

Nanjing University of Information Science and Technology, Nanjing, China
luyong@nuist.edu.cn, librawangyan@163.com,
18252088166@163.com, 13584703270@163.com,
15351731658@163.com, chenmanyu98@163.com

Abstract. Cloud computing develop quickly, which has powerful computing ability and allows authorized users to store and transmit data on cloud servers. Therefore, the security of applications in the cloud environment becomes an inevitable challenge. Therefore, many scholars at home and abroad have studied how to improve the security in cloud environment. The emergence of attribute-based encryption (ABE) has made it a better choice to improve cloud security. Subsequently, since ciphertext attribute-based encryption (CP-ABE) is more suitable for cloud storage than key attribute-based encryption (KP-ABE). Therefore, in view of the efficiency and security of CP-ABE, the CP-ABE's access structure and revocation mechanism are studied in depth. Finally, we summarizes the weaknesses of the existing ABE schemes and points out the future research directions. So the paper provides a reference for further research.

Keywords: Cloud computing · ABE · CP-ABE · Access structure · Revocation mechanism

1 Introduction

Cloud storage [1] provides storage services to a large number of users through pay-as-you-go methods, eliminating the burden of users managing resources and spending a lot of money to purchase hardware. Cloud storage brings great convenience to people because of its low price and convenient use [2]. But it also poses a serious threat to users' data privacy requirements because of the data out of users' actual control [3].

The traditional public key infrastructure (PKI) [4] function as protecting the confidentiality, nevertheless, there are still three notable weaknesses. Firstly, the public key must be obtained, otherwise not be encrypted. Secondly, the resource provider needs the message which is encrypted each user's public key in every receiving group, and the ciphertext is separately sent to the corresponding user, leading to large processing overhead and occupying a large amount of bandwidth. Thirdly, the broadcast encryption technology [5–7] partially solves the efficiency problem. Nevertheless, when encrypting, we should have gotten the user list. This will create two other secondary problems: it is difficult to obtain the size and membership of the receiving

© Springer Nature Singapore Pte Ltd. 2020
J. Shen et al. (Eds.): IC3 2019, CCIS 1227, pp. 375–384, 2020.
https://doi.org/10.1007/978-981-15-6113-9_43

group at one time; the distributed application enumerates the user and impairs the user's privacy.

In order to solve the above weaknesses, Shamir [8] and Boneh et al. [9] brought out the concept of identity-based encryption (IBE) [10]. In the scheme, the public key is the user's identity, so that the resource provider online does not need query the user's public key certificate [11]. Sahai and Water [12] proposed ABE based on IBE technology to implement attribute-based encryption and decryption, which can further solve the second and third major defects.

The complexity of ABE leads to some important problems that need to be solved by itself. Firstly, user key is related to attribute in ABE, the dynamic of attribute increases the cost and difficulty of key revocation. Secondly, the authority generate the user private key, which may cause the authorized institution and the user to disclose the user's private key [13], and cannot distinguish the responsibility of the key leakage. Thirdly, multi-authority ABE can sharing the responsibilities of the authorized organizations and meeting the needs of multi-agency collaboration for cloud environment. It has also challenged the design of ABE. Therefore, the ABE mechanism has become a hot topic for scholars recently. A lot of good research results have been published in journals and academic conferences in the field of passwords and security protocols.

The scheme of the paper can be concluded as follows. Firstly, in Sect. 2, we describe the key properties of ABE. In Sect. 3, we discuss the difficult issues of ABE. In Sect. 4, we discuss the CP-ABE's access structure and revocation mechanism in view of the efficiency and security of CP-ABE. The next Sect. 5, we compare and analyze the schemes from two aspects of access structure and revocation mechanism. Finally, we summarized our work and completed the survey.

2 Key Properties of ABE

ABE has four key properties. This section will give a brief introduction to the four key properties of ABE.

2.1 Efficient

In ABE, attribute collections or access policies often need to be uploaded to the cloud along with the ciphertext. At this point, the resource provider only needs to encrypt the message according to the provided attributes, and does not need to pay attention to the number and identity of the members in the group, which greatly reduces the overhead in the data encryption process and improves the efficiency.

2.2 Confidentiality

When decrypting data, only members of the group that meet the ciphertext attribute requirements can decrypt the message and obtain the information. And members of the group that do not meet the ciphertext attribute requirements cannot decrypt. This guarantees data confidentiality.

2.3   Anti-collusion

The user key in the ABE is related to a random polynomial [14] or a random number. This randomness causes the keys of different users to be unjoined, and the enemy cannot decrypt by the key of the joint user, which can prevent the user from collusion attacks [15].

2.4   Strategic Flexibility

In ABE, the access structure describes the logical composition of the access control policy [16] and determines the expressive ability of it. And ABE supports attribute-based flexible access control policies.

3   Difficult Issues of ABE

In ABE, the dynamic nature of the key increases the complexity of the key revocation and the attribute key is independent of the user ID, which makes it impossible to prevent and track the private key of the illegal user, but in the cloud environment applications require ABE to support multi-agency collaboration to meet the needs of scalability and fault tolerance [17]. These factors have brought challenges to ABE research, which are as follows.

3.1   The Attribute Key Revocation Overhead Is Large

In ABE, user keys are related to attributes, and dynamic changes in the system often cause attribute failures or affiliation changes. Therefore, the revocation of the ABE attribute key becomes the research focus [18]. The attribute key revocation of ABE is divided into three cases: the revocation of the entire user, the partial revocation of the user and the revocation of the system attribute. The revocation user needs to invalidate the user's key, and does not affect unrevoked users. The revocation user must invalidate the user's key without affecting the unrevoked user. All users with this attribute are affected when the system attribute is revoked. In ABE, the many-to-many relationship between attributes and users increases the design difficulty of the attribute key revocation mechanism that supports the above three revocation requirements.

3.2   Key Abuse

In ABE, the user private key is only related to the user attribute and has nothing to do with any specific information of the user. The generation of pirated keys can not prevented. In addition to the user's disclosure of his private key, authorities that hold all user private keys may also disclose the private key of a legitimate user. Therefore, when the pirated key appears, it is impossible to determine whether the user or the authorized organization has leaked the private key, so it has difficulties in account-ability. The pirate key is difficult to prevent and difficult to define the responsibility, so the key abuse [19] problem in the ABE mechanism is especially prominent and difficult to solve.

3.3 User Authorization Under Multiple Agencies

The basic ABE belongs to the single-licensing organization and cannot meet the needs of cloud environment. Authorized organizations manage all the attributes in the system, issue keys to users, and have a large workload, which becomes a performance bottleneck of the system. The multi-authority ABE can not only meet the needs of cloud environment, but also distribute the trust and workload of a single authority to all authorized organizations of the system. ABE in a multi-agency situation is necessary. However, the need for each authority to independently issue key and user key accuracy poses a challenge to multi-authority ABE [20] research.

4 ABE Overview

According to access structure, the ABE can be classified into two types, they are KP-ABE and CP-ABE. In the KP-ABE, the key corresponds to an access control, decrypted if and only if the attributes in the attribute set satisfy the access structure. In CP-ABE, the encryption party can encrypt data by specifying the access structure of the attribute set. When the attribute possessed by the user satisfies the access structure of the ciphertext, the ciphertext can be decrypted and resist the joint attack. And CP-ABE is more suitable for cloud storage than KP-ABE. So CP-ABE is an ideal solution to solve cloud storage data confidentiality and fine-grained access control.

Therefore, this section combs the basic CP-ABE scheme. And in view of the efficiency and security of CP-ABE, we study the access structure and revocation mechanism of CP-ABE.

4.1 Access Structure

In CP-ABE, the cipher controls the access policy. As the complexity of the strategy increases, the complexity of the system public key design and the difficulty of proving the security of mechanism increase. According to access structure, CP-ABE is divided into three categories, namely the AND gate, the access tree and the LSSS matrix.

AND Gate
Cheung and Newport [21] used the AND gate to represent the access policy. However, only the AND and NOT operations of the attribute can be implemented. And is low. Later, Nishide et al. [22] proposed a collusion-resistant and hidden policy CP-ABE based on the Cheung's scheme. Emura et al. [23] first proposed CP-ABE with the same ciphertext length. These two schemes implement policy hiding and efficiency improvement, but they only support attribute and operation.

Access Tree
The CP-ABE proposed by Bethencourt [24] uses a tree structure to represent a flexible access control strategy, but its security proof is based on the general group assumption. In view of DBDH, Goyal et al. [25] proposed a bounded CP-ABE that supports any bounded polynomial size formula (including AND, OR and threshold operations) in

order to implement a policy-flexible CP-ABE under the DBDH assumption. However, the encryption overhead is increased, so this method is not practical.

Liang et al. [26] improved Goyal's scheme and shortened the system PK, user private key and ciphertext length. The scheme also improved the efficiency of the encryption/decryption. In addition, it uses DBDH assumptions and unforgeable one time signature (OTS) technology to extend to CCA security.

LSSS Matrix

For the first time, Waters [27] directly implements the CP-ABE that supports attribute and/or threshold operations under strong numerical assumptions, and uses LSSS access structure [28]. The CHK [29] technology can be extended to CCA security. However, The more complex the access structure, the more ciphertext length and encryption/ decryption time. Both of them have a linear relationship with the increase of access structure.

4.2 Revocation

According to the different executors, the current research work direction of the researchers mainly includes direct revocation, indirect revocation.

Indirect Revocation

Pirretti et al. [30] first proposed a method for the attribute revocation of ABE. The schemes is simple, but there are many disadvantages. Firstly, the encrypting party needs to negotiate the validity period of the attribute with the organization. Secondly, the user needs to save the key of each time period, because the finer the granularity of the revocation date, the larger the key storage overhead. Thirdly, users interact with the organization online in the attribute key update stage, and the workload of the authorized organization grows linearly with the number of users, so it can be seen that the scalability of the system is not good. Meanwhile, the attributes cannot be revoked before expiration. After that, Ibraimi et al. [31] introduced a semi-trusted third party as a CP-ABE-based arbiter, because Bethencourt's idea [24] of CP-ABE key update, while eliminating coordination between the cryptographic and authorized organizations and reducing user key storage overhead, it does not support immediate revocation attributes.

Direct Revocation

In 2007, Ostrovsky et al. [32] first proposed the direct revocation of CP-ABE. The user identification (ID) was used as an attribute to associate the "non" of the revoked user identification with the ciphertext, so that the revoked user could not decrypt the ciphertext. However, not only the size of the ciphertext is increased, but the user's private key is also increased. Attrapadung et al. [33] adopt the same idea which reduce the overhead of revocation. In the direct revocation, the unrevoked user does not need to periodically update the key. However, Ostrovsky's scheme [32] and Attrapadung and Imai's scheme [33] both adopted the user ID to support the revocation of the entire user. It does not solve the situation of user attribute revocation, and the length of PK is increased instead.

5   Comparison

5.1   Comparison of Access Structure

In Table 1, we compares the access structure, supported policies, system public key, ciphertext length. And in Table 2, we compares the computational overhead (encryption and decryption time). According to the two table, the user PK and ciphertext of Emura's scheme are the shortest and the encryption/decryption overhead is the lowest, but only AND is supported. In general, the advantage of the AND gate is that the structure is simple, so it has advantages in the length of PK, ciphertext length and computational overhead. Nevertheless, not only that the strategy expression ability is weak, which is only applicable to simple policy semantic design, but also that the application scenario is limited. The access tree and the LSSS matrix are complex, so the computational overhead are higher than the AND gate and have rich policy expression capabilities, so the tree access structure is more intuitive and convenient than the LSSS matrix.

Table 1. Comparison of the access structure

Scheme	Access structure	Support policy	PK	Ciphertext
Cheung et al. [21]	AND gate	And, not	$(3k+1)l_{G_1}+l_{G_2}$	$(k+1)l_{G_1}+l_{G_2}$
NiShide et al. [22]	/	And	$(2I+1)l_{G_1}+l_{G_2}$	$(2I+1)l_{G_1}+l_{G_2}$
Emura et al. [23]	/	And	$(I+2)l_{G_1}+l_{G_2}$	$2l_{G_1}+l_{G_2}$
Bethencourt et al. [24]	Tree	And, or, threshold	$3l_{G_1}+l_{G_2}$	$(2|A_1|+1)l_{G_1}+l_{G_2}$
Goyal et al. [25]	Tree	Bounded and, or, threshold	$(nc^{d-1}+c^d-1)l_{G_1}+l_{G_2}$	$(|A_1|+|\sum T_n|)l_{G_1}+l_{G_2}$
Waters et al. [27]	LSSS matrix	And, or, threshold	$(k+2)l_{G_1}+l_{G_2}$	$(2|A_1|+1)l_{G_1}+l_{G_2}$

Table 2. Comparison of computational overhead

Scheme	Encrypt	z
Cheung et al. [21]	$(k+1)G_1 + 2G_2$	$(k+1)P + (k+1)G_2$
NiShide et al. [22]	$(2I+1)G_1 + 2G_2$	$(3k+1)P + (3k+1)G_2$
Emura et al. [23]	$(k+1)G_1 + 2G_2$	$2P + 2G_2$
Bethencourt et al. [24]	$(2|A_1|+1)G_1 + 2G_2$	$2|A_2|P + (2|N|+2)G_2$
Goyal et al. [25]	$(2|A_1|+|\sum T_n|)G_1 + 2G_2$	$(|A_1|+|\sum T_n|)P + 2(|N|+|\sum T_n|)G_2$
Waters et al. [27]	$(4|A_1|+1)G_1 + 2G_2$	$(2|A_2|+1)P + 3|A_2|G_2$

G_i: group or operation in group; P: bilinear pairing operation; k: number of attributes
I: the total number of possible value of attributes; A_1: attributes of ciphertext;
N: least interior nodes satisfying an access structure; A_2: attributes of user;
l_*: bit-Length of element in *; d: the maximum height of the access tree;
T_n: a (d, c) finite standard access tree.

5.2 Comparison of Revocation Mechanisms

In Table 3, we compares and analyzes the above revocation mechanism. AA represents the attribute authority. For systems that do not have online requirements, users get updated information through AA. For systems with online requirements, users need to interact with the online party to obtain information. The executor of the direct revoke is the sender and the executor of the indirect revoke is AA. The revoke speed is related to the executor. The comparison shows that although the revocation mechanism currently executed by the sender eliminates the online constraint and realizes the immediately revocation, it does not solve the revocation of the user attribute. Therefore, it is still necessary to study CP-ABE without online interaction to achieve all revocation requirements and to realize immediately revocation in the future.

Table 3. Comparisons of revocation mechanisms

Scheme	Executor	Online party	Speed	Revoke		
				User	User's attribute	System attribute
Piretti et al. [30]	AA	AA	Expiry	√	√	√
Bethencourt et al. [24]	AA	AA	Expiry	√	√	√
Ibraimi et al. [31]	Third party	Third party	Immediate	√	√	√
Ostrovsky et al. [32]	Sender	/	Immediate	√	×	√
Attrapadung et al. [33]	Sender	/	Immediate	√	×	√

6 Conclusion

ABE as a new type of cryptographic scheme, it can be widely used in many fields such as politics, military, commerce, etc. Especially, it can also solve the problems of data security sharing in the cloud environment.

Presently, although the research on ABE has achieved outstanding results, But there are still many problems that require further research. The research focus after this is mainly on the following aspects: a) Efficiency needs to be improved greatly. b) Improve the efficiency of communication among authorized agencies. c) The validation of outsourced data remains the focus. d) The search schemes supporting fuzzy search, relational operation and search results ranking are still the research contents in the future. e) Ensure the security of the system even if part of the key is leaked. In the survey, we read a lot of papers and discussed the major ABE schemes. This paper first discusses the key properties and the difficult issues of ABE. Then, we discuss the access structure of CP-ABE and revocation mechanism are studied in depth. Finally, the weaknesses of existing research on ABE are summarized, and then we pointed out the future research directions.

References

1. Vernik, G., et al.: Data on-boarding in federated storage clouds. In: 2013 IEEE Sixth International Conference on Cloud Computing, Santa Clara, CA, pp. 244–251 (2013). https://doi.org/10.1109/cloud.2013.54
2. Feng, D.G., Zhang, M., Zhang, Y., et al.: Cloud computing security research. J. Softw. **22** (1), 71–83 (2011)
3. Zhang, P.F.: Research on data security in cloud storage. Sci. Guide (6) (2016)
4. An Overview of Public Key Infrastructures (PKI). Techotopia. Accessed 26 March 2015
5. Fiat, A., Naor, M.: Broadcast encryption. In: Stinson, D.R. (ed.) CRYPTO 1993. LNCS, vol. 773, pp. 480–491. Springer, Heidelberg (1994). https://doi.org/10.1007/3-540-48329-2_40
6. Naor, D., Naor, M., Lotspiech, J.: Revocation and tracing schemes for stateless receivers. In: Kilian, J. (ed.) CRYPTO 2001. LNCS, vol. 2139, pp. 41–62. Springer, Heidelberg (2001). https://doi.org/10.1007/3-540-44647-8_3
7. Boneh, D., Gentry, C., Waters, B.: Collusion resistant broadcast encryption with short ciphertexts and private keys. In: Shoup, V. (ed.) CRYPTO 2005. LNCS, vol. 3621, pp. 258–275. Springer, Heidelberg (2005). https://doi.org/10.1007/11535218_16
8. Shamir, A.: Identity-based cryptosystems and signature schemes. In: Blakley, G.R., Chaum, D. (eds.) CRYPTO 1984. LNCS, vol. 196, pp. 47–53. Springer, Heidelberg (1985). https://doi.org/10.1007/3-540-39568-7_5
9. Boneh, D., Franklin, M.: Identity-based encryption from the weil pairing. In: Kilian, J. (ed.) CRYPTO 2001. LNCS, vol. 2139, pp. 213–229. Springer, Heidelberg (2001). https://doi.org/10.1007/3-540-44647-8_13
10. Au, M.H., Carminati, B., Kuo, C.-C.J. (eds.): Network and System Security. LNCS, vol. 8792. Springer, Cham (2014). https://doi.org/10.1007/978-3-319-11698-3
11. Xu, J.J., Hong, H.H., Lin, G.F., Sun, Z.X.: A new inter-domain information sharing smart system based on ABSES in SDN. IEEE Access **6**, 12790–12799 (2018). https://doi.org/10.1109/ACCESS.2017.2788443

12. Sahai, A., Waters, B.: Fuzzy identity-based encryption. In: Cramer, R. (ed.) EUROCRYPT 2005. LNCS, vol. 3494, pp. 457–473. Springer, Heidelberg (2005). https://doi.org/10.1007/11426639_27

13. Barolli, L., Zhang, M., Wang, X.A. (eds.): Advances in Internetworking, Data & Web Technologies. Lecture Notes on Data Engineering and Communications Technologies. Springer, Cham (2018). https://doi.org/10.1007/978-3-319-59463-7

14. Hammersley, J.M.: The zeros of a random polynomial. In: Proceedings of the Third Berkeley Symposium on Mathematical Statistics and Probability. Contributions to Probability Theory, vol. 2, pp. 89–111. University of California Press, Berkeley (1956)

15. Yaseen, Q., Jararweh, Y., Al-Ayyoub, M., AlDwairi, M.: Collusion attacks in Internet of Things: detection and mitigation using a fog based model. In: 2017 IEEE Sensors Applications Symposium (SAS), Glassboro, NJ, pp. 1–5 (2017)

16. Han, F., Qin, J., Zhao, H.W., Hu, J.K.: A general transformation from KP-ABE to searchable encryption. Future Gener. Comput. Syst. **30**, 107–115 (2013)

17. Goyal, V., Pandey, O., Sahai, A., et al.: Attribute-based encryption for fine-grained access control of encrypted data. In: Proceedings of the 13th ACM Conference on Computer and Communications Security, pp. 89–98. ACM (2006)

18. Yu, S., Wang, C., Ren, K., et al.: Attribute based data sharing with attribute revocation. In: Proceedings of the 5th ACM Symposium on Information, Computer and Communications Security, pp. 261–270. ACM (2010)

19. Yu, S., Ren, K., Lou, W., Li, J.: Defending against key abuse attacks in KP-ABE enabled broadcast systems. In: Chen, Y., Dimitriou, T.D., Zhou, J. (eds.) SecureComm 2009. LNICST, vol. 19, pp. 311–329. Springer, Heidelberg (2009). https://doi.org/10.1007/978-3-642-05284-2_18

20. Cramer, R., Gennaro, R., Schoenmakers, B.: A secure and optimally efficient multi-authority election scheme. Eur. Trans. Telecommun. **8**(5), 481–490 (1997)

21. Cheung, L., Newport, C.: Provably secure ciphertext policy ABE. In: Proceedings of the 14th ACM Conference on Computer and Communications Security, pp. 456–465. ACM (2007)

22. Nishide, T., Yoneyama, K., Ohta, K.: Attribute-based encryption with partially hidden encryptor-specified access structures. In: Bellovin, S.M., Gennaro, R., Keromytis, A., Yung, M. (eds.) ACNS 2008. LNCS, vol. 5037, pp. 111–129. Springer, Heidelberg (2008). https://doi.org/10.1007/978-3-540-68914-0_7

23. Emura, K., Miyaji, A., Nomura, A., Omote, K., Soshi, M.: A ciphertext-policy attribute-based encryption scheme with constant ciphertext length. In: Bao, F., Li, H., Wang, G. (eds.) ISPEC 2009. LNCS, vol. 5451, pp. 13–23. Springer, Heidelberg (2009). https://doi.org/10.1007/978-3-642-00843-6_2

24. Bethencourt, J., Sahai, A., Waters, B.: Ciphertext-policy attribute-based encryption. In: 2007 IEEE Symposium on Security and Privacy (SP 2007), pp. 321–334. IEEE (2007)

25. Goyal, V., Jain, A., Pandey, O., Sahai, A.: Bounded ciphertext policy attribute based encryption. In: Aceto, L., Damgård, I., Goldberg, L.A., Halldórsson, M.M., Ingólfsdóttir, A., Walukiewicz, I. (eds.) ICALP 2008. LNCS, vol. 5126, pp. 579–591. Springer, Heidelberg (2008). https://doi.org/10.1007/978-3-540-70583-3_47

26. Liang, X., Cao, Z., Lin, H., et al.: Provably secure and efficient bounded ciphertext policy attribute based encryption. In: Proceedings of the 4th International Symposium on Information, Computer, and Communications Security, pp. 343–352. ACM (2009)

27. Waters, B.: Ciphertext-policy attribute-based encryption: an expressive, efficient, and provably secure realization. In: Catalano, D., Fazio, N., Gennaro, R., Nicolosi, A. (eds.) PKC 2011. LNCS, vol. 6571, pp. 53–70. Springer, Heidelberg (2011). https://doi.org/10.1007/978-3-642-19379-8_4

28. Beimel, A.: Secure schemes for secret sharing and key distribution. Technion-Israel Institute of Technology, Faculty of Computer Science (1996)
29. Canetti, R., Halevi, S., Katz, J.: Chosen-ciphertext security from identity-based encryption. In: Cachin, C., Camenisch, J.L. (eds.) EUROCRYPT 2004. LNCS, vol. 3027, pp. 207–222. Springer, Heidelberg (2004). https://doi.org/10.1007/978-3-540-24676-3_13
30. Pirretti, M., Traynor, P., McDaniel, P., et al.: Secure attribute-based systems. J. Comput. Secur. **18**(5), 799–837 (2010)
31. Ibraimi, L., Petkovic, M., Nikova, S., Hartel, P., Jonker, W.: Mediated ciphertext-policy attribute-based encryption and its application. In: Youm, H.Y., Yung, M. (eds.) WISA 2009. LNCS, vol. 5932, pp. 309–323. Springer, Heidelberg (2009). https://doi.org/10.1007/978-3-642-10838-9_23
32. Ostrovsky, R., Sahai, A., Waters, B.: Attribute-based encryption with non-monotonic access structures. In: Proceedings of the 14th ACM Conference on Computer and Communications Security, pp. 195–203. ACM (2007)
33. Attrapadung, N., Imai, H.: Conjunctive broadcast and attribute-based encryption. In: Shacham, H., Waters, B. (eds.) Pairing 2009. LNCS, vol. 5671, pp. 248–265. Springer, Heidelberg (2009). https://doi.org/10.1007/978-3-642-03298-1_16

Finding the Most Reliable Maximum Flow in Transport Network

Jie Wang[1($\boxtimes$)], Wei Cai[1], Sihai Zhou[1,2], Yundi Liu[1,2],
Weicheng Liao[1,2], and Baili Zhang[1,3]

[1] School of Computer Science and Engineering, Southeast University,
Nanjing 211189, China
220174309@seu.edu.cn
[2] Key Laboratory of Computer Network and Information Integration of Ministry
of Education, Nanjing, China
[3] Research Center for Judicial Big Data, Supreme Count of China,
Nanjing 211189, China

Abstract. This paper intends to solve the most reliable maximum flow problem (MRMF) on transport network. A subgraph path division algorithm (SPDA) is proposed to get the most reliable maximum flow distribution, which avoid the negative impact of the number of simple paths and its bottleneck capacity. SPDA divides the sub-graph space of a transport network into a set of disjoint closed intervals, which satisfies the maximum flow constraints. Among the lower bounds of all the intervals, the one with discovered probability has proven to be the most reliable maximum. Finally, experimental results reveal the effectiveness and efficiency of the proposed algorithm.

Keywords: Transport network · Maximum flow · Flow reliability

1 Introduction

Transport networks are the realization of space networks, describing structures that allow vehicles to move or certain commodities to flow. Examples include but are not limited to road networks, railways, routes, pipelines, aqueducts and power lines [1]. Uncertainty has been an inherent feature of the actual transport network system. For instance, transportation network has the probability of congestion, etc. When these uncertainties appear, the uncertainty graph can describe the complex data relationships between objects in the transmission network well. Studies on theories and applications of uncertain graphs have emerged a considerable number of significant problems and the solutions to them have been proposed [2–11]. Xu et al. conduct a comprehensive study on the use of adjacency matrices and weight, mining uncertain maximum frequent subgraphs, and so on [5]. They also propose many effective algorithms aiming at such problems as mining model construction, reduction in the computation complexity of subgraph isomorphism. Parchas et al. use a single representative instance in an indeterminate graph to solve the exact query processing of an indeterminate graph [6]. Héctor Cancela et al. discuss the reliability estimation problem of high-reliability random flow networks [7]. Yuan and Wang adopt an effective random algorithm to

© Springer Nature Singapore Pte Ltd. 2020
J. Shen et al. (Eds.): IC3 2019, CCIS 1227, pp. 385–395, 2020.
https://doi.org/10.1007/978-981-15-6113-9_44

quickly estimate the reachability and improve the algorithm with the conditional probability [8]. In addition, for transportation networks, Oded Cats and Erik Jenelius consider loopholes in connectivity reliability and increased the robustness of the traffic network by increasing system capacity to absorb unplanned outages [10]. Xu, M. research on road network improvement methods [11].

The maximum flow problem on transport networks is the natural extension of the traditional maximum flow problems along with some new issues. Two most straight-forward problems are listed as follows.

(1) How is the reliability of a transport network with uncertainties evaluated when it passes the maximum flow or rated flow?

This is to measure the reliability of the transport network in carrying (maximum) flow. It is a classical issue in stochastic flow networks and has proven to be an NP-hard problem [12, 13]. The algorithms in this area can be divided into two categories: accurate algorithm and approximate algorithm respectively. The most basic accurate algorithm is the complete enumeration algorithm, which directly enumerates all pos-sible state combinations to obtain the reliability of the network. The papers [12–15] adopt different state-division methods to divide the state space into three state sets, which are qualified state sets that meet the flow requirements, the unqualified ones, and the ones including the previous two sets. And the probabilities of all qualified state sets are gradually obtained by dealing with the state set to be divided iteratively. Some researchers [16–18] propose a method based on path set or cut set to filter the state space, and then calculate the network reliability under the inclusive-exclusive principle. But for a complex system, the efficiency of accurate algorithms is often unsatisfactory. Therefore, some approximate algorithms have been proposed successively. For instance, the Monte-Carlo approximate algorithm is proposed by Ramirez-Marquez Coit [19], and Rocco and Muselli [20] adapt the methods of machine learning to get network reliability.

(2) Which maximum flow distribution is the most reliable and the preferred solution to flow delivery since one maximum flow of a transport network is likely to correspond to multiple maximum flow distributions?

This is also a very important issue concerning decision-making to maximize the existing network to choose the most reliable flow implementation plan. As shown in Fig. 1, according to the Ford-Fulkerson Maximum Flow Algorithm [21], the maximum flow value from the source point s to the sink point t in the original graph is 3, which corresponds to 3 different maximum flow distributions (They are referred to as Distribution 1, 2, 3). The probability of these flow distributions is not identical, so their reliability is different. The known literature [2–24] shows that there is little research on the reliability of flow distribution in uncertain graphs. But this issue is quite valuable and can effectively help solve a series of practical problems such as the construction of a reliable network, the selection of reliable transmission paths, and the analysis of system weaknesses.

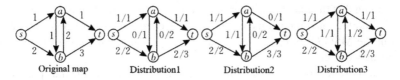

Fig. 1. Original map and corresponding maximum flow distribution

Therefore, based on the possible world model, this paper defines the most reliable maximum flow problem for transport network firstly, and gives a probability calculation model for maximum flow reliability. Next, this paper proposes a most reliable maximum flow algorithm SPDA (Subgraph Path Division Algorithm) based on state space division. Finally, experiment results have revealed the effectiveness and efficiency of the proposed algorithm.

2 Finding the Most Reliable Maximum Flow

This paper studies a simple two-state transport network, that is, the capacity of each edge in the network is 0 or C, and the sum of the possibilities of two kinds of capacities is 1. (Assuming that the edge probability of the graph is statistically independent. The flow and capacity values on the edge are non-negative integers, and the flow must satisfy the conservation of the flow [18]).

A transport network G is a quadruples G (V, E, Σ, Γ), where V is a set of vertices of a directed graph; E is an edge set; Σ is a set of tuple (c, p), c represents capacity, p represents the probability of capacity; Γ is a mapping: $E \rightarrow \Sigma$, for $\forall e \in E$, $\Gamma(e) = (c, p)$ means that when the capacity of edge e is c, the corresponding probability is p. The range of the corresponding tuple for each edge is $\{(c, p), (0, q)\}$, and $p + q = 1$.

For a transport network with $|E|$ edges, the number of deterministic subgraphs is $2|E|$, and the probability of each subgraph $PG(g) = \{\prod e\, p\,(e, c) \mid e \in E\}$ (where $p\,(e, c)$ represents the probability that edge e takes capacity c). If and only if each edge in G takes the maximum capacity, the corresponding determinant subgraph is the maximum subgraph of G, denoted as MSG(G) (Max Sub Graph).

A one-to-one mapping can be established between the space formed by the $2|E|$ deterministic subgraph implicated in the transport network G and the $|E|$ dimensional 0–1 vector V $(y1, y2, \ldots, ym)$ $(m = |E|)$. For V, 0–1 vector probability can be computed as:

$$P(V) = \prod_k p_k \qquad (1)$$

where $p_k = \begin{cases} p(e_k, c_k), y_k = 1 \\ 1, y_k = 0 \end{cases}$, $p(e_k, c_k)$ indicates the probability of e_k (the k-th edge of G)'s capacity taking c_k ($c_k > 0$).

Assuming that the maximum deterministic subgraph implicated in the transport G is MSG(G), and the maximum value of the flow value from the source point s to the sink point t in the MSG(G) is F_{max}, then the F_{max} is the maximum value of the s-t of the transport network G.

For transport network G, the maximum subgraph contained in the transport network G is MSG(G). If the maximum flow from the source streams to the sink point t is F_{max}, the vector formed by the flow passing on each edge is FV $= (v_1, v_2, \ldots, v_m)$ (where m represents the number of edges of G and vi represents the value of the flow passing on the edge e_i, which does not exceed the capacity of the edge, Such vector FV is a maximum flow distribution of G from s to t, which called as the maximum flow for short, and the reliability of this maximum flow FV is PG(FV) $= \sum PG(g)$ (where g is a subgraph contained in G, and there exists a maximum flow FV in g).

Maximum flow reliability calculation model. According to the above, the reliability of the maximum flow FV has the following formula:

$$P_G(FV) = \sum_g P_G(g) \tag{2}$$

Where g is the sub-graph contained in G, and there is a maximum flow FV in g. Through analysis, it can be found that the sum of the probabilities of such sub-graphs $\sum PG(g)$ is actually equal to the product of the edge probabilities that v_k is greater than 0 in FV. Therefore:

$$P_G(FV) = \sum_g P_G(g) = \prod_k x_k \tag{3}$$

where $x_k = \begin{cases} p(e_k, c_k), 0 < v_k < c_k \\ 1, v_k = 0 \end{cases}$, $p(e_k, c_k)$ indicates the probability of e_k (the k-th edge of G)'s capacity taking c_k ($c_k > 0$).

Obviously, If FV $= (v_1, v_2, \ldots, v_m)$ is mapped to 0–1 vector $V(y1, y2, \ldots, ym)$, where $y_k = \begin{cases} 0, v_k = 0 \\ 1, v_k > 0 \end{cases}$, PG(FV) $=$ PG(V) can be known from Eqs. (1) and (3).

Given the transport network G, source point s and sink point t, let $FV_1, FV_2, \ldots, FV_k$ be all possible maximum flows from s to t, and PG(FV_i) be the reliability of the maximum flow of FV_i in G, the maximum flow FV_i with the largest PG(FV_i) value is called the s–t most reliable maximum flow of G.

3 Subgraph Path Division Algorithm

From previous section, we can see that there is a one-to-one mapping relationship between the subgraphs implied by the transport network and the 0–1 vector. That is, the subgraphs implied by a transport network G can be described as subgraph V. The graph space can be described as $\Omega = [(0, 0, \ldots, 0), \ldots, (1, 1, \ldots, 1)]$.

Definition 1. Partial order relationship. Set the partial order relationship $\geq$ and $>$, for two 0–1 vectors $V_1(y_{11}, y_{12}, \ldots, y_{1m})$ and $V_2(y_{21}, y_{22}, \ldots, y_{2m})$, if for any i, $i \in \{1, \cdots, m\}$, $y_{1i} \geq y_{2i}$, then $V_1 \geq V_2$; if $V_1 \geq V_2$, and there is at least one i, $i \in \{1, \cdots, m\}$, so $y_{1i} > y_{2i}$, then $V_1 > V_2$.

Based on the definition above, this section proposes the SPDA algorithm. The algorithm consists of four steps:

Step 1 is to get the max flow value F_{max} from s to t of G by running the max flow algorithm;

Step 2 is to decompose the state space of G to a series of disjoint and closed intervals, and the acceptable intervals which can transmit the maximum flow are identified;

Step 3 is to evaluate the probability of the lower bounds of the intervals and among those lower bounds the one LB_{max} with the greatest probability is picked out;

Step 4 is to run max flow algorithm in the state subgraph corresponding to LB_{max}, then a max flow FV is gotten, and that is MRMF.

Here referring to literature [3], the decomposing method is used to compute the disjoint and closed intervals. The detail procedure is as follows:

For a given closed set C [L, U] of 0–1 vectors, where $L = (l_1, l_2, \ldots, l_{|E|})$ and $U = (u_1, u_2, \ldots, u_{|E|})$, $F(L^C)$ is the max flow value on the lower bound state L and $F(U^C)$ is the max flow value on the upper bound state U. If $F(L^C) \geq F_{max}$, it indicates that C [L, U] is an acceptable set, that is, all instances in C [L, U] can transmit the maximum flow. If $F(U^C) < F_{max}$, it indicates that C [L, U] is an unacceptable set, that is, no instance in C [L, U] can transmit the maximum flow. If $F(L^C) < F_{max} \leq F(U^C)$, it indicates that C [L, U] is an unspecified set and is needed to divided continuously.

Rule 1. Assuming that C [L, U] is an unspecified, $FV = (f1, f2, \ldots, f|E|)$ is a max flow on the upper bound state subgraph U, $V = (b1, b2, \ldots, b|E|)$ is the 0–1 vector corresponding to FV, where bi = 1 if fi > 0, and bi = 0 if fi = 0. Let $IC = \{i \mid bi > li \wedge i \in \{1, \ldots, |E|\}\} = \{i1, i2, \ldots, iq\}$, where q = |IC|. According to I_C, C can be divided into $q + 1$ closed and no empty intervals, denoted by $C_0, C_1, \ldots, C_q$, and C_0 is acceptable, where $C_{k=}[(\alpha_1, \alpha_2, \ldots, \alpha_{|E|}), (\beta_1, \beta_2, \ldots, \beta_{|E|})]$. If $k = 0$, $\alpha_i = \beta_i = u_i$ for $i \in I_C$, $\alpha_i = l_i$, $\beta_i = u_i$ for $i \notin I_C$; If $0 < k \leq q$, $\alpha_{ij} = \beta_{ij} = u_{ij}$ for $1 \leq j < k$, $\alpha_{ij} = \beta_{ij} = l_{ij}$ for $j = k$, $\alpha_i = l_i$, $\beta_i = u_i$ for $i \in \{1, 2, \ldots, |E|\} \setminus \{i_1, i_2, \ldots, i_k\}$ [14].

Based on the decomposition method above, the pseudo of the SPDA algorithm to discover MRMF is as following:

Algorithm 1. SPDA algorithm

Input: an transport network G, source s, sink t

Output: the max flow value F_{max}, the MRMF FV and its probability P

---

1. Init $P = 0$, $left \leftarrow (0, 0, ..., 0_{|E|})$;
2. $F_{max} = getMaxFlow(G,s,t)$;
3. Push $\{[(0, 0, ..., 0_{|E|}), (1, 1, ..., 1_{|E|})], \Phi, I=0, j=0\}$ into stack;
4. While stack is not empty
5.   Get current state space $[\alpha, \beta]$ according to j in the top of stack;
6.   If $j < I$, then j++; else pop stack;
7.   Get the max flow value f on low subgraph α,
8.   If $f \geq F_{max}$, then
9.   Calculate the possibility $p(\alpha)$
10.   If $p(\alpha) > P$, then $P = p(\alpha)$ and $left \leftarrow \alpha$
11.   Else
12.   Get max flow value f and its distribution f_w on upper subgraph β
13.   If $f \geq F_{max}$, then
14.   Use fv to get pivot intervals I_C by rule 1 and push $\{\alpha, \beta, I_C, |I_C|, 1\}$ into stack;
15.   Get $C_0=[\alpha', \beta]$ by $\{\alpha, \beta, I_C, |I_C|, 1\}$ according to Rule 1;
16.   Calculate the possibility $p(\alpha')$;
17.   If $p(\alpha') > P$, then $P = p(\alpha')$ and $left \leftarrow \alpha'$;
18. Get current flow solution FV on subgraph $left$;
19. Return (F_{max}, FV, P).

Assume that the iteration number of the space decomposition of SPDA is k and the Dinic algorithm (the time complexity of it is $O(mn^2)$) is adopted to get maximum flow, then the time complexity of SPDA is $O(kmn^2)$, where $m = |E|$, $n = |V|$.

In order to demonstrate that SPDA algorithm is able to find out the MRMF, the following theorem is given.

Theorem 1. Let F_{max} be the max flow value from s to t of G, and all states (possible subgraph) which can untake(reach) the max flow value F_{max} are divided into $A_1, A_2, ..., A_r$, where A_i is a closed set $[\alpha_i, \beta_i]$ with $\alpha_i = (\alpha_{i1}, \alpha_{i2}, ..., \alpha_{i|E|})$, $\beta_i = (\beta_{i1}, \beta_{i2}, ..., \beta_{i|E|})$, and $A_i \cap A_j = \Phi$. Let $P(\alpha_i)$ be the greatest one among $P(\alpha_1), P(\alpha_2), ..., P(\alpha_r)$, then the following two conclusions are true.

Observation 1. If removes any one edge from α_i, the max flow value of the rest graph must be less than F_{max}.

Observation 2. There must exists a MRMF from s to t of G in α_i. (== $P(\alpha_i)$ is Max).

Proof. Assume that $\alpha_{i'}$ is the state deriving from α_i by removing one edge, and the max flow value from s to t of $\alpha_{i'}$ is still F_{max}, then $\alpha_{i'}$ must belong to a A_j, where

$j \in \{1, 2, \ldots, r\}$ and $j! = i$, i.e. $\alpha_{i'} \geq \alpha_j$, so $P(\alpha_{i'}) \leq P(\alpha_j)$. While $P(\alpha_{i'}) > P(\alpha_j)$, then $P(\alpha_j) > P(\alpha_i)$, it is contradicted to the condition that $P(\alpha_i)$ is the greatest one, so Observation 1 is correct.

Observation 1 shows that the reliability of state α_i is $P(\alpha_i)$, so Observation 2 is equivalent to proof that $P(\alpha_i)$ is equivalent to $PG(FV)$ of MRMF. Firstly, assume that $P_G(FV)$ is greater than $P(\alpha_i)$. Let $FV = (v_1, v_2, \ldots, v_{|E|})$, mapping FV into to 0–1 vector $V = (y_1, y_2, \ldots, y_{|E|})$, where V is corresponding to a sub graph of G. Since FV is MRMF, so V must belong to an $A_j (j \in \{1, 2, \ldots, r\})$, then $P(V) \leq P(\alpha_j)$. While $P(\alpha_j) \leq P(\alpha_i)$, so $P(V) \leq P(\alpha_i)$. As $P_G (FV) = P(V)$, so $P_G (FV) \leq P(\alpha_i)$, it is contradicted to the condition that $P_G (FV)$ of MRMF FV is greater than $P(\alpha_i)$, so Observation 2 is proven.

4 Experiments

In order to verify the operating efficiency of the algorithm proposed in this paper and analyze various factors affecting the performance of the algorithm, we conducted a series of experiments. All the algorithms were implemented with Visual C++ under the support of the STL library. This experiment used an ordinary PC as the platform and basic configuration. For: processor Intel (R) Core (TM) i3, CPU 2.93 GHz, memory 4 GB, 64-bit Windows7 operating system (The next step will be based on the graph segmentation strategy, research algorithms are extended from stand-alone to multi-machine parallel).

Since the most reliable maximum flow problem is the new problem proposed in this paper, there is no universally widely recognized data test set. The experiments in this paper are based on a certain directed graph generator NETGEN [25] that is commonly used in the related research of graphs. Test data sets synthesized according to certain rules are mainly divided into three categories:

(1) Generate five sets of directed graphs by a directed graph generator (V_6E_{10}, V_8E_{14}, $V_{10}E_{18}$, $V_{12}E_{22}$, $V_{14}E_{26}$), where V_nE_m represents a graph set consisting of n vertices and m edges (in this experiment, the set size is 5), and the edge capacity and corresponding possibility in the graph are assigned by combination of random, uniform distribution, and normal distribution (σ = 0.2, 1.0, and 1.8). Their combinations are shown in Table 1.

Table 1. Edge capacity and corresponding probability combination

Capacity c	Probability p				
	Random distribution	Uniform distribution	Normal distribution (0.5, 1), $\mu = 0.75$		
Random distribution	$c \in [1, 40]$	$c \in [1, 40]$	$c \in [1, 40]$	$c \in [1, 40]$	$c \in [1, 40]$
	$p \in (0.5, 1)$	$p \in (0.5, 1)$	$\sigma = 0.2$	$\sigma = 1.0$	$\sigma = 1.8$
Uniform distribution	$c \in [1, 40]$	$c \in [1, 40]$	$c \in [1, 40]$	$c \in [1, 40]$	$c \in [1, 40]$
	$p \in (0.5, 1)$	$p \in (0.5, 1)$	$\sigma = 0.2$	$\sigma = 1.0$	$\sigma = 1.8$

(2) Under the condition of the number of vertices in the graph is fixed (the vertex in the experiment is 15) and the number of edges is determined according to the graph density defined in [26] ($d = 2|E|/|V| \times (|V| - 1)$). The graph set (the experimental set size is 5) is generated by the directed graph generator and then assigned 10 to each edge capacity of the graph. The probability of the corresponding capacity is randomly chosen between (0.5, 1). The source and sink point selection strategy of this kind of data set as same as (1) in the experiment.

(3) On the basis of the directed graphs with 15 vertices and 30 sides in [14], sequentially assign the capacity (the assigned capacity in this experiment is 5, 10, 15, 20, 25, 30 in order) and corresponding probabilities (probabilities is randomly chosen between (0.5, 1)) to produces a graph set of size 6, and continues to use s, t (s = 1, t = 15) in the literature [14] as the source and the sink points in this experiment.

Experiment 1. The influence of the capacity distribution and probability distribution on the edge of transport networks on the running time of the SPDA is investigated. The experiment uses the data set of type (1). The results are shown in Fig. 2.

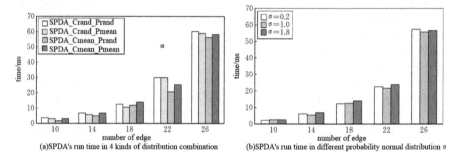

(a)SPDA's run time in 4 kinds of distribution combination   (b)SPDA's run time in different probability normal distribution σ

Fig. 2. The influence of capacity probability distribution on SPDA

Figure 2(a) shows that when the number of edges is greater than or equal to 22 and the capacity is uniformly distributed, the running time of the SPDA will be slightly lower than the case of capacity is randomly distributed when the capacity is uniformly distributed. Compared with the case of possibility is uniformly distributed, the algorithm runs at a relatively short time when possibility is randomly distributed; when the capacity is randomly distributed, compared with the case that possibility is randomly distributed, the algorithm runs at a relatively short time when the probability is uniformly distributed. Figure 2(b) illustrates that Under the same conditions, the probability obeys the normal distributions of the same mean μ, and different mean square deviations σ, which has negligible impact on the running time of the SPDA.

Experiment 2. The influence of the density of the graph and the value of the edge capacity on the running time of the SPDA is investigated. Experiments use the data sets of types (2) and (3). The results are shown in Fig. 3.

From Fig. 3(a), it can be seen that the running time of the SPDA increases as the graph density d increases, mainly because the density of the graph directly affects the state space of the state partitioning algorithm. The higher the density, the higher the state space. The larger the number of iterations the algorithm needs, the greater the running time of the algorithm is. Figure 3(b) shows that under the same conditions, the capacity of the edge has little effect on the running time of the SPDA, so it could be ignored.

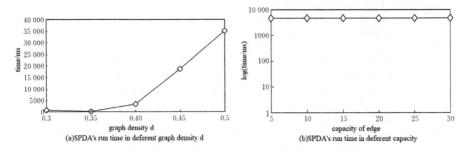

(a)SPDA's run time in deferent graph density d

(b)SPDA's run time in deferent capacity

Fig. 3. The influence of density and capacity on SPDA

5 Conclusion

This paper studies the most reliable maximum flow problem and reliability calculation model for transport networks based on the possible world model. Then aiming at the problems concerning the availability and efficiency of basic algorithms. An efficient and applicable algorithm based on space state division called SPDA is proposed. The experiment results show that the proposed algorithm can solve the most reliable maximum flow problem of transport networks effectively. The algorithm is not affected by the number of simple paths and its bottleneck capacity, and its performance is comparatively favorable.

Acknowledgements. This work was partly supported by the National Key R&D Program of China (2018YFC0830200), the Fundamental Research Funds for the Central Universities (2242018S30021 and 2242017S30023) and Open Research Fund from Key Laboratory of Computer Network and Information Integration In Southeast University, Ministry of Education, China.

References

1. Geoff, B.: OSMnx: new methods for acquiring, constructing, analyzing, and visualizing complex street networks. Comput. Environ. Urban Syst. **65**, 126–139 (2017)
2. Lin, L., Xu, L., Zhou, S., Wang, D.: The reliability of subgraphs in the arrangement graph. IEEE Trans. Reliab. **64**(2), 807–818 (2015)
3. Liu, L., Jin, R., Aggarwal, C., Shen, Y.: Reliable clustering on uncertain graphs. In: IEEE International Conference on Data Mining (2013)

4. Liu, Z., Wang, C., Wang, J.: Aggregate nearest neighbor queries in uncertain graphs. World Wide Web **17**(1), 161–188 (2014). https://doi.org/10.1007/s11280-012-0200-6

5. Xu, M., Wang, G., Grant-Muller, S., Gao, Z.: Joint road toll pricing and capacity development in discrete transport network design problem. Transportation **44**(4), 731–752 (2017)

6. Parchas, P., Gullo, F., Papadias, D., Bonchi, F.: Uncertain graph processing through representative instances. ACM Trans. Database Syst. **40**(3), 1–39 (2015)

7. Cancela, H., Murray, L., Rubino, G.: Highly reliable stochastic flow network reliability estimation. In: Computing Conference (2017)

8. Yuan, Y., Wang, G.R.: Answering probabilistic reachability queries over uncertain graphs. Chin. J. Comput. **33**(8), 1378–1386 (2010)

9. Hua, M., Pei, J.: Probabilistic path queries in road networks: traffic uncertainty aware path selection. In: EDBT 2010, Proceedings of the 13th International Conference on Extending Database Technology, Lausanne, Switzerland, 22–26 March 2010 (2010)

10. Cats, O., Jenelius, E.: Planning for the unexpected: the value of reserve capacity for public transport network robustness. Transp. Res. Part A: Policy Pract. **81**, 47–61 (2015). https://www.sciencedirect.com/science/article/abs/pii/S0965856415000300

11. Xu, M., Wang, G., Grant-Muller, S., Gao, Z.: Joint road toll pricing and capacity development in discrete transport network design problem. Transportation **44**(4), 731–752 (2017)

12. Doulliez, P., Jamoulle, E.: Transportation networks with random arc capacities. RAIRO **6**(3), 45–59 (1972)

13. Alexopoulos, C.: Note on state-space decomposition methods for analyzing stochastic flow networks. IEEE Trans. Reliab. **44**(2), 354–357 (1995)

14. Jane, C.C., Laih, Y.W.: A practical algorithm for computing multi-state two-terminal reliability. IEEE Trans. Reliab. **57**(2), 295–302 (2008)

15. Chin-Chia, J., Yih-Wenn, L.: Computing multi-state two-terminal reliability through critical arc states that interrupt demand. IEEE Trans. Reliab. **59**(2), 338–345 (2010)

16. Peixin, Z., Xin, Z.: A survey on reliability evaluation of stochastic-flow networks in terms of minimal paths. In: International Conference on Information Engineering & Computer Science (2009)

17. Lin, J.S.: Reliability evaluation of a multicommodity capacitated-flow network in terms of minimal pathsets. Int. J. Inf. Manag. Sci. **27**(3), 13 (2016)

18. Lin, Y.K.: System reliability evaluation for a multistate supply chain network with failure nodes using minimal paths. IEEE Trans. Reliab. **58**(1), 34–40 (2009)

19. Ramirez-Marquez, J.E., Coit, D.W.: A Monte-Carlo simulation approach for approximating multi-state two-terminal reliability. Reliab. Eng. Syst. Saf. **87**(2), 253–264 (2005)

20. Claudio, M.R.S., Muselli, M.: Approximate multi-state reliability expressions using a new machine learning technique. Reliab. Eng. Syst. Saf. **89**(3), 261–270 (2005)

21. Ahuja, R.K., Magnanti, T.L., Orlin, J.B.: Network Flows: Theory, Algorithm and Applications. China Machine Press, Beijing (2005)

22. Jane, C.C., Lin, J.S., Yuan, J.: Reliability evaluation of a limited-flow network in terms of minimal cutsets. IEEE Trans. Reliab. **42**(3), 354–361 (1993)

23. Lin, Y.-K.: A simple algorithm for reliability evaluation of a stochastic flow network with node failure. Comput. Oper. Res. **28**(13), 1277–1285 (2001)

24. Lee, S.H.: Reliability evaluation of a flow network. IEEE Trans. Reliab. **R-29**(1), 24–26 (2009)

25. Klingman, D., Napier, A., Stutz, J.: NETGEN: a program for generating large scale capacitated assignment, transportation and minimal cost flow network problems. Manag. Sci. **20**(5), 814–821 (1974)

26. Han, W.S., Lee, J., Pham, M.D.: iGraph: a framework for comparisons of disk-based graph indexing techniques. In: Proceedings of the 36th International Conference on Very Large Data Bases (VLDB), Singapore, pp. 449–559 (2010)

Evaluation of the BeiDou Regional Service with the iGMAS

Zhao Dayong[✉] and Xie Yong

Beijing, China

Abstract. The BeiDou navigation satellite system (BDS) has been set up and in operation by China itself. Its service performance has an important impact on China's military and economy. As a global GNSS monitoring and evaluation system, the iGMAS (international global monitoring and assessment system) is designed and promoted by China and play a important role of a basic approach to monitor the performance of the BeiDou navigaiton system service. In this paper, the iGMAS is used to monitor and evaluate the performance of the BeiDou system service in a specific region. The analysis shows that the positioning accuracy of the BeiDou system in this region is 1.1 m in horizontal, 2.8 m in vertical, and that the speed accuracy is 0.024 m/s. It indicates that the system can provide users with a high-quality navigation and positioning service in this region.

Keywords: iGMAS · BeiDou navigation satellite system · Monitoring · Assesment

1 Introduction

BeiDou navigation satellite system is an important national infrastructure and also the important component part of the international satellite navigation systems [1]. With the development of science and technology, the application of BeiDou navigation system is more and more extensive and gradually expands to all fields of national life. The performance of BeiDou navigation mainly includes three aspects: constellation status, broadcast ephemeris and service performance. IGMAS is an important platform for BeiDou navigation performance monitoring [2]. By monitoring and analyzing the navigation data from the monitoring stations, the service performance of the BeiDou system in a certain region can be obtained. In this paper, the constellation status, broadcast ephemeris and service performance are analyzed with iGMAS data, and quantitative conclusion is obtained.

2 Introduction of IGMAS

IGMAS is a global satellite navigation monitoring and evaluation system led and promoted by China, including globally distributed monitoring stations, centralized data centers and analysis centers, etc. [3]. It is a comprehensive processing platform for monitoring and evaluation of navigation signals and navigation information. The

J. Shen et al. (Eds.): IC3 2019, CCIS 1227, pp. 396–405, 2020.
https://doi.org/10.1007/978-981-15-6113-9_45

monitoring and evaluation of GNSS services by iGMAS platform can be divided into the following levels: constellation layer, spatial signal layer, navigation information layer and service performance layer, to provide different levels of monitoring and evaluation products for BDS and other classified users and serve the construction and operation of BDS [4].

3   Evaluation Model

3.1   Positioning Accuracy

The positioning accuracy is divided into horizontal positioning accuracy and vertical positioning accuracy. By acquiring the distribution information of navigation satellites at the epoch time and corresponding observation data, the pseudo-distance equation is constructed for solving, and the transmission error caused by troposphere and ionosphere is considered.

Based on the measurements, the error of the pseudo-range observation equation can be expressed as:

$$V_k = A_k \hat{X}_k - L_k \tag{1}$$

Where A_k is the design matrix, V_k is the residual vector of the observation vector L_k, and $\hat{X}_k$ is the estimation of the system state parameter vector. Generally, the least square method, kalman filter and the improved algorithm are adopted for $\hat{X}_k$ calculation.

Based on Eq. (1), the root-mean-square error of positioning accuracy could be calculated [5]:

$$\begin{bmatrix} \Delta e_{rms} \\ \Delta n_{rms} \\ \Delta u_{rms} \end{bmatrix} = \begin{bmatrix} \sqrt{\frac{\sum_{k=1}^{n} \Delta e_k^2}{(n-1)}} \\ \sqrt{\frac{\sum_{k=1}^{n} \Delta n_k^2}{(n-1)}} \\ \sqrt{\frac{\sum_{k=1}^{n} \Delta u_k^2}{(n-1)}} \end{bmatrix} \tag{2}$$

Equation (2) can be used to calculate the pseudo-distance positioning accuracy of a single test point.

3.2   Accuracy of Speed Measurement

The velocity measurement is to obtain the three-dimensional velocity of the station by calculating the change rate of distance between satellites and stations in unit time, and further solve the acceleration, acceleration jerk, and so on.

The formula for calculating the root-mean-square error of velocity measurements is as follows:

$$
\begin{bmatrix} \Delta de_{rms} \\ \Delta dn_{rms} \\ \Delta du_{rms} \end{bmatrix} = \begin{bmatrix} \sqrt{\sum_{k=1}^{n} \Delta de_k^2 \Big/ (n-1)} \\ \sqrt{\sum_{k=1}^{n} \Delta dn_k^2 \Big/ (n-1)} \\ \sqrt{\sum_{k=1}^{n} \Delta du_k^2 \Big/ (n-1)} \end{bmatrix} \tag{3}
$$

3.3   Service Continuity

Service continuity refers to the capability of navigation satellite system to provide continuous service performance over a period of time and in the service area.

Assuming that in region L, the test period is $[t_{start}, t_{end}]$, and the sampling interval of the user machine is denoted as T, then the calculation formula of the continuity index of system service con_l is [6]:

$$
Con_l = \frac{\sum\limits_{t=t_{start},inc=T}^{t_{end}-Top} \left\{ \prod\limits_{k=t,inc=T}^{t+Top} bool(EPE_k \le f_{Acc}) \right\}}{\sum\limits_{t=t_{start},inc=T}^{t_{end}-Top} bool(EPE_k \le f_{Acc})} \tag{4}
$$

In formula (4), if k, the positioning error $EPE_k \le f_{Acc}$, the Boolean function is 1, otherwise it's 0. For navigation satellite systems, the continuity index of system service per hour is generally calculated, that is, Top is usually taken as 1 h.

Formula (4) is used to calculate the continuity of positioning accuracy for a single test point. If the service accuracy of the whole service area is counted, the spatial-temporal correlativity of the test points in the covered area should be considered overall. The weight method is used to calculate the service continuity in the covered area:

$$
\overline{Con} = \frac{a_1 Con_1 + a_2 Con_2 + \cdots a_n Con_n}{a_1 + a_2 + \cdots a_n} \tag{5}
$$

Where a_n represents the number of valid data collected in each region.

3.4 Service Availability

Service availability is the percentage of the promised accuracy that can be provided in the servant region. Service availability is divided into three levels: instantaneous, regional and service area availability. This paper uses service area availability as an evaluation indicator.

Assuming that the test period is $[t_{start}, t_{end}]$, and the sampling interval of the user machine is denoted as T, then the calculation formula for the availability index Ava_l of the service in a specific region (single point) is [7]:

$$Ava_l = \frac{\sum_{t=t_{start}, inc=T}^{t_{end}} bool\{EPEk \leq f_{Acc}\}}{1 + \frac{t_{end} - t_{start}}{T}} \tag{6}$$

In formula (6), if the positioning error is $EPE_k \leq f_{Acc}$ at time k, then the Boolean function is set as 1; otherwise, it is set as 0.

Then the calculation formula of system service availability in the covered area is as follows:

$$\overline{Ava} = \frac{a_1 Ava_1 + a_2 Ava_2 + \cdots + a_l Ava_l}{a_1 + a_2 + \cdots + a_l} \tag{7}$$

In formula (7), a_l represents the number of valid data collected in each region.

4 Performance Evaluation

Constellation status, broadcast ephemeris and service performance were evaluated by processing according to observation data and ephemeris from iGMAS data center.

4.1 Constellation State Simulation

Constellation status includes satellite health status, number of health satellites and DOP value, etc. [8]. In this paper, only the satellite health status and number of health satellites were evaluated.

4.1.1 Satellite Health Status

In this paper, iGMAS monitoring data of a region in December 2018 were used to simulate the BeiDou navigation system satellites health status. As can be seen from Fig. 1, the health status of C01–C14 is in good condition, and the unhealthy satellites are BeiDou-3 satellites.

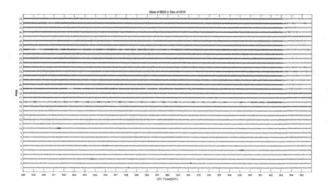

Fig. 1. Satellites health status

4.1.2 Number of Healthy Satellites

As can be seen from Fig. 2, the number of healthy satellites is around 15.

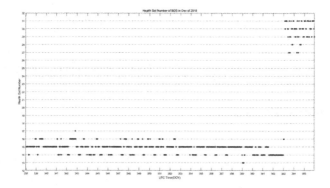

Fig. 2. Number of healthy satellites

Since December 29, the BeiDou-3 satellites has been found in a healthy state, with a total number of about 30 healthy satellites, which indicates that the BeiDou-3 has been put into operation.

4.2   Broadcast Ephemeris Evaluation

Broadcast ephemeris include broadcast orbit and clock error, broadcast orbit and clock error jump, URE, URRE, URAE, etc. [9]. This paper only evaluates broadcast orbit and clock error.

4.2.1   Broadcast Orbit Error

It can be seen from Fig. 3 that, except for C08 and C13, the broadcasting orbit error is all below 3 m.

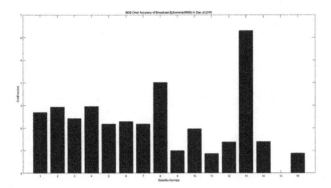

Fig. 3. Broadcast orbit error

4.2.2 Broadcast Clock Error

It can be concluded from Fig. 4 that the broadcast clock error of C01– C05 is large, while that of C06–C16 is small.

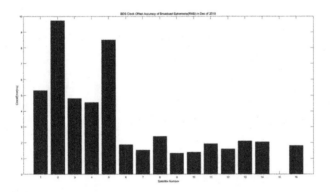

Fig. 4. Broadcast clock error

4.3 Service Performance Evaluation

Service performance includes positioning accuracy, velocity accuracy, positioning continuity and availability, velocity continuity and availability, etc. [10].

4.3.1 Positioning Accuracy

As can be seen from Fig. 5, the horizontal positioning accuracy is mainly distributed within the range of 0–2 m, and the vertical positioning accuracy is mainly distributed within the range of −5–0 m, and the horizontal positioning accuracy is concentrated.

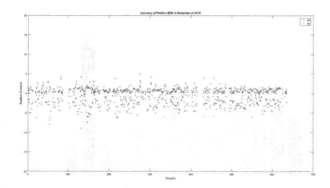

Fig. 5. Positioning accuracy

4.3.2   Velocity Measurement Accuracy

It can be seen from Fig. 6 that the velocity measurement accuracy is mainly distributed in the range of 0–0.03 m/s.

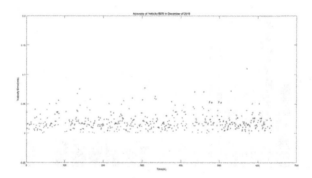

Fig. 6. Velocity measurement accuracy

4.3.3   Positioning Continuity

It can be concluded from Fig. 7 that the positioning continuity of a certain area is close to or reaches 100%.

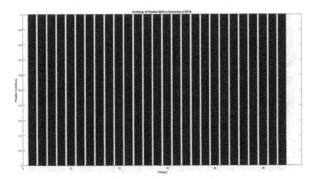

Fig. 7. Continuity of positioning

4.3.4 Positioning Availability

It can be concluded from Fig. 8 that the positioning availability of BeiDou in a certain region in December is close to or reaches 100%

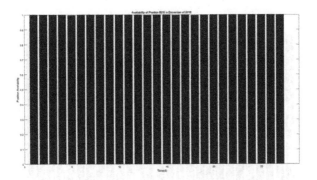

Fig. 8. Positioning availability

4.3.5 Velocity Continuity

It can be concluded from Fig. 9 that the measured velocity continuity of BeiDou in a certain region in December is close to or reaches 100%.

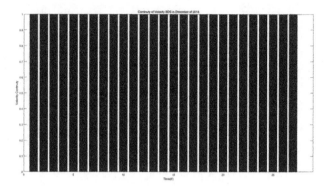

Fig. 9. Velocity continuity

4.3.6 Velocity Availability

It can be seen from Fig. 10 that the measured velocity availability of BeiDou in a certain region in December is above 90%.

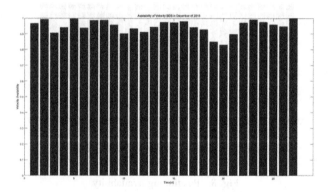

Fig. 10. Velocity availability

4.3.7 Service Performance Summary

See Table 1 for statistical indexes of service performance of BeiDou in a certain region.

Table 1. Service performance statistics

Test item	Positioning accuracy		Velocity accuracy	Positioning continuity	Positioning availability	Velocity continuity	Velocity availability
	Horizontal	Vertical					
Results	1.099	2.826	0.024	1.000	0.998	1.000	0.946

It can be concluded from Table 1 that the horizontal positioning accuracy and velocity accuracy are good, while the vertical accuracy is lower than the horizontal accuracy, which is consistent with the inherent characteristics of the satellite navigation system. The continuity of positioning and velocity measurement are 100%, and the availability of positioning and velocity measurement is good.

5 Conclusion

IGMAS is an important means to monitor the performance of the navigation satellite system. By analyzing the observation data from a certain region, it can be seen from the monitoring and evaluation results of constellation status, broadcast ephemeris and service performance that the performance of the BeiDou navigation satellite service in a certain region meets the relevant requirements and can provide guaranteed services.

References

1. Qiangwen, Y.: BeiDou navigation satellite system construction and application. Aerosp. China **14**(1), 10–14 (2013)
2. Li, X., Yuan, Y., Zhu, Y., Huang, J., Wu, J., Yun, X., et al.: Precise orbit determination for BDS3 experimental satellites using iGMAS and MGEX tracking networks. J. Geodesy **7**, 1–15 (2018)
3. Bingfeng, T., Yunbin, Y., Mingyue, W., Yafei, N., Xifeng, L.: Initial results of the precise orbit determination for the new-generation BeiDou satellites (BeiDou-3) based on the igmas network. ISPRS Int. J. Geo-Inf. **5**, 196 (2016)
4. International GNSS Monitoring & Assessment System. http://en.igmas.org/Home/Index/homedetail.html. Accessed May 2019
5. Weijie, W., Yanmin, L.: Analysis of the mean absolute error (mae) and the root mean square error (rmse) in assessing rounding model. IOP Conf. Series Mater Sci. Eng. **324**, 012049 (2018)
6. Zhang, X., Lu, X., Han, T.: Quantitative analysis of improvement of availability and continuity in service performance for users under interoperable GNSS. J. Time Freq. **3**, 1173–1180 (2014)
7. Li, Z., Jiao, W., Huang, X., Geng, C., Liu, X.: Comparison and Analysis of Signal Availability in the GNSS Service Volume. J. Astronaut. **34**, 1605–1613 (2013)
8. Xu, W., Xu, M., Yan, C.: Evaluation of the impact of BDS Satellite failure on regional positioning performance. GNSS world **38**, 1133–1136 (2018)
9. Wang, E., Wang, S., Lei, H., Pang, T., Qu, P., et al.: On methods for evaluation of GNSS signal-in-space accuracy. Electr. Opt. Control. **25**, 78–82 (2018)
10. Zhang, P., Chen, G., Zhang, X., Shao, S., Hao, J., et al.: Accuracy evaluation of BDS spatial signal based on iGMAS. Commun. Technol. **5**, 1820–1827 (2018)

A Mixed Model for Privacy Preserving and Secure Sharing of Medical Datasets

Franck Seigneur Nininahazwe[(✉)]

School of Computer and Software, Nanjing University of Information Science
and Technology, Nanjing, Jiangsu, China
seigneurinuyasha777@yahoo.fr

Abstract. Data mining has been a huge success from the beginning because of what it can offer and do. But there are some concern about the privacy of people in the used data. The problem here is being able to share datasets without putting privacy of the concerned people at risk and without being accessed by unauthorized people. That's where the different anonymization techniques like suppression and generalization can be employed to safeguard privacy of people in the datasets. Privacy preserving data mining (PPDM) has been researched for some years now, but there still many things to do. Privacy concerns are everywhere, but here the author only considered privacy issues with medical dataset. How to protect privacy of people in those dataset while keeping the data in them useful. In this paper, the author present a work which combines anonymization in order to tackle privacy issues in a medical dataset and secure sharing in order to control the access to the datasets. In the end, it is clear that the combination of anonymization and secure sharing offers not only protection against re-identification but also against unauthorized access to a given dataset.

Keywords: Anonymization · Secure sharing · Encryption · Access control

1 Introduction

We are in the era of electronics, internet, IOT, data mining and so on. In this era, we need to protect things more than before. We have many protections possibilities; encryption techniques, authentication techniques, electronic signature… Data mining researchers also developed many techniques which would help protect the privacy of people in the datasets. In privacy preserving data mining, we have many techniques like k-anonymity, l-diversity, t-closeness, k-map and many more.

In this research, the author focuses on the patient privacy when sharing data for research purposes or just between two healthcare centers.

Medical research is really one of the most important field, but that involves many people manipulating medical data records. Some records are made by the researchers themselves with the help of volunteers, for example when tests for a new drogue are needed. The second type of records are made by researchers who use medical datasets to perform statistical research over a population sample, a region or any other criteria.

Some proposition have been done about how to improve those techniques [1, 2], or how to use them in another way by proposing a software oriented model [3].

© Springer Nature Singapore Pte Ltd. 2020
J. Shen et al. (Eds.): IC3 2019, CCIS 1227, pp. 406–415, 2020.
https://doi.org/10.1007/978-981-15-6113-9_46

In this paper, the author concentrated on the anonymization part of privacy preserving in data mining, namely generalization, suppression and diversity but also on the access control on the anonymized file, and if the file would be intercepted by someone else, it would be impossible for that person to read the file.

2 Related Work

In the world, there are many people who conduct research on different topics. Regarding privacy on the web, we have got some improvement like RSA encryption, AES encryption, VPN, private networks for example Tor network and i2p, some tools and algorithms which send fake request and many other systems or tools. As you can see, we have come a long way since the time we couldn't protect ourselves online. Then comes data mining.

Data mining has brought a lot of advantages in machine learning, artificial intelligence... but it has also brought some issues, like for example how to mine data without damaging the privacy of people the data are mined from. Privacy preserving data mining area is the one in charge of conducting research in that area, in order to make sure that even though data are mined, sensitive attributes will be protected, so the privacy of those people won't be violated.

Researchers like Ren-Jie have proposed to improve already existing methods like k-anonymity [10], l-diversity or any other method for privacy preserving [1, 2], others like Ding propose a model-driven application-level or new protocols [3, 8]. But not all researchers propose new things. Some prefer to research about how things are so far and what could be done in the future; either it's all PPDM in general [4, 5] or just by studying one technique, it's risks and possibilities [6, 7, 9]. With that list, you can see all the main existing methods and what they are capable of. Although none of them is perfect, you can notice that they keep being improved.

And then there is encryption methods which are used to encrypt files and keep them from being read by someone without a decryption key [11, 14], or encryption methods to control the access to the file and share keys [12, 13].

3 The Proposed System

The proposed system includes a first part, which is in charge of anonymizing the tuples in a given medical dataset so the privacy of the people in it would be protected. It consist of generalization, suppression and diversity. The second part is in charge of controlling the access to the anonymized file and encrypting it as it will be presented in more details later.

3.1 Anonymization

General Knowledge. To put it briefly, data mining is the operation of uncovering patterns in datasets and drawing out those patterns, it is also the process of drawing out details from a dataset and change it into a comprehensible form for farther use. The final objective of data mining is to predict, and predictive data mining is the most regular type of data mining and also is the one with more business applications [4, 5].

For the purpose of mining data, people needs procedures but also a course of action to protect delicate information; that's why safeguarding of privacy in data mining has come out as an out and out precondition for trading private information with regard to data categorization, validation, and publishing.

There are two leading analysis of PPDM.

First, private raw data like identifiers, names, addresses, ..., should be changed or clipped out from the initial database, so that the possessor of the data would not be able to infer anyone sensitive information or be put at risk by that type of information. The sensitivity of a function, symbolized Δ f is stated by:

$$\Delta f = \max \|f(D_1) - f(D_2)\| \tag{1}$$

Furthermore, if by employing data mining you can extract some private information then those elements must also be kept out, because those kind of information would be able to damage data privacy. With that understanding, we may say that privacy preservation has two main groups: users' individual information and information regarding their common activities. The former is allude to as individual privacy preservation and the latter is allude to as collective privacy preservation.

Privacy preserving data mining is also separated in three different kind of methods: Randomization based techniques (value-based perturbation, multidimensional perturbation, ...), cryptographic based techniques (secure multiparty computation, homomorphic encryption, ...) and anonymization based techniques (k-anonymity, l-diversity, t-closeness, ...). Here, the author only focused on anonymization.

As a general rule, the major advantages of anonymization techniques are scalability and simplicity but they are unsuccessful in protecting data against some attacks and hinder the deduction of information.

Types of Attacks. Privacy of datasets can be decreased or demolished by several kind of attacks. Here we concentrate on three main attacks, and those are the prosecutor model, the journalist model and the marketer model.

Prosecutor Model. We presume that the invader is trying to re-determine the record belonging to a particular individual. This particular individual is known to the invader. For example, this particular targeted individual may be the invader's neighbor or a prominent individual. The invader has some background information about that prey, and then makes use of this background information to look for a corresponding record in the uncovered dataset [4, 5].

Journalist Model. The invader is not interested in which person is being uncovered, but only care about being able to assert that it can be accomplished. In this instance the invaders desire to uncover a single person to disgrace the company revealing the data [9].

Marketer Model. The intruder doesn't aim at a specific individual. The intruder wishes to uncover a large amount of people. It is not important who is uncovered as long as all tuples that could be uncovered are uncovered then that's the only important thing that the invader cares about. This model is only seen as a success if a large amount of tuples can be uncovered.

How It Works. The anonymization part of the system focuses on protecting the tuples while keeping the sensitive attribute diverse enough to confuse an attacker. The author uses generalization, suppression and diversity in order to ensure that the data would be protected but also stay utile for further use. Suppression works by adding '*' to the tuples according to a given hierarchy. Generalization uses interval on attribute for example age 24 can become 20 >= age <= 30. Diversity makes sure that the sensitive attributes are at least diverse according to the l index. Let a q*-*block* be a set of tuples so that its non-sensitive values derive to q*. A q*-*block* is diversified if it has l well symbolized values for the sensitive attribute S.

Hierarchy. Suppression and generalization use hierarchy in order to achieve their purpose. The hierarchy consist of different level depending on the chosen attribute. The type of hierarchy is also different in case it's suppression or generalization with intervals or else. But if we consider the hierarchy alone, we can say that suppression is part of generalization. In that case, for an attribute A there is two types of generalization with suppression, domain generalization hierarchy (DGH_A) and value generalization hierarchy (VGH_A) [10].

DGH_A can be defined as follow: Given an attribute A, it can be said that a generalization of an attribute is a function on A. That is, each $f : A \rightarrow B$ is a generalization. It can also be said that:

$$A_0 \xrightarrow{f_0} A_1 \xrightarrow{f_1} \ldots \xrightarrow{f_{n-1}} A_n \tag{2}$$

is a generalization sequence or a functional generalization sequence. Given an attribute A of a private table *PT*, DGH_A for A can be defined as a set of functions $f_h : h = 0, \ldots, n-1$ such that formula (2) is right. $A = A_0$ and $|A_n| = 1$. DGH_A is over: $\bigcup_{h=0}^{n} A_h$. In this presentation, it can be assumed that $A_h, h = 0, \ldots, n$, are disjoint; if an application is to the opposite and there are shared elements, then DGH_A is over the disjoint summation of A_h's and definitions become different consequently. Given a DGH_A for an attribute A, if $v_i \in A_i$ and $v_j \in A_j$ then it can be said $v_i \leq v_j$ if and only if $i \leq j$ and:

$$f_{j-1}(\ldots f_i(v_i)\ldots) = v_j \tag{3}$$

This define an incomplete ordering $\leq$ on: $\bigcup_{h=0}^{n} A_h$. Such association suggest the existence of a value generalization hierarchy VGH_A for an attribute A. The depiction of generalization can be increased to include suppression by forcing on each value generalization hierarchy a new maximal piece, atop the old maximal piece. The new maximal piece is the attribute's deleted value.

Let's consider a dataset we would want to anonymize. The dataset is considered to have quasi-identifiers and sensitive fields too. The system would proceed as follow:

- Get the data.
- Define attributes types, separate quasi-identifiers (*QI*) from sensitive attributes (*SA*) and non-sensitive attributes (*N-SA*).
- Define hierarchies and diversity; generalization and suppression for quasi-identifiers and diversity for sensitive fields.
- Anonymize; apply hierarchies and diversity.
- Get result.

Here is a figure of the main steps (Fig. 1):

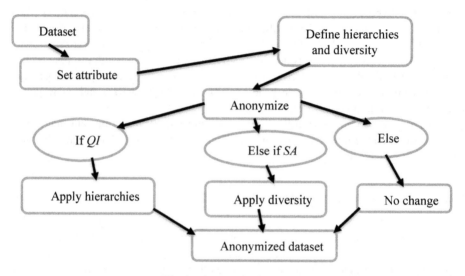

Fig. 1. Anonymization steps

The following is a graphic showing the average results when calculating the success rate of the anonymized datasets against the three type of attack mentioned before. The experimentations were done using java IDE eclipse and ARX open source libraries with small, medium and large datasets on a computer managing windows with a memory of 8 GB and double core processor of 2.30 GHz made by Intel (Fig. 2).

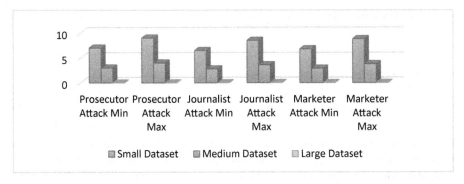

Fig. 2. Attacks success rate

Discussion. We got the results of the anonymization experimentations in Fig. 2, which is the first part of the system and as you can see, the system is able to protect the tuples against the 3 main attacks even if it is not 100%. Here, the author considered security but without omitting the utility of the anonymized dataset. The success rate for each of the three attack is pretty much the same, no matter if it's prosecutor model, journalist model or the marketer model. With the experimentations, we came to notice something. The larger a dataset becomes the more the success rate of each attack diminish. So depending on the size of the dataset the level of security is different, which we tested by using datasets with different size in our experimentations. But the method is far from perfect because it's difficult to ensure security and utility at the same time, the more you improve the security level the more you reduce the utility of the dataset.

3.2   Access Control

Encryption Methods. There are three well-known techniques (Data Encryption Standard, Advanced Encryption Standard and Rivest-Shamir-Adleman). But the author focused on AES, RSA and ABE.

AES: Advanced Encryption Standard (AES) algorithm is well known due to its speed and security capabilities. Its software and hardware implementation are still fast. It's a new encryption standard suggested by NIST to replace DES. AES is composed by three block ciphers: *AES-128, AES-192* and *AES-256.* The same secret key must be used and known by both the receiver and the sender. The first modification in the AES encryption cipher is to use a substitution table for data substitution; the second modification moves data rows, the third merges columns. The last modification is a normal exclusive or (*XOR*) operation accomplished on every column using a distinct part of the encryption key; lengthier keys need more rounds to finalize.

RSA: In RSA cryptography, a message can be encrypted by both the private and the public keys; in other to decrypt the message the opposite key from the one utilized to encrypt a message is employed.

To encrypt a message M and send a cipher text C:

$$c = m^e \bmod n \tag{4}$$

And the receiver can decrypt it using:

$$m = c^d \bmod n \tag{5}$$

ABE: Attribute-based encryption is a kind of algorithm of public key cryptography in which the private key employed to decrypt information is dependent on certain user attributes such as position, place of residence, type of account [12, 13]. The general scheme consists of four stages, for each of them has its own algorithm:

Generating the Public Key and Master Key: Trusted center selects randomly $t_1, \ldots, t_n, y$ from finite fields Z_q and calculates the master key MK and the public key PK.

Generate Private Keys: A collection of user attributes is provided to the input of the algorithm that generates the private key, and the user's private key is given at output of the algorithm. The reliable center generates a private key for every user U. A_U is a set of user attributes.

Encryption: The message which it is necessary to be encrypted is fed to the encryption algorithm input, a set of attributes, the owner of which will have the means to decipher the data, and arbitrary selected number, and the output of the algorithm is encrypted data.

Decryption: A set of user attributes A_U and the encrypted data are provided to the input of the decryption algorithm, and the algorithm output is a decrypted message.

How It Works. The second part of the system focuses on sharing the anonymized dataset with approved centers or people. The author proposes to control who accesses the file by using different encryption techniques and a defined step by step process.

The different steps are as follow:

- The receiver asks the server for the owner of the file public key. The authority produces Master Secret Key (MSK) and the public variable Public Key (PK) employing non-zero arbitrary value α, β from Z_p and uses AT a set of user attributes and MSK to create the private key SK.

$$PK = \left(G_1, g, h = g^\beta, f = g^{\frac{1}{\beta}}, 1(g, g)^\alpha\right) \tag{6}$$

- Encrypts a file request and his attributes with the owner public key $c = m^e \bmod n$ and sends it
- The owner checks the receiver attributes; if the attributes are linked to an approved Id. It takes AT a set of attributes and PK of the sender and checks for an identifier ID in the database, it returns 0 if none and ID_n if any user match.

- Encrypts the anonymized data to get cypher-text (CT), it takes the anonymized data and the AES-192, using symmetric encryption, and returns CT.
- Encrypts CT (M) and the AES key using a combination of the receiver public key and attributes (Final CT) and sends it. Let $q_x(0) = q_{parents(x)}(index(x))$ and $q_{r0}(0) = s$, where $s \in Z_p$. Let LN represent the collection of leaf nodes. The encrypted text Final CT(E) is determined as:

$$\tilde{E} = Ml(g,g)^{\alpha s}, E_1 = h^s, \forall i \in LN, E_y = g^{qi(0)},$$
$$E_y' = H(att(i))^{qi(0)} \tag{7}$$

- The receiver decrypts the final CT using his private key and AT a set of attributes and then the decrypt anonymized file (CT) using the AES key as symmetric decryption. Let $v = w = att(x)$ and determine CT (M) if $w \in AT$ as:

$$M = \tilde{E}\Big/ \frac{l(D_w,E_v)}{l(D_{w'},E_{v'})} = \tilde{E}\Big/ \frac{l\left(g^r.H(w)^{ra}, g^{qv(0)}\right)}{l\left(g^r, H(w)^{qv(0)}\right)}$$
$$= \tilde{E}/l(g,g)^{rq_v(0)} \tag{8}$$

The following figure is a summary of the different steps (Fig. 3):

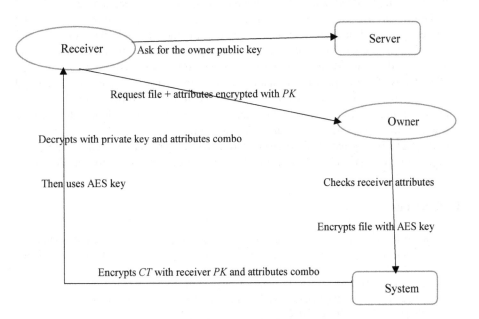

Fig. 3. Secure sharing

Discussion. For the second part, which consist of being able to share safely the anonymized dataset and control who can access it; the algorithm is very laborious for invaders because it requires several steps including checking the identity of who receives the file and multiple encryption level. The proposed algorithm supplies security from the malevolent insiders and risks during the handling of the data. Although, it offers a pretty strong protection nothing is perfect and there is always a way to hack a system, all one can do is protect it as much as possible.

4 Conclusion

We started by talking about privacy and what other researchers have done, what was their point of view. Either for creating new methods, improving the existing ones or just by doing study about the existing ones, their weaknesses and strong points.

In the second part, we talked about the different privacy preserving and encryption methods, then the author presented the system by stating how the anonymization part works step by step, by using generalization and suppression on quasi-identifiers which helps protect against re-identification but also adding diversity on sensitive attributes which strengthen more the anonymization; and then how the secure sharing and the access control work by using a multiple steps process, which encrypts the anonymized dataset using AES, but also for a final encrypted file, the author used an attribute based method; and then added some figures for a comprehensive understanding.

The last part was about testing. Showing the results of the experimentations we did on different type of datasets, and we noticed that the model would be really advantageous, since it offers more protection than using only generalization and suppression; also discussed the anonymization and encryption work of the system.

The focus of the work was on establishing a system which can anonymize medical dataset and also share the anonymized data in a secure way. In order, not only to make sure that an unauthorized person won't access it, but also to be able to safeguard the privacy of the people whose data are in the dataset.

Although, the system isn't perfect, it offers some protections against tuples re-identification and an access control on who would access the anonymized file.

References

1. Song, R.J., Lei, Z.Y., Feng, L.T.: an improved k-anonymity algorithm model. In: 2009 1st International Conference on Information Science and Engineering (ICISE), pp. 1659–1661. IEEE (2009)
2. Liu, F., Jia, Y., Han, W.: A new k-anonymity algorithm towards multiple sensitive attributes. In: 2012 IEEE 12th International Conference on Computer and Information Technology (CIT), pp. 768–772. IEEE (2012)
3. Ding, Y., Klein, K.: Model-driven application-level encryption for the privacy of e-health data. In: 2010 International Conference on Availability, Reliability, and Security. ARES 2010, pp. 341–346. IEEE (2010)

4. Li, X., Yan, Z., Zhang, P.: A review on privacy-preserving data mining. In: 2014 IEEE International Conference on Computer and Information Technology (CIT), pp. 769–774. IEEE (2014)
5. Qi, X., Zong, M.: An overview of privacy preserving data mining. Procedia Environ. Sci. **12**, 1341–1347 (2012)
6. Panackal, J.J., Pillai, A.S., Krishnachandran, V.N.: Disclosure risk of individuals: a k-anonymity study on health care data related to indian population. In: 2014 International Conference on Data Science & Engineering (ICDSE), pp. 200–205. IEEE (2014)
7. Machanavajjhala, A., Gehrke, J., Kifer, D., Venkitasubramaniam, M.: l-diversity: privacy beyond k-anonymity. In: 2006 Proceedings of the 22nd International Conference on Data Engineering. ICDE 2006, pp. 24–24. IEEE (2006)
8. Zhou, J., Cao, Z., Dong, X., Lin, X.: PPDM: a privacy-preserving protocol for cloud-assisted e-healthcare systems. IEEE J. Sel. Top. Signal Process. **9**(7), 1332–1344 (2015)
9. El Emam, K., Dankar, F.K.: Protecting privacy using k-anonymity. J. Am. Med. Inform. Assoc. **15**(5), 627–637 (2008)
10. Sweeney, Latanya: Achieving k-anonymity privacy protection using generalization and suppression. Int. J. Uncertainty Fuzziness Knowl. Based Syst. **10**(05), 571–588 (2002)
11. Mahajan, P., Sachdeva, A.: A study of encryption algorithms AES, DES and RSA for security. Glob. J. Comput. Sci. Technol. **13**(15), (2013). version 1.0. Online ISSN: 0975-4172 & Print ISSN: 0975-4350
12. Sukhodolskiy, I.A., Zapechnikov, S.V.: An access control model for cloud storage using attribute-based encryption. In: 2017 IEEE Conference of Russian on Young Researchers in Electrical and Electronic Engineering (EIConRus), pp. 578–581. IEEE (2017)
13. Kumar, N.S., Lakshmi, G.R., Balamurugan, B.: Enhanced attribute based encryption for cloud computing. Procedia Comput. Sci. **46**, 689–696 (2015)
14. Zhou, X., Tang, X.: Research and implementation of RSA algorithm for encryption and decryption. In: 2011 6th International Forum on Strategic Technology (IFOST), no. 2, pp. 1118–1121. IEEE (2011)

Code Multipath Analysis of QZSS by Time-Frequency Representation

Chao Yan[1] 🆔, Qing Wang[1(✉)], Fuyang Ke[2(✉)], Yuan Yang[1], and Fen Liu[1]

[1] School of Instrument Science and Engineering, Southeast University, Nanjing 210096, China
wq_seu@seu.edu.cn
[2] School of Remote Sensing and Geomatics Engineering, Nanjing University of Information Science and Technology, Nanjing 210044, China
ke.fuyang@qq.com

Abstract. The Quasi-Zenith Satellite System (QZSS) is a system capable of regional time transmission and satellite-based enhancement for Global Positioning System (GPS) receivable in the Asia-Oceania regions, and the main service focus is within Japan. QZSS has 4 on-orbit service satellites, including three quasi-zenith orbits (QZO) satellites and one geostationary earth orbit (GEO) satellite. This paper is to study the multipath performance of QZSS L1, L2 and L5 signals. Multipath performance has always been one of the research hotspots to assess GNSS signals. For all visible QZSS satellites, the data of six International GNSS Service (IGS) stations located at unequal latitudes in the regions of Asia-Oceania over three days is analyzed. The code multipath was estimated by using pseudorange multipath (MP) method. A time-frequency representation was performed to strictly account for the existence of multipath based on the use of continuous wavelet transform (CWT). The experimental results showed that the correlation coefficient of code multipath of two consecutive days of low-latitude stations is higher than that of high-latitude stations, and the correlation coefficient is over 80%. As for the suppression of code multipath, the L2 signal is significantly superior to other QZSS signals, and the GEO (now only J07) satellite is superior to the QZO satellite.

Keywords: Code multipath · Time-frequency representation · QZSS · Pseudorange multipath methods · Continuous wavelet transform

1 Introduction

Quasi-zenith satellite system (QZSS) is a satellite positioning system operated by Japan Aerospace Research and Development Agency (JAXA). In Japan, especially in urban canyons and mountains, the use of QZSS as a GPS auxiliary system has improved the usability, reliability, integrity and positioning accuracy of the Asia region [1, 2]. At present, four quasi-zenith satellites (QZs) are in orbit. Apart from QZS-3 (geostationary orbit) satellites, the other three QZSS satellites are in quasi-zenith orbit (QZO), with an inclination of about $43 \pm 4°$. Octagonal track with similar shape, the QZO satellites

© Springer Nature Singapore Pte Ltd. 2020
J. Shen et al. (Eds.): IC3 2019, CCIS 1227, pp. 416–427, 2020.
https://doi.org/10.1007/978-981-15-6113-9_47

stays longer in regions with high elevations above Japan, and the time interval passing the same region is 8 h [3]. The details of the satellites are given in Table 1.

Multipath is still one of the most important challenges in GNSS positioning, which is the same as QZSS, because multipath is often considered to be the main source of ranging error [5]. Urban conditions are particularly affected by this phenomenon, resulting in some errors in measurement, resulting in unacceptable errors in navigation solutions [6]. Multipath is caused by the reflection of multiple signals from different objects in the environment; multipath signals are always delayed than line-of-sight signals. For many years, the quantification of multipath error for a given pseudorange observation has been studied. The methods to solving multipath errors before can be roughly divided into two categories: methods for improving receiver hardware and methods for data post processing. The former mainly focuses on the improvement of the antenna structured internal carrier tracking loop, as well as processing method of the delay locked loop performance and the receiver signal. For most users, solving multipath errors mainly concentrates on processing methods of the latter-data. However, in multipath error analysis, the biggest drawback is the lack of a model that can accurately describe the multipath error. The use of more flexible analysis tools, such as wavelet transforms, is considered necessary. At present, the application of wavelet in the field of GNSS has achieved good results in the application of cycle slip detection, multipath analysis and observable noise reduction.

Souza [7] and Satirapod and Rizos [8] applied a wavelet decomposition technique is used to extract multipath signals from GPS observation data, and then the extracted multipath signals are directly applied to GPS observation data to correct multipath effects., and the results showed that this method could obviously weaken the multipath effect.. Mosavi and Azarbad [9] applied stationary wavelet transform (SWT) to double difference (DD) residuals, the multipath error is extracted and used to correct DD observations. Wang et al. [10] synthesized the advantages of EMD and wavelet and proposed a GPS baseline calculation method based on EMD wavelet system error suppression model. Pugliano et al. [11] and Robustelli and Pugliano [12] applied continuous wavelet transform (CWT) to analyze CMC (Code-minus-carrier) residuals or pseudorange multipath (MP) residuals, and proposed a scale map for recognizing the time-frequency variation of multipath signals. CWT provides the ability to properly decompose signals into different scales (or frequencies), which is a useful help for this decomposition. The main advantage of CWT is that it reveals signal components in more detail than Fourier analysis or Discrete Wavelet Transform (DWT).

Table 1. Information of QZSS satellite [4]

Satellite	PRN	Orbit type	Launch data	Operation period
QZS-1	J01	QZO	September 2010	23 h 56 min
QZS-2	J02	QZO	June 2017	
QZS-3	J07	GEO	August 2017	
QZS-4	J03	QZO	October 2017	

Based on above analysis, data of all visible QZSS satellites on three different dates at the 6 IGS stations located at distinct latitudes in the Asia-Oceania regions were analyzed. Code multipath was estimated by using the MP method. A time-frequency representation was performed to rigorously account for the presence of multipath based on the use of CWT.

2   Methodology

Due to signal propagation of multiple path, the GNSS receiver signal is reflected by the reflector near the station entering the receiver antenna, the interfering signal is directly from the satellite, the observation value deviates from the true value, and the delay effect is called the multipath effect. Having greater impact on the pseudorange observations, the multipath effect is related to the spatial relationship between the satellite and the receiver antenna and the environment around the station. This paper mainly uses the MP observation to achieve code multipath estimation [13, 14].

For GNSS triple-frequency data, the pseudorange and carrier phase observation equations can be abbreviated as [15, 16]

$$P_i = \rho + c(\delta_{tr} - \delta^s) + \text{Trop} + ion_i + M_i + \varepsilon_{P_i} \tag{1}$$

$$\lambda_i \varphi_i = \rho + c(\delta_{tr} - \delta^s) + \text{Trop} - ion_i - \lambda_i N_i + M_{\varphi_i} + \varepsilon_{\varphi_i} \tag{2}$$

where i is satellite signals L1, L2 and L5 for QZSS; P_i and φ_i are pseudorange and carrier phase observations on the signal i, respectively; δ_{tr} and δ^s are receiver clock error and satellite clock error, respectively; c is the speed of light and Trop is the Tropospheric delay; ion_i is Ionospheric delay on the signal i, the sign is the opposite in the pseudorange and carrier equation; λ_i and N_i are the wavelength and the integer ambiguity of the φ_i carrier phase, respectively; M_i and M_{φ_i} are multipath error of pseudorange and carrier phase observations on the signal i, respectively; ε_{P_i} and ε_{φ_i} are observations noise of pseudorange and carrier phase observations on the signal i, respectively.

Existing researches show that pseudorange multipath is m-level, while carrier multipath is cm-level [17]. ε_{P_i} and ε_{φ_i} are m-level and cm-level, respectively. So $|M_{\varphi_1}| \ll |M_{P_1}|$ and $|\varepsilon_{\varphi_1}| \ll |\varepsilon_{P_1}|$ exist for L1, pseudorange minus carrier phase observation equations can be written as

$$P_1 - \lambda_1 \varphi_1 = 2ion_1 + \lambda_1 N_1 + M_1 + \varepsilon_{P_1} \tag{3}$$

The relationship of the ionospheric delay between the carrier phase L1 and L2 is as follows

$$ion_2 = \frac{f_1^2}{f_2^2} \cdot ion_1 \tag{4}$$

where f_i is frequency on the signal i.

Carrier phase observation L1 minus carrier phase observation L2 equations can be written as

$$\lambda_1\varphi_1 - \lambda_2\varphi_2 + \lambda_1 N_1 - \lambda_2 N_2 + M_{\varphi_1} - M_{\varphi_2} + \varepsilon_{\varphi_1} - \varepsilon_{\varphi_2} = ion_2 - ion_1 \qquad (5)$$

Considering Eq. (4) and ignoring $M_{\varphi_1} - M_{\varphi_2}$ and $\varepsilon_{\varphi_1} - \varepsilon_{\varphi_2}$, we can get the Eq. (6)

$$ion_1 = \frac{f_2^2}{f_1^2 - f_2^2}(\lambda_1\varphi_1 - \lambda_2\varphi_2 + \lambda_1 N_1 - \lambda_2 N_2) \qquad (6)$$

By introducing Eq. (6) into Eq. (3), code multipath combined observations on carrier phase L1 can be obtained.

$$M_{P_1} = M_1 + \varepsilon_{P_1} = P_1 - \frac{f_1^2 + f_2^2}{f_1^2 - f_2^2}\lambda_1\varphi_1 - \frac{2f_2^2}{f_1^2 - f_2^2}\lambda_2\varphi_2 - B_1 \qquad (7)$$

with

$$B_1 = \frac{f_1^2 + f_2^2}{f_1^2 - f_2^2}\lambda_1 N_1 - \frac{2f_2^2}{f_1^2 - f_2^2}\lambda_2 N_2 \qquad (8)$$

Similarly, code multipath combined observations on carrier phase L2 and L5 can be obtained.

$$M_{P_2} = M_2 + \varepsilon_{P_2} = P_2 - \frac{2f_2^2}{f_1^2 - f_2^2}\lambda_1\varphi_1 - \frac{f_1^2 + f_2^2}{f_1^2 - f_2^2}\lambda_2\varphi_2 - B_2 \qquad (9)$$

$$M_{P_3} = M_3 + \varepsilon_{P_3} = P_3 - \frac{2f_3^2}{f_1^2 - f_3^2}\lambda_1\varphi_1 - \frac{f_1^2 + f_3^2}{f_1^2 - f_3^2}\lambda_3\varphi_3 - B_3 \qquad (10)$$

with

$$B_2 = \frac{2f_2^2}{f_1^2 - f_2^2}\lambda_1 N_1 - \frac{f_1^2 + f_2^2}{f_1^2 - f_2^2}\lambda_2 N_2 \qquad (11)$$

$$B_3 = \frac{2f_3^2}{f_1^2 - f_3^2}\lambda_1 N_1 - \frac{f_1^2 + f_3^2}{f_1^2 - f_3^2}\lambda_3 N_3 \qquad (12)$$

Code multipath combined observations contains receiver internal noise and pseudorange multipath error for pseudorange observations; B1, B2 and B3 are combinations of ambiguities of the carrier phase. When no cycle slip occurs, it is a constant term. In a continuous arc without cycle slip, the constants in M_{P_1}, M_{P_2} and M_{P_3} are partially removed when the code multipath effect is calculated, and then the code multipath effects of each satellite are changed with the epoch.

$$MP_i = M_{P_i} - \overline{M}_{P_i} \qquad (13)$$

where $\overline{M}_{P_i}$ is the mean of a continuous arc without cycle slip M_{P_i} [18]. This technique removes the ionosphere error by means ionosphere-free carrier measurements. The noise introduced is at millimeter level, well below code thermal and multi-path noise.

3   Data Processing

For all visible QZSS satellites, the data of six IGS stations located at latitudes with ±33° in the Asia-Oceania regions over three different days is analyzed. Table 2 lists the details of the stations and their global locations are shown in Fig. 1. The experiment was performed by RINEX 3.0 file data collected from three pairs of different antenna-receiver couples at a rate of 30 s. The data of HKWS and HKSL in 3 days (from DOY 218 to DOY 220 of 2018) are processed, the data of AIRA, GMSD, ALIC and CUT0 in 3 days (from DOY 088 to DOY 090 of 2019) are also processed.

Table 2. The information of IGS stations used

Site	Country	Latitude (°)	Longitude (°)	Receiver	Antenna
AIRA	Japan	31.8241	130.5596	TRIMBLE NETR9	TRM59800.00
GMSD		30.5564	131.0156	TRIMBLE NETR9	TRM59800.00
HKWS	China	22.4342	114.3354	LEICA GR50	LEIAR25.R4
HKSL		22.3720	113.9280	LEICA GR50	LEIAR25.R4
ALIC	Australia	−23.6701	133.8855	LEICA GR25	LEIAR25.R3
CUT0		−32.0039	115.8948	TRIMBLE NETR9	TRM59800.00

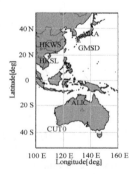

Fig. 1. Stations position, they are CUT0, ALIC, HKSL, HKWS, GMSD and AIRA respectively from south to north

MP multipath estimations of PRN J01 and J02 satellite in HKWS site on DOY 218 of 2018 are shown in Fig. 2, respectively. It could be told from Fig. 2 that, MP multipath estimations for signal L1, L2 and L5 are at m-level. To analyze the characteristics of pseudorange multipath, Table 3 counts the mean of RMS (Root Mean Square) values of the six stations' pseudorange multipath for signals L1, L2 and L5 on DOY 088-090 of 2019 (HKWS and HKSL in DOY 218-220 of 2018). The RMS of each site is the mean of all visible satellites, QZO satellites include J01, J02, J03, and GEO satellites currently contain J07.

As could be seen from Table 3, the multipath results of six stations show that the RMS value of code multipath of the L2 signal is the smallest; The results of AIRA, GMSD and ALIC show that the RMS value of pseudorange multipath for GEO satellite is lower than that for QZO satellite. Therefore, it can be confirmed that, for the suppression of code multipath, the L2 signal is significantly superior to other QZSS signals, and the GEO (now only J07) satellite is superior to the QZO satellite.

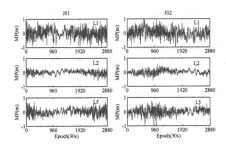

Fig. 2. MP multipath estimation for signal L1, L2, L5 for J01 (left) and J02 (right) at site HKWS on DOY 218

Table 3. The mean of RMS of each site's code multipath for signal L1, L2 and L5 in DOY 088-090 of 2019 (HKWS and HKSL in DOY 218-220 of 2018). HKWS, HKSL and CUT0 didn't observe J07

Site	Orbit type	L1 (m)	L2 (m)	L5 (m)
AIRA	QZO	0.2809	0.2455	0.3302
	GEO	0.2755	0.1434	0.2377
GMSD	QZO	0.2697	0.2167	0.2574
	GEO	0.2681	0.1264	0.1227
HKWS	QZO	0.2946	0.1433	0.2154
	GEO	–	–	–
HKSL	QZO	0.2799	0.1438	0.2352
	GEO	–	–	–
ALIC	QZO	0.2508	0.1046	0.1621
	GEO	0.0903	0.04620	0.0463
CUT0	QZO	0.5937	0.3778	0.3181
	GEO	–	–	–

According to Table 1, it is known that the operation periods of J01, J02, J03 and J07 are 23 h and 56 min. A preliminary analysis has been carried out in the time domain. In Fig. 3, the multipath for L1, L2 and L5 transmitted by PRN J01 during DOY 218 (in blue), 219 (in green) and 220 (in red) in the HKSL site is shown. From the figure below, the figure confirms that the multipath error peak appears approximately 240 s per day. For readability, the multipath sequences of DOY 219 and 220 are translated by 2 m and 4 m, respectively. Since the period of J01 satellite is 23 h and 56 min, DOY219 and DOY220 take 8 and 16 epoch data at the last moment of DOY218 and DOY219 as the beginning time. In Fig. 3, it shows that there is a strong similarity in the time series of code multipath for two consecutive days. According to statistics, the correlation coefficient between DOY 218 and 219, DOY 219 and 220 are 79.9% and 82.0% for L1 signal, respectively, is 82.7% and 80.3% for L2 signal, respectively, and is 78.4% and 79.6% for L5 signal, respectively. The results of the correlation coefficients of the code multipath for two consecutive days of the six stations are shown in Table 4.

As can be seen from Table 4, the correlation coefficient of HKSL, HKWS and ALIC stations is the largest, which could be up to 80%. The correlation coefficient of QZO satellite is higher than that of the GEO satellite, which also confirms that GEO satellite has better suppression effect on code multipath than QZO satellites. Combined with Table 2, we find that the correlation coefficient of code multipath of two consecutive days of low-latitude stations is higher than that of high-latitude stations.

To compare the pseudorange multipath of six stations, the relationship between multipath and satellite elevation angle is analyzed. Figure 4 shows elevation-dependent MP models of signal L1, L2 and L5 for J01, J02, J03 and J07 for AIRA site at DOY 088 of 2019. In Fig. 5, code multipath for each site is shown. The mean of code multipath are computed for that of the absolute value for elevation bins of 10° for all visible satellites at each site.

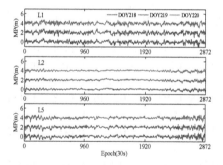

Fig. 3. Pseudorange multipath observable for PRN J01 in HKSL site plotted versus 30 s of the day for DOY 218 (in blue), 219 (in green) and 220 (in red), and the top is signal L1, the median is signal L2, the bottom is signal L5. For readability, multipath values for DOY 219 and 220 are shifted by 2 and 4 m, respectively. Since the operation period of J01 is 23 h and 56 min, in order to more intuitively display the similarity of the pseudorange multipath magnitude between two consecutive operating periods, the data of last 8 epochs on the first day is used as the starting data for the next day, and the data of the last 16 epochs on the second day is used as the starting data for the third day. (Color figure online)

As can be seen from Fig. 4 and 5, The results show that the multipath decreases as the desired elevation angle increases, which seems to be a constant. Code multipath values for four stations AIRA, GMSD, ALIC and CUT0 are higher than those for statins HKWS and HKSL. In particular, the code multipath stays steady at elevations above 50°, and the correlation with the elevation angle is lowered.

Table 4. Correlation coefficients of time series of code multipath, the statistical correlation coefficient is the mean of two consecutive two-day correlation coefficients, while the continuous two-day correlation coefficient is the mean of all visible satellites

Site	Orbit type	L1 (%)	L2 (%)	L5 (%)
AIRA	QZO	26.1	43.3	64.4
	GEO	2.6	3.0	23.8
GMSD	QZO	23.5	30.0	83.0
	GEO	2.4	5.1	74.0
HKWS	QZO	87.4	87.0	89.8
	GEO	–	–	–
HKSL	QZO	82.9	83.9	81.5
	GEO	–	–	–
ALIC	QZO	87.8	85.6	83.8
	GEO	30.1	61.6	69.6
CUT0	QZO	25.9	30.0	55.9
	GEO	–	–	–

4   CWT Analysis

The idea of Wavelet Transform (WT) is to use a basis function that does not have an infinite duration, such as a sine wave with a finite duration, so the wavelet is a waveform with a finite duration and a mean of zero. Unlike smooth and predictable sinusoids, wavelets tend to be irregular and asymmetric [11]. The CWT of signal $f(t)$ is reported in Eq. (14) [11, 12]

$$C_j(s,p) = \int_{-\infty}^{+\infty} f(t)\psi^*(\frac{t-p}{s})dt \tag{14}$$

Where C is coefficient that is resulted by the CWT of signal $f(t)$; j is the j-th CWT coefficient; ψ^* is the complex conjugate function of the mother wavelet function $\psi(t)$; s is the scale used to change the frequency or shape of the wavelet function, and p is the time shift used to move the wavelet function to a position.

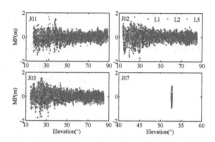

Fig. 4. Elevation-dependent MP models for AIRA site at DOY 088 of 2019. Blue, green and red represent code multipath for signal L1, L2 and L5, respectively. The J07 is a geostationary orbit satellite, the elevation angle varies from 52.25° to 53.25° in a day for AIRA. (Color figure online)

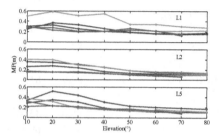

Fig. 5. Satellite code multipath plotted versus elevation, each graph contains six lines representing code multipath for a particular site, respectively.

The scalogram represents the percentage of energy for each wavelet coefficient in the time-scale plane calculated according to:

$$S_{C_j} = \frac{\left|C_j(s,p)\right|^2}{\sum_{i=1}^{N}\left|C_j(s,p)\right|^2} \cdot 100 \tag{15}$$

where S_{C_j} is the percentage of energy associated with CWT coefficient C_j at scale s at translation time p. The scalogram is used to divide the signal's information content in both time and frequency domains.

We used CWT to analyze all visible satellites at each site and selected a subset of them for discussion. Firstly, we analyzed the L1 code multipath of the J03 satellite of the CUT0 site on DOY 089 of 2019, the result is as shown in Fig. 6, the top is the time series of L1 code multipath and the lower box is bump CWT scalogram. From Fig. 6, notice that the early part of the time series of L1 code multipath for J03 is noisier than the later part. This phenomenon also exists in the time-frequency representation.

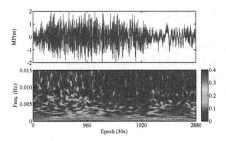

Fig. 6. J03 satellite code multipath and bump CWT scalogram for L1 signal at CUT0 site for DOY 089 of 2019

Secondly, we plotted the bump CWT scalogram for L1 code multipath of DOY218, 219 and 220 of J01 in HKSL site in Fig. 7, with time domain analysis recorded at the top of Fig. 2. Time information can provide strong evidence by conducting this analysis within 3 days. By observing Fig. 7, the processed three-day data energy peak time is identical, the magnitude is essentially the same, and the upper box, middle box and lower box are similar, confirming that the correlations between DOY 218 and 219, DOY 219 and 220 are strong.

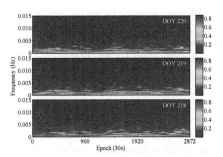

Fig. 7. L1 multipath estimation bump CWT scalogram for the J01 in HKSL site DOY 220 upper box, 219 middle box and 218 lower box

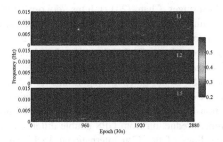

Fig. 8. L1, L2 and L5 multipath estimation bump CWT scalogram for the J07 in AIRA site for DOY 090, L1 upper box, L2 middle box and L5 lower box

Finally, we used J07 satellite data in AIRA site for DOY 090 to analyze their abilities of signal L1, L2 and L5 to suppress multipath. In Fig. 8, the L1, L2 and L5 code multipath scalograms are plotted. By observing the upper, middle and lower boxes, a comparison of L1, L2 and L5 code multipath error can be done. It can be seen that the L2 signal shows a very low multipath error. Therefore, the L2 signal can greatly reduce the code multipath.

5 Conclusion

The pseudorange multipath results of six different IGS stations from different latitudes in Asia-Oceania were analyzed for three different days of signals L1, L2 and L5. In particular, time-frequency analysis was performed on all visible QZSS satellites. The procedure involves the use of pseudorange multipath (MP) observables and the continuous wavelet transform analysis. Through analysis, the following conclusions are drawn: (1) Correlation coefficient of code multipath of two consecutive days of low-latitude stations is higher than that of high-latitude stations, and the correlation coefficient is over 80%; (2) the L2 signal shows a significant suppression of multipath as compared to the other QZSS signals; (3) Considering suppression of code multipath, the GEO satellite is superior to the QZO satellite.

Acknowledgments. This work was supported by the projects of the National Key Research and Development Plan of China (Grant Number: 2016YFB0502103), the National Natural Science Foundation of China (Grant Number: 61601123,41674036), the Natural Science Foundation of Jiangsu Province of China (Grant Number: BK20160696).

References

1. Zaminpardaz, S., Wang, K., Teunissen, P.J.G.: Australia-first high-precision positioning results with new Japanese QZSS regional satellite system. GPS Solutions **22**(4), 101 (2018)
2. Overview of the Quasi-Zenith satellite system (QZSS). Cabinet Office, National Space Policy Secretariat. http://qzss.go.jp/en/overview/services/sv01_what.html. Accessed Apr 2018
3. Teunissen, P.J.G., Montenbruck, O. (eds.): Springer Handbook of Global Navigation Satellite Systems. SH. Springer, Cham (2017). https://doi.org/10.1007/978-3-319-42928-1
4. Wang, K., Chen, P., Zaminpardaz, S., et al.: Precise regional L5 positioning with IRNSS and QZSS: stand-alone and combined. GPS Solutions **23**(1), 10 (2019)
5. Elie, A., Karim, D., De Boer, J., et al.: Correlator-based multipath detection technique for a global positioning system/GNSS receiver. IET Radar Sonar Navig. **12**(7), 783–793 (2018)
6. Angrisano, A., Gaglione, S., Gioia, C.: RAIM algorithms for aided GNSS in urban scenario. In: 2nd International Conference and Exhibition on Ubiquitous Positioning, Indoor Navigation and Location-Based Service (UPINLBS). IEEE, Helsinki (2012)
7. Souza, E.M.D.: Multipath reduction from GPS double differences using wavelets: how far can we go? In: Proceedings of the 17th International Technical Meeting of the Satellite Division of the Institute of Navigation, pp. 2563–2571. ION, Long Beach (2004)
8. Satirapod, C., Rizos, C.: Multipath mitigation by wavelet analysis for GPS base station applications. Empire Surv. Rev. **38**(295), 2–10 (2005)

9. Mosavi, M.R., Azarbad, M.R.: Multipath error mitigation based on wavelet transform in L1 GPS receivers for kinematic applications. AEU Int. J. Electron. Commun. **67**(10), 875–884 (2013)
10. Wang, J., Wang, J.L., Roberts, C.: Reducing carrier phase errors with EMD-Wavelet for precise GPS positioning. In: Proceedings of the National Technical Meeting of the Institute of Navigation NTM, vol. 6682, no. 1, pp. 919–928 (2007)
11. Pugliano, G., Robustelli, U., Rossi, F., et al.: A new method for specular and diffuse pseudorange multipath error extraction using wavelet analysis. GPS Solutions **20**(3), 499–508 (2016)
12. Robustelli, U., Pugliano, G.: Code multipath analysis of Galileo FOC satellites by time-frequency representation. Appl. Geomatics **11**, 69–80 (2019)
13. Defraigne, P., Bruyninx, C.: On the link between GPS pseudorange noise and day-boundary discontinuities in geodetic time transfer solutions. GPS Solutions **11**(4), 239–249 (2007)
14. Seepersad, G., Bisnath, S.: Reduction of PPP convergence period through pseudorange multipath and noise mitigation. GPS Solutions **19**(3), 369–379 (2015)
15. Leick, A., Rapoport, L., Tatarnikov, D.: GPS Satellite Surveying, 4th edn. Wiley, Hoboken (2015)
16. Zhou, F.: Theory and methodology of multi-GNSS undifferenced and uncombined precise point positioning. East China Normal University, Shanghai (2018)
17. Yan, C., Wang, Q., Yang, G., et al.: EMD-RLS combination algorithm and its application in weakening BDS multipath error. J. Chin. Inertial Technol. **27**(2), 190–198 (2019)
18. Feess, W., Cox, J., Howa, R.D.E., et al.: GPS inter-signal corrections (ISCs) study. In: Proceedings of the 26th International Technical Meeting of the ION Satellite Division, ION GNSS+ 2013, pp. 1244–1248. The Institute of Navigation, Nashville (2013)

An Identity-Based Anonymous Signcryption for Vehicular Ad Hoc Networks

Yong Lu[1(✉)] and Huijie Yang[2,3,4]

[1] School of Management Science and Engineering,
Nanjing University of Information Science and Technology, Nanjing, China
luyong@nuist.edu.cn
[2] Guizhou Provincial Key Laboratory of Public Big Data, Guizhou University,
Guiyang, China
[3] School of Computer and Software, Nanjing University of Information Science
and Technology, Nanjing, China
[4] Guangdong Provincial Key Laboratory of Data Security and Privacy
Protection, Guangzhou, China

Abstract. The vehicular ad hoc networks (VANETs) can share information of vehicles' location, speed and route within a certain range by interconnecting vehicles, roadside units (RSU) and the cloud. As people's daily traffic tools, vehicles reflect users' daily routines and other privacy. Therefore, privacy protection is very critical in VANETs. However, in the existing schemes, a user's temporary identity (TID) is generated by the user himself, which is inconvenient to be managed and can be easily forged. The reputation values of users also need to be considered. In this paper, an identity based signcryption scheme for VANETs is proposed. In the novel scheme, TID is generated by key generation center (KCG) and a personal reputation system is produced. The security analysis of the scheme shows that our scheme is practical.

Keywords: Vehicular ad hoc networks · Signcryption · Identity-based

1 Introduction

In recent years, with the development of Internet of things (IoT) [1], people have become increasingly demanding in terms of intelligent transportation [2]. Due to the increase of the number of vehicles, urban traffic has become more and more congested. In particular, in the first-line developed cities, people driving at the peak stage are even stuck on the road for hours, they spend too much time on the road every day. Self-driving vehicles [3] and vehicular ad hoc networks (VANETs) [4] can alleviate this situation. Users will use and generate a lot of personal privacy when using the VANETs, so a secure VANETs is necessary [5]. Self-driving vehicles can take over the vehicles via smart computers, which can greatly reduce the congestion time and traffic accidents caused by human factors. VANETs connect vehicles to roadside units (RSU) to realize data intercommunication between vehicles, roads, and the cloud, then obtain an intelligent transportation network. With VANETs, a self-driving vehicle can quickly acquire the data sensed by other vehicles and shares the road conditions it

© Springer Nature Singapore Pte Ltd. 2020
J. Shen et al. (Eds.): IC3 2019, CCIS 1227, pp. 428–437, 2020.
https://doi.org/10.1007/978-981-15-6113-9_48

perceives with other vehicles. At present, there are many types of networks that make up the VANETs [6], such as vehicles to vehicles (V2V), vehicles to RSU (V2R), and the interconnection between RSU and the cloud. However, cause there is no unified industry standard, these interconnections have many limitations [7, 8]. Communication security between users [9], trust management [10, 11] and the privacy protection are the issues need to be solved. In this paper we discuss the VANETs of star network environment and propose a secure signcryption scheme.

Motivation of Our Work: In the existing schemes, a user's identity is easily to be obtained and then the corresponding routines and other privacy information will be leaked. The temporary identity (TID) generated by a user himself is easily forged. The method of sign-encrypting also reduces the timeliness of messages. The novel scheme solves these problems with the utilization of signcryption and TID selected by the key generation center (KCG). Each vehicle will send its own location and monitored weather, road conditions and other information to the RSU with a TID randomly selected by KGC. The RSU uploads the valid messages to the cloud immediately to achieve transparency of the regional traffic conditions. Then vehicles can plan the best travel routes and reduce travel time and other costs based on the real-time traffic conditions.

1.1 Our Contributions

In this paper, a novel ID-based signcryption scheme for VANETs is proposed to implement authentication and secure communication between vehicles and RSU.

- **The secure communication between the vehicles and the RSU can be achieved.** All the vehicles connect with the RSU is more reliable than the vehicle-to-vehicle interconnected network cause the RSU verifies the identity of each vehicle and the legitimacy of the message. Vehicles collect data of nearby environment and their vehicle conditions, then signcrypt these data and send to the RSU. The RSU verifies the validity of the messages. Only the valid messages will be uploaded to the cloud.
- **Privacy of users is effectively protected.** In our scheme, the KGC is completely trustworthy and a vehicle only provides its real ID to KGC. The KGC will verify the authenticity and reputation of the ID. If the user fails the verification, he will not be able to obtain the TID. The KGC randomly selects a TID to correspond to the valid user's real ID, then the user communicates with the RSU with the TID so that his real ID is hidden and his personal privacy can be protected.
- **The reliability of VANETs is increased with triple legality verification.** If a vehicle wants to access the VANETs, it first has to send its real ID to KGC to obtain a legal TID. Its authenticity and reputation will be verified by KGC, only the authenticated user can obtain a legal TID. Second, when a vehicle with a TID sends a message, RSU will check whether the received message exceeds the maximum transmission delay threshold Δt. If the transmission delay exceed Δt, the message will be rejected. Finally, the message will be checked by the RSU for validity. Only messages that pass triple-authentication will be accepted and uploaded to the cloud.

1.2   Organizations

The remainder of this paper is organized as follows. The related works are given in Sect. 2. Some preliminaries of this paper are presented in Sect. 3. The threat models are given in Sect. 4. The proposed scheme is presented in Sect. 5 in detail. The security analysis of the novel scheme is provided in Sect. 6. Section 7 provides the conclusion of the paper.

2   Related Works

With the popularity of VANETs, some security issues have also emerged [12, 13]. The privacy, such as when the user passed a route, where he stayed for a long time, and what messages the he sent to the RSU during driving, may be leaked. By analyzing these data, the adversary can obtain much privacy of the user such as his daily routines and personal journeys. Therefore, the privacy protection of users is very important in the VANETs. Some protocols have been proposed, including network route improving [14–17], secure communication protocols [18, 19] and cloud secret sharing [20].

Kamat et al. [21] proposed a security framework for VANETs, provided the authentication, confidentiality, non-repudiation and message integrity by identity-based cryptography. Sun et al. proposed an identity-based security system for user privacy in vehicular ad hoc networks [22], which to achieve privacy desired by vehicles and traceability required by law enforcement authorities, in addition to satisfying fundamental security requirements including authentication, nonrepudiation, message integrity, and confidentiality. Moreover, a privacy-preserving defense technique was proposed for network authorities to handle misbehavior in VANET access, which considering the challenge that privacy provides avenue for misbehavior. Lu et al. [23] proposed a novel ID-based authentication framework with adaptive privacy preservation for VANETs and divided the authentication process into offline and online phases. Based on [23–25] were proposed. However, it is very difficult for a user to obtain a signature in the offline phase in practical application because the receivers are always changed with the high mobility of vehicles. Many details of the protocol in [21, 23] are not given. Mishra et al. [26] proposed a secure and efficient protocol for VANETs to ensure both message authentication and privacy preservation. In their protocol, a user's TID is generated by the user himself, which may cause the malicious user to forge a TID without being discovered. It is a security risk for these protocols which TID is generated by a user himself. Most of the protocols also do not take account of a user's reputation.

3   Preliminaries

3.1   Bilinear Pairing

The KGC chooses an additive group $\mathbb{G}_1$ and a multiplicative group $\mathbb{G}_2$, both the two groups have the same order q. q is a sufficiently large prime number. P is a generator of

$\mathbb{G}_1$. There is a bilinear pairing map $e : \mathbb{G}_1 \times \mathbb{G}_1 \to \mathbb{G}_2$. The map e should satisfy the following properties:

- **Bilinearity.** For all $P, Q \in \mathbb{G}_1$, $a, b \in Z_q^*$, $e(aP, bQ) = e(P, Q)^{ab}$.
- **Non-degeneracy.** P is a generator of $\mathbb{G}_1$, $e(P, P)$ is a generator of $\mathbb{G}_2$, and $e(P, P) \neq 1$.
- **Computability.** e can be computed efficiently in polynomial time.

3.2 Personal Reputation System

The personal reputation system [27] is a set of registration and inquiry system that records the user's reputation activity in detail. The system evaluates a user's reputation based on the penalties and lawsuits [28] and records it. A user's ID is unique and associated with the user's personal items, including the his vehicles, credit cards and criminal records. Once the user is punished for bad reputation behavior, the system will record the demerit points. If a user's score is lower than the threshold, he will be included in the reputation blacklist, and his reputation will be questioned. In this paper, the KGC will check the reputation of a user via his ID before randomly selects the TID. A user can obtain a TID only if he pass the reputation inspection.

4 Threat Model

It is assumed that an adversary can intercept the communication between the vehicle and the RSU, then tries to crack the message m, tampers with the message or collects the user's private information in m.

An adversary can locate the real-time location of a vehicle and speculates on the user's real-time activity range by searching for the vehicle's ID. The adversary can guess the user's driving route through the RSU path which the vehicle passes, and analyzes the user's personal habits and daily schedules. Using these information, the adversary can steal the user's home during the period of the user's departure, or creates traffic accidents on the sections that the user passes through every day, and endangers the personal safety of the user. On the other hand, the adversary can intercept legitimate messages sent by the vehicle, then sends these messages to the RSU again at another time. Once these messages are accepted, the user's reputation value will be reduced, the real-time traffic conditions will be misjudged by the cloud, and the urban traffic may be paralyzed.

It is worth noting that in our scheme the KGC is fully trusted. The KGC can check the user's reputation value before selects a TID for the user.

5 The Proposed Scheme

We propose a novel identity-based signcryption scheme for VANETs. In VANETs, vehicles and RSU are interconnected to form a star network to share real-time traffic conditions. Here we take the vehicle i as an example. Suppose i's identity is ID_i and the RSU's identity is ID_R.

Setup. With a security parameter k, the KGC chooses an additive group $\mathbb{G}_1$ and a multiplicative group $\mathbb{G}_2$. Both $\mathbb{G}_1$ and $\mathbb{G}_2$ have the same order prime q. $\mathbb{G}_1$ has a generator P. There is a bilinear maps $e : \mathbb{G}_1 \times \mathbb{G}_1 \to \mathbb{G}_2$. Three hash functions are donated as follows: $H_1 : \{0,1\}^{l_{ID}} \to \{0,1\}^{l_1}$, $H_2 : \mathbb{G}_2 \to \{0,1\}^{l_2}$, $H_3 : \{0,1\}^{l_2} \to \{0,1\}^{l_3}$. Here l_{ID} is the number of ID's bits, l_1, l_2, l_3 are also the number of bits. The master secret key s is selected randomly from Z_p^* by KGC, then KGC calculates the master public key $P_{pub} = sP$ and a public parameter $r = e(P,P)$. The system parameters will be published by KGC as $\{\mathbb{G}_1, \mathbb{G}_2, q, e, P, P_{pub}, \mathrm{r}, H_1, H_2, H_3, l_{ID}, l_1, l_2\}$. The master secret key s is kept by KGC itself.

KG. This part is divided into two cases.

The first case is that the key generation request is sent by a RSU. After receiving the ID_R, KGC will calculate the private key

$$S_R = \frac{1}{sH_1(ID_R)}P$$

and the public key

$$PK_R = H_1(ID_R)P_{pub}$$

then returns S_R and PK_R to the RSU via a secret channel.

The second case is that the key generation request is sent by a vehicle i. The KGC will first query i's reputation value through the personal reputation system after receiving ID_i from the vehicle. If i is included in the reputation blacklist, KGC will reject the request, otherwise the KGC randomly selects a TID_i and calculates the private key

$$S_i = \frac{1}{sH_1(TID_i)}P$$

and the public key

$$PK_i = H_1(TID_i)P_{pub}$$

then returns TID_i, S_i and PK_i to the vehicle via a secret channel.

The process of i's key generation is presented in Fig. 1. Notice that and the KGC is fully trusted in our scheme.

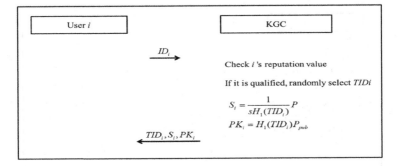

Fig. 1. User's key generation phase

SC. i chooses two random numbers $\xi, \gamma \in Z_p^*$. The algorithm calculates $\alpha_1 = r^\xi$, $\alpha_2 = r^{\xi+\gamma}$,

$$W = \xi PK_R,$$
$$c = m \oplus H_2(\alpha_1),$$
$$V = \gamma S_i \frac{1}{H_3(m)},$$

where m represents the plaintext message.

A ciphertext $\lambda = (c, \alpha_2, V, W, t)$ will be sent to the RSU after this step. t is the sending time stamp of λ.

USC. When the RSU receives λ, it first checks whether $t^* - t \leq \Delta t$, here t^* is the receiving time stamp of λ, λ will be rejected directly if the formula does not hold. Otherwise, the RSU calculates

$$\alpha_1 = e(S_R, W) \tag{1}$$

and unsigncrypts λ by computing $m = c \oplus H_2(\alpha_1)$. At last, the RSU computes $V^* = VH_3(m)$ and checks whether the equation

$$\alpha_2 = e(V^*, PK_i)\alpha_1 \tag{2}$$

is established. m can be accepted only if Eq. (2) is established.

The communication process of our scheme are presented in Fig. 2.

6 Security Analysis

6.1 Correctness

In the unsigncryption step, the Eq. (1) can be proved by the following formula:

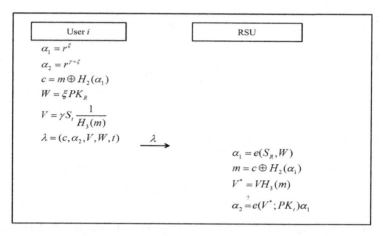

Fig. 2. The communication process between i and RSU

$$e(S_R, W) = e\left(\tfrac{1}{sH_1(ID_R)}P, \xi PK_R\right)$$
$$= e\left(\tfrac{1}{sH_1(ID_R)}P, \xi H_1(ID_R)P_{pub}\right)$$
$$= e(P, \xi P)$$
$$= e(P, P)^{\xi}$$
$$= r^{\xi}$$
$$= \alpha_1$$

If the message is valid, then Eq. (2) can be proved by the following formula:

$$e(V^*, PK_i)\alpha_1$$
$$= e(\gamma S_i, PK_i)\alpha_1$$
$$= e(\gamma \tfrac{1}{sH_1(TID_i)}P, H_1(TID_i)P_{pub})\alpha_1$$
$$= e(\gamma P, P)\alpha_1$$
$$= e(P, P)^{\gamma} r^{\xi}$$
$$= r^{\gamma} r^{\xi}$$
$$= r^{\gamma + \xi}$$
$$= \alpha_2$$

6.2   Security Against the Man-in-the-Middle Attack

An adversary may intercept and tamper with the message during the communication process. However, these operations need time cost. In our scheme, after receiving the λ, RSU will first check whether $t^* - t \leq \Delta t$, if the transmission delay exceeds the maximum transmission delay Δt, λ will be rejected directly. Assume that the attack operations take little time that λ passes the transmission delay check, the RSU will verify λ by calculating $\alpha_2 = e(V^*, PK_i)\alpha_1$. If the message was tampered during transmission, RSU cannot obtain the correct V^* by computing $VH_3(m)$ cause m has been changed.

With a wrong V^*, the equation $\alpha_2 = e(V^*, PK_i)\alpha_1$ will not hold. The message will be accepted only if Eq. (2) is established. Thus in our scheme, the integrity of the message can be guaranteed. Our scheme can resist the man-in-the-middle attacks.

6.3 Anonymity

In many existing protocols, users can be easily tracked and positioned through his ID. An adversary can guess the range of user's activities by locating his vehicle or obtain the user's daily journeys by recording the user's driving route. A user can trick the system by forging a TID to evade the violation check. In our scheme, the TID is selected by KGC randomly. The TID is hard to be speculated because it is updated by KGC irregularly. It is very difficult for the adversary to track a user, cause only KGC and the user himself know the correspondence between TID and the real ID. And tracking the user by TID is meaningless because TID are updated from time to time.

6.4 Backward Security and Forward Security

The adversary may obtain some security parameters by decrypting a message and tries to decrypt the previous or future messages with these security parameters. It is almost impossible for an adversary to obtain the correct m in this way cause he cannot know the private keys and the random numbers ξ, γ for each communication are different.

6.5 Security Against the Malicious User Attack

We assume that the adversary is a malicious user, and then discuss the situation in two cases. In the first case, the adversary has a legal TID and tries to send some incorrect information to mislead real-time traffic condition updating. Although this incorrect message may be accepted by RSU, the cloud will update real-time traffic information only after comprehensive analysis of all received messages. During this process, the incorrect information will be easily identified and not taken into consideration. Once the adversary is found to send incorrect information, his reputation value will be reduced, which will seriously affect his life cause the personal reputation system involves a lot of public resource applications. The cost is very heavy, so the adversary is not motivated to carry out such attacks. In the second case, the adversary is a malicious user with low reputation value and is included in the blacklist of the personal reputation system. When receiving the adversary's ID, KGC will refuse to provide him with a TID. Any message sent by the adversary will be rejected without a legal TID.

7 Conclusion

Vehicles share real-time traffic information to ease traffic congestion via the VANETs. In this paper, we propose an identity-based signcryption scheme for VANETs which can achieves this function and protects users' privacy. By introducing the TID selected randomly by KGC, users do not have to worry about being tracked. Moreover, the novel scheme has little overhead while protecting privacy.

Acknowledgment. This work is supported by the National Natural Science Foundation of China under Grant No. 61672295, No. 61672290, No. U1405254 and No. 61772280, Foundation of Guizhou Provincial Key Laboratory of Public Big Data No. 2018BDKFJJ003 and the Opening Project of Guangdong Key Laboratory of Data Security and Privacy Protection No. 2017B030301004.

References

1. Gubbi, J., Buyya, R., Marusic, S., Palaniswami, M.: Internet of Things (IoT): a vision, architectural elements, and future directions. Future Gener. Comput. Syst. **29**(7), 1645–1660 (2012)
2. Xiong, Z., Sheng, H., Rong, W., Cooper, D.E.: Intelligent transportation systems for smart cities: a progress review. Sci. China Inf. Sci. **55**, 2908–2914 (2012). https://doi.org/10.1007/s11432-012-4725-1
3. Guizzo, E.: How google's self-driving car works. IEEE Spectr. Online **18**(7), 1132–1141 (2011)
4. Zeadally, S., Hunt, R., Chen, Y.-S., Irwin, A., Hassan, A.: Vehicular ad hoc networks (VANETS): status, results, and challenges. Telecommun. Syst. **50**(4), 217–241 (2012). https://doi.org/10.1007/s11235-010-9400-5
5. Raya, M., Hubaux, J.P.: Securing vehicular ad hoc networks. In: International Conference on Pervasive Computing & Applications (2007)
6. Sutariya, D., Pradhan, S.: An improved AODV routing protocol for VANETs in city scenarios. In: 2012 International Conference on Advances in Engineering, Science and Management (ICAESM), pp. 575–581. IEEE (2012)
7. Sharma, R., Choudhry, A.: An extensive survey on different routing protocols and issue in VANETs. Int. J. Comput. Appl. **106**(5), 23–28 (2014)
8. Abumansoor, O., Boukerche, A.: A secure cooperative approach for nonline-of-sight location verification in VANET. IEEE Trans. Veh. Technol. **61**(1), 275–285 (2012)
9. Pathan, A.-S.K.: Security of Self-Organizing Networks: MANET, WSN, WMN, VANET. CRC Press, Boca Raton (2016)
10. Huang, Z., Ruj, S., Cavenaghi, M., Nayak, A.: Limitations of trust management schemes in VANET and countermeasures. In: 2011 IEEE 22nd International Symposium on Personal Indoor and Mobile Radio Communications (PIMRC), pp. 1228–1232. IEEE (2011)
11. Perrig, A.: Securing VANETs: industry approaches and current research directions. In: International Workshop on Vehicular Ad Hoc Networks, VANET 2009, Beijing, China, September 2009, pp. 1–2 (2009)
12. Al-Kahtani, M.S.: Survey on security attacks in vehicular ad hoc networks (VANETs). In: International Conference on Signal Processing and Communication Systems, pp. 1–9 (2013)
13. Yousefi, S., Mousavi, M.S., Fathy, M.: Vehicular ad hoc networks (VANETs): challenges and perspectives. In: 2006 6th International Conference on ITS Telecommunications Proceedings, pp. 761–766. IEEE (2006)
14. Shen, J., Wang, C., Wang, A., Sun, X., Moh, S., Hung, P.C.K.: Organized topology based routing protocol in incompletely predictable ad-hoc networks. Comput. Commun. **99**(C), 107–118 (2017)
15. Fiore, M., Harri, J., Filali, F., Bonnet, C.: Vehicular mobility simulation for VANETs. In: 2007 40th Annual Simulation Symposium. ANSS 2007, pp. 301–309. IEEE (2007)

16. Xiao, B., Yu, B., Gao, C.: Detection and localization of Sybil nodes in VANETS. In: Proceedings of the 2006 workshop on Dependability Issues in Wireless Ad Hoc Networks and Sensor Networks, pp. 1–8. ACM (2006)
17. Qian, Y., Moayeri, N.: Design of secure and application-oriented VANETs. In: 2008 IEEE Vehicular Technology Conference. VTC Spring 2008, pp. 2794–2799. IEEE (2008)
18. Choi, J., Jung, S.: A security framework with strong non-repudiation and privacy in VANETs. In: IEEE Conference on Consumer Communications and Networking Conference, pp. 835–839 (2009)
19. Ashritha, M., Sridhar, C.: RSU based efficient vehicle authentication mechanism for VANETs. In: 2015 IEEE 9th International Conference on Intelligent Systems and Control (ISCO), pp. 1–5. IEEE (2015)
20. Shen, J., Zhou, T., Chen, X., Li, J., Susilo, W.: Anonymous and traceable group data sharing in cloud computing. IEEE Trans. Inf. Forensics Secur. 13(4), 912–925 (2018)
21. Kamat, P., Baliga, A., Trappe, W.: An identity-based security framework for VANETs. In: International Workshop on Vehicular Ad Hoc Networks, pp. 94–95 (2006)
22. Sun, J., Chi, Z., Zhang, Y., Fang, Y.: An identity-based security system for user privacy in vehicular ad hoc networks. IEEE Trans. Parallel Distrib. Syst. 21(9), 1227–1239 (2010)
23. Lu, H., Li, J., Guizani, M.: A novel ID-based authentication framework with adaptive privacy preservation for VANETs. In: Computing, Communications and Applications Conference, pp. 345–350 (2012)
24. Li, J., Lu, H., Guizani, M.: ACPN: a novel authentication framework with conditional privacy-preservation and non-repudiation for VANETs. IEEE Trans. Parallel Distrib. Syst. 26(4), 938–948 (2015)
25. Jenefa, J., Anita, E.A.M.: Secure vehicular communication using ID based signature scheme. Wireless Pers. Commun. 98(1), 1383–1411 (2018)
26. Mishra, B., Panigrahy, S.K., Tripathy, T.C., Jena, D., Jena, S.K.: A secure and efficient message authentication protocol for VANETs with privacy preservation. In: Information and Communication Technologies, pp. 880–885 (2012)
27. Chen, Y.M., Wei, Y.C.: A beacon-based trust management system for enhancing user centric location privacy in vanets. J. Commun. Netw. 15(2), 153–163 (2013)
28. Shen, J., Wang, C., Castiglione, A., Liu, D., Esposito, C.: Trustworthiness evaluation-based routing protocol for incompletely predictable vehicular ad hoc networks. IEEE Trans. Big Data (2017)

The Privacy-Preserving Data Publishing in Medical Application: A Survey

Chieh-Lin Chuang[1(✉)], Pang-Chieh Wang[2], Ming-Shi Wang[1], and Chin-Feng Lai[1]

[1] National Cheng Kung University, No. 1, Daxue Rd., Tainan 70101, Taiwan (R.O.C.)
n96074162@mail.ncku.edu.tw
[2] No. 195, Sec. 4, Zhongxing Rd., Zhudong Township, Hsinchu County 310, Taiwan (R.O.C.)

Abstract. As the time goes by and the development of science and technology, medical issues are becoming part of everyone's life. People are paying much more attention to their own rights. When people transfer from one hospital to another for treatment, they may need to repeat multiple examinations, resulting unnecessary expenses and waste of medical resources. The Ministry of Health and Welfare promotes a system that uploads all patients' medical files to an online database allowing them to check their own medical information and share it also, but it probably makes some privacy problem. In this paper, we found several methods that might be useful for image encryption, including, privacy-preserving data publishing (PPDP), scale invariant feature transform (SIFT), convolutional neural network (CNN), explored their algorithms and compare their strengths and weaknesses in the field of medical imaging encryption. Hoping to find a method for people to use the system without doubt.

Keywords: PPDP · SIFT · CNN

1 Introduction

A comprehensive health examination could cost more than twenty-thousands TWD. To reduce waste, in January 2018, Taiwan's Ministry of Health and Welfare promotes a new database system. The doctor can read and check patients' medical history through the database even though it is their first visit. This system is expected to save 2 billion TWD per year from healthcare expenditure.

The idea of sharing medical information through an online database is great. However, it may produce some new problems for those who cares about their own personal privacy being shared. The British government's health department, announced in July 2017, patients have the right to refuse to share their medical records. The right can also be applied to the health and social care system starting from March 2018. Based on the development of this new system, the British government and its citizen seems to care a lot about their personal information being shared, which seems

© Springer Nature Singapore Pte Ltd. 2020
J. Shen et al. (Eds.): IC3 2019, CCIS 1227, pp. 438–447, 2020.
https://doi.org/10.1007/978-981-15-6113-9_49

reasonable. Therefore, we propose information sharing encryption to protect privacy, which can also improve the security and reliability of the medical information sharing system. The new system also improves public's willingness to share medical information, and further reduce healthcare expenditure.

For the privacy part, using Computed tomography of the chest [1, 2] as an example, chest muscle, breast, lung, ribs and other human organs are taken in the chest CT photos. The shape and location of organs in the chest CT photos taken from different patients can be really different. According to doctors, if the shape and the location of the patients is special, then doctors might have a chance to identify patients' identities if they have seen it before which will violate the privacy of patients. Therefore, we hope only essential medical information are kept in the system, then the rest photos will not be able to identify after special security treatment. Using this kind of encryption to protect the privacy of citizens can reassure people sharing their medical information to the internet.

Medical image reports are divided into three main stage: image encrypting, image processing and medical analysis. First of all, patients' first medical information is encrypted so that it can be used correctly by the image processor. Image processor then used this encrypted medical information in machine learning. Machine learning implies model for searching suspicious lung tumor location, model for identifying the lung tumor is either benign or malignant. The encrypted medical information should not affect the result of machine training. When medical analyst is facing new patients, they will be able to use the model provided, quickly and accurately diagnose the symptoms for patients. These help assisting doctors in diagnosis, and further reduce medical expenditure.

After encrypting the image provided by the image provider, the user can simply use the medical information for machine learning, and cannot identify the identities of the medical information provider, thus protecting the patient's privacy. Image processors can also safely use the medical information for training, and then submit the model to medical inspectors. We divide the encryption behavior into two parts: one is to encrypt the file, which does not affect the data content; the other is to modify the image content to get inconsistent images.

2   Related Research

2.1   PPDP

In the privacy publishing process, it can be divided into two steps: data collection and data publishing, as shown in Fig. 1 below:

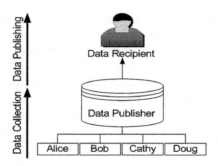

Fig. 1. Data collection and data publishing.

Therefore, the method to achieve privacy protection is also divided into two parts. There are many mature research methods for the privacy of data collection. It can be traced back to the Randomized response proposed by Warner, S. L. in 1965 [3].

This approach ensures the privacy of the data provider by hiding the questions from the data publisher, thus protect data provider's identity. In 1969, the method of Greenberg et al. was based on Warner, which improved the data collection process of data publishers, and increased the willingness of data providers to provide private data [4].

Warner's method is assuming the population is divided into A part and B part, he designs a disk divided into two sectors, and writes A and B on the sector respectively. There is a pointer on the disk, and the data provider turns the pointer and gives the answer "yes" or "no" according to the position where the pointer naturally stops (e.g. Because the publisher does not know where the pointer is, he will not know the true category of the data provider, whether the data provider answers "yes" or "no"). In this way, the data provider's privacy is guaranteed under protection.

non-sensitive. The data provider is randomly assigned to answer sensitive or non-sensitive questions. For example, to find out if a college student has ever stolen from a store, write one question on each piece of paper: "have you ever stolen from a store? "And" is the last digit of your student number 3? Before answering the questions, the data provider will see two questions and decide which one to answer by drawing lots or other random methods. This approach increases the willingness of data providers to provide private information while protecting privacy.

In addition to the manipulation of data collection methods, many encryption services have also made it difficult for publishers to keep track of data providers as technology advances. Chaum put forward the concept of Mix network in 1981 [5]. The data publisher will not be able trace the information of the data provider after encryption by many trusted third-party encryptions, as shown in Fig. 2 below:

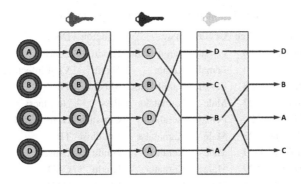

Fig. 2. Example diagram for mix network

We can observe that when the data publisher obtains the privacy information of the data provider, he does not know who is the provider of this privacy information because many third party encryption. It helps protect the privacy of the data provider.

However, in Chaum's method, a large number of trusted third-party encryption is required. In order to improve this, Yang et al. proposed in 2005 that no trusted third party is required and the privacy of data providers can still be guaranteed [6]. In his paper, zero knowledge proof is proposed to allow data publishers to provide data required by data receivers without disclosing the privacy of data providers.

In addition to the research on the privacy of data collection, there are also many researches on the privacy protection of data providers after obtaining their privacy information. For example: The Randomization method, K - anonymity, L-diversity, T - closeness, these are all common method.

According to [7], the Randomization method is a method to apply noise to the original data. Assuming that the distribution of the original data is X, we can add it to the distribution of Y to get the Z data set, which provides a certain degree of privacy protection. Another way to add noise is to multiply the data by a certain ratio. Assuming that the original data distribution is X, we can multiply X by any value between 0.8 and 1.2 to become the Z 'data set. In the case of the Randomization method, the receiver of the data is not in a position to accurately know the information of the provider without knowing the allocation and the ratios.

K - anonymity, L - diversity, and T - closeness are series of improvement methods. These methods all aims on privacy protection for data sets with multiple fields. Suppose we now have a medically relevant dataset, as shown in Table 1 below:

Table 1. Medical data examples (original data).

Name	Age	Gender	State	Religion	Disease
Ramsha	29	Female	Tamil Nadu	Hindu	Cancer
Yadu	24	Female	Kerala	Hindu	Viral infection
Salima	28	Female	Tamil Nadu	Muslim	TB
Sunny	27	Male	Karnataka	Parsi	No illness
Joan	24	Female	Kerala	Christian	Heart Attack
Bahuksana	23	Male	Karnataka	Buddhist	TB
Rambha	19	Male	Kerala	Hindu	Cancer
Kishor	29	Male	Karnataka	Hindu	CAD
Johnson	17	Male	Kerala	Christian	CAD
John	19	Male	Kerala	Christian	Viral infection

Using the generalization and the suppression technique in k-anonymity [8], we can generalize the numerical data to classes (for example, age in the example data) and remove the sensitive data (for example, names and religions in the example data). The data after generalization and removal are shown in Table 2 below:

Table 2. Medical data examples (privacy protected).

Name	Age	Gender	State	Religion	Disease
*	20–30	Female	Tamil Nadu	*	Cancer
*	20–30	Female	Kerala	*	Viral infection
*	20–30	Female	Tamil Nadu	*	TB
*	20–30	Male	Karnataka	*	No illness
*	20–30	Female	Kerala	*	Heart Attack
*	20–30	Male	Karnataka	*	TB
*	<20	Male	Kerala	*	Cancer
*	20–30	Male	Karnataka	*	CAD
*	<20	Male	Kerala	*	CAD
*	<20	Male	Kerala	*	Viral infection

Although this method can achieve a certain degree of privacy protection, privacy may be partially disclosed when prior knowledge is available, and the generalization ratio is unevenly distributed. For example, if John is one of them in the above data, it can be inferred that he has cancer, heart disease or viral infection. Therefore, the L-diversity method [9] was proposed, hoping to solve such a problem.

In the L-diversity method, every category must have diversity, which means that there was no way to get private information through a single category. For example, in the data in Table 2, as long as John's age is known, it can be determined that John is sick, but this situation can be avoided if there is no disease data under the age of 20 in the data.

However, L-diversity has its own small defects. If the category itself is highly homogeneous, and if we also want to increase the diversity at the same time then the classification is non-significant. For example, Heart attack and coronary artery disease (CAD) are both Heart related diseases. To test homogeneity, Li et al. put forward a T - closeness method [10].

2.2   SIFT

SIFT was originally published by David Lowe in 1999 [11] and improved in 2004. At first, this algorithm is mainly used as a machine vision algorithm to detect and describe local features in the image. The algorithm extracts the location of the extremum from the spatial scale and records the scale and rotation invariants.

By extracting these extreme points and relevant information, the image system can perform more complex identification. When the algorithm is actually applied to image comparison, it goes through four processes, including extreme value detection in scale space, location of key points, direction orientation and generation of key point descriptors [12].

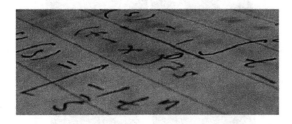

Fig. 3. Example of SIFT.

Figure 3 is the feature points obtained after the actual operation of the algorithm. We can see that the feature points of handwritten points are all endpoints, so this algorithm can also be used to extract the features in image. For example, techniques such as edge detection, corner detection, spot detection ridge detection, hough trans- form, the structure tensor, feature description and so on various computer vision areas can all be based on SIFT algorithm. The above figure shows the output using typical angle detection.

This algorithm has been applied in various fields of computer vision, and has shown very good results in various types of comparison or detection after feature extraction. This is not only because of the high utility of extracted feature points, but also because of its scale-invariant characteristics.

Warren Cheung and Ghassan Hamarneh proposed N-SIFT (n-dimensional Scale Invariant Feature Transform) for n dimensions [13]. The algorithm extends the concept of SIFT in computer vision for two-dimensional scalar graphs and enables it to extract feature points from other dimensions. Different from the original SIFT, they used the hyperdimensional spherical coordinates to calculate the gradient, and added the feature histogram of this multidimensional image to generate the feature vectors, and finally compared through these feature vectors. The experiment includes 3D MRI images and sequential 3D CT data. The following pictures are examples of three dimensions (Fig. 4).

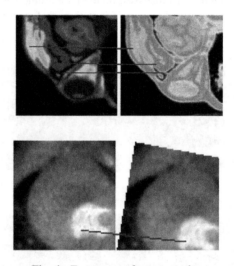

Fig. 4. Feature transform examples.

2.3 CNN

CNN has been a very popular in the field of machine learning in recent years. The concept of prototypes is proposed in 1989 by the earliest Lecun in [14], and proposed the weight updating method in [15]. Most of today's CNN model is similar to Alex's in [16], in the model using the Dropout [Improving neural networks by preventing co-adaptation of feature detectors to avoid overfitting. This improves the accuracy of CNN, and also extend to many other improved versions. For example, R-CNN was proposed in order to solve the image that has many specific targets [17].

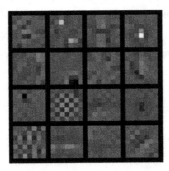

Fig. 5. Kernel visualization for hidden layer.

The use of CNN in the medical field is usually the identification of symptoms through classification [18]. It helps doctors judge the patient's' condition more quickly. Images processed by neural networks are usually unrecognizable to humans, so an alternative privacy protection can be achieved. The following figure is the kernel visualization (Fig. 5).

3   Comparison

3.1   PPDP

The main focus of PPDP is encryption technology. Either encryption by some third party to cause confusion, or adding noise to the data can both cause the receiver almost impossible to know who the owner of the file is. However, the method does not change the image pixels. In the case of medical imaging of rare disease cases, such an approach would not be effective strategy in confusing of the receiver.

3.2   SIFT

For SIFT, we simply flip or filter images to cause confusion. By the SIFT algorithm, feature can be found between processed image and the originals. In another way, we can simply use the gaussian blur used in the first half of the algorithm to mark feature points, which tells us which parts of the image may be important. Then we carry out actions on the image such as image cutting to remove the useless parts, so as to reduce the probability of recognition of patients' identities.

3.3   CNN

The original image will be greatly reduced after multi-layer convolution and pooling. We can ideally filtrate out the result we want, and the processed image will be different from the original version, so that the data receiver cannot know the original appearance.

Table 3. Comparison on three methods.

	PPDP	SIFT	CNN (convolution)
For machine-learning	Yes	Yes	Yes
Data change	No	Depend on method	Yes
Reversible	Yes	Depend on method	No
Recognizable	Yes	Yes	No

3.4   Summary

It can be seen from the table that the file formats are still pictures after processed by the three modes. However, the contents are different, so that they are still applicable to machine learning. PPDP is the easiest to identify because it makes no changes to the image. For SIFT, if the feature point density is used as the basis to partially discard the image, but it cannot be recovered. The method of convolution will use pooling layer. As in result, there will be actions of deleting and it is also not recoverable. In neural network, the way of how machine identifying images is usually different from how we human identifies. The numerical visualization of the hidden layer is usually unrecognizable for human beings (Table 3).

4   Conclusion

The goal of the research is looking for a method to protect the privacy of patients. We discussed PPDP for data encryption, SIFT algorithm for possible contribution in medical image, and CNN for image processing. In conclusion, it can be seen that these methods all trying to achieve privacy protection. However, by comparing the advantages and disadvantages of the three, we find that when all information is blocked, the convolution of the image should be the best way to achieve our goal. Not only because of its irreversible, people also can not recognize the graph by intuitive judgment is the most important reason.

References

1. Alakwaa, W., Nassef, M., Badr, A.: Lung cancer detection and classification with 3D Convolutional Neural Network (3D-CNN). Int. J. Adv. Comput. Sci. Appl. **8**, 409 (2017)
2. Sun, W., Zheng, B., Qian, W.: Computer aided lung cancer diagnosis with deep learning algorithms. In: Medical Imaging 2016. Computer-Aided Diagnosis, vol. 9785, p. 97850Z (2016)
3. Warner, S.L.: Randomized response: a survey technique for eliminating evasive answer bias. J. Am. Stat. Assoc. **60**(309), 63–69 (1965)
4. Greenberg, B.G., Abul-Ela, A.L.A., Simmons, W.R., Horvitz, D.G.: The unrelated question randomized response model: theoretical framework. J. Am. Stat. Assoc. **64**, 520–539 (1969)
5. David, C.: Untraceable electronic mail, return addresses, and digital pseudonyms. In: Secure Electronic Voting, pp. 84–90 (1981)

6. Yang, Z., Zhong, S., Wright, R.N.: Anonymity-preserving data collection. In: Proceedings of the eleventh ACM SIGKDD International Conference on Knowledge Discovery in Data Mining, pp. 334–343 (2005)
7. Mendes, R., Vilela, J.P.: Privacy-preserving data mining: methods, metrics, and applications. IEEE Access **5**, 10562–10582 (2017)
8. Samarati, P., Sweeney, L.: Protecting privacy when disclosing information: k-anonymity and its enforcement through generalization and suppresion. In: Proceedings of the IEEE Symposium on Research in Security and Privacy, pp. 384–393 (1998)
9. Aggarwal, C.C., Yu, P.S.: A general survey of privacy-preserving data mining models and algorithms. In: Aggarwal, C.C., Yu, P.S. (eds.) privacy-preserving data mining, pp. 11–52. Springer, Boston (2008). https://doi.org/10.1007/978-0-387-70992-5_2
10. Li, N., Li, T., Venkatasubramanian, S.: t-closeness: privacy beyond k-anonymity and l-diversity. In: 2007 IEEE 23rd International Conference on Data Engineering, pp. 106–115 (2007)
11. Lindeberg, T.: Scale invariant feature transform. Scholarpedia **7**, 10491 (2012)
12. Lowe, D.G.: Object recognition from local scale-invariant features. In: Proceedings of the Seventh IEEE International Conference on Computer Vision, pp. 1150–1157 (1999)
13. Cheung, W., Hannarneh, G.: N-SIFT: N-dimensional scale invariant feature transform for matching medical images. In: 2007 4th IEEE International Symposium on Biomedical Imaging: From Nano to Macro, pp. 720–723 (2007). Bioinformatics University of British Columbia Medical Image Analysis Lab
14. LeCun, Y., et al.: Backpropagation applied to handwritten zip code recognition. Neural Comput. **1**, 541–551 (1989)
15. LeCun, Y.: Generalization and network design strategies. In: Connectionism in Perspective, pp. 143–155 (1989)
16. Krizhevsky, A., Sutskever, I., Hinton, G.: ImageNet classification with deep convolutional neural networks. In: Advances in Neural Information Processing Systems, pp. 1097–1105 (2012)
17. Girshick, R., Donahue, J., Darrell, T., Malik, J.: Rich feature hierarchies for accurate object detection and semantic segmentation. In: Proceedings of IEEE Computer Society Conference on Computer Vision and Pattern Recognition, pp. 580–587 (2014)
18. Li, Q., Cai, W., Wang, X., Zhou, Y., Feng, D.D., Chen, M.: Medical image classification with convolutional neural network. In: 2014 13th International Conference on Control Automation Robotics and Vision, ICARCV 2014, pp. 844–848 (2014)

Research on Natural Language Processing in Financial Risk Detection

Wei-Yu Chen[1,4(⊠)], Shing-Han Li[2], and Yung-Hsin Wang[3]

[1] Department of Mass Communication, Chinese Culture University,
Taipei, Taiwan
cwy4@pccu.edu.tw
[2] Department of Accounting Information,
National Taipei University of Business, Taipei, Taiwan
[3] Department of Information Management, Tatung University, Taipei, Taiwan
ywang@ttu.edu.tw
[4] Department of Computer Science and Engineering, Tatung University,
Taipei, Taiwan

Abstract. With the rise of electronic financial transactions, illegal financial activities have emerged in an endless stream. People have used illegal funds to conceal or cover up illegal sources of funds through small-value transfers, cash orders, traveler's checks and other gold trading channels to evade supervision by government units. It isn't easy to trace the information of these golden streams, because the flow of funds includes the source and destination of the wire transfer, the nature of the wire transfer and the relationship between the sender and the bank are very complicated and difficult to check. Natural language processing understands the meaning of people's commands and inputs in a seamless and simplified way. Further, it can eliminate the mistakes caused by human beings and enable financial risk control personnel to find problematic transactions in a short period of time in a more efficient manner. This study uses BERT's TensorFlow open source code and the test data set provided by Paysim to conduct risk model construction research.

Keywords: Financial risk detection · Natural language processing · Anti money laundering

1 Introduction

In recent years, the prevention and control of money laundering has been valued by Taiwan's financial institutions, mainly because the US Financial Services Agency (DFS) has conducted investigations on money-laundering prevention and control against well-known banks at home and abroad, and imposed fine fines on those who have suffered serious losses. In addition, the Asia-Pacific Money Laundering Prevention Organization (APG) has evaluated Taiwan's financial industry, and the results of the evaluation have affected the competitiveness and international image of the financial industry's overseas market operations. However, it is not so easy to prevent money laundering. Financial institutions need to spend a lot of time and money to deal with them. The counters of the bank's counters need to repeatedly ask questions and

© Springer Nature Singapore Pte Ltd. 2020
J. Shen et al. (Eds.): IC3 2019, CCIS 1227, pp. 448–455, 2020.
https://doi.org/10.1007/978-981-15-6113-9_50

investigate, and if the customers are willing to answer, they can obtain the source of funds and funds. Information on the flow, use, and relationship with politicians, these actions are likely to trigger customer dissatisfaction. Secondly, under the issue of privacy of data analysis, major banks are unable to quickly identify and identify the source and use of funds after the identification of personal data. Finally, the data acquisition and analysis cost problem, this part requires a lot of manpower and money to analyze, because if the customer is not willing to provide the correct information, the bank has no way to know the correct information about the fund, which will become bank money laundering. Prevent important burdens.

The use of artificial intelligence in the prevention and control of money laundering has been carried out in Europe and the United States for many years. The traditional method is to fragment a large amount of financial data for a long time, fragment it, continuously carry out pairing analysis, and import the collected data or models into financial institutions. In the risk management platform, monitoring and observation to identify the possibility of transactions may be money laundering and fraud, but such applications will take a lot of manpower and time. As the complexity of neural networks increases and data sets continue to expand, the cost of completely retraining a model continues to increase.

In October 2018, deep learning made a major breakthrough in natural language processing. Google researchers trained 3.3 million text corpora into language models and then fine-tuned them in different application scenarios. After testing these models, the best results were obtained in different application scenarios, and some of the results were better than the previously learned models. Google's Bidirectional Encoder Representations from Transformers allows users to quickly train question and answer systems and other types of models on the cloud TPU or GPU. In general, the biggest challenge in natural language processing is the lack of training materials, because it is not easy to obtain such a large amount of training materials, and pre-training techniques use a large amount of unmarked text on the Internet to train the general language representation model, and You can then use the small specific datasets such as sentiment analysis or Q&A to fine-tune the pre-training model, so that you can use the dataset of a particular collar to train at the beginning, which can significantly improve the accuracy of the model, and the data size is also Not so big.

2 Literature Review

2.1 Natural Language Processing

The most important thing about people-to-person communication is the language, the meaning of language, which allows people to understand each other's minds and needs. To make the computer a machine that only recognizes 0 and 1, to let the computer have the ability to understand human language, you must first let the computer learn how to break words and understand the meaning of words. In the process of human self-learning language, the first step is to memorize and memorize the meaning of the vocabulary. The second step is to understand the smallest unit of use in the language-vocabulary through the actual practice and writing of the practice words. Among them,

Chinese is different from other languages in that there is no limit between words and words. Sentences can be kept down all the time. Unlike English, spaces can be broken with spaces. Therefore, when you want to understand a Chinese article, you need to learn the word break, understand the syntactic structure and the meaning of the word, and then have a way to understand the meaning of the sentence.

Natural language processing is mainly to convert complex language into a computer-calculated computing form. The processing method used in 1950 is to build a vocabulary database, write artificial rules in the programming language, and let the computer follow the rules. Make relevant reactions. The main research direction from 1980 to 2017 is to establish an algorithmic model that allows the computer to learn the characteristics of the data from the training materials. Using machine learning algorithms, the computer learns to automatically summarize the characteristics of the language from the training materials. 2018 is a year of major breakthroughs in natural language processing. In general, the problem of natural language processing is the lack of training materials. Since natural language training is a diverse field that combines different tasks, most task-specific data sets Containing only thousands or hundreds of thousands of training paradigms, but based on the natural language of deep learning techniques of the time, millions or billions of examples of tag training data are needed to have good results. In practice, it is very difficult to obtain such a large amount of training, so the pre-training technology is developed. The pre-training mainly uses a large amount of unmarked text on the network to train the general language representation model, and this type can use sentiment analysis or It is a small specific data set such as question and answer to fine-tune, so that training with a specific field data set can be used to improve the accuracy of the model. The evolution of natural language processing is shown in Table 1.

Table 1. Evolution of natural language processing

Age	Processing method	Computing power
1950	Establish a vocabulary database, write artificial rules in the programming language, and let the computer respond according to the instructions. However, there is no way to handle the different meanings according to the lexical context	General CPU
1980	Combining the algorithm of machine learning, the algorithm model is built, and the computer learns to find out the specific patterns and trends contained in the data from the training materials, so that the computer can automatically summarize the characteristics of the language from the training materials	GPU
2018	The pre-training context representation is a deep two-way unsupervised model that can be used to train advanced question and answer systems through TPU and GPU. In the way of question and answer, the parameters in the model are precisely adjusted to increase the accuracy of the context in the language identification	TPU and GPU

After completing the training of the model, natural language processing can be applied at a very wide range, such as: more accurate detection of fraudulent emails, finding people's sentiment analysis of things, suggestions and corrections to search engines, marking of words in sentences, machines Translation, speech recognition, syntactic analysis, name recognition, and an outline of an automated abstract article. These need to let the computer understand the language used by human beings, master the syntactic structure, analyze the emotions between lines, and then count the characteristics and understand what is being said in the article.

2.2 Bidirectional Encoder Representation from Transformers

The Bidirectional Encoder Representations from Transformers is built on Google's TensorFlow, allowing users to quickly train question and answer systems and other types of models through the cloud TPU or GPU. In addition to the source code, there are many pre-trained language representation models in the program. There will be pre-training techniques, and it is very difficult to obtain a large amount of training materials to narrow the gap between demand and actual data. Among them, pre-training can use a large amount of unmarked text on the network to train the general language representation model, and then use a small specific data set such as sentiment analysis or question and answer to perform pre-training model fine-tuning. Technically, pre-training can be divided into Contextual or Contextless, where the context can be further divided into one-way or two-way. The two-way context model is very powerful, but training the model is not easy, so there is no system to use the bidirectional model before BERT. Google uses an intuitive approach to cover some of the input words with a mask and predicts the covered words bi-directionally for each word. Although this method has been around for a long time, BERT is the first successful technology to train deep learning neural networks. The BERT two-way context model uses the words before and after the words in the sentence to make guesses. For example, "I have accessed" and "account" in the sentence indicate that it may be related to "bank".

According to the framework proposed by Google, there are two steps in implementing Bert: pre-training and fine-tuning. During the pre-training phase, the model trains unlabeled data on different pre-training tasks. During the fine-tuning phase, the BERT model is initialized with pre-trained parameters and all parameters are adjusted using marker data from downstream tasks. Each downstream task separates the exact models, even if they are initialized with pre-trained parameters. As shown in Fig. 1.

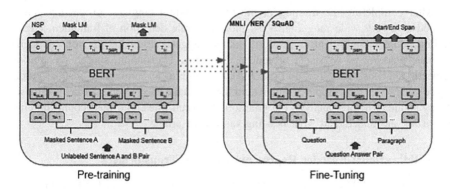

Fig. 1. Pre-training and fine-tuning procedures for BERT

Pre-training. Google uses two unsupervised tasks to pre-train BERTs, Masked LM and Next Sentence Prediction.

- Masked LM: In order to train a deep bidirectional representation, we simply mask some percentage of the input tokens at random, and then predict those masked tokens. We refer to this procedure as a "masked LM" (MLM).
- Next Sentence Prediction: This stage is mainly to understand the meaning between the two sentences through question and answer and natural language reasoning. When choosing sentences and predictive training, the 50% chance is that the B sentence follows the next sentence of the A sentence and is labeled Is Next, and the other 50% chance is from the random sentence of the corpus and is labeled Not Next. As we show in Fig. 1, C is used for next sentence prediction (NSP).

Fine-Tuning. Fine-tuning is straight forward since the self-attention mechanism in the Transformer allows BERT to model many downstream tasks—whether they involve single text or text pairs—by swapping out the appropriate inputs and outputs. The BERT model first encodes the input, converts it to the encoding format required by the model, and uses the auxiliary markers [CLS] and [SEP] to indicate the beginning and separation of the sentence. Then according to the input to get the corresponding embedding, here embedding is the sum of three embedding, which are token, segment, position. As shown in Fig. 2.

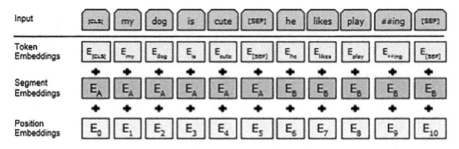

Fig. 2. Fine-tuning input representation

2.3   Anti-money Laundering Activity Detection

Money laundering refers to the process of obtaining cash in illegal activities and making cash appear to be the income of legitimate business activities. Used to describe the process by which criminals conceal the original ownership and control of the proceeds of a criminal act by making these proceeds appear to come from legitimate sources. These methods range from very simple to very complex. One of the most common methods is to launder money through legal cash operations owned by criminal organizations. An important part of the prevention and control of money laundering is that financial institutions report abnormal gold flows, so that illegal funds cannot distort the illegal sources of their money through legal channels. A common method in Taiwan is to investigate the relationship between the source and the destination and the related person affairs when the bank has a large amount of money circulating, so as to avoid a large amount of funds to be bleached by this method.

3   Bert-Based Anti-money Laundering Model

3.1   Research Model

This study refers to Google's BERT-Base, Chinese provided on November 3, 2018 for pre-training and the establishment of a generic model. In the direction of fine-tuning, this study used GTX1080 to train and evaluate on a local computer.

3.2   Data Source

A recent version of Google's BERT has been able to import traditional Chinese texts into the computer for deep learning, pre-training to create a model of suspected money laundering or fear trading, and let the computer know what "money laundering" is. First of all, this study will transfer 115 case stories from the "Money Laundering Case Compilation" published by the Taiwan Ministry of Justice's Investigation Bureau from 2001 to 2018 to the BERT for pre-training and establish a general model. Next, according to the "suspected money laundering or terrorism transaction status abbreviation comparison table" published by the Ministry of Justice of Taiwan, according to the financial industry classification, the phenomenon of money laundering of the suspected money laundering statement, this study converts these patterns For the coding format required by the model, fine-tune the general model according to various situations. The finishing is shown in Table 2.

Table 2. Sources of money laundering research data

BERT data project	Data source
Pre-training data	Money Laundering case compilation, 115 cases
Fine-tuning data	Suspected money laundering or terrorist trading situation comparison table

3.3   Fine-Tuning Process

First, you need to perform some pre-processing, which is to label the training set, verification set, and test set. Then we will call our custom MyPro class that inherits the DataProcessor class. This step is to convert our training data into a standard input format that the model can obtain. Here is an InputExamples format that is converted into a paper definition. As shown in Fig. 3. Then call convert_examples_to_features() to convert all InputExamples to a train_features format. The latter is the related operation in pytorch, first transform the train_features into the TensorDataset format, and then use the DataLoader to send the TensorDataset to the model for training.

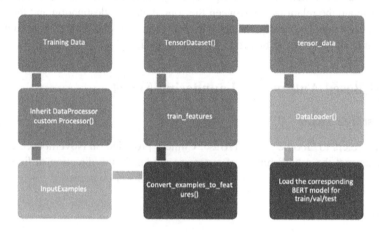

Fig. 3.   Fine-tuning process

3.4   Parameter Setting

Main related parameters in the main program are set as follows. Data_dir: Enter the directory of the data file, including training, verification, and test, respectively, train, val, and test. Bert_model: bert pre-training model, here is bert-base-chinese. Task_-name: The name of the training task. Model_save_pth: the saved address of the trained model parameters. Max_seq_length: The maximum length of the string. The longer the calculation, the more calculations are required. Generally, 64 or 128 is set. Do_train/do_eval: Whether to train or verify. Train_batch_size: The size of the batch at training, which is generally set to 64. Learning_rate: Learning rate, Google paper recommended several, 5e−5, 3e−5, 2e−5. No_cuda: Whether to use GPU acceleration, this study uses GTX1080 acceleration, which is set to TRUE. Local_rank: This study uses a default value of −1.

4   Conclusion

This study introduces the money laundering case into BERT and draws the following conclusions. For the BERT Chinese model, each sentence can only have 512 words, so the content in the assembly needs to be sorted before being imported. Pay attention to the head and tail mark characters [CLS] and [SEP] when using model.get_sequence_output() to get the word vector for each word. The BERT model requires a high level of memory and capacity. If it is not possible, try to reduce the batch_size and max_seq_length, or send it to the TPU for calculation. This study trains the general model, but still needs to fine-tune the items to fill in the accuracy. The follow-up needs to combine the web crawlers to judge the relevant financial activity statements and find out the activities that may be money laundering.

References

1. Jernite, Y., Bowman, S.R., Sontag, D.: Discourse-based objectives for fast unsupervised sentence representation learning. CoRR, abs/1705.00557 (2017)
2. Peters, M., et al.: Deep contextualized word representations. In: NAACL (2018)
3. https://github.com/google-research/bert. Accessed 05 Nov 2018
4. Salehi, A., Ghazanfari, M., Fathian, M.: In India, data mining techniques for anti money laundering. Int. J. Appl. Eng. Res. **12**(20), 10084–10094 (2017)
5. Devlin, J., Chang, M.-W., Lee, K., Toutanova, K.: BERT: pre-training of deep bidirectional transformers for language understanding. cs.CL/1810.04805v2 (2019)
6. Akbik, A., Blythe, D., Vollgraf, R.: Contextual string embeddings for sequence labeling. In: Proceedings of the 27th International Conference on Computational Linguistics, pp. 1638–1649 (2018)

Artificial Intelligence Theory and Technology Related to Cognitive City

Correlation Analysis Between Deep Displacement and Multi-source Landslide Monitoring Data

Genwang Li[1] and Fuyang Ke[2(✉)]

[1] Jiangsu Kebo Space Information Technology Co., Ltd.,
Nanjing 210000, China
[2] School of Remote Sensing and Geomatics Engineering,
Nanjing University Information of Science and Technology,
Nanjing 210044, China
ke.fuyang@qq.com

Abstract. The landslide geological disasters have many hazard factors, and the data indicators for monitoring geological disasters are not the same. Through the use of various intelligent sensors, multi-angle and multi-source monitoring of landslide geological disasters can be carried out. The deep displacement is an important parameter to reflect the deformation depth and range of the landslide body. The surface displacement, groundwater level and pore water pressure can all react to the stability of the landslide body. In this paper, the experimental data can be used to study the correlation between different depths of deep displacement and surface displacement, groundwater level and pore water pressure. First, qualitative research is carried out in the form of graphs; then, quantitative research is carried out by using Pearson correlation coefficient method using MATLAB software; finally, the model is established by multivariate linear regression method. Through comparative analysis, it can be found that the established multivariate linear regression model can well predict surface displacement, groundwater level, pore water pressure and deep displacement.

Keywords: Deep displacement · Multi-source data · Landslide monitoring · Correlation analysis

1 Introduction

China is a country with complex geological conditions, fragile geological environment and frequent geological disasters. The development of geological disasters has many types (collapse, landslide, mudslide, ground fissure, ground subsidence, ground collapse, etc.) and wide area (collapse, landslide and the distribution of debris flow accounts for 44.8% of the country's land area) [1], large scale, high frequency and long time [2, 3]. Frequent geological disasters not only bring serious economic losses and casualties to mountainous and urban residents, but also become a very prominent problem in China's economic development and sustainable development.

There are many factors affecting the occurrence and development of geological disasters, such as topography, geological structure, engineering geological rock group,

© Springer Nature Singapore Pte Ltd. 2020
J. Shen et al. (Eds.): IC3 2019, CCIS 1227, pp. 459–468, 2020.
https://doi.org/10.1007/978-981-15-6113-9_51

ground deformation, slope structure, vegetation coverage, degree of fissure development, existing dynamic geological effects, seismic activity, etc. [2]. These factors change little in a certain period and can be regarded as static factors. In contrast to static factors, there are also dynamic factors, which are often important factors in inducing collapse, landslides, and debris flows. Dynamic factors include groundwater levels associated with precipitation, pore water pressure, surface displacement, and deep displacement.

There are many influencing factors causing landslide geological disasters. Although some organizations and personnel have established correlation analysis of targeted geological disaster hazard factors for different landslide geological disasters, there is still no complete research on geological disasters. There is still a big gap between the factors and the actual expectations in the relationship between the factors and the predictions [4, 5]. Therefore, the majority of scientific workers engaged in disaster prevention and mitigation work study geological disasters from various geological and geological disaster mechanisms, mathematical models, and data collection.

Based on the engineering example of a geological disaster monitoring in Nanjing, China, this paper monitors the deep displacement, surface displacement, groundwater level and pore water pressure by using various geological disaster monitoring sensors, and collects and analyzes the data through parameter analysis and monitoring. Comprehensive comparative analysis of various hazard factors for advice and advice in monitoring landslides.

2 Correlation Analysis

Correlation analysis refers to the analysis of two or more related variable elements to measure the closeness of the two variable factors. The correlation coefficient (Correlation coefficient) is a statistical indicator of the close relationship between the reaction variables, and the correlation coefficient ranges from −1 to 1. [6] Generally, we think that the correlation coefficient is micro-correlation between 0 and 0.3. It is a real correlation between 0.3 and 0.5. It is significantly correlated between 0.5 and 0.8. It is highly correlated between 0.8 and 1 [7]. In practical applications, there are five commonly used methods for correlation analysis [8]. In this study, we chose to use the graph and correlation coefficient method to study the correlation between deep displacement and multi-source landslide monitoring data [9].

This study used the deep displacement data, surface displacement data, groundwater level data and pore water pressure data of the "Nanjing Landslide Geological Hazard Monitoring Project" to study the correlation between deep displacement and multi-source landslide monitoring data. The time is from October 2018 to March 2019, totaling 180 days, and the data monitored on the first day is analyzed as the initial value. Among them, deep displacement data, surface displacement data, groundwater level data and pore water pressure data are obtained by fixed inclinometer, Beidou/GNSS receiver, water level gauge and osmometer.

2.1   Correlation Analysis Between Deep Displacement and Surface Displacement

Graphical Analysis

In the experiment, a total of 180 days of deep displacement (underground 4.5 m, 9.0 m, 13.5 m, 18.0 m) and surface displacement raw data were extracted from October 2018 to March 2019, and the average value of the two was obtained. The data of the first day is the original initial value, and the subsequent data is accumulated on the basis of the original initial value. Finally, the processed data is graphically displayed by using MATLAB software, as shown in Fig. 1.

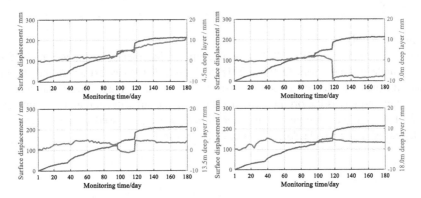

Fig. 1. Trend map of deep displacement and surface displacement of each layer

From Fig. 1, we can see that, in general, the change trend between the surface displacement and the depth displacement of each layer tends to be the same, and the depth displacement at 4.5 m is more consistent with the surface displacement.

Correlation Coefficient Analysis

Correlation analysis was carried out on the data of deep displacement and surface displacement of each layer by using MATLAB based on Pearson algorithm. The results show that (Table 1), the correlation coefficient between deep displacement and surface displacement at 4.5 m is 0.96, which is highly correlated; the correlation coefficient between deep displacement and surface displacement at 9.0 m is −0.77, which is significant correlation; deep displacement at 13.5 m. The correlation coefficient of surface displacement is 0.26, which is micro-correlation; the correlation coefficient between deep displacement and surface displacement at 18.0 m is 0.49, which is a real correlation.

Table 1. Correlation coefficient between deep displacement and surface displacement of each layer

Deep displacement layer depth/m	Pearson correlation coefficient
4.5	0.96
9.0	−0.77
13.5	0.26
18.0	0.49

2.2   Correlation Analysis Between Deep Displacement and Groundwater Level

Graphical Analysis

In the experiment, a total of 180 days of deep displacement (4.5 m, 9.0 m, 13.5 m, 18.0 m underground) from October 2018 to March 2019 was extracted and the raw data of the groundwater level was processed to obtain the average value of the two. The data of the first day is the original initial value, and the subsequent data is accumulated on the basis of the original initial value. Finally, the processed data is graphically displayed by using MATLAB software, as shown in Fig. 2.

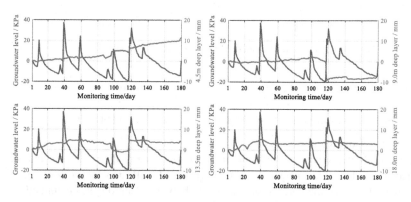

Fig. 2. Deep displacement and groundwater level change trend of each layer

From Fig. 2, we can see that in general, the change trend between the groundwater level and the deep displacement of each layer tends to be the same, but the correlation is not strong.

Correlation Coefficient Analysis

Correlation analysis was carried out on the data of deep displacement and surface displacement of each layer by using MATLAB based on Pearson algorithm. The results show that (Table 2) the correlation coefficient between deep displacement and groundwater level at 4.5 m is 0.02, which is micro-correlation; the correlation coefficient between deep displacement and groundwater level at 9.0 m is −0.27, which is micro-correlation; deep displacement at 13.5 m. The correlation coefficient of groundwater level is 0.31, which is a real correlation; the correlation coefficient between deep displacement and groundwater level at 18.0 m is 0.17, which is micro-correlation.

Table 2. Correlation coefficient between deep displacement and groundwater level of each layer

Deep displacement layer depth/m	Pearson correlation coefficient
4.5	0.02
9.0	−0.27
13.5	0.31
18.0	0.17

2.3 Correlation Analysis Between Deep Displacement and Pore Water Pressure

Graphical Analysis

In the experiment, a total of 180 days of deep displacement (underground 4.5 m, 9.0 m, 13.5 m, 18.0 m) from October 2018 to March 2019 were extracted and the raw data of pore water pressure were processed to obtain the average of both. value. The data of the first day is the original initial value, and the subsequent data is accumulated on the basis of the original initial value. Finally, the processed data is graphically displayed by using MATLAB software, as shown in Fig. 3.

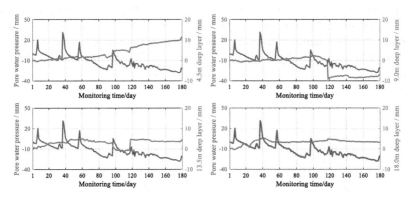

Fig. 3. Trend of deep displacement and pore water pressure in each layer

From Fig. 3, we can see that, in general, the variation trend between pore water pressure and deep layer displacement tends to be the same, and the depth displacement at 4.5 m is more consistent with the pore water pressure.

Correlation Coefficient Analysis

Correlation analysis was carried out on the data of deep displacement and surface displacement of each layer by using MATLAB based on Pearson algorithm. The results show that (Table 3), the correlation coefficient between deep displacement and pore water pressure at 4.5 m is −0.72, which is a significant correlation; the correlation coefficient between deep displacement and pore water pressure at 9.0 m is 0.55, which is significantly correlated; deep layer at 13.5 m The correlation coefficient between displacement and pore water pressure is −0.21, which is micro-correlation; the correlation coefficient between deep displacement and pore water pressure at 18.0 m is −0.27, which is micro-correlation.

Table 3. Correlation coefficient between deep displacement and pore water pressure of each layer

Deep displacement layer depth/m	Pearson correlation coefficient
4.5	−0.72
9.0	0.55
13.5	−0.21
18.0	−0.27

2.4   Deep Correlation Analysis of Deep Displacement Layers

Graphical Analysis

In the experiment, a total of 180 days of deep displacement (underground 4.5 m, 9.0 m, 13.5 m, 18.0 m) data from October 2018 to March 2019 was extracted for daily average calculation. The data of the first day is the original initial value, and the subsequent data is accumulated on the basis of the original initial value. Finally, the processed data is graphically displayed by using MATLAB software, as shown in Fig. 4.

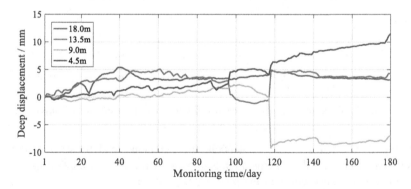

Fig. 4. Trend pattern of deep displacement in each layer

It can be seen from Fig. 4 that, in general, the trends of the deep layer displacements of the layers tend to be uniform, and the consistency between the deep layer displacements of the adjacent layers is stronger.

Correlation Coefficient Analysis

Correlation analysis between deep displacements of each layer was performed by using MATLAB based on Pearson algorithm. The results show that (Table 4), the maximum correlation coefficient between deep displacement at 4.5 m and other layer depths is −0.85, which is the depth of adjacent layers; the maximum correlation coefficient between deep displacement and other layer depths at 9.0 m is −0.85, is the depth of the adjacent layer; the maximum correlation coefficient between the deep displacement at 13.5 m and the depth of other layers is −0.47, which is the depth of the adjacent layer; the maximum correlation coefficient between the deep displacement at 18.0 m and the depth of other layers is 0.38, It is deep for adjacent layers.

Table 4. Table of correlation coefficients of deep layer displacement of each layer

Pearson correlation coefficient		Deep displacement layer depth/m			
		4.5	9.0	13.5	18.0
Deep displacement layer depth/m	4.5	1	−0.85	0.22	0.37
	9.0	−0.85	1	−0.47	−0.22
	13.5	0.22	−0.47	1	0.38
	18.0	0.37	−0.22	0.38	1

3   Model Establishment

3.1   Modeling Method

Through the graph and correlation analysis of the "correlation analysis of deep displacement and multi-source monitoring data", it can be found that the deep displacement at 4.5 m is highly linearly correlated with the multi-source monitoring data, and the multivariate linear regression method is adopted to establish the model. In this paper, the MATLAB multiple regression method is used to model the linear relationship between surface displacement data (x_1), groundwater level data (x_2) and pore water pressure data (x_3) and deep displacement at 4.5 m.

By using MATLAB, the correlation coefficient R in stats is 0.91, which indicates that the correlation coefficient of the established multiple linear regression equation is larger and the fitting degree is better. At the same time, the coefficient b1 of the multiple linear regression equation is $b_1(1)$ is −1.773, $b_1(2)$ is 0.048, $b_1(3)$ is −0.006, and $b_1(4)$ is 0.011.

The multivariate linear regression equation is obtained as:

$$Z = b_1(1) + b_1(2)x_1 + b_1(3)x_2 + b_1(4)x_3 \qquad (1)$$

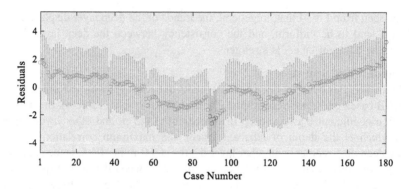

Fig. 5. Residual case order plot (Color figure online)

Bringing the regression coefficient b1 obtained above into Eq. (1):

$$Z = 0.048x_1 - 0.006x_2 + 0.011x_3 - 1.773 \tag{2}$$

To test whether the established multiple regression model is appropriate, the residual map (Fig. 5) is used for testing.

Through the residual graph, we can find that the distribution of residuals is concentrated between −4 and 4, and the scatter is mainly concentrated near 0, indicating that the establishment of this regression model is reasonable. The green line indicates that the confidence interval passes through the origin and fits the better point of the equation; the red line indicates that the confidence interval does not pass the origin, and the point is poorly fitted to the equation. The value of the part is an abnormal value and is not eliminated.

3.2   Experimental Result

Based on the previous analysis data, the prediction model is built. By comparing the predicted values obtained by the prediction model with the actual values, the following results are obtained (Fig. 6):

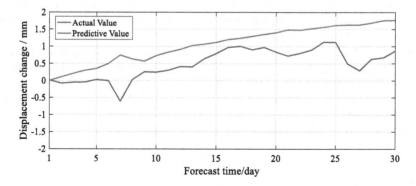

Fig. 6. Deep displacement change prediction map

4   Conclusions

In this paper, the landslide geological disaster monitoring area in Nanjing is used as the experimental area to study the correlation between surface displacement, groundwater level, pore water pressure and deep layer displacement. At the same time, the correlation model is used to analyze and predict the deep displacement. The trend of change is thus analyzed to predict trends in landslides. The main conclusions of the paper are as follows:

(1) When analyzing the correlation between surface displacement, groundwater level, pore water pressure and deep displacement layers, it can be found through graph and correlation coefficient analysis:

> ①With the increase of layer depth, the correlation coefficient between surface displacement and deep displacement is smaller and smaller, indicating that the correlation between surface displacement and deep displacement is smaller with the increase of layer depth;
> ②With the increase of layer depth, the correlation coefficient between groundwater level and deep displacement is larger and larger, indicating that the correlation between groundwater level and deep displacement is increasing with the increase of layer depth;
> ③As the depth of the layer increases, the correlation coefficient between the pore water pressure and the deep displacement becomes smaller and smaller, indicating that the correlation between the pore water pressure and the deep displacement becomes smaller as the depth of the layer increases;
> ④Through graph analysis, the correlation coefficients between the deep displacement layers (4.5 m, 9.0 m, 13.5 m, 18.0 m) are: -0.85, -0.47, 0.38, and the largest correlation coefficient is obtained between adjacent layers. The layer depth with a correlation coefficient of -0.85 is 4.5 m and 9.0 m, indicating that the shallower the layer depth, the stronger the correlation.

(2) Using the surface displacement, groundwater level and pore water pressure as the variation factors, the deep displacement of 4.5 m is modeled by establishing multiple regression equations. By comparing the actual value with the predicted value, it can be found that the predicted deformation curve and the actual deformation The curves tend to be consistent, indicating that the multiple linear regression model established by multi-source data can effectively predict deep displacement monitoring.

Acknowledgements. This study is supported by the National Natural Science Foundation of China (grant no. 41674036).

References

1. Xue, J., Xu, J., Zhang, F., et al.: Study on meteorological forecast methods for regional geological hazards. Meteorology **31**(10), 24–27 (2005)

2. Chen, W., Xu, Q.: Research on early warning benchmark of geological disaster rainfall. Earth Environ. **39**(3), 393–397 (2011)
3. Xiao, W., Huang, D., Li, H., et al.: Research on meteorological forecasting and early warning methods for geological disasters. Geol. Resour. **14**(4), 274–278 (2005)
4. Wei, F., Hu, K., Cui, P., et al.: Decision support system for debris flow mitigation in mountainous cities. J. Nat. Disasters **11**(2), 31–36 (2002)
5. Yue, J., Tu, B., Liu, G., et al.: Application of geological disaster warning and forecasting and information management system. Nat. Disaster Rep. **17**(6), 60–63 (2008)
6. Liu, S., Qiang, F., Nie, S.: Correlation analysis of geological disaster distribution and influencing factors in Jixian County. J. Water Resour. Archit. Eng. **15**(01), 165–170 (2017)
7. Qiang, F., Zhao, F., Dang, Y.: Correlation analysis of geological hazards and influencing factors in Qinba mountain area of Southern Shaanxi. South-to-North Water Transf. Water Sci. Technol. **13**(03), 557–562 (2015)
8. Yang, Q., Yao, C., Liu, S., Gao, F.: Analysis of the relationship between geological disaster development and topography in mountainous areas of Shandong Province. Chin. J. Geol. Hazard Control **26**(02), 93–96 (2015)
9. Zeng, W., Zhang, Z.: Development characteristics and formation conditions of geological disasters in Suining County. Geol. Disasters Environ. Prot. Environ. **29**(01), 17–22 (2018)

Integrating Artificial Intelligence into STEAM Education

Yu-Shan Chang and Chia-hui Chou[(⊠)]

National Taiwan Normal University, Taipei, Taiwan
selina.chiahui@gmail.com

Abstract. The development of artificial intelligence has revolutionized impact on education. Cramming education will no longer exist, and students have to learn more than memorizing. Secondly, artificial intelligence can provide a variety of effective learning methods, not only students can record learning content, but also make learning more effective. Teachers can also analyze the students' learning and get feedback from the students so that they can learn from each other.

STEAM education is increasingly valued by many countries, such as the ITEEA's Education by Design, 6E Learning by DeSIGN STEM courses, and NASA-sponsored robot STEAM courses. South Korea have further promoted STEAM education (such as Incheon University) to propose the Wheel Model (STEAM & HUG). STEAM's goals combining with design thinking, cross-domain learning, and teamwork form the main spirits of Taiwan's 12-year national curriculum, which are "taking the initiative, engaging the public, and seeking the common good". Those main components of artificial intelligence are knowledge reasoning, planning, machine learning, natural language processing, computer vision, and robotics. Artificial intelligence becomes an important learning and educational tool for students. Meanwhile, students learn through artificial intelligence products. Based on artificial intelligence components and STEAM education, how to develop instruction model and learning modules will be a most important theme. Through effectiveness artificial intelligence STEAM instruction, students' higher-order thinking ability, creativity, problem solving ability, and the literacy of artificial intelligence will be improved effectively.

Keywords: Artificial intelligence · STEAM · Teaching effectiveness

1 Introduction

Artificial Intelligence (AI) has revolutionized not only science and technology but also the industries and ways of life of the entire humanity. Its scope of application encompasses retail, financial services, biotechnology and medicine, autopilot, robots, and smart living [1]. In light of technological development, industrial development, impact on everyday life, human resource development, and educational development, AI has been regarded as the fulcrum of the fourth Industrial Revolution. In contrast to the previous three industrial revolutions, it will have even more tremendous impact on the forms of human life as well as industrial development in the future [1]. Seizing the opportunity of AI development, the government announced that 2017 is the inaugural

© Springer Nature Singapore Pte Ltd. 2020
J. Shen et al. (Eds.): IC3 2019, CCIS 1227, pp. 469–474, 2020.
https://doi.org/10.1007/978-981-15-6113-9_52

year of AI in Taiwan, and quickly started to promote major programs including AI Scientific Research Strategies and the Taiwan AI Action Plan [2].

Being rapidly developed, AI has reached various levels of education and a disciplines. STEAM education is a current focus in the international community. Will it be more effective in inspiring creativity and improving problem-solving ability and AI knowledge acquisition if AI is introduced into STEAM education?

2   The Development of AI Education

Artificial Intelligence (AI) refers to the technology of human-made mechanical intelligence. Through computing, it is able to perform rational and human thinking as well as moves. AI study is regarded as a new discipline outside science and engineering, encompassing fields including Neural Network, Machine Learning, Deep Learning, Natural Language Processing, Computer Vision [5].

The concept of artificial intelligence has been hotly debated in the computer industry since its introduction in the 1950s. Various algorithms have been proposed one after another. It is expected that artificial intelligence can simulate human thinking and make machines intelligent agents. However, due to the lack of computing power and can only solve problems in specific areas, it gradually declined in the 1980s. Although neural network-like, speech recognition, and mechanical translation technologies were proposed in the mid-1980s, they are still limited by the ability of machine computing to meet expectations. However, since 2010, computer computing command cycle has increased, and machine capabilities have begun to meet the calculation needs of artificial intelligence. Artificial intelligence has once again become a hot topic. The concept of big data and deep learning has also expanded the research and practicality of artificial intelligence.

To prepare for a future in which AL becomes universally accessible, the humanity should also possess proper knowledge to understand the workings of technological products based on AI. The model of AI teaching, especially for high school students, should be combined with learning through experience and problem-solving processes, thereby allowing students to experience the operation of AI and apply it to problem-solving (by means of question-oriented or topic-oriented teaching), and finally encouraging students to develop various ideas to be tested.

(1) Defining problems and collecting information: Discovering potential problems within scenarios, analyzing the items that can be processed by AI, and collecting relevant cases and processing methods.

(2) Constructing models: Developing solutions and basic structures for system analysis and design.

(3) Choosing appropriate algorithms: Performing algorithms and object designs according to system planning.

(4) Learning in depth: Selecting items to be analyzed, feature processing and in-depth learning according to system plans,

(5) Assessing and explaining results: Interpreting the results of calculations, comparing the differences, and analyzing and summarizing the causes.

(6) Constructing and testing innovative ideas: Exploring and implementing ways to improve or innovate and assessing their effectiveness.

3 STEAM Teaching

U.S. scholars have put forward an educational policy that encompasses science, technology, engineering, and mathematics (STEM), which has been included in the key policies of then U.S. President Barack Obama. Later, arts were included in the policy to form STEAM, the "A" in which encompassing "Arts" as a wide range of cultural subjects including design, arts and humanities, rather than "art" in a narrower sense.

From the perspective of design thinking, we will find that from the needs and wants of people, we will find and solve problems. From empathy, definition of needs, creative ideas, making prototypes, actual The process of "testing" has reached the goals of people-oriented, cross-domain teamwork, learning in progress, empathy, rapid prototyping and correction, and also integrates STEAM's interdisciplinary learning to apply what you have learned to actual situations and achieve literacy improvement the goal of. Therefore, the importance of the STEAM course includes:

(1) Connection with the real world: Textbooks start from life and are also used in life. The content design of STEAM courses is mostly based on units or themes. It is also suitable for starting from problems or situations and combining with real life situations. Students' acquired solutions and problem solving skills can also be applied to the same or different situations in life.

(2) Focus on the learning process: In addition to the transfer of knowledge, hands-on implementation, and innovative thinking, more importantly, the deeper participation in the learning process and the enhancement of learning interest.

(3) Emphasis on implementation: Whether it is design innovation or inquiry implementation, STEAM learning activities emphasize interdisciplinary, hands-on, trial and error, teamwork, problem solving, and practical application.

(4) Integrate the study of arts and humanities: the main axis of design innovation, emphasizing design thinking, that is, taking people as the starting point. Under the integration characteristics of STEAM, the related arts, society, and humanities will also be meaningfully integrated into activities.

(5) Cultivate design thinking skills of problem-solving: from real problem discovery, group research, collecting data, analyzing data, designing, testing, and improving the solutions produced, so that students can acquire design thinking skills in the process of design thinking and solve problems In the process, learn problem solving skills.

STEAM education has attracted attention from many countries. For instance, in the U.S., the International Technology and Engineering Educators Association (ITEEA) offers STEAM courses such as education by design and 6E learning by design, while NASA promotes STEAM courses on robots [7]. South Korea even promotes STEAM education on a massive scale (for instance, Incheon National University has proposed Wheel Model, STEAM and HUG) [4]. In general, the currently promoted STEAM Maker courses and material strategies include:

(1) Themed integration: Design practice is incorporated into individual subjects: In music, design and production of ukulele can be included; in mathematics, rolling toys can be made and angles and angular deviations can be calculated; in physics, toys for experimentations on gravity, slopes, and leverages; in history, the developments of weaponry in different periods can be studied.

(2) Interdisciplinary teaching: When introducing transportation mechanics in technology classes, teachers can also relate it to history by introducing historical transportation vehicles. When introducing mechanical toys in technology classes, teachers can relate them to the concepts in physics such as moment, leverage, torque, and axles.

(3) Multi-disciplinary integration: Multiple subjects can be combined in teaching centering on a common theme. For example, technology can be related to the design and production of cultural and creative products. In arts classes, visual design and commercial design for product appearance and product packaging can be taught.

(4) Thematic courses: Focusing on a main theme, such as energy issue, air pollution, greenhouse effect, and traffic congestion, around which the design of course material for all subjects will be centered.

Therefore, a STEAM Maker course combines design thinking and exploratory learning based on exploratory practice and design innovation. It integrates STEAM's disciplinary knowledge and allows students to conduct active, in-depth, application-oriented and integrated learning, as shown in Fig. 1.

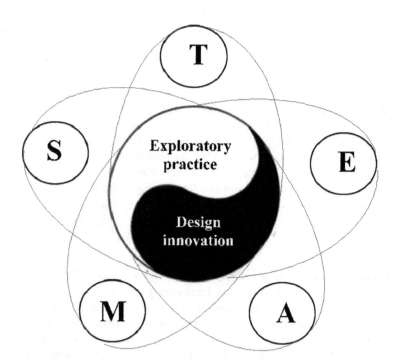

Fig. 1. The idea of a STEAM course

4   Integrating AI into STEAM Teaching

This study develops a STEAM teaching design based on the ADDIE (Analysis, Design, Development, Implementation, and Evaluation) model. This section offers an example of integrating AL into STEAM teaching. In this activity, the AI smart car provided by VIA Technologies is used as a teaching aid, and the smart car is integrated into the interdisciplinary teaching that encompasses science and technology, physics, information technology, and arts.

(1) Introducing software and hardware kits: Students are acquainted with preliminary knowledge about the software and hardware of smart cars.
(2) Introducing the program user interface and basic syntax: Teachers introduce the program user interface and basic syntax to familiarize students with the interface.
(3) Executing the sample program: Students practice with sample programs to become familiarized with the entire program.
(4) Explanation and sample of AI functions: Teachers teach AI functions such as speech recognition, and have students practice with sample programs.
(5) Autonomous car production practice: Students perform smart car productions and write relevant programs. These classes are the focus, because students are allowed to practice (thus integrating technology), in which they can learn mechanical concepts such as axle, torque, shifting, etc. (thus integrating physics), and finally write computer program to make the car move (thus integrating information technology).
(6) Creative autonomous car: Students will exercise their creativity and design unique autonomous cars, during the process of which they experience artistic learning in terms of design and use of colors.

5   Conclusion

Artificial intelligence will become an important learning and educational tool for students to achieve the goals of their learning through AI products. It will be important for AI research and development to explore the ways to integrate STEAM teaching through AI to achieve teaching effects, and equip students with AL knowledge and high-level thinking ability such as problem-solving, and develop their creativity.

References

1. Executive Yuan News and Communications Office. "Taiwan AI Action Plan - Mastering the opportunity to fully launch the industry's AI" (2019). https://www.ey.gov.tw/Page/ 5A8A0CB5B41DA11E/a8ec407c-6154-4c14-8f1e-d494ec2dbf23
2. Executive Yuan News and Communications Office. "Using artificial intelligence education to enhance students' competitiveness and creativity" (2017). https://www.ey.gov.tw/Page/ 9277F759E41CCD91/70882f5c-5b3f-4a4e-8ff5-5ec1148ef830

3. Helmstaedter, M.: The mutual inspirations of machine learning and neuroscience. Neuron **86**(1), 25–28 (2015)
4. Kim, P.W.: The wheel model of STEAM education based on traditional Korean scientific contents. Eurasia J. Math. Sci. Technol. Educ. **12**(9), 2353–2371 (2016)
5. Kunioshi, N., Noguchi, J., Tojo, K., Hayashi, H.: Supporting English-medium pedagogy through an online corpus of science and engineering lectures. Eur. J. Eng. Educ. **41**(3), 293–303 (2016)
6. National Education Radio Station. "The era of AI artificial intelligence is coming" (2018). https://www.ner.gov.tw/program/5acc6f86b026920005579844/5b77bad2214b200007ec1d0a
7. Quigley, C.F., Herro, D., Jamil, F.M.: Developing a conceptual model of STEAM teaching practices. Sch. Sci. Math. **117**, 1–12 (2017)

An Intelligent Detection and Notification (iDN) System for Handling Piglet Crushing Based on Machine Learning

Whai-En Chen[1(✉)], Li-Xian Chen[1], and Yi-Chich Chiu[2]

[1] Department of CSIE, National Ilan University, Yilan 26047, Taiwan
wechen@niu.edu.tw
[2] Department of Biomechatronic Engineering, National Ilan University, Yilan 26047, Taiwan

Abstract. Piglet crushing that causes the piglet mortality is an important issue for hog (pig) farmers. Average 0.05 piglet per hour is crushed by the sows. To consider the animal welfare and reduce the piglet mortality, this paper utilizes the Internet of Things (IoT) and machine learning technologies to develop an intelligent detection and notification (iDN) system for handling piglet crushing. If any piglet crushing occurs, the iDN will inform the farmer to handle the crushing events. This paper introduces the architecture and components of iDN system, elaborates the development of the machine learning model and analyzes the relation between the accuracy and different feature-enhancement methods and different parameters of the machine learning model. In addition, this paper investigates the optimal parameters of the machine learning model.

Keywords: CNN · Crushing · IoT · Machine learning · Piglet

1 Introduction

Piglet crushing that causes the piglet mortality is an important issue for hog (pig) farmers. About 15% piglets are dying in the pre-weaning stage. Around 50% of the losses are caused by sows and occurred within the first three days of birth [1]. The study [2] indicates that average 0.05 piglet per hour is crushed by the sows. The piglets are crushed when the sow is lying down or turning the body over while lying [3]. There are two ways (i.e. prevention and remedy solutions) to solve the piglet crushing issue.

The article [4] indicates that the weaker piglets spend more time than normal ones to stay around with their mother sow for suckling. Keeping piglet away from malnutrition is one way to reduce piglet crushing. According to Edwards' work [5], low temperature is also a factor that causing piglet crushing. Therefore, heating up the environment is also a useful way to prevent piglet crushing.

Recently, the major way to prevent piglet crushing is to reduce the living space of the sows, such as using a farrowing cage [6]. The restricted space can slow down the posture changes of sows, and provide more safety space to piglets. Base on the farrowing cage, the hog farmer should manually supervise to solve the piglet crushing. The skillful farmers can recognize the screaming vocalization from the crushed piglet

J. Shen et al. (Eds.): IC3 2019, CCIS 1227, pp. 475–484, 2020.
https://doi.org/10.1007/978-981-15-6113-9_53

[7]. When the screaming is detected, farmers would force the sow to stand up or separate the crushed piglet from the sow. The farrowing cage results in an impairment of the sows' welfare, which requests the sow to have more space to be active [8].

In addition, supervising the farrowing cage in whole day by human is impossible and costs expensive. Thus, several vocalization-based methods [7, 9, 10] are proposed to automatically detect the piglet crushing event. The related work [7] utilizes the directional microphone and webcam to record the vocalizations and video for labeling and detecting the screaming, respectively. The article [9] examined whether piglet's distress vocalizations vary with the piglet's age, weight and health status. To analyze the piglet's vocalizations, the related work [10] transforms the vocalizations into spectrogram, extracts 8 indicators from the spectrogram, and use K-means clustering method to classify different piglet's vocalizations.

MFCCs (Mel-Frequency Cepstral Coefficients) are used to extract the features of the vocalizations. The related work [11] uses MFCCs and CNN (Convolutional Neural Network) to detect the infants' crying. This method not only considers the peak frequency of the vocalizations, but also considers the frequency change over time.

Moreover, in the farrowing hose, there are various environmental sounds, such as human voice, the colliding sound of metals, and noise from working fans. The frequency range of human voice is 300 Hz to 3400 Hz [12], which is overlap with that of the screaming vocalizations of the crushed piglets (523.57 Hz to 1418 Hz [13]). These sounds cause impairment to the conventional detection methods.

To consider the animal welfare and reduce the piglet mortality, this paper utilizes the Internet of Things (IoT) and machine learning technologies to develop an intelligent detection and notification (iDN) system for piglet crushing. If any piglet crushing occurs, the iDN will inform the farmer to handle the crushing events. The rest of the paper is organized as follows. The Sect. 2 introduces the architecture and components of the iDN system. The Sect. 3 elaborates the development of the machine learning model. The Sect. 4 analyzes the results on different feature-enhancement methods and different parameters. The conclusions and future work are given in the last section.

2 The Intelligent Detection and Notification (IDN) System

The iDN system is deployed in the farrowing house (see Fig. 1). There are several farrowing cages (Fig. 1. (1)) in a farrowing house. The heating devices (Fig. 1. (2)) are deployed in the cages to heat the environment for piglets. The microphone (Fig. 1. (3)) and IP cam are installed on the top of the cages to record the vocalizations and videos.

To detect the piglet crushing and notify the farmer, this paper proposes an intelligent detection and notification (iDN) system for handling piglet crushing illustrated in Fig. 2.

Fig. 1. The farrowing house environment.

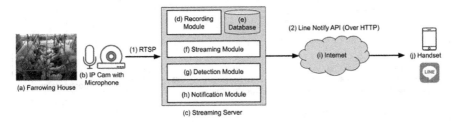

Fig. 2. The iDN system architecture.

A microphone (Fig. 2 (b) and Fig. 1 (3)) is installed in the farrowing house (Fig. 2 (a)) and used to record vocalizations (e.g., environmental sounds and piglet's screaming). The microphone can be omnidirectional or directional. The omnidirectional microphone can receive the vocalizations from all farrowing cages. When the piglet crushing occurs, the system cannot easily identify the cage while using the omnidirectional microphone. Thus, in this paper, we adopt the directional microphone to detect the vocalizations in one cage. The microphone connects to an IP Cam, which connects to the network through an Ethernet cable. The RTSP (Real Time Streaming Protocol, Fig. 2 (1)) is used to transmit the streaming audio to the *Streaming Module* (Fig. 2 (f)) in the *Streaming Server* (Fig. 2 (c)). The Streaming Module duplicates the streaming audio and forwards the audio streams to the *Recording Module* (Fig. 2 (d)) and the *Detection Module* (Fig. 2 (g)). The Recording Module stores the audio into the Database (Fig. 2 (e)). The Detection Module performs the CNN classification and determines whether the audio contains the piglet's screaming. If the screaming vocalization is detected, the Detection Module invokes the *Notification Module* (Fig. 2 (h)) to send a message to the farmer's handset through the **LINE notification API**.

3   The Development of Machine Learning Model

In the previous study [14], MFCC is used to extract the frequency features of the vocalizations and CNN (Convolutional Neural Network) is used to classify the vocalizations. In the related studies [11, 15, 16], using CNN to classify time-frequency domain audio signal (such as MFCCs, Mel-Frequency Cepstral Coefficients) can obtain a great performance. Based on MFCC and CNN, we develop the Detection Module (Fig. 2 (g)). The pre-processing flow is shown in Fig. 3.

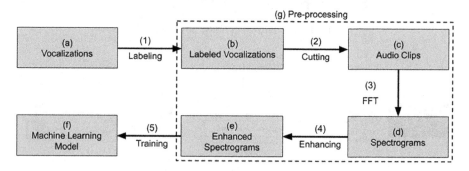

Fig. 3. The Pre-processing flow.

The vocalization (Fig. 3 (a)) and video is collected by the microphone of the IP Cam installed in the farrowing house. The vocalization files are stored in the database. Then, the expert (e.g., skillful farmer) accesses the database and labels the vocalization (Fig. 3 (1)). For training, the labeled vocalizations (Fig. 3(b)) are retrieved from the Database. Then, we cut it into the audio clips with small and fixed length (i.e., 1 s duration). Fast Fourier Transforms (FFT) is performed to transform the audio clips into the spectrograms (Fig. 3(d)). Before training, this paper performs the feature enhancement to obtain the enhanced spectrogram (Fig. 3(e)). Specifically, this paper utilizes the MFCC, min-max scaling, min-max scaling with threshold methods. The threshold is defined based on the piglet's screaming frequency (i.e., 1,418 Hz [13]). We analyze these methods by evaluating the experimental result in the Sect. 4. After training, we obtain the well-trained Machine Learning Model (Fig. 3(f)).

The vocalizations collected from the farrowing cage are divided into normal and abnormal labels. The abnormal label is tagged while the vocalizations include the piglet's screaming. Otherwise, the environmental sounds and the other vocalizations are tagged the normal labels. In this paper, we have 848-second abnormal vocalizations and 43,200-s normal vocalizations.

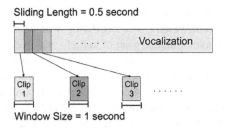

Fig. 4. Audio clip generation.

The number of normal vocalizations are much more than that of the abnormal vocalizations. To extend the abnormal dataset (audio clips), we slide the window 0.5 s and cut a one-second audio clip repeatedly (see Fig. 4). The window size is 1 s. Finally, we obtain 1,696 audio clips by this method. We also apply this method to the normal vocalizations, and we get 86,400 audio clips.

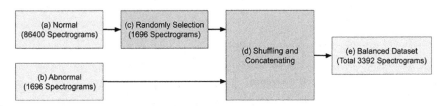

Fig. 5. Balancing the amount of different types spectrograms.

By performing FFT, the audio clips are transformed into 86,400 spectrograms labeled with "Normal" (Fig. 5(a)) and 1,696 spectrograms labeled with "Abnormal" (Fig. 5(b)). The spectrograms labeled normal are much more than that labeled abnormal. The imbalance training datasets cause a negative impact on the CNN model [17]. In other words, if these spectrograms are used to train the CNN model without extra processing, the CNN model will be biased by the large-amount (normal) spectrograms. Before training the CNN model, the amount of the spectrograms with different labels should be balanced. Specifically, the 1,696 normal spectrograms are randomly selected (Fig. 5(c)). Then, both types spectrograms are shuffled and concatenated (Fig. 5(d)) into the balanced dataset (Fig. 5(e)). Note that the dataset contains total 3,392 spectrograms. The dataset is divided into the training subset and the testing subset by 80% and 20%, respectively. In the training process, the epoch number is 8 and the batch size is 40.

Based on the detection model in [11], we develop the CNN model in Fig. 6.

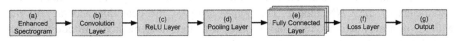

Fig. 6. The CNN model for piglet screaming classification.

The CNN model contains five major layers, including the *Convolution Layer*, *Rectified Linear Units (ReLU) Layer*, *Pooling Layer*, *Fully Connected Layer* and *Loss Layer*. The convolution layer contains a set of kernels, which extracts the features from input. In each convolution layer, the number of kernels and kernel size should be configured. The number of kernels defines the number of features to be retrieved, and the kernel sizes identifies the size of features. Note that the more kernels or the smaller kernel size conduct the more calculation time. The ReLU layer replaces the negative value with 0. This way reduces the calculation time and improves the accuracy. The Pooling Layer summarizes the data from the closed region. Typically, the Max-Pooling is adopted and achieves the great performance [14, 18]. The window size in the Pooling Layer should be defined. The Fully Connected Layer is similar to the Multi-Layer Perceptron and classifies the output from previous layers. The Dropout rate in the Fully Connected Layer should be defined. The Loss Layer estimates the difference between the predicted result and the target result. *Softmax* is a classic loss function for multiple exclusive classes. In the Sect. 4, this paper evaluates the results while setting different parameters such as kernel number, kernel sizes, pooling window size, and dropout rates.

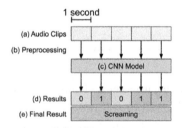

Fig. 7. The majority voting mechanism (n = 5).

To classify the audio streaming, we apply a majority voting mechanism (Fig. 7). In this example (n = 5), the vocalization is divided into 5 audio clips with 1-s length (Fig. 7 (a)). Then, the pre-processing elaborated in Fig. 3 is performed on these audio clips (Fig. 7 (b)) to produce the spectrograms. The spectrograms are input into the CNN model (Fig. 7 (c)), and the CNN model outputs 5 results (Fig. 7 (d)). The results are [0, 1, 0, 1, 1], where "1" means the abnormal event is detected. Based on the majority voting mechanism, the final result is screaming (i.e. the abnormal event) in Fig. 7 (e).

4   Performance Analysis and System Deployment

In this section, we discuss the effect of using three pre-processing methods and different parameters of the CNN model. This paper analyzes the detection accuracy of the MFCC, min-max scaling, min-max scaling with threshold methods. In addition, the kernel number, kernel sizes, pooling window size, and dropout rates, and number of fully connected layers in the CNN model are also studied to find the optimal parameters for the iDN system. In the experiment, Nvidia GEFORCE GTX 1080 Ti is used for training and validation, and a Intel Core i5-6600 CPU is used for preprocessing.

The effect of kernel size on the CNN model accuracy is illustrated in Fig. 8. The data sizes of the MFCC, the Min-Max Scaling 1 and the Min-Max Scaling 2 (with threshold) are 20 × 88, 513 × 100 and 33 × 100, respectively. The Min-Max scaling 2 only extracts the frequency below 1418 Hz, and the data size is small.

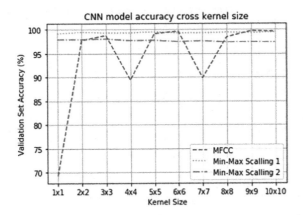

Fig. 8. The effect of kernel size on the CNN model accuracy.

The accuracy values of Min-Max Scaling methods are not affected by the kernel size, but the accuracy values of the MFCC are not stable. Among these methods, the Mix-Max Scaling 1 with the largest data size outperforms the other two methods.

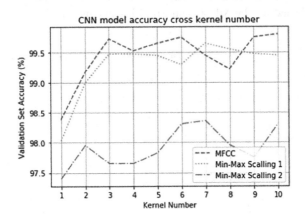

Fig. 9. The effect of kernel number on the CNN model accuracy.

The effect of kernel number on the CNN model accuracy is shown in Fig. 9. The larger kernel number means that the CNN model can extract more features. The accuracy values of all methods are more than 97% with different kernel numbers. The accuracy values of Min-Max Scaling method do not increase with the kernel number. The accuracy values of MFCC and the Min-Max Scaling methods increase when the kernel numbers from 1 to 3. The MFCC method outperforms the other methods in most cases (kernel numbers).

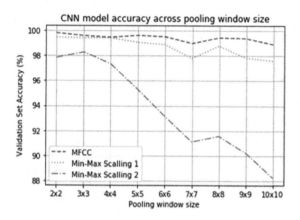

Fig. 10. The effect of pooling window size on the CNN model accuracy.

The effect of pooling window size on the CNN model accuracy is presented in Fig. 10. The pooling window is used to extract to reduce the size of data. The larger window size reduces more data. The accuracy of the Min-Max Scaling 2 decreases dramatically with the window size increasing. On the contrary, the MFCC and the Min-Max Scaling 1 are not affected obviously. Based on Fig. 10, the pooling window size 4 × 4 can be selected for the MFCC and Min-Max Scaling 1.

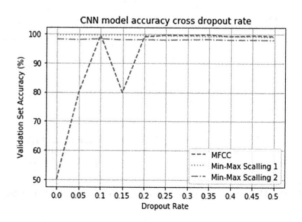

Fig. 11. The effect of dropout rate on the CNN model accuracy.

The effect of dropout rate on the CNN model accuracy is illustrated in Fig. 11. The dropout is used to reduce overfitting. The dropout rate p means the nodes are dropped out with probability p. According to Fig. 11, the Min-Max Scaling methods are almost not affected by the dropout rate. In other words, the dropout can be omitted for the Min-Max Scaling methods. On the contrary, the dropout rate affects the MFCC method obviously when the rate is less than 0.2. Thus, the dropout rate for the MFCC are suggested to set more than 0.2.

Table 1. The result of three preprocessing methods

Method	Data size	Accuracy	Parameters	Average time
MFCC	20 × 88	99.26%	kn = 10, ks = 9, pw = 2, dr = 0.35	192.4 ms
Min-Max scaling 1	513 × 100	99.41%	kn = 7, ks = 5, pw = 3, dr = 0.05	187.6 ms
Min-Max scaling 2	33 × 100	98.38%	kn = 7, ks = 3, pw = 2, dr = 0.1	187.0 ms

Note: ks: kernel size, kn: kernel number, pw: pooling window size, dr: dropout rate.

The optimal accuracy values of the MFCC, Min-Max Scaling 1, and Min-Max Scaling 2 methods are listed in Table 1. The Min-Max Scaling 1 method has the largest data size and provides the highest accuracy. The MFCC method has the smallest data size and high accuracy (2nd high). However, the MFCC method consumes more pre-processing time. The Min-Max Scaling 2 is the fastest method and the accuracy reaches 98.38%. By applying the majority voting mechanism, the accuracy values all reach 100% if $n \geq 3$. Thus, the fastest method (i.e., Min-Max Scaling 2) is suggested to adopt.

5   Conclusion

This paper utilizes Internet of Things (IoT) and Machine learning technologies to develop an intelligent Detection and Notification (iDN) system for handling the piglet's crushing. This paper elaborates the architecture of the iDN system, three pre-processing methods, and the development of CNN model. Then the paper discusses the impacts on the accuracy by setting different parameters and identifies the optimal parameter sets. The iDN System is deployed at Fu-Chang pig farm in Yi-Lan, Taiwan. The accuracy of the proposed model may be influenced by various environmental parameters. In the feature work, we will improve the model to be adaptive to different environments.

Acknowledgement. The work of Dr. Whai-En Chen was sponsored in part by MOST 107-2221-E-197   006-MY3,   108-2321-B-197-003,   107-2218-E-007-004,   107-2218-E-009-046, 1072218-E-007-004, 107-2218-E-009-046 projects and ITRI project.

References

1. Device designed to reduce devastating piglet crushing, Thefencepost.com (2019). https://www.thefencepost.com/news/device-designed-to-reduce-devastating-piglet-crushing/. Accessed 31 May 2019
2. Weary, D.M., et al.: Sow body movements that crush piglets: a comparison between two types of farrowing accommodation. Appl. Anim. Behav. Sci. **49**(2), 149–158 (1996)
3. Matheson, S.M., et al.: Relationships between sow conformation, accelerometer data and crushing events in commercial piglet production. In: 51st Annual Meeting of the International Society for Applied Ethology. Newcastle University (2017)
4. Fraser, D.: Behavioural perspectives on piglet survival. J. Reprod. Fertil. **40**, 355–370 (1990). Supplement
5. Edwards, S.A.: Perinatal mortality in the pig: environmental or physiological solutions? Livestock Prod. Sci. **78**(1), 3–12 (2002)
6. Weber, R., et al.: Piglet mortality on farms using farrowing systems with or without crates. Anim. Welfare-Potters Bar Wheathampstead **6**(2), 277 (2007)
7. Manteuffel, C., et al.: Online detection and localisation of piglet crushing using vocalisation analysis and context data. Comput. Electr. Agric. **135**, 108–114 (2017)
8. "Prevent Piglet Crushing", Successful Farming (2019). https://www.agriculture.com/podcast/successful-farming-radio-podcast/prevent-piglet-crushing. Accessed 31 May 2019
9. Illmann, G., et al.: Calling by domestic piglets during simulated crushing and isolation: a signal of need? PLoS ONE **8**(12), e83529 (2013)
10. Tallet, C., et al.: Encoding of situations in the vocal repertoire of piglets (Sus scrofa): a comparison of discrete and graded classifications. PLoS ONE **8**(8), e71841 (2013)
11. Zabidi, A., et al.: Detection of asphyxia in infants using deep learning convolutional neural network (CNN) trained on Mel frequency cepstrum coefficient (MFCC) features extracted from cry sounds. J. Fundam. Appl. Sci. **9**(3S), 768–778 (2017)
12. "Voice frequency", En.wikipedia.org (2019). https://en.wikipedia.org/wiki/Voice_frequency. Accessed 13 May 2019
13. Chapel, N., et al.: Comparison of vocalization patterns in piglets which were crushed to those which Underwent human restraint. Animals **8**(8), 138 (2018)
14. Tompson, J., et al.: Real-time continuous pose recovery of human hands using convolutional networks. ACM Trans. Graph. (ToG) **33**(5), 1–10 (2014)
15. Bozkurt, B., Germanakis, I., Stylianou, Y.: A study of time-frequency features for CNN-based automatic heart sound classification for pathology detection. Comput. Biol. Med. **100**, 132–143 (2018)
16. Hershey, S., et al.: CNN architectures for large-scale audio classification. In: 2017 IEEE International Conference on Acoustics, Speech and Signal Processing (ICASSP), pp. 131–135. IEEE (2017)
17. Hensman, P., Masko, D.: The impact of imbalanced training data for convolutional neural networks. Degree Project in Computer Science, KTH Royal Institute of Technology (2015)
18. Nagi, J., et al.: Max-pooling convolutional neural networks for vision-based hand gesture recognition. In: 2011 IEEE International Conference on Signal and Image Processing Applications (ICSIPA), pp. 342–347. IEEE (2011)
19. Krizhevsky, A., Sutskever, I., Hinton, G.E.: Imagenet classification with deep convolutional neural networks. In: Advances in Neural Information Processing Systems, pp. 1097–1105 (2012)
20. Jiang, C., et al.: Speaker verification using IMNMF and MFCC with feature warping under noisy environment. In: 2018 Chinese Automation Congress (CAC). IEEE, pp. 2583–2588 (2018)

Improvement of ADHD Behaviors with AI Perception Technology

Ying Hsun Lai[1(✉)], Yao Chung Chang[1], Yi Wei Ma[2],
Shih Yun Huang[3], and Han Chieh Chao[3]

[1] Department of Computer Science and Information Engineering,
National Taitung University, Taitung, Taiwan
yhlai@nttu.edu.tw
[2] Department of Electrical Engineering,
National Taiwan University of Science and Technology, Taitung, Taiwan
[3] Department of Electrical Engineering, National Dong Hwa University,
Hualien, Taiwan

Abstract. Attention Deficit Hyperactivity Disorder (ADHD) is an attention deficit disorder that includes excessive activity and impulsive symptoms in children, which causes behavioral, emotional, and related learning disabilities, and it takes considerable time for teachers and parents to counsel such children. This study aims to introduce AI perception technology to assist teachers in solving the behavioral problems of children with ADHD. The AI perception technology was introduced into the perceptual system to assist tutors to record children's functional assessments in the early and middle stages, in order to improve the time spent by tutors in implementing behavioral functional observation and assessment, and to solve the difficulties of assessments caused mostly by post observations rather than direct observation, thus, tutors can record the functional assessment scale more accurately and formulate relevant treatment strategies for the children. During the intervention, AI perception is used to observe the emotions and attention of the schoolchildren, in order that the real-time strategies can be provided when schoolchildren are unconscious of their emotions or fail to focus on learning, and the effectiveness of the strategies are recorded with the help of interactive robots to identify the best assistant processing strategies and construct the best personalized strategy activities to assist instructors to improve the students' behavioral problems and emotional control in the classroom. This study has closely examined the effect of this system on the behavioral problems of ADHD children.

Keywords: ADHD · Behavioral problems · AI perception technology

1 Introduction

Attention-deficit Hyperactivity Disorder (ADHD) is a common disorder among school-age children. School-age children with ADHD are more likely to suffer from inattention, hyperactivity, and emotional impulsion than normal school-age children. According to the "Diagnostic and Statistical Manual of Mental Disorder" Fifth Edition, as published by the American Psychiatric Association (APA), ADHD includes various symptoms, such as

© Springer Nature Singapore Pte Ltd. 2020
J. Shen et al. (Eds.): IC3 2019, CCIS 1227, pp. 485–491, 2020.
https://doi.org/10.1007/978-981-15-6113-9_54

inattention, hyperactivity, and impulsion, which last for more than six months. Children with ADHD are more difficult to integrate into general social life, and have related learning disorders due to attention deficit; as such symptoms affect their learning and social behaviors, they can be judged as having ADHD (DSM-5, 2015). Children with ADHD are accompanied by behavioral characteristics, such as inattention, hyperactivity, and impulsion [1–3]. In recent years, although some studies have found that drug therapy can temporarily improve the potential neuropsychological function of children and patients with ADHD, and they have made progress in behavior after taking drugs, parents still have doubts about drug use, and for ADHD children, teachers, parents, and the overall school teaching environment are all critical factors impacting their development.

The purpose of this study is to develop and import AI perception technology to assist ADHD children to improve their behavioral problems. In schools, the AI perception module was introduced to observe ADHD children's related emotional and physiological information, and the AI perception platform was used to assist teachers to analyze their related information relationships, and organize different environments or events with an impact on ADHD children [4, 5]. In order to facilitate the establishment of professional strategies and activities, and further construct a cognitive learning network and record the actual improvement benefits for the children of the intervention plans designed by the teachers, which will allow teachers to accurately revise the implementation of the intervention plan. The AI cognitive learning network can record the environmental information of ADHD schoolchildren when their problem behaviors occur, and establish early warning learning perceptions of their problem behaviors, and 7thus, quickly identify problem behaviors or emotions [6, 7]. When schoolchildren's problematic behaviors or emotions occur, or are about to occur, it can provide simple voice questions-and-answers or inform teachers in real time, thus, improving the probability of children's behavior problems through real-time early warning and introducing pre-intervention, in order that children can adapt to group learning life and improve their interpersonal relationships.

2   Literature Review

2.1   Attention Deficit Hyperactivity Disorder (ADHD)

According to the "Diagnostic and Statistical Manual of Mental Disorders" Fifth Edition, as published by the APA, the standard diagnostic criteria for ADHD include the following:

1. The behaviors of inattention, impulsion, and hyperactivity have lasted for more than six months. The behaviors no longer conform to the development stage, and have negative impact on academic and social activities, such as maladjustment.
2. The age of onset is usually earlier than 12 years old.
3. The environment for its onset needs to be cross-situational, such as school, family, work, etc., with related diseases occurring.
4. The symptoms have resulted in maladjustment or dysfunction in school, family, work, and other environments.
5. Extensive developmental disorders, schizophrenia, or other psychiatric and emotional disorders should be excluded.

The accompanying behavioral problems of the three main characteristics of ADHD include poor academic achievements, disobedience, and aggression, and the resulting poor interpersonal relationships and low self-esteem make it more difficult for ADHD students to integrate into the existing normal learning or social system [8]. According to Barkley's statistics, ADHD students have obvious aggressive, destructive, disruptive, and noisy behaviors in the learning environment, and especially fighting, aggressive behavior, and students' excessive agitation, resulting in an inability to participate quietly in learning activities in various areas, which in turn disturbs other students' studies [9].

2.2 AI Emotional Perception-Cognitive Learning

Emotion is a kind of response to the changes of external or internal environments, which produces organized psychological and behavioral tendencies. Emotion generation is an important social tool for human communication and social interaction. In human interaction, emotions and internal emotions will also be reflected in facial and physiological reactions, which are directed by the brain, and then, affect human facial expressions, intonation, heartbeat, and blood pressure [10–12]. As people's internal state is related to their growth experience and innate environmental impact, in the face of the same external changes, different people will have different emotions, and the physiological information affected by these same emotions will be different [13].

3 Research Method

3.1 Teaching Situation of the AI Perception System

This study mainly establishes an AI perceptual fusion learning system shown as Fig. 1, which can assist teachers to record the physiological and emotional responses of ADHD children through long-term collocation and a direct recording method via a robotic imaging device, in order to help teachers formulate appropriate intervention strategies to improve the behavioral problems of children with ADHD, which are used for continuous observation and feedback for teachers to confirm the effectiveness of intervention strategies, and then, improve them. This system introduces AI cognitive and assistant robots during the intervention and maintenance periods, which can predict the emotions of students according to the data of previous training, inform teachers when ADHD behavioral problems occur, and provide simple interventional voice and images, which can reduce the occurrence of children's problem events through immediate interventional behavior, and help students to improve their relevant learning achievements and integrate them into teaching groups.

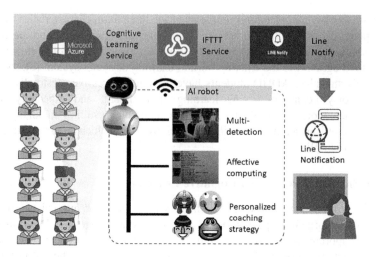

Fig. 1. AI perceptual fusion learning system

3.2 AI Emotional Perception Technology

As mentioned above, ADHD school children often suffer from inadequate attention, anger, hyperactivity, and poor interpersonal relationships, as they are unconscious of or unable to control their emotions or concentrate. In this study, Face Recognition technology was provided by the Microsoft Azure platform, and this perception service is embedded into the APP application through its API. Microsoft Azure provides an account for the facial recognition service to be used for one-year free of charge, which can be used for user recognition and identify different faces. Therefore, different tutoring strategies can be established for different students. Through its recognition function, it can return the judgement of hair, glasses, emotions, and other characteristic values. For emotional recognition, the return parameters include different emotional scores, such as anger, contempt, disgust, fear, happiness, neutral, sadness, and surprise, as shown in Fig. 2.

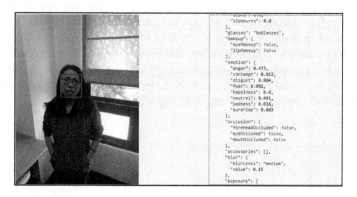

Fig. 2. The emotion parameter of recognition model

Finally, emotional recognition results can be obtained by establishing emotional recognition actions according to their emotional scores. After AI perception technology is used to detect the emotional problems of these target behaviors, the plan is expected to adopt appropriate notification or simple intervention methods, which include message warning instructors, assistant voice management, relevant songs, and video playback reminders, in order that ADHD children can be strengthened and trained in this aspect.

4   Results and Discussion

The experience analyzed the situation of emotional improvement. The control object was to introduce AI counseling into teaching, and the numbers of the occurrences of Sad and Angry in the experiment and the control group were counted. This experiment required teachers to observe emotions for more than 1 min before recording, and teachers were asked not to give counseling in the first 30 s after emotional events occurred. H1 suggests that AI counseling can reduce the times of negative emotion occurrence, while null hypothesis H0 suggests that the increase of AI counseling may increase the occurrence of the variable or make it remain the same. ANCOVA statistics was used as the statistical method, and the results are shown in the table below (Tables 1 and 2).

Table 1. Summary of descriptive statistics

Descriptive statistics						
Group	Number	Pre-test		Post test		Adjustment average
	n	M	SD	M	SD	M'
Experience group	6	16.17	11.63	10.33	8.59	9.32
Control group	6	13.50	9.29	13.00	8.10	14.01

Table 2. Description statistics analysis summary

共變數考驗分析摘要表					
變異來源	SS	df	MS	F	p
組間	64.657	1	64.657	9.507	0.013
組內	61.207	9	6.801		
全體	125.864	10			

Its p value is 0.013, which negates the null hypothesis and means that the introduction of AI counseling strategy can effectively improve students' emotional induction.

According to the above statistical results, this study mainly focused on the impact of AI emotional recognition on ADHD children's recognition rate and emotional improvement. The overall research results are presented, as follows.

S1: AI recognition results had partial recognition rate for ADHA children: The results show that AI emotional recognition resulted in poor recognition for some children, while analysis and discussion with teachers show that some children with more serious emotional disorders have different facial expressions. Detailed discussions of emotional recognition are mainly based on mouth angle and eyes. If the balance angle of the mouth is inclined, it will be the main factor affecting the recognition results. However, for students with mild emotional disorders, the correct rate was about 81%. According to the machine vision algorithm, the recognition degree of Sad was higher than that of Angry. The reason is that Angry needs more obvious expression, while the situation of sulking or a slight expression cannot always be recognized.

S2: AI emotional counseling could improve students' emotions: According to the results, the use of teaching strategies with AI counseling could effectively reduce the occurrence of students' anger or sadness. The average number of times in the experimental group was reduced from 16.17 to 10.33, and 13.5 to 13.0 in the control group. According to the results of class tutors' discussions, AI assistive devices can provide timely counseling strategies to improve students' emotional control. In addition, the encouragement strategies provided by AI aids normal emotional performance, and can effectively improve the students' situations.

5   Conclusion

Aiming at the performance of ADHD students' emotional disorders in school curriculum learning, this study introduced AI emotional recognition and robotic AIDS as curriculum learning counseling, integrated AI emotional recognition service through robotic aids to detect students' emotional performance, and introduced personalized emotional counseling strategies to improve or reduce students' emotional occurrence, in order to reduce the need for teachers to engage in pacifying or counselling students. The results show that the introduction of robotic aids can effectively reduce the number of emotional occurrences of students, meaning that a guidance strategy with robotic AIDS has certain effect. In the future, different sensing methods can be integrated or emotional recognition methods can be adjusted for students with severe emotional expressions to improve the overall recognition performance.

Acknowledgment. The authors would like to thank the Ministry of Science and Technology of the Republic of China, Taiwan for supporting this research under Contract MOST 107-2511-H-143-004 –.

References

1. Fernando, M., Claudia, B., Nimrod, G., Juan, G.: KAPEAN: understanding affective states of children with ADHD. Educ. Technol. Soc. **19**(2), 18–28 (2016)
2. Brodeur, D., Pond, M.: The development of selective attention in children with attention deficit hyperactivity disorder. J. Abnorm. Child Psychol. **29**(3), 229–239 (2001)

3. Bikic, A., Leckman, J.F., Lindschou, J., Christensen, T., Dalsgaard, S.: Cognitive computer training in children with attention deficit hyperactivity disorder (ADHD) versus no intervention: study protocol for a randomized controlled trial. Trials. **16**, 480 (2015). https://doi.org/10.1186/s13063-015-0975-8

4. Daróczy, G., Artificial intelligence and cognitive psychology applications, models. In: Proceedings of the 8th International Conference on Applied Informatics, vol. 1, pp. 61–69. Eger, Hungary, (2010)

5. Horner, R.H.: Positive behavior supports. Focus Autism Other Dev. Disabil. **15**, 97–105 (2000)

6. Lee, M.J., Shin, M.: Fear versus humor: the impact of sensation seeking on physiological, cognitive, and emotional responses to antialcohol abuse messages. J. Psychol. **145**(2), 73–92 (2011)

7. Posner, J., Russell, J.A., Peterson, B.S.: The circumplex model of affect: an integrative approach to affective neuroscience, cognitive development, and psychopathology. Dev. Psychopathol. **17**(03), 715–734 (2005)

8. Neef, N.A., Iwata, B.A.: Current research on functional analysis methodologies: an introduction. J. Appl. Behav. Anal. **27**(2), 211–214 (1994)

9. Strickland, E.: Brain-controlled game helps kids with ADHD improve mental focus. Blog – IEEE Spectrum (2017). https://spectrum.ieee.org/the-human-os/biomedical/devices/brain-controlled-game-helps-kids-with-adhd-improve-mental-focus

10. Bolls, P.D., Lang, A., Potter, R.F.: The effects of message valence and listener arousal on attention, memory, and facial muscular responses to radio advertisements. Commun. Res. **28**(5), 627–651 (2001)

11. Brown, K.W., Ryan, R.M.: The benefits of being present: mindfulness and its role in psychological well-being. J. Pers. Soc. Psychol. **84**(4), 822–848 (2003)

12. Laparra-Hernández, J., Belda-Lois, J.M., Medina, E., Campos, N., Poveda, R.: EMG and GSR signals for evaluating user's perception of different types of ceramic flooring. Int. J. Ind. Ergon. **39**(2), 326–332 (2009)

13. Van der Heijden, H.: Factors influencing the usage of websites: the case of ageneric portal in The Netherlands. Inf. Manag. **40**(6), 541–549 (2003)

Classification of Intrusion Detection System Based on Machine Learning

Hsiu-Min Chuang[(⊠)] [iD], Hui-Ying Huang, Fanpyn Liu,
and Chung-Hsien Tsai

Department of Computer Science and Information Engineering,
Chung Cheng Institute of Technology, National Defense University,
Taoyuan, Taiwan
showmin1205@gmail.com

Abstract. In order to detect abnormal network behaviors early, it is common to build an intrusion detection system (IDS) by recording logs and analyzing active processes on the host. In this way, mining host behavior patterns from massive logs plays an important role in identifying anomalies in order to provide corresponding courses of action, such as blocking or tracking threats. Because of the ever-changing nature of cyber-attacks, it is critical to identify previously unknown threats. In this paper, we propose the hierarchical multi-class classifier (HMC) approach to intrusion detection, which combines multiple binary classifiers into a hierarchy architecture. In addition, we extract the characteristics of data distribution using a k-means algorithm to append new features to the original NSL-KDD public dataset to use as our experimental dataset. The experimental results show that our HMC approach outperforms other classifiers to reach 78% of F1-measure. This paper provides a preliminary research direction for detecting unseen and new types of abnormal activities in IDS. For future work, we will consider the feature representation by deep learning algorithms to improve their performance in practical applications.

Keywords: Intrusion detection system · Multi-Class classification · Clustering

1 Introduction

With Convenience and security are two important factors that people often consider the trade-off when using the Internet. To ensure the security of the internal network, the traditional method is to set up a firewall to implement security rules. However, once the firewall mechanism is applied to a large network, it may cause network congestion since a large number of network packets need to be filtered by complicated rules. Because the accumulated rules can lead to management difficulties, the intrusion detection system (IDS) is used to alleviate some of this filtering. When the network packets pass through the IDS, it judges whether it displays abnormal behavior according to the features of the network packet.

The detection methods of the IDS are divided into *misuse detection* and *anomaly detection*. Misuse detection establishes known abnormal behaviors by creating a list of such behaviors in the database, and then compares new network packets with these of

© Springer Nature Singapore Pte Ltd. 2020
J. Shen et al. (Eds.): IC3 2019, CCIS 1227, pp. 492–498, 2020.
https://doi.org/10.1007/978-981-15-6113-9_55

the database. Relative to the anomaly detection method, it builds a model of normal patterns to identify abnormal behaviors. Thus, misuse detection is more difficult than anomaly detection for unknown abnormal behaviors because all behaviors besides those defined specifically as abnormal are considered normal.

Historically, a traditional IDS mostly used rule-based methods to detect abnormal behaviors. In recent years, due to the development of machine learning, research has begun to prepare data for training models and to predict abnormal behaviors based on these models. There are three types of machine learning approaches: supervised learning, semi-supervised learning and unsupervised learning. Supervised learning methods are usually more accurate because the training data is labeled by experts. However, in most real cases the prepared data is not labeled because of the huge cost of manual oversight, so semi-supervised and unsupervised methods are employed as practical methods to identify unseen and new types of attack behaviors. Depending on the cyber-tracks, different response measures are taken. This requires that the IDS not only needs to identify abnormal behaviors, but also needs to be able to distinguish between the types of attacks. Commonly known attack behaviors can be easily detected since the amount of training data is large enough to develop accurate model judgments, but for lesser known classes of attacks, the amount of related data can be insufficient and hence lead to misjudgment by the model.

In this paper, we propose the HMC approach to the multi-class classification problem. First, we adopt a clustering method to group clusters for extracting the characteristics of data distribution. Then, the HMC approach is used, which combines multiple binary classifiers based on a hierarchical architecture. In detail, each class is identified by a binary classifier for each layer. Normal behaviors are eliminated after the first layer to solve the multi-class classification problem. We adopted F1-measure for evaluating the performance. With complete records in IDS, there are many features, including network protocols, destination addresses, amount of data, frequency, connection time, among others. The experimental results show that our HMC approach outperforms other classifiers to reach 78% of F1-measure. Based on our proposed, this paper contributes in two ways in facing the challenges of IDS:

- We propose a hierarchical multi-class classifier and improve the multi-class classification problem in stratification.
- Based on clustered features, all classifiers can improve the performance for detecting new types of behaviors.

In the next section, we introduce related work in detail. In Sect. 3, we introduce our HMC approach and the new corpus. In Sect. 4, we present the experimental results. We end with our conclusions in Sect. 5.

2 Related Work

The concept of IDS was developed in the 1980s. In the 1990s, IDS often used rule-based methods, such as snort [9], based on preexisting attack rules. Each network packet is compared with the rules of the IDS. With the increase in the number of cyber-attack types, the number of rules is also increasing, and these rules must be updated immediately. New attacks are difficult to identify as no rule exists for them. There are two types of IDS: network-based IDS (NIDS) and host-based IDS (HIDS) [7] The former mainly monitors the audit records of the terminal host and is deployed hosts in the internal network. The latter focuses on monitoring network packets and is deployed at the network gateway.

Due to the popularity of machine learning and deep learning technology since 2011, several researchers have started adopting neural networks in the IDS. Sabhnani and Serpen [10] found that machine learning technology is not suitable for misuse detection when testing data containing unseen or new types of data. To detect anomalies, Kruegel et al. [6] used the Bayesian network to determine the probability distribution of OS command in order to identify whether a specific behavior is abnormal. Bilge et al. [2] used the decision tree algorithm to detect malicious domains using passive domain name systems (DNS). On the other hand, Anwer et al. [1] presented a feature selection framework for network anomaly detection via different machine learning classifiers and using filter and wrapper features selection methodologies. With the development of deep learning, Javaid et al. [5] proposed the self-taught learning (STL) method, a deep learning-based technique, to solve the multi-class classification problem. Nguyen et al. [8] adopted the convolutional neural network (CNN) to detect denial of service (DoS) attack. Tang et al. [11] used a gated recurrent unit recurrent neural network (GRU-RNN) enabled IDS for software defined networking (SDN) which has emerged as a key enabler for future agile Internet architecture. Vinayakumar et al. [14] proposed a deep neural network (DNN) to detect and classify unforeseen and unpredictable cyber-attacks, and evaluated several datasets, such as KDD Cup 99, NSL-KDD, UNSW-NB15, Kyoto, WSN-DS, and CICIDS 2017, to conduct the benchmark. In contrast to supervised learning, Thang and Pashchenko [13] proposed a semi-supervised method by combing the incremental graph-based clustering and multistage machine learning for outlier detection.

With regard to the multi-class classification problem, Bishop [3] mentioned that such a problem can be divided into multiple binary classification problems before the final results are consolidated. Three strategies for labeling currently being used are: one vs. one(OvO), one-vs.-all (OvA) and a similar method, one-vs.-rest (OvR). The first labeling method trains $K*(K-1)/2$ binary classifiers for a K-way multi-class classification problem, and then each classifier trains samples of a pair of classes from the original training data. Finally, a voting scheme is applied in which: all $K*(K-1)/2$ classifiers combine to predict the class of a new sample, and the result is the highest number of the class. The second labeling method involves training a single classifier per class, with the samples of that class as positive samples and all other samples as negatives. The slight difference between OvA and OvR is the exclusion of the previously classified data after classification.

3   System Architecture

3.1   Hierarchical Multi-Class Classifiers (HMC)

In order to identify which type of abnormal behaviors requires immediate response, multi-class classification is required. Due the poor performance of common multi-class classifiers, we convert the multi-class classification problem into multiple binary classification problems. That is, we use a divide-and-conquer strategy based on a top-down hierarchical architecture. There are two strategies to design the conversion: OvR-HMC and OvA-HMC. The former selects the class with the largest number, marks this as 1, and marks the remaining classes as 0 at each layer. Subsequently, the previous classified samples are removed. The latter strategy selects a class and marks as 1 for each layer, with the others marked as 0. Next, it retains the previous classified abnormal samples. The architecture of IDS can be applied to on-line or off-line systems. The online system can use historical data as the training data, which requires experts to label whether the behaviors are abnormal, as well as newly collected data for developing predictions. In the next subsection, we go more into detail on the dataset.

3.2   C-NSLKDD Dataset

The NSL-KDD dataset [4] is publicly available from the Canadian cyber security institute to conduct intrusion detection classification research. It is an improvement on the KDD99 dataset [12] which was developed for the 1999 network intrusion detection competition. The NSL-KDD dataset contains 125,973 training samples and 25,543 testing samples. There are 41 features in the dataset, including network protocols, destination addresses, amount of data, frequency, connection time, among others. There are five dataset label categories: normal, DoS which uses a large number of packets to block the network of the system, probe which scans the whole network architecture of the system, remote to local (R2L) which unauthorized accesses to control through the network from remote ends, and user to root (U2R) which fully controls the system permission.

To detect unseen abnormal behaviors, we increase two features from the characteristics in the data distribution. We assume that if the distribution of the new behavior is farther away from the general behaviors, then the behavior is more likely to be abnormal. Thus, we can use the common clustering algorithm, i.e., k-means, to group clusters. The sum of squared error (SSE) is used to measure the quality of the number of clusters. When the number of clusters is equal to 2, the result is ideal. After the number of clusters is determined, two indicators are calculated as new features: Cluster c, which describes the cluster to which the sample belongs and the Euclidean distance $D(x, \mu)$, which describes the distance between the sample and the mean of the nearest cluster. Thus, two clustered features are added to NSL-KDD dataset, bringing the total number of features to 43. This modified dataset we have called C-NSLKDD.

4   Experiments

Using the C-NSLKDD dataset and the F1-measure we evaluate the whole performance and positive class (i.e., abnormal behavior). The formula is listed as follows:

$$F1 - \text{measure} = \frac{2 \times P \times R}{P + R} \qquad (1)$$

where P is the number of correct positive results divided by the number of all positive results, and R is the number of correct positive results divided by the number of all relevant samples. The experiments are divided into two parts: the performance of clustered features and the performance HMC approach for multi-class classification.

First, we compare the performance of original dataset and new dataset which contains clustered features. As shown in Fig. 1, the performance of C-NSLKDD outperforms NSL-KDD dataset by all classifiers, including support vector machine (SVM), Naive Bayes, logistic regression, Bayes net, K nearest neighbor (KNN), multi-layer perceptron (MLP) and decision tree C4.5. Because the distribution of training data and testing data is different, we can validate that the clustered features enable us to recognize the previously unseen abnormal behaviors.

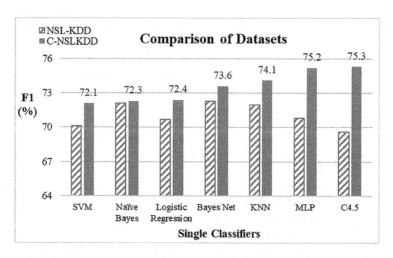

Fig. 1. Performance comparison between C-NSLKDD and NSL-KDD.

Next, we compare the performance of four types of multi-class classifiers: Ada-Boost, Bagging, ensemble classifier and our HMC approach as shown in Fig. 2. Because C4.5 achieved the best performance in the previous experiment, for AdaBoost, Bagging, and our HMC approach, the kernel algorithm all used C4.5. For ensemble classifiers, we mix *k* classifiers into three types of combinations, where *k* is the number of classifiers: *Ensemble*(3), which includes C4.5, MLP and KNN, *Ensemble*(5), which includes Ensemble(3), Bayes Net and logistic regression, *Ensemble*(7), including *Ensemble*(5), Naive Bayes and SVM.

The result shows that our OvR-HMC and OvA-HMC approaches outperform other classifiers. Moreover, OvA-HMC is superior to the OvR-HMC approach because OvA-HMC retains other types of abnormal behaviors, enabling learning quite similar to the distribution of real dataset. Bagging algorithm performs the third best. Although *Ensemble*(7) contains 7 types of classifiers, the performance is not better than the other combinations. This means that more classifiers do not improve performance. This may be due to conflicting classifiers in the voting mechanism.

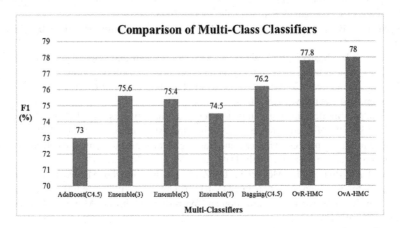

Fig. 2. Performance comparison of multi-class classifiers

5   Conclusions

In this paper, we propose the HMC approach to solve the multi-class classification in IDS. The experimental results show the HMC approach outperforms other classifiers. In addition, clustered features can detect unknown abnormal behaviors different from those of training data. For future work, we will consider the feature representation by deep learning algorithms to improve the performance in practical applications.

Acknowledgments. This work is partially sponsored by the Ministry of Science and Technology, Taiwan under grant 108-2221-E-606-013-MY2.

References

1. Anwer, H.M., Farouk, M., Abdel-Hamid, A.: A framework for efficient network anomaly intrusion detection with features selection. In: Proceedings of the 9th International Conference on Information and Communication Systems (ICICS), IRBID, Jordan, 3–5 April 2018 (2018)
2. Bilge, L., Kirda, E., Kruegel, C., Balduzzi, M.: EXPOSURE: finding malicious domains using passive DNS analysis. In: Proceedings of the Annual Network and Distributed System Security Symposium (NDSS), California, USA, 31 August 2011 (2011)

3. Bishop, C.M.: Pattern Recognition and Machine Learning. Springer, New York (2006)
4. Chandrashekar, G., Sahin, F.: A survey on feature selection methods. Comput. Electr. Eng. **40**(1), 16–28 (2014)
5. Javaid, A., Niyaz, Q., Sun, W., Alam, M.: A deep learning approach for network intrusion detection system. In: Proceedings of the 9th EAI International Conference on Bio-inspired Information and Communications Technologies (formerly BIONETICS), New York, USA, 3–5 December 2015 (2015)
6. Kruegel, C., Mutz, D., Robertson, W., Valeur, F.: Bayesian event classification for intrusion detection. In: Proceedings of IEEE the 19th Annual Computer Security Applications Conference, Las Vegas, USA, 8–12 December 2003 (2003)
7. Mukherjee, B., Heberlein, L.T., Levitt, K.N.: Network intrusion detection. IEEE Netw. **8**, 26–41 (1994)
8. Nguyen, S.N., Nguyen, V.Q., Choi, J., Kim, K.: Design and implementation of intrusion detection system using convolutional neural network For DoS detection. In: Proceedings of the 2nd International Conference on Machine Learning and Soft Computing, Phuoc Island, Vietnam, 2–4 February 2018 (2018)
9. Roesch, M.: Snort: lightweight intrusion detection for networks. In: LISA 1999 Proceedings of the 13th USENIX conference on System administration, pp. 229–238 (1999)
10. Sabhnani, M., Serpen, G.: why machine learning algorithms fail in misuse detection on KDD intrusion detection data set. Intell. Data Anal. **8**(4), 403–415 (2004)
11. Tang, T.A., Mhamdi, L., McLernon, D., Zaidi, S.A.R., Ghogho, M.: Deep recurrent neural network for intrusion detection in SDN-based networks. In: Proceedings of the 4th IEEE Conference on Network Softwarization and Workshops (NetSoft), Montreal, Canada, 25–29 June 2018 (2018)
12. Tavallaee, M., Bagheri, E., Lu, W., Ghorbani, A.A.: a detailed analysis of the KDD CUP 99 data set. In: Proceedings of the IEEE Symposium on Computational Intelligence for Security and Defense Applications(CISDA), Ottawa, Canada, 8–10 July 2009 (2009)
13. Thang, V.V., Pashchenko, F.F.: Multistage system-based machine learning techniques for intrusion detection in WiFi network. J. Comput. Netw. Commun. **2019**, 4708201:1–4708201:13 (2019)
14. Vinayakumar, R., Alazab, M., Soman, K.P., Poornachandran, P., Al-Nemrat, A., Venkatraman, S.: Deep learning approach for intelligent intrusion detection system. IEEE Access **7**, 41525–41550 (2019)

The Ideas of Robot Design and Application from the First-Year Undergraduate Students

Tzu-Hua Ho[(⊠)]

Department of Early Childhood Education, Asia University, Taichung, Taiwan
otjuliaho@gmail.com

Abstract. The purpose of this research was to understand college students' perspectives of robot design and robot application. This study invited 53 first-year college students to participate. Participants were invited to draw the robots which they want to design, and to describe the ideotype, target group, and the function of the robot. All information of robot characteristics was coded and analyzed. In the results, four robot ideotypes were presented, including: humanoid style, android style, pet/animal style, and others. The five target populations were baby and children, college students and young people, family and all people, elderly or single person, and others. Ten categories of robot functions were suggested, including: accompanying and chatting, personal assistant, educational function, babysitter, dance and exercise, pet function, elder care, housework, entertaining, and other specific functions. More relationships between robot characteristics were discussed in the study. The results can help the instructors to develop artificial intelligence and robot courses to establish better knowledge and competencies for students in the college of social sciences. This information may also help the robot designers to think human needs from different perspectives and to develop robots with more friendly functions for improving user's experiences and life quality in future.

Keywords: Artificial intelligence · Robot design · Robot application · Robot function · Robot ideotype · Robot appearance

1 Introduction

With the progress of science and technology in the 21st century, the applications of artificial intelligence (AI) and big data played more and more important roles in various aspects of human world, such as health care, education, communication, finance, transportation, or service industries, etc. Robot is one of the applications of artificial intelligence (AI) and advanced technologies. In response to the demands of different industries and populations, many kinds of robot have been invented and produced to help with peoples' tasks and daily living. For example, a robot can be a mechanical arm controlled by a surgeon in an operating room. Tourists may find robots in hotels to help with the check-in/check-out service. More and more robots are designed to socially interact with children and families with the function of chatting or storytelling. The robot companions can accompany with elder people, connect them with friends, and help to improve an active and healthy lifestyle.

© Springer Nature Singapore Pte Ltd. 2020
J. Shen et al. (Eds.): IC3 2019, CCIS 1227, pp. 499–506, 2020.
https://doi.org/10.1007/978-981-15-6113-9_56

Since the robots will be available in many human oriented environments and with more human interaction features, Walters et al. [1] suggested that a robot companion must satisfy two main criteria. First, the robot must be able to perform a range of tasks or functions. Second, it must perform the tasks in a manner which is socially acceptable and comfortable for the users. Researchers has studied individuals' preferences and perceptions of robot appearance. According to literature [2–4], the robot appearances can be classified to three types: mechanoid (relatively machine-like in appearance), humanoid (not realistically human-like in appearance, but will possess some human-like features), and android (exhibits appearance or behavior which is close to a real human). When investigating individuals' preferences of robot appearance and robot height, researchers found that there was no significant overall preference for either the factors of robot appearance or robot height. Peoples' preferences for robot appearance or behavior may be related to their own personalities [2, 5]. In a cross-cultural study, Li et al. [6] found that the interaction of cultural background and the sociability of a task can affect the human-robot interaction. Thus, users' acceptance of robots and their engagement in human-robot interaction would be the complicated results associated with the interactions of a wider range of factors. When developing robots to benefit human life, it is important to include different perspectives from professionals and potential users for designing the social robot or service robot which can be better adapt to the needs of future users [7].

As the artificial intelligence getting more connected to human society and life, our future generation will need to learn the knowledge of artificial intelligence, to know how to interact with artificial intelligence, and to apply artificial intelligence technologies appropriately for improving people's quality of life. In Taiwan, the Ministry of Education has proposed the updated Curriculum Guidelines of 12-Year Basic Education in 2014 [8], which will be officially implemented in September 2019. In the new curriculum guideline, the technology and information literacy are part of the core competencies which a student should prepare for becoming a lifelong learner. Students will learn to possess the competency of using information and technology effectively and appropriately [8]. In higher education, universities have begun to provide the courses about big data and artificial intelligence and listed these courses as the required core courses in the colleges of humanities and social science. Students who major in social science may have opportunities to collaborate with experts of artificial intelligence to develop services or products for their target populations. The knowledge and perspectives of social science college students toward artificial intelligence will be important to the professors for developing and teaching the courses of artificial intelligence. Thus, this research tended to understand college students' perspectives related to the application of artificial intelligence. Robot is one of the products and applications of artificial intelligence. This research focused on collecting the information of students' ideas of robot design and robot application. The results of this study can help the instructors to design artificial intelligence courses to develop better competencies of applying artificial intelligence for students in the college of humanities and social sciences.

2   Research Method

In order to collect information of students' ideas of robot design and robot application, an investigation was conducted in a group of college students.

Participants. This study invited 53 first-year college students to participate. All the participants are the first-year college students in the department of early childhood education.

Data Collection. The participants were invited to think and answer an open-ended question: "If you have a chance to design a robot, what kind of the robot you will design? Please draw the robot, and describe the ideotype, target group, and the function of this robot." After collecting the participants' robot picture and description, two researchers coded the robot characteristics of robot ideotype, target group, and robot function to various categories. All data and information were analyzed according to the following research questions.

Research Questions

(1)   What kinds of robot ideotype were designed?
(2)   Who are the target groups that the robots can provide service to?
(3)   What are the functions that the robots were expected to have?
(4)   Are there any relationships between the ideotype, target group, and function of the robots designed by student participants?

3   Result

3.1   Robot Ideotypes

Four robot ideotypes were found from the 53 robot pictures, including: humanoid robot (28%), android robot (28%), pet/animal robot (27%), and others (such as mechanical boxes, arms, screen, smart house, and egg style robots) (17%). Figure 1 presented the examples of four robot ideotypes.

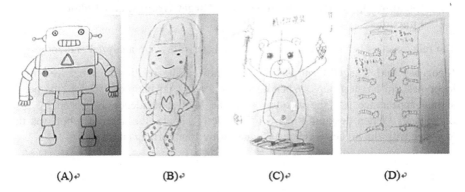

(A)↵   (B)↵   (C)↵   (D)↵

Fig. 1. Examples of four robot ideotypes: (A) humanoid, (B) android, (C) pet/animal, and (D) others.

3.2   Target Groups

The target populations included five groups of people who need robot services in the results, such as baby and children (35%), college students and young people (26%), others (military, or people with specific interest or needs) (16%), families and all people (12%), and elderly or single person who lives alone (11%).

3.3   Robot Functions

Most participants expected robots to have multiple functions. The results showed ten categories of robot functions, including: accompanying and chatting, personal reminding (searching information, answering, reminding, and booking, etc.), educational function (storytelling, play, teaching and learning), housework (cooking, cleaning), other specific functions (military, smart house, librarian, auto-driving, and repairing), entertaining (singing, joking), babysitter (baby care, appeasing, brewing milk), dance and exercise, pet function, and elder care and taking medicine (Fig. 2).

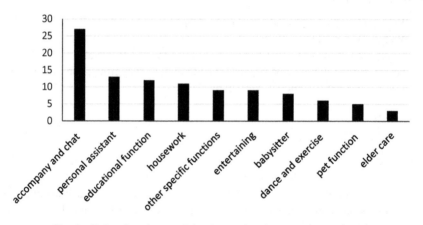

Fig. 2.   Robot functions and the times of each category mentioned.

3.4   Relationships Between the Ideotypes, Target Groups, and Robot Functions

The relationships between different robot characteristics were analyzed and compared.

Ideotypes and Target Groups. Figure 3 showed the relationships between robot ideotypes and target groups. When designing a robot for baby or children, the pet or animal appearance was the ideotype with the highest incidence suggested by nine participants. When designing a robot for elderly people, the android robot was the ideotype with the higher incidence suggested by four participants.

Robot Functions and Target Groups. Figure 4 demonstrated the relationships between robot functions and target groups. When designing robots for baby or children, they were expected to have multiple functions appropriate to young children, such as accompanying and chatting, educational function (storytelling, play, or teaching), babysitter (baby care, brewing milk, or appeasing), entertaining function (singing or joking), and pet function. When providing services to elderly people, the function of accompanying and chatting was the most needed function than other functions (take medicine or housework). When designing robots for college students or young people, the participants suggested the robot functions which reflecting the needs in their daily life, such as personal assistant (reminding, booking, and searching information), chatting, entertaining, dance and exercise, or housework.

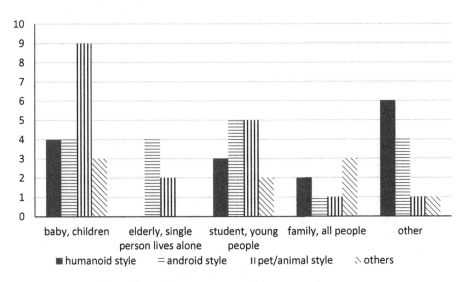

Fig. 3. Relationships between robot ideotypes and target groups.

Ideotypes and Robot Functions. Figure 5 showed the relationships between robot functions and target groups. The accompanying and chatting functions of three types of robots (humanoid, android, and pet/animal) were suggested by most participants. The humanoid style robots were expected to provide many kinds of services except pet function and elder care. The android robots were expected to have the functions close to human life, such as accompanying and chatting, personal assistant, babysitter, elder care, and housework. The pet/animal style robots were expected to have more functions than just to be a pet. For example, an intelligent pet robot needs to accompany and chat with people, or to provide educational programs to children.

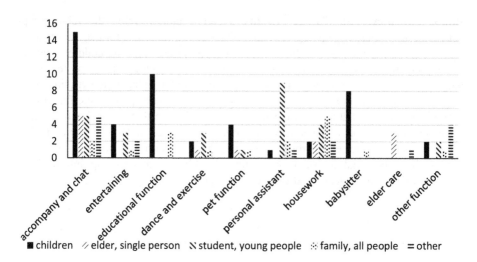

Fig. 4. Relationships between robot functions and target groups.

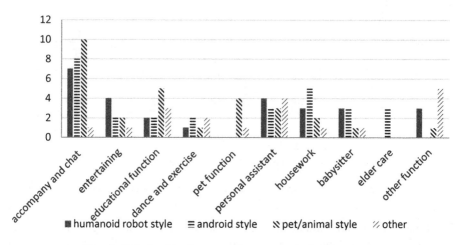

Fig. 5. Relationships between ideotypes and robot functions.

4   Discussion

The present study collected the ideas of robot design and application from 53 first-year college students in the department of early childhood education. Researchers analyzed the information of the robot ideotype, target group, and robot function. In the results, four robot ideotypes were presented, including: humanoid robot, android robot, pet/animal robot, and others (boxes, arms, screen, smart house, and egg style robot). The five target populations were baby and children, college students and young people, others (military, and people with specific interest or needs), families and all people, and elderly or single person who lives alone. In addition, ten categories of robot functions were suggested, including: accompanying and chatting, personal assistant (searching information, answering, reminding, and booking, etc.), educational function (storytelling, play, teaching and learning), housework (cooking and cleaning), other specific functions (military, smart house, librarian, auto driving, and repairing), entertaining (singing and joking), babysitter (baby care, appeasing, brewing milk), dancing and exercise, pet function, and elder care (taking medicine).

The results presented participants' perspectives and concerns about robot application. Since all participants in this study were the first-year college students in the department of early childhood education, their responses reflected their concerns about the needs of baby and young children. Thus, robots were expected to accompany young children, to be a babysitter, and to provide educational functions, such as programs of storytelling, teaching, and learning. The ideas of robot design also came from the personal experience and daily life of college students. The robot with the functions of personal assistant can help young people to make their busy and messy life easier.

Regarding the robot ideotype and robot function, three types of robot design (humanoid, android, and pet/animal style) were mentioned by similar number of participants. It was noticed that regardless the robot ideotype, the accompanying and chatting functions were suggested by many participants and required in all three types of robots (mechanical, humanoid, and pet/animal style). This finding suggested that socially interacting behaviors are always important human needs. Corresponding to the previous studies [9], the robot appearance may affect people's expectation or perceptions of the robot function. The robot with android or pet ideotype, or which can present a social manner as a cute baby, may help to initiate or maintain user's interest of interacting with the robot [10]. This study also found that robots with the appearance of cute pet/animal or young child were expected to demonstrate the basic social skills (such as accompanying and chatting) and may get better acceptance from the users.

The study recruited participants from one department in Social Science College. The sample size of this research was small and maybe not representative to all college students. However, the results can provide instructors information about students' knowledge and perspectives toward artificial intelligence (AI) and robot application. According to this information, the instructors can develop the lecture and class discussion in a more creative and interactive way to enrich students' knowledge and learning experience. College students will not only learn the basic concepts of AI, but also try to update the information of technological advancement. As the potential users and developers of assistive robots, students need to understand that the users' preferences of robots may be associated with various factors and to consider the needs of different populations more comprehensively. We hope the AI and robot courses can help students who major in social science to get closer to modern technology. As the educators for young children, they can integrate the knowledge of AI with their professional competencies and collaborate with engineers or designers to develop effective AI or robot programs. Further, we expect these college students may apply AI technologies appropriately to meet users' needs and to improve the quality of human life.

5 Conclusion

This research collected the college students' perspectives of robot design and robot application. The participants demonstrated their understanding and imagination to human needs and robot features. The behaviors of social interaction were regarded as the essential function of robots for different populations. The relationships between robot ideotypes, robot function, and target populations were discussed. The findings of this research will provide researchers and instructors for developing courses of artificial intelligence and robot application to students who major in social science. Through exploring students' ideas about robot design, we also got some inspirations and understandings about the needs of different populations. This information may help robot designers to think human needs from different perspectives and to develop robots with more friendly functions for improving users' experiences in future.

References

1. Walters, M.L., Syrdal, D.S., Dautenhahn, K., te Boekhorst, R., Koay, K.L.: Avoiding the uncanny valley: robot appearance, personality and consistency of behavior in an attention-seeking home scenario for a robot companion. Auton. Robots **24**(2), 159–178 (2008). https://doi.org/10.1007/s10514-007-9058-3
2. Walters, M.L., Koay, K.L., Syrdal, D.S., Dautenhahn, K., te Boekhorst, R.: Preferences and perceptions of robot appearance and embodiment in human-robot interaction trials. In: Proceedings of New Frontiers in Human-Robot Interaction, AISB 2009, Edinburg, Scotland, pp. 136–143 (2009)
3. Gong, L., Nass, C.N.: When a talking-face computer agent is half-human and half-humanoid: human identity and consistency preference. Hum. Commun. Res. **33**(2), 163–193 (2007)
4. MacDorman, K., Ishiguro, K.: The uncanny advantage of using androids in cognitive and social science research. Inter. Stud. **7**(3), 297–337 (2006)
5. Syrdal, D.S., Walters, M.L., Koay, K.L., Woods, S.N., Dautenhahn, D.: Looking good? appearance preferences and robot personality inferences at zero acquaintance. In: Proceedings of AAAI - Spring Symposium 2007, Multidisciplinary Collaboration for Socially Assistive Robotics, pp. 86–92. Stanford University, Palo Alto (2007)
6. Li, D., Rau, P.L.P., Li, Y.: A cross-cultural study: effect of robot appearance and task. Int. J. Soc. Robot. **2**(2), 175–186 (2010). https://doi.org/10.1007/s12369-010-0056-9
7. de Graaf, M.M.A., Allouch, S.B., van Dijk, J.A.G.M.: Why would I use this in my home? a model of domestic social robot acceptance. Hum.-Comput. Inter. **34**(2), 115–173 (2019). https://doi.org/10.1080/07370024.2017.1312406
8. Ministry of Education: Curriculum of guidelines of 12-year basic education- General guidelines. Ministry of Education, Taiwan (2014)
9. Powers, A., Kiesler, S.: The advisor robot: tracing people's mental model from a robot's physical attributes. In: Proceedings of the 1st ACM SIGCHI/SIGART Conference on Human-Robot Interaction, pp. 218–225. ACM, New York (2006)
10. Breazeal, C.: Sociable machines: expressive social exchange between humans and robots. Doctor of Science Thesis, Massachusetts Institute of Technology, Boston (2000)

Internet of Things for Cognitive City

Characteristics of the Ionospheric Disturbances Caused by Typhoon Using GPS and Ionospheric Sounding

Jiujing Xu[1], Fuyang Ke[2(✉)], Xingwang Zhao[3], and Xiaoman Qi[2]

[1] School of Instrument Science and Engineering, Southeast University, Nanjing 210000, China
[2] School of Remote Sensing and Geomatics Engineering, Nanjing University Information of Science and Technology, Nanjing 210000, China
ke.fuyang@qq.com
[3] School of Geodesy and Geomatics, Anhui University of Science and Technology, Huainan 232001, China

Abstract. The regularity and coupling mechanism of typhoon-induced ionospheric disturbances are still unclear. In this paper, three typhoons that made landfall over China in 2016 are selected as typical cases. The morphological characteristics of ionospheric disturbances affected by typhoons are comprehensively analyzed using ionospheric TEC extracted from ground-based GPS, ionospheric scintillation data, and digital ionosonde data. The results show that the ionospheric TEC shows positive anomalies and the ionospheric scintillation intensity increases before typhoon's landfall. On the vertical scale, anomalies have occurred in E, F1 and F2 layers of the ionosphere too. It is analyzed that the movement of the turbulent layer and the gravity waves generated by the interaction between the typhoon and the ground cause changes in the electric field and then cause ionospheric disturbances.

Keywords: GPS · Typhoon · Ionospheric disturbances · Scintillation

1 Introduction

Since the 1950s, many scholars have carried out related research on the morphological characteristics and coupling mechanism of ionospheric disturbances in typhoon processes (Davies and Jones 1971; Chou et al. 2017; Song et al. 2017; Ke et al. 2019). In 1958, Siegfried J. Bauer (1958) of the University of Graz, Austria, first discovered that the ionosphere would be disturbed when the hurricane transited. When the hurricane approached the station, the critical frequency of the F2 layer began to increase; when the hurricane was closest to the station, the ground pressure dropped to the lowest, foF2 increased to the maximum. In 1978, Hung et al. (1978) of NASA in the United States observed the existence of gravity waves and mesoscale disturbances in the F layer of the ionosphere during the tornado eruption using a high-frequency Doppler detector, and considered that the gravity wave may be the main cause of ionospheric disturbance. However, Huang et al. (1985) found that high-frequency Doppler detectors are less effective in detecting gravity waves excited by typhoons that can disturb the

© Springer Nature Singapore Pte Ltd. 2020
J. Shen et al. (Eds.): IC3 2019, CCIS 1227, pp. 509–517, 2020.
https://doi.org/10.1007/978-981-15-6113-9_57

ionosphere. Xiao et al. (2007) found that the ionosphere disturbances response to typhoon is with obvious periodicity and the ionospheric disturbances are linearly related to gravity waves. Vanina-Dart and Sharkov (2016) analyzed the ionospheric parameters obtained by ground-based and satellite sensing over the TC and at a certain distance and got the conclusion that internal gravity waves are the main factors that influence the ionosphere from the active cyclones. Regarding the mechanism of typhoon-ionospheric disturbances, there are still some differences between the research results of different scholars. It was indicated by Shen (1982) that the turbopause motion is a possible mechanism for the interaction of the lower layers of the atmosphere and ionosphere. Wang (2005), and Liu (2006a; 2006b) used one-dimensional ionospheric physical model and numerical model to simulate and verify Shen 's view that the rise of turbulent layer top during typhoon may be a very effective mechanism of Typhoon affecting ionospheric region.

Using GPS to study the ionospheric disturbance response to typhoon, with all-weather, high-resolution and large-scale that other observation techniques do not have (Wang et al. 2018). Ionospheric TEC extracted from ground-based GPS, ionospheric scintillation data, and digital ionosonde data is used in this article to describe the morphological characteristics of ionospheric disturbances affected by Typhoon Meranti, Sarika and Haima that landed on China in 2016.

2 Data and Methodology

2.1 Typhoon and Ionospheric Dataset

Typhoon Meranti formed as a tropical depression on September 10, 2016 near the island of Guam. It reached its peak intensity on September 13 with winds of 75 m/s. By September 14, it struck Xiamen China with the winds of 52 m/s; Typhoon Sarika was noted as a tropical disturbance on 11th October, 2016, while it was located about 1050 km to the southeast of Philippines. Early on October 16, Sarika had made its first landfall over in Baler, Philippines. After moving for 2 days, Sarika weakened to a severe tropical storm with winds of 45 m/s as it made landfall over in Hainan, China; Impacting Hainan less than 3 days after Typhoon Sarika, Typhoon Haima was developed into a tropical storm southwest of Luzon Philippines on October 15. Haima made landfall over Luzon Philippines on October 19 as a super typhoon with winds of 60 m/s and made landfall over Guangdong China on October 21 as a weak typhoon with winds of 42 m/s. Figure 1 shows the tracks of three typhoons and the location of GPS stations (GPS-FJXM and GPS-HNWZ belong to China Meteorological Administration, GPS-HKST belongs to Hong Kong Satellite Positioning Reference Station Network), digital ionosonde (FKT-DPS belongs to Chinese Meridian Project) and ionospheric Scintillation Monitor (SZT-ISM belongs to Chinese Meridian Project). Table 1 shows the time, location, winds, level and radius about Typhoon Meranti, Sarika and Haima while they made landfall over China.

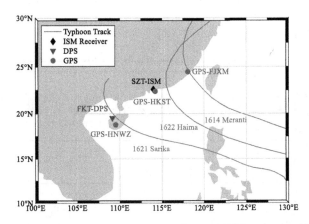

Fig. 1. Typhoon track and distribution of GPS, ISM Receiver and DPS.

Table 1. Information about typhoon when they made landfall over China.

No.	Time (UT)	Lat. °	Lon. °	Winds m/s	Level	Radius (km)
1614	19 h, 14th, Sep.	24.5	118.3	52	15	200
1621	1 h, 18th, Oct.	18.8	110.4	45	14	260
1622	6 h, 21st, Oct.	22.8	115.1	42	14	350

2.2   Solar and Geomagnetic Activity

In general, the solar activity index F10.7 represents low, medium and high levels of solar activity during [70 sfu 100 sfu], [100 sfu 150 sfu] and [150 sfu 250 sfu], respectively. The geomagnetic activity Dst index at [−50 nT −30 nT], [−100 nT −50 nT], [−200 nT −100 nT], and Dst less than −200nT represent small, moderate, large, and intense geomagnetic storms, respectively. The Kp index at [0 2], [3 4], 5, 6, and [7 9] represents quiet, unstable, small, large, and severe geomagnetic storms. As shown in Fig. 2, the solar activity during Typhoon Meranti, Sarika and Haima were at low level and some moderate geomagnetic storms occurred on 13th October before Sarika and Haima formed. The geomagnetic activities were all quiet when Typhoon Meranti, Sarika, and Haima made landfall over China. Hence, it can be inferred that the solar and geomagnetic activities might not trigger ionospheric disturbances.

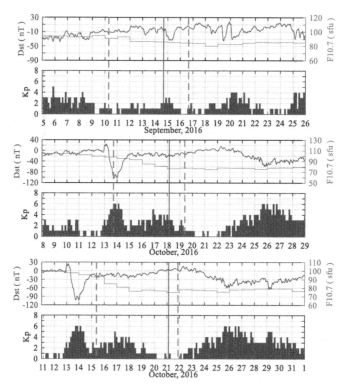

Fig. 2. Geomagnetic activity Dst index, Kp index and solar activity F10.7 index. (The red line denotes the time point when Typhoon Meranti, Sarika, and Haima land on China. The two pink lines denotes the time points of typhoons (Meranti, Sarika, and Haima) formed and dissipated.)

3　Results and Discussions

3.1　GPS TEC Response to Typhoon

Figure 3 demonstrates the ionospheric TEC sequences before and after typhoons' landfall extracted from GPS stations FJXM, HNWZ and HKST dual observations and the abnormal TEC using the correlation coefficient method. The details of the TEC derivation from the GPS dual observations (Sezen et al. 2013; Arikan et al. 2008) and the anomaly detection method (Ke et al. 2018) will not be discussed here. The ionospheric TEC occurred a large positive abnormal about 20TECU before Typhoon Meranti struck Xiamen, while the solar and geomagnetic activities are all at low level. When the anomaly occurred, Meranti had just passed through the southern part of Taiwan, and the distance between typhoon eye and Xiamen was about 300 km. At this time, Meranti had a wind speed of 65 m/s and its seven-level impact radius was about 350 km. On 14th October, a large anomaly of TEC occurred because of the moderate geomagnetic storms been displayed by Fig. 2. As same as Typhoon Meranti, Positive abnormal of ionospheric TEC occurred before Sarika and Haima made landfall. However, a negative abnormal of TEC occurred after Sarika's landfall and a positive abnormal of TEC occurred after Haima's landfall.

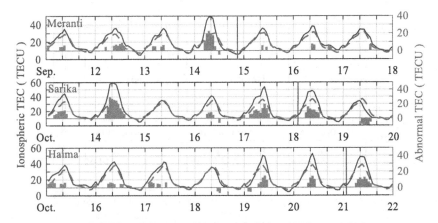

Fig. 3. Ionospheric TEC anomaly sequence during Typhoon Meranti, Sarika and Haima. (The blue lines indicate the ionospheric TEC extracted from FJXM, HNWZ and HKST GPS data. The pink lines and brown histogram indicate the background value of TEC and Abnormal TEC calculated by the correlation coefficient method respectively.). (Color figure online)

3.2   GPS Ionospheric Scintillation Response to Typhoon

When the GPS signal passes through the ionosphere, it is affected by the non-uniformity of the ionospheric structure, resulting in irregular changes in signal amplitude and phase. Based on GPS single data from ZET-ISM as shown in Fig. 1, the ionospheric amplitude scintillation index S_4 of all GPS satellites calculated (Luo et al. 2018). Figure 4 shows the distribution and quantity of the ionospheric puncture points of GPS satellites in region (22°N–25°N, 117°E–120°E) for Meranti, region (17°N–20°N, 109°E–112°E) for Sarika and region (20°N–23°N, 115°E–117°E) for Haima.

On 13th September, the quantity of S4 > 0.1 in region (22°N–25°N, 117°E–120°E) was 101, when Typhoon Meranti was about 500 km away from Taiwan. The next day, Meranti moved from Taiwan to Xiamen, and landed on Xiamen at night. The quantity of S4 > 0.1 increases to 127 in this region. On 15th September, the typhoon had already made landfall over Xiamen and continued to move inland. The quantity of S4 > 0.1 on this day reduced to 102 in the same region.

Typhoon Sarika affected area (17°N–20°N, 109°E–112°E) was closer to the Earth's equator than Meranti affected area, so the intensity and possibility of ionospheric scintillation were also higher. On 17th October, the quantity of S4 > 0.2 was 54 when Sarika moved to Hainan and made landfall at night. The quantity was more than the before day and the next day.

Since the area (20°N–23°N, 115°E–117°E) affected by Typhoon Haima, is very close to SZT-ISM station, the satellite elevation angle in this range is very high, and the probability of occurrence of S4 > 0.1 is very low. On 20th and 21th October, the quantity of S4 > 0.1 in this region is 0. At 0:00 21st October Haima was 150 km away from Guangdong, and after 6 h Haima made landfall over Guangdong. On this day, the quantity of S4 > 0.1 is 7, and they were distributed around the typhoon path.

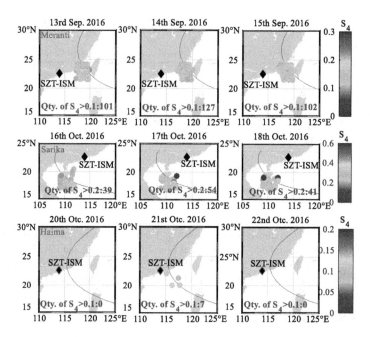

Fig. 4. Distribution of the ionospheric puncture point of S4 > 0.2 or 0.1

3.3   The Characteristics in E/F1/F2 Layer Response to Typhoon

The ionosphere is divided into layers D, E, F1 and F2, and the morphological characteristics of each layer of ionosphere are different. Although the ionospheric TEC and scintillation data have the advantages of spatial distribution, they cannot detect the characteristics of each layer of the D, E, F1 and F2 layers of the ionosphere in the vertical direction. Using the digital ionosonde installed in Fuke, Hainan, to detect the morphological changes of the E, E1, F1 and F2 layers of the ionosphere before and after the Typhoon Sarika made landfall over Hainan. The result is shown in Fig. 5.

On 12th, 13th and 14th October, the critical frequency foF1 of the ionospheric F1 layer fluctuated significantly. The critical frequency foF2 of the ionospheric F2 layer had a positive anomaly about 5 MHz at 12 o'clock on 13th October. The critical frequency foE of the ionospheric E layer showed a positive anomaly about 2 MHz on 12th October. The three days of the ionospheric E, F1 and F2 layers all showed abnormal disturbances, but at this time Typhoon Sarika just formed near the southeast of Philippines, so the abnormal of ionospheric E, F1 and F2 was not associated with the typhoon. It can be seen from Fig. 2 that the three-day geomagnetic activity Kp index was at level 4, so the occurrence of low-level geomagnetic storms led to abnormal of the E, F1 and F2 layers observed by the digital ionosonde at the Fuke station in Hainan. On 15th, 16th and 17th October, the critical frequency foF1 of the F1 layer was still higher than the background value about 0.8 MHz, but the change was stable. The value of the critical frequency foE of the E layer was also higher than the background value about 1.5 MHz, and the change was stable too. The value of the critical frequency foF2

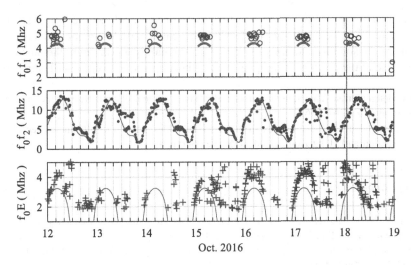

Fig. 5. Variation in the ionosphere foF1, foF2 and foE from October 12 to 19, 2016

of the F2 layer was basically consistent with the background value. With the Typhoon Sarika landing on Hainan, the E, F1 and F2 layers above the Hainan had experienced small-scale anomalies. The F2 layer foF2 increases abnormally before the typhoon's landfall, and tended to be normal when the typhoon landed on Hainan. Then there was a small increase in abnormality after typhoon's landfall.

4   Conclusions

Based on ground-based GPS, ionospheric scintillation, and digital ionosonde data, this paper selects three typhoons that struck China in 2016, and analyzes the morphological characteristics of ionospheric anomalies response to typhoon. The results are as follows:

1) The day before Typhoon Meranti Sarika and Haima made landfall over china, positive anomaly all occurred of ionospheric TEC over their landfall point. And the day after Typhoon Sarika and Haima made landfall over china, the ionospheric TEC occurred positive anomaly over their landfall too.

2) Before the Typhoon Meranti, Sarika and Haima made landfall, the probability and intensity of ionospheric scintillation of GPS satellites in the affected areas increased.

3) With Typhoon Haima striking Hainan, the critical frequency of ionospheric E, F1 and F2 layers over Hainan had disturbances of meso-micro scale.

Typhoon is a strong convective weather in the lower atmosphere. The downdraft at the center and around the typhoon indirectly leads to the upward rise of the top of the turbulent layer at 100 km, which leads to the increase of neutral particles in the ionosphere. With the direct radiation of the sun, neutral particles are ionized that lead to irregular ionospheric anomalies. When GPS signals pass through the anomalous ionosphere to the receiver, the signal receives interference or even scintillation occurs.

Acknowledgements. This study is supported by the National Natural Science Foundation of China (grant no. 41674036).

We acknowledge the use of data from the Chinese Meridian Project, China Meteorological Administration and Hong Kong Geodetic Survey Services.

References

Arikan, F., Nayir, H., Sezen, U., et al.: Estimation of single station inter frequency receiver bias using GPS-TEC. Radio Sci. **43**(4), 1–13 (2008)

Bauer, S.J.: An apparent ionospheric response to the passage of hurricanes. J. Geophys. Res. **63**(1), 265–269 (1958)

Chou, M.Y., Lin, C.H., Yue, J., Chang, L.C., Tsai, H.F., Chen, C.H.: Medium-scale traveling ionospheric disturbances triggered by super typhoon Nepartak (2016). Geophys. Res. Lett. **44**, 7569–7577 (2017)

Davies, K., Jones, J.E.: Ionospheric disturbances in the F2 region associated with severe thunderstorms. J. Atmos. Sci. **28**, 254–262 (1971)

Huang, Y.N., Cheng, K., Chen, S.W.: On the detection of acoustic-gravity waves generated by typhoon by use of real time HF Doppler frequency shift sounding system. Radio Sci. **20**(4), 897–906 (1985)

Hung, R.J., Phan, T., Smith, R.E.: Observation of gravity waves during the extreme tornado outbreak of 3 April 1974. J. Atmos. Terr. Phys. **40**(7), 831–843 (1978)

Ke, F.Y., Wang, J.L., Tu, M.H., et al.: Characteristics and coupling mechanism of GPS ionospheric scintillation responses to the tropical cyclones in Australia. GPS Solutions **23**(2), 34 (2019)

Ke, F.Y., Wang, J.L., Tu, M.H., et al.: Enhancing reliability of seism-ionospheric anomaly detection with the linear correlation between total electron content and the solar activity index F10.7: Nepal earthquake 2015. J. Geodyn. **121**, 88–95 (2018)

Liu, Y.M., Wang, J.S., Xiao, Z., Suo, Y.C.: A possible mechanism of typhoon effects on the ionospheric F2 layer. Chin. J. Space Sci. **26**(2), 92–97 (2006)

Liu, Y.M.: The influence of typhoon on the F2 layer of the ionosphere and the integral difference method for predicting the ionospheric TEC. Peking University (2006b)

Luo, X., Lou, Y., Xiao, Q., et al.: Investigation of ionospheric scintillation effects on BDS precise point positioning at low-latitude regions. GPS Solutions **22**(3), 63 (2018)

Sezen, U., Arikan, F., Arikan, O., et al.: Online, automatic, near-real time estimation of GPS-TEC: IONOLAB-TEC. Space Weather **11**(5), 297–305 (2013)

Shen, C.S.: The correlations between the typhoon and the foF2 of ionosphere. Chin. J. Space Sci. **2**, 335–340 (1982)

Song, Q., Ding, F., Zhang, X., Mao, T.: GPS detection of the ionospheric disturbances over China due to impacts of Typhoon Rammasum and Matmo. J. Geophys. Res. Space Phy. **122**, 1055–1063 (2017)

Vanina-Dart, L.B., Sharkov, E.A.: Main results of recent investigations into the physical mechanisms of the interaction of tropical cyclones and the ionosphere. Izvestiya Atmos. Oceanic Phys. **52**(9), 1120–1127 (2016)

Wang, J.S.: Chronic or Permanent coupling (CoP coupling) between the lower and upper martian atmospheres. Geophys. Res. Abs. **7**, 05855 (2005)

Wang, X., Ke, F., Cao, Y.C., et al.: Combination of GPS, HY-2A and COSMIC observations to establish global ionospheric map. Indian J. Geo-Mar. Sci. **47**(05), 1000–1010 (2018)

Xiao, Z., Xiao, S., Hao, Y., et al.: Morphological features of ionospheric response to typhoon. J. Geophys. Res. Space Phys. **112**(A4) (2007)

A Mutual Authentication Lightweight RFID Protocol for IoT Devices

Yong Lu[1]($\boxtimes$), Anxi Wang[2,3,4], and Shuai Liu[3]

[1] School of Management Science and Engineering, Nanjing University of Information Science and Technology, Nanjing 210044, China
luyong@nuist.edu.cn
[2] Guizhou Provincial Key Laboratory of Public Big Data, GuiZhou University, Guiyang 550025, Guizhou, China
anxi_wang@126.com
[3] School of Computer and Software, Nanjing University of Information Science and Technology, Nanjing 210044, China
shuai_liu@nuist.edu.cn
[4] Guangdong Provincial Key Laboratory of Data Security and Privacy Protection, Guangzhou 510632, China

Abstract. The IoT data security is a hot topic at a data time. Personal privacy data may be easily leaked to data collectors in an open network environment. If the collectors get enough data, they can analyze the habit and interest of every IoT user, which may give helpful advice or cause endless harass. RFID authentication protocol in IoT is a powerful way to avoid the essential data leaked to data collectors. The previous protocols protect the security of RFID system. But they cannot guard the privacy of RFID system. The protocol we proposed achieves both the privacy and security.

Keywords: Authentication · Anonymity · Radio frequency identification (RFID) · Internet of Thing (IOT)

1 Introduction

Internet of Thing is an architecture where everything can be connected to the Internet and communicate with one another through special devices. IoT is rapidly applied into in many fields such as smartphones, wearable devices, asset management, vehicle [1, 2]. Due to IoT approaching people's daily lives gradually, people pay more attention to the privacy security of IoT. At an open environment, lack of necessary protection, the information of personal devices can be collected by everyone. The malicious attackers may use the collected information to obtain the habit of people and guess the bank account password. Thus, people may suffer from malicious harassment or property

Supported by the Foundation of Guizhou Key Laboratory of Public Big Data (No.2018BDKFJJ003), the Opening Project of Guangdong Key Laboratory of Data Security and Privacy Protection (No.2017B030301004).

J. Shen et al. (Eds.): IC3 2019, CCIS 1227, pp. 518–525, 2020.
https://doi.org/10.1007/978-981-15-6113-9_58

damage. By utilizing the mechanism of authentication protection, the IoT system at least protect one kind of user's privacy in a certain degree [3–5].

Radio frequency identification (RFID) is one of the most important basic technologies in IoT application [6]. As we all know, a simple RFID system usually consists of three parts, namely tag, reader, and server. We can attach the tag to the surface of an object or insert the tag into one object. The tag plays an important role when we need to collect information and help an object communicate with the reader or server [7]. To avoid the illegal attacker gets private data the and damages RFID system, an authentication is applied into the RFID system. In the authentication of RFID system, the tag is a crucial role. However, the tag is constrained by resources and only provides lightweight operation.

We refer to the work of our predecessors and propose our scheme. We make the following three contributions in this paper. We proposed an authentication protocol that can provide a secure mutual authentication. In our scheme, the server can be used to authenticate the tag and reader and the tag also can be used to confirm the identity of reader and server, which is a departure from previous work on RFID security. Our scheme achieves strong security, such as tag anonymity, mutual authentication, replay attack resistance, forward security, Anti-Dos attack. Our scheme will be used in large scale RFID system in our expectation. In addition, we improve the data table [8] in our scheme to obtain efficient authentication.

2 Related Work

In previous literature, there are a lot of RFID authentication protocols which all utilize public key infrastructure or lightweight mechanism.

Protocols based on public key cryptography need to improve RFID tag hardware to compute the complex and large data. The RFID hardware improvements can be find at [9, 10]. That is not easy. Lightweight protocols can be deployed into current RFID tag hardware [11, 12]. We make a brief discussion of RFID lightweight protocols. Weis et al. proposed Hash-lock [13] which uses a hash value to identify tags. Their scheme requires reader to try all keys in the database to validate a tag's replay, which causes the slow authentication. Chien proposed a mutual authentication protocol [14], which achieves the standard of EPC Class 1 Generation 2 to defend synchronization and anti-replay attacks. But their protocol lacks a crucial anonymity which ensures the privacy of user's identity. Sarah's RFID protocol is based on cloud [15], which has large storage and computation performance. However, Sarah's protocol lacks tag anonymity. Tian's protocol [16] just uses three kinds lightweight bit operation to achieve several security privacy protocol in a degree, which can be enhanced by us. [16] uses three new different kinds secret values and other three old different kinds secret values to resist de-synchronization attack. That protocol has a bad efficiency to authenticate the tag. To meet large-scale authentication requirements, we need an efficient scheme.

The protocol we proposed needs less computing resources and can provide several secure protections including tag anonymity, mutual authentication, forward security, replay attack resistance.

3   Lightweight RFID Scheme

3.1   Notations and Index Data Table

In order to introduce the proposed protocol, it is necessary to show some of the notations defined or used in this scheme and their implication which all will be presented in Table 1.

Table 1. Notation.

Notation	Description
R	Indicates an RFID reader's identity
T	Indicates an RFID tag's identity
Q	Indicates some necessary initial information
K, K_{new}	Indicates a session number shared by the reader and tag
sk	Indicates the reader's private key preallocated by server via a secure channel
N_R	A random number generated by an RFID reader
N_T	A random number generated by an RFID tag
$W(y)$	Indicates the number of non-zero bits in y
$Rot(x, y)$	Indicates the cyclic left shift $W(y)$ bits
$Hash()$	Indicates a secure one-way hash function
$PRNG()$	Indicates the pseudo-random noise generation function
$\oplus$	Indicates a XOR operation by the bitwise
$\|$	Indicates a concatenation operation
$Mark$	Indicates the current status in a session

In this scheme, in order to achieve the efficient information retrieval in the reader and server, we employ a table [6] called index data table (IDT). Especially, we need to check the index value firstly and then get index content exactly after we successfully search the matched index value in the reader or server.

In reader, we issue a table shown in Table 2 which contains the index $Rot(R, T) \oplus K$ and the index value content K. In addition, we issue a table shown in Table 3 to server which contains the index value $Hash(sk \oplus Rot(R, T))$ and the index value content $Rot(T, R)$.

Table 2. Reader's index data table (RIDT).

Index	Index content
$Rot(R, T) \oplus K$	K
...	...

Table 3. Server's index data table (SIDT).

Index	Index content
$Hash\,(sk \oplus Rot(R,T))$	$Rot\,(T,R)$
...	...

3.2 Proposed Protocol

Mutual authentication lightweight RFID protocol is depicted in the Fig. 1. We describe its details as follows.

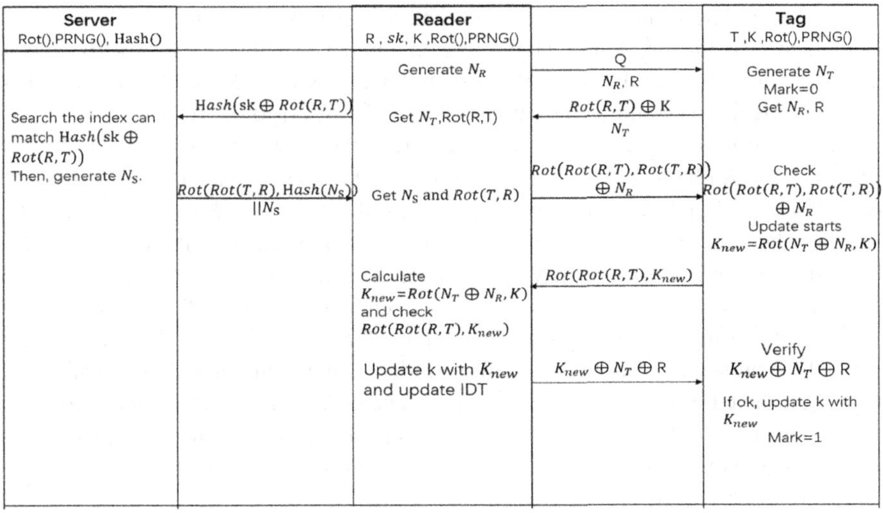

Server		Reader		Tag
Rot(),PRNG(), Hash()		R , sk, K ,Rot(),PRNG()		T ,K ,Rot(),PRNG()
		Generate N_R	$\xrightarrow{\quad Q \quad}$ $\xrightarrow{\quad N_R, R \quad}$	Generate N_T Mark=0 Get N_R, R
Search the index can match $Hash(sk \oplus Rot(R,T))$ Then, generate N_S.	$\xleftarrow{Hash(sk \oplus Rot(R,T))}$	Get N_T,Rot(R,T)	$\xleftarrow{Rot(R,T) \oplus K}$ $\xleftarrow{\quad N_T \quad}$	
	$\xrightarrow{Rot(Rot(T,R), Hash(N_S)) \parallel N_S}$	Get N_S and $Rot(T,R)$	$\xrightarrow{Rot(Rot(R,T), Rot(T,R)) \oplus N_R}$	Check $Rot(Rot(R,T), Rot(T,R)) \oplus N_R$ Update starts $K_{new}=Rot(N_T \oplus N_R, K)$
		Calculate $K_{new}=Rot(N_T \oplus N_R, K)$ and check $Rot(Rot(R,T), K_{new})$	$\xleftarrow{Rot(Rot(R,T), K_{new})}$	
		Update k with K_{new} and update IDT	$\xrightarrow{K_{new} \oplus N_T \oplus R}$	Verify $K_{new} \oplus N_T \oplus R$ If ok, update k with K_{new} Mark=1

Fig. 1. The authenticated protocol which we propose.

In the first step, the reader will generate N_R which is a random number, and sends N_R, Q as well as R to the tag. Then the tag will get N_R and set the value of *Mark* to "0" that means it is a new session. The tag computes $Rot\,(R,T) \oplus K$ and sends it as well as N_T which is generated by itself to the reader.

In the second step, the reader searches the corresponding index content in its RIDT basing on the received the index $Rot\,(R,T) \oplus K$ If it can be found, that means the previous session was executed correctly and the current session will be executable. At the same time, obtain N_T and $Rot\,(R,T)$. It is noted that $Rot\,(R,T)$ can be computed by $Rot\,(R,T) \oplus K$ XOR K. After those operations has been done, the reader uses its key sk and the value $Rot\,(R,T)$ to compute $Hash\,(sk \oplus Rot(R,T))$ And then the reader will send the message containing $Hash\,(sk \oplus Rot(R,T))$ to the server. However, if the received value is not matched in RIDT, the protocol will stop for the wrong index value.

In the third step, the server will firstly match the index value according to the received value $Hash(sk \oplus Rot(R,T))$. If there is no matched value, the server will stop the protocol. Since the index values are computed by using the valid values of tags and readers, the failed match retrieval indicates the tag or reader is fake. If there is a matched index, the server will generate a random number N_S. It means that the reader and tag is authenticated by the server. Then the server uses that index's content value $Rot(T,R)$ and the random number N_S to calculate the $Rot(Rot(T,R), Hash(N_S))$. The server sends $Rot(Rot(T,R), Hash(N_S))||N_S$ to the reader.

In the fourth step, N_S is obtained by the reader. Then the reader can calculate the value $Rot(T,R)$ according to the received value $Rot(Rot(T,R), Hash(N_S))||N_S$. The reader then sends $Rot(Rot(R,T), Rot(T,R)) \oplus N_R$ to the tag. After receiving the value, the tag will check $Rot(Rot(R,T), Rot(T,R)) \oplus N_R$ by using the local parameter R, T, N_R to calculate the value. If the value is right, it indicates the reader and the server is authenticated by the tag. After that, the session number K will be updated with the new value K_{new}. The tag calculates the new session number $K_{new} = Rot(N_R \oplus N_T, K)$. Then the tag sends the message including $Rot(Rot(R,T), K_{new})$ to the reader.

In the fifth step, the reader will calculate the new session number $K_{new}^* = Rot(N_R \oplus N_T, K)$ by using its local parameter N_R, N_T, and K. Then the reader uses the local $Rot(R,T)$ and K_{new}^* to calculate the local value $Rot(Rot(R,T), K_{new})^*$ for checking the validity of message from tag. If that value is equal to the received value, the reader will update the K with K_{new} and the index with $Rot(R,T) \oplus K_{new}$ in its Index Data Table. After those operations, the reader sends $K_{new} \oplus N_T \oplus R$ to the tag.

After the fifth step, through the operation of $K_{new} \oplus N_T \oplus R \oplus N_T \oplus R$, we can check the new session number K_{new} from reader. If the value of K_{new} is equal to the local K_{new}, the tag will update old K with the value of K_{new} and set the value of $Mark$ to be "1", which indicates the authentication and update are successfully completed. Our scheme also takes some strategy to resist de-synchronization attack, which is introduced in Security analysis.

4 Security Analysis

In this section, we will show some necessary analysis of our protocol's security, against many different types of common attacks in such an open RFID system.

- **Tag Anonymity:** The anonymity of the tag can protect the privacy of the tag and avoid the illegal attacker to imitate the valid tag. For the attackers, they cannot obtain or imitate the valid identities of many tags even if they may illegally obtain the relevant information of one valid tag. Because the identity T is only stored in the local. Even sending authentication information, the identity of the tag is mixed with other parameter and transmitted in the form of ciphertext. So, the anonymity of tag is achieved in our scheme.
- **Mutual Authentication:** In the wireless communication environment, some attackers can pretend a legal party to receive or send information, which may cause privacy leaks or break the RFID system. So, guaranteeing the privacy security, it is necessary to authenticate the party in our scheme. For the server, it is vital to ensure

the validity tag and the reader. The server needs to process large and different data in time, so it does not process and give a respond to message from illegal users, which can save the storage and calculation resource. For the reader it is same as server. Upon receiving $Rot(R, T) \oplus K$, the reader can check the message and send message to server after ensuring the message is right. The server can verify the message from the reader, which means the tag and reader can be authenticated by the server. Because the reader's private key sk and $Rot(R, T)$ is never public. In addition, we assume the channel between reader and server is secure and against replay-attack. The tag can use local parameters to authenticate the message from reader, which indicates the server and the reader can be authenticated by the tag. Because that message value $Rot(Rot(R, T), Rot(T, R)) \oplus N_R$ is calculated by using the parameter from reader and server. In addition, the reader can authenticate the tag by checking $Rot(Rot(R, T), K_{new})$.

- **Replay Attack Resistance:** Replay attack is a kind of common attacks, which may be avoided by adding a random number or timestamp. In our protocol, the random N_T, N_R and N_S are generated by the tag, reader, and server respectively. Those random numbers and session number K will change or update in every new session. Even if the attackers get some messages about current session, they still cannot use that information to attack future session. So the proposed protocol can resist replay attacks.

- **Forward Security:** If an attack illegally gets any secret knowledge from current session, the attack cannot guess any useful knowledge about the previous communication. The random numbers N_T, N_R and N_S used in our protocol are just used once for current session and changed in every different session. So it is impossible to guess the previous secret values using some current message value. Moreover, session number K shared between reader and tag also is changed for updating $K_{new} = Rot(N_R \oplus N_T, K)$. Therefore, proposed protocol achieves the forward security.

- **Anti-DoS Attack:** In the proposed protocol, a data table is used in the reader and a data table is used in the sever, which balances the performance overhead of traversal search. When the received value is not valid, the reader or server can stop the protocol, which avoids to exhaust the computing and storage resources that is named as denial of service attack (DoS).

- **Resist De-synchronization Attack:** Synchronization attack is a common attack in different update operations. When the update operation is broken, the later or next session may fail. So, it is essential to resist that attack. In our scheme, we will store K_{new} in tag even the bad check received value, which indicates we will not update the value of K. In next session, when the first attempt is failed, the tag can use the store K_{new} to try this protocol again. So, this protocol can defend de-synchronization attack. In addition, the update of K_{new} or K will be executed after successful checking $K_{new} \oplus N_T \oplus R$.

5　Performance Analysis

What is known to all, the computation and communication of passive tag is constrained. In order to design an efficient and secure protocol, it is necessary for us to account the performance of the proposed protocol.

In our proposed protocol, it just uses some lightweight operations, XOR, the cascade operation, the left cyclic shift [14] and hash operation. But the hash operation is used in reader and server. Comparing to the protocol [15] containing hash operations in tags, it costs less computation resources and storage. If the max length of communication data block is denoted as L in the authentication protocol [6], the communication cost of this protocol is 5*L. The communication cost of [6] is 8*L and the communication cost of [15] is 7*L. So, we achieve better communication performance.

6　Conclusions

This paper shows that we can achieve mutual authentication and defend different attacks. We propose that the tag authenticate the reader and server, which is important to achieve the security. Other schemes just achieve the server to authenticate the reader and tag, but they do not help the tag authenticate both server and reader. The improving index table can raise the efficiency of searching key information. We also need to give a formal proof to confirm our protocol's security strongly, which is the weakness of the paper. That is our next work, which can help us to authenticate large scale authentication and management in the future.

Acknowledgments. This work is supported by the Foundation of Guizhou Key Laboratory of Public Big Data No. 2018BDKFJJ003, the Opening Project of Guangdong Key Laboratory of Data Security and Privacy Protection No. 2017B030301004 and MOE (Ministry of Education in China) Youth Foundation Project of Humanities and Social Sciences No. 11YJC870018.

References

1. Chen, D., et al.: S2M: a lightweight acoustic fingerprints based wireless device authentication protocol. IEEE Internet Things J. **4**(1), 88–100 (2017)
2. Jia, X., et al.: RFID technology and its applications in Internet of Things (IoT). In: International Conference on Consumer Electronics. IEEE (2012)
3. Juang, W.S., Chen, S.T., Liaw, H.T.: Robust and efficient password-authenticated key agreement using smart cards. IEEE Trans. Ind. Electron. **15**(6), 2551–2556 (2008)
4. Sun, D.Z., et al.: Improvements of Juang's password-authenticated key agreement scheme using smart cards. IEEE Trans. Ind. Electron. **56**(6), 2284–2291 (2009)
5. Li, X., et al.: Anonymity enhancement on robust and efficient password-authenticated key agreement using smart cards. IEEE Trans. Ind. Electron. **57**(2), 793–800 (2010)
6. Fan, K., et al.: Lightweight and ultralightweight RFID mutual authentication protocol with cache in the reader for IoT in 5G. Secur. Commun. Netw. **9**(16), 3095–3104 (2016)
7. He, D., et al.: Lightweight and confidential data discovery and dissemination for wireless body area networks. IEEE J. Biomed. Heal. Inf. **18**(2), 440–448 (2017)

8. Fan, K., et al.: Lightweight RFID protocol for medical privacy protection in IoT. IEEE Trans. Ind. Inf. **14**(4), 1656–1665 (2018)
9. Juels, A.: RFID security and privacy: a research survey. IEEE J. Sel. Areas Commun. **24**(2), 381–394 (2006)
10. Rieback, M., et al.: The evolution of RFID security. IEEE Pervasive Comput. **5**(1), 62–69 (2006)
11. Czeskis, A., et al.: RFIDs and secret handshakes: defending against ghost-and-leech attacks and unauthorized reads with context-aware communications. In: ACM Conference on Computer & Communications Security, pp. 479–490 (2008)
12. Sakai, K., et al.: Dynamic bit encoding for privacy protection against correlation attacks in RFID backward channel. IEEE Trans. Comput. **62**(1), 112–123 (2013)
13. Weis, S.A., et al.: Security and privacy aspects of low-cost radio frequency identification systems. Lect. Notes Comput. Sci. **28**(2), 201–212 (2003)
14. Chien, H.Y., et al.: Mutual Authentication Protocol for RFID Conforming to EPC Class 1 Generation 2 Standards. Elsevier Science Publishers, Amsterdam (2007)
15. Abughazalah, S., Markantonakis, K., Mayes, K.: Secure improved cloud-based RFID authentication protocol. In: Garcia-Alfaro, J., et al. (eds.) DPM/QASA/SETOP -2014. LNCS, vol. 8872, pp. 147–164. Springer, Cham (2015). https://doi.org/10.1007/978-3-319-17016-9_10
16. Tian, Y., et al.: A new ultralightweight RFID authentication protocol with permutation. IEEE Commun. Lett. **16**(5), 702–705 (2012)

Decentralized E-Learning Marketplace: Managing Authorship and Tracking Access to Learning Materials Using Blockchain

Patrick Ocheja[1(✉)], Brendan Flanagan[2], and Hiroaki Ogata[2]

[1] Graduate School of Informatics, Kyoto University, 36-1 Yoshida-Honmachi,
Sakyo-Ku, Kyoto, Japan
ocheja.ileanwa.65s@st.kyoto-u.ac.jp
[2] Academic Center for Computing and Media Studies, Kyoto University,
Yoshida-Nihonmatsu, Sakyo-Ku, Kyoto 606-8501, Japan

Abstract. The difficulty in protecting and enforcing Intellectual Property (IP) rights has been a major obstacle to sharing intellectual works in digital forms. In this work, we present a prototype design for a decentralized e-learning market-place where teachers, authorized publishers and authors can publish their learning materials, establish conditions for allowing access, and grant or revoke access based on adherence or infringement of their rights. Using the Blockchain of Learning Logs (BOLL) and a digital book reader (BookRoll), we demonstrate how authors can be empowered to deploy smart contracts that protect and enforce these rights on their intellectual works in a distributed manner. We particularly use the blockchain in order to enable trust, trace-ability, rights protection, transparency and collaboration between authors and users of their work with no third party interference. Finally, we examine the implications of our proposed design, its limitations and directions for future work.

Keywords: Intellectual Property · Copyright elearning · Education privacy · Security · Blockchain · Smart contract · BOLL · Bookroll

1 Introduction

As the amount of data in the digital space continue to grow leading to more meaningful use cases, it is important to ensure appropriate use, reward ingenuity and foster collaboration among diverse parties. Intellectual Property Rights (IPR's) are rights that allow creators or owners of industrial properties (patents for inventions, trademarks, etc.) or copyrighted works (books, poems, artistic works, etc.) to benefit from their own work or investment in a creation by defining terms of usage which potential users of their work should comply with [1]. With many works on the use of technology to solve is-sues relating to IPR's protection and enforcement such as [2–7], we focus on specific issues on how educators including students and teachers can share learning materials in a secure, privacy-enabled, intellectual rights-aware and collaborative environment. new resources that other students or the teacher might find helpful. With more knowledge resulting from simple interactions like this, we consider it necessary to have a system that supports exchange of these resources, reward ingenuity, increase distribution,

© Springer Nature Singapore Pte Ltd. 2020
J. Shen et al. (Eds.): IC3 2019, CCIS 1227, pp. 526–535, 2020.
https://doi.org/10.1007/978-981-15-6113-9_59

foster collaboration, and protect the intellectual rights of the authors. Thus, this paper is inspired by the need to solve these problems:

1. How do we ensure trust and transparency between an author of a work that is made available to students and a sponsoring organization that pays for the author's work based on the usage quota of each student without using any third-party?
2. How can students generate and share learning materials with their peers across different schools with IPR's protection?
3. For companies, other learning organizations, and publishers, how can we establish a trusted and transparent network where these actors can co-exist and provide a wide pool of educational resources to students?.

We provide solutions to the above problems by extending the framework for a blockchain-based learning analytics platform proposed in [8] and implemented in [9] as a Blockchain of Learning Logs (BOLL). BOLL is a decentralized platform that enables logical movement of students and their academic records from one institution to another. Different from certificates or transcripts issuing systems, BOLL provides a mechanism to share learning logs of students on the various learning tools they interacted with while studying at different institutions. Our main contributions are:

1. We engender trust between sponsors, authors, and users of their work by providing transparent auditing of access to learning materials on a decentralized network.
2. We propose algorithms for programming smart contracts that enforce privacy and IPR's.
3. We design and discuss a framework for realizing a decentralized e-learning marketplace for a healthy co-existence among parties with varied interests.

The rest of this paper is organized as follows. The next section reviews related works and how our idea differ from existing solutions. This is followed by the section on our proposed framework and its components. Our discussions and ideas to solving identified problems and potential challenges are provided in the discussions section. Finally, we conclude this paper and provide potential directions for future work.

2   Related Work

There are many previous works on the need to protect IPR's in a digital world including [2, 10–13]. Anderson et al. [2] proposed an eXtensible Access Control Markup Language (XACML) geared towards achieving more usability of digital assets over a broad spectrum of applications and to also ensure security policies defined by asset owners are adhered to. Lorch, Proctor, Lepro, Kafura and Shah [3], demonstrated how XACML can be used by distributed systems to achieve a more robust access control. However, XACML and the implementation in [3] does not provide a mechanism for engendering trust between two or more potentially distrustful parties without the need for a central authority to act as a mediator.

To solve the problem of lack of trust and eliminate the need for a third-party, Zhu et al. [5] proposed a Transaction-based Access Control (TBAC) assets management sys-tem on blockchain which is fundamentally built on an Attribute-based Access Control (ABAC) model [14]. Using the Bitcoin blockchain, Zhu et al. showed how a digital asset can be escrowed on the blockchain and protected with policies defined in state functions. While the ideas proposed by Zhu et al. are similar to ours, we find their work limited in handling multi-party scenarios such as a sponsoring organization providing access to learning resources to a learner and only pays for what the learner actually uses (parties involved: sponsor-author-learner). Another difference is a sce-nario in academic where one or more authors may write a learning resource together but each of the authors would like to manage access or changes to their contributions differently. Thus, an education-specific implementation of IPR's management becomes even more necessary as educational assets are frequently accessed, updated, and constitute different kinds of data that engender further analytics by not just the asset owner but also the accessor (learner or her institution).

Also, we consider implementations of e-learning systems and/or marketplaces such as these [15–17] to be limited in facilitating interactions between potentially distrustful parties and the lack of transferability of learning footprints across different institutions. Hoffman et al. [7] and Janowicz et al. [6] also identified the possibility of using a de-centralized network to offer IPR's protection in education but focused on using the blockchain to manage journal management workflows.

The Blockchain of Learning Logs (BOLL) proposed in [9] enables the realization of lifelong learning logs for students as they move from one learning environment to another. The BOLL framework forms a fundamental background for our work. Our pro-posed framework allows broad auditing by concerned parties on the network and also permits digital content owners to decide how their contents from the DDS are served to other users in order to facilitate better policy violation tracking. Also, to improve learning outcomes, we introduce a mechanism for users to rate and recom-mend useful contents to one another.

3 Proposed Framework

Figure 1 shows our proposed framework for enabling a decentralized e-learning market-place for managing authorship and tracking access to digital contents on BOLL. BOLL Marketplace (BOLL-M) comprises of two groups of stakeholders; authors and users. Authors refer to actors on BOLL-M who own intellectual rights to learning materials made available in the marketplace. While users refer to members of the BOLL network who wish to access learning materials made available in the market and/or organizations that provide sponsorship for students to access learning materials (e.g. a government education ministry or other funding organizations). A student or teacher on BOLL-M can also be an author of a learning material in the marketplace. In this scenario, the student or teacher can rely on the learning material publishing tool made available to them by their institution. For publishers who do not belong to an

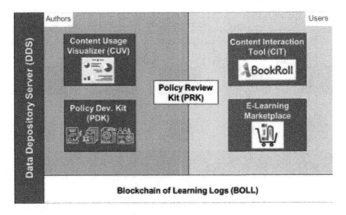

Fig. 1. Decentralized e-learning marketplace.

academic institution, it is required for them to be authorized by the BOLL Consortium proposed in [9]. After such an authorization is acquired, the publisher can setup a node on the BOLL network as show in Fig. 2. We will now describe each of the components shown in Fig. 1.

3.1 Policy Development Kit (PDK)

To enable appropriate use of learning materials on BOLL-M, it is necessary to define policies that accessors should comply with. We represent these policies as state transition functions in the smart contracts. Due to the technical skills required to write smart contracts, we provide multiple templates as a PDK which authors can choose from, adapt to their use case and install on BOLL to protect access to their learning materials. We represent these smart contracts in four broad categories.

One-time Signatory Policy (OSP). This refers to smart contracts that can be installed once and contain clauses on how a learning material can be accessed and used with the permission of the author. When an OSP is issued on BOLL-M, it is irrevocable and the issuer either grants a limited or lifetime access to a learning material depending on the duration specified. An example of a useful application is where students are given a one-time limited access to a professional or degree examination provided by another organization. In Algorithm 1, we show a pseudo-code for issuing an OSP by an author identified by public key, Pkauthor to a learner with public key, Pklearner. The implementations of the get Signer(message) and notify(message) are not shown in this work as one could easily use the public key resolution and event emitting features of the blockchain as well.

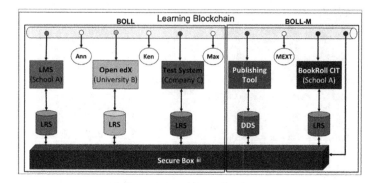

Fig. 2. Decentralized e-learning marketplace on BOLL

Dual Party Signatory Policy (DPSP). This is a revocable version of OSP where two parties can agree or disagree on the terms of access to a learning material. In a DPSP, terms of access can be modified by the issuer and such modified version becomes valid only when the accessor of the learning material agrees to the new terms. DPSP is useful in scenarios where an author maintains a continuously improved version of a learning material (e.g. lecture slides being updated regularly) and does not wish to create an entirely new version with the new changes. Although, smart contracts once installed are immutable, we achieve versioning of terms of access by allowing the execution of sets of instructions within the contract until all parties, S Pk append their signatures, SPk. The learner will be notified when this happens and only after that can the learner access such learning material. Algorithm 2 gives an illustration of a typical DPSP.

Multi Party Signatory Policy (MPSP). The MPSP is a collaboration enabled smart contract that allows multiple parties to determine the conditions for accessing a learning material. To enable multi party arbitration, MPSP starts off with the proposed clauses of the originating party. Another party can review these proposals and either refuse or accept them by invoking the state transitions functions contained in the initial MPSP. The originating party is tasked with initializing the MPSP with some settings including the participating parties (Pkvoter1 ...Pkvotern $\in$ VPk), the wining strategy (wining ratio) and the tie breaker (Pkarbiter) as shown in Algorithm 3. For example if a simple majority wining strategy is specified (wining ratio > 50%), the smart contract becomes valid if a simple majority agrees with the stated terms. In a case where a tie occurs, the parties can propose one party (Pkarbiter) whom they think should be the final arbiter. This party is then given the ability to override all votes and either accept or deny the approved installation of the MPSP terms. For instance, we find the MPSP useful in a three-party scenario where one party owns and provides the learning material (e.g. publisher), the second party pays for the learning material (e.g. government) and the third party is the consumer of the learning material at no cost (e.g. students). This solves the particular problem where an organization sponsors access to a learning material on behalf of the students. The tie breaker is useful in a case where the sponsoring organization is unable to ascertain the usefulness of a learning material to the student. In this case, both the sponsoring organization and the author can delegate the student to adjudge whether they find such learning material useful or not. Algorithm 4 provides a typical demonstration of the voting procedure on an MPSP.

Algorithm 1: Procedure for issuing a One-time Signatory Policy (OSP)

Pk_{author} : author's public key, $Pk_{learner}$: learner's public key Pk_{owner} : public key of the policy recipient

$getSigner(message)$: returns public key of the signer $notify(message)$: emits an event or sends a broadcast

1 **procedure issueOSP** (Pk_{author}, $Pk_{learner}$, $message$)
2 **if** $getSigner(message) = Pk_{author}$ **then**
3   **if** $Pk_{owner} = Pk_{author}$ **then**
4          $Pk_{owner} \longleftarrow Pk_{learner}$
5   notify($Pk_{learner}$)
6 **end procedure**;

Algorithm 2: Procedure for issuing a Dual Party Signatory Policy (DPSP)

S_{Pk} : public keys of stakeholders S'_{Pk} public keys of stakeholders who've approved DPSP

$access_{grant}$: indicates if DPSP is approved

1 **procedure issueDPSP** (Pk_{author}, $Pk_{learner}$, $message$)
2 **if** $access_{grant} = false$ **then**
3   **if** $Pk_{author} \in S_{Pk}$ and $getSigner(message) = Pk_{author}$ **then**
4   **if** $Pk_{author} \notin S'_{Pk}$ **then**
5             $S'_{Pk}[Pk_{author}] \longleftarrow 1$
6   **if** $length(S_{Pk}) = length(S'_{Pk})$ **then**
7             $Pk_{owner} \longleftarrow Pk_{learner}$
8             $access_{grant} \longleftarrow true$
9   notify($Pk_{learner}$)
10 **end procedure**;

Discovery Policy (DP). In order for an author or a publisher's learning material to show in the e-learning marketplace on BOLL-M, the author is required to install a DP smart contract. This contract contains a basic information about the learning material such as title, date published, version, description, applicable smart contracts (at least one of OSP, DPSP, MPSP). Because the DP smart contract does not contain the actual learning material or pointers to it, it is publicly available to anyone on the network to access but not modify.

Algorithm 3: Procedure for initializing a Multi Party Signatory Policy (MPSP) V_{Pk} : public keys of stakeholders who can vote $Pk_{arbiter}$: public key of arbiter (tie-breaker)

$arbitrate_{start}$: indicates if arbitration should/has started $Poll_{open}$: indicates if voting is still open $Votes_{Pk}$: votes cast $wining\_ratio$: the minimum fraction of total votes required for victory

1 **procedure initializeMPSP** (V_{Pk}, $Pk_{arbiter}$, $wining\_ratio$)
2 $V_{Pk} \longleftarrow V_{Pk}$
3 $arbiter \longleftarrow Pk_{arbiter}$
4 $arbitrate_{start} \longleftarrow false$
5 $Poll_{open} \longleftarrow true$
6 $Votes_{Pk} \longleftarrow \{\}$
7 $wining\_ratio \longleftarrow wining\_ratio$
8 **end procedure**;

Algorithm 4: Procedure for issuing a MPSP

Pk_{voter} : voter's public key $message$: a message signed by the voter $vote$: 1 (for) or -1 (against)

$sgn(value)$: signum function

1 **procedure** issueMPSP (Pk_{voter}, $message$, $vote$)
2 **if** $Poll_{open}$ **then**
3 | **if** $Pk_{voter} \in V_{Pk}$ **and** $getSigner(message) = Pk_{voter}$ **then**
4 | | $Votes_{Pk}[Pk_{voter}] \longleftarrow vote$
5 | | $totalVotes \longleftarrow \sum_{i=0}^{length(V_{Pk})} \begin{cases} Votes_{Pk}[V_{Pki}] & \text{if } V_{Pki} \in Votes_{Pk}. \\ 0 & \text{otherwise.} \end{cases}$
6 | | **if** $\dfrac{length(Votes_{Pk})}{length(V_{Pk})} \geq wining\_ratio$ **then**
7 | | | $no\_tie = |\dfrac{totalVotes}{length(Votes_{Pk})}| \geq wining\_ratio$
8 | | | **if** no_tie **then**
9 | | | | $approve \longleftarrow sgn(totalVotes)$
10 | | | **else**
11 | | | | $arbitrate_{start} \longleftarrow true$
12 | | | | $notify(arbiter)$
13 | | | **end**
14 | | | $Poll_{open} = false$
15 | | | $notify(V_{Pk})$
16 **else if** $arbitrate_{start}$ **then**
17 | **if** $getSigner(message) = arbiter$ **then**
18 | | $approve \longleftarrow vote$
19 | | $arbitrate_{start} \longleftarrow false$
20 | | $notify(V_{Pk})$
21 **end procedure**;

3.2   Policy Review Kit (PDK)

The PDK contains a set of useful tools for reviewing proposed as well as installed policies or smart contracts. This include policy modifying tools like acceptance, refusal or
arbitration, and learning material rating tools. The policy modifying tools are pro-vided
to ensure that other parties understand the defined terms before accepting them.
Learning material rating tools are useful for helping students find contents that might be
appropriate for different scenarios based on the perception of their peers or teachers.

3.3   Content Usage Visualizer (CUV)

We propose an interface for authors and sponsors to visualize the interactions users
have made with their learning materials. Since all transactions on the blockchain are
written to a public ledger whose contents are immutable, we realize the CUV by
querying this public ledger. However, because some functions in the installed smart
contracts do not modify state and thus do not lead to transactions, we consider it a
necessity that all request to view a learning material should invoke at least, a payable
transaction so that access histories can also be written to the ledger. This can be
achieved by mandating that all functions used to check access authorizations before
responding with the learning material should write on the ledger a message signed by
the accessor.

3.4   Data Depository Server (DDS)

We recommend that authors or publishers should store their learning materials on a DDS. For students and teachers who might not be able to setup the publishing tool shown in Fig. 2 (Consisting of CUV, PDK, and a part of PRK), we envisage that their schools would setup a shared publishing tool and a DDS. The DDS is connected to the SecureBox proposed in [8] and all requests sent to the DDS are verified with BOLL through the SecureBox.

3.5   E-Learning Marketplace

The e-learning marketplace is an interface that lists all learning materials published on BOLL-M. For an author's learning material to be displayed in the marketplace, it is required that the author should install a DP smart contract. This contract can be retrieved from the PDK and adapted to the author's use case. An author may also specify that their learning material can be discovered in the marketplace by only selected users.

3.6   Content Interaction Tool (CIT)

To ensure that intellectual rights of authors are not violated, we recommend that the tool for viewing escrowed learning materials, here referred to as Content Interaction Tool (CIT), should be connected to BOLL. In Fig. 2, we use BookRoll, a digital book reader as our CIT. BookRoll traditionally logs user interactions with digital books including bookmarking, highlights, page turns, etc. We consider these interactions enough to know when a user accesses an escrowed learning material. For recording a simple interaction on BOLL-M, one can simply log an access event when the content is being served for the first time. In a case where monitoring more interactions is desired, we can listen to specific events of the CIT. As BookRoll stores user logs on a Learning Record Store (LRS), it is possible to listen to page turn events and subsequently notify BOLL-M of these interactions. We note that monitoring of the user's interactions can be an invasion of privacy. Hence, we recommend that this should only be done according to the terms of the smart contracts.

4   Discussion

What Should Authors Track? By default, authors should only be aware of direct access such as a request to serve a given learning material. But in a case where detailed interactions such as page views are required to calculate cost, users should be informed during the policy review phase by selecting an appropriate smart contract. In turn, the CIT can then query BOLL-M before feeding forward any interaction events to the concerned smart contracts if required.

Collaborative Content Authoring. In a situation where two or more authors want to in-dependently improve a particular learning material, BOLL-M should provide a medium for such collaboration. This can be achieved through a version control mechanism with each author ascribing a particular smart contract to their own section. A simple approach might be to consider these versioned sections as either preceding or succeeding learning material depending on the changes time-line.

Rewarding Intellectual Contribution. Students who interact with certain learning materials, contribute useful learning materials and/or solve quiz problems could be rewarded with points. These points can then be traded for other learning materials or digital assets on BOLL-M or on other platforms.

5 Limitations

When a learning material is illegally reproduced outside the CIT, the reproduced version is no longer within the control of BOLL-M to manage its authorship rights. While this is a challenge, we recommend the development of interactive features within the CIT that renders any illegal reproduction unattractive and deficient in serving the original purpose. Also, in our proposed framework, we assume that authors and/or publishers will provide high quality learning materials. To detect content quality and/or plagiarism on BOLL-M, it is required to analyze contents of submitted learning materials. While we consider this to be outside the scope of our current framework, we suggest that users should take advantage of the PRK and report suspected plagiarized works through it.

6 Conclusion and Future Work

In this work, we proposed a framework for enabling decentralized e-learning marketplace on BOLL. This framework facilitates managing of intellectual rights, tracking access and fostering collaboration between different users, authors and publishers. We described how authors can define terms of use on their learning materials and how students can access these learning materials on the blockchain where their privacy is not violated. Alongside other smart contracts, MPSP smart contract plays an important role in facilitating collaborative policy formulation, learning material sponsorship and verifiable proof of learning material consumption. Future work will be focused on providing a concrete implementation of this framework on BOLL towards enabling BOLL as a wide-reaching system.

Acknowledgement. This work was partly supported by JSPS Grant-in-Aid for Scientific Research (S)16H06304 and NEDO Special Innovation Program on AI and Big Data 18102059-0.

References

1. May, C.: World Intellectual Property Organization (WIPO): Resurgence and the Development Agenda. Routledge, Abingdon (2006)
2. Anderson, A., et al.: Extensible access control markup language (xacml) version 1.0, OASIS (2003)

3. Lorch, M., Proctor, S., Lepro, R., Kafura, D., Shah, S.: First experiences using XACML for access control in distributed systems. In: Proceedings of the 2003 ACM Workshop on XML Security, pp. 25–37 (2003)

4. Cantor, S., Scavo, T.: Shibboleth architecture. Protoc. Prof. **10**, 16 (2005)

5. Zhu, Y., Qin, Y., Zhou, Z., Song, X., Liu, G., Chu, W.C.: Digital asset management with distributed permission over blockchain and attribute-based access control. In: 2018 IEEE International Conference on Services Computing (SCC), pp. 193–200 (2018)

6. Janowicz, K., et al.: On the prospects of blockchain and distributed ledger technologies for open science and academic publishing. In: Semantic Web. Preprint, pp. 1–11 (2018)

7. Hoffman, M.R., Ibáñez, L., Fryer, H., Simperl, E.: Smart papers: dynamic publications on the blockchain. In: European Semantic Web Conference, pp. 304–318 (2018)

8. Ocheja, P., Flanagan, B., Ogata, H.: Connecting decentralized learning records: a blockchain based learning analytics platform. In: LAK 2018: Proceedings of the 8th International Conference on Learning Analytics and Knowledge, pp. 265–269 (2018)

9. Ocheja, P., Flanagan, B., Ogata, H.: Managing lifelong learning records through blockchain. Res. Pract. Technol. Enhan. Learn. **14**(1), 4 (2019)

10. Foroughi, A., Albin, M., Gillard, S.: Digital rights management: a delicate balance between protection and accessibility. J. Inf. Sci. **28**(5), 389–395 (2000)

11. Chuang, J.C., Sirbu, M.A.: Network delivery of information goods: optimal pricing of articles and subscriptions. In: Proceedings Internet Publishing Beyond: Economic Digital Information Intellectual Property. Kennedy School of Government, Harvard University, Cambridge (2000)

12. National Research Council and others: The digital dilemma: Intellectual property in the information age, National Academies Press (2000)

13. Liu, Q., Safavi-Naini, R., Sheppard, N.P.: Digital rights management for content distribution. In: Proceedings of the Australasian Information Security Workshop Conference on ACSW Frontiers, vol. 21, pp. 49–58 (2003)

14. Hu, V.C., et al.: Guide to attribute based access control (ABAC) definition and considerations (draft). NIST Spec. Publ. **800**(162) (2013)

15. Emanuel, E.J.: Online education: MOOCs taken by educated few. Nature **503**(7476), 342 (2013)

16. Abelson, H.: The Creation of OpenCourseWare at MIT. J. Sci. Educ. Technol. **17**(2), 164–174 (2008)

17. Thompson, C.: How Khan Academy is changing the rules of education. Wired Mag. **126**, 1–5 (2011)

Business Application and Management
for Cognitive City

A Study on the Measurement
of the Development Level of Urban Exhibition
Industry in China and the Driving Effect
Towards International Trade in Goods

Te-Hsin Hsieh[(✉)] and Zhen Ye

School of International Business, Xiamen University Tan Kah Kee College,
Zhangzhou, China
thsieh@xujc.com

Abstract. The exhibition industry is one of the fastest growing sectors in China. At present, the evaluation methods and measurement process of the competitiveness of the urban exhibition industry in the domestic academic circles are still blank. This paper will use the Principal Component Analysis (PCA) method to establish the evaluation index system which measures the development level of urban exhibition industry. The exhibition industry is inseparable from the commodity trade. Based on the theory of international trade in goods, this thesis establishes an OLS regression model to analyze the relationship between the two empirically. The results of this study show that the development level of the urban exhibition industry plays a significant role in promoting international trade in goods, and the role of promoting imports are greater than exports. To further strengthen the promotion of the exhibition industry to the international trade of goods, the paper puts forward corresponding reasonable countermeasures and effective suggestions.

Keywords: Exhibition industry · International trade in goods · Exhibition competitiveness

1 Introduction

According to the China Convention and Exhibition Society (CCES), the GDP of China's tertiary industry accounted for 56.5% of the total in 2018. Among tertiary sectors, exhibition is a sunrise industry in China, featuring high income, environmental friendliness and high output and becoming a new economic driving force. The relevant literature shows that most economists regard exhibition industry as a catalyst for economic growth and international trade in goods. Given the strong capability of exhibition industry to promote trade, this study starts from the perspective of international trade and conducts empirical research on the development of exhibition industry, aiming to provide a reference for the urban areas that intend to boost exhibition industry. In doing so, the economic income generated by foreign trade can rise and the economic and social development of cities can be materialized. This marks the significance of this paper. This paper will make an empirical study on the relationship

© Springer Nature Singapore Pte Ltd. 2020
J. Shen et al. (Eds.): IC3 2019, CCIS 1227, pp. 539–544, 2020.
https://doi.org/10.1007/978-981-15-6113-9_60

between the development of China's urban exhibition industry and international trade in goods, analyzes the results and draws conclusions and proposes corresponding suggestions.

2 Definition of Exhibition Industry and Discussion on Relevant Literature

Exhibition is a kind of social activity that was produced and developed by economic exchange as a result of the development of social labor. Literally, exhibition has the dual functions of "demonstration" and "appreciation". The scale and date of an exhibition are fixed. Exhibitors show their products and sell them to the market, while the visitors know the real objects by attending exhibition. Exhibition aims is to provide a space where exhibitors interact with visitors. In terms of function, exhibitions can be divided into trade exhibitions and consumption exhibitions; regarding category, exhibitions can be divided into comprehensive exhibitions and professional exhibitions; with respect to scale, there are international, national and regional exhibitions, as well as the exclusive exhibition of a certain company; there are also exhibitions on a regular or irregular basis. According to the location, there are indoor, outdoor, travelling and mobile exhibition. Technically there are physical and online exhibitions.

3 Development Index of China's Urban Exhibition Industry

A representative evaluation indicator system can objectively and accurately reflect and evaluate the objects, and influence the authenticity and accuracy of the evaluation results. In order to ensure the authenticity, accuracy, comparability and operability of variable selection in this study, this paper adopts the literature analysis method. By studying the analysis of the development of Macao's exhibition industry conducted by Liu (2018) and the indicator system of exhibition industry competitiveness built by Wang (2009), this paper divides the urban exhibition industry development evaluation indicator system into three standard indicators: macro-economic environment, internal resources of exhibition industry and external industrial support for exhibition industry. Based on the data availability and quantitative analysis, this paper selects the indicators in Table 1 for the principal component analysis (PCA) of related variables, which helps to obtain the development index of exhibition industry in 30 cities within 5 years. The data of each index from 2012 to 2016 are obtained from *Statistic Report on China's Exhibition*, *China City Statistical Yearbook* and *China Statistical Yearbook for Regional Economy*.

Table 1. Evaluation indicator system of urban exhibition industry development

Standard indicator	Specific indicator	Indicator code
Macro-economic environment	GRP per capita (RMB)	S1
	GRP growth rate (%)	S2
	Proportion of tertiary industry in GRP (%)	S3
Internal resources of exhibition industry	Number of exhibitions	S4
	Exhibition area (ten thousand m2)	S5
	Number of professional exhibition halls	S6
	Indoor area of professional exhibition hall (ten thousand m2)	S7
	Number of exhibition management agencies	S8
External industrial support for exhibition industry	Number of users of bus and public electrical vehicles in the whole year (ten thousand person times)	S9
	Consumer product retailing (RMB ten thousand)	S10
	Number of telephone users by the end of year (ten thousand households)	S11
	Number of mobile phone users by the end of year (ten thousand households)	S12
	Number of broad band users by the end of year (ten thousand households)	S13

Source: Compiled by this study

4 Empirical Research on China's Urban Exhibition Industry Development and International Trade

4.1 Empirical Testing Result Analysis

By analyzing the impact coefficient of the urban exhibition industry development on the total foreign trade in goods (0.2455711), the paper concludes that the urban exhibition industry development will influence the international trade in goods of a city, and the better urban exhibition industry development of a city can correspondingly increase the total foreign trade in goods of the city.

By dividing the foreign trade in total imports of goods and total exports of goods, it can be concluded that the urban exhibition industry development has a positive impact on both imports and exports, and the better urban exhibition industry development of a city can correspondingly increase its total exports and imports of goods. Moreover, by comparing the impact coefficients of the urban exhibition industry development on exports and imports, it is found that the impact coefficient of exhibition industry on imports (0.278389) is greater than that on exports (0.2136542), indicating that the urban exhibition industry development will promote the exports of goods of a city, and the effect of promotion on exports is stronger than that on imports.

4.2 Policy Suggestions

The study of this paper proves that the active development of exhibition industry in cities will play a positive role in the international trade of goods. Ensuring the sustainable and sound development of exhibition industry is a prerequisite for the development of international trade of goods and provides a new way for China to promote the transformation and upgrading of international trade of goods. In addition, exhibition industry serves as a bridge. Apart from promoting the international trade of goods, the exhibition industry can enhance the sustainable regional economic development. Considering the inevitability of exhibition industry development, this study, referring to the experience of developed countries in promoting exhibition industry, as well as the internal (internal resources of exhibition industry) and external (support of external industries on exhibition industry) influencing factors mentioned in the empirical research, this paper proposes the following policy suggestions:

1. Referring to the Experience of Exhibition Industry Development in Developed Countries

(1) Introducing international talents and high-end exhibition facilities
In recent years, although the number of exhibition venues in China has been increasing, the management of the exhibition industry remains uneven. The lack of the concept of internationalized operation and professional and technical management personnel will not be conducive to the further internationalization of China's exhibition industry. It is not enough to build large-scale exhibition venues only. We should also learn more from the experience of countries with a mature exhibition industry. We can directly introduce international talents and high-end exhibition facilities, which can effectively shorten the time to explore the development path of the exhibition industry.

(2) Holding city-oriented exhibitions to avoid competition
The international exhibition industry has a long history, and the famous exhibition cities in foreign countries have their own characteristics, such as the International Music Products Exhibition in Ahnam, USA, the Medical Design and Manufacturing Exhibition, the International Radio Exhibition in Berlin, Germany, and the Automobile Exhibition. In recent years, due to the role of the exhibition industry in promoting urban economy, the governments of major cities in China are intensifying their support for the exhibition industry, resulting in the fiercer competition of the exhibition industry among cities. According to the above ranking of the exhibition industry development index of 30 cities from 2012 to 2016, Shanghai, Beijing, Guangzhou and Chongqing have been among the top cities steadily. To maintain competitive advantages, emerging exhibition cities must create leading exhibition brands and hold exhibitions that show the characteristics of this city, so as to avoid the vicious competition of exhibition industry among cities.

(3) Enhancing the Market Operating Ability of the Exhibition Industry
Exhibition is not a government action, but a commercial action. The experience of advanced exhibition cities in foreign countries shows that trade associations and professional companies have great advantages as exhibition organizers. The exhibition

industry development depends largely on the development of trade associations and professional companies. In the case of China, most exhibitions currently are dominated by the government. In order to enhance the market operation and professionalism of exhibition industry, the government should step back by strengthening the guidance for enterprises and associations and fully tapping the potential of these two to promote the marketization and specialization of exhibition industry, and to further enhance the innovation and service management of exhibition enterprises.

2. Improving Internal Resources for Exhibition Industry

(1) Establishing a sound management system for exhibition associations

China's urban exhibition industry is still at the stage of growth, with scattered resources, inefficient management and resource waste that are not in line with the rapid social development. In order to better coordinate the exhibition industry development, we must break through the bottleneck of the existing management system and establish an integrated management organization for unified management. China can refer to the supervisory systems of international exhibition associations, such as UFI, BIE, IAEM and SISO, to perfect the coordination and management of the industry associations in China, so that they can organize better exhibitions at home.

(2) Promoting the international recognition of exhibition certification agencies

At present, the four authoritative certification agencies in the exhibition industry, UFI, FKM, OJS and Eventgold, have their own mature evaluation system to evaluate exhibitions level. Eventgold provides certification services for exhibitions held in China, but the most authoritative organization for exhibition evaluation and certification is UFI worldwide. Our government should draw on the experience of UFI to further enhance Eventgold's international recognition.

3. Coordinated Development of External Industries that Support Exhibition Industry

(1) Promoting the common development of exhibition industry and external industries

This paper holds that the related industries that support the development of exhibition industry include transportation, retail, communication and information industries, and exhibition industry can promote the development of urban economy and related industries through its own development. The exhibition is often accompanied by a large number of people flow, which can promote the construction of transportation facilities; the rigid demand of non-local visitors for daily necessities and their flexible demand for special products provide a deluge of business opportunities for retail industry; exhibitions need better dissemination to attract more exhibitors and visitors from all over the world, which can encourage the host cities to further develop their communications and information industries.

(2) Taking advantage of e-commerce to promote online exhibitions

The emergence of e-commerce is based on the development of the Internet. With the popularization of e-commerce, the international exhibition industry has begun to pay attention to the combination of exhibition industry and information technology, and the Internet-based exhibition is being actively promoted. PROJECT SYNDICATE of the United States published an article saying that China is the largest e-commerce market in the world, accounting for more than 40% of the global total transaction and becoming the leader of digital consumption. Some small trade exhibitions in China find it difficult to attract foreign investment because of their small scale and lack of brand effect. The government can provide information technology assistance for this type of exhibitions and promote online exhibitions to improve economic efficiency and the influence of small exhibitions inside the industry. Compared with traditional physical exhibitions, online exhibitions are more convenient and rapid. The Interest-based exhibition industry is conducive to promoting online product transactions and expanding the space for trade of goods.

References

Wang, F.H., Kuo, C.J., Chang, Y.L.: Developing exhibition industry to improve competitiveness of cities. Commer. Res. **9**, 116–119 (2009)

Liu, Y.: Research on the measurement of the development of macao's exhibition industry and its industrial driving effect. National Chi Nan University (2018)

Study on the Key Items of a Maker Project Course Design in Higher Vocational Engineering

Chih-Chao Chung[1,2] and Chun-Chun Tung[1,3(✉)]

[1] Fortune Institute of Technology, Kaohsiung, Taiwan
t03050@fotech.edu.tw
[2] National Pingtung University of Science and Technology, Pingtung, Taiwan
[3] National Kaohsiung University of Science and Technology,
Kaohsiung, Taiwan
i107109115@nkust.edu.tw

Abstract. The purpose of this study is to discuss the key items of the Maker project course design for higher vocational engineering. By using a literature review and the Fuzzy Delphi method expert questionnaire, 8 experts in the Maker field were invited to help design the expert questionnaire to determine the key items of the Maker project course design. The results show that the Maker project course includes 6 major design items: student-centered, real situation topics, learning strategies, Maker Space, Internet community, publication of results, and teaching practice research. The implementation methods are specifically listed in detail, which can be used as a reference for Maker teaching application and future studies.

1 Introduction

The growing popularity of the Maker Movement abroad in recent years has also gradually received attention in Taiwan as well. The Executive Yuan launched the vMaker Project in 2014, which aims to enhance Maker power in three stages: first, look for vMaker to expose high school students to hands-on culture; second, "Make for All" digital manufacturing competition, which encourages Taiwanese Makers to come up with creative ideas and solve problems by hand; and finally, Fab Lab Asia Annual Meeting as a conclusion to enhance the visibility of Taiwanese Makers [1]. Therefore, many people have recently tried to bring Maker Movement into the field of education, such as introducing it in summer camps or after-school courses through teachers with Maker characteristics, etc. [2]. As Maker Movements are being implemented in school fields, Maker education has become more and more important.

Taiwan's 12-year National Basic Education curriculum outline is based on core literacy, and its concept of "spontaneity, interaction and common good" coincides with the spirit of the Maker Movement that attaches importance to sharing and co-creating. In the 12-year National Basic Education curriculum reform, new fields of science and technology have been added, including information technology and life science and technology, which emphasize hands-on course content [3, 4]. Based on this, Wang [5] proposed that schools should be encouraged to plan Maker project courses and

J. Shen et al. (Eds.): IC3 2019, CCIS 1227, pp. 545–552, 2020.
https://doi.org/10.1007/978-981-15-6113-9_61

integrate Maker education into interdisciplinary subjects. Schools at all levels can make good use of Maker space, plan Maker project courses in school-based courses, establish school characteristics, and encourage students to cultivate Maker expertise [6].

When Maker enters the educational system and becomes a formal or informal course, it is necessary to ensure the direction and benefit of Maker education through systematic planning and evaluation. In view of this, according to the Maker blueprint drawn by the Ministry of Education, this study explores the key design items for the construction of a Maker project course for higher vocational engineering. It is expected to specifically list the key points for the content design and teaching activities of a Maker project course, so as to help students realize creativity, make finished products according to their own designs, and enhance students' Maker mentality and skills.

2   Literature Review

2.1   Maker Education

In view of the fact that there are no clear indicators for Maker education in the formal field of schools, Yeh, Cheng, Lo, and Shih [7] attempted to demonstrate and integrate the "core concept of literacy orientation", the "concept of Maker promoters", the "interpretation of Maker by educators", and the "results of empirical research on Maker education". They presented three core concepts of: (1) hands-on practice; (2) team-work; and (3) knowledge sharing and putting forward corresponding operational definitions. Furthermore, Chang [8] pointed out that the creator education includes: (1) the sense of achievement in practice, the establishment of self-confidence; (2) experiential learning, deepening learning, and active learning; and (3) creative entrepreneurship and the cultivation of human quality. Maker education emphasizes that students "do it by hand", which can cultivate their key abilities of innovation, criticism, problem-solving, cooperation, and communication in the 21st century [9].

2.2   Maker Course Design

The learning content of Maker is mainly project-based science, and its learning type belongs to problem-based learning. This kind of learning content and type is a typical "learning through making" method. Graves [10] pointed out that starting to operate a Maker space in schools can be roughly divided into the following six steps. First, there should be promoters dedicated to Maker education. The second is to invite similar people to join. The third is to purchase resources and equipment for Maker space. The fourth is to establish Maker communities. The fifth is to hold workshops or plan and design tasks. The sixth is to integrate Maker education and formal courses. Chang [8] noted that the practice of creator education includes the four steps of playing, doing, thinking, and creating: (1) playing: playing or doing something; (2) doing: making finished products from materials; (3) thinking: thinking about the related problems of products in materials, tools, processing, and operating principles; and (4) creating: innovating, changing, extending, expanding, etc. There are more changes in innovation.

Chu and Tseng [11] proposed that the creator education should start from the campus and take students as the main body. Through the hands-on process, students can learn to constantly carry out trial and error, learn to think and make with their own hands, and train themselves to apply knowledge in real life situations and to realize a sense of accomplishment they create.

3 Research Design

According to the purpose of this study and the results of literature research, our research design is divided into the following parts.

3.1 Research Process

Through a literature review, this study integrates Maker spirit and Maker Space elements into project courses of higher vocational engineering, adopts the expert Fuzzy Delphi method, and invites 8 experts in the Maker field to help design expert questionnaires to determine the key items of a Maker project course design, which can serve as a reference for Maker project course planning.

3.2 Research Subjects

According to the research objective, the subjects of this study are experts and scholars of the Fuzzy Delphi method. In order to achieve reliability and validity of the research, this study invited 8 experts and scholars from Maker, Maker Space, innovative teaching, and course design fields to participate and provide suggestions on course integration planning and questionnaire development. The basic data of these 8 experts are shown in Table 1. They all have more than six years of rich practical and teaching experience in their fields of expertise.

Table 1. Summary of expert background.

No.	Gender	Teaching experience	Educational background	Title	Field of expertise
Expert 1	Male	18	Doctor	Professor	Maker space, Innovative teaching
Expert 2	Male	16	Doctor	Professor	Maker, Innovative teaching, Action learning
Expert 3	Female	15	Doctor	Professor	Maker, Innovative teaching, Course design
Expert 4	Male	6	Doctor	Associate professor	Maker, innovative teaching
Expert 5	Female	7	Doctor	Associate professor	Maker, Course design
Expert 6	Male	10	Master	Higher vocational teacher	Maker, Innovative teaching
Expert 7	Male	6	Master	Higher vocational teacher	Maker, Innovative teaching
Expert 8	Female	8	Master	Higher Vocational teacher	Maker, Innovative teaching

3.3   Research Method

Fuzzy Delphi Method (FDM) is a combination of the Delphi Method and Fuzzy Theory. The use of triangular fuzzy numbers not only can improve the shortcomings of the traditional Delphi Method, but can also solve the limitation of fuzziness of human nature. It is an effective method for index construction [12]. FDM represents the concentration trend of data in the form of intervals. According to the concept of membership function in Fuzzy Theory, the opinions of experts are integrated. The range of membership functions is between 0 and 1. The greater the degree of membership is, the closer the membership value is to 1, and vice versa (the smaller the degree, the closer it is to 0) [13]. Therefore, this study adopts the Fuzzy Delphi method to determine the key items of Maker project course design for higher vocational engineering.

3.4   Research Tools

The research tool of this study is the "Questionnaire on Key Items of Maker Project Course Design for Experts" compiled by ourselves. We adopted the Fuzzy Delphi method expert questionnaire, which was compiled by 3 experts and scholars, and then developed it into a formal questionnaire after revision. The reliability of the questionnaire was pre-tested by 50 higher vocational students. The pre-test conducted the Cronbach's α value test, and the α values of the sub-tables of Maker Spirit, Maker Space application, and Learning Outcome were .913, .867, and .844, while the α value of the total table was .896, indicating that the table had internal consistency.

4   Results and Discussion

According to the implementation of the research design, the results of the expert questionnaire survey on the key items of the Maker project course design for higher vocational engineering are as follows.

4.1   Analysis of Key Items in a Maker Project Course Design

This study integrates the suggestions on Maker education by Dougherty (2012), Kurti, Kurti and Fleming (2014), Liu (2016), Yeh, Cheng, Lo, and Shih (2017), Chu and Tseng (2018), Lin (2018), and Chang (2018) [2, 7–9, 11, 14, 15], refers to the 10 ways of introducing the Maker Movement into education in the Maker Space Work Manual-School Edition [16], and summarizes the design focus of a Maker project course for higher vocational engineering. The results of the questionnaire for experts with the Fuzzy Delphi method are shown in Table 2. The scores of each key item in course design are between 0.714 and 0.877. Among them, "design student-centered Maker course" has the highest score with a weight value of 0.877, followed by "create a friendly Maker space environment" with a weight value of 0.813, and "apply learning strategies into Maker teaching" with a weight value of 0.797.

The threshold value is mainly determined by the researcher subjectively, in order to obtain an appropriate, important, and sufficient number of evaluation indices, which are generally between 0.6 and 0.8 [17]. After analysis by the fuzzy Delphi method, the threshold value of 0.70 is used as the screening criterion in this study, and the consensus factors of experts on the key points of Maker project course design are as follows.

(1) Design a student-centered Maker course
(2) Set real situation issues
(3) Apply learning strategies into Maker teaching
(4) Create a friendly Maker Space environment
(5) Build a Maker learning network community platform
(6) Hold the publication of Maker's entity works

Table 2. Results of fuzzy delphi expert questionnaire.

Item (threshold = 0.70)	Number	Weight value	Ranking
(1) Design a student-centered Maker course	8	0.877	1
(2) Set real situation issues	8	0.783	4
(3) Apply learning strategies into Maker teaching	8	0.797	3
(4) Create a friendly Maker Space environment	8	0.813	2
(5) Build a Maker learning network community platform	8	0.714	6
(6) Hold the publication of Maker's entity works	8	0.749	5

4.2   Implementation Description of Key Items in a Maker Project Course Design

This research develops "6 key design items of Maker project courses" to further confirm its meaning and implementation focus, which are explained in sequence as follows.

(1) Design student-centered Maker courses

Maker project courses should take student-centered Maker spirit as the main objective and integrate the needs of knowledge, ability, learning, and application of engineering related majors in higher vocational colleges as the main axis. Based on the situation of creator education, students have the autonomy to complete learning tasks and resource selection, which naturally generates in-depth learning and stimulates creativity. As a result, students can develop the ability to discover problems, analyze problems, and solve problems [14]. Therefore, the scope of project courses has a high correlation with what students learn and is in line with students' interests. It enables students to actively collect data, discuss in groups, and learn cooperatively, and it emphasizes the importance of their learning experience.

(2) Set real situation issues

The theme of the project should integrate the current development trend of science and technology, carry out the theme design of Maker project courses, and enable students to interact with the environment to generate a learning experience. In the course, students are required to collect topics related to a theme in real life, and students in open groups are required to set topics that can be brought into play by themselves. In this way, students can make full use of what they have learned to solve problems in daily life with their knowledge and skills.

(3) Apply **learning strategies into Maker teaching**

Referring to Dougherty's [2] suggestion, Maker sports should be brought into the educational field and learning strategies should be integrated. Therefore, Maker project courses can use learning strategies such as STEAM, 6E, PBL, etc. to design Maker educational activities, encourage students to bring their creativity into play, and create their own stories of implementation processes [15]. Project learning tasks are planned and students need to complete them in sequence, which include literature discussion, theme setting, design drawing, creative design and thinking, practical problem solving, writing of written reports and publication of results, etc., which attach importance to the process and input in students' exploration.

(4) Build **learning platforms in Internet communities for creators**

In order to give full play to the characteristics of Maker education in the digital era, such as hands-on, creativity, sharing, customization, and from-bottom-to-top [18], Maker project courses should establish "learning community platforms for creators" to facilitate students to discuss and share knowledge and experience, so that students can have effective group discussions, exchanges, sharing, and learning, jointly think about solutions to problems, show creativity, and make tools or products that can solve problems by their own hands, regardless of the limitations of environment, region, and time.

(5) Create **a friendly Maker Space environment**

Maker project courses should give full play to the nature of cultivating students with their environment. Through activating Maker Space, a friendly environment for students can be created to meet and discuss, to share the use of digital equipment, manufacturing tools, programming techniques, and skills, and to combine cross-field knowledge and skills to stimulate everyone's creativity [19]. Maker Space should provide rich and diverse equipment for students to use, including laser engraving machines, 3D printing machines, digital inkjet cutting machines, drilling machines, milling machines, lathes, grinding machines, etc., so as to enable students to think and solve problems efficiently through the application and hands-on implementation of scientific and technological products that can help them achieve their goals.

(6) Hold publications **of Maker entity works**

The Maker project courses should plan "Maker entity work and achievement presentation meetings". Through achievement presentation meetings, each group of students can display their works and the functions they produce and share their creative design ideas as well as problems encountered in the production process and their solutions. Through creative sharing and mutual explanation among groups, the purpose of exchanging knowledge and practical experience is achieved, and the spirit of sharing and creating is brought into play.

5 Conclusion and Suggestions

Based on the discussion of Maker's related literature, this study concludes the "six key items of Maker's project course design" and applies the Fuzzy Delphi method to conduct expert questionnaire analysis. The consensus of expert opinions is calculated with the Fuzzy Delphi method, and it is confirmed that the key items of Maker's project course design include: (1) designing Maker courses with students as the main body; (2) setting up real situation topics; (3) integrating learning strategies into Maker teaching; (4) creating a friendly Maker Space environment; (5) building Maker learning Internet community platforms; and (6) holding publications of Maker entity works, etc., so as to confirm their meaning and implementation focus, to build a learning process with clear learning objectives and a Maker Space environment, to give full play to the nature of cultivating students' professional knowledge with the environment, to help students show creativity and create finished products, and to enhance their Maker attitude and knowledge.

References

1. Li, S.Y.: vMaker Plan. Business Next Homepage (2015). http://www.bnext.com.tw/article/view/id/35888. Accessed 12 May 2019
2. Dougherty, D.: The maker movement (2012). Accessed 1 Dec 2017. https://www.mitpressjournals.org/doi/pdf/%2010.1162/INOV_a_00135
3. Ministry of Education: Senior Secondary School Creative Maker Promotion Program. Ministry of Education, Taipei (2015)
4. National Academy for educational Research: The 12-year Basic Education Curriculum Outline - Science and Technology (2017). http://www.bnext.com.tw/article/view/id/35888. Accessed 12 May 2019
5. Wang, L.Y.: The enlightenment of the united states to promote the makerspace. Pulse Educ. **7**, 163–169 (2016)
6. Yang, M.S., Lin, Y.S.: The theory and practice of maker education. Taiwan Educ. Rev. **7**(2), 29–38 (2018)
7. Ye, J.Y., Cheng, Y.M., Lou, S.J., Shih, R.C.: Analysis of empirical research on maker education in Taiwan. Taiwan Educ. Rev. **7**(5), 180–188 (2018)
8. Chang, Y.S.: STEAM maker cross-domain integration, practice 12-year basic education. Taiwan Educ. Rev. **7**(2), 1–5 (2018)
9. Liu, M.C.: The concept and practice of maker education - the supporting design that should be concerned. Taiwan Educ. Rev. **5**(1), 158–159 (2016)
10. Graves, C.: Starting a School Makerspace from Scratch (2015). https://www.edutopia.org/blog/starting-school-makerspace-from-scratch-colleen-graves
11. Zhu, P.Z., Tseng, S.H.: An analysis of the practice of maker education in the 12-year basic education. Taiwan Educ. Rev. **7**(3), 160–163 (2018)
12. Ishikawa, A.: The max-min delphi method and fuzzy delphi method via fuzzy integration. Fuzzy Sets Syst. **55**, 241–253 (1993)
13. Pedrycz, W., Ekel, P., Parreiras, R.: Fuzzy Multicriteria Decision-Making: Models, Methods and Applications. John Wiley & Sons, Hoboken (2011)
14. Kurti, R.S., Kurti, D.L., Fleming, L.: The philosophy of educational makerspaces: part 1 of making an educational makerspace. Teach. Libr. **41**(5), 8–11 (2014)

15. Lin, K.Y.: The reflections and suggestions on promoting maker education in Taiwan. Taiwan Educ. Rev. **7**(2), 6–9 (2018)
16. Maker Media: Makerspace Playbook: School Edition (2013). http://makered.org/wp-content/uploads/2014/09/Makerspace-Playbook-Feb-2013.pdf

A Case Study of E-government Website Affinity Design

Yen-Chieh Huang[1]($\boxtimes$), Chung-Chien Wu[2], and Jen-Her Wu[2]

[1] Department of Information Management, Meiho University, Pingtung, Taiwan
x00003199@meiho.edu.tw
[2] Department of Information Management, Sun Yat-Sen University,
Kaohsiung, Taiwan

Abstract. With the rapid development of information and Communication Technologies (ICTs) and a wide range of mobile devices, the government website must provide rich information to adopt multi-mobile devices and response the public questions quickly. In Taiwan, the National Development Council (NDC) has established the website-checking system, then help each government organization to improve the website service. Therefore, the purpose of this study is to apply the design research method. To solve the current issues of the old website design, the case study was discussed based on theories of four main operation performance indicators by NDC, ten major digital service designs by UK Government, as well as six main principles of the user-friendly web design. The case study of government website, the old website used the checking system was 88 score points, but the new website got 99 points, the only one item didn't get is the website rank must under 1000 in Taiwan. The methodology developed by the process of this research provided appropriated solutions for the same issues, which county and municipal government may encounter with in the future. In response to the ever-changing web service, service innovations and future designs can be brought into institutions by applying it. In addition, it achieved goals, such as improving website performance, enhancing the transparency of government administrations, and strengthening the power of public supervision of governments.

Keywords: Website affinity design · Website performance assessment indicators · E-government

1 Introduction

In recent years there has been a dramatic proliferation of research concern with E-Government website. Considerable interest has arisen over effective and efficient networks that can deliver messages, two-way communication, share experiences and knowledge, and improving government organizations to respond to public needs quickly. With the rapid development of information and Communication Technologies (ICTs) and a wide range of mobile devices, popularity of internet usage has been growing exponentially. However, with growing innovation and evolution for Web technology and design, and with rapid development of website function towards modern, international, high efficiency and security standard, as well as fast-growing

© Springer Nature Singapore Pte Ltd. 2020
J. Shen et al. (Eds.): IC3 2019, CCIS 1227, pp. 553–562, 2020.
https://doi.org/10.1007/978-981-15-6113-9_62

mobile application service and users, the old web version with passive front-end features and lacked of innovation were unable to meet users' need. Therefore, the introduction of Response Web Design by county government has become a very important point, strengthening of user-friendly design, and creating user-friendly public websites.

By the development of Web User Interactive Service, more service of E-Government was expected. Thus, providing a variety of real-time information, improving the overall service and encouraging communications via the network, and providing the innovative digital service became top priority for E-Government. To improve the quality of E-Government and to enhance efficiency of central government, its institutions and each county and municipal government, the real-time checking system was established in 2008 by NDC (National Development Council). The web-checking system provided references for improving quality of the E-Government service, so that government could keep the maintenance of the websites on track, maximizing efficiency of the digital service. If the government website was checked by the tool, and didn't reach 90 points, the NDC will help them to improve the functions.

Nowadays, the Internet and mobile communications are booming, government websites have become an important conduit for public access to government information and services. And the county and municipal governments are committed to implementing mobile features to optimize public service. Therefore, how to use technology to solve problems and strengthen the government's website, for instance, issues of accessibility, user-friendly, user satisfaction and service quality, are also topics discussed in this case study. To solve the current issues of the old website design, the case study was discussed based on theories of four main operation performance indicators by NDC, ten major digital service designs by UK Government, as well as six main principles of the user-friendly web design. Finally, to improve situations through inspections of the websites by the real-time checking system, tests of the website platforms, services and participation of users etc., furthermore, developing future web design and service, strengthening innovation of the agency services.

2 Literature Review

2.1 The Government Website Operation Performance Indicators

Since 2003, the NDC operated by Government Rating Indicators of Brown University in the US. And since 1994, the suitable web checking indicators were established by referring E-Government Indicators of Waseda University, Japan [1]. To continuously reach international development trend level, many times, the performance indicators were revised and the government website were checked, adding perspectives about how to improving our E-Government service quality [2]. This study researched the website operation performance and the scope of indicators were mainly included, the Web interface, Web services, E-participation, Web future services design, based on four major and ten sub-item indicators. As shown in the Table 1.

Table 1. The website operation performance defined by this research

Indicator	Sub-indicator	Rating
Web interface	Layout planning, path link function, site navigation, disable welcome screen	13
Web services	Search function, site optimization rankings, formalities services, cross-platform	24
E-participation degree	Interactive service, interactive level	25
Web future service design	Cross-platform Fat Footer API	5

2.2   Ten Major Design Principles of Government UK

The UK Government portal was created by the UK Government Digital Services team (GDS) led by chief designer Ben Terrett, which has been rebuilt the design [3]. The focus was not only on the integration of thousands of UK Government websites into an entrance network. The core idea was to focus on the user's needs, rather than Government demands, making it easy and intuitive for users to use the site, creating a Government Digital Service that favors the popular choice.|In this study, the research aimed at Government UK design contents and services, which focused on User-centric design, developing ten principles of good designs.

2.3   The Principle of User-Friendly Web-Design

This study excerpted the six major website design principles defined by its specifications, corresponding to the thirteenth norm version. Its goal was to achieve design improvement, in terms of user-centric, interface-friendly and user-friendly, as well as, improvement for content selection and classification of govt. websites. And to emphasize that to the different user needs, the govt. can provide the best accessibility and usability, making it more credible, reliable and accessible, in order to improve user satisfaction and service quality.

2.3.1   Six Major Design Principles

The NDC [2] defined the Website design principles into "Home page use-friendly design, task-oriented, navigation and architecture, web and content design, search mechanism and service credibility, six major principles"

(1) Web user-friendly design: Enhance the design and functionality of the site to provide everyone using the service and to clearly communicate the purpose of the Govt's website.
(2) Task orientation: To understand the main tasks of the user. And in response to Web service needs, to provide friendly operational functions, assisting user in achieving specific tasks without setbacks.

(3) Navigation and structure: Establishing website navigation design and information architecture, so that users can more quickly find what their queries, site or information.

(4) Web content and design: For the form, content and text, page layout and visual design content, etc., establishing the standardized website specifications and visual consistency to achieve the best visual picture.

(5) Search mechanism: Improving the search mechanism to enhance interface availability to quickly and effectively help users finding the services and information they need.

(6) Service credibility: Maintaining information transparency of the content, real-time function, correctness to enhance the government's website professionalism and credibility.

2.3.2 NDC 13 Norms

The National Development Committee [1] considered that the clarity and usability of the website structure, which directly affected the user, whether they could successfully obtain information. Using particularly the user-displayed device, web page elements, navigation, home design, text style and links, pictures and multimedia, forms, search, essential contents, content presentation format, content management, mobile version, foreign language version of the website, 13 norms, to correspond to the above definition of the six user-friendly web design principles, guiding the Government Web developers to follow.

2.4   Responsive Web Design

The response web design is abbreviated as RWD. In Chinese it is also called self-adaptive, adaptive or responsive web design, corresponding web design etc. It enables smart phones and pads to obtain the best visual and interactive experience on websites and it is a frequently used method for web design technology practices. The design allowed the site to read and navigate on a wide variety of browsing devices, while reducing user actions such as scaling, panning, and scrolling [4].

2.5   Introduction and Application Web 2.0

The development of social network had become an important trend of electronic government, and the introduction and application of WEB 2.0 social media had become the best practical tool of Social Networking for Government policy marketing and measures [5]. Common government agencies websites were combined with Web 2.0 apps, social media applications such as Facebook, Twitter, Google, line, LinkedIn, Gmail, Weibo, MySpace, bloggers; Website self-development services such as polling, referral forwarding, tag bookmarks, etc., "Web2.0 helps public organizations deliver highly effective services" by its ability to produce social guidance, to serve the public interest, to create common values and to strengthen the Government's accountability and transparency."

3   Research Methodology

The methodology of this research is to apply the design research method [6]. To solve the problems of user experiences and mobile service on the old websites, this study using the website operating performance indicators developed by the NDC and the ten major principles of UK Govt. Digital Services Design combined with the analysis of benchmark websites domestic and foreign, developed Information technology solutions and found a basis for improving the quality of Web services. Finally, through the real-time detection system testing the new websites, the situation in Web interface, Services, E-participation (Web 2.0 Community Services), Web future services design and other problems would be improved.

3.1   Definition of the Problem and Motivation

This study focused on the web service quality of the global information network case, i.e. Web interface, service, E-participation level, etc. As there were issues on the old web version, i.e. complex and user-unfriendly web interface, low search efficiency, lack of two-way interactive sharing mechanism, etc., it caused problems, like poor public browsing rate, E-service did not meet public expectation, maintenance difficulty (parallel maintenance of PC and mobile version required) and so on, which resulted in poor web performance, and then, low public satisfaction and expectation problems of E-Government service.

3.2   Defining the Objectives of the Solution

This study is based on theories of four major performance rating indicators and ten major design principles of UK Govt. Digital Service design. Discussed were issues facing old website and how to use benchmark websites inland and abroad to analyze its advantage, evaluating and designing websites, developing a new version of global information network system. At last, validation acquired through the real-time inspection of system tools, enabling maximum web service effectiveness of this government case. The research results and development in practice served as reference and supplied other counties and cities government, when facing the same problems in the future.

3.3   Design and Development Solutions

According to operating performance indicators set by the NDC to define the problem points sorted out from this study and involved in it. First, the study foundations were based on theories of Web Performance Indicators of the NDC, the ten major principles of UK Gov Digital services, six major principles of web user- friendly design. Then with forward-looking benchmarking website analysis inland and abroad, it listed the introduction of response design technology according to inspection indicators, respectively.

Website key service would be strengthened and intelligent search mechanism, integration community platform tools, user-oriented one-column design, design pattern of information type on end page were provided.

It provided an improved approach to optimizing web user-friendly design, i.e. open API Tandem services, developing an integrated solution for cross-platform information technology, and mapping out practices in detail.

Finally, through the Government web real-time inspection system of the NDC, and after testing new websites, improvements of problems and in interface, service, E-participation degree (Web 2.0 community Service), website future service design etc. were examined to make sure whether new websites were sufficient to address problems raised in the motives of this study.

3.4   Show the Solution

This study weighed in six major problems before improvements, according to four major indicators, which were web interface, service, E-participation, web future service design, and showed the method of improvement. With images of its before and after development of information system, the extent of the resolution was shown.

3.5   Evaluation Solutions

After introducing of new Global Information Network of government case, measured data were tested by real-time inspection system of NDC Government website, recognizing resolution degree and its benefits of solutions listed in this study for case govt's external service.

4   Research Results

This study aimed to solve the problem in the case of old version of global Information network. According to web performance inspection guidelines, the part covered by this study were defined. Through in-depth analysis of domestic and foreign benchmarking site, optimization of improvement methods for web user-friendly design were listed, starting planning and designing. Gradually, old version of site layout, function, operation was improved, optimizing user browsing experience. Finally, for improvement of new website, performance of the site projects was reviewed, checking system test, verification solution level and effectiveness of the government's external web service.

According to "Standard for Govt. Website Edition and Content Management" and integration of web user-friendly Web Design Indicators which had six principles: "Friendly Homepage Design", "Task-oriented", "Navigation and Architecture", "Web page and Content Design", "Search Mechanism", "Service Credibility". These principles defined common norms of govt. web design and structure, platform design and content management, reaching goal of usability and providing web administrator quick guidance for design and maintenance.

4.1   Real-Time Inspection System on Government Website

In recent years, with the rapid development of information technology, changes of people's behavior accessing information occurred. Demands for websites has greatly increased. Government agencies facing problems of crossing browsers, data update frequency, web user-friendly and interactive services etc.

"The Government Website Real Time Inspection System" currently carried on meeting of online promotion explanation. In March 2016, it has been officially online to provide testing services. This study will use this stand-alone version of the test tool to detect improvements of each performance indicator of new web, verifying solutions listed in this case study of govt's external services for global web information and its benefits.

The ranges of detection and description were shown as follows:

1. Description of scoring rules for the inspection systems
   Seven major and nineteen sub-item indicators of "Government Website Operation Performance Indicators" included Website Interface (13%), Content (15%), Dimension Management (15%), Service (24%), E- Participation Degree (25%), Future Service Design (5%) self-testing on foreign language websites (3%) and so on. A total of 100 points. All were integrated into "Management Norms of the Government Website Version and Content" and "Reference Guides of Government Web Operation" which were related to each other, carrying out system automation inspection.
2. Introduction of functions of the Government Website Inspection System
   The government website Inspection system mainly provided four services, i.e. website- inspection, self-assessment, intelligent inspections and warnings, flow meter panels, etc. which conducted inspections of performances of website inde-pendent operations for organizations, enabling them to regularly review website operating mechanisms and service suitability, as well as implementing mechanisms of observation learning and self-management.

Name of Software: Real-Time Inspection system of Government Website

URL: http://webassessment.hamastar.com.tw/Default.aspx
Type of Tool: Website Inspection Service
Date of release: 2016 March 7

(1) Website Inspection: After setting up of basic web information, system would run tests automatically, gave feedback reports of inspections and listed recommen-dations for improvement and optimization for organizations.
(2) Website Self-evaluation: provides Authority Managers to browse rules of inspections and carries out manual self-assessments.
(3) Early Warning of Intelligent Inspections: provide agency managers to set web information classes.

According to these levels set, system would be scheduled to check if pages were updated. If it was not updated, the system would automatically send notification letters to managers. The case study of government website, the old website used the checking system was 88 score points, but the new website got 99 points, the only one item didn't get is the website rank must under 1000 in Taiwan.

5   Presentations and Evaluations

5.1   Introduction to the Case

In this section, the actual case would be used to demonstrate the solution. The case study of Global Information Network was domestic and county governments. Their current systems contained Chinese, English, Vietnamese and Indonesian websites of Global Information Networks, as well as 66 sub-websites, a total of 70 websites. The development environment of current systems was ASP.net 3.5. The database was Microsoft SQL Server 2005. In user context, the original Web system supported only some of browsers on the market, such as Internet Explorer version 8, Google Chrome, and the old website only supported desktop PCs. Principles for use of system's websites were to install separately Java and Flash play components, although the browser's original functions for data processing could be fully used, but it must download and install plug-in components.

5.2   Basis of New Website Planning

To address the problems faced by the previous web version, the study mainly based on "The Inspection Program of Government Web Operating Performance" set up by the NDC as main body. It combined Ten principles of UK Digital Services and in-depth analysis of domestic and foreign benchmarking site, joining service Innovation of Web IT Applications, in order to improve quality of web services.

5.2.1   Purpose of Improving Government Web Service Quality

As standards for IT and Government Web services continue to rise, in recent years the NDC has regularly conducted Performance Inspections of web operation, targeting central ministry and affiliated agencies, as well as county Government and affiliated tourism websites. It mainly assisted agencies to strengthen web information real-time, user-friendly operation and interactive designs, exerting maximum service efficiency of electronic Government website. But the results of inspections were only for internal reference improvements. And announced would agencies which has reached higher than 90 points of the inspection results, as learning samples.

5.2.2   To Identify the Needs of Redesign Opportunities

The case study of global Information network was launched in year 2009, providing public information bulletins and services of county offices and township city offices. But with updating and evolution of Web technology and design concepts and increase of web user numbers on mobile devices, the front page layouts and functions of legacy system could not meet the needs of users. Also, with rapid development of today's web technology, functions, efficiency and security are moving forwards to be more compliant with modernization of international standards. And it has long replaced the traditional passive websites. Contents are very innovative.

5.2.3 To Understand the Old Web Issues of the Case

The case of old version of the front page layouts and features of the Global Information Website, according to the "Inspection Rating of Government web operational performance" on Nov. 2014, has reached a total of 88 points (Date of inspection: Nov. 24, 2014) Referring to audit reports, first, it should be to improve web layouts and functions and to plan and design new solutions, the priority of improvements was marked.

5.3 Responsive Design Principles of the New Version

According to the contents of Waseda [6] and responsive web design advantages of this research, this is currently the best technical solution for solving problems related to multiple types of screen.

Technical features include no fixed page size, no mm or inches, no physical limitations, no hardware limitations. And with the website's establishment, there are more and more gadgets and template frameworks available. Pixel design, which is limited to the desktop and mobile, and has become history. The following instructions are the basic principles for how to use responsive web design to achieve a smooth web browsing experience.

1. Analysis of web resolution and recommendations of webpage
   Depending on the mobile device, three layout resolutions are proposed for each device, as illustrated in the following illustrations.
2. Focus on Web Content Design and less of User Interface
   Different from previous web design concepts, the first priority of this responsive web design is the readability of website information. Visitors to the website can quickly get the information they want.
3. To maintain Image contents readability and visual aesthetic
   With different resolutions by different browsing device, after changing of the pages, it keeps remaining highly readable web and the overall web visually appealing. It also reduces the user's handling, such as dragging, zooming in and out.
4. Focus on text readability
   On different browsing devices, the user can change the font size of the webpage without destroying the font.
5. Suitable for finger touch operation
   Depending on the interface size of the mobile vehicle, clicking on the link or button must be suitable for finger touch operation.
6. No use of FLASH
   Mobile device does not support Flash, other ideas need to be conceived for the web design effects, avoiding not displaying of contents.
7. Menu design
   According to the user's practical convenience, common Methods of menu design include sidebar menu, sliding menu, floating menu, etc., three presentation methods.

6 Conclusions

This study used the process steps of the Design Science Research Process to develop integrated solutions for planning cross-platform IT systems, responsive web design, enhanced website focus services, smart search mechanisms, integrated community platform tools, and Fat Footer end-page design. And open API Cascade services, etc., to improve the design of the website's affinity design, to produce the details of the implementation, and to provide an academic field to understand the process of promoting the electronic government service innovation.

Based on the background and motive of this research, goals and benefits of the new solution expected to achieve were listed below.

I. to improve web performance and service quality ratings within 99–95 scores.
II. to significantly improve the search rankings and visibility close to 50%.
III. to achieve over 50% increase of visitors of mobile device.

This study develops the methodology of process, other counties and city government websites in the future will provide a solution to the same problem. Enhance a friendly user experience, provide smart search services, and strengthen interaction and communication between the government and citizen, strengthen government mobile service innovation applications and forward-looking design, and improve the performance of the website and enhance the government's fast services. This study uses the website operation performance check index and the forward-looking benchmark website analysis at domestic and foreign to clearly define the relationship between interface design and user experience. The results of this study can be used as the basis and reference for future academic research on website affinity design.

References

1. Gardner, B.S.: Responsive web design: enriching the user experience. Sigma J. Inside Digit. Ecosyst. **11**(1), 13–19 (2011)
2. Government Digital Service: GDS, GOV.UK Design Principles, OGL: Open Government License 2.0, July 2012. https://www.gov.uk/design-principles. Accessed Nov 2015
3. National Development Council: Web guide Service, January 2015. http://www.webguide.nat. gov.tw/index.php/ch/read_file/home/id/104/app/downloads.html. Accessed Jan 2015
4. O'reilly, T.: What is web 2.0: design patterns and business models for the next generation of software. Commun. Strateg. **1**, 17–20 (2007)
5. Peffers, K., et al.: A design science research methodology for information systems research. J. Manag. Inf. Syst. **24**(3), 45–77 (2007)
6. Waseda University Institute of e-Government: The 2014 Waseda-IAC International E-Government Ranking, May 2014. http://www.e-gov.waseda.ac.jp/ranking2014.htm. Accessed Feb 2016

The Requirement Analysis for Developing the Assisted Living Technology for the Elderly

Sui-Hua Ho and Chiuhsiang Joe Lin$^{(\boxtimes)}$

Department of Industrial Management, National Taiwan University of Science and Technology, Taipei, Taiwan
cjoelin@mail.ntust.edu.tw

Abstract. The aging issues have become critical in the world and also in Asia society. In order to develop useful and effective assisted living technology to help the elderly users, the user-centered design process should include the requirement analysis. This research collected the experts' opinions through the multidisciplinary focus group to develop the personas from the perspectives of the elderly and caregivers. Based on the description of these two personas, the needs of the elderly users and the caregivers were identified. The possible features of the assisted living technology and the service plan were therefore developed by the identified needs of the elderly and caregivers. The finding of this research will provide future researchers and designers for developing the assisted living technologies and services for the elderly living in the community. Through the improved user experience of using technology by the elderly users, the elderly can interact with the assisted living technology independently and enhance their quality of life. Therefore, the caregivers' loads will be reduced. Then, the goal of aging in place will accomplish through the well-designed assisted living technologies and services for the elderly users.

Keywords: Aging · Assisted living technology · User experience

1 Research Background and Motivation

The population aging is a global issue. The proportion of older adults is particularly notable in Asia, and the aging population is still increasing rapidly [1]. According to the population projection reported by the National Development Council in Taiwan, the population ages 65 and above will reach over 20% in 2026. The health promotion and long term care are considered as important issues in the aging society [2]. Meanwhile, the assisted living technology can also provide support for the elderly and to help the caregivers in the community. For developing the assisted living technology and supporting services for the elderly, it is important to consider the elderly users' needs and requirements in their everyday life. This research focused on investigating the elderly's needs in their daily life. The potential solutions were developed for providing the assisted living technology and supporting services to enhance the elderly's independence and to lighten caregivers' loads.

© Springer Nature Singapore Pte Ltd. 2020
J. Shen et al. (Eds.): IC3 2019, CCIS 1227, pp. 563–568, 2020.
https://doi.org/10.1007/978-981-15-6113-9_63

2   Research Method

In order to develop the user centered assisted living technology and the supporting services for the elderly users, the following steps were carried out to collect information for the development of the elderly's requirements to support their healthy life.

2.1   Summary of Current Literatures

For the thorough understanding of the elderly's requirements in their daily living, the current literatures were searched and reviewed. The possible difficulties the elderly and their caregivers might face were also considered in the searching process. Based on the literature review and the interview with the elderly and caregivers, Christophorou, Georgiadis [3] summarized a list of twenty ICT (information and communication technology) services for aging well. The expected functions of robot in elderly care which was developed from the interview of 166 participants (including 35 elderly and 131 caregivers) in Cylkowska-Nowak, Tobis [4] research. Parsa, Rezapur-Shahkolai [5] summarized 7 themes of medication difficulties in elderly care from the elderly's perspectives. In the area of home care, Talarska, Kropińska [6] outlined the most common problems for improving independence of the elderly in community. For considering the cognitive declines in the elderly, Salatino, Gower [7] proposed the user requirements for the seniors with mild cognitive impairment. Based on the above literatures, three common needs, including medication service, meal preparation, and the management of daily necessities, were selected to be key issues in this research for developing the elderly's services.

2.2   Focus Group

In order to develop proper personas to describe the elderly's and caregivers' requirements, this research collected opinions and recommendations from the experts of the related disciplines through conducting the focus group. The focus group consisted of 4 experts from disciplines of psychology, management, ergonomics, and the occupational therapy in health science. Since these experts obtained the background knowledge of the aging issues in different fields, they could provide the perspectives in a multidisciplinary way. Among them, one expert came from psychology background and could provide her knowledge of elderly's psychosocial, and emotional needs. One expert obtained knowledge of management in her bachelor's and graduate study, and she could provide the points of view in the management of the elderly care. There was also one expert who had experiences of being an occupational therapist and specialized in the area of elderly care in hospital and community. All these experts had obtained at least one year experiences of studying courses or conducting researches in the field of user experience and the ergonomic design.

In the focus group, the experts could check the discussing issues on the projected screen simultaneously, and they were encouraged to provide their opinions through the process of brainstorming. The finding from the focus group would benefit to the construction of personas. The focus group consisted with the following steps: introduction, issue identification, share of related literatures, the development of subtopics, confirmation of the elderly's needs, and the confirmation of the caregivers' difficulties.

Step 1- Introduction. The experts, who participated in the focus group, introduced themselves about their backgrounds and the understanding of the elderly's issues.

Step 2- Issue identification. The focused issues in this focus group were summarized and outlined to be related to medication, meal preparation, and the management of daily necessities, which were the common issues the elderly needed to deal with.

Step 3- Share of related literatures. The current literatures collected by the research team were shared among the experts. These were the references the experts might but not be required to use.

Step 4- Development of subtopics. In this step, the experts were invited to share their opinions for developing the subtopics under the common issues, including medication, meal preparation, and the management of daily necessities. The subtopics developed were the specific difficulties the elderly might face in their daily life.

Step 5- Confirmation of the elderly's needs. Based on the experts' professional knowledge and experiences, they discussed and shared their opinions to develop the possible difficulties from the elderly's perspectives. The elderly's needs and requirements were developed and identified under the subtopics, in order to develop the matched persona for the elderly users.

Step 6- Confirmation of the caregivers' difficulties. Based on the discussions of the experts in the focus group, the caregivers' needs and requirements were also developed and identified under the subtopics, in order to develop the matched persona for the caregivers.

2.3   Development of Persona

The research team considered the results from the focus group and the literature review to develop the personas. According to the developed needs of the elderly and the difficulties of the caregivers, the matched personas for the elderly and caregivers were developed in this stage.

2.4   Summary of Needs Analysis and the Service Plan

Based on the personas for the elderly and caregivers, the research team constructed the needs analysis for the elderly users and the caregivers. The needs analysis was the basis for the further development of the service plan.

3 Result and Discussion

3.1 The Personas for the Elderly and Caregivers

Through conducting the focus group, this research collected the perspectives from the experts from the backgrounds of psychology, management, ergonomics, and the health science in occupational therapy. The issues focused on the areas of medication, meal preparation, and the management of daily necessities. Based on the discussion of the experts, the major features were developed on the basis of the elderly's motor, mental, and emotional conditions, and the subtopics included cognition, physical condition, social relationship, and the technology use. In the subtopic of cognition, the memory problem was considered as the most important issue for the elderly. The common medical problems of controlling the body sugar and blood pressure were two key considerations in the subtopic of physical condition. In addition, the emotional support was considered as the focused part in the social relationship, and the interaction of the mobile devices was considered as the major part in elderly's technology use.

After the focus group, the personas of elderly and caregiver were developed according to the summary of the needs of the elderly and caregivers in their daily life. The persona of the elderly was shown in Fig. 1, and the persona from the perspectives of caregivers was shown in Fig. 2.

Grandma Lin

Age: 72 years old
Gender: female
Occupation: retired teacher
Habits: go hiking
Residence: Taipei, Taiwan
Marriage: her husband passed away recently, lives with son currently
Education: B.S.

Mood changes: She previously liked to help others, optimistic and usually hanged out with husband to enjoy nice food and tourist spot. However, she becomes lonely and sad after her husband passed away.

- **Life:**

After retiring from high school, she lived happily with his family. She usually went to many tourist spots and went hiking with her husband to enjoy their wonderful life. However, after her husband passed away two years ago due to heart attack, she became sad and lonely. Her body condition changed a lot during these two years.

- **Body condition:**

She has been diagnosed with diabetes and hypertension, which were controlled by medication. She also got mild memory problems. Her son mentioned that she could not find out some important things at home recently. She sometimes forgets to have drugs and even forgets to eat meals. The meal preparation is also difficult for her.

Fig. 1. The persona from the perspectives of the elderly.

Susan Wang

Age: 37 years old	**Mood changes:**
Gender: female	- Her life changed a lot after getting married.
Occupation: housekeeper	
Habits: shopping	- She becomes emotional since too much loads of taking care for the family.
Residence: Tainan, Taiwan	
Marriage: married	
Education: B.S.	
Family: live with husband, 4-year-old-child, and husband's parents	

- **Life:** She needs to take care for the 4-year-old daughter and the parents of her husband, therefore, she can not have time for herself.
- **Difficulties as a caregiver:** Because her father-in-law and mother-in-law have different diseases, she needs to prepares different meals and medications for them. Sometimes she gets confused of the different needs of them. In addition, because she has to take care for the child simultaneously, she feels too busy to finish all tasks by herself.

Fig. 2. The persona from the perspectives of the caregivers.

3.2 The Needs Analysis and the Service Plan

According to the developed personas, the needs of the elderly and caregivers were identified for developing the assisted living technology and service plans. The identified needs of the elderly included to remind for taking medication, to arrange the balanced diet, to keep accompanied, and to manage personal belongings. Therefore, the assisted living technology and the service plan developed for the elderly would consist of the system to remind medication, to detect the condition of taking medicine, to provide records of having meals, and to give emotional support for elderly. The system to help the users organize personal belongings would also be important. There should also be a system to provide support of caregivers for taking care for the family.

4 Conclusion

This research collected the professional experiences from the experts from the multi-disciplinary focus group to develop the personas of the elderly and caregivers for identifying the users' needs of three key issues, including the medication services, meal preparation, and the management of daily necessities. The finding will contribute to the future development of the effective assisted living technology and service plans for the elderly users. It will benefit to enhance the independence of the elderly in their daily life and to reduce the caregiver's burden through the effective utilization of the assisted living technology. The ultimate goal will be to enhance the quality of life and accomplish the concept of aging in place for the elderly population.

References

1. Peng, D.: An overview of aging in the Asia/Oceania region: demography, projections, unique elements. Innov. Aging **1**(Suppl. 1), 999 (2017)
2. Kazawa, K., Rahman, M.M., Moriyama, M.: An investigation of factors influencing high usage of medical and long-term care services in an aging society in Japan. Asia Pac. J. Public Health **30**(2), 95–106 (2018)
3. Christophorou, C., et al.: ICT systems and services for ageing well: identification and assessment of an important set (package) of ICT services for active ageing and independent living. In: Kyriacou, E., Christofides, S., Pattichis, C.S. (eds.) XIV Mediterranean Conference on Medical and Biological Engineering and Computing 2016. IP, vol. 57, pp. 903–908. Springer, Cham (2016). https://doi.org/10.1007/978-3-319-32703-7_176
4. Cylkowska-Nowak, M., et al.: The robot in elderly care. In: The 2nd International Multidisciplinary Scientific Conference on Social Sciences and Arts SGEM2015, Albena, Bulgaria, book 1, vol. 1, pp. 1007–1014 (2015). https://doi.org/10.5593/SGEMSOCIAL2015/B11/S2.130
5. Parsa, P., et al.: Medication problems from the perspective of the elderly: a qualitative study. Elder. Health J. **4**(1), 29–34 (2018)
6. Talarska, D., et al.: The most common factors hindering the independent functioning of the elderly at home by age and sex. Eur. Rev. Med. Pharmacol. Sci. **21**(4), 775–785 (2017)
7. Salatino, C., et al.: The EnrichMe project: a robotic solution for independence and active aging of elderly people with MCI. In: Miesenberger, K., Bühler, C., Penaz, P. (eds.) ICCHP 2016. LNCS, vol. 9758, pp. 326–334. Springer, Cham (2016). https://doi.org/10.1007/978-3-319-41264-1_45

The Business Model of Maker Space – A Case Study of Taiwan Experience

Syuan-Chen Jhou[✉] and Sheng-Yi Wu

Nation Pingtung University, Pingtung City, Taiwan
a845697@gmail.com

Abstract. Since the word maker was introduced to Taiwan, it has caused a great wave of education and activities. The maker movement has been rapidly launched in Taiwan. Both government units and the private sector are building maker space, and also refer to foreign makers. Space all the tools, design courses and publicity Maker education. This study is a study of the operation of each of the founding centers. After waves of the maker movement, the two centers of the Maker Center, which can continue to operate, discuss the operational difficulties and business models, and conduct research on the nine aspects of the business model, trying to analyze the key ways in which it operates to make recommendations.

Keywords: Maker space · Business model 3 by 3 grid

1 Research Background and Motivation

Since the beginning of 2016, the culture of makers has been introduced to Taiwan from the United States. In the same year, Taiwan also spurred the wave of maker education. Therefore, many schools began to purchase a large number of manufacturing equipment, including 3D printers and laser engraving. Machines, a variety of maker space have arisen, hope to let more Taiwanese people experience the part of the maker culture, sharing, discussion, and self-made. Today, three years later, the trend of makers has gradually eased, and digital manufacturing tools have become more and more affordable. Some of the booming maker bases have already quietly closed down, and of course many bases still exist. Therefore, I hope to understand the maker bases that are still operating, their business experience, and the business model as the basis of the interview questions, investigate the business model of Taiwan's maker center, and understand the makers who are still in operation. The center, which operating model is used to support the operation of the maker center.

© Springer Nature Singapore Pte Ltd. 2020
J. Shen et al. (Eds.): IC3 2019, CCIS 1227, pp. 569–577, 2020.
https://doi.org/10.1007/978-981-15-6113-9_64

2 Literature Review

2.1 The Maker Movement

In 2005, Dale Dougherty founded "Make:" magazine, which gave birth to the maker movment, began to use the microcontroller and 3D printer to create works, and in 2006 held the first Maker Faire, invited people around the world who like to create, develop a platform for multiple exchanges. After the makers share their own works, in addition to learning new technologies and ideas, they can also have different creations or cooperation in different fields. This is the two key points in the maker movement. Collaborate with others. (Li 2015); (Peng 2015) Another reason for the rise of the maker movement came from the Media Lab of the Massachusetts Institute of Technology (MIT), which was founded in 1985 and both of which they studied with architecture or science and engineering subjects would not teach And irrelevant topics, they believe that "the identification of digital technology will induce (force) art and architecture across existing boundaries, and will also change the working patterns and methods of various professional fields, so it has been in the broadest sense from the beginning. Understanding the word "media" not only includes all the possibilities of the past, but also focuses on the future development. "By breaking the framework to solve social problems, and thus making cross-border cooperation, just like the current co-creators.

2.2 Business Modal

Since the emergence of e-commerce in the 1990s, the business model has begun to produce the phenomenon of middleware and retailer virtualization, which has been widely discussed and used by the public. The interpretations of various experts are also different, but roughly refers to the enterprises used to establish and provide valuable goods. Business activities with services to customers and thereby creating profits and corporate version values.

This research uses the "Business Model Canvas" as the basis for the design of this problem. The "Business Model Map" was proposed by Alexander Osterwalder, author of "Business Model Generation", and his team. It is a systematic organization of the "business model" through nine elements, and focuses on market demand. To understand how companies make money.

Osterwalder and Pigneur (2010) describes the business model as a way of how a company creates, delivers and acquires value for its customers in the book Profitable Generation. At the same time, the analysis mode of the business model is proposed, which provides a set of standards for all enterprises to evaluate the feasibility of commercial projects (Fig. 1).

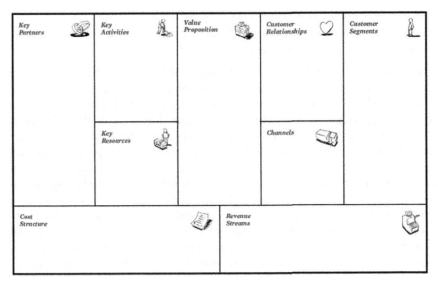

Fig. 1. Business model

3 Research Methods

The research tools of this research are based on the business model and develop access problems. Question contains

1. Maker space name:
2. How long have you been in this maker center?
3. Is there any major activity in this maker space, like the Maker Carnival? (key activities)
4. What are the costs in this space, such as the purchase of machines, the rent of the venue, the salary of the staff, the maintenance fee, etc.? (cost structure)
5. Do you have no important partners? (key partners)
6. What is the purpose of your establishment in this space? (value proposition)
7. What are the important resources in your team? Like a machine, a special job or a plan? (key resources)
8. Who are your target customers? (customer segments)
9. How do you usually interact with customers? It is like giving a course and so on. (customer relationships)
10. What methods would you use to promote your maker center, like on the internet or in magazines? (channels)
11. What is the source of funding for this maker space, such as membership fees, venue rentals, etc.? (revenue streams)
12. Is there a creative culture or work culture in the Maker Center?

13. What is the biggest dilemma you have encountered?
14. In the business model, what kind of marketing do you use to recruit creators or attract creators to join your team?

In the research subject part, this study takes Taiwan's maker base as the research subject, and the public and private maker space, which is the research business model, so it is based on the profitable maker space. At present, Taiwan's maker space, according to the Executive Yuan vMaker (2019) data, Taiwan currently (2019) the total number of maker space is about 88, and according to the nature of its establishment funds, divided into three maker spaces, including (a) Private: privately run maker space; (b) government-run private, government-sponsored, or coached transformation bases, and (c) school-attached, school-based or school-based maker spaces. This research mainly focuses on the profitable maker space, so we selected the Fablab STMC (Southern Taiwan Maker Center) and the Pàng de PanPlace for analysis.

Finally, in terms of research and analysis, this study analyzes the business model, and analyzes the nine dimensions of its key partners, target customers, and capital flow to understand how these maker spaces support the present after the makers retreat.

4   Results and Discussion

This study selected Fablab STMC (Southern Taiwan Maker Center) and Pàng de PanPlace for analysis based on the research purpose. Firstly, it was established in 2016 in the Fablab STMC. It was one of the maker bases set up in five locations in Taiwan after the government planned. It is currently managed by the Workforce Development Agency, MOL and operated by a private organization (PanMedia). It is a privately-run private base. It is transformed from a vocational training institute. Therefore, the target is the general public. Later, the spirit of the maker is added. That is to share. Discuss, create, and share ideas, make ideas visible to people, or share the work styles and experiences shared by others, and then discuss them so that ideas can collide with each other and finally create their own. After the discussion, I created it and shared it with others.

The maker space is a platform for people who have ideas to provide it with creative sharing, but it is also a stage. By showing, the public can see more people join. In the early days of the development of the base, there were no young people who needed to use the way of self-seeking or workshops to share with each other's life and reach out to all kinds of creators. At the same time, they also entered the enthusiasm of the southerners. In the crowd, people want to stay more, do not charge membership fees in the business, and provide free equipment borrowing, creative space, so that the creators have a development stage, while opening lectures, workshops and other courses. It will also be a monthly creator course with different themes. Try to use life as a starting point and stay close to the public life circle to achieve the resonance effect.

From the business model nine squares analysis as shown below (Table 1).

Table 1. Fablab STMC

Key partners: 1. PanMedia 2. Tainan City Government	Key activities: 1. Course	Value proposition: Everyone in the maker space is treated like a family. Through a platform like the maker center, more people can see different creators and make the creators more competitive	Customer relationship: 1. Family-like interaction	Customer segments: 1. The general public is interested in creation 2. Those who have already created the ability to be unexplored
	Key resources: 1. Machine equipment		Channel: General public	
Cost structure: 1. Machine purchase 2. Machine maintenance			Revenue streams: Most of the income is free or charged a fee, and the funds come from the PanMedia and the Tainan City Government	

1. Customer Segments: For the general public, including people who are interested in creating a variety of professionals after work, or people who are already engaged in creation but no one knows.
2. Value Proposition: create the feeling of a big family. Through cooperation and projects, the platform of maker space can enable more people to learn knowledge different from their own profession by sharing knowledge, and finally let the creative creators have the ability. Start your own business or do what you want to do.
3. Channel: Originally, I was doing vocational training, so most of them are based on the government and they are looking for themselves.
4. Customer Relationship: classifying customers, it is more like family members, renting studios is working partners, and the general public is like friends.
5. Revenue streams: It belongs to publicly-run private organizations, so part of the funds is provided and operated by pan-technical knowledge, plus the support of most Tainan municipal governments.
6. Key Resources: The use of equipment and equipment will be taught and assessed after joining the membership, and the equipment will be used after passing.
7. Key Activities: At the end of each month, the team at the maker base will start thinking about the theme to be started next month, such as a table or a stadium, and then branch out from this theme, so you can keep the theme. The ministry will repeat.

8. Key Partners: Pan-Knowledge knowledge, established in 2014 to invite Taiwanese scientific researchers, educators, enthusiasts, and all people affected by science to talk about science and relocate deep and complex scientific development back to the Taiwan Public Forum. And use rational thinking about the scientific orientation in social issues, and strive to provide the best occasions for scientific discussion, both online and offline.

9. Cost Structure: Space is the space of institutional units, mainly spent on the purchase and maintenance of machine facilities.

And about the Pàng de PanPlace, the Pàng de was established in 2013. At that time, it was applied for by FabLab Tainan. When you apply, you will need 3D printing, laser engraving and so on. There is also a space to apply and It is audited by two major US maker bases and has a party every year, like the fifth FAN5.

Every year, results are published, and these come from the three major trends of the maker space, general courses, activities, lectures, and then re-education and citizenship technology, in which nurturing counseling is a space, technology or machine for the new team. Support, guided by cultural creation and digital manufacturing, followed by citizen technology, this is a part of citizen participation, in the case of digital work, this is a plan for the master, in the traditional craft, by There is only one piece of work made by man-made, it is difficult to imitate it. It is more difficult to save the cultural skills. Therefore, the digital work plan is to save traditional skills and crafts by means of digital manufacturing. The other is digital electronic control. In the past, the use of machine tools may be used in the middle of the night, so it may cause disgust of neighbors. It is also the management of the machine. It manages the user's use time in the machine in a digitally controlled way. It can effectively maintain equipment, or it can also apply digital electronic control to other industries.

There is another group of people operating in Pàng de PanPlace, that is part of the community. Based on the spirit of makers, I hope to achieve Do it with others. I can do one thing with a group of people. This is the community. The party in the park is on Tuesday night, called "MakerTuesday", in the community business model. Let the people in the maker center have more technology to share, and it is an important partner for the fat land. If you want to continue cooperation after the general technical courses, you will let the general public join the community, and the society. The group will complete various projects together. After the cooperation, such people will start to have ideas. Maybe they want to mass production, start a company, etc., they will turn into entrepreneurship, enter the breeding stage, or become a sharer and enter the part of public technology.

"Playing new ideas in the old house." "There are a group of madmen here, thinking about how to make fat places better every day." This is probably a special element in Tainan, making some different changes in the old house.

From the business model nine squares analysis as shown below (Table 2).

Table 2. Pàng de PanPlace

Key partners: 1. PanMedia 2. Tainan City Government 3. Community	Key activities: 1. Course	Value proposition: A group of people who have made new ideas in the old house, by combining the old house features of Tainan, let the past technology talk to the current technology	Customer relationship: 1. Family-like interaction	Customer segments: 1. The general public is interested in creation
	Key resources: 1. Machine equipment		Channel: 1. General public 2. Internet	2. Those who have already created the ability to be unexplored
Cost structure: 1. Machine purchase 2. Machine maintenance			Revenue streams: Most of the income will be charged for some expenses, and the funds come from the Pan-Knowledge Knowledge and the Tainan Municipal Government	

1. Customer Segments: For the general public, including various occupations, people who are interested in creating after work, or who are already engaged in creation but no one knows.
2. Value Proposition: A group of people who play new ideas in the old house, through the combination of Tainan's old house features, let the past technology and the current technology dialogue.
3. Channel:
   (1) The general public: When the annual results exhibition is held, the public will be contacted to let the public see the works of the maker space.
   (2) Operate the official Facebook account, provide a space for makers to communicate, and let the community partners extend the opportunity to meet.
4. Customer Relationship: In the customer group, it is divided into community, studio partner, and general public. The community is the backbone of the base. The space in the base and the large part of it are completed by the community. They will also complete large projects together to realize the idea of DO IT Together".
5. Revenue streams: It belongs to publicly-run private organizations, so most of the funds are provided and operated by pan-technical knowledge, plus some income when doing activities.
6. Key Resources: The use of equipment and equipment will be taught and assessed after joining the membership, and the equipment will be used after passing.
7. Key Activities: There will be MakerTuesday's maker gatherings every week. People in the community will get together, share ideas, ideas, or sometimes hold workshops on Saturday to try to practice ideas.
8. Key Partners: PanMedia, established in 2014 to invite Taiwanese scientific researchers, educators, enthusiasts, and all people affected by science to talk about science and relocate deep and complex scientific development back to the public.

And use rational thinking about the scientific orientation in social issues, and strive to provide the best occasions for scientific discussion, both online and offline.

9. Cost Structure: Space is the space of institutional units, mainly spent on the purchase and maintenance of machine facilities.

The maker space interviewed by this institute is a public-owned private customer base. Therefore, most of the base costs are sufficient to run the funds. Almost all government or PanMedia supports the salary and equipment purchase. Most of these maker spaces are of a promotional nature, or assist in employment, so that the general public can have the ability to work. With the different levels of stimulation of the curriculum, people can have new ideas to make a living. In these two spaces, there will be so-called community gathering time, which is composed of people other than the staff of the maker base. They all come from different industries and form their own community. Most of the ordinary nights are their own creations. At the gathering day, everyone will share the working methods, techniques, new ideas, and project creations that they want to work together. By inspiring new ideas and absorbing new experiences with creators of different backgrounds. This is a "Do it Together" in the maker culture. After creating it, you can complete a project with different people, such as a doll machine, an arcade, and so on.

Most of the bases in Taiwan have major promotion targets. The object of this interview is that they are almost locked in the general public, not in the student population, mainly because of the background of the creation, and the goal is to target the public rather than the students. At the same time, they will also add elements of culture to make the base closer to the society. By approaching life, the people who come to the base have some links to create a longer-term operation.

5   Conclusions and Recommendations

Since the introduction of the term "Maker" in Taiwan, it has brought a big wave in Taiwan, including maker education, maker activities, hands-on, self-created, and all kinds of new ways of learning to join the teaching system. 3D printing, laser engraving, woodworking, enamel printing, etc. At the same time, the government assisted the schools to promote the concept of Maker education, and established five different maker spaces in Taiwan to assist in the development of local Maker education. Schools at all levels have also begun to purchase and build a maker space, allowing students to have the space to play their imagination and create a variety of creations in the maker space. After three years of time, the trend of makers has gradually declined, and the attention of various media in the makers has gradually decreased, and the public is no longer fresh to makers. However, there is still a group of people who are still on the road of makers, but at the same time there are slight changes. The enjoyment of enjoyment in Taichung is due to business problems, and most of the other maker spaces have some units behind them. Therefore, this study is to find the business model of the maker space in Taiwan and understand the way of operation. Can support the operation of the maker space.

In the above two maker space, we can see that the funds is not a problem to the public private organization, but there are so-called communities in this two spaces. It is an informal group composed of the same good people in the maker base. Each of them is a professional leader who came to the base to create. However, they will combine them when they are working on large projects. They are the key partners of these bases. When the base needs to do interior decoration, design, project production, etc., use the technical skills of the company to complete it with other creators, just like the extension of the base as a home, with such a maker In addition to being a driving force for the spiritual practice of makers, the spirit can also achieve the spirit of "Do it Together" and enable the Maker base to continue its operations.

The maker space in this study is a form of public private, so there are some restrictions, such as the study of revenue streams, cost structure, etc., which cannot be reflected in this study. Therefore, in the future research, you can join the private The maker base, which understands the actual flow of funds, the management of the operation, or whether it has undergone transformation or combined with different industries to support the operation of the maker base after the turmoil, is the future research direction.

References

Lin, T.-X.: Research on the Construction of Business Model of Makerspace (2018)

Yang, P.-Y.: Innnovation Business Model of Fashion Style Idols, Celebrities, and Clothing Designers: A Case Study of BLENDER (2017)

Chang, J.-L.: 3D Printer and Makers Business Model (2014)

Benjes-Small, C., Bellamy, L.M., Resor-Whicker, J., Vassady, L.: Makerspace or Waste of Space: Charting a Course for Successful Academic Library Makerspaces (2017)

Yang, M.-S., Lin, Y.-S.: Maker education theory and practice. Taiwan Educ. Rev. Monthly 7(2), 29–38 (2018)

Peng, M.-H.: Independent Review – Common Wealth, Maker Spirit and University Bot System. https://opinion.cw.com.tw/blog/profile/30/article/3581. Accessed 30 Nov 2015

Li, X.-Y.: Business Next, the Executive Yuan launched the vMaker project and created a three-stage initiative. https://www.bnext.com.tw/article/35888/BN-2015-04-07-222857-109. Accessed 08 Apr 2015

Li, X.-Y.: Business Next, Maker economy. https://www.bnext.com.tw/article/36387/BN-2015-05-28-162337-36. Accessed 30 May 2015

Li, X.-Y.: Business Next, The predecessors did not sow, and it is difficult for Taiwan's self-creaters to harvest. https://www.bnext.com.tw/article/36512/BN-2015-06-12-133616-36. Accessed 22 June 2015

Cases of Hunger Marketing in Digital Era

Yue-Nuo Yan, Pei-Ting Huang, Yi-Fang Li, Chun-Yu Chuang,
and Shyang-Yuh Wang[✉]

Chinese Culture University, Taipei City 11114, Taiwan
wxy6@g.pccu.edu.tw

Abstract. In the digital era, market competition has become more complicated and comprehensive. In addition, the marketing means of enterprises are also changing significantly. When the traditional methods cannot meet the needs for changing market, some new concepts and means emerge should take place. Hunger marketing strategies are wildly adopted for fashion and consumer electronics products could be a good example. In order to create an impression of supply shortage to reinforce consumers to buy the product, providers intentionally reduce production or supply less products to regulate supply and demand. While maintaining the image of the product, it also maintains higher retail prices or higher profit margin of products. This paper expounds some concepts and characteristics of hunger marketing, and analyses some well-known hunger marketing campaigns. A survey instrument was utilized obtain data form consumers to find out their feelings and feedbacks in participating those hunger marketing sales campaigns.

Keywords: Hungry marketing · Production · Brand value

1 Introduction

In our daily life, we often encounter some actions, such as buying a new mobile phone, registering for a time-limited membership, or signing up for a limited-edition merchandise.

Marketing messages like limited-time, limited edition, countdown price are always around us. In today's abundant material, why is there a long queue of goods in short supply? This is precisely because businesses have been using hunger marketing strategies to a certain extent. It is important to sell products to customers, and it is essential to make customers willing to accept the products.

Nowadays, hunger marketing is not a conventional marketing strategy, and it is not focus on thinking about how to sell products to customers or carry out various conventional sales promotions. It is more wildly adopted by innovating consumer products, or services improvement to provide customers with better products and services. Therefore, customers are willing to take the initiative to pursue, and obtain a high-level need to meet [2].

According to the general understanding, the higher the output, the greater the profit; and he better the benefit, the faster the pace of enterprise development. Subsequently, after a large number of products were put into the market, it was found that the products

© Springer Nature Singapore Pte Ltd. 2020
J. Shen et al. (Eds.): IC3 2019, CCIS 1227, pp. 578–583, 2020.
https://doi.org/10.1007/978-981-15-6113-9_65

put in were larger than the demand of customers, which caused a vicious circle and wasted the enterprise's early investment. It actively controls the market and strictly controls the scale of production within the range of less than 10–20% of the specific market capacity. In the long-term interests of enterprises, such a way to promote the first restraint is a conscious strategy of reducing production and achieving the goal of product better selling.

2   Case Discussion and Literature Review

Starbucks is a popular brand which is not only for famous coffee, but also for various souvenirs of the treasures of town stores every year. In this wave of brand awareness, Starbucks has made great efforts. As everyone familiar with Starbucks knows, selling cups has become another Starbucks business besides coffee, and Starbucks cups have been welcomed by consumers for their novel shape and unique creativity. Starbucks cup has played a huge role in promoting the cultural communication of Starbucks brand, and is an indispensable carrier of cultural symbols for Starbucks. Apart from drinking coffee at Starbucks, it is also very fashionable for people to own a Starbucks cup.

2.1   Brand Value Management

The brand name is considered as an important factor that has been running through the implementation process of hunger marketing strategy. The brand's appeal in the market is a strong backing for continuous promotion. Well-known brands usually have good cultural connotations. Consumers not only choose the efficacy and quality of products or services, but also choose the cultural taste of products or services when they buy products or services.

In the process of brand value management, culture plays a role of cohesion and catalysis. For a long time, Starbucks, as the representative of foreign investment in brand chain drinks, has occupied a dominant position in the market. Starbucks has always been famous for its coffee worldwide. Its product orientation is based on high quality and elegant catering. In this era of rapid development, Starbucks has always positioned the public at a higher level of consumption. Therefore, the choice of limited-edition souvenir release has become the reason for many Starbucks fans to pursue.

2.2   Starbucks' Hunger Marketing Case

Starbucks utilized a campaign for this "Cat's Claw Cup" on Weibo, and that attracted over 150 million readers and 116,000 discussions posted. In Little Red Book website, over 5700 notes posted for "Starbucks Cat's Claw Cup", and over 8000 notes posted for "Cat's Claw Cup". In addition, there has been more 110 million audiences watched related film clip in Douyin.com. It was a successful sales campaign that attracted massive attentions on the internet.

Users take the initiative to generate content under the unpaid driving force. Similar to the band float propaganda, consumers unconsciously jumped on the band float driven by Starbucks. Consequently, increasing brand value has created brand hunger that everyone wants. In addition to Starbucks "limit" and "first come, first buy, first buy unrestricted rules of the game", essentially is to operate a sense of hunger! Through online detonation (online video) offline cooperation (price competition) online hot search keyword "Holy Grail" war.

2.3   Price-Added Sales

In the case of shortage in supply, when consumers want to obtain products or services in the earliest time, they must pay a higher amount than the retail price to meet their needs. Because consumers are influenced by the propaganda, in order to satisfy their puzzlement and interest, they prefer to spend more money to achieve it.

3   Purpose of Research

Hunger marketing strategies wildly used in digital ear, and many 3C products, such iPhone and Xiaomi also utilize it to generate higher social media discussions. However, it may also have negative effects. Therefore, the purpose of this research is to understand respondents' perceptions in the participations of hunger marketing activities. Based on the research purpose, this study proposed the following research questions.

1. What are the reasons would increase consumers' desires to buy new products?
2. What are the positive and negative effects for utilizing hunger marketing campaigns?

4   Methodology

This research utilized a survey instrument to collect consumers' perceptions in their participations in huger marketing sales campaigns. This research used a purposive sampling technique to ensure that the most appropriate participants would respond to the study's survey items. The survey instrument with 34 items, including three questions for demographic data were distributed online in June 2019.

5   Research Results

A total of 401 usable surveys were collected form respondents, including 127 males (31.67%) and 274 females (68.33). In addition, 22 (5.49%) respondents were under 18 years old, 170 (42.39%) were between 19–22 years old, 36 (8.98%) were between 22–25 years old, 43 (10.72%) were between 25–35 years old, 73 (18.20) were between 35–45 years old, and 57 (13.28%) were over 45 years old. Moreover, among the respondents, 213 (53.12%) were students, 177 (44.14) were full-time employees, and 11 (2.74%) were retired.

Among the respondents, 128 (31.92%) have participated in time-limited online shopping activities, 99 (24.69%) have participated in food and merchandise promotion activities, 93 (23.19%) have participated in online TV drama series programs, and many people have participated in various hunger marketing activities, such as Unique 49 (12.22), Xiaomi Cellphone 46 (11.47%) and Starbucks 39 (9.73%).

In the survey instrument, 5-point likert-type scale questions were used to find out what would be the most important aspects to attract people's desire to buy, and what issues would affect customer's satisfaction. In the likert-type scale, 5 point means strongly agree, 4 point means agree, 3 point means no opinion, 2 point means disagree, and 1 point means strongly disagree.

Among the 401 respondents, the top three reasons would increase their desires to buy new products are quality of the product (M = 4.16, Md = 4, Mo = 5, SD = 1.0), cost-performance ratio of the products (M = 3.98, Md = 4, Mo = 4, SD = 0.94), and innovation of the products (M = 3.86, Md = 4, Mo = 5, SD = 0.95) (Table 1).

Table 1. Reasons of increasing desires to buy *(N = 401)*

Variables	M	Md/Mo	SD	Agree & S. Agree
Quality	4.16	4/5	1.00	327(81.55%)
Cost-performance	3.98	4/4	0.94	290(72.32%)
Innovation	3.86	4/4	0.95	275(68.58%)
Brand name	3.83	4/4	0.92	271(67.58%)
Endorser	2.84	3/3	0.96	78(19.45%)
Popularity	3.42	3/3	0.90	192(47.88%)
F&F recommendation	3.46	4/4	0.85	206(51.37%)

Among the 401 respondents, the top three effects of hunger marketing are increasing revenue (M = 3.85, Md = 4, Mo = 4, SD = 0.88), increasing consumers desires to buy (M = 3.83, Md = 4, Mo = 4, SD = 0.91), and increasing brand's charismatic (M = 3.68, Md = 4, Mo = 4, SD = 0.89) (Table 2).

Table 2. Positive effects of hunger marketing *(N = 401)*

Variables	M	Md/Mo	SD	Agree & S. Agree
Value of brand	3.66	4/4	0.89	257(64.09%)
Desire to buy	3.83	4/4	0.91	281(70.07%)
Brand's charismatic	3.68	4/4	0.89	253(63.09%)
Increase revenue	3.85	4/4	0.88	282(70.32%)
Brand image	3.39	4/3	0.91	190(47.38%)

Utilizing hunger marketing would also generate negative images to the consumers. Out of the 401 respondents, 264 (65.58%) responders agreed or strongly agreed that would increase the possibility of sales scalping, 236 (58.85%) responders agreed or strongly agreed that would disturb market order, and 226 (56.36%) responders agreed or strongly agreed that would affect on rational spending (Table 3).

Table 3. Negative effects of hunger marketing ($N = 401$)

Variables	M	Md/Mo	SD	Agree & S. Agree
Brand image	3.13	3/3	0.85	125(31.17%)
Lost royalty	3.17	3/3	0.88	140(34.91%)
Cash flow	3.09	3/3	0.82	123(30.67%)
Consumer dispute	3.28	3/3	0.89	165(41.15%)
Sales scalping	3.78	3/3	1.03	264(65.58%)
Disturb Mkt order	3.66	3/3	0.99	236(58.85%)
Rational spending	3.62	3/3	0.95	226(56.36%)

In this study, 78 (18.95%) responders agreed or strongly agreed that hunger marketing would affect their desires to buy products (Table 4).

Table 4. Hunger marketing effect ($N = 401$)

Variable	M	Md/Mo	SD	High & very high
Hunger Mkt effect	2.87	3/3	0.88	76(18.95%)

6 Conclusion and Discussion

With the rapid development of modern internet, hunger marketing is being widely used as a popular marketing strategy. In order to catch up with the new wave, new forms of advertising attract more and more people. According to our survey results, quality of the product is the key to marketing success. From the perspective of hunger marketing strategy, although it attracts customers with a shortage of quantity supply, it cannot always maintain a small number of products or sell inferior products in order to meet the demand of quantity. When a thing is scarce, it is precious.

Only when the product itself has equal value can it attract consumers. Hunger marketing in this case will become a long-term solution. Moreover, brand influence is very important. If a brand is not popular and does not have enough social influence, it will not be able to attract a certain number of consumers to pay attention to new products. Therefore, in the early stage of product promotion, we should pay more attention to customer experience to attract customers' attention. If the seller blindly continues hunger marketing, there is a risk of customer churn. The lack of attractive products is a disruption to the brand image itself. Businessmen need to think carefully when utilizing hunger marketing. According to the performance of the product, adequate preparation for the marketing plan can ensure the smooth realization of hunger marketing. While it brings more profits, it also increases customers' needs on brands.

References

1. Zhang, X.: Introduction to Xiaomi hunger marketing. Modern Commerce, 18 January 2019
2. Yong, T.: Hunger marketing does not give the market too much. Public Relations World, 01 March 2007

Motivation and Characteristics of Social Media Use Behavior of New Generation Entrepreneurs

Qing-Jie Sun[✉]

The Chinese University of Hong Kong, Hong Kong, Hong Kong
papa_uwin@yahoo.com

Abstract. From the beginning of the 21st century, the birth of social media, such as Friendster, LinkedIn, and Facebook, completely subverted the one-way information communication mode of traditional media. It is the technology breaking through the time and space restrictions of interpersonal interaction, and has become the most mainstream application form in the Internet world. Social media provides people with diversified services and gradually changes the way how people live and interact. For example, it can connect users' online and real-life relationships, which can help users to communicate real-time, improve public relations, and build up social network on social media platform. With its advantages of instant, convenient and interactive, social media has become an indispensable media carrier in modern social life.

In recent years, many news media put spotlight on "New engine of entrepreneurship and innovation" proposed by Premier Li Keqiang in the "Government Work Report", a national policy in China to support young entrepreneurs. Young people's enthusiasm for innovation has also spurred the fourth wave of entrepreneurship, which is an entrepreneurial trend mainly based on Internet and social network. Their social media use which accounts for a large proportion of Internet use behavior is worth exploring in depth. Therefore, this study focuses on the new generation entrepreneurs in the fourth wave of entrepreneurship in mainland China, and explores the behavior characteristics of such a group of entrepreneurs in the use of social media in their daily lives, as well as the intrinsic motivation behind their use. Based on the theory of social capital, the study will also analyze the value that social media brings to the career of the new generation entrepreneurs.

Keywords: Social media · User behavior · User motivation · Social capital · Social support

1 Introduction

With the rapid development of Web technology, the information revolution has completely and profoundly changed the way of human's production, lifestyle and social interaction, then social media began to emerge [1]. Social media is an interactive computer media technology that provides users with a virtual community that is free to create, share and exchange information, and flexibly publish ideas, images, and audio

© Springer Nature Singapore Pte Ltd. 2020
J. Shen et al. (Eds.): IC3 2019, CCIS 1227, pp. 584–590, 2020.
https://doi.org/10.1007/978-981-15-6113-9_66

and video. The emergence of social media can be seen almost as a revolution, created through user-participatory communication, community building, knowledge creation and shared information [2].

Although many social media applications grow up in recent years, they have two things in common: 1. sharing - people sharing experiences, opinions and information; 2. communication - people communicate with business, family, friends or new people [3]. Social media plays an indispensable role in the social and professional lives of billions of people around the world, not only in forming the new way that organizations, communities and individuals communicate, but also in changing the relation of society. In addition, social media is also an important source of information. The rapid development of social media has changed the past process of information dissemination and knowledge creation, and accelerated the sharing of knowledge [4].

Unlike the website based on Web 1.0 that restricts people from watching content in a passive manner, social media which established on Web 2.0 allows users to interact, collaborate, and exchange information through social conversations as a creator of UGC, in a virtual community. In addition, social media differs in many ways from traditional paper media and traditional electronic media (television, broadcasts, etc.), such as quality, coverage, frequency, and immediacy [5].

Social media allows users to develop online relationships that are different from face-to-face relationships, and maintain the warmth of these relationships; social media creates a form of social communication that enables individuals to stay in touch with people who have a common interest beyond time and space [6]. It can be seen that the emergence of social media has subverted the one-way information dissemination mode, time and space restrictions of traditional media, and established a new form of social interaction communication for human society, which has become the crucial application forms in the world.

2   Study on Motivation of Social Media Use

Some scholars take in the concept of the Uses and Gratifications Theory to study the motivations or reasons for the use of social media by the public, thereby defining how people with different purposes can use social media to meet their own needs. As early as the Internet appeared, communication researchers Eighmey and McCord (1998) summarized four usage needs in Internet web usage research, which is communication, interaction, information acquisition, personal participation and maintenance of interpersonal relationships [7]. Clark, Lee. and Boyer (2007) summarized the needs of American college students using social software Facebook, in the book called "A Place of Their Own: An Exploratory Study of College Students Uses of Facebook": information sharing, maintenance of interpersonal relationships, social interactions and recreational entertainment. Krishnamurthy & Dou (2008) divided the reasons for using social media into two broad categories: rational reasons (sharing information, searching for information and seeking support, etc.) and emotional reasons (social interaction, self-expression, self-realization, socialization, etc.) [8]. Smock et al. (2011) found that people think that when they use Facebook, it can help them get job security, manage relationships in a low-cost way, and promote professionalism [9].

Researcher conducted in-depth interviews with six new generation entrepreneurs who joined the fourth wave of entrepreneurship, in mainland China. Two of them earn network flow on Weibo by becoming opinion leaders, and the other two operate Public Accounts on WeChat. The others launch the business in their own studio. Among the entrepreneurs interviewed, most of them think that the main purpose of using social media is to conduct "community link" and "recreation", and the part of "community link" is mainly to maintain contact with familiar friends. Less cases are meant to create new friendships. However, a small number of entrepreneurs also play the role of contacting customers and managing business at work. They believe that social media such as WeChat is used to exchange resources and promote career development, which can help them obtain more resources.

Some of the entrepreneurs interviewed believe that the emergence of social media has "information value" and "social value" for entrepreneurs, and social media can bring the latest industry dynamics as well as more accurate and transparent information to entrepreneurs, which is convenient for them to find the corresponding customers. Some other interviewees believe that the use of social media can bring more "social value" and actual "social support" to entrepreneurs. For entrepreneurs in several new media industries, the social media itself is the "foundation" of their entrepreneurship. With such a social platform, entrepreneurs have more opportunity to establish a career, gain attention and funds.

3   Study on Behavior of Entrepreneurs as Social Media User

Since the 1980s, some scholars have recognized the multiple roles of Internet users, and explored users and usage behaviors with terms such as "prosumer" or "co-creators." José Van Dijck (2009) proposed concepts such as "producer", "consumer" and "data provider" [10].

Many scholars also make different classifications for the use of social media. Jiang Mengqi (2018) believes that there are currently seven main kinds of social media use behavior: watching, joining, collecting, commenting, sharing and creating, plus negative use behavior [11]. Shao (2009) divides the activities of social media users into three categories: Consumer (this behavior is limited to reading the content of other users, in other words, users just watch or read, but they did not join; Participator (This behavior includes user interaction with the user and content interaction, for example, joining a group, adding favorite content to a playlist, sharing with others, publishing comments, and this behavior does not include real creation); Creator (This behavior includes user-generated content and published content, such as text, image and video). All of these productions can achieve their own goals of expression and self-fulfillment [12].

Among the six new generations of entrepreneurs interviewed, researcher found that most of them deem when they use social media, they often read information in a "bystander" manner, and also record the helpful information during reading. Less entrepreneurs belong to "participator" or "creator" on social media platform. However, two of them believe that commenting on or forwarding some meaningful content is because they are eager to get different voices or new ideas about an issue, and are willing to understand people in different social sectors, which can broaden their breadth of thinking. For entrepreneurs who have just entered the mainland market, in addition to reading, interacting with friends in the circle of social network is also an important way to lay a foothold for their careers, so they will often participate and join.

In terms of the categories of reading content, most of the interviewees said that they prefer to browse some relaxed entertainment content and also read articles about their career-related industries. For the operators of the WeChat public account, news, biographies, youth attitudes and other types of content will give him inspiration and career nutrition with the subtle influence. For entrepreneurs in the field of custom design, they will pay more attention to the information dynamics of entrepreneurial and Internet, and try to understand the market in different fields. In addition, entrepreneurs in the new media industry believe that social news and online "hot issues" are quite needed by entrepreneurs in this industry.

4 Social Capital and Social Sport Accumulation of Entrepreneurs on Social Media Platform

Social capital is a resource embedded in a personal social network. These resources are not fortunate assets owned by a certain member. Instead, they provide some convenience when individuals make actions through social network relationships, which is an indispensable support for personal survival and development. Social capital is a kind of social network resource, which is established by individuals. The position of individuals in the social network is ultimately manifested as embedded resources in the social network that can be mobilized and used by this location [13].

Scholars in different fields have given different definitions of social capital. Some of them analyze from a structural point of view, emphasizing the value of the network structure to individuals. In an interactive social structure, the contact of a member's location provides the member's specific interests, and people can use their contacts to get work, get information, or access certain resources. Coleman (1990) pointed out that the concept of social capital pays more attention to the level of relationship. If the level of relationship between the individual is higher, the more network is formed, the stronger ability to obtain information and resources, and more abundant resources to help achieve the goal. Putnam (1995) believes that social network relations can increase social capital [14]. The division of "strong tie" and "weak tie" proposed by Mark S. Granovetter (1973) is of great significance for the study of social capital. Among them, strong tie means that the individual's social network is more homogenous, the relationship between people is close, and there are strong emotional factors to maintain interpersonal relationship; on the contrary, the weak tie is characterized by personal social network heterogeneity. That is, a wide range of contacts, which means the objects of interaction may come from all walks of life [15].

The social network orientation regards the whole composition of individuals in society as a network system. Under this analysis mode, "social support" is regarded as the key to the connection of social network nodes. Each individual or group constitutes a node in a network of relationships, and the links between nodes depend on the flow of information and resources. Scholar Kahn Antonucci (1980) defines social support as human-computer interaction, which involves emotions, affirmation, aid, encouragement, and emotional confirmation [16]. In summary, many research orientations of social support are mainly divided into two dimensions: first, objective, visible or actual social support, including material and informational help; second, subjective, experienced emotional support, such as respect, an emotional experience of support and understanding.

During interviews, most entrepreneurs believe that the use of social media can help them to build a wider social network, accumulate social capital, enhance the popularity and exposure of entrepreneurs' careers in society, and thus help them gain more social resources. Some of them added contacts from the group chat in the early stage of their business. After a certain period of accumulation, they will reduce the cumulative behavior of this "weak ties" and turn to focus on maintaining "strong ties", or keep in touch with people who are under the same social structure. And entrepreneurs know that the behavior of their contacts has changed from "active" to "passive" because they believe that, the accumulation of social capital in the use of social media depends on the power of the entrepreneur themselves.

Some of the entrepreneurs who owned a more successful business believe that they will gain more social resources while gaining social capital in the social media, because the social class in which they live brings the same high quality social capital. Another part of the interviewees who are still in the exploration stage of business, believe that social media does help to accumulate social capital, but it does not directly lead to actual social support. Most of what can really help the entrepreneurship is the "social structure" capital in social capital, not the "inter-relationship" capital. Some interviewees believe that the premise that entrepreneurs can transform their social connections into social capital is that, entrepreneurs need to have higher socioeconomic status than these networks, or at least on the same social structure. With the interest interactivity, it is possible to activate static network into a real "social support".

5   Conclusion

According to the study, in the aspect of the frequency and time of social media use, most new generation entrepreneurs have high viscosities on social media such as WeChat. They usually use social media for more than 10–18 h per day which occupy nearly 50%–70% of their daily life. This group of people has always been concerned about the dynamics on social media, and is in a state of responsiveness in order to chase social hotspots and connect with business partners.

This study initially found that WeChat is the most popular social media application for the new generation of entrepreneurs in China. Different from the Weibo which features information explosion, the content on the WeChat platform is not only deeper and of high quality, but also has informational and social value. Besides, it facilitates the internal communication between "strong ties" and strengthens the social capital built on the social structure. In addition, WeChat aggregate the functions of various applications to meet the needs of entrepreneurs, such as: entertainment, work, financial management, etc. Many new generation entrepreneurs usually read the Internet dynamics related to their own industry on social media.

In terms of the use behavior, the study found that more entrepreneurs would choose to read the information in a "stand-by" manner and take in the useful information. Few entrepreneurs may "participate" or "create", mainly because they need to accumulate social capital in a certain market or industry in the early stage of the venture. The behavior of new generation entrepreneurs accumulating social capital will change with the various stages of entrepreneurship. In the early stage of entrepreneurship, entrepreneurs will take the initiative to add some contacts from the group chat or friend recommendation. After a certain period of accumulation, they will reduce the cumulative behavior of this "weak ties" and turn to focus on maintaining "strong ties", or keep in touch with people who are under the same social structure. And the behavior of accumulating social capital has changed from "active" to "passive."

During the study, researcher found that for the new generation of entrepreneurs, the main motivation for using social media is "community link" and "recreation". And the "community link" part is mainly maintaining contact with "strong ties", and less often to establish new relationships. At the same time, entrepreneurs believe that social media can also bring them information value (learning fresh information) and social value (social connection).

This study initially confirms that Baker's viewpoint of limiting social capital to the structure of the relationship network in 1990 and the definition of social capital that participants obtain resources from special social structures. Studies have shown that social media does help to accumulate social capital, but it does not directly lead to actual "social support". Most of the social capital that can really bring entrepreneurial help is the "social structure" capital, not the "relationship" capital. Therefore, the interpersonal relationship that users develop on social media only through a period of interaction does not bring actual benefits and resources in most cases. At the same time, the network is divided into "active" connections and "static" connections. When the social structure or hierarchy of social media user is in equal or similar social relations, they can provide active resources for each other.

References

1. Chandler, D.: A Nation Transformed by Information: How Information Has Shaped the United States from Colonial Times to the Present (2008)
2. Postman, J.: Social Corp: Social Media Goes Corporate (2008)
3. Kurtuluş, S., Özkan, E., Öztürk, S.: How Do social media users in turkey differ in terms of their use habits and preferences? Int. J. Bus. Inf. (IJBI) 10(3), 337–364 (2015)
4. Jie, P., Zhou, H.-C.: Research on the value, mechanism and governance strategies of social media. Peking University Press, Peking, China (2015)
5. Definition of Web 2.0. https://en.wikipedia.org/wiki/Web_2.0. Accessed 01 June 2019
6. Hemsley, J., Mason, M.: The Nature of Knowledge in the Social Media Age: Implications for Knowledge Management Models (2012)
7. Eighmey, J., McCord, L.: Adding value in the information age: uses and gratifications of sites on the World Wide Web. J. Bus. Res. 41, 187–194 (1998)
8. Krishnamurthy, S., Dou, W.Y.: Note from special issue editors: advertising with user-generated content: a framework and research agenda. J. Interact. Advert. 8(2), 1–4 (2008)

9. Smock, A.D., Ellison, N.B., Lampe, C., Wohn, D.Y.: Facebook as a toolkit: a uses and gratification approach to unbundling feature use. Comput. Hum. Behav. **27**, 2322–2329 (2011)

10. Dijck, J.V.: Users like you? Theorizing agency in user-generated content. Media Cult. Soc. **31**, 41–58 (2009)

11. Jiang, M.-Y.: The exploration of the use of social media behavior. Master's thesis, National Taipei University Information Management Institute, Taipei City, Taiwan (2018)

12. Shao, G.-S.: Understanding the appeal of user-generated media: a uses and gratification perspective (2009)

13. Lin, N.: Introduction to social capital theory and its research. Soc. Sci. Ser. **1**, 1–32 (2007)

14. Putnam, R.: Tuning in, tuning out: the strange disappearance of social capital in America. J. Democr. **6**(1), 65–78 (1995)

15. Granovetter, M.S.: The strength of weak ties. Am. J. Sociol. **78**(6), 1360–1380 (1973)

16. Kahn, R.L., Antonucci, T.C.: Convoys over the life course: attachment, roles, and social support. In: Baltes, P.B., Grim, O.G. (eds.) Life Span Development and Behavior, vol. 3, pp. 253–286. Academic Press, New York (1980)

A Book-Finding Application Based on iBeacon-A Case Study of CCU Library

Yao-An Sui and Yih-Jiun Lee[✉]

Department of Information Communications, Chinese Culture University,
Taipei, Taiwan
lyjl5@ulive.pccu.edu.tw

Abstract. Finding a book or a thesis in a large library is never an easy job, even though librarians and researchers provides a call number system or an on-line webcat system. Since indoor positioning technologies are getting popular and cost-reasonable, it might be useful in the library to assist. In order to help readers finding books, this paper aims to design a book-finding application with iBeacon. Provide readers with more convenient and effective services to help them locate their books quickly in the library.

Keywords: iBeacon · Book-finding system

1 Introduction

Although on-line library service is getting more popular and convenient, finding a Ph. D. dissertation or a Master thesis are still required to present on site in Taiwan. Since the authors may not allow the electronic version of the paper to release until five years after the publication date, students still need to find the paper-based copy in the library on-site. Even though a web-based self-service book-finding system, shown in Fig. 1, can assist us to find where the books (thesis) might be, it is still difficult to find the accurate bookshelf in a large university library. In order to provide effective book-finding services, libraries are dedicated to developing information systems that can help readers quickly find the books such as the use of WIFI or Radio Frequency Identification (RFID) positioning technology [1, 6]. Although they are all possible from the technologies point of view, the financial or computational cost might be relatively high.

IBeacon operates as a signal provider. It continuously sends signals so that the phone can receive signals within the signal range [2, 3]. Once the signal is received, the pre-installed application can execute a specific corresponding process [5, 7]. One of the important applications of iBeacon is indoor positioning and integrated marketing system. Using iBeacon in libraries has not been discovered, but it can be very useful.

This research aims to design and implement a book-finding assistant application based on mobile communication and iBeacon Technology in a reasonable cost to provide an effective and efficient service for book finding.

© Springer Nature Singapore Pte Ltd. 2020
J. Shen et al. (Eds.): IC3 2019, CCIS 1227, pp. 591–596, 2020.
https://doi.org/10.1007/978-981-15-6113-9_67

Fig. 1. Library webcat in CCU

2   Current Process of Finding a Book or Thesis

The library of Chinese Culture University is a seven-story building with more than 400,000 volumes of collections. To find a book in the library, a student might follow the following process:

a. Log into the library's book-finding system (shown in Fig. 1) to find the call number of the book.
b. Find the proper bookshelf after he or she finds the right direction
c. At the correct bookshelf, using the call number to get to the book. Usually, the books are placed in order (Fig. 2).

Fig. 2. Library bookshelf in CCU

Graduate students to conduct a simple experiment. They are giving a book title or a thesis title, and have to find the book or thesis. The average time to locate the object is 5 min and 30 s. The students agree that a book-finding system can be very helpful.

3 System Designing

This research aims to design a book-finding system in the library based on iBeacon Technologies. Therefore, iBeacon(s) must be pre-installed in the library and their locations must be pre-configured, so that the system can correctly operates.

The system is composed of a mobile application, a set of web services and a cloud data center. The structure of the system is shown in Fig. 3 and the functionalities of each component is described as follows:

a. A mobile app: A mobile application provides an ease of use interface. Users can search for a book and the correspondent information, such as the call number and where it might be found, is displayed in the app. In the background service, the app is always sensing the signal of iBeacon(s), which has been pre-installed in the library (as shown Fig. 4). Once a single is picked up, the location of users can be estimated and the direction between the user and the book can be calculated.

b. A set of web services: Similar with the web cat, the web services provide the backbone to the app. There are several fundamental functions, such as authentication and location services. The former checks users' identities and the latter find the location of the book through its title. Other services might be provided to support the book-finding system.

c. A Cloud data center: The data uploaded to the server is analyzed and stored in the database system to maintain data security and integrity.

An iBeacon enabled environment: The mobile phone will receive messages or connect commands to the device when it senses the signal from iBeacon pre-installed in the library (Figs. 4 and 5) [4].

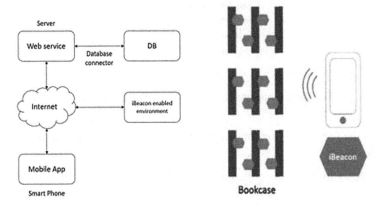

Fig. 3. System design   **Fig. 4.** iBeacon placed

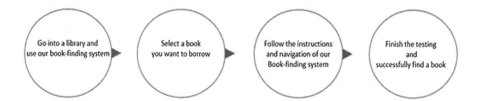

Fig. 5. The process of testing the users

Record the testing results, including:

a. The user's responds and how they feel when they are completing the test.
b. Is each step of the iBeacon instructions clear?
c. How long does it take for each user?
d. What can we improve by incorporating the replies?
e. Find out what the users have replied in common (Fig. 6).

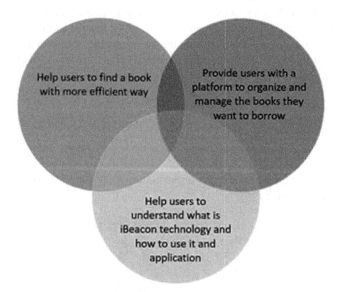

Fig. 6. The opportunity areas of book-finding system

Based on the features of iBeacon, we defined the opportunity areas of the app. The main opportunity areas are:

a. Help users to find a book with more efficient way, so they can save time on searching.
b. Provide the newest information as fast as possible, and help them to organize and manage the books they want to borrow.
c. Make a process of finding a book easier.

d. Help users to understand what iBeacon is and how it is used in a helpful way in an application.
e. Remind the users of how many you have already borrowed and a deadline for returning a book (Fig. 7).

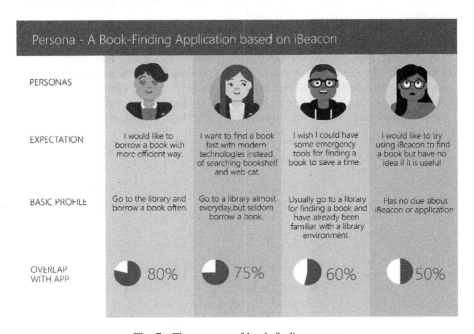

Fig. 7. The persona of book-finding system

4   Preliminary Conclusion

Finding a book in a large library is difficult. In the experiment, finding a random book requires approximately 5 min for graduate students, so the subjects agree that a book-finding system can be very useful and helpful. Similar researches have been proposed by using RFID, NFC and AR technologies. However, they either cost too much or have different limitations. We believe iBeacon is a better solution.

iBeacon technology has a strong potential to make unique contributions to our lives. As the storage center of human knowledge, the library has a massive collection such as books and periodicals. The more collection a library has, the more difficult finding a book is. The call number and the webcat system provide limited help to locate the approximate location, but we still have to find the book physically.

The iBeacon-enabled environment and the proposed system can fill in the blank. Therefore, the location of the queried book can be directed through the user's phone. Finding a book can be more effectively and efficiently.

References

1. Li, H.S.: Implementation of indoor positioning system based on iBeacon bluetooth device. Master thesis, TungHai University, Taiwan, pp. 1–14 (2017)
2. Wikipedia. https://zh.wikipedia.org/wiki/IBeacon. Accessed 15 June 2019
3. Peerbits. https://www.peerbits.com/blog/the-most-comprehensive-guide-beacon-installation-maintenance.html. Accessed 15 June 2019
4. Beacon Marketing in 2018. https://medium.com/@the_manifest/a-beginners-guide-to-beacon-marketing-in-2018-15ac361d4226. Accessed 15 June 2019
5. Library views. https://libraryview.me/2016/05/02/10068. Accessed 15 June 2019
6. Chang, J.F.: The application of radio frequency identification technology to library book accessing service. Master thesis, National Cheng Kung University, Taiwan, pp. 5–32 (2008)
7. Hong, J.M.: A Localization system based on RFID and iBeacon technology for elderly people. Master thesis, ChaoYang University of Technology, Taiwan, pp. 1–23 (2016)

Exploring the Impact Variables of Mobile Device Users' Continuous Use of Mobile Payment with a Commitment to Trust

Huei Wen Wu and Shyang-Yuh Wang[✉]

Chinese Culture University, Taipei City 11114, Taiwan
wxy6@g.pccu.edu.tw

Abstract. In the modern era of the popularity of mobile phones and mobile services, the basic requirements of people's lives can be processed through the screen that these needs are more closely linked to online and offline for mobile payment services. This study explores the formation of a commitment-trust relationship between users and mobile payment services in the perspective of relationship commitment and trust, and moreover, further, observe whether the committed3f relationship and trust affect the loyalty performance and customer stickiness of user.

Keywords: Mobile payment · Customer stickiness · FinTech · Relations marketing

1 Introduction

The year of 2018 has been recognized as the initiate year of mobile payment in Taiwan [1]. In recent years, various mobile payment services have sprung up introducing to the market. Through the popularity of mobile devices, the needs for people's daily life will be resolved between fingers with screen. Financial services, such as savings, loans, settlements, financial management, asset management, and personal financial business are included in the Apps. Today, people tend to operate easily and distribute own property. According to a research, China largest third payment service corporation Alipay has reached 54.26% market share, and nearly 2.8 trillion U.S. dollars transition in the 4th quarter of 2017 [2].

By taking advantage of the high development of online payment system and service platform, most importantly China's government policies reinforcement on the third part payment, all those reasons encourage people to put the embrace of action to pay. Therefore, action payments have a high degree of customer popularity in China [2].

1.1 Current Mobile Payment Penetration Rate in Taiwan

According to a research conducted in the third quarter of 2018 by Institute of Information Industry, 50.3% of people in Taiwan have used mobile payment, and the

© Springer Nature Singapore Pte Ltd. 2020
J. Shen et al. (Eds.): IC3 2019, CCIS 1227, pp. 597–602, 2020.
https://doi.org/10.1007/978-981-15-6113-9_68

penetration rate of users aged 18 to 25 increased from 39.2% in 2017 to 63.3% in 2018, while the penetration rate of users aged 56 to 65 increased from 26.3% to 41.4%. The top five mobile payment platforms are LINE pay (22.3%), Apple Pay (19.9%), Jkopay (19.7%), Google Pay (9.1%), and Taiwan Pay (4.7%). In addition, nearly ninety percent of people used 1∼3 mobile payment platforms. The Taiwan government has announced the policy to promote mobile payment to reach the policy goal of increasing the penetration rate to 90% by 2025. The top three keys success points of mobile payment are accessibility, concessions and system stability [3].

In 2019, the penetration rate of mobile payment reached 86%, which was in the leading position in the world [4]. Comparing with daily action payment development in China, Taiwan is still in the midst of a gradual cooling cycle after the craze has receded. Marketing activities cause Taiwanese successfully start to use Mobile payment. However, when incentives in marketing campaigns are weakened, the frequency of use of action payments begins to decline and the continued use intentions are also reduced. Therefore, mobile payment is unable to reach a real application.

2   Purpose of Study

This study intends to modify Promise-trust model originally proposed by Morgan and Hunt. By modifying the key mediating variables (KMV) based on the reverent research, this research tends to develop a survey instrument to examine if proposed factors would positively influence people's commitment and trust in the proposed modified model. The results can be adopted to increase loyalty and stickiness of people while using a mobile payment applications.

3   Research Question and Variables

Commitment-trust theory is a key mediating variable (KMV) model in relational marketing field proposed by Morgan and Hunt [5]. They believe that relational commitment and trust is a key indicator to determine the success of relationship marketing, which can encourage enterprises to cooperate and maintain long-term cooperation [5].

Commitment-trust theory is one of the most commonly used theories in the field of relational marketing. Morgan and Hunt [5] are based on the B2B relationship between tire industry suppliers. Because of the scope of relationship marketing, it is not limited to B2B [6]. Therefore, the theory can modify or expand the variables according to different hypothetical situations (Fig. 1).

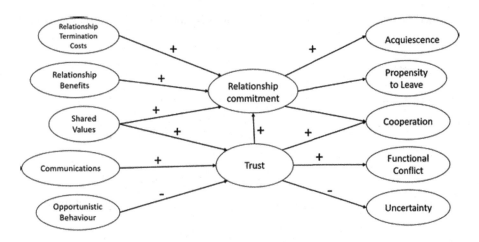

Analysis of Morgan & Hunt (1994) Key Mediating Variables Model

Fig. 1. Original commitment-trust model by Morgan and Hunt.

3.1   Modification of Key Mediating Variables

The modification of the Key Mediating Variables (KMV) of the commitment-trust theory proposed by Morgan and Hunt [5], this study removed numbers of factors that do not meet the use situation of the mobile payment based on reverent literature. Furthermore, as shown in Fig. 2, two antecedent variables, two dependent variables, and two extraneous variables were added to the model. The users focus on two aspects of the security mechanism and the additional function, so that the antecedent variables are closer to use situation of the mobile payment.

3.2   Security Mechanism

According to the MIC (Market Intelligence & Consulting Institute) of Taiwan report published in February 2017, among the top five factors in the Taiwanese people's consideration of whether to use mobile payments, the security (83.3%) is the top factor of the list [7], indicating that when people use mobile payment the security is the most important consideration. Therefore, when the government wants to increase the penetration rate of mobile payments to above 90% of the expectations, the primary solution is to minimize security concerns.

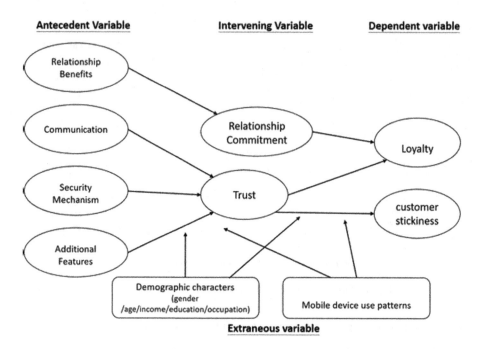

Fig. 2. Modified commitment-trust model

3.3   Additional Features

Hu, the senior industry analyst at MIC, pointed out that consumers, in addition to transaction payment functions, also expect mobile payment to be applied to more life-oriented functions such as "billing payment", "transfer service" and "consumption" [1].

3.4   Loyalty and Customer Stickiness

Loyalty can represent the user's reuse of specific actions. Stickiness is defined as "the ability of an enterprise to retain customers and allow customers to visit and browse the site again." [8] In the implementation of mobile payment, the repeated use of behavior is to present the mobile payment to the daily performance of the day.

4   Research Problems

Based on the purpose of this research, this research proposes a research question to exam if there statistically significant exist among the six dimensions proposed in the modified commitment-trust model. Based on the research question, researchers of this study proposed the following hypotheses:

H1: When using mobile payment services, relationship commitments positively affect loyalty.

H2: When using mobile payment services, a trust will positively affect loyalty.

H3: When using mobile payment services, trust affects customer stickiness.

H4: When using mobile payment services, relationship benefits will positively affect relationship commitments.

H5: When using mobile payment services, communication positively affects trust

H6: When using mobile payment services, security mechanisms positively affect trust.

H7: When using mobile payment services, additional features affect trust.

H8: The use of mobile devices has an interference effect on the commitment and trust relationship of using mobile payment services.

H9: Demographic characteristics have an interference effect on the commitment and trust relationship of using mobile payment services.

5   Research Design

This study intends to modify Promise-trust model originally proposed by Morgan and Hunt. After the modification, a survey instrument will be developed and utilized to collect data from selected samples to examine if proposed factors would positively influence people's commitment and trust in the proposed model.

5.1   Population

This research design employs in this study will be a cross-sectional survey research design. The survey instrument will be developed and utilized to collect data form at least 400 mobile payment users of various platforms to find out their perception and satisfactions. In addition, selected a panel of experts will be invited to a focus group meeting to discuss the finding of this research.

5.2   Data Analysis Techniques

The SPSS and AMOS programs will be used to construct a Structural Equation Modeling to verify the model fit to the collected data and the overall magnitude of the relationships between and among the proposed variables. Also, structural equation modeling will be used to detect the effects of proposed variables on stickiness, trust and loyalty.

References

1. Department of Information Services, Executive Yuan, Mobile payment platform targets 90% penetration by 2025. Executive Yuan, Republic of Chain (Taiwan). https://english.ey.gov.tw/News_Content2.aspx?n=8262ED7A25916ABF&s=856ACD24C9691379
2. Wang, P.B.: The transaction scale of China's Third-party Mobile Payment report in 2017 Q4. https://www.analysys.cn/article/analysis/detail/1001257. Accessed 02 Apr 2018
3. Ho, P.S.: MIC survey: Taiwan mobile payment penetration rate breaks 50%, LINE Pay usage rate is highest, 09 January 2019. https://www.businesstoday.com.tw/article/category/80392/post/201901090048/

4. Shen, J., Lin Q-Z., Hu, Z-Q., Zhang, Q., Cai, Y., Xie, M.: Fintech Trends and Prospects - Research on Taiwan Mobile and Third-Party Payment Trends, p. 41 (2016)
5. Morgan, R.M., Hunt, S.D.: The commitment-trust theory of relationship marketing. J. Mark. **58**(3), 20–38 (1994). https://doi.org/10.2307/1252308/
6. Lin, T-C.: Users' Participation in Business Micro-blogging Community: From Relationship Commitment Perspective. Doctoral dissertation, Institute of Marketing Communication of Management at National Sun Yat-Sen University (2012)
7. Mobile Payment Consumer Survey"80% of consumers are willing to use mobile payment (2017). https://mic.iii.org.tw/IndustryObservations_PressRelease02.aspx?sqno=457
8. Beddoe-Stephens, P.: Yahoo: Gettin' sticky with it (1999). http://www.wired.com/culture/lifestyle/news/1999/03/18229

Big Data for Cognitive City

Educational Big-Data Practice: A Model for Combining Requirements and Technologies

Sheng-Kuei Hsu[✉]

Zhaoqing University, Zhaoqing, China
johnhsu.tw@gmail.com

Abstract. Institutional research (IR) has revealed the need for data processing in a university, and big-data technology can be regarded as a technical approach. The combination of the two methods can help universities introduce data-driven decision-making models. On the demand side of big-data processing on campus, we proposed three groups of university stakeholders—university, student, and society—with student learning outcomes as the main research topic. On the technical side, we proposed a data processing model from the perspective of big-data processing, including data gathering, pre-processing, storage and integration, analysis and exploration, and visual presentation. We applied the proposed learning outcomes and the big-data processing model to Tzu-Chi University, exploring student learning outcomes with big-data technology. In an initial experiment, this application model is feasible. Finally, we proposed several relevant conclusions to promote educational big-data research as a reference for related research.

Keywords: Educational big-data · Institutional research (IR) · Learning outcomes

1 Introduction

Institutional research (IR) is an activity undertaken from the perspective of university needs. It originated in the United States from the 1940s to the 1950s. It is different from the traditional decision-making model and introduces a "data-driven" decision-making model, which entails finding useful information and knowledge from data to help universities solve problems arising from the rapid development of higher education at the time, thereby driving the rise of institutional research [1, 2].

"Big data" is a term developed from a technical point of view, referring to large or complex data sets that traditional data-processing applications are not sufficient to handle [3, 4]. The data types it includes contain a large amount of unstructured or structured data from a variety of sources. Combining the big-data processing technology (technical) and institutional research (demand) is an important element of this paper.

To effectively combine the above two viewpoints, this study is an attempt to use the theory of stakeholders and the theme of student learning so that universities' big-data processing has a clear direction, and we proposed the processing mode of education big data to process related data. Finally, we applied the former two to Tzu-Chi University

© Springer Nature Singapore Pte Ltd. 2020
J. Shen et al. (Eds.): IC3 2019, CCIS 1227, pp. 605–610, 2020.
https://doi.org/10.1007/978-981-15-6113-9_69

(where the author previously worked) in Taiwan, which has been initially verified as feasible, and provide our conclusions and recommendations.

2   Identify Research Topics Based on Stakeholder Theory and Student Learning Outcomes

Peterson divides the development of IR in the United States into three phases according to specialization and institutionalization [5]: The first phase was the rise of IR in the 1950s and 1960s, when advanced education became popular in the US and the number of universities increased dramatically. To more effectively formulate relevant policies and thereby manage student affairs, IR was explored. The second stage lasted from the 1960s to the mid-1970s, when IR was gradually developed for specialization. The third stage lasted from the mid-1970s to the mid-1980s, and the evaluation of learning outcomes became one of the most important research tasks for IR.

Another study revealed that although the direction and tasks of academic research in American universities are not the same, the development experience can be summarized in five directions [6]: (1) to physically examine campus pulsations and changes, such as analysis of student affairs, curriculum design and teaching, and faculty and staff affairs to discover the problems therein and deal with them in real time; (2) to examine the development trend in university education through the consolidation of literature, participation in international conferences, and comparison with peer universities or standard universities; (3) to evaluate the university's strengths and weaknesses through external self-evaluation, systematic and objective analysis, and comparison with peer universities or standard universities; (4) to respond to special issues and plan improvement and development strategies to help universities become more outstanding; and (5) to organize and disseminate university information to provide a relevant reference for government units.

In Japan, since 2004, universities have set up IR centers, some of which are dedicated to internal investigations and some to self-assessment reports [7]. Since then, the Japanese IR Strategic Alliance and IR Research Association have been established, and some universities have also adopted IR as one of the important strategies to improve the quality of education. Among them, the University of Tokyo's survey of more than 700 universities across Japan revealed the following facts: Most Japanese public and private universities have implemented institutional research. The purposes of setting up an IR unit are (1) to determine whether the teaching results have improved, (2) to respond to university evaluations, (3) to assist in university operations, (4) to serve as a reference for student support, and (5) to address the university's performance responsibility.

After summarizing the tasks and development of the aforementioned countries in institutional research, we used the stakeholder theory in university governance to examine the relationship between students, **universities** (boards, managers, and teachers), and society. With the concerns of all parties, we can more clearly summarize the multi-disciplinary issues of IR and the tasks that should be in place. The views of various stakeholders and the possible topics of concern are as follows:

Student: ways to strengthen learning and other issues, such as learning outcome tracking and management, automated early warning, and counseling intervention.

University: ways to improve the university's professional management issues, such as new student entrance analysis and course-cost analysis.

Society: the provision of information about the various facets of the university as a basis for understanding and selection.

Institutional research, which focuses on learning-outcome issues, is not only the most relevant to students but also concerns the school and parents. Therefore, the theme of learning outcomes can be the main topic of IR.

3   A Big-Data Processing Model

From the perspective of data processing, IR is a process of statistical analysis or data mining. Hui & Jha proposed that the data mining process consists of seven phases [8]: setting goals, selecting data, pre-processing data, data conversion, data warehousing, data mining, and evaluation results. In this study, we emphasize the application of technology and tools in each stage and consider the IR information system a decision-support system (DSS), so it is combined with the stage of visualization. Finally, we propose IR data processing procedures as follows: (1) data gathering, (2) pre-processing, (3) storage and integration, (4) analysis and mining, and (5) visual presentation. In Fig. 1, the data processing procedure for the IR outlines the purpose of each processing stage. The tasks and available tools for each stage are described below:

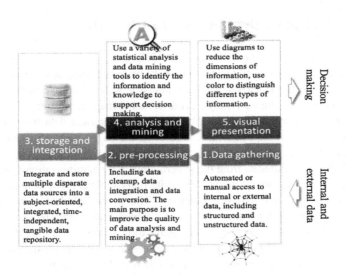

Fig. 1. The data processing procedure for IR

Data Gathering. Automated or manual access to internal or external data, including structured and unstructured data. Three common types of data acquisition are available:

1) XML + Web Service, 2) JSON + Resful, and 3) Excel. When the information inside or outside the campus cannot be obtained through the above methods, such as the information on the Manpower Bank website, tools such as Web Spider, Web Crawler, and HTML Parser are necessary.

Pre-processing. Including data cleanup (including noise, inconsistency, omission, and duplication), data integration, and data conversion, the main purpose is to improve the quality of data analysis and exploration. At this stage, due to different data analysis/mining purposes and diverse data sources, most of them require custom development of pre-processing tools.

Storage and Integration. Integrate and store disparate data in a subject-oriented, integrated, time-dependent data warehouse.

Analysis and Mining. Use the techniques and tools of statistical analysis and data mining to identify the information and knowledge to support decision making. The tools that can be applied at this stage can be sorted into three categories: (1) statistical analysis tools, such as SAS, SPSS, Lisrel, AMOS, Matlab, and R; (2) data mining tools, such as Weka, SAS Enterprise Miner, IBM Intelligent Miner, and SPSS Clementine; and (3) some OLAP tools.

Visual Presentation. Use diagrams to reduce the dimensions of information, colors to distinguish types of information, and proportions to present the degree of importance, etc., to be easily understood. Tools such as Microsoft Power BI, Tableau Software, Watson Analytics, and Analytics Cloud are available.

4   Case: Education Big Data at Tzu-Chi University

Since the establishment of the IR Office in 2015, Tzu-Chi University has established an IR information platform, conducted university-wide analysis, and analyzed student learning outcomes. In the early stage, the main issue was to improve students' learning outcomes and enhance the university's professional-management ability. In the end, we hope to create a decision-making culture based on empirical data through scientific investigation. The first important task is to establish an IR information platform and import data related to the issue.

The IR system is different from the general university administration system, which is mainly used to support the university in its daily business and is mainly used by general operators or middle-level managers. The processed data is biased toward current or immediate information. The system's back end mainly receives the school database; the IR system is more like an organization's DSS, mainly used for decision support by analysis or decision makers or to process history or multi-dimensional data. The back end also often receives data warehouse. In this consideration, Tzu-Chi University has set up another university research and analysis system to meet the needs of IR and initially completed 10 major analysis modules (2018). Figure 2 shows the student-analysis module, including the enrolled students and the correlation analysis of their entry mathematics scores and school performance.

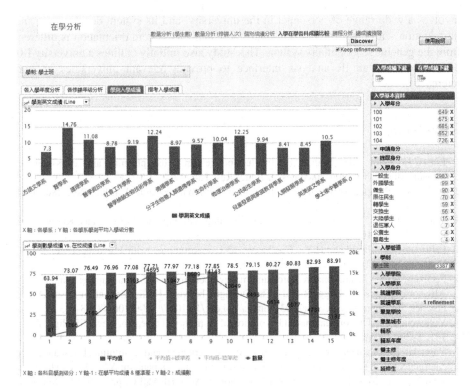

Fig. 2. The student-analysis module of IR at Tzu-Chi University

5 Conclusions

Applying the Viewpoint of University Stakeholders to the Search for IR Issues. IR topics are diverse and difficult to classify. This study is based on the perspective of university stakeholders, and the research topics can be clearly summarized. This view consists of students, universities, and society, and it is based on the student's learning outcomes and should meet the university's requirements.

Building and Applying Various Technologies and Tools Related to IR From the Data-Processing Perspective. The IR system is not the same as the general school administration system, but from the data-processing perspective, it can immediately distinguish its differences. Therefore, this study is an attempt to classify the technologies and tools involved in the IR into five processing steps, including data gathering, pre-processing, storage and integration, analysis and mining, and visual presentation. With the presentation of this division, the roles and timings of various technologies, tools, and applications become clearer.

Providing an Example of Actual IR Planning and System Development to Assist Relevant Personnel or Universities. Development of the general school administrative system usually only involves business-related units or personnel, but the IR system involves a wide range of personnel in the university, and its system development and introduction with data warehousing and timely analysis system orientation is different from the general school affairs system. This study also initially outlines a university IR-driven step and an IR analysis interface to provide relevant universities or staff references.

References

1. Lin, C.H., Chen, J.H., Shih, C.L.: Institutional research: use planning and assessment to measure student learning outcomes. J. Educ. Res. **280**, 17–29 (2017)
2. Hsu, C.H.: Prospect of big data analysis in institutional research. J. Educ. Res. **280**, 4–16 (2017)
3. Wu, X., Zhu, X., Wu, G.Q., Ding, W.: Data mining with big data. IEEE Trans. Knowl. Data Eng. **26**(1), 97–107 (2013)
4. Labrinidis, A., Jagadish, H.V.: Challenges and opportunities with big data. Proc. VLDB Endowment **5**(12), 2032–2033 (2012)
5. Peterson, M.W.: Institutional research and management in the U.S. and Europe: some EAIR - AIR comparisons. In: Begg, R. (ed.) The Dialogue between Higher Education Research and Practice. Springer, Dordrecht (2003). https://doi.org/10.1007/978-0-306-48368-4_3
6. Volkwein, J.F.: The foundations and evolution of institutional research. New Dir. High. Educ. **141**, 5–20 (2008)
7. Yamada, R., Yamada, A.: Higher education governance and institutional research: the emergence of a new role in the post-massification era in Japan. In: Wu, A.M., Hawkins, John N. (eds.) Massification of Higher Education in Asia. HEAQEG, pp. 129–147. Springer, Singapore (2018). https://doi.org/10.1007/978-981-13-0248-0_10
8. Hui, S.C., Jha, G.: Data mining for customer service support. Inf. Manag. **38**(1), 1–13 (2000)

Trends and Research Issues of Online Dating: A Review of Academic Publications from 2005 to 2019

Wan Zhen Hong[✉] and Chih Chao Lia

Graduate Institute of Applied Foreign Languages,
National Yunlin University of Science and Technology, #123 University Road,
Section 3, Douliou 64002, Yunlin, Taiwan
eunice19960320@gmail.com

Abstract. With the progress of the technology, online dating has become one of the most popular ways to meet new partners in recent years. The study aims to understand the perspective of the studies published in academic journals from 2005 to 2019. A total of 43 journals were conducted to analyze the research design, research purpose, countries, continent, and the platform of online dating. From the review results, it was found that both apps and website in online dating have made great progress in the past decades. In addition to the changes in relationship and the increasing number of online daters in the new era, the strategies of self- disclosure in internet and dating life have also become more diverse in recent years.

Keywords: Online dating · Motivation · Relationship · Communication

1 Introduction

In the early 2000s, made up a relationship with the people you met through phone would be difficult to imagine. However, the situation had changed recently, this has become one of the most popular ways to meet new partners. (Couch and Liamputtong 2008). Online dating refers to practice of using dating software to develop a relationship. By operating the platform to connecting the daters with database of potential romantic partners (Vardelle et al. 2016), the new technology plays an essential role in current life, it has changed the life in dating and the view of relationship. Since 2005, the study conducted by Cacioppo et al. (2013) indicated over a third of marriages in the United State occurred after online dating. Moreover, the study conducted by Sparrow et al. (2016) shows 50 million individuals used one of the most popular dating apps is called Tinder, the users spent approximately 90 min per day and check it frequent times in a day. By connecting and communicating and the chance face to face with potential partners, the appealing part of the new trend is that it allows daters to strategically choose the aspects of identity to present. Nevertheless, it makes deception as a common strategy for ensure a date in reality with online partners (Sharabi and Caughlin 2019). McCornack and Levine (1990) define deception as the "deliberate falsification or omission of information by a communicator, with the intent being to mislead the

© Springer Nature Singapore Pte Ltd. 2020
J. Shen et al. (Eds.): IC3 2019, CCIS 1227, pp. 611–619, 2020.
https://doi.org/10.1007/978-981-15-6113-9_70

conversation partner" (p. 120). The relevant studies broke new prospect in understanding of the online dating development and perspective in the new dating life. Online dating has gradually been widely discussed around the globe; however, the development and trends of mobile dating apps and websites is still lack systematic analysis. Therefore, a meta review of the studies published in academic journals from 2005 to 2019 was conducted to analyze the research design, research purpose, countries, continent, and the platform been analysis. From the review results, it was found that both apps and website in online dating have made great progress in the past decades. In addition to the changes in relationship and the increasing number of online daters in the new era, the strategies of self- disclosure in internet and dating life have also become more diverse in recent years. It was also found that mobile dating software has mainly been used by young adults for finding potential partners, some previous study examines the popular apps and goals for online daters, while a few or even no studies are related to other different classification of categories. The past few decades have dramatically changed the dating behavior owing to the rise of the online dating.

2 Literature Review

The use of the dating sites and apps specifically focus on helping people looking for the relationship with potential partner is increasing rapidly and has widely use in current society. As the previous research shows, there are no gender difference in the characteristic, that both male and female they want their partner that are kind, reliable, outgoing and smart (Botwin et al. 1997). Nevertheless, there still exist the difference in the preference. Men were generally considered playing a more active role in sexual encounter, being involved in multiple relationship. While women were expected more passive compared to men, tended to invest in stable relationship. Specially, men approach women from online dating platform more than women approach men (Tolman et al. 2003). For instance, a previous study indicated that 57% of male verse 23% of female never got a single email form a prospective date (Hitsch et al. 2010). There was various difference with communicating with others. People tend to express themselves and sometimes exaggerate or fabricate their characteristic. The previous investigation focuses on the type of self-disclosure and deception in nature. Additionally, the literature indicates that both men and women have the behavior using deceptive self- presentation to enhance different traits. The study by Camire (1991) specify male and female willingness to attract a mate. Men were reported tend to appear more dominant, resourceful, and more kind than they usually were. In contrast, women were shows that they were willing to use deception to their physical appearance as more favorable than it actually were. Overall, the research on deceptive self- presentation shows that both the interaction and the gender difference matter in the online dating society. During the last 10 to 15 years, the internet has become an essential platform to connect people together. With the rise of the mobile devices, smartphones play an increasingly important role in our daily lives and people nearly consistently connected to their devices. Several applications (apps) and social networking sites have been released which allows the Internet users to keep in touch, share information or develop relationship. Dating websites and apps have flourished in the market and enjoy a lot of popularity worldwide. The new trends make mobile dating software become a way for emerging adults to initiate committed romantic relationships. In addition, several widely adopted online dating purpose, such as relationship satisfaction, platform analysis, self-disclosure, deception risk, and the motivation have seldom been adopted in communication of online dating. This also reflects the fact that most of these studies focused on influence and relationship satisfaction, while few were conducted in the domains aimed at deception risk, such as misrepresenting and trustworthiness. On the other hand, it was found that the number of studies using the nonexperimental design and the qualitative research has no significant difference in recent years; moreover, the amounts of studies reported the platform analysis, while motivation were seldom analyzed. Accordingly, the research trends and potential research issues of online dating are proposed as a reference for researchers, instructors and policy makers.

3   Research Method

3.1   Resources

The journal papers related to online dating between 2005 to 2019 were searched in the Web of Science database on April 1st, 2019. There were 294 papers including "Online dating" in the paper title, abstract, or keywords list. Among those papers, 45 were related to communication. By removing 2 redundant journal papers, a total of 43 papers were selected in the final list for analysis, as shown in Fig. 1. The researcher then read and categorized the papers based on the coding scheme. During the coding process, if there were inconsistent coding values, the researchers were asked to discuss until an agreement was reached.

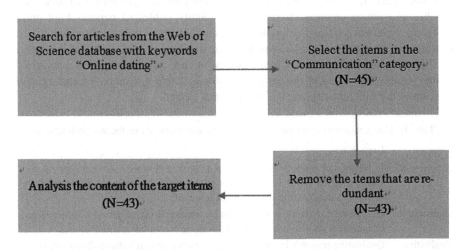

Fig. 1. Web of Science database searching steps

3.2   Data Distribution

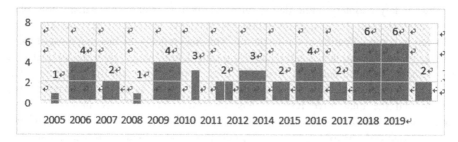

Fig. 2. Published papers applying online dating from 2005 to 2019

Figure 2 shows the publication situation of online dating in communication papers from 2005 to 2019. The earliest paper was written by Alapack et al. (2005) and investigated the online dating behavior and interaction on internet flirting. The number of the paper had no relevant difference in research on online dating in 2005 to 2016. It was not until 2017 that it started to receive more attention from researchers

3.3   Coding Schemes

Open coding served as a reference to analyze the contents in this study, including the authors, journals, research design, research purpose, countries and continents, the platform. The following items explain the coding schemes of each dimension:

- Nationalities, authors, and journals: The basic information of those published papers is discussed, including authors, nationality, and journals. The aim is to understand who, and which countries have more frequently published papers about online dating. Relevant journals for publishing communication are also provided.
- Research design: The strategies that integrate in different components of the studies. The set of the methods and procedures used in collecting and analysis measures of the variables specified in the research problem. Table 1. Categories and explanations of the different approach of the research design.

Tab. 1. Categories and explanations of the different approach of the research design.

Strategy	Explanation
Experimental	Experimental research is any research conducted with a scientific approach, where a set of variables are kept constant while the other set of variables are being measured as the subject of experiment
Quantitative	Quantitative research is the systematic empirical investigation of observable phenomena via statistical, mathematical, or computational techniques
Qualitative	Qualitative research is a type of social science research that collects and works with non-numerical data and that seeks to interpret meaning
Mixed methods	Mixed methods research is a methodology for conducting research that involves collecting, analyzing and integrating quantitative and qualitative
Analytical	Analytical research is a research that involves critical thinking skills and the evaluation of facts and information relative to the research being conducted

- Research purpose: The study categorized the purpose refer to the research into five aspects. Relationship satisfaction, platform analysis, self-disclosure, deception risk and the influence.
- Continents: There are five large land surfaces, involved Africa, Europe, Asia, Oceania, American (North and South) referred in the paper. On one hand to be easier to define which part of the world are engage in the new technology, on the other hand it will be easier to compare with different continents. It would be more complex and meaning less to compare with countries.
- Platforms: Online dating can be divided into two dimensions, dating application on the mobile devices and website-oriented dating platform. Dating apps are similar to online dating websites in that they provide access to potential romantic partners (Finkel et al. 2012).

4   Research Result

4.1   Nationalities, Authors, and Journals

Only the nationalities of the first authors of the published papers on online dating were counted in this study. From the results, it can be found that there were many researchers from different countries attempting to apply online dating research. Figure shows significant difference on the papers the countries published. A large amount of research were conducted by Americans (Fig. 3).

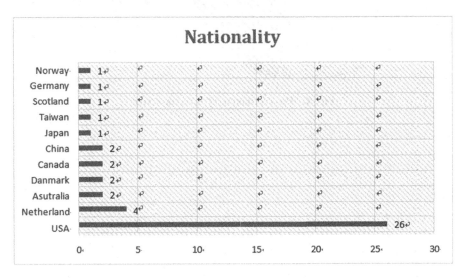

Fig. 3. Countries publishing papers on online dating during 2005 to 2019

4.2   Research Design and Research Purpose

Figure 4 shows the research design of the online dating in communication by receiving the literature from 2005 to 2019. The largest amount of the research design is quantitative studies, it contains 46% of the design. The second greatest number is qualitative research 44%. The difference of the two aspects is that qulitative research is a method for in-depth learning from daters' behaviors. While by statistic were able to acquire more data and the correlation of online dating. Mixed method and Analytical design only contain 5% each in the reviews. Figure 5 is the distribution of research purpose. The result shows the researchers preferred to study the motivation and effect on online dating more than focus on the individuals behavior, reveals the motivation of understanding the influence is the most common issues for the studies.

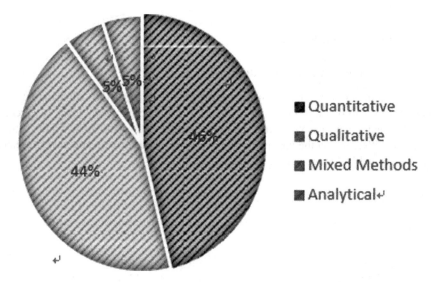

Fig. 4. The distribution of research design

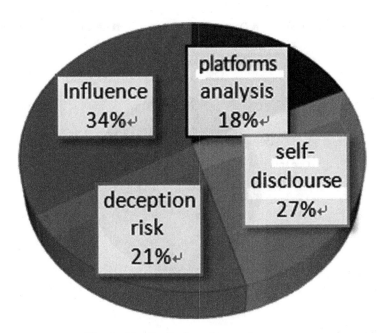

Fig. 5. The distribution of research purpose.

4.3   Continents

In the online dating research, distribution of the continents in the world is shown in the Fig. 6. There are referred in these continents: America (27), Europe (6), Asia (5). No study was found investigating Africa and Oceanina. Half of the research were conducted in America. Asia, Europe and the places not mentioned contain nearly equally distriubuted. The researchers point out the reason they were interested in American is that there were difference in grouping human self- identified as Asian American, African American, Native American and Caucasian. The dissimmar position is worth investigate, making the popular trends for the online dating research.

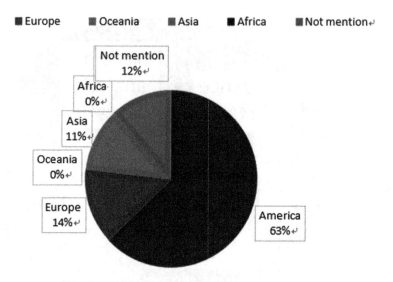

Fig. 6. The distribution of continents.

4.4   Platforms

The platforms in the research investigation involved the applications, websites, both application and website, and not mentioned in the journals. From the Fig. 7, it shows that the distribution of the platform in the studies. Apparently, most of the research conducted with website as the online dating means. The dating website have been refferd in the papers included Facebook, American single, Webdate, Match.com, and many other current dating website. The most used application contain Tinder, Okcupid, Bumble as the top three rank for daters.

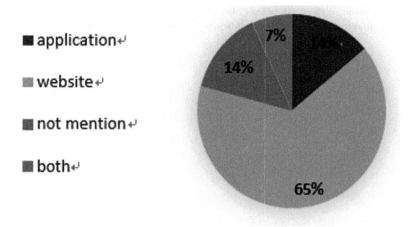

Fig. 7. The distribution of dating platform.

5 Conclusion and Discussion

In this study, a meta-review was conducted by analyzing the online dating studies in communication published in academic journals from 2005 to 2019. It was found that the number of studies gradually increased in recent years. Despite the first country started to investigated the issues was from Eurpoe, the majority of the researchers were American. Both quantitative and qualitative design were wildly used to examine the theme of online dating. In addition, mixed method was also being conducted owing to get the statistic data and the semi-structure response from the participants for the accuracy. A large amount of the research conducted the study by the platform of website, the researcher found that application was less than site can be affect by the flow of technology. The smartphone apps are just become popular not until 2015 (Smith and Anderson 2016). Addtionally, the websites were considered more easier to build and manage by the administrator. However, the apps are now gradually replacing the website fiercely. The future studies can put the effort on the different countries, most of the research were American- oriented that different countries with different culture may not be generalize with the results. The results presented may arise people's attention on the online dating.

References

Botwin, M.D., Buss, D.M., Shackelford, T.K.: Personality and mate preferences: five factors in mate selection and marital satisfaction. J. Pers. **65**(1), 107–136 (1997). https://doi.org/10.1111/j.1467-6494.1997.tb00531.x

Couch, D.: Liamputtong, P: Online dating and mating: the use of the internet to meet sexual partners. Qual. Health Res. **18**(2), 268–279 (2008)

Finkel, E.J., Eastwick, P.W., Karney, B.R., Reis, H.T., Sprecher, S.: Online dating: a critical analysis from the perspective of psychological science. Psychol. Sci. Publ. Interest **13**(1), 3–66 (2012)

Hitsch, G.J., Hortaçsu, A., Ariely, D.: Economics: what makes you click?—mate preferences in online dating. Quant. Mark. Econ. **8**(4), 393–427 (2010). https://doi.org/10.1007/s11129-010-9088-6

Sharabi, L.L., Caughlin, J.P.: Deception in online dating: significance and implications for the first offline date. New Med. Soc. **21**(1), 229–247 (2019). https://doi.org/10.1177/1461444818792425

Smith, A., Anderson, M: 5 facts about online dating, vol. 29 (2016)

Tolman, D.L., Striepe, M.I., Harmon, T.: Gender matters: constructing a model of adolescent sexual health. J. Sex Res. **40**(1), 4–12 (2003). https://doi.org/10.1080/00224490309552162

Vardelle, A., et al.: The 2016 thermal spray roadmap. J. Therm. Spray Technol. **25**(8), 1376–1440 (2016). https://doi.org/10.1007/s11666-016-0473-x

Sparrow, E., Friede, M., Sheikh, M., Torvaldsen, S., Newall, A.T.: Passive immunization for influenza through antibody therapies, a review of the pipeline, challenges and potential applications. Vaccine **34**(45), 5442–5448 (2016)

Alapack, R., Blichfeldt, M.F., Elden, A.: Flirting on the internet and the hickey: a hermeneutic. Cyberpsychol. Behav. **8**(1), 52–61 (2005). https://doi.org/10.1089/cpb.2005.8.52

McCornack, S.A., Levine, T.R.: When lies are uncovered: emotional and relational outcomes of discovered deception. Commun. Monogr. **57**(2), 119–138 (1990)

The Influence of Reading of Various Genres on Writing Enhancement

Chia Ju Ho[✉] and Shyh Chyi Wey

Graduate Institute of Applied Foreign Languages,
National Yunlin University of Science and Technology,
#123 University Road, Section 3, Douliou, Yunlin 64002, Taiwan
lulu40725lulu40725@gmail.com

Abstract. Busy with daily works, people choose to relieve intensive pressure through reading. A growing number of language instructors and curriculum designers also believe that students' language proficiency will be effectively enhanced when novel reading practices are applied. Therefore, this study aims to investigate the influence of reading of various genres on students' written English. The research reviewed 30 papers on relevant topics between 2016 to 2018. They were categorized based on several aspects such as years, research design, levels of reading as well as research participants. A majority of the papers reviewed in this study employed experimental approach to conduct their researches. The results suggested that experimental approach is relatively more reliable than qualitative approach; choosing proper course materials plays a significant role when processing a research.

Keywords: Reading or writing · Writing performance · Experimental approach

1 Introduction

Due to widespread Internet, people have developed a heavy dependence on cyber spaces to acquire current affairs. As a result, many students in Taiwan tend to demonstrate lack of writing proficiency. Extensive reading of various genres is considered helpful to avoid the common writing problems such as redundancy (Ferry 2006). Therefore, this study aims to identify the impacts of reading of diverse genres on writing. İn the past, the importance of cultivating reading habit was highlighted in many previous studies, many of which ignored the significance of reading various genres and topics. From the present study, we have found that cultivating a reading habit of diverse genres is fundamental to an individual's writing advancement.

A majority of papers simply emphasized the necessity of cultivating reading habit of language materials, whereas few of them had identified the effectiveness of reading different genres and how it would impact an individual's writing. The present paper is aimed to discuss the significance of reading various topics.

© Springer Nature Singapore Pte Ltd. 2020
J. Shen et al. (Eds.): IC3 2019, CCIS 1227, pp. 620–625, 2020.
https://doi.org/10.1007/978-981-15-6113-9_71

2 Literature Review

Reading has become more prevalent since the advent of Internet, and a wide variety of benefits are introduced to rebuild the reading preference of the EFL students (Ivins 1992). In addition, according to (Tammeus 2001), ten or twenty years ago, it was not unusual to find opinion and editorial columns in the 850 to 1,000 word range, while now 700 words is a rough max. Therefore, many students have reshaped a reading preference of various genres, including columns, to improve either reading or writing performance. In order to better understand the characteristics of the influence of reading of various genres, this chapter begins with common writing problems of the EFL writers in Taiwan. Contrastive analysis will be the following emphasis. In the last section of this chapter, the scoring criteria will be reviewed.

3 Research Method

3.1 Resources

The journal papers related to novel reading in writing enhancement between 2016 and 2018 were searched in the Web of Science on November 29th, 2018. There were 190 papers including "English writing" or "reading" in the paper title, abstract, or keywords list. Among those papers, 190 were related to writing enhancement. By removing 60 non-journal papers and 70 redundant journal papers, a total of 60 papers were selected in the final list for analysis.

3.2 Implementation Method

In order to transfer the results of virtual environment training to the real environment, we use the programmable uav as the real uav, which can control the aircraft by command. On this side we use the pyparrot bebop 2 quadcopter.

Figure 1 shows the publication situation of papers discussing the influence of reading English novels on writing enhancement from 2016 to 2018. The earliest paper was written by Nielsen (2016), and investigated the influence of reading quarterly. There was no abundant journal on such field published by the year of 2016. Despite a limited number of journals by 2016, Fig. 1 shows a stable growth of journals published every year that investigate the correlation between reading novel and writing proficiency. Seven papers were found in 2016, and more dedications were also made in the next two years, with 10 and 13 papers were released respectively.

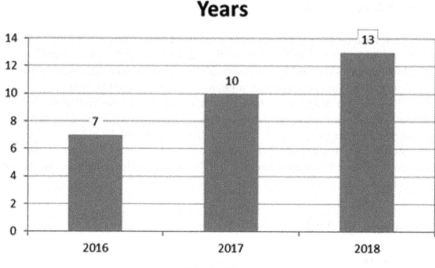

Fig. 1. Years.

3.3   Coding Schemes

Previous coding schemes served as a reference to analyze the contents in this study, including the years, research design, level of reading, research participants. The following items explain the coding schemes of each dimension:

(1). Years: The basic category of those papers is the year when they were published. The aim is to understand when the paramount period is of research of relevant topics.

(2). Research design: Among the 30 papers collected, half of them were published in 2016 and based on experimental research which included pre-tests and post-tests. Another 8 papers were also published in the same year but based on non-experimental research, such as descriptive or questionnaire approaches. 3 papers were found to employ qualitative research and be published in 2017; 4 papers were based on strategic or historic analysis and published in the same year. On the top of that, the other 30 papers "mixed" both qualitative and quantitative approaches which were not presented in this category.

(3). Level of reading: 30 papers were categorized based on the current level of reading proficiency observed from participants who were measured by a pre-test to fit into appropriate lelve of class. The scale was ranged from simple, intermediate, intermediate and advanced as well as advanced. Firstly, 5 research papers were based on simple level, with story books and teenager literatures being distributed in class. Furthermore, 6 research papers were based on intermediate level, with short passages of reading comprehensive tests being offered to assess students' reading performance. In addition, 9 research papers were based on intermediate and advanced, with short passages adopted from magazines or any authentic materials being given in class for reading tasks. Finally, the other 10 papers were based on advanced level, with thematic or professional journals being employed in class for reading challenges.

(4). Research participants: Participants may vary based on different topics in each papers. Among the 30 papers, 3 papers published in 2017 were conducted in primary schools, with young kids being assessed by giving reading assistance. From 2016 to 2018, 3 papers were done in middle and high schools. Furthermore, 14 research papers published in 2017 and 2018 were processed in universities, with college students being academically assessed in class. There were also 6 papers published in the same year aimed to process the research by studying people with high education such as master or doctorate degrees. Finally, 4 papers were conducted by studying other groups of subjects not mentioned in original studies.

4 Research Results

4.1 Years

There are abundant research papers on the relevant topic. From the results, it can be found that there were many researchers aware of the influence of reading novels on writing advancement. It is also concluded that reading and writing proficiencies are highly correlated. From the Fig. 1, we can infer that, from 2016 to 2018, there is a stable growth on awareness of the close relations between reading and writing performances. As a result, it is also convinced that there will be more papers released in the future which are dedicated to identifying the correlation between reading ability and writing proficiency.

4.2 Research Design

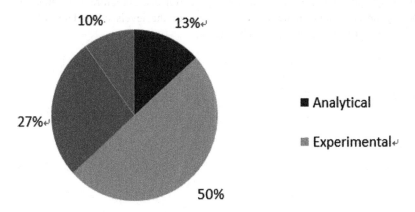

Fig. 2. Research design.

Figure 2 indicates that many scholars employed experimental approach to conduct their researches, half of which being completed in such way. Therefore, we can postulate that experimental approach is relatively more reliable and trustworthy. In contrast to experimental research, qualitative research is less popular when it comes to relevant topics.

4.3   Level of Reading

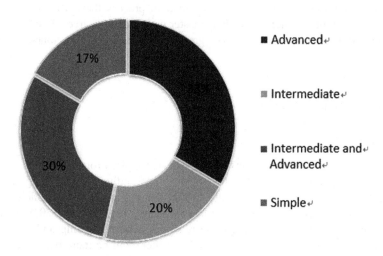

Fig. 3. Level of reading.

From Fig. 3, it suggests an obviously even distribution of course materials employed in each class with different levels. Course materials taught in class will vary, owing to disparity of educational levels of each group of subjects. Therefore, we can assume that choosing proper course materials customized for the levels of students plays a significant role in processing a research (Fig. 4).

4.4   Research Participants

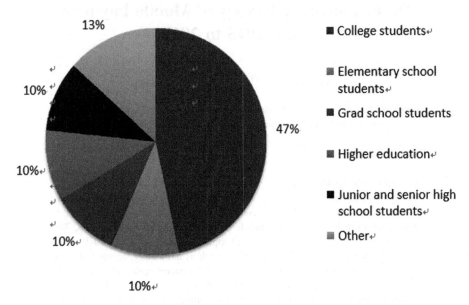

Fig. 4. Research participants.

5   Conclusion and Conclusion

The main study focused on examining the influence of reading of various genres on EFL learners' writing enhancement. In the study, it is commonly believed that, in the future, more papers will be published to identify the correlation between reading and writing performance. İn the past, a majority of papers simply emphasized the necessity of cultivating reading habit of language materials, whereas few of them had identified the effectiveness of reading different genres and how it would impact an individual's wiring. The present paper is aimed to discuss the significance of reading various topics, motivating more EFL students to reshape their reading behaviors.

References

Ferry, T.: Your Guide to English News Language (20 K), vol. 5 (2006)

Ivins, M.: Molly Ivins Can't Say That, Can She? Vintage (1992)

Chen, Y.-m.: The problems of university EFL writing in Taiwan. Korea TESOL J. **5**(1), 59–79 (2002)

James, C.: Contrastive Analysis (1980)

Tammeus, B.: A Gift of Meaning. University of Missouri Press, Columbia (2001)

Trends and Research Issues of Technology Development: A Review of Mobile Payment from 2015 to 2019

Yu-Jhu Guo$^{(\boxtimes)}$ and Ching-Pu Chiao

Graduate Institute of Applied Foreign Languages, National Yunlin University of Science and Technology, Douliou 64002, Yunlin, Taiwan
M10741013@yuntech.edu.tw

Abstract. The mobile payment plays an important role in this convenience society. By the growing number of the mobile payment users, the mobile payment has been use in different area and different countries. Therefore, this study aims to make a review of mobile payment during recent five years. The research reviewed 33 papers on relevant topics between 2015 and 2019. They were categorized based on several aspects such as nationality, research design, participates, and research theme. A majority of the papers reviewed in this study employed nonexperimental approach to conduct their researches. Because the mobile payment will become the trend in the future, the result showed that the security field can be investing in the future.

Keywords: Mobile payment · User intention

1 Introduction

With the development of smart phones and the e-commerce system, mobile payment has been gaining popularity in the world. Compared with traditional offline payment, mobile payment can help customers and merchants complete various types of transactions through mobile devices without any time and place limit. (Shao et al. 2019) Mobile payment represents a technical innovation of traditional payment, which is defined as "initiating, authorizing and confirming the exchange of financial value in exchange for any payment for goods and services using mobile devices (Au and Kauffman 2008). There are many researches aim to different approaches that related to mobile payment. This research reviews the relevant topic between 2015 and 2019 in order to know the development of mobile payment in the recent year.

2 Literature Review

Mobile payment services are the forms of combinative technologies that provide consumers with the ability to complete a financial transaction in which monetary value is transferred over mobile terminals to the receiver via the use of a mobile device. (Park et al. 2019) Mobile payment has been extensively discussed in recently years. During

© Springer Nature Singapore Pte Ltd. 2020
J. Shen et al. (Eds.): IC3 2019, CCIS 1227, pp. 626–631, 2020.
https://doi.org/10.1007/978-981-15-6113-9_72

these years, mobile payment has been used in many places such as convenience stores, public transportation, online shopping, restaurants, and daily fee payment. There were many researches that related to mobile payment and aimed to different fields, such as business, telecommunications, computer science information…etc. Also, there were many different research topics, such as users' intention, usage of mobile payment, users' acceptance, and the influence.

3   Research Method

3.1   Resources

The journal papers related to mobile payment between 2015 and 2019 were searched in the Web of Science on April 24, 2019. There were 412 papers including "mobile payment" in the paper title, abstract, or keywords list. Among those papers, 60 papers were related to business. By removing 27 non-journal papers, a total of 33 papers were selected in the final list for analysis (Fig. 1).

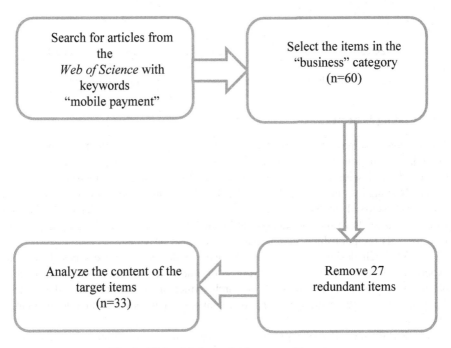

Fig. 1. Web of Science database searching steps

3.2   Data Distribution

Figure 2 shows the publication situation of mobile payment papers from 2015 to 2019. The earliest paper was written by (Slade et al. 2015), and investigated the consumers' adoption intentions of mobile payment. There were 7 papers published in 2016, and more dedications were also made in the next three years, with 6, 10 and 4 papers were released. Figure 2 shows a stable growth of journals published every year that investigate the correlation of mobile payment.

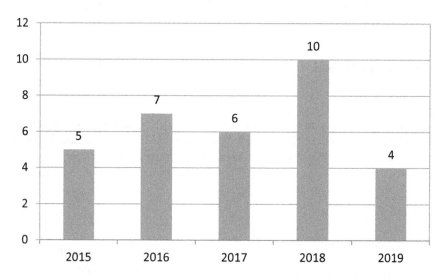

Fig. 2. Published papers applying mobile payment from 2015 to 2019

3.3   Coding Schemes

The coding schemes served as a reference to analyze the contents in this study, including the nationality, authors, journals, research design, participants, and research theme. The following items explain the coding schemes of each dimension:

(1) Nationality, authors, and journals: The basic information of those published papers is discussed, including authors, journals. The aim is to understand who and which countries have more frequently published papers about mobile payment. Relevant journals for publishing mobile payment are also provided.

(2) Research design: Among the 33 papers collected, 15 papers based on non-experimental research such as descriptive or questionnaire approaches. Another 4 papers were based on experimental research, which included pre-test and post-test. 3 papers were based on strategic or historic analysis. 5 papers were found to qualitative research.

(3) Participants: Participants may very base on different topics in each paper. Among the 33 papers, half of them, participants were consumers who use the mobile payment. However, there were different research approaches, and the participants were different. Participants of this paper (Lee et al. 2019) were included consumer and retailer. Participants of this paper (Park et al. 2019) were divided into different gender, males and females.

(4) Research theme: The category of research themes was based on the usage, the acceptance, the evaluation, the security, the influence. The usage means participants'

using habits of mobile payment. The acceptance means the participants' perceptions of mobile payment. The evaluation discusses the benefits that mobile payment brings to the society and people. The security that investigated the safety of mobile payment. The influence aspect means the effects that mobile payment brings to the society.

4   Research Result

4.1   Nationalities

Only the nationalities of the first authors of the published papers were counted in this study. From the result, it can be found that there were many researchers from different countries attempting to investigate mobile payment in different approaches. Figure 3 shows the distribution of the top 10 countries and areas. The top three countries and areas are the Spain (5), the Denmark (4), and United States (3).

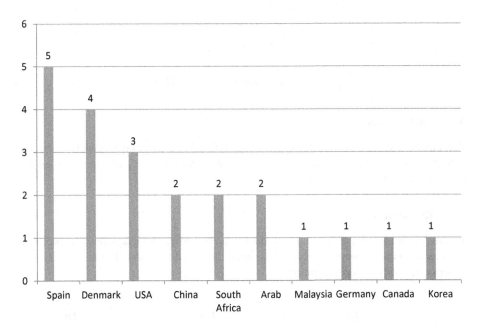

Fig. 3. Top ten countries publishing papers on mobile payment during 2015 to 2019

4.2   Research Design

Figure 4 indicates that many scholars employed non-experimental approach to conduct in mobile payment researches, half of which being completed in survey, use questionnaires to make a survey and make data analyze. The second proportion is qualitative research. The third proportion is experimental research. The fourth proportion is strategic or historic analysis approaches.

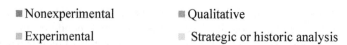

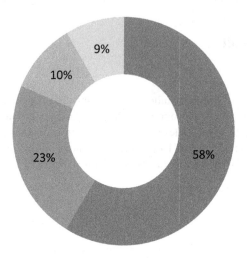

Fig. 4. The distribution for the research design

4.3 Participants

Participants are different from different research theme. Among the 33 papers, indicates that most of participants are mobile payment users. Different research topic decided the different participants.

4.4 Research Theme

Figure 5 indicates the distribution for the research theme. The usage has 6 papers and the evaluation has 6 papers, which have been discussed the most. In the contrary, the security has only 1 paper mentioned.

	The usage	The acceptance	The evaluation	The security	The influence
Total	6	5	6	1	4
2015	1	1	0	0	1
2016	2	1	2	0	1
2017	1	0	2	1	2
2018	1	3	2	0	0
2019	1	0	1	0	2

Fig. 5. The distribution for the research theme

5   Conclusion

Mobile payment will become the new trade in the recently years, there will be more and more researches related to mobile payment this filed. As the result, it shows that the usage and the evaluation these two themes have been discussed a lot, on the contrary, the security field has not been discussed actively. The security of mobile payment will become an important part that people concern in the future. Therefore, the security part of mobile payment is worth more investigating in the future.

References

Au, Y.A., Kauffman, R.J.: The economics of mobile payments: Understanding stakeholder issues for an emerging financial technology application. Electron. Commer. Res. Appl. **7**(2), 141–164 (2008). https://doi.org/10.1016/j.elerap.2006.12.004

Lee, J., Ryu, M.H., Lee, D.: A study on the reciprocal relationship between user perception and retailer perception on platform-based mobile payment service. J. Retail. Consum. Serv. **48**, 7–15 (2019). https://doi.org/10.1016/j.jretconser.2019.01.007

Park, J., Ahn, J., Thavisay, T., Ren, T.: Examining the role of anxiety and social influence in multi-benefits of mobile payment service. J. Retail. Consum. Serv. **47**, 140–149 (2019). https://doi.org/10.1016/j.jretconser.2018.11.015

Shao, Z., Zhang, L., Li, X.T., Guo, Y.: Antecedents of trust and continuance intention in mobile payment platforms: the moderating effect of gender. Electron. Commer. Res. Appl. **33** (2019). https://doi.org/10.1016/j.elerap.2018.100823

Slade, E.L., Dwivedi, Y.K., Piercy, N.C., Williams, M.D.: Modeling consumers' adoption intentions of remote mobile payments in the United Kingdom: extending UTAUT with innovativeness, risk, and trust. Psychol. Mark. **32**(8), 860–873 (2015). https://doi.org/10.1002/mar.20823

Trends and Research Issues of Exploring the Role of Social Media in Adolescents from 2010 to 2018

I. Chia Liu[✉] and Shyh Chyi Wey

Graduate Institute of Applied Foreign Languages,
National Yunlin University of Science and Technology,
#123 University Road, Section 3, Douliou 64002, Yunlin, Taiwan
a9989999@gmail.com

Abstract. Social media is becoming a vital part of adolescents in these years. More and more studies are doing research bases on social media. The researcher based on 30 journal papers to analyze the trends in social media in recent years. The researcher used analytical method to analyze 30 papers, including resources, data distribution and coding schemes. The results were divided into 5 categories, including types of social media, the first purpose of using, using times, research method and different dimensions. In the future, social media will still exist in adolescents' life. Therefore, the study of social media will still appear.

Keywords: Social media · Adolescents

1 Introduction

Social media plays a vital role in adolescents' peer relationship, Eleuteri et al. (2017) indicated social media is a platform which can make people share content, connect with each other, interaction, and cooperation. Either in the past or present, social media are considered as a platform which can do interaction, keep connect, receive some information and share somethings. However, social media is as well as regarded as a place to keep peers connect, understand peer's life and make peer can social now. Moreover, Nesi and Prinstein (2015) indicated that it is difficult to neglect the effect on the omnipresence of the technology that surrounding the modern adolescents and the technology accompany with the progress of the times, technology modify adolescents social universe rapidly. Therefore, with the statement illustrated above, it can discover social media is gradually transforming adolescents' life.

Besides, it was found that adolescents were progressively using social media to be a tool to connect with their peers. Lenhart et al. (2015) showed there were many adolescents often use the Internet, cellphones, and video games to gain information and communicate with each other everywhere in the United States.

However, at adolescent about 15–20 years old stage, friends are more significant than family. They are more pay attention to the peer relationship. Consequently, if adolescents do not have a social media among peers, they may be edged out or be

© Springer Nature Singapore Pte Ltd. 2020
J. Shen et al. (Eds.): IC3 2019, CCIS 1227, pp. 632–641, 2020.
https://doi.org/10.1007/978-981-15-6113-9_73

bullied by their friends. To realize the trend of the role of social media in adolescents, literature on social media in adolescents was analyzed in the study which was from 2010 to 2018.

2 Literature Review

There are various studies showed social media is becoming a necessary part of people's life. One study pointed in particularly, as deliberating whether use social media or not, Internet use is the most vital factor. Then, it spends about one half young people's time to use online social media (Thompson and Lougheed 2012). According to these study, they apparently illustrated social media is invading into people's daily life now, including adolescents.

There is a large volume of published studies describing the different role of social media in adolescent. For example, Beyens et al. (2016) indicated adolescents have a strongly feel that they need to belong to their peer and keep good connection with their peer, besides, they feel that they need to be favorite among their peer. Therefore, social media is becoming a role which would affect peer relationships and a role which could increase them to use it. Besides, Garmy et al. (2012) showed there were a thing in adolescents which was the relationship with use more Internet and slighter sleep time, tardy to go to the bed and raise daytime fatigue. It demonstrated social media was a negative role among adolescents which would influence on their health.

An increasing number of literatures are undertaking to find negative issues arising from social media. To understand the role of social media in adolescents deeply, the research trends in social media is becoming increasingly important. However, the research trend analysis of how to guide adolescents use social media more correctly then avoid their mental and physical were damaged is exiguous. In the future study, it can explore more research on how to prevent adolescents from using social media incorrectly.

3 Research Method

3.1 Resources

The journal papers related to the role of social media on adolescents between 2010 and 2018 were searched in the Website of Science database on November 10th, 2018. The total journal papers were searched for 101. Then there were some keywords of these journal papers' title were including "Social Media", adolescents" and "peers". After removing 16 non-journal papers and 55 unrelated journal papers. After figuring up, there were 30 papers were chosen to analyze finally. Subsequently, the researcher read and used coding scheme to categorize the paper. When the researcher was doing coding scheme, the researcher would be asked to revise if there were discordant coding.

3.2   Data Distribution

Figure 2 presents the publication of the relationship between social media and adolescent's papers from 2010 to 2018. The earliest paper was published in 2010 and the author is Stephanie M REICH. At 2010, the social media was not an important role of adolescents; therefore, the paper of studying social media and adolescents was not popular, however, the paper was written by Stephanie M REICH that is the only one paper about social media and adolescents in 2010. Gradually, from 2013 to 2015, the social media was becoming a vital part of adolescents. Consequently, in 2015, there are 5 papers related to social media and adolescents. In 2016, there were a high peaked that the studies were about social media and adolescents. Since the social media was formally invading into adolescents' daily life. Accordingly, there were some problems emerging that social media caused and influenced on adolescents. However, in 2017 to 2018, the studies about social media and adolescents were little by little decreasing for social media has been universal (Fig. 1).

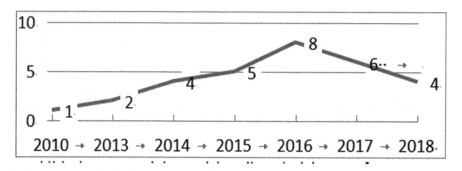

Fig. 1. Published papers applying social media and adolescents from 2010 to 2018.

3.3   Coding Schemes

The coding schemes mentioned above are to analyze the contents in this study, including the types of social media, the first purpose of using, using times, research design and measurement issue. The following items explain the coding schemes of each dimension:

(1) Types of social media: Nowadays, more and more social media is appearing. Accordingly, using the coding scheme is to explore what kinds of social media the most influences on adolescents. There are 5 categories of the coding scheme, including Facebook, Instagram, Twitter, mixed and not specified.

(2) The first purpose of using: Some adolescents using social media is to learn, however, some adolescents using social media is to entertain. Consequently, using the coding scheme is to explore the adolescents' first purpose of using. There are 3 categories of the coding scheme, including for learning, for fulfill one's heart and for socializing.

(3) Using times: Some adolescents are fear of missing out something, so he/she uses social media for all the time. Even in the bed time, he/she is still using. Therefore, using the coding scheme is to explore the adolescents' using time. There are 1 category is 1 day more than 2 h.

(4) Research design: The research method categories are based on those proposed by Johnson and Christensen (2000), including mixed methods, experimental method, non-experimental method, and qualitative analytical.

(5) Measurement issue: Social media can cause three-dimension issues, including the effect of adolescent, the cognition of adolescents and the physical effect on adolescents. First, in the affect, it divides into 4 categories, including depressive tendency, family relationship, degree of anxiety and fear of reality. Next, in the cognition, it sorts for 4 categories, including decreasing concentration, decreasing grades, decreasing social and narcissism. Finally, there is a category in the physical part, that is, poorer sleeping quality.

4 Research Results

4.1 Types of Social Media

From the results, Facebook was the most types of social media which was adopted to research in the field of social media and adolescents. There were 23 papers use Facebook to investigate. Obviously, Facebook still played a vital role among adolescents. Figure 3 presented the types of social media in the field of social media and adolescents. There were 3 papers adopted mixed social media to conduct the research. Besides, there were 2 papers not use certain social media to investigate the research. Then, Instagram was adopted to do the research was only showed in 1 paper. Finally, Twitter was the same as Instagram, only showed in 1 paper.

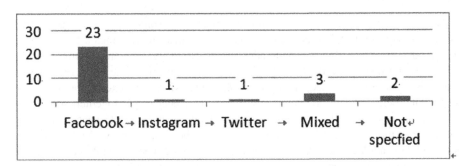

Fig. 2. Types of social media in the field of social media and adolescents from 2010 to 2018.

4.2 The First Purpose of Using

Figure 4 show that there were 9 papers mentioned that the first purpose of using social media in adolescents is for socializing. Nowadays, social media is invading into adolescents' life. Therefore, in their peer relationship, they always use social media to connect each other and make friends. Afterward, using social media for socializing is becoming a basis phenomenon in adolescents' peer relationship. Moreover, there were 4 papers presented that the first purpose of using social media in adolescents is for fulfill one's heart. Social media is a place that can reveal personal information, including images and videos. Consequently, it will cause adolescents for attracting others attention and post images or videos to show themselves. When someone commented to the adolescent's post, he/she would feel satisfy with someone was care about him/her. It will cause their mental feel well-being. In addition, there are 3 papers indicate that some adolescents using social media is for learning. In the technological generation, much information is from social media since it is quite convenient. For example, some courses which need adolescents to set up a group to discuss the course content and post some course information to inform course participants. Accordingly, the purpose of some adolescents of using social media is for learning.

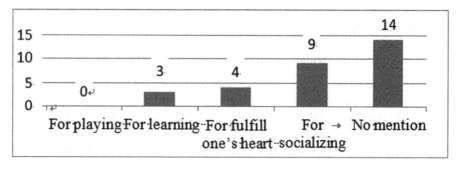

Fig. 3. Types of social media in the field of social media and adolescents from 2010 to 2018.

4.3   Using Times

Figure 5 indicate that there are 11 papers indicate that some adolescents use social media 1 day more than 2 h. Nowadays, because of smartphone brings a convenience, hence, social media is always around adolescents. No matter they are at home or at the school, social media is anywhere. Even before bed time or in the sleep time, social media is a role that can deeply impact adolescents. Moreover, except for the above statements, when adolescents have a meal with their peer or get together, some adolescents are always looking at social media. Consequently, adolescents use social media 1 day more than 2 h is becoming a common phenomenon now. On the contrary, less and less adolescents use social media less than 2 h since adolescents have a reliance on the social media to get the information about anything. No matter to get news or to understand their peers' things, adolescents are through social media to obtain.

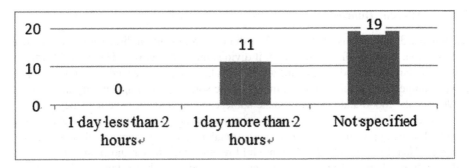

Fig. 4. Types of social media in the field of social media and adolescents from 2010 to 2018.

4.4   Research Method

There are many types of research methods are adopted, including mix methods, experimental methods, non-experimental methods, qualitative methods and analytical method.

There are 3 papers adopt mix methods, these papers use qualitative and quantitative to investigate adolescents' pre bed time use social media. Moreover, there is 1 paper adopt experimental method to conduct the study, and then it focuses on 1 experimental group and 1 control group to investigate adolescents' learning effect. Figure 6 present that most papers adopt non- experimental method to conduct studies; there are 20 papers focus on questionnaire to investigate adolescents' physical and mental differences. In addition, there 4 papers use qualitative method to conduct papers; and then they focus on interview and case study to investigate the depression with adolescents. Finally, there are 2 papers adopt analytical method to analyze recent articles about social media impact on adolescents.

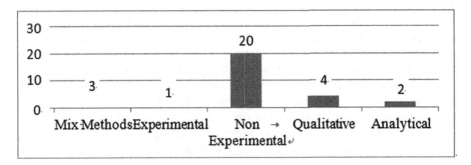

Fig. 5. Types of social media in the field of social media and adolescents from 2010 to 2018.

4.5 Different Dimensions

There are 3 dimensions, including affect dimension, cognition dimension and physical dimension. First, in affect dimension, it divides into 4 categories. There are 11 articles indicate that social media can make adolescents have depressive tendency. For example, when adolescents receive bad comments or see some worst things, it will influence on adolescents' mood and gradually make adolescents have depressive tendency.

Afterward, there are 2 articles show that social media can keep family relationship well. For example, parents can through social media to understand their children's things. Therefore, it can make parent-child relationships better and more intimate. On the contrary, there is 1 article show that social media can break family relationship.

There are 11 papers show that social media can make adolescents have anxiety. For example, when adolescents are limited to do not use social media, they will feel anxiety. Since modern adolescents are used to have social media to get information, if they cannot use it, they might feel anxiety. Consequently, social media can make adolescents have a high degree of anxiety. On the contrary, there is only 1 article show that social media would not make adolescents have anxiety. In fact, social media is being a necessary part of adolescents. Therefore, few articles show social media would decrease the anxiety of adolescents.

There is 1 article indicate social media can make adolescents fear of reality. For example, social media can make adolescents meet stranger who can make adolescents fulfill their satisfaction. Afterward, it will let adolescents cannot know the facts and visual then make adolescents are fear of reality.

Next, in the cognition dimension, it divides into 4 categories. There are 2 articles show that social media can decrease adolescents' concentration. For example, smartphone is always around adolescents, that is, they can use social media anytime. No matter during the class or during the break time, they always use social media. Therefore, it will decrease adolescents' concentration. Besides, there is 1 article show that social media would decrease adolescents' grades. Without concentration, the grades will go down naturally.

There are 9 articles show that social media can decrease adolescents' social ability. Nowadays, through social media can connect with adolescents' peer relationship, it will cause adolescents lack of communicating to others by face to face. Consequently, adolescent with decreasing social ability is influenced by social media. However, there is 1 article indicate that social media would not decrease adolescents' social ability.

There are 3 articles show that adolescents use social media is because of narcissism. Social media is a place that adolescents can post their images, videos et al. However, some adolescents are due to narcissism then post something to attract others' attention. All the factors are caused by narcissism. Therefore, using social media will cause narcissism for adolescents.

Finally, there is 1 category in physical dimension. There are 4 articles indicate that social media will cause poor sleep quality for adolescents. Since some adolescents are fear of missing out, so they cannot truly have a good sleep. In addition, for not missing anything that they want to know, they always stay up. Consequently, with these reasons, social media is a thing that breaks adolescents' sleep quality.

Main Dimension	Sub-dimension	Positive	Negative	No difference
Affect	Depressive Tendency	11	0	1
	Family relationship	1	2	1
	Degree of anxiety	11	1	0
	Fear of reality	0	1	0
Cognition	Decreasing concentration	2	0	0
	Decreasing grades	1	0	0
	Decreasing social	9	1	1
	Narcissism	3	0	1
Physical	Poorer sleeping quality	4	0	0

Fig. 6. Different dimensions.

5 Conclusion and Future Work

A review and analysis of the role of social media in adolescents from 2010 to 2018 was conducted in the study. In these literatures, the researcher discovered there was seldom research adopted Instagram and Twitter to conduct the research. Most studies adopted Facebook to conduct was because Facebook was the most common social media platform in the past that adolescents used. However, according to Anderson and Jiang (2018), the study indicated Facebook is not any longer as popular as before among adolescents and Instagram is becoming the most familiar social media platform that adolescents use now. Therefore, it can do more research on Instagram among adolescents in the future study.

Furthermore, the researcher found there were numerous studies showed their first purpose of using social media was for socializing in these literatures. Vernon et al. (2015) showed technology makes adolescents submerge. With various social media emerging gradually, social media is be a necessary part of people's life, including adolescents. Therefore, adolescents are used to social media to make friends and their first purpose of using social media for socializing is gradually clear. However, the first purpose of adolescents to use social media for learning was seldom be discussed.

Moreover, the researcher as well as discovered there were many studies presented adolescents used social media 1 day more than 2 h. With ever-changing technology, modern people use the Internet and social media is increasing, including adolescents. According to Lenhart et al. (2010), the study demonstrated about 86% adolescents would put their cell phones near them, such as on the bed, in their hands or on the nightstand. All these situations would cause the convenience of them and increase them to use social media. Accordingly, the situation that adolescents used social media 1 day more than 2 h is increasingly common. Nevertheless, there were numerous studies didn't discuss how many times do adolescents use social media 1 day.

In addition, there were numerous different dimensions statistics based on adolescents to analyze in the study, including depressive tendency, family relationship, anxiety, fear of reality, decreasing concentration, decreasing social, narcissism and poor sleeping quality. Although most dimensions above were negative and the statistics based on adolescents. However, for the future research, it can collect more positive statistics of adolescents who use social media to analyze. In addition, it can investigate not only adolescents but also different ages children to conduct the review research as well as.

Analyze and review relevant issues about social media in adolescents was the primary purposes and contribution of the study. Besides, the suggestions of future research have been proposed as well as. With advances in technology, social media have gained popularity among people, including adolescents. Therefore, there are numerous negative problems that caused by social media. Social media can have serious influences on the mental and physical health in adolescents. Consequently, how to prevent adolescents from using social media incorrectly is worth researching these issues in greater depth.

References

Anderson, M., Jiang, J.: Teens, social media & technology 2018. Pew Res. Cent. **31** (2018)

Baumeister, R.F., Leary, M.R.: The need to belong: desire for interpersonal attachments as a fundamental human motivation. Psychol. Bull. **117**(3), 497 (1995)

Beyens, I., Frison, E., Eggermont, S.: "I don't want to miss a thing": adolescents' fear of missing out and its relationship to adolescents' social needs, Facebook use, and Facebook related stress. Comput. Hum. Behav. **64**, 1–8 (2016)

Eleuteri, S., Saladino, V., Verrastro, V.: Identity, relationships, sexuality, and risky behaviors of adolescents in the context of social media. Sex. Relat. Ther. **32**(3–4), 354–365 (2017)

Garmy, P., Nyberg, P., Jakobsson, U.: Sleep and television and computer habits of Swedish school-age children. J. School Nurs. **28**(6), 469–476 (2012)

Ji, Y., Wang, G.-J., Zhang, Q., Zhu, Z.-H.: Online social networking behaviors among Chinese younger and older adolescent: the influences of age, gender, personality, and attachment styles. Comput. Hum. Behav. **41**, 393–402 (2014)

Lenhart, A., Duggan, M., Perrin, A., Stepler, R., Rainie, H., Parker, K.: Teens, social media & technology overview 2015. Pew Res. Cent. [Internet Am. Life Proj.] (2015)

Lenhart, A., Ling, R., Campbell, S., Purcell, K.: Teens and mobile phones: text messaging explodes as teens embrace it as the centerpiece of their communication strategies with friends. Pew Internet Am. Life Proj. (2010)

Nesi, J., Prinstein, M.J.: Using social media for social comparison and feedback- seeking: gender and popularity moderate associations with depressive symptoms. J. Abnorm. Child Psychol. **43**(8), 1427–1438 (2015)

Santor, D.A., Messervey, D., Kusumakar, V.: Measuring peer pressure, popularity, and conformity in adolescent boys and girls: predicting school performance, sexual attitudes, and substance abuse. J. Youth Adolesc. **29**(2), 163–182 (2000)

Thompson, S.H., Lougheed, E.: Frazzled by facebook? an exploratory study of gender differences in social network communication among undergraduate men and women. Coll. Student J. **46**(1), 88–99 (2012)

Vernon, L., Barber, B.L., Modecki, K.L.: Adolescent problematic social networking and school experiences: the mediating effects of sleep disruptions and sleep quality. Cyberpsychol. Behav. Soc. Netw. **18**(7), 386–392 (2015)

The Role of Technology in Chemistry Experiment Learning: A Review of Academic Publications from 1993 to 2018

Shu-Hao Wu[1] and Chiu-Lin Lai[2(✉)]

[1] Graduate Institute of Information and Computer Education,
National Taiwan Normal University, Taipei, Taiwan
[2] Department of Education, National Taipei University of Education,
Taipei, Taiwan
jolen761002@gmail.com

Abstract. In this study, a review of technology-enhanced chemistry experiment learning was conducted. The selected studies were published in SSCI journals from 1993 to 2018, and a coding scheme was employed that included types of technology, roles of technology, learning domains, learning places and participants. From the review results, it was found that researchers frequently employed personal computers in their studies and applied technology to deliver learning knowledge to students. On the other hand, studies were frequently conducted in Inorganic Chemistry courses in the classroom. In addition, the participants in the studies were generally senior high school and higher education students. According to the review, it was found that most of the studies employed technologies for lower level implementation that is, providing supplementary materials for students. They rarely discussed the effects of technology on providing students with learning guidance or helping students solving complex problems. Accordingly, the research trends and potential research issues of technology-enhanced chemistry experiment learning are proposed as a reference for researchers, instructors and policy makers.

Keywords: Technology-enhanced learning · Chemistry education · Chemistry experiments · Research trends

1 Introduction

In recent years, students' ability of solving scientific problems in their lives has been regarded as an important issue. Some researchers and educational organizers have proposed some educational strategies and learning modes for cultivating students' scientific abilities [1]. For example, [2] developed a mobile learning context with self-regulated learning mechanisms. They employed this approach to help students conduct scientific inquiry and make effective reflections. [1] also integrated a collaborative learning model to help students learn science and enhance their collaborative learning skills. Scientific learning has already produced an important topic of current education [3, 4]. According to previous studies' conclusions, it was found that the issue of cultivating students' scientific abilities, such as inquiry, investigation, induction and data

© Springer Nature Singapore Pte Ltd. 2020
J. Shen et al. (Eds.): IC3 2019, CCIS 1227, pp. 642–651, 2020.
https://doi.org/10.1007/978-981-15-6113-9_74

screening [5, 6] has been regarded as a good strategy for improving the concept of national science [7, 8]. Although science education research has long been discussed, most studies have focused on general science education, since most research has been conducted in primary schools [9, 10]; Some studies have considered the reason for this distribution as being due to the difficulties of sampling or subject knowledge [11, 12]. In the case of general science education, it is easy to present its specific scientific phenomena in teaching, and the instruments or scientific methods used are simple. On the other hand, studies conducted in complex science or specific science-related subjects (e.g., physics or chemistry) need to put more time and effort into preparing and designing complex learning strategies and activities [13, 14]. An example is the activities that guide students to observe the precipitation, the change of color and the acidity and alkalinity of the acid–base titration. In the activity, teachers need to provide step-by-step guidance, the concept of the complex chemistry reaction, and the observation tips for avoiding failed experiments.

Thanks to advances in information technology, students can improve their learning outcomes, the efficiency of learning, and the overall quality of teaching [15–17]. Scholars have confirmed that through appropriate technology and considerate activity designs, students can improve their learning outcomes [18, 19]. Especially in chemistry education, many technologies have also been implemented since they can assist students in learning and help teachers explain abstract scientific concepts more effectively. For example, [20] employed mobile devices to assist inexperienced researchers in practicing single-crystal X-ray diffraction operations. With the guidance information provided by the mobile devices, those science researchers operated the equipment while understanding the steps. Moreover, this technology-supported guidance further increased their efficiency of operating the equipment. On the other hand, [21] integrated microscopic laboratories to help students learn the concept and the use of pH indicators. They found that the technology's level of information affected the students' observations. However, chemistry education is complex and it requires teachers to design rigorous activities [13], especially for the activities that guide students to conduct chemistry experiments. In supporting students' learning in chemistry experiments, researchers should provide students with adequate learning opportunities, effective tools and useful strategies [14, 22]. For understanding effective technology-enhanced chemistry experiment learning modes, reviewing the research trends and issues in the research field is important [23]. Therefore, this study analyzed the research related to chemistry experiments, and further discussed their applications and related issues to provide useful references for future scholars related to chemistry education.

2 Method

2.1 Resources

According to the research purpose, a review of technology-enhanced chemistry experiment learning was conducted. The Boolean expression ("education" or "instruction" or "learning" or "teaching") and ("chemical" or "chemistry") and ("experiment" or "laboratory") and ("e-learning" or "technology") was used to search for publications from the Web of Science database (WOS). In addition, the category was limited to educational research, and the literature type was limited to "article." Finally, 128 articles were selected. To ensure the papers were consistent with the research purposes, two researchers with more than 5 years' experience of conducting technology-based learning and chemistry education were asked to filter the papers. By excluding the irrelevant studies, a total of 58 papers were included in the final list for analysis.

2.2 Data Distribution

Figure 1 presents the distribution of technology-enhanced chemistry experiment learning from 1993 to 2018. The results showed that the number of papers applying technologies in chemistry experiment learning grew steadily. From 2013 to 2017, the number of papers published was 3–4 times higher.

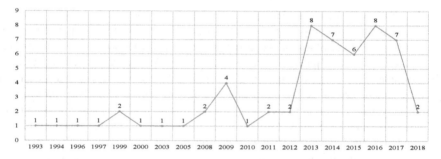

Fig. 1. The distribution of technology-enhanced chemistry experiment learning from 1993 to 2018

2.3 Coding Scheme

A coding scheme was developed to cover different aspects, including types of technology, roles of technology in learning, learning environment, learning domains and participants. The two researchers manually read and categorized the papers based on the coding scheme. They were asked to discuss any inconsistent coding values until they reached agreement on them. Detailed descriptions are provided as follows:

(1). Types of technologies: The coding scheme of the types of learning devices is based on [24] and [25]. The items included personal computers, tablets, smart phones, traditional mobile devices, wearable devices, mixed, not-specified, no use of devices, and others.

(2). The roles of technology in learning: The coding scheme of the roles of technology in activities is based on [26] and included: accessing learning materials only, accessing learning materials and taking assessments, learning across contexts, not specified, and no activities.

(3). Learning places: The coding scheme of the learning places referred to [27] and included classroom, laboratory, school campus, homes, real-world contexts related to learning content, across contexts, not-specified, and none.

(4). Learning domains: The coding scheme of the learning domains is divided into several sub-domains based on [28]'s definition of chemistry sub-disciplines: organic chemistry, inorganic chemistry, physical chemistry, analytical chemistry, laboratory training, others, mixed, and none. Laboratory training refers to the training content such as laboratory safety and health education, introduction of laboratory equipment and so on.

(5). Participants: The coding scheme of participants is divided based on [29]. The participants are divided into elementary school students, junior and senior high school students, higher education, teachers, mixed and none. Mixed refers to an activity comprising two or more groups of participants at the same time.

3 Result

In this study, a review of the research related to technology-enhanced chemistry experiment learning was conducted. A total of 58 papers were selected through the WOS database. This study also developed a coding scheme to explore the research trends of technology-enhanced chemistry experiment learning from different perspectives. The coding scheme in this study included types of technology, roles of technology in learning, learning environment, domains and participants, and measurement issues.

3.1 Analysis of the Integration of Technologies

The distribution pie chart of the types of technologies is shown in Fig. 2. It was found that more than half (64%) of the studies used personal computers, 3% used tablets, 2% used traditional mobile devices, and 2% used other technologies (e.g., an electronic tool that students can physically interact with). On the other hand, 7% of the studies mentioned that they adopted two different technologies in their research (e.g., personal computers and smart phones or tablets and wearable devices). In addition, 10% of the studies did not mention the type of technology they implemented in their research, while 12% did not use technology. According to the results, it was found that no studies integrated smart phones or wearable devices independently in their studies.

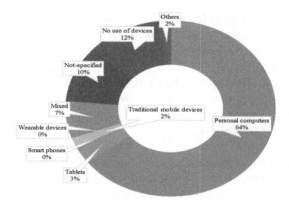

Fig. 2. Proportion of types of technologies of technology-enhanced chemistry experiment learning

The study also investigated the roles of technology in learning. It represented how researchers used technologies in teaching and learning. In Fig. 3, it showed that 79% of research used technology as the tool for accessing learning material only, and 2% adopted technologies that help learners access learning materials and take assessments on the e-learning equipment. Meanwhile, the percentages of learning across contexts is 2%, indicating that few studies conducted research that supported learners learning across different learning environments (e.g., classroom, laboratory, and the context in the field). Lastly, 2% of studies did not clearly specify the activity modes in their research, and 15% did not conduct activities.

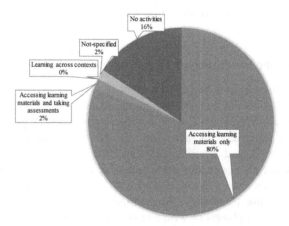

Fig. 3. Proportion of roles of technology of technology-enhanced chemistry experiment learning

3.2   Analysis of the Contexts and Participants

This study not only evaluated the integration of technologies in the research related to technology-enhanced chemistry experiment learning, but also investigated the contexts and the participants involved in their research. In terms of the learning places, Fig. 4 shows that most of the research took place in the classroom (37%), 34% of the studies did not mention their learning places, and few studies took place in a laboratory (10%), across contexts (8%), or in the home (2%). All of the across context studies conducted activities across classroom and laboratory, while 9% of studies did not conduct activities. In addition, none of the studies conducted activities on the school campus or in real-world contexts related to the learning content. This study concludes that the research related to technology-enhanced chemistry experiment learning seldom conducted activities in real-world environments.

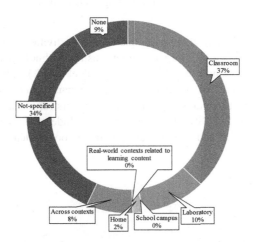

Fig. 4. Proportion of learning places of technology-enhanced chemistry experiment learning

In terms of learning domains, Fig. 5 shows that 32% of the articles are on inorganic chemistry, 9% on organic chemistry, 6% on physical chemistry, and 8% on analytical chemistry. Laboratory training constituted 11%. On the other hand, 17% conducted activities across different domains, 2% conducted studies with other domains, such as general chemistry, and environmental chemistry, and lastly, 15% of the studies did not conduct activities in their research.

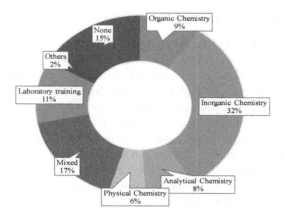

Fig. 5. Proportion of learning domains of technology-enhanced chemistry experiment learning

This study also investigated the participants of the activities. According to Fig. 6, it was found that most of the target learners using technology-assisted chemistry experiments were junior and senior high school students (33%) and in higher education (41%). Few studies enrolled teachers (4%) as the participants, and 5% conducted activities with mixed participants (e.g., including learners form senior high schools and higher education). Finally, 18% of studies did not include participants in their studies, and no studies conducted activities for elementary school students.

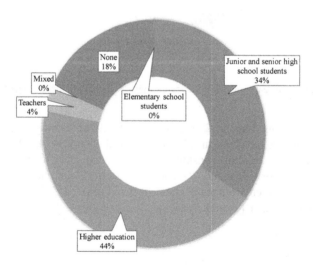

Fig. 6. Proportion of learning domains of technology-enhanced chemistry experiment learning

4 Discussion and Conclusions

Chemistry experiment learning generally requires learners to synthesize what they learned and what they observed in the laboratories [30]. Researchers have pointed out the difficulty students face in successfully combining multiple perspectives due to the weak support of technologies and learning strategies [31]. Therefore, the aim of this study was to review the literature related to technology-assisted chemistry experiment learning from 1993 to 2018. By analyzing the employment of technologies for chemistry experiment learning, it is expected that researchers can understand the research trend and innovative issues in chemistry experiment learning. Therefore, a total of 58 studies related to chemistry experiment learning were systematically analyzed.

In the analysis of the integration of technologies, it was found that most of the studies used personal computers for research activities, and up to 80% of the studies used technologies to provide students with digital learning content. From the scope of the application of technologies, it was concluded that most of the studies considered technologies as a channel for delivering learning knowledge. However, studies related to educational technologies have mentioned that technologies can also be an approach to helping learners to conduct inquiry, collect data when making observations, organize and analyze data, and then summarize the phenomena learners found [27, 32]. These activities were considered as the strategies for cultivating people's scientific abilities [33]. Therefore, some complex application or tight integration of technology for chemistry experiment learning is encouraged.

In the application domains, nearly 30% of the research was conducted in Inorganic Chemistry, and most in the field of VSEPR. This is because the learning knowledge of VSEPR consists of complex spatial knowledge; students are frequently confused if they do not have a physical model in their hands [34]. In this case, the digital 3D structure can help students to understand the concepts [35]. Among the participants, 40% of the research was conducted in higher education, and 30% was in secondary education (including junior and senior high schools). This might be because of the educational policy of learning chemistry; therefore, studies have mainly focused on secondary and higher education. However, it is worth noting that the support of technology in chemistry experiment learning can be extended to adult learning, especially for novice chemistry researchers [20]. They often need to operate complex equipment and solve various problems during the research process; therefore, the support of technologies is essential. On the other hand, in the learning places, 37% of the research was conducted in the classroom, and only 10% was carried out in a laboratory environment. It can be inferred that the research generally used technology-assisted teaching to assist students in understanding the chemistry experiments procedure or the concepts before entering a laboratory. Few studies asked students to conduct experiments together with technologies. Moreover, few studies conducted activities in real-world contexts related to the learning content. For improving students' learning and helping them to connect knowledge from the textbook to the real-world, researchers are encouraged to allow technologies to be used to help students in other places.

Through a systematic review of the research in this study, it was found that the research on technology-enhanced chemistry experiment learning generally remained at a relatively lower level of application, such as delivering learners' learning knowledge through technologies. In the future, it is suggested that relevant chemistry experiments research can introduce relevant technologies commonly used in current educational technology, and aim to provide students with more learning guidance, assessment and even analytical tools [20] to enhance the learning outcomes of students in the chemistry experiments course.

References

1. Baser, D., Ozden, M.Y., Karaarslan, H.: Collaborative project-based learning: an integrative science and technological education project. Res. Sci. Technol. Educ. 35(2), 131–148 (2017)
2. Lai, C.L., Hwang, G.J., Tu, Y.H.: The effects of computer-supported self-regulation in science inquiry on learning outcomes, learning processes, and self-efficacy. Educ. Technol. Res. Dev. 66(4), 863–892 (2018). https://doi.org/10.1007/s11423-018-9585-y
3. Hofstein, A., Lunetta, V.N.: The laboratory in science education: Foundations for the twenty-first century. Sci. Educ. 88(1), 28–54 (2004)
4. Osborne, J., Collins, S., Ratcliffe, M., Millar, R., Duschl, R.: What "ideas-about-science" should be taught in school science? - a Delphi study of the expert community. J. Res. Sci. Teach. 40(7), 692–720 (2003)
5. Marx, R.W., et al.: Inquiry-based science in the middle grades: assessment of learning in urban systemic reform. J. Res. Sci. Teach. 41(10), 1063–1080 (2004)
6. Sandoval, W.A., Reiser, B.J.: Explanation-driven inquiry: integrating conceptual and epistemic scaffolds for scientific inquiry. Sci. Educ. 88(3), 345–372 (2004). https://doi.org/10.1002/sce.10130
7. Edelson, D.C.: Learning-for-use: a framework for the design of technology-supported inquiry activities. J. Res. Sci. Teach. 38(3), 355–385 (2001)
8. Linn, M.C.: Technology and science education: starting points, research programs, and trends. Int. J. Sci. Educ. 25(6), 727–758 (2003)
9. Niess, M.L.: Preparing teachers to teach science and mathematics with technology: developing a technology pedagogical content knowledge. Teach. Teach. Educ. 21(5), 509–523 (2005)
10. Pelgrum, W.J.: Obstacles to the integration of ICT in education: results from a worldwide educational assessment. Comput. Educ. 37(2), 163–178 (2001)
11. Chang, C.Y., Lai, C.L., Hwang, G.J.: Trends and research issues of mobile learning studies in nursing education: a review of academic publications from 1971 to 2016. Comput. Educ. 116(Supplement C), 28–48 (2018)
12. Fu, Q.K., Hwang, G.J.: Trends in mobile technology-supported collaborative learning: a systematic review of journal publications from 2007 to 2016. Comput. Educ. 119, 129–143 (2018)
13. Kaya, E., Erduran, S.: Integrating epistemological perspectives on chemistry in chemical education: the cases of concept duality, chemical language, and structural explanations. Sci. Educ. 22(7), 1741–1755 (2013)
14. Johnstone, A.H.: Multiple representations in chemical education. Int. J. Sci. Educ. 31(16), 2271–2273 (2009)
15. Hensberry, K., Moore, E., Perkins, K.: Effective student learning of fractions with an interactive simulation. J. Comput. Math. Sci. Teach. 34(3), 273–298 (2015)
16. Kim, M.C., Hannafin, M.J.: Scaffolding problem solving in technology-enhanced learning environments (TELEs): bridging research and theory with practice. Comput. Educ. 56(2), 403–417 (2011)

17. Papastergiou, M.: Digital game-based learning in high school computer science education: impact on educational effectiveness and student motivation. Comput. Educ. **52**(1), 1–12 (2009)
18. Ip, H.H.S., et al.: Enhance emotional and social adaptation skills for children with autism spectrum disorder: a virtual reality enabled approach. Comput. Educ. **117**, 1–15 (2018)
19. Rachels, J.R., Rockinson-Szapkiw, A.J.: The effects of a mobile gamification app on elementary students' Spanish achievement and self-efficacy. Comput. Assist. Lang. Learn. **31**(1–2), 72–89 (2018)
20. Hwang, G.J., Yang, T.C., Tsai, C.C., Yang, S.J.H.: A context-aware ubiquitous learning environment for conducting complex science experiments. Comput. Educ. **53**(2), 402–413 (2009)
21. Nakhleh, M.B., Krajcik, J.S.: A protocol analysis of the influence of technology on students' actions, verbal commentary, and thought processes during the performance of acid-base titrations. J. Res. Sci. Teach. **30**(9), 1149–1168 (1993)
22. Frailich, M., Kesner, M., Hofstein, A.: Enhancing students' understanding of the concept of chemical bonding by using activities provided on an interactive website. J. Res. Sci. Teach. Off. J. Natl. Assoc. Res. Sci. Teach. **46**(3), 289–310 (2009)
23. Brewer, R., Movahedazarhouligh, S.: Successful stories and conflicts: a literature review on the effectiveness of flipped learning in higher education. J. Comput. Assist. Learn. **34**(4), 409–416 (2018)
24. Lin, H.C., Hwang, G.J.: Research trends of flipped classroom studies for medical courses: a review of journal publications from 2008 to 2017 based on the technology-enhanced learning model. Inter. Learn. Environ. **27**(8), 1–17 (2018)
25. Ozdamli, F., Uzunboylu, H.: M-learning adequacy and perceptions of students and teachers in secondary schools. Br. J. Educ. Technol. **46**(1), 159–172 (2015)
26. Hwang, G.J.: Definition, framework and research issues of smart learning environments - a context-aware ubiquitous learning perspective. Smart Learn. Environ. **1**(1), 4 (2014)
27. Hwang, G.J., Tsai, C.C., Yang, S.J.H.: Criteria, strategies and research issues of context-aware ubiquitous learning. Educ. Technol. Soc. **11**(2), 81–91 (2008)
28. Laidlaw, W., et al.: Chemistry subdisciplines. In: The Canadian Encyclopedia (2019). https://www.thecanadianencyclopedia.ca/en/article/chemistry-subdisciplines
29. Hwang, G.J., Tsai, C.C.: Research trends in mobile and ubiquitous learning: a review of publications in selected journals from 2001 to 2010. Br. J. Educ. Technol. **42**(4), E65–E70 (2011)
30. Bernholt, S., Broman, K., Siebert, S., Parchmann, I.: Digitising teaching and learning - additional perspectives for chemistry education. Isr. J. Chem. **59**(6–7), 554–564 (2019)
31. Seery, M.K., Agustian, H.Y., Zhang, X.C.: A framework for learning in the chemistry laboratory. Isr. J. Chem. **59**(6–7), 546–553 (2019)
32. Elyakim, N., Reychav, I., Offir, B., McHaney, R.: Perceptions of transactional distance in blended learning using location-based mobile devices. J. Educ. Comput. Res. **57**(1), 131–169 (2019)
33. Shin, S., Brush, T.A., Glazewski, K.D.: Designing and implementing web-based scaffolding tools for technology-enhanced socioscientific inquiry. Educ. Technol. Soc. **20**(1), 1–12 (2017)
34. McCollum, B.M., Regier, L., Leong, J., Simpson, S., Sterner, S.: The effects of using touch-screen devices on students' molecular visualization and representational competence skills. J. Chem. Educ. **91**(11), 1810–1817 (2014)
35. Merchant, Z., Goetz, E.T., Cifuentes, L., Keeney-Kennicutt, W., Davis, T.J.: Effectiveness of virtual reality-based instruction on students' learning outcomes in K-12 and higher education: a meta-analysis. Comput. Educ. **70**, 29–40 (2014)

Mobile Technology Facilitated Chemistry Learning in School: A Systematic Review from 2010 to 2019

Sasivimol Premthaisong[1(✉)], Pawat Chaipidech[3],
Patcharin Panjaburee[5], Sumalee Chaijaroen[4],
and Niwat Srisawasdi[2(✉)]

[1] Demonstration School of Khon Kaen University,
Nong Khai Campus, Nong Khai 43000, Thailand
[2] Division of Science, Mathematics, and Technology Education, Faculty
of Education, Khon Kaen University, Khon Kaen 40002, Thailand
niwsri@kku.ac.th
[3] Science Education Program, Faculty of Education, Khon Kaen University,
Khon Kaen 40002, Thailand
[4] Division of Professional Education, Faculty of Education, Khon Kaen
University, Khon Kaen 40002, Thailand
[5] Institute for Innovative Learning, Mahidol University,
Nakhon Pathom 73170, Thailand

Abstract. Over the last ten years, mobile learning issue in chemical education have been discussed around the world. However, the trend of applying mobile technology in chemical education still lack systematic analysis. In this study, a meta review of the studies published in academic journals, indexed by Scopus, from 2010 to 2019 was conducted to analyze nationalities, authors, journals, learning strategies, and research methods. The results revealed that the use of mobile technologies in chemical education have been increased in the past decade. It was also found that mostly mobile technologies have been applied in scientific experiment for chemistry learning as a learning tool. In addition, mobile learning strategies have seldom been adopted in inquiry learning, contest, and collaborative learning. In contrast, it was found that the number of studies using a system development has increased in recent years. Besides, most studies reported the process of using mobile devices in a laboratory, while students' psychomotor domain were rarely analyzed.

Keywords: Mobile learning · Mobile device · Mobile application · Chemical education · School science

1 Introduction

Currently, mobile devices are becoming a popular technology in our life. Especially in education, these devices provided educators with the opportunity to transform teaching and learning for addressing 21st century education. This transformed instruction creates a more flexible learning model that give advantages to students who could access to multiple information sources and shifted from an authority-based learning structure to a

© Springer Nature Singapore Pte Ltd. 2020
J. Shen et al. (Eds.): IC3 2019, CCIS 1227, pp. 652–662, 2020.
https://doi.org/10.1007/978-981-15-6113-9_75

structure based upon the concept of a community of learners [1]. It also gives educators the capability to connect with learners in many ways with devices that they use on a regular basis [2].

In this 21st century education, the advancement of mobile technology have brought a transformation to the education in all subjects. In particular, implementing mobile technology in chemistry-oriented education is also an interesting issue. Mobile technologies was not only integrated as innovative techniques to assist the teaching and learning of chemical theory contents, but also the learning of scientific laboratory investigation in real-world situation. For instances, [3] explored preservice chemistry teachers' perception of mobile augmented reality called Element 4D application which could represent atom of 36 natural elements of the periodic table, the findings revealed that the preservice teachers gave positive feedback and considered the possible way to integrate this technology in chemical education. Furthermore, mobile technology can be used to engage students in learning chemistry content by transforming it to mobile game application [4, 5].

Although there have been numerous valuable syntheses of previous studies on mobile learning, there are areas that need further examination. For example, there is possible for using mobile learning in the area of chemistry education due to the aspects that make it unique and well fitted to features and functions of mobile technology. Most of chemistry-related phenomena occur outside of the classroom and is arguably better studied in its natural environment and daily life, while other science content is impossible to see with naked eyes and requires graphical visualizations for assisting students to be able to construct completely scientific understand. In addition, scientific system and models cannot be comprehended without an immersive experience that demonstrates how the variables interact. These distinct aspects of science learning are well bringing into line with the mobility of devices as well as their ability to display interactive, three-dimensional graphics and simulations. However, there have been no reviews of research conducted to date on mobile learning in school chemistry. To understand the application and trends of mobile technology in chemical education, literature on mobile devices in chemistry learning in school level from 2010 to 2019 was analyzed in this study.

2   Literature Review

Numerous studies about the use of mobile and wireless communication technologies in education have been reported, in which these technology-enhanced learning approaches [6]. Mobile learning definitions have been recognized by researchers, such as "learning that happens learner takes advantage of learning opportunities offered by mobile technologies" and "learning that happens without being limited at a fixed location by using mobile technologies (e.g., mobile phone or Personal Digital Assistant, PDAs)" [7]. On the other hand, several researchers suggest that to develop effective learning activities and plans for helping students learn across contexts [8].

There have been many published studies of applying mobile technology in chemical education. For instance, [9] used smartphone-based hands-on guided laboratory to support science learning about solution in chemistry. The findings indicated that the instructional intervention can promote students' conceptual understanding and their ability to explain solution phenomena scientifically. In addition, to conduct the learning activity more engaging and meaningful, [10] integrated smartphone into science teaching to help their students develop a procedure to evaluate the corrosion rate of Iron in simulated seawater. The result shown that after participated with the technology and problem-based approach, the students could develop the experimental procedure themselves. In order to foster students' science process skills, a virtual chemical laboratory was developed by [11] using a hand movement recognition system. The results reveals that students working with a virtual lab had a better performance in terms of remembering information, showed a greater durability of remembering information and also had better results in solving problematic laboratory tasks.

According to the literature review, an increasing number of researchers who are struggling to apply mobile technology to improve students' learning, provided educators information to prepare the learning activities suitable for their students. To enable the research and development in chemistry in school level to become more enlightened, analyzing previous application and research trends in mobile technology in chemical education has become important. To provide a more detailed, the literature was analyzed to understand the findings of mobile technology in chemical education in the past, the research trends and issues are then proposed.

3   Research Methodology

3.1   Resource

This research study intend to serve as a basis of the implementation of mobile learning in school chemistry education. As such, the researchers examined papers from the SCOPUS database from 2010 to 2019 by searching for the publications whose titles, abstracts, or keywords met the logical condition ("mobile" or "smartphone") and ("chemistry") and ("school"). A total of 90 papers published in SSCI/SCI journals were appropriate for this study. By removing 42 non-article and non-English papers, 48 papers were comprised in the present study by deleting 20 which were not related to mobile-based chemistry learning (see Fig. 1).

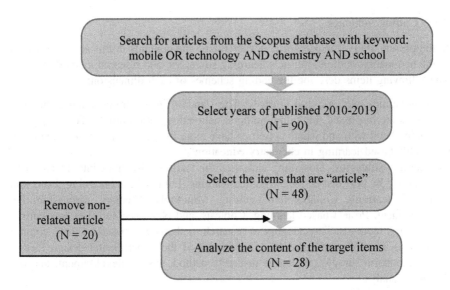

Fig. 1. Scopus database searching steps

3.2   Data Distribution

There were 90 papers in this study. The papers were classified and reviewed by three researchers based on the coding scheme. If there were inconsistent coding results, they would discuss until agreement was reached.

Figure 2 demonstrates the papers on the application of mobile technology in chemistry learning from 2010 to 2019. There were no literature reviews on mobile-based chemistry learning in 2010; after 2010, no more than 10 papers on mobile technology applied in chemistry were published each year. Since 2017 and 2018, academics have paid more attention to this field, with 6 papers published in 2017 and 2018.

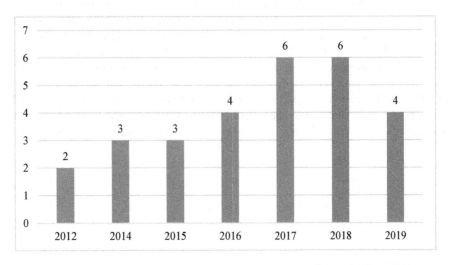

Fig. 2. Published paper using mobile technology in school from 2010 to 2019

3.3   Coding Schemes

In the present study, the categories for analyzing the contents in this study, consisting of the nationality, authors, journals, learning strategies, and research methods [12, 13]. The following items describe the coding schemes of each dimension:

1. Nationalities, authors, and journals: The standard information of those published papers are discussed, including authors, nationality, and journals. The purposes to comprehend who and which countries have more frequently published papers about mobile-based learning in chemistry education.
2. Learning strategies: This study classified the learning strategies into 11 categories proposed by [14] that is, Direct-guided learning, Inquiry-based learning, Contextual mobile learning, Collaborative learning, Mindtools, Thematic discussion, Peer assessment, Project-based learning, Contests, and Non-specified (i.e., laboratory).
3. Research methods: The category of research methods was based on the 6 common research methods presented by [15], consist of the experimental design method, questionnaire survey, qualitative research method, system development, and document analysis.
4. Research issues: The research issues investigated in the mobile-based learning in chemistry education studies were also analyzed, including the aspects of cognition, affect, psychomotor, and scientific experiment.

4   Research Results

4.1   Nationalities, Authors, and Journals

In this study, we only examined the nationality of the first author of the papers on mobile technology applied in the field of chemistry. The results indicated that many countries have already tried applying mobile technology-supported learning in chemistry teaching. The top country is the United states (7 papers) (See Fig. 3).

The journals which published are: Journal of Chemical Education (JCE), International Journal of Computer-Assisted Language Learning and Teaching, International Journal of Mobile and Blended Learning, Eurasia Journal of Mathematics, Science and Technology Education, British Journal of Educational Technology and Lab on a Chip. The top international journal with the highest productivity in this area is Journal of Chemical Education (JCE). The statistical results of the authors and journal titles could be a good reference to those who intend to publish mobile-based chemistry learning studies or host relevant workshops or conferences in the future (See Fig. 4).

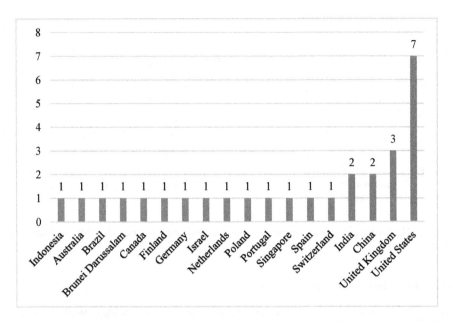

Fig. 3. Countries publishing papers on mobile technology in chemical learning during 2010 to 2019

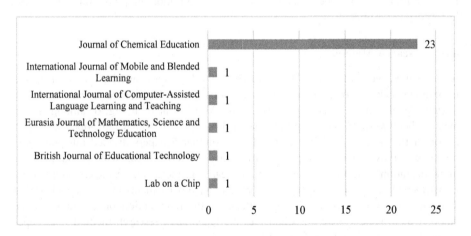

Fig. 4. Journals publishing on mobile learning in chemistry education from 2010 to 2019

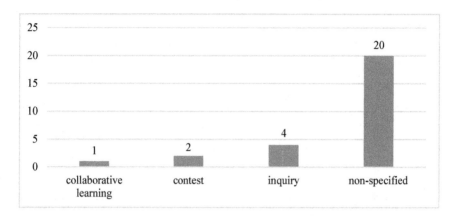

Fig. 5. The learning strategies applied in mobile technology-supported chemistry learning from 2010 to 2019.

4.2 Learning Strategies

The distribution of learning strategies applied in mobile technology-supported chemistry learning from 2010 to 2019 is indicated in Fig. 5. The greatest proportion is non-specified (i.e. laboratory), with a total of 20 papers, while the second greatest is inquiry learning, with a total of 4 papers. The third greatest is contest, with a total of 2 papers. It can be found that mobile-based chemistry education more emphasis on usage in the laboratory environment.

4.3 Research Method

In this study, we investigated the research methods in each article, for instance, the Experimental design method, Questionnaire survey, the Qualitative research method, System development or Document analysis. As illustrated in Fig. 6, among all 28 papers, there were 16 adopting the system development, which developed an application platform and then verified its effects. Another 5 papers divided into the questionnaire survey, which examined participants' preference for widespread tools or implementation of technology in chemistry learning. there were 3 papers adopted the Experimental design method, which refers to engage participants in system or learning strategies, and then investigating the effects of the intervention on the participants. Another three papers were classified into the Qualitative research method; one paper adopted the method of Mixed method.

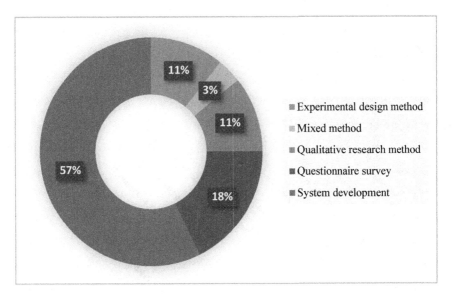

Fig. 6. Ratio of methods adopted in mobile-based learning chemistry education from 2010 to 2019

4.4   Research Issues

The research issues were investigated in the mobile chemical education studies, including the aspects of cognitive, affective domain, psychomotor, and scientific laboratory. Figure 7 shows the number of each issue discussed in the literature. It can be seen that studies on the scientific experiment (15 papers) and on the affective domain (9 papers) constitute the majority of the studies. In contrast, the research issues of the cognitive aspect (5 papers) and psychomotor (1 paper) were rarely discussed throughout the period from 2010 to 2019 in mobile-based learning chemistry education. Only one study investigated participants' psychomotor [5]. To summarize, scientific experiment was the main concern of most of the mobile learning studies among the chemistry education research. Many researchers intended to integrate mobile devices into science laboratory since it was a convincing way to bring students' mobile devices as a learning tool in their own learning way.

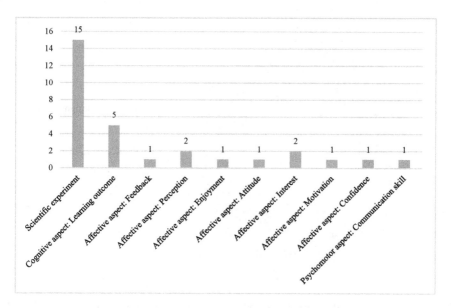

Fig. 7. Research issues in mobile chemical education

5   Conclusion and Discussion

A meta-review and analysis of using mobile technology in chemistry learning from 2010 to 2019 were performed in this study. This result indicated that the quantity of studies increased over many years. Moreover, it was found that the number of publications which integrated the mobile technology into chemical education are greatly increased over the decades. This result is consistent with Crompton et al. that the use of mobile learning in science education is growing at an exponential rate [16]. It was also found that many studies used system development in the methodology. This implied that numerous researchers have considered to develop the application of mobile devices in chemistry learning which focuses on laboratory.

Meanwhile, it was found that issues related to "psychomotor" were rarely investigated. Most studies used mobile devices in scientific laboratory for chemistry subject. This reveals that more studies are required to develop learners' scientific process during perform the experiment for learning science. This implies that investigating the impacts of mobile learning approaches on learners' scientific process skills in integration of this technology into chemistry learning remains a challenging and important issue.

On the other hand, it can be found that many learning strategies, for example direct-guided learning, peer assessment, thematic discussion, mindtools, project-based learning, and contextual mobile learning, were hardly adopts in mobile chemical education. In the many years, several studies have reported the success of using those learning strategies in mobile learning applications [17]; consequently, it is trying to examine the probability of applying them to mobile learning for chemical education.

Especially, inquiry-based learning, contextual mobile learning, mindtools, project-based learning and peer assessment could be helpful to the learners in terms of their higher order thinking, such as critical thinking performance and problem-solving.

References

1. Hamm, S., Satsman, G., Jones, B., Baldridge, S., Perkins, S.: A Mobile Pedagogy Approach for Transforming Learners and Faculty. In: Berge, Z., Muilenburg, L., (eds.). Routledge, New York (2013)
2. Ward, D.N., Finley, J.R., Keli, G.R., Clay, G.: Tansy.: benefits and limitations of ipads in the high school science classroom and a trophic cascade lesson plan. J. Geosci. Educ. 1(61), 378–384 (2013)
3. Yang, S., Mei, B., Yue, X.: Mobile augmented reality assisted chemical education: insights from elements 4D. J. Chem. Educ. 6(95), 1060–1062 (2018)
4. Jones, A.H.O., Spichkova, M., Spencer, J.S.M.: Chirality-2: development of a multilevel mobile gaming app to support the teaching of introductory undergraduate-level organic chemistry. J. Chem. Educ. 7(95), 1216–1220 (2018)
5. Koh, B.K.S., Fung, M.F.: Applying a quiz-show style game to facilitate effective chemistry lexical communication. J. Chem. Educ. 11(95), 1996–1999 (2018)
6. Chu, H.-C., Hwang, G.-J., Tsai, C.-C., Tseng, C.R.J.: A two-tier test approach to developing location-aware mobile learning system for natural science course. Comput. Educ. 4(55), 1618–1627 (2010)
7. O'Malley, C., Vavoula, G., Glew, J. P., Taylor, J., Sharples, M. https://hal.archives-ouvertes. fr/hal-00696244. Accessed 07 June 2019
8. Hwang, G.-W., Lai, C.-L., Wang, S.-Y.: Seamless flipped learning: a mobile technology-enhanced flipped classroom with effective learning strategies. J. Comput. Educ. 2(4), 449–473 (2015)
9. Prasongsap, B., Srisawasdi, N.: Investigating the impact of smartphone-based guided inquiry laboratory on middle school students' science learning performance. In: 26th International Conference on Computers in Education, pp. 626–633, Philippines (2018)
10. Moraes, P.E., Confessor, M.R., Gasparotto, H.S.L.: Integrating mobile phones into science teaching to help students develop a procedure to evaluate the corrosion rate of iron in simulated seawater. J. Chem. Educ. 10(92), 1696–1699 (2015)
11. Wolski, R., Jagodzinski, P.: Virtual laboratory—using a hand movement recognition system to improve the quality of chemical education. Br. J. Educ. Technol. 1(50), 218–231 (2019)
12. Chang, C.-Y., Hwang, G.-W.: Trends in digital game-based learning in the mobile era 20 from : a systematic review of journal publications 2007 to 2016. Int. J. Mobile Learn. Organ. 1(13), 68–90 (2019)
13. Chang, C.-Y., Lai, C.-L., Hwang, G.-J.: Trends and research issues of mobile learning studies in nursing education: a review of academic publications from 1971 to 2016. Comput. Educ. 116, 28–48 (2018)
14. Lai, C.-L., Hwang, G.-J.: Effects of mobile learning time on students' conception of collaboration, communication, complex problem-solving, meta-cognitive awareness and creativity. Int. J. Mobile Learn. Organ. 4(8), 276–291 (2014)
15. Burke, J., Larry, C.: Educational Research: Quantitative and Qualitative Approaches. 5th edn. SAGE, Needham Heights, MA, US (2000)

16. Crompton, H., Burke, D., Gregory, K.H., Gräbe, C.: The use of mobile learning in science: a systematic review. J. Sci. Educ. Technol. **25**(2), 149–160 (2016). https://doi.org/10.1007/s10956-015-9597-x

17. Hwang, G.J., Wu, P.H.: Applications, impacts and trends of mobile technology-enhanced learning: a review of 2008–2012 publications in selected SSCI journals. Int. J. Mobile Learn. Organ. **2**(8), 83–95 (2014)

Engineering Technology and Applied Science for Cognitive City

Design of a Trajectory Control with Minimum Energy Consumption for a Kite Power System

Yung-Chia Hsiao[✉]

School of Materials Science and Engineering, Baise University, Baise, China
1879320336@qq.com

Abstract. A kite power system is an airborne wind energy conversion system of a ground system and the kite in altitudes of about 800–1000 m above the ground that are mechanically connected by tethers. The system generates electricity through that the circled kite pulls the tethers to drive an electrical generator installed on the ground. To keep electrical output, the kite continuously encircles under control. Hopf bifurcations were observed when the kite is in some flight postures. This phenomenon demonstrates that the kite could circle by adjusting the bridle angle. This study designed a trajectory control algorithm with minimum energy consumption via applying the dynamics of the kite. The kite firstly takes off and steadily hovers in a specific altitude under the control. Then the algorithm forced the kite into self-excitation motions which draws the tethers to rotate the generator. A simulation about the trajectory control confirms that the kite could successfully hover in an assigned altitude and then fly a limit cycle which originally exists in the kite. The controller consumes little electricity as the kite steadily flies. The use of the trajectory control with low power consumption increases the efficiency of the kite power system.

Keywords: Airborne wind energy · Hopf bifurcation · Trajectory control

1 Introduction

In the last decades there has been a lot of pollution that proceeds from the use of fossil fuels, such as carbon dioxide and nitric oxide, brings about global warming and the change of climate which results in many disasters. Furthermore, continuous increase in the price of the fossil fuels adversely affects the economic development in recent years. The condition forces countries to realize the importance of slowing down the global warming and propels people to pay great attention to renewable energy that are clean and abundantly available in nature, such as solar power, wind power, and biomass. Among them, the wind energy has a huge potential of becoming a major source of renewable energy.

A windmill converts the kinetic energy of wind into shaft energy to drive an electrical generator for a wind turbine system. The electricity from the generator is conveyed to the grid via a grid-tide inverter, or to power storages such as batteries. Large wind turbine systems are the most widespread type because of their large power more than 500 kW, high efficiency, and low cost per kWh. Meanwhile, high cut-in wind speed of the systems and noise from the windmill give rise to the need of the best

© Springer Nature Singapore Pte Ltd. 2020
J. Shen et al. (Eds.): IC3 2019, CCIS 1227, pp. 665–672, 2020.
https://doi.org/10.1007/978-981-15-6113-9_76

wind sites those with steady reasonably wind of high speed and far away from urban areas. The thing that is interesting is that the outside 30% of the blades of a windmill generate more than half of the total power while they are much thinner and lighter than the inner parts of the blades [1]. The large wind turbines were evolved rapidly over the last three decades with increasing rotor diameters and the height of towers to capture more wind power. The larger the power is, the heavier the inner parts of the blades and the tower are. Size increase of the blades and the towers would dramatically increase the installed costs for the wind turbines because the percentage of total cost for them is up to 40% [2].

Based on the previous description, the idea of kite power systems is to replace the outer parts of the blades by a fast flying kite, and to substitute a tether for the inner parts of the blades as well as the tower [3, 4]. The kite flies in altitudes of about 800–1000 m above the ground that are mechanically connected by tethers. The system generates electricity through that the circled kite pulls the tethers to drive an electrical generator installed on the ground. To keep electrical output, the kite continuously encircles under control [5]. However, the controllers which consume some power would decrease the efficiency of the kite power system. Fortunately, Adomaitis observed the existence of a Hopf bifurcation for a kite in flight [6]. The kite could fly in a self-excitation motion with no excitation of the tether. Besides, Sánchez studied that the kite is self-excited at specific bridle angles [7, 8]. The kite could encircle without consuming energy under the existence of the limit cycle attractor.

In this context, this study designed a trajectory control algorithm with minimum energy consumption via applying the bifurcations of the kite. The kite firstly takes off and steadily hovers in a specific altitude under the control. Then the algorithm forced the kite into self-excitation motions which draws the tethers to rotate the generator. Simulation about the trajectory control is applied to confirm that the kite could successfully hover in an assigned altitude and then fly along a limit cycle which originally exists in the kite. The controller consumes little electricity as the kite steadily flies. The use of the trajectory control with low power consumption increases the efficiency of the kite power system.

2 Nonlinear Model of a Single-Line Kite

A dimensionless state differential equation for a single-line kite shown in Fig. 1, derived from the model which Sánchez demonstrated [7], is showed as follows,

$$
\begin{Bmatrix} \frac{dx_1}{d\tau} \\ \frac{dx_2}{d\tau} \\ \frac{dx_3}{d\tau} \\ \frac{dx_4}{d\tau} \end{Bmatrix} = \begin{Bmatrix} x_2 \\ \frac{1}{|S|}[(\widehat{r}_g^2 + \widehat{r}^2)\cdot g_1 + \widehat{r}\cdot f_2 \cdot g_2] \\ x_4 \\ \frac{1}{|S|}[\widehat{r}\cdot f_2\cdot g_1 + g_2] \end{Bmatrix} \tag{1}
$$

where the state variables $x_1 = \Gamma$, $x_2 = \frac{d\Gamma}{d\tau}$, $x_3 = \theta$, $x_4 = \frac{d\theta}{d\tau}$, Γ is the azimuth angle of the line at the ground, θ is the pitch angle of the kite, the dimensionless time $\tau = \sqrt{\frac{g}{l}}\cdot t$. The symbols used in Eq. (1) are defined as follows,

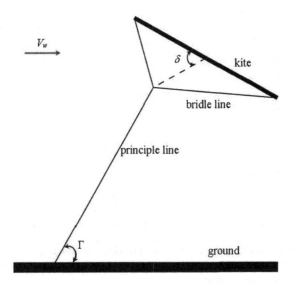

Fig. 1. A single-line kite referred from the study by Sánchez [7].

$$|S| = \widehat{r}_g^2 + \widehat{r}^2 \cdot f_1^2 \tag{2}$$

$$g_1 = \widehat{r} \cdot \left(\frac{d\theta}{d\tau}\right)^2 \cdot f_1 - \cos\Gamma + \mu \cdot \widehat{V}_A^2 \cdot C_N \cdot \cos(\Gamma + \theta) \tag{3}$$

$$g_2 = \widehat{r} \cdot \left(\frac{d\Gamma}{d\tau}\right)^2 \cdot f_1 + \widehat{r} \cdot \cos(\delta - \theta) + \mu \cdot \widehat{V}_A^2 \cdot C_N \cdot (\widehat{x}_{cp} - \widehat{r} \cdot \cos\delta) \tag{4}$$

$$f_1 = \sin(\delta - \theta - \Gamma) \tag{5}$$

$$f_2 = \cos(\delta - \theta - \Gamma) \tag{6}$$

where $\widehat{r} = \frac{r}{l}$, $\widehat{r}_g = \frac{r_g}{l}$, $\widehat{x}_{cp} = \frac{x_{cp}}{l}$, $\widehat{V}_A = \frac{V_A}{\sqrt{g \cdot l}}$, $\mu = \frac{\rho \cdot A \cdot l}{2m}$, $x_{cp} = (x_G - x_{cop})$, r is the bridle length, r_g is the radius of gyration, l is the length of the principle line, x_{cp} is the distance to centre of mass from centre of pressure, V_A is the kite aerodynamic velocity, g is acceleration due to gravity, ρ is air density, A is the area of the kite, m is the kite's mass, x_G is the distance to centre of mass from leading edge, x_{cop} and C_N are respectively the distance to centre of pressure from leading edge and the aerodynamic normal force coefficient shown in Fig. 2, δ is the bridle angle of the kite. Table 1 shows the parameters for the previous equations.

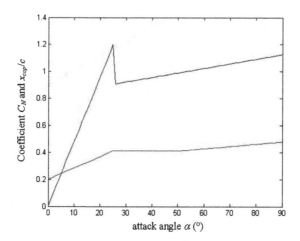

Fig. 2. Normal force coefficient and centre of pressure position proposed from the study by Sánchez [7]. The blue and red lines are the normal force coefficient C_N and the centre of pressure position x_{cop}/c. (Color figure online)

Table 1. Parameters for the single-line kite. The data are referred from the investigation by Sánchez [7].

Parameters	Values
ρ	1.293 (kg/m^3)
A	0.48 (m^2)
l	100 (m)
m	0.3 (kg)
c	0.8 (m)
r	1 (m)
r_g	0.19 (m)
x_G	0.4 (m)

3   Analysis and Control of the Single-Line Kite

An equilibrium point $x^* = \left(x_1^*, x_2^*, x_3^*, x_4^*\right)$ of the kite is determined through zeros of the equation given below,

$$\begin{cases} x_2 = 0 \\ (\widehat{r}_g^2 + \widehat{r}^2) \cdot g_1 + \widehat{r} \cdot f_2 \cdot g_2 = 0 \\ x_4 = 0 \\ \widehat{r} \cdot f_2 \cdot g_1 + g_2 = 0 \end{cases} \tag{7}$$

To perturb the point x^*, this study substitutes $x = x^* + \delta x$ into Eq. (1). $\delta x = (\delta x_1, \delta x_2, \delta x_3, \delta x_4)$ represents small perturbation of the point. Preserving only the linear terms of the equations, the perturbed system can be described as follows,

$$\delta \dot{x} = \mathbf{M}_J \cdot \delta x, \tag{8}$$

where $\mathbf{M}_J$ is the Jacobin matrix of the equilibrium point. The characteristic equation of $\mathbf{M}_J$ is written as follows,

$$|\lambda, \cdot \mathbf{I} - \mathbf{M}_J| = 0 \tag{9}$$

where $\mathbf{I}$ is an unit matrix, λ is a eigenvalue for the point x^* which is numerically evaluated [9]. According to the bifurcation theory [10], the equilibrium point is stable if real parts of all eigenvalues of its Jacobin matrix are negative; otherwise it is unstable. A bifurcation occurs once either a simple real eigenvalue approaches zero or a pair of simple complex eigenvalues reaches the imaginary axis of the complex plane. Two types of instabilities are shown as follows: (i) $\lambda = 0$, saddle-node bifurcation, pitchfork bifurcation or transcritical bifurcation occurs; (ii) $\lambda = j\omega_0$ or $-j\omega_0$, $\omega_0 > 0$, $j = \sqrt{-1}$, Hopf bifurcation occurs.

Figure 3 depicts the algorithm of the trajectory control of the kite. The controller firstly takes off the kite to the specific height via using a P control to adjust the bridle angle and then hoods the bridle angle to keep the kite at a steady state. As the kite stably flies, the algorithm forces the kite into a self-excitation motion according to the amplitude of the limit cycle trajectory.

4 Nonlinear Dynamics and Trajectory Control of the Single-Line Kite

This study varied the bridle angle to observe the self-excitation motions of the kite. The equilibrium points of the kite are detected using the Newton's method in different bridle angles at a fixed wind speed. In addition, the stability of the equilibrium points is obtained using the equations illustrated in Sect. 3. The bifurcation points can be found for the stability analysis. Figure 4 depicts the root locus for the kite at $V_w = 6.5$ m/s. The limit cycles exist between $\delta = 63°$ and $\delta = 73°$ due to the occurrence of two Hopf bifurcations which the trajectory control could use.

A simulation is applied to confirm that the kite successfully hovers in an assigned altitude and then fly along a limit cycle which originally exists in the kite. Figures 5(a), (b), and (c) demonstrate the simulation results under $k_p = 0.1$. The kite rapidly took off as the controller adjusted the bridle angle δ to 62°. When the kite flight is stable at 94 m height, the control algorithm continuously increased the value of δ to 65.24° and then to force the kite into the self-excitation motion. The control did not consume the electricity if the kite flied along the trajectory of the limit cycle. The simulation result confirms that the kite could successfully hover in an assigned altitude and then encircle in a limit cycle which originally exists in the kite. The controller consumes little electricity as the kite steadily flights. The use of the trajectory control with low power

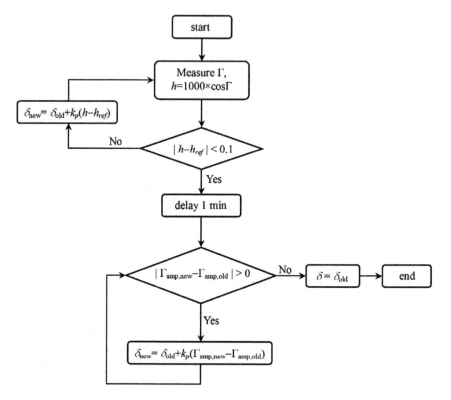

Fig. 3. Flow chart of the trajectory control of the kite.

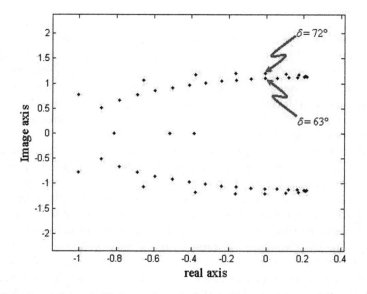

Fig. 4. Loot locus of the equilibrium points as a function of the parameter δ for the single-line kite. (Color figure online)

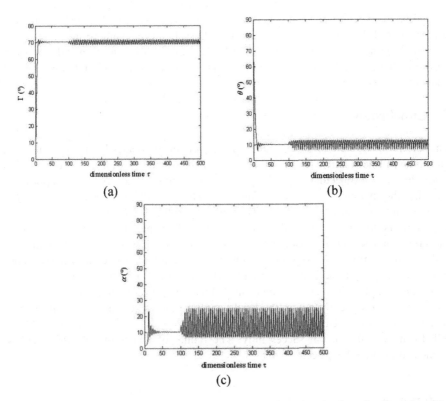

Fig. 5. Simulation for the trajectory control of the single-line kite: (a) the azimuth angle of the principle line Γ; (b) the pitch angle of the kite θ; (c) attack angle of the kite α. Red lines in Figs. 4 (a) and 4(b) are the desired values of Γ and θ as steady kite flight, respectively.

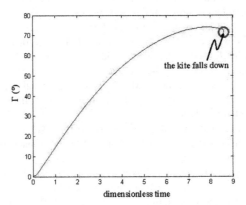

Fig. 6. Simulation for the trajectory control of the single-line kite as straightly adjusting the bridle angle to the target value.

consumption increases the efficiency of the kite power system. Meanwhile, another way to control the kite flight is to straightly adjust the bridle angle to the target value without keeping steady kite flight a while. However, this algorithm did not work according to the simulation shown in Fig. 6. The kite would suddenly fall down even it takes off successfully.

5 Conclusion

The kite power system is to replace the outer parts of the blades by a fast flying kite, and to substitute a tether for the inner parts of the blades as well as the tower. This study designed a trajectory control algorithm with minimum energy consumption via applying the dynamics of the kite. The kite firstly took off and steadily hovers in a specific altitude under the control. Then the algorithm forced the kite into a self-excitation motion which draws the tethers to rotate the generator. Simulation about the trajectory control confirms that the kite could successfully hover in an assigned altitude and then fly a limit cycle which originally exists in the kite. The controller consumes little electricity as the kite steadily flights. The use of the trajectory control with low power consumption increases the efficiency of the kite power system. Besides, another algorithm is to straightly adjust the bridle angle to the target value without keeping steady flight a while. However, this algorithm did not work because the kite suddenly fell down even it took off successfully. The failure of undetermined origin will be studied to modify the trajectory control.

References

1. Cherubini, A., Papini, A., Vertechy, R., Fontana, M.: Airborne wind energy systems: a review of the technologies. Renew. Sustain. Energy Rev. **51**, 1461–1476 (2015)
2. Lan, W.-T.: World Wind Energy Industry Outlook. In: ITIS of Ministry of Economic Affairs, pp. 1–6. Hsinchu County (2007). (in Chinese)
3. Loyd, M.L.: Crosswind kite power. J. Energy **4**(3), 106–111 (1980)
4. Diehl, M.: Airborne wind energy: basic concepts and physical foundations. In: Ahrens, U., Diehl, M., Schmehl, R. (eds.) Airborne Wind Energy, pp. 3–22. Springer, Heidelberg (2014). https://doi.org/10.1007/978-3-642-39965-7_1
5. Zgraggen, A.U., Fagiano, L., Morari, M.: Real-time optimization and adaptation of the crosswind flight of tethered wings for airborne wind energy. IEEE Trans. Control Syst. Technol. **23**(2), 434–448 (2015)
6. Adomaitis, R.A.: Kites and bifurcation theory. SIAM Rev. **31**(3), 478–483 (1989)
7. Sánchez, G.: Dynamics and Control of Single-Line Kites. Aeronaut. J. **110**(1111), 615–621 (2006)
8. Losantos, L.S., Sánchez-Arriaga, G.: Flight dynamics and stability of kites in steady and unsteady wind conditions. J. Aircr. **52**(2), 660–666 (2015)
9. Press, W.H., Teukolsky, S.A., Vetterling, W.T., Flannery, B.P.: Numerical Recipes: The Art of Scientific Computing, 3rd edn., pp. 1092–1093. Cambridge University Press, Cambridge (2007)
10. Kuznetsov, Y.A.: Elements of Applied Bifurcation Theory, 3rd edn., pp. 77–78. Springer, New York (2004). https://doi.org/10.1007/978-1-4757-3978-7

Improve the Properties of Anti-reflective Film by Silica Nano Solution

Yaw-Nan Shieh[(✉)]

Department of Materials Science and Energy Engineering, Ming Dao University,
Pitou Township, Taiwan
ynshieh@mdu.edu.tw

Abstract. In this paper, glass was dipped coating by nano-solution of silica to prepare an SiO2/glass anti-reflection film layer. The optical properties and adhesion of the anti-reflection film layer were compared between acidic and basic silica oxide solution. UV-visible spectrometer was used to measure the transmittance of the film, and the scanning electron microscope was used to observe the microstructure of the film. According to the experimental results, it was found that the pulling speed of the coating increased resulting in the thickness of the film increased. When the pulling speed was 75 mm/min have the best average transmittance, the average transmittance in the visible wavelength range of 400–800 nm is 96.5%, which is 6.32% higher than that of blank glass which was 90.2%. The highest transmittance is 98.2% at 540 nm wavelength.

Keywords: Deep coating · Silica. nano solution · Anti-reflection film · Transmittance

1 Introduction

In recent years, global warming has caused climate change, and climate anomalies around the world have caused serious economic losses. The carbon dioxide generated by petrochemical energy such as oil and coal is the main cause of the greenhouse effect, so the world has launched an energy-saving and carbon-reducing and clean energy source. The trend of oil, natural gas, coal and other petrochemical energy shortages, prices rise, however solar energy sources are inexhaustible for human beings. If the energy of solar that illuminates the earth for one day can be collected and utilized, it can be used by humans for 236 years. Therefore, the development of solar cell technology has arisen, and it is expected to replace today's non-renewable energy sources as the main energy source in the future, and prevent the expansion of the greenhouse effect and solve environmental pollution problems. Sample Heading (Third Level). Only two levels of headings should be numbered. Lower level headings remain unnumbered; they are formatted as run-in headings.

The solar cell is made of a semiconductor. The semiconductor has a P-type and N-type PN junction semiconductor. After illuminating the sunlight, it absorbs sunlight energy to excite electrons in the valence band, so that the P-type semiconductor and the N-type semiconductor generate electron hole pairs. The current is guided out and connected to the load, so the sunlight enters more or less affects the power generation

© Springer Nature Singapore Pte Ltd. 2020
J. Shen et al. (Eds.): IC3 2019, CCIS 1227, pp. 673–680, 2020.
https://doi.org/10.1007/978-981-15-6113-9_77

efficiency. Therefore, the solar cell needs to coat a layer of anti-reflection layer to increase the light entering, so that the component absorbs more sunlight and enhances the efficiency of the solar cell.

Anti-reflective coating (ARC) is an essential process in the preparation of solar cells [1]. The commonly used low refractive materials are MgF2 (n = 1.38), SiO2 (n = 1.46), and the medium refractive index material is Al2O3 (n = 1.7), SiNXOY (n = 1.7 ~ 1.9), there are many types of high refractive index materials. The commonly used materials are Ta2O5 (n = 2.1), TiO2 (n = 2.3), ZrO2 (n = 2.05), ITO (n = 2.0), ZnS (n = 2.3) and other materials, the common material combination for the preparation of double-layer anti-reflection film is MgF2/ZnS [2], MgF2/TiO2 [3], MgF2/SiNX [4], MgF2/CeO2 [5], SiO2/SiNX [6].

2   Experimental Method

S in this study, glass was used as the substrate, and a single layer of silica oxide was coated on the glass substrate as an anti-reflection film by deep coating. The center wavelength was selected from 550 nm and 630 nm, and the thickness of the film was four-quarters of wavelength.

Designed with wavelengths, the design conditions must meet the following two conditions:

1. $n = \sqrt{n_0 n_S}$
2. $\lambda = 4nd$

Where n is the refractive index of the film, n_0 is the refractive index of the air, n_S is the refractive index of the substrate, λ is the preset center wavelength, and d is the required thickness of the film. The sketch is shown in Fig. 4.

In this study, glass was used as the substrate, and a single layer of silica oxide was coated on the glass substrate as an anti-reflection film by deep coating. The center wavelength was selected from 550 nm and 630 nm, and the thickness of the film was four-quarters of wavelength.

Designed with wavelengths, the design conditions must meet the following two conditions:

1. $n = \sqrt{n_0 n_S}$
2. $\lambda = 4nd$

Where n is the refractive index of the film, n_0 is the refractive index of the air, n_S is the refractive index of the substrate, λ is the preset center wavelength, and d is the required thickness of the film. The sketch is shown in Fig. 4.

In this study, glass was used as the substrate, and a single layer of silica oxide was coated on the glass substrate as an anti-reflection film by deep coating. The center wavelength was selected from 550 nm and 630 nm, and the thickness of the film was four-quarters of wavelength.

Designed with wavelengths, the design conditions must meet the following two conditions:

1. $n = \sqrt{n_0 n_S}$
2. $\lambda = 4nd$

Where n is the refractive index of the film, n_0 is the refractive index of the air, n_S is the refractive index of the substrate, λ is the preset center wavelength, and d is the required thickness of the film. The sketch is shown in Fig. 4.

In this study, glass was used as the substrate, and a single layer of silica oxide was coated on the glass substrate as an anti-reflection film by deep coating. The center wavelength was selected from 550 nm and 630 nm, and the thickness of the film was four-quarters of wavelength.

Designed with wavelengths, the design conditions must meet the following two conditions:

1. $n = \sqrt{n_0 n_S}$
2. $\lambda = 4nd$

Where n is the refractive index of the film, n_0 is the refractive index of the air, n_S is the refractive index of the substrate, λ is the preset center wavelength, and d is the required thickness of the film. The sketch is shown in Fig. 4.

The glass substrate is a glass piece with an diameter of 25.4 mm × 76.2 mm × 1.0 mm. The cleaning process of the glass piece affects the uniformity, compactness and adhesion of the solution on the test piece. Therefore, special attention should be paid to the cleaning of the glass test procedure. The glass test piece cleaning procedure as follows:

A. The glass test piece matter was placed in acetone and ultrasonically shaken for 30 min to remove organic
B. The glass subtract was placed in deionized water and shaken for 30 min to remove acetone.
C. The glass piece was placed in an ethanol solution and shaken for 30 min to remove grease.
D. Place glass subtract in deionized water and shake for 30 min to remove ethanol.
E. Put it in deionized water, wash it for 30 min, and dry it with nitrogen to prepare for coating.

For the solution preparation, two different silica oxide solutions was selected, there were, acidic and basic, silica oxide solution. These two solutions were diluted to a solid content of 1% in order to make the coated film have better adhesion and stability on the glass.

In order to enhance the film formation and adhesion, polyvinyl alcohol Polyvinyl Alcohol (PVA) was added.

The volume percentage of 5% of PVA were added into these two solutions.

The experimental parameters of the solution are shown in Table 1.

Table 1. Experimental parameters

Samples no.	A (Acidic Sol)	B (Alkaline Sol)
Solid content (wt%)	1	1
PVA content (V%)	5	5
Polling up speed (mm/min)	50–150	50–150
Heat treatment temperature (°C)	550	550
Heat treatment time (min)	30	30
Deeping no.	2	2

In this experiment, we used a deep coating process to prepare an anti-reflection layer of silica oxide, and changed the polling speed from 50 to 150 mm/min, also observed the relative film thickness at the fixed polling up speed coating

Using UV-visible spectroscopy the transmittance of the film was measured, and the microstructure and thickness of the film were observed by field emission scanning electron microscopy (SEM), and the relationship between the film thicknesses of various polling up speeds on the SiO2 solution were compared.

3   Results and Discussion

Figure 1 is the relationship between the coated film thickness and the polling up speed of two different kinds of SiO2 solution. Pulling speed was changed from 50–150 mm/min, then annealing at 550 °C after deep coating, heat treatment for 30 min. The heating temperature is raised to 5 °C per minute until 150 °C then keeping for 10 min, after then carry on same heating rate to 550 °C for 30 min keeping, and finally cooled to room temperature.

It can be seen from Fig. 1 that the film thickness increases with the increase of the pulling speed, and the film thickness of sample B is slightly thicker than that of the sample A film.

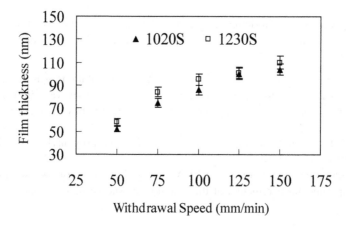

Fig. 1. Relationship between SiO2 film thickness and pulling up speed.

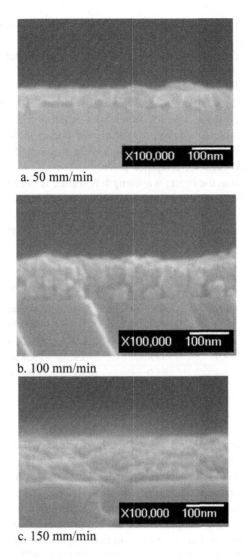

a. 50 mm/min

b. 100 mm/min

c. 150 mm/min

Fig. 2. Film thickness relative to different polling up speed

Figure 2 shows the actual film thickness of sample B observed under SEM. a, b and c are the film thicknesses of 50 mm/min, 100 mm/min and 150 mm/min, polling up speed, respectively.

The thickness of a is 58 nm, b. thicknes 95 nm, the thickness of c is 110 nm, which can be estimated by Fig. 1.

When the pulling speed is controlled, then the thickness of film can be speculate.

We design the anti-reflective layer at, the two required film thicknesses 94 nm and 108 nm, respectively, the pull-up speed of 100 and 150 mm/min is selected.

The anti-reflection effect is measured by UV-visible, and its spectrum is shown in Fig. 3.

From this figure, the A curve is an anti-reflection layer prepared by the sample B solution. The center wavelength of the design falls on the 630 nm, but the actually center wavelength is falls on 626 nm.

B curve is the same situation as the sample B solution. The center wavelength of the design is 550 nm, but the actually center wavelength is 558 nm.

C curve is the sample A solution to prepare the anti-reflection layer. The design center wavelength is 550 nm, but the actually center wavelength is at 557 nm.

D curve is a blank glass for reference piece.

The phenomenon that the center wavelength is shifted is because the film thickness is slightly different from the ideal thickness. When the film thickness is thicker than design ideal thickness, the spectral pattern will shift to the right, and vice versa.

Table 2, is the comparison of transmittance for various samples for anti-reflection layer.

Table 2. The transmittance of different samples for anti-reflection layer

Sample	400–800 nm T(%)	Increase T (%)	400–1200 nm T(%)	Increase T (%)	Center wavelength	Maximum T (%)
A	95.6	5.2	94.0	5.9	626 nm	97.1
B	96.3	5.9	93.8	5.9	558 nm	97.9
C	95.3	4.9	93.0	5.1	557 nm	96.8
D	90.4	–	87.9	–	–	–

It can be clearly seen from Fig. 3 that after the single-layer anti-reflective coating is applied, the transmittances rate will increase greatly.

As shown in Table 2, the increase rate is almost more than 5%, and the best transmittance rate is curve B. The penetration rate is 96.3% that is 5.9% higher than that of the blank glass test piece (90.4%) in the wavelength range of 400–800 nm

Curves B and C are the comparison of the transmittance rate of the anti-reflective layer coating by alkaline and acidic SiO_2 solution respectively. It can be seen that the transmittance rate of the anti-reflective layer of the alkaline SiO_2 solution is higher than that of the acidic SiO_2 solution.

The reason for this phenomenon may be that the difference in the adhesion of the two solution which causes unevenness film formation.

The film form Sample A solutions, has a slight scattering of the film during the UV-visible spectrum measurement.

This resulting in the antireflection layer of the an alkaline SiO_2 solution (sample B) is better than that of acidic SiO_2 solution(sample A).

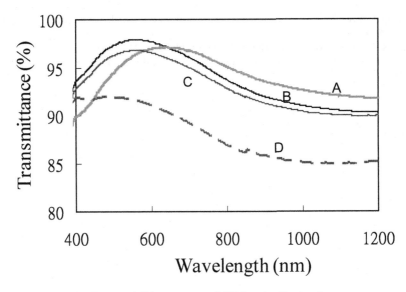

Fig. 3. UV-visible spectrum of SiO2 anti-reflection layer

4   Conclusion

In this experiment, the relationship between the thickness of the acidic SiO2 solution and the alkaline SiO2 solution immersed on the glass substrate by deep coating, and the relationship between the film thickness and the pulling speed is obtained.

From the results, it can be found that the film thickness increases with the increase of the pulling up speed. The alkaline SiO2 solution (sample B) is immersed at a similar pulling speed, and the thickness of the film is thicker than that of the acidic SiO2 solution (sample A).

The effect of the transmittance rate relative to anti-reflective layer prepared by the alkaline SiO2 solution is better than that of prepared by acidic SiO2 solution.

The transmittance of the anti-reflective layer of the SiO2 solution is better than that of blank glass test piece in the wavelength of 400–800 nm which increase 5.98%.

The maximum transmittance rate is 97.9% at wavelength of 558 nm.

The deep coating process used in the preparation of the antireflection layer has the advantages of low deposition cost, large area deposition and simple operation.

References

1. Hovel, H.J.: Solar Cells, Semiconductors and Semimetals, vol. 11. Academic Press, New York (1975)
2. Zhao, J., Green, M.A., Trans, I.E.E.E.: Electron Devices **38**, 1925–1934 (1991)
3. Woo, S.H., Hwangbo, C.K.: Appl. Opt. **45**(7), 1447–1455 (2006)

4. Dhungel, S.K., Yoo, J., Kim, K., Jung, S., Ghosh, S., Yi, J.: J. Korean Phys. Soci. **49**(3), 885–889 (2006)
5. Lee, S.E., Choi, S.W., Yi, J.: Thin Solid Films **376**, 208–213 (2006)
6. Chen, Z., Sana, P., Salami, J., Rohatgi, A.: IEEE Trans. Electron Devices **40**(6), 1161–1165 (1993)

Re-Trace: Relive and Share Your Story

Yih-Jiun Lee[1(✉)], Yu-Ting Su[1], and Kai-Wen Lien[2]

[1] Chinese Culture University, Taipei, Taiwan
lyjl5@ulive.pccu.edu.tw
[2] Chienkuo Technology University, Changhua City, Taiwan

Abstract. Memories fade with time, so in the past we use photographs to keep memories alive. However, with the development of technology, taking photos is so easy that users no longer cherish them. In this study, we built a platform for users to tell and share their stories in multimedia. A story can be written in text, a picture, an audio recording, or a video file. Once the story is saved, it can be accessed and shared easily. Users can share their stories with families or friends, who share the same memories or even to everyone who is intrigued. People can save others' story in the collections and add a comment to create their own version. By crowd-creating stories, the family can be bound, and the community of neighborhood might be more connected.

Keywords: Digital humanities · Crowdsourcing · Mobile application

1 Introduction

When you were kids, parents or grandparents often hold you in their arms and tell you your family stories. How much do you remember? One of my students once shared a story. He found a 20 years photo showing his father's scary face because he tried to grab his father's new camera which was an expensive gift back to the date. He did not recall until he saw the picture. Memory can be easy vague, but through a photo, it came back again.

Photographs carry people's memories. Taking a photograph was a luxury thing, which could only be done on a special event. Photos were kept carefully in the albums and might be often taken out to review.

With the development of smart cellular phones, taking photo seems to be an easy job. The user takes a photo with his phone in one second and the picture is uploaded immediately to a cloud-based space. The cloud space might be free to store, so users would not care to organize it. Time by time, there are hundreds of thousands of pictures on the cloud, but no one really appreciates them. A photograph does not tell a story and memory is gone with the wind.

We believe you have stories that matter, at least to you, so we want you to tell them. However, with technologies, storytelling can be done in different ways. In addition, social media, such as Facebook or Instagram, also play an important role in keeping our memories or moments. But are social media posts telling stories we remember, or are they just other people's stories?

© Springer Nature Singapore Pte Ltd. 2020
J. Shen et al. (Eds.): IC3 2019, CCIS 1227, pp. 681–688, 2020.
https://doi.org/10.1007/978-981-15-6113-9_78

What kinds of stories matter to users? We found that an aged story usually matters when users are at a certain location or a specific time and date. Locations and timestamp often help to bring memory alive.

This research tries to design and build a platform, called "Re-Trace" to allow users to tell a story and access it when necessary. One can easily tell a story, share it with someone and relive it when he wants. Moreover, a story does not only matter to its creator but also significant to its stakeholders, for instance, for a family or a neighborhood. Similar research shows this kind of group wisdom helps to form the community. Therefore, designing a proper mechanism to share the story with the community is also a research objective in this study.

2 Literature View

2.1 Crowdsourcing

Crowdsourcing is a sourcing model, in which people can get what they want or ask from a large and relatively open group of internet users. Advantages of using crowdsourcing may include improved costs, speed, quality, flexibility, scalability, or diversity [1–3]. The adaptability of crowdsourcing allows it to work in an effective and powerful way to solve problems [4]. Based on Geiger and Schader [5], crowdsourcing can be divided into four categories: crowd-solving, crowd-creation, crowd-rating and crowd-processing. Crowd-solving is often used to solve a complex problem. Crowd-creation mainly focuses on cooperative creation of a content or artifacts based on heterogeneous contribution. Crowd-rating is commonly used to collect data and perform predictions. Crowd-processing relies on the crowd to perform large quantities of homogeneous tasks.

2.2 Historypin

Historypin, a crowdsource platform for historical materials, is a digital, user-generated archive of historical photos, videos, audios recordings [6, 7]. It aims to connect communities with local history. It also collects stories based on their local communities. A user does not need to be an IT expert to upload their content through the website and is able to see world-wide stories on the map [8]. Figure 1 shows the stories in Kyoto, Japan. There are 15 uploaded stories when we zoom in the map and each of them can be read by further drilled down. Most of them are photos, and only a few provide text. Users read the text and see the photos, but they don't feel the story.

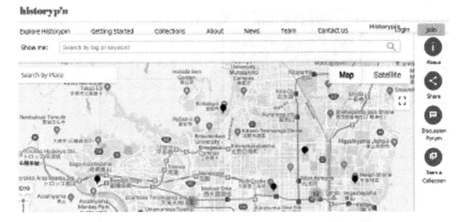

Fig. 1. Mapview of historypin (screenshot from historypin)

3 System Design

The system is composed of two components: a cloud center and a mobile application. The cloud center acts as a data storage center and provides a set of web services to allow users to input and keep their stories while privacy and security remains.

The mobile application provides a unique and elegant user interface for both writers (authors) and readers (audients). Therefore, one can write a story. A story can be told in different ways, such as text, audio, image or video. It also consists of a location marker and a timestamp. A location is a geographic location, which can be either latitude and longitude or an address. The current location, where the story is written, is set by default. However, if an ancestor's story is told, the location can be moved to the correct one. Similar strategic is used to set up timestamp, the current time is set by default, but manually configuration is always allowed. Table 1 presents the structure in the Backus–Naur form (BNF).

Table 1. Backus–Naur Form (BNF)

\<Story\>	::=	\<author\>\<Location\>\<Timestamp\>\<Narrative\>
\<Narrative\>	::=	(\<text\> | \<audio\> | \<video\> | \<image\>) \<Narrative\>
\<Location\>	::=	where the story happens | where the story is told
\<Timestamp\>	::=	when the story happens | when the story is told

Stories can be written in several methods, such as an article, an audio file, a picture or a video (Fig. 2). Since it is written in different ways and consists of different contents, how to display a story is varied. Therefore, there are 8 different layout templates to be used to carry out the best present. Figure 3 shows the layout of a story with all kinds of contents.

Fig. 2. New a story

Fig. 3. One of the story template

When users like to review their story, they can either spin the timeline interface (Fig. 4) or check through a map view (Fig. 5). In the timeline view, the thumbnail in the center shows the current chosen story, and we use the magnification effect to highlight. With spinning the wheel (timeline), stories are moved up and down. It seems that the user literately goes back to the old time as a time traveler. During the preliminary test, users show their appreciation for this design.

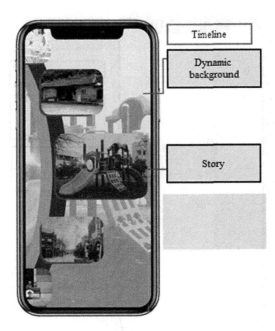

Fig. 4. Timeline view

Map view is the layout being designed to be activated both actively and proactively. A user can actively read the map for stories at any time. However, the layout is also able to enable when the context fits.

Each story has a marker site from which a radius of 500 m is considered a geographic fence. When a user enters a geofence, the app is awakened and moves into the prompt mode and the map view is shown. In the map view, the user's current location, and nearby locations with stories are shown. User can click on a "story landmark" and the story mode is activated. If the story were AR-enabled (Augmented Reality), the mark is different. In an AR-enabled story, the camera on the phone turns on and an object must be detected to show an AR story.

The stories, shown in the map view, are diversity. They might not be your stories but from the community of location. When uploading a story, users can set up privacy, which can be private, sharable specifically or fully sharable. Once the story is fully sharable, anyone can read it through the map view.

For every story a user has read, he or she can add it into "my collection" and add his unique feeling to the saved story.

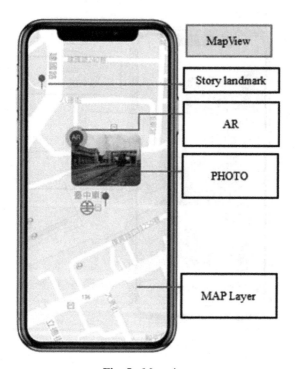

Fig. 5. Map view

Since we might want to share stories with others, "sharing" is necessary. Once the user completed the personal stories, he/she can choose the "share" function. A one-time QRCODE is generated for receivers to scan (Fig. 6). When the receivers receive and read the code, there are two kinds of possible processes. If the user has not installed the application yet, he is directed to the app store or google play. However, if he had installed the application in prior, the application is automatically activated and marked the shared story. The receiver cannot change the content of the story, but he can add his thoughts and keep the commented story in the "my collection", which can be accessed through the main screen.

Fig. 6. Sharing via a QR code

4   Conclusion and Future Work

In Taiwan, family ties are very tight, so the origination of this research is to document family stories. Therefore, your children can know their grand-grandparents. However, during the process, the team has learned that everyone has stories to tell, and the eager cannot be done in the current approach. Re-Trace fits the requirements to keep everyone's story. By providing an ease of use user interface, users do not require training to be able to use the app. The storage and cloud services are hiding in the backend without bothering users. The pilot test and the preliminary study shows that most of the interviewees agree the system is usefulness and ease of use. Further questionnaire survey and implementation will be conducted in the summer.

Reference

1. Buettner, R.: A systematic literature review of crowdsourcing research from a human resource management perspective. In: 2015 Hawaii International Conference on System Sciences, Hawaii, USA, pp. 4609–4618 (2015)

2. Prpić, J., Taeihagh, A., Melton, J.: The fundamentals of policy crowdsourcing. Policy Internet **7**(3), 340–361 (2015). https://doi.org/10.1002/poi3.102

3. Brabham, D.C.: Crowdsourcing as a model for problem solving: an introduction and cases. Convergence **14**(1), 75–90 (2008). https://doi.org/10.1177/1354856507084420

4. Estellés-Arolas, E., González-Ladrón-de-Guevara, F.: Towards an integrated crowdsourcing definition. J. Inf. Sci. **38**(2), 189–200 (2012). https://doi.org/10.1177/0165551512437638

5. Geiger, D., Schader, M.: Personalized task recommendation in crowdsourcing information systems - current state of the art. Decis. Support Syst. **65**, 3–16 (2014)

6. Historypin. https://www.historypin.org/en/. Accessed 10 June 2019

7. Bakker, R., Du, Z., Kass, M., Krefft, J.V., Rogers, J.: Digital Initiatives Newsletter, Issue 3. Florida International University. Accessed 12 June 2019

8. Harris, k., Harris, A.: Data visualization tools for archives and special collections. MAC Newslett. **46**(3), 26–29 (2019)

Detail-Preserved Tone Mapping Based on Joint Global and Local Histogram Equalization

Kuo-Hua Hsu[1], Ting-Chi Liu[1], Kai-Lung Hua[2],
and Yung-Yao Chen[3(✉)]

[1] Graduate Institute of Automation Technology,
National Taipei University of Technology, Taipei 106, Taiwan
gggpppooo2266@gmail.com, inhail0819@gmail.com
[2] Department of Computer Science and Information Engineering,
National Taiwan University of Science and Technology, Taipei 106, Taiwan
hua@mail.ntust.edu.tw
[3] Department of Electronic and Computer Engineering,
National Taiwan University of Science and Technology, Taipei 106, Taiwan
yungyaochen@mail.ntust.edu.tw

Abstract. This paper presents a tone mapping method to generate a high-dynamic-range (HDR) image, in which intensity values are smoothly allocated to a final low-dynamic-range (LDR) image. First, a global histogram equalization scheme is applied to obtain an image histogram with an equalized redistribution. In addition, the image is divided into blocks, and transformation functions are performed using the cumulative distribution function of these blocks. To resolve the seam artefacts that typically arise in the local tone mapping operation, the two tone-mapped images are blended using a multiscale pyramid-based structure. The experimental results show the validity of the proposed method.

Keywords: High Dynamic Range Imaging (HDRI) · Tone mapping · Detail preserving

1 Introduction

Tone mapping techniques are widely applied in fields such as remote sensing and surveillance. Although there are many researches regarding image enhancement or detail-preserving [1–9] proposed in the recent decades, most of them they are designed for the LDR images. As a result, most of them are no suitable in HDR tone mapping applications. Dynamic range is basically the difference between the lightest light and the darkest dark which we can capture in a photo by human's eye or any other electronic imaging system. A higher bit resolution results in more realistic scenes. However, the dynamic range of a display is 8 bits, which is incompatible with images captured using modern equipment. Once subject's luminance exceeds the camera's dynamic range, it results in the loss of details in either highlight or darkest region.

Therefore, a good tone mapping operator is needed to map the contrast and details of HDR images to LDR images while maintaining good quality. Numerous tone mapping techniques have been studied and utilized in recent years, such as logarithmic

© Springer Nature Singapore Pte Ltd. 2020
J. Shen et al. (Eds.): IC3 2019, CCIS 1227, pp. 689–694, 2020.
https://doi.org/10.1007/978-981-15-6113-9_79

transformation, histogram equalization (HE) and gamma correction methods. A novel approach based on combining global and local tone mapping has also received increasing interest, as reported in [10]. This work takes advantage of the local and global HE method by applying a multi-resolution blending technique to obtain good contrast and fine details in the tone mapping results.

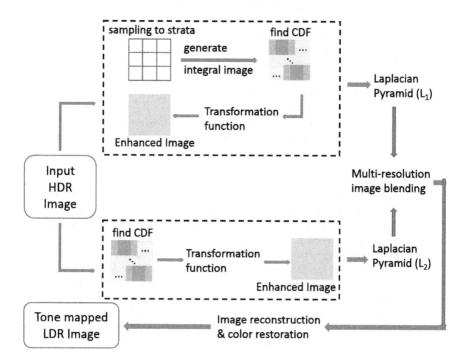

Fig. 1. Flowchart of the proposed method.

2 Proposed Method

2.1 Performing the HE Methods

To achieve contrast enhancement, in the method reported in [11], the image histogram is first stretched locally and then globally. Although directly stretching the image's histogram can be performed rapidly, defining intervals for local regions is difficult. This problem in defining local regions can be resolved using the algorithm proposed in [12], which linearly separates a logarithm-domain histogram to generate a cumulative distribution function (CDF) curve. However, this approach may lead to seam effects in the resulting image as the CDF curve is separated piecewise.

A flowchart of the proposed method, aiming to address this issue, is shown in Fig. 1. First, the input HDR image is normalized and transformed from the luminance to the logarithm domain. Two enhanced images are generated: one via global HE and the other via local HE. For the former, the method used in [13] is applied:

$$L_d(i,j) = f(L_\omega(i,j)), \tag{1}$$

and

$$f(D_k) = D_0 + (D_{k-1} - D_0) \sum_{j=0}^{k} \frac{N_k}{N}, k \in [0, k-1], \tag{2}$$

where L_ω and L_d represent the logarithmic and display luminance values, respectively. The symbol $[D_k, D_{k+1}]$ indicates the interval of the histogram. For local HE, the CDF function is utilized to stretch the histogram, in which the transformation function of each pixel is based on the concept of block-based processing. In local HE, the transformation function of each pixel is independent and related to its neighboring region's pixels. Inspired by [14], Fig. 2 presents the block definition employed in this work, where the parameters (M, N) define the block size, and parameters (α, β) define the sub-block size. For example, for $(\alpha = 2, \beta = 4)$, there are 4×4 sub-blocks within a block, and individual 2×2 sub-blocks form a population to calculate the corresponding CDF.

2.2 Multi-Resolution Image Blending

The image pyramid scheme is used to fuse two contrast-enhanced images. First, Laplacian pyramids of both enhanced images are constructed. For each pixel, we average the values from the two pyramids to adjust the control parameter C. The final Laplacian pyramid contains those pixels whose intensity is closer to C. Finally, we reconstruct the Laplacian pyramid to obtain an image and restore the color.

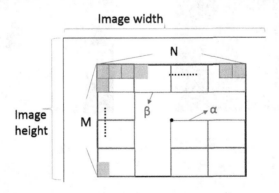

Fig. 2. Block definition of the local HE.

3 Experimental Results

Figure 3 shows an example application of the proposed method. As shown in Fig. 3(e), the luminance of pixels exceeding the dynamic range limitation becomes too dark or too bright. After global HE is performed, the image histogram has an equalized distribution, and the image has more levels of visual light intensity (Fig. 3f). Although the histogram for the local HE (Fig. 3c) exhibits a fine distribution, the wall in the output image displays some abnormal shadowing. Nevertheless, after the results of global/local HE are blended using an image pyramid, the abnormal shadowing decreases, and the details are preserved (Fig. 3h). In addition, the histogram of the proposed method's output (Fig. 3d) appears to have a more equalized distribution than that in Fig. 3(a), i.e. the input image's histogram.

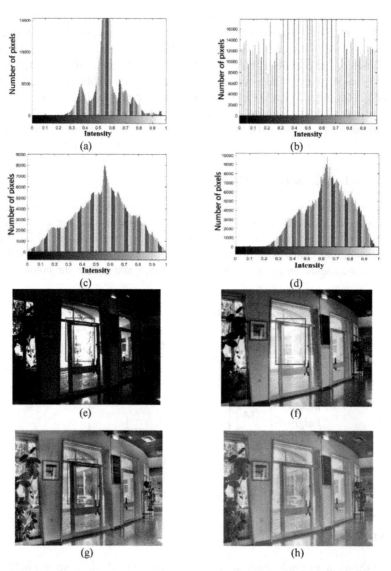

Fig. 3. Visual comparison 1. (a)–(d) Histograms; (e)–(h) resultant images. (a) and (e) present the input image; (b) and (f) display the results of global HE; (c) and (g) present the results of local HE; (d) and (h) display the results of the proposed method.

Figure 4 presents a visual comparison of the proposed method and the method used in [1]. In [1], the HDR image is decomposed into base and detail layers via a self-defined filter. However, the filter is based on approximation, which may lead to noise or loss of details during filtering. In contrast, this study maintains good contrast in not only bright but also dark regions.

4 Conclusion

This paper proposes an HE-based tone mapping algorithm. The results show that the proposed method resolves the issue of defining local regions and avoids seam effects. Furthermore, as shown in Fig. 4, the proposed algorithm outperforms the comparative method in terms of contrast enhancement and detail preservation.

(a)   (b)

Fig. 4. Visual comparison 2. (a) Result from the proposed method. (b) Result from [1].

References

1. Hsia, C., Yang, J., Chiang, J.: Complexity reduction method for ultrasound imaging enhancement in Tetrolet transform domain. J. Supercomput. **76**, 1438–1449 (2018). https://doi.org/10.1007/s11227-018-2240-x
2. Tu, H., Hsia, C., Giang, H.: An efficient adaptive image enhancement method in wavelet domain for handwritten document. J. Appl. Sci. Eng. **19**(3), 357–370 (2016)
3. Chen, Y., Hsia, C., Lu, C.: Multiple exposure fusion based on sharpness-controllable fuzzy feedback. J. Intell. Fuzzy Syst. **36**(2), 1121–1132 (2019)
4. Hsia, C.: New verification method for finger-vein recognition system. IEEE Sens. J. **18**(2), 790–797 (2018)
5. Hsia, C., Lin, T., Chiang, J.: An adaptive binarization method for cost-efficient document image system in wavelet domain. J. Imaging Sci. Technol. **64**(3) (2020)

6. Hsia, C., Guo, J., Wu, C.: Finger-vein recognition based on parametric-oriented corrections. Multimedia Tools Appl. **76**(23), 25179–25196 (2017)
7. Guo, J., Hsia, C., Shih, M., Liu, Y., Wu, J.: High speed multi-layer background subtraction. In: Proceedings of IEEE International Symposium on Intelligent Signal Processing and Communications Systems, pp. 74–79 (2012)
8. Hsia, C.: A new VLSI architecture for symmetric mask-based discrete wavelet transform. J. Internet Technol. **15**(7), 1083–1090 (2014)
9. Hsia, C., Chiang, J., Li, H., Lin, C., Chou, K.: A 3D endoscopic imaging system with content-adaptive filtering and hierarchical similarity analysis. IEEE Sens. J. **16**(11), 4521–4530 (2016)
10. Gu, B., Li, W., Zhu, M., Wang, M.: Local edge-preserving multiscale decomposition for high dynamic range image tone mapping. IEEE Trans. image Process. **22**(1), 70–79 (2013)
11. Pathak, S., Dahiwale, P., Padole, G.: A combined effect of local and global method for contrast image enhancement. In: Proceedings of IEEE International Conference Engineering and Technology, pp. 1–5 (2015)
12. Yang, J., Hore, A., Shahnovich, U., Lai, K., Yanushkevich, S.N., Yadid-Pecht, O.: Multi-Scale histogram tone mapping algorithm enables better object detection in wide dynamic range images. In: Proceedings of IEEE International Conference Advanced Video and Signal Based Surveillance, pp. 1–6 (2017)
13. Husseis, A., Mokraoui, A., Matei, B.: Revisited histogram equalization as HDR images tone mapping operators. In: Proceedings of IEEE International Symposium Signal Processing and Information Technology, pp. 144–149 (2017)
14. Liu, Y., Guo, J., Yu, J.: Contrast enhancement using stratified parametric-oriented histogram equalization. IEEE Trans. Circ. Syst. Video Technol. **27**(6), 1171–1181 (2017)

Performance Analysis of Linear Regression Based on Python

Gongxin Shen[1,2(✉)] and Qihe Liu[1,2]

[1] School of Information Engineering, Nanjing Polytechnic Institute,
Nanjing 210048, China
sgx0554@163.com
[2] Jiangsu Province Fluid Sealing and Measurement and Control Engineering
Technology Research and Development Center, Nanjing 210044, China

Abstract. Python language has become the most popular machine learning language because of its simplicity, readability and expansibility. By expanding the library NumPy, it can achieve fast array processing. At the same time, Python can directly implement machine learning algorithm by extending TensorFlow framework, but there is a lack of quantitative analysis among different methods. This paper simulates different amounts of data and then realizes linear regression with NumPy library and TensorFlow framework respectively. By comparing the calculation time of the same number of iterations and the analysis of the same number of iterations with the same accuracy, A quantitative data analysis is given, which provides some reference for the practical application of NumPy library and TensorFlow framework.

Keywords: Python · NumPy · TensorFlow · Linear regression

1 Introduction

1.1 Python Development Status

At present, Python has become one of the most popular programming languages. In December 2017, it surpassed C# language, second only to Java, C and C++ language, ranking fourth. Because of the simplicity, readability and expansibility of Python language, there are more and more research institutes using Python to do scientific computing abroad. Some well-known universities have adopted Python to teach programming courses. Python language has become the most popular machine learning language. Many open source scientific computing software packages provide Python's call interface. The classical extended library of scientific computing: NumPy provides Python with fast array processing function, similar to the partial matrix processing function of MATLAB in Python. With the continuous development of machine learning, many companies and organizations have introduced the Python open source framework of machine learning. At present, there are dozens of open source libraries of machine learning based on Python, including TensorFlow, Caffe, Theano and Scikit_learnt, etc. [1]. TensorFlow is the open source machine learning framework of

© Springer Nature Singapore Pte Ltd. 2020
J. Shen et al. (Eds.): IC3 2019, CCIS 1227, pp. 695–702, 2020.
https://doi.org/10.1007/978-981-15-6113-9_80

Google. The most widely used number of stars in Github in 2017 is far beyond that of other frameworks.

1.2   Research Methods

The research idea of this paper is to generate different amounts of data through Python. On the one hand, the linear regression algorithm is realized by NumPy library matrix operation programming to view computing time. On the other hand, the TensorFlow machine learning framework is introduced to realize regression to view computing time. By using the same hardware, under the same gradient. Reduction algorithm, the same learning rate, and the same accuracy to compare the calculation time and their sensitivity to the number of data, to provide a certain reference for the practical application of machine learning.

2   Linear Regression

2.1   Linear Regression Theory

Given the independent variable x and function f, the solution is obtained through function processing. Similar to f (x) = y, machine learning is that there are a lot of X (eigenvalues) and Y (target variables) in the sample and then the function f is obtained in turn.

The idea of linear regression is to assume that h(x) = theta_0*x^0 + theta_1*x^1 + theta_2*x^2 + theta_n*x^n + ... = y, only considering theta_0 and theta_1, and that x^0 = 1, the original formula is simplified to: h(x) = theta_0 + theta_1*x^1 = y. If h (x) is the closest to f(x), it is to find (h(x) − y)^2 at the minimum. Assume that there are m x and y values in total, It is to find the minimum value of $\sum_{i=1}^{m} (h(x_i) - y_i)^2$. The function h(x) = theta_0 + theta_1*x^1 obtained under this minimum value is the hypothetical function closest to the real function. The definition of the loss function is defined.

$$J(\theta_0, \theta_1) = \frac{1}{2m} \sum_{i=1}^{m} (\theta_0, \theta_1 * x_i - y_i)^2 \tag{1}$$

The problem is described to getting the value of theta (0), theta (1) when the function J (theta _0, theta _1) is the smallest.

2.2   Linear Regression Calculation Process

The linear regression method is achieved through gradient descent.

Step 1: is to get any theta _0, theta _1 value.

Step 2: The function of J (theta _0, theta _1) is derived from theta _0 and theta _1 respectively.

$$\frac{\partial J(\theta_0, \theta_1)}{\partial \theta_0} = \frac{1}{m} \sum_{i=1}^{m} (\theta_0 + \theta_1 * x_i - y_i) \tag{2}$$

$$\frac{\partial J(\theta_0, \theta_1)}{\partial \theta_0} = \frac{1}{m} \sum_{i=1}^{m} (\theta_0 + \theta_1 * x_i - y_i) \times x_i \tag{3}$$

Step 3: Modify the values of theta_0 and theta_1, and the derivative is to get a changing trend and a small variable, we can Cost loss value repeatedly until no theta_0, theta_1 value can be founded or theta_0, theta_1 value is too small to be neglected, then theta_0, theta_1 values are what we want, where a is the learning rate, generally set to 0.01.

$$\theta_0 = \theta_o - \frac{\alpha}{m} \sum_{i=1}^{m} (\theta_0 + \theta_1 * x_i - y_i) \tag{4}$$

$$\theta_1 = \theta_1 - \frac{\alpha}{m} \sum_{i=1}^{m} (\theta_0 + \theta_1 * x_i - y_i) \times x_i \tag{5}$$

Step 4: Calculate the difference between J (theta_0, theta_1) and the last J (theta_0, theta_1) each time, less than a certain value that theta_0, theta_1 is the solution they need, otherwise repeat the third step, pay attention to gradient decline, every calculation update theta_0, theta_1 need to use all samples, such an update is also known as training once, to be Making h (x) closest to f (x) can be trained many times until the error meets its own needs.

3 NumPy and TensorFlow Achieve Linear Regression

3.1 NumPy Realizes Linear Regression

NumPy is an open source numerical computation extension library of Python. It can be used to store and process large matrices, which is more efficient than Python's nested list structure. The core is N-dimensional array object Array and many special operation libraries. NumPy is used to realize linear regression [2]. Firstly, read in M sets of X and Y data, initialize theta_0 and theta_1, set training times and learning rate, read in all data in each training, calculate new theta_0 and theta_1 according to gradient descent, calculate loss function with new theta_0 and theta_1, and stop training if it meets the requirements, otherwise train to set. The number of times. The core code of Python is as follows:

```
def gradientDescent(X, y, theta, alpha, num_iters):
m, n = X.shape
# M and N represent rows and columns respectively.
J_history = []
for i in range(num_iters):
temp1 = 0.0
temp2 = 0.0
```

```
for j in range(m):
temp1 += list((np.dot(X[j, :], theta) - y[j]) * X[j, 0])[0]
temp2 += list((np.dot(X[j, :], theta) - y[j]) * X[j, 1])[0]
# Temp1, temp2 is already an array after computation,
# [temp1 and temp2] are column vectors.

theta = theta - alpha * np.array([temp1, temp2]) / m
if (computeCost(X, y, theta) < 0.01):
print("num_iters = ", i)
break
J_history.append(computeCost(X, y, theta))
return theta, J_history
```

In the gradientdescen function, theta value is calculated according to the gradient descent, the parameters X and y are training data, the initial value of theta is 0, alpha is the learning rate, the default value is set to 0.01, num_iter is the number of training, and the initial value is 0.01. The process value of each iteration is stored in J_history. In the code, matrix multiplication is used instead of one cycle training of all data, and the dot method in NumPy is needed.

3.2 TensorFlow Achieves Linear Regression

TensorFlow is a second-generation machine learning system developed by Google. It has greatly improved flexibility and portability, speed and scalability. It uses Symbolic programming. The front of the programming is to define the symbol, which is executed in the session. When planning unified memory allocation and considering the efficiency of calculations, the Python core code is as follows:

```
#Calculate the w and b values according to the gradient dscent,
#w and b are equivalent to theta1 and theta0, respectively
#The parameter x_data placement is the value of x,
#the learning rate is set to 0.01 by default,
#and the number of training is 100.
W = tf.Variable(tf.random_uniform([1], -1, 1), name = 'W')
b = tf.Variable(tf.zeros([1]), name = 'b')
y = W * x_data + b
loss = tf.reduce_mean(tf.square(y - y_data), name = 'loss')
optimizer = tf.train.GradientDescentOptimizer(0.01)
train = optimizer.minimize(loss, name = 'train')
sess = tf.Session()
init = tf.global_variables_initializer() sess.run(init)
for step in range(1000):
sess.run(train)
```

Where W is equivalent to theta_1, b is equivalent to theta_0, loss is the loss function, optimizer adopts gradient descent algorithm, learning rate is set to 0.01, the previously defined parameters are always symbols, until the program runs to sess.run (init) code, TensorFlow is allocated Memory, the latter code is optimized based on parameters.

4 Linear Regression Performance Comparison

4.1 Experimental Computer Hardware and Software Configuration

The computer hardware configuration used in the experiment includes: CPU is Intel Core(TM) i5-6500, memory is 4 GB, no GPU is configured, software platform configuration includes: WINDOWS SERVER2012 64 operating system, and python developing language based on Anaconda integrated environment. Anaconda is essentially a package management. The device and environment manager support a variety of open source packages and also supports the python language. If you don't want these open source packages, you can install Miniconda to install the desired packages yourself via command: conda install PACKAGE. The current version of python3 is Anaconda34.4.0-Windows-x86_64.exe. Mainly include NumPy, Scipy, Matplotlib, Pandas (data analysis), Seaborn (statistical visualization), Bokeh (web visualization), Scikit-Learn (machine learning and data mining), NLTK (natural language), Notebook (web interactive computing environment). This regression experiment has a Python version of 3.6 and a NumPy version of 1.13.1. The version of TensorFlow is 1.2.0-rc2. When installing TensorFlow, first configure the corresponding TensorFlow virtual environment [3], then activate the TensorFlow virtual environment by using the command: Pip install–upgrade–ignore-installed TensorFlow. This command implements the installation of the CPU version of TensorFlow. The installation is completed to test the TensorFlow environment. We start the TensorFlow environment in Anaconda Prompt, and enter the python environment, test the environment through the following code: import TensorFlow as tf, if the compilation does not go wrong, then the TensorFlow environment configuration is normal.

4.2 Linear Regression Data Generation

The experimental data is generated using a linear function plus a random perturbation. The x coordinate uses a Gaussian distribution with $\mu = 0$, $\sigma = 0.5$, the y value is 2 multiplied by x plus 5, implemented in Python programming, writes the generated data to the file according to test1 $\sim$ test4, and then reads the same data by NumPy and TensorFlow respectively to perform linear regression analysis. The generated data samples are defined as 20, 100, 500 respectively. 2500, you can use Python's Matplotlib library to draw data on the graph to see [4, 5]. The core code is as follows:

```
#Python code Generate 100 points, and send the generated
#points data to the corresponding text file at the same time,
#then call the points data separately with NumPy code
#and TensorFlow code.
#and the number of training is 100. num_points = 100
data_set = []
```

```
for i in range(num_points):
x1 = np.random.normal(0.0,0.5)
y1 = x1*2 + 5+np.random.normal(0.0,0.5)
data_set.append([x1,y1]) np.savetxt("C:\\test2.txt", data_set)
x_data = [v[0] for v in data_set]
y_data = [v[1] for v in data_set]
plt.subplot(222) plt.ylim(0,10) plt.xlim(-2,2)
plt.scatter(x_data,y_data,c = 'r', marker = "+")
plt.title('points = 100')
```

In the following, Python draw analog data graphs with data points of 20, 100, 500, and 2500 respectively by the drawing library [6, 7] (Fig. 1).

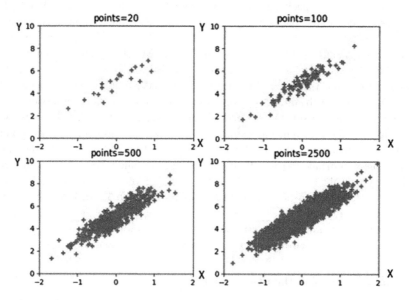

Fig. 1. 20, 100, 500, and 2500 corresponding analog data point X-Y coordinates

4.3   Linear Regression Performance

Calculation Time Required for the Same Number of Iterations

In Python programs, there are three commonly used methods for calculating the running time of a Python program. Here, the DATETIME library is used to calculate, and the clock method is used to obtain the running time of the program [8, 9]. The calculation time is more accurate, regardless of I/O time and other. Time. Only considering the nuances of each calculation time. The parameters involved in the calculation include: Analog Points, Number of iterations, learning rate. In order to ensure that the number of iterations is completed, the threshold value of the loss value is not considered in the program to terminate the program. The calculation time is based on the average of 50 calculations, and the statistical results are shown in Table 1.

Table 1. Different analog data points correspond to frame runtime.

Python methods	Analog points			
	20 points	100 points	500 points	2500 points
NumPy	14(ms)	14(ms)	18(ms)	30(ms)
TensorFlow	13(ms)	14(ms)	15(ms)	18(ms)

Note: iterNum = 1000, alpha = 0.01

The Number of Iterations Required for the Same Regression Precision

Since the linear regression calculation has two parameters, the accuracy is divided into one parameter, 5% error range, two parameters, 5% error range, one parameter, 2% error range, and two parameters, 2% error range, for statistical analysis. The number of data points is 2500 points, the learning rate is 0.01, and the calculation time is also based on the average of 50 calculations. The program does not consider the threshold of loss value to terminate the program, only considering the set of parameter deviations. The statistical results are shown in Table 2.

Table 2. Different precision corresponding frame training times.

Python methods		Accuracy			
		Single parameter < 0.05	Two parameters < 0.05	Single parameter < 0.02	Two parameters < 0.02
NumPy	Iterations	429 times	1307 times	523 times	1535 times
	runtime	30 ms	88 ms	34 ms	103 ms
Tensor Flow	Iterations	213 times	640 times	243 times	738 times
	runtime	189 ms	490 ms	212 ms	558 ms

Note: pointNum = 2500, alpha = 0.01

5 Conclusions

Through the comparative analysis of the generated data, the analysis Table 1 shows that the operation time and the data amount of the NumPy library increase quickly in the same training times and learning rates, and the use of TensorFlow is not sensitive to the change of the data amount. In table two, the computation of two parameters is much larger than that of one parameter. With the increase of parameter precision, Although TensorFlow has fewer iterations than NumPy, it consumes more time. Since the hardware configuration of the machine is consistent, Due to the introduction of TensorFlow framework, iteration takes much more time than NumPy. The regression time efficiency of NumPy is high. In summary, this paper compares the efficiency of the NumPy library and the TensorFlow framework through quantitative data analysis. Although the TensorFlow framework uses the optimized calculation method, there is a certain gap in computational efficiency compared with the NumPy library. Comprehensive Table 1, Table 2, the same accuracy, the same amount of data, NumPy is more than times efficiency than the TensorFlow framework, but TensorFlow framework also has certain advantages in Programming efficiency.

References

1. Chun, W.J Song, J.: Python Core Programming. Beijing: People's Posts and Telecommunications Press, pp. 1–22 (2008). translation
2. Ivan, I., Zhang Y.: Python Data Analysis Basic Tutorial. Beijing: People's Posts and Telecommunications, pp. 126–144 (2014). translation
3. http://wiki.jikexueyuan.com/project/TensorFlow-zh/
4. Chudoba, R., Sadílek, V.: Using Python for scientific computing: efficient and flexible evaluation of the statistical characteristics of functions with multivariate random inputs. Comput. Phys. Commun. **184**(2), 414–427 (2013)
5. Harrington, P., Li, R., et al.: Machine Learning in Actual Combat. Beijing: People's Posts and Telecommunications Press, pp. 73–84 (2013). translation
6. Paweł, P.: Measures and visualization methods of map projection distortions with the use of "python matplotlib library" as an example. Polish Cartographical Rev. **48**(3), 104–114 (2016)
7. Ryan, V.: ExoData: a Python package to handle large exoplanet catalogue data. Comput. Phys. Commun. **207**, 298–309 (2016)
8. https://pythonhow.com/measure-execution-time-python-code/
9. https://www.w3resource.com/python-exercises/python-basic-exercise-57.php

Maker, CT and STEAM Education for Cognitive City

Design and Implementation of Green Energy Teaching Modules for Elementary School

Sheau-Wen Lin[1(✉)], Wan-Lin Yang[1], Hua-Shu Hsu[1],
Kelvin H.-C. Chen[1], Jang-Ho Son[2], and Satoko Ishikawa[3]

[1] National Pingtung University, Pingtung, Taiwan
linshewen@mail.nptu.edu.tw
[2] Daegu National University of Education, Daegu, Korea
[3] Osaka Kyoiku University, Kashiwara, Japan

Abstract. This study designed and implemented green energy teaching modules for elementary school. An international curriculum development committee were built to identify key issues and trends in "Green energy". Green energy curriculum was developed based on the guideline from Japan, Korea, and Taiwan. The purpose of course objectives was to cultivate grade 5–6 students' green energy literacy. Student active learning in authentic context was base for design modules. Local and international teaching resource and materials were identified to assist with course implementation. Students' performance criteria were set for evaluation. Five participant teachers' teaching preparation and practices were explored. Learning difficulties and teaching adjustment were described and interpreted. Classroom observations, teacher interviews, and questionnaires were adopted to collect data. Data was classified and coded. Then, triangulation was used to enhance the validity. It was found that the participant teachers showed neutral responses to STEM instruction and teaching efficacy. They spent time to clarify green energy concepts, learned new green energy technology, and selected or made some local materials for instruction during preparation stage. They covered most of the content of modules, used materials suggested by the booklet or selected by themselves (for example, simple movie, local materials), and rewarded students for their engagement frequently during teaching. Time limitation led to surface learning instead of deep learning. Assigning some tasks as homework could make students have enough time to assimilate and accumulate knowledge, then to complete following comprehensive works successfully. Suggestions were made for teaching and curriculum design.

Keywords: Green energy · Curriculum design · Teaching practices

1 Research Background

Energy is one of the major global issues. Many countries tried to develop new energy to protect environment from being persecuted and to reduce the impact on the environment. Being friendly to the environment, green energy is considered to be the most effective renewable energy source. However, during developing green energy, it also caused many problems, such as over-cultivation of biomass plant, destruction of local

© Springer Nature Singapore Pte Ltd. 2020
J. Shen et al. (Eds.): IC3 2019, CCIS 1227, pp. 705–711, 2020.
https://doi.org/10.1007/978-981-15-6113-9_81

ecology and agricultural land, and high cost in solar modules recycling. The science of green energy has become an issue to the public.

Due to growing attention on environmental sustainability, the need for proper environmental education is emphasized globally. Environmental education could promote people's efforts and proper knowledge to solve environmental problems. A more global perspective on curriculum design instead of a single regional or national perspective could enhance successfully student environmental literacy. Elementary level education is the beginning and base for further learning. It need more researchers and teachers to deal with it. The teaching modules in this study was designed by scholars from Taiwan, Japan, and South Korea that lacked energy resources. It is hoped to cultivate elementary students' energy literacy through this module teaching. So that students can get better green energy literacy and develop the world views on green energy [1].

2   Research Purposes and Questions

Teachers play an important role for curriculum implementation. This study draws on the perspective of hermeneutics, observes the practices of green energy modules taught by the participant teachers, problems encountered and solutions in practical teaching. Research problems that lead to inquiry are: (1) What were the practices of green energy teaching modules? (2) What problems did teachers encounter when conducting teaching practice? And how to solve them?

3   Literature Review

3.1   Elementary School Green Energy Education

Green energy is a socially controversial technology [2]. Experts and scholars have not reached a consensus on this technology application in the society, and the evidence and information to judge the dispute are incomplete, and the results and predictions presented are not absolutely certain. However, green energy has a certain meaning in education. Lin [3] pointed out that discussing controversial science and technology issues in the science classroom would help student nurture their democratic literacy and social responsibility. Especially elementary schools are the foundation of basic education. Conducting green energy education in elementary level will inspire future learning and citizenship. It is very important to teach green energy issues in elementary school classrooms.

3.2   Interdisciplinary Nature of Green Energy Instruction

Green energy has an interdisciplinary nature of Science, Technology, Engineering and Math (STEM) education program. STEM teaching is a relatively important teaching mode in the 21st century. Ei-Deghaidy and Mansour [4] indicate that teacher's view on STEM instruction can help and promote the skills required in the 21st century, including thinking skills, collaboration, problem solving, and research skills, are all useful for future science career. Meanwhile, teachers link STEM to school science with the authentic life context, which is necessary for the students' choice in their future career. Therefore, if the teacher effectively uses the green energy teaching modules in their classes, it will be very helpful for teacher to reflect their own teachings. As Wallace and Louden [5] believe, one of the ways to enrich professional knowledge of teachers is to promote teachers to learn new educational rationales or to teach less familiar content. Therefore, implementation of green energy teaching modules will enhance teachers' professional knowledge.

4   Research Methods

4.1   Green Energy Booklet Design

A cross-county curriculum development committee were built to identify key issues and trends in "Green energy". Green energy curriculum was developed based on the guideline from Japan, Korea, and Taiwan. Elementary school curriculum and textbook content from three counties were analyzed. The purpose of course objectives, learning theory, teaching resource and materials, performance rubric were identified as bases for design modules.

4.2   Participants and Situations of Implementation

Five teachers from an elementary schools taught five topics of green energy teaching modules. Two of five teachers cooperated with each other as a group to teach one unit. The participant teachers had teaching experience on STEM in their science classes, respond with medium to high self-efficacy on STEM teaching, would like to provide opportunities to cultivate students future learning attitude. However, they are not sure about STEM education and career awareness.

The participant 19 students were 5th or 6th graders. They were divided into five groups, three to four people per group, each with a large table, where the group members can discuss and design.

The students had two hours a week class that lasted for a total of five weeks and ten hours. The booklet with ten modules used in this study were designed by Taiwan, Japan, and South Korea scholars. Due to time limitation, the participant teachers selected five themes, introduction of green energy, solar energy, biomass energy, hydropower energy, and hydrogen energy, for teaching.

4.3   Data Collection and Analysis

With the consent of the teachers and the students, classroom observations with video recording and two teacher interviews were conducted before and after the teaching. The teachers took a questionnaire on "Self-Efficacy and STEM Teaching Attitude" [6] to describe teachers' existing practices, self-efficacy, and attitude about STEM. The purposes of interviews were mainly aimed at the preparation and modification made by the teachers for module teaching and problems they encountered in the implementation and their solutions. Data was classified and coded according the question framework. Then, triangulation was used to enhance the validity.

4.4   Roles of the Researchers

The researchers in this study was both an "observer" and a "teaching assistant" On the one hand, observed the teacher's teaching behavior, on the one hand, gave the teacher assistance that he/she needed during instruction.

5   Results and Discussion

5.1   Green Energy Teaching Modules

Through analysis elementary school curriculum and textbook content from three counties, nine easy to understand types of Green Energy at the elementary school students' were identified. The topics included: solar energy, bio-energy, wind energy, hydro power, electrical energy, ocean, waste, geothermal, and hydrogen. The purpose of course objectives were to cultivate grade 5–6 students' green energy literacy. Student active learning in authentic context was base for design modules. Local and cross-county teaching resource and materials were identified to assist with course implementation. Students' performance criteria were set for evaluation.

5.2   Instruction Preparation

Before instruction, the teachers first spent time to understand science concepts and technology of the whole module. Then, the teachers tried to clarify the partially incomplete or difficult to implement part of the module. The teachers modified and adjusted some of the module and search relevant materials as a substitute teaching plan. Researchers discussed and prepared teaching materials with teachers together to facilitate smooth teaching of the classroom. The participant teachers played as "learners" in this teaching context that was similar to Lin's [3] research that indicated that preparatory stage was the most difficult part for the teachers to incorporate and organize related knowledge and experiences for teaching. The teachers' unfamiliarity with the contents and procedures made the teachers unconfident to teach green energy.

For example, in the "introduction of green energy" module, teachers worried about students' ability of "definition of green energy". Teachers and researchers exchanged their ideas and decided to let students have a brainstorm to define "green energy" for further learning activity. Great attention is paid to the student's initial ideas on green energy. Another discussion was about biomass energy, which led students to use orange peel instead of candle to demonstrate flame and energy. The researcher helped teachers to set up the experiment of orange peel as an energy sources. Meanwhile, the teachers searched easier, simpler, and more interesting video materials than the provided, such as bio-energy-produced biodiesel, and local TV programs. The teachers indicated that the local films was closer to Taiwanese everyday life that can initiate student interest and motivation.

Teachers rearranged some teaching procedure suggested by modules. The teaching activity flowed in a mode of "introduction → development activities → comprehensive activities". In the "solar energy" modules, the teachers arranged outdoor activities, such as using solar energy stoves, solar car competitions, observing the solar panels, etc., to let the students have physical and hands-on experience first. The activities initiated students' curiosity and engagement on following inquiry guided by teachers.

Teachers also felt that it was too difficult to teach all the content of one module within two hours. Some activities such as planning maps of hydrogen energy cities, making hydropower books, and hand-on activities were cut off because of time limitation.

Teachers spent lots of time on steps of each hands-on activity. Sometimes, the teachers would change the materials to make it easy to carry out. For example, in the solar energy module, the teachers used a magnifying glass together with the solar cooker to heat water. Another example was in hydrogen energy module, the teachers planned to add a "making a hydrogen car" activity to provide an exciting hand-on activity to promote students learning interest.

5.3 Implementation

The progress of the class activities followed the suggested steps, observation → question → response → telling → questioning → discussion → summarizing. Teachers used questions to guide learning, to attract attention, to thinking, and to lead to the follow-up activities. Meanwhile, teachers used strategies that encourage, praise, and respond at the right time to let students speak and answer questions.

Teachers provided opportunities for group discussion and whole class discussion to express their thoughts and listened to others' ideas. Students showed their attitude towards future learning, for example, respecting different opinions of their peers and including others' perspectives when making decisions.

From class observation, it was found that teachers did not proceed or proceed incompletely some activities to prepare students creativity. For example, making brochures and drawing energy comics and assembled a hydroelectric generator were deleted and drawing green energy booklet was carried out without sharing and summary. Teachers indicated that modification was based on the consideration that it was too difficult for the fifth and sixth grade students to finish in limited time.

5.4 Teacher Reflection

Throughout the process of preparation, implementation, and reflection, the teachers developed a greater insight into the consequences of their instruction [3]. It was found that during the preparation period, the teachers added many hands-on activities to attract students' attention. Students who were interested in hand-on activities than watching films or lectures was observed during instruction. In after-class interviews, the participant teachers confirmed the effectiveness of hands-on activities. Teacher's reflection led their professional knowledge growth [5].

Teachers mentioned that this green energy teaching experience made them more confident of green energy instruction, especially on biomass energy, solar energy, hydropower, and hydrogen. The five teachers had gradually improved their understanding of green energy concepts and enhanced their professionalism. Teachers could teach green energy in more multiple and diverse ways to cultivate the fifth and sixth graders' energy literacy.

All five teachers pointed out that two hours for a topic was too hasty to teach the modules to the best. Time limitation made surface learning and students could get fragment only and lack the structure of the green energy knowledge.

6 Conclusions and Recommendations

This study explored the design and implementation of green energy modules. The participant teachers' instruction made us understand teaching difficulties encountered and how they struggled with these problems. From the above results and discussions, the following conclusions and recommendations were proposed.

6.1 Conclusions

The participant teachers linked existing experience and knowledge to the green energy modules teaching, adjusted concepts, activities, and sequence of teaching activities. The experience made teacher professional growth. Time limitation seemed to be the biggest problem to cover all content of the modules.

6.2 Recommendations

It is found in this study that difficulty of concept learning and time is a major factor affecting teaching, this could be a good base for modification of the green energy modules. Green energy knowledge and technology were not familiar to teachers, it was a good way to enrich teachers' professional knowledge. Support and resources are needed to help teachers teach new topics. The cooperation between researchers and elementary teachers would be an important factor influence effectiveness of teaching. In-service teacher preparations program is suggested for further modules implementation and extension.

References

1. Lin, S.-W., Hsu, H.-S., Chen, K.H.-C., Son, J.-H., Ishikawa, S.: Green Energy Guide Book for Elementary School Teachers. National Pingtung University, Taiwan (2019)
2. Millar, R.: Science education for democracy: what can the school curriculum achieve? In: Levinson, R., Thomas, J. (eds.) Science Today - Problem or Crisis? pp. 87–101. Routledge, London (1997)
3. Lin, S.-S.: Interpretative research on the roles of the science teacher in instruction of a controversial issue in science and technology-a case study. Chin. J. Sci. Educ. **14**(3), 237–255 (2006)

4. El-Deghaidy, H., Mansour, N.: Science teachers' perceptions of STEM education: possibilities and challenges. Int. J. Learn. Teach. **1**(1), 51–54 (2015)
5. Wallace, J., Louden, W.: Teachers' Learning: Stories of Science Education, vol. 7. Springer, Heidelberg (2000). https://doi.org/10.1007/0-306-47218-X
6. Friday Institute for Educational Innovation: Teacher Efficacy and Beliefs Toward STEM Survey. Author, Raleigh (2012)

The Case Study of Learning Effectiveness of STEAM Education-Take "Variety Origami" as an Example

Cheng-Hung Wang[1]([⊠]), Chih-Yi Lin[1], and Sheng-Yi Wu[2]

[1] National University of Kaohsiung, Kaohsiung, Taiwan
wang101@nuk.edu.tw
[2] National Pingtung University, Pingtung, Taiwan

Abstract. In response to the rapid development of science and technology in recent years and the enthusiasm for cultivating popular aesthetics, the emphasis on cultivating problem-solving abilities and integrating STEAM education in practical applications in various fields has become a trend of promotion today.

Based on STEAM education, this study designed and produced a briefing booklet with origami as the main axis for learners to learn. Using the quasi-experimental research method to observe the difference in performance of learners before and after the briefing, using the "Learning Effectiveness Assessment" scale. Investigate learners. It is used to explore whether the application of STEAM education to origami-related teaching plans has a significant impact on learners' learning. In addition to analyzing the results and presenting the findings, the authors are working hard to apply the research results to future design-related teaching areas.

Keywords: STEAM education · Learning effectiveness · Origami

1 Research Background and Motivation

In the 1990s, the United States promoted its national science ability and promoted STEM education that emphasized science and technology. However, the STEM education policy has been in progress for many years, and it has gradually been found that its content lacks the motivation of learners to have an interest in scientific learning. To this end, after several exchanges and discussions in various countries, Yakman, a professor at Virginia University of Technology in the United States, proposed in 2011 to include the "A" of Art in the education curriculum. Since then, the STEAM education for art design has been merged. Health.

After the evolution of STEAM education has the characteristics of cross-domain, integrated learning, hands-on operation, and the addition of artistic concepts, learners can understand and integrate knowledge in various fields through the process of exploration and artistic creation (Connor et al. 2015), and art education is widely used in various types of courses, among which "origami" is highly respected by American children's enlightenment education. Origami is a hand-made activity in which paper is folded into various forms. Common works such as paper cranes and paper planes are mainly folded on a single sheet of paper. It is a kind of leisure for all ages.

This study produced a STEAM education and teaching briefing to test the learner's relevant influence on learning, and explored the STEAM model different from the traditional teaching model. Is it positive for the learner's learning outcome? In addition, after trying to find out, the case study of the "variable change" teaching case of this research design can assist the relevant learning areas, in order to promote the interdisciplinary teaching application and related research in the future.

2 Research Purposes and Problem Assumptions

Based on the content emphasized by STEAM Education, this study designed a set of origami teaching lesson plans called "Amazing Folding" to compare with traditional origami teaching methods, and conducted experiments in an open and guided way, hoping to improve the learning of adult learners. Results. The purpose of this research study is as follows:

(1) Planning a set of origami teaching lesson designed by STEAM, "various origami", and traditional origami Teaching methods are compared.
(2) Exploring the impact of the learning outcomes of design students in the "variable origami" curriculum.
(3) Based on the results of the research and analysis, make specific recommendations for design education related units or cross-cutting a reference to the design and implementation of the curriculum.

Based on the above problems and the extension of the research purpose, the research hypothesis is summarized as follows: The implementation of origami teaching integrated into STEAM will help improve the learning outcomes of design college students.

3 Research Scope and Limitations

This study is based on 50 design college students in Kaohsiung City in 2019. Using the "Learning Effectiveness Assessment" and "Learning Attitudes and Learning Motivation Questionnaire" questionnaires, the experimental research and analysis of STEAM teaching and traditional cramming teaching were conducted, and qualitative data-assisted research was collected.

The research is integrated into STEAM's origami teaching, which is supplemented by a briefing film that integrates fairy tale plots. The content combines the plot problems to challenge and timely teaching. Due to the time limit of the test, both traditional teaching and STEAM teaching are planned into five chapters. The first chapter aims to recognize the characteristics of origami; the second chapter aims at the correlation between origami and mathematics; the third chapter aims to experience the origami. With the physical sciences, the fourth chapter aims at origami and artistic aesthetics; the fifth chapter aims to solve problems and creative thinking; both of the lesson plans provide the learning focus of the learners' chapters, but the traditional cramming teaching and STEAM teaching. The teaching methods are not the same as the teaching methods. In order to avoid the confusion of the purpose of the test teaching method due to the setting of too complicated challenges, the teaching method is based on the basic entry method, and this study has collected various combinations of origami techniques books and screened, and finally decided to refer to "Sonobe module". The project is the main content of technical teaching.

4   Literature Discussion

The purpose of this study is to explore the impact of learning motivation and learning outcomes of origami teaching and traditional cramming teaching combined with STEAM education. According to the purpose of the research, this chapter summarizes the theoretical framework of the research through the collection and analysis of the literature. The first section of this chapter is the analysis of the STEAM education teaching case; the second section is the form and technique of collecting origami, which will be detailed below.

4.1   STEAM Education Teaching Case

The STEAM concept focuses on the mutual integration of interdisciplinary disciplines, fosters people's ability to solve problems, and increases people's interest in learning modern science and technology, thereby enhancing self-competitiveness. When STEAM implements teaching, it should not only emphasize the five subject knowledge separately, but also focus on innovative teaching and learning methods (Xiaotao et al. 2016). There have been many successful teaching cases since the implementation of STEAM Education. The following two cases are selected and discussed in this case:

(1) STEAM-oriented Maker teaching (Yu-Hung et al. 2017).
The experimental process is divided into four weeks, which are introduction, collection, group discussion, publication and competition. One of the research tools uses the Creative Product Genre Scale. One of the results of the study is that there is no significant difference in the learning of STEAM knowledge between high school students and design college students, and the average score of high school students in group discussion is slightly better than that of design college students. This conclusion also seems to point out that STEAM education is suitable. The general public is not just for specific ethnic groups. Therefore, this study attempts to refer to the development and verification model of its research curriculum. It is expected that STEAM can be applied to origami-related teaching, which proves that adult use of STEAM teaching materials has significant learning results.

(2) STEAM theory is integrated into the design of high school technology implementation activities (Bo-Wei 2017).

This study draws on some of the activity design process of this experiment, and replaces the scientific knowledge part of the teacher with the engineering part of the process design into the film teaching of the origami technique, retains the use of the technology tools and the cultivation part of the innovative thinking, and deletes the size matching description. Partly, the prototype of the STEAM experimental course design of this study was formed.

Based on the above STEAM teaching case, this study designs PowerPoint presentations for the basic teaching of origami, allowing learners to think about the basic components, how to design and achieve the preset goals in a limited material and time, and stimulate Its creativity and learning ability to make a problem-solving and aesthetically pleasing finished product.

4.2 Origami Form

Origami is widely used in various fields. As long as you master the basic forms and techniques, a variety of skill applications can create many useful and interesting objects like magic. According to the classification of British origami writer David Mitchell, the origami form can be divided into the following three types:

(1) Single sheet designs

Designed on a single sheet of paper, most of them use square paper, and traditional origami designs fall into this category. This is done by folding the paper into the proper position to form the desired result. For example, a horse has four legs, a tail and a head, but a square has only four corners. How to achieve the desired rendering under limited conditions is a challenge of this single design.

(2) Multiple sheet designs

An origami design formed by placing or connecting a sheet of paper or more. The advantage of this form is that each part can be folded in an easier way, but at the same time the challenge is lower, and the final result of the finished product is usually more concise than the single design.

(3) Modular origami

This form is literally translated into a special case of modular origami (translated into "composite origami" in China) in multiple designs. It uses multiple sheets of paper folded into simple geometric shapes called cells or modules, which are then combined to form a more complex design.

The top three models are based on the amount of paper used and the way the results are presented. In addition, David Mitchell has used the purpose of origami to classify origami. In the following study, the origami genealogy drawn by it is redrawn (Fig. 1):

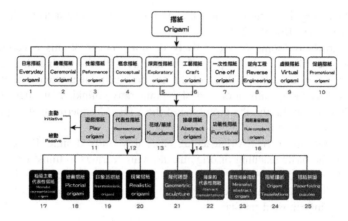

Fig. 1. Origami genealogy (Source: David Mitchell, redrawn in this study)

5 Research Process and Architecture

The research process of this study is divided into five phases, namely "Research Preparation Phase", "Research Tool Development Phase", "Experimental Phase", "Data Analysis Phase" and "Drawing Conclusion Phase". The researchers will draw the five phases in Study flow chart, as shown in Fig. 2:

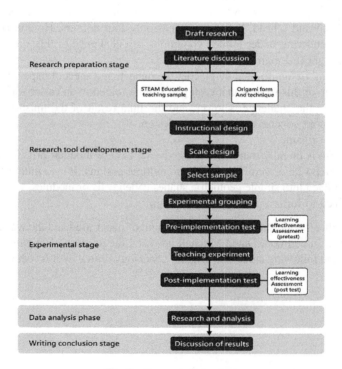

Fig. 2. Research flow chart

6   Research Design

The experimental design content of this research is based on the spirit of STEAM education. The overall experimental application includes the cross-domain learning, self-learning, problem-solving skills, hands-on production and life application emphasized by STEAM.

This study refers to Mayer's multimedia learning design principles and attempts to present the origami steps in the form of chapter stories. Table 1 below shows the chapter content description and teaching scope of the two lesson plans for this study:

Table 1. Teaching plan chapter content and teaching scope.

Chapter	Traditional cramming lesson plan (Group A)	STEAM lesson plan (Group B)	Teaching category
1	How many times can a piece of paper be folded in multiple times? It indicates that the area, thickness and softness of the paper may be the influencing factors of the number of folds, and the learner can think in combination with the life application questions	Little Red Riding Hood's grandmother has to cross the birthday of this year, so she needs to buy a candle for the age to visit her grandmother, and the number of times the magic color paper can be folded to the minimum is just the number of grandma's age	Origami and science
2	Directly tell the principle principle of beauty, and ask learners to use color paper to make "symmetry" and "gradation."	Little Red Riding Hood enters the mountain to collect flowers and send grandma, but there are big wolves in the mountains. I heard that the big wolf is afraid of conforming to the repeated, gradual, symmetrical, balanced, harmonious, contrast, proportion, rhythm, uniform window decoration, please help to avoid the big wolf	Origami and aesthetics

(continued)

Table 1. (*continued*)

Chapter	Traditional cramming lesson plan (Group A)	STEAM lesson plan (Group B)	Teaching category
3	Use the origami to prove the formula of the Pythagorean theorem: In a right triangle, the sum of the squares of the two squares is equal to the square of the hypotenuse	Little Red Riding Hood picked up the flowers to wrap them up, and the way she wrapped the flowers could prove the Pythagorean theorem	Origami and mathematics
4	Let the learner know that the paper can change its structure through folding, etc., so as to achieve the effect that it can not bear the weight	Go to the grandmother's path, please use magical color paper to build a bridge to help Little Red Riding Hood not fall off the bridge	Origami and mechanics
5	Introduce Sonobe's origins and techniques, and ask learners to combine a container based on their basic skills	Grandma got the flowers very happy, so I taught Little Red Riding Hood "Sonobe" to upgrade the magic, and asked Little Red Riding Hood to use this magic to make the flower ware, so that the flowers can be stored	Origami creativity and independent thinking

(*continued*)

Table 1. (*continued*)

Chapter	Traditional cramming lesson plan (Group A)	STEAM lesson plan (Group B)	Teaching category

7 Research Analysis and Conclusion

This chapter examines the impact of "learning effectiveness" on learners in classes A and B (experimental and control) using different textbooks. Exploring whether the traditional cramming materials and STEAM teaching materials will affect the learner's learning effect on the origami course, so the experimental group and the control group's learners will conduct experimental analysis on the origami topic, and compare the two groups of learners before and after the origami test. Performance. The researchers used SPSS software to perform independent sample t-tests on the pre-test scores of the two classes of learners to detect whether there were significant differences between the two classes of learners on the cognitive starting point of the origami project. If there is no significant difference, the two classes start. If the points are similar, then the follow-up study and analysis can be continued. After that, the two test scores of the two classes are tested independently. It is analyzed whether the two classes of learners have significant influence on the learning outcome of the origami course after the experiment of different textbooks.

7.1 Independent Sample t-Test of Pre-test Scores

First, the scores of the online test questions made by the experimental group (Class A) and the control group (Class B) before the formal teaching are taken as the pre-test scores of the two groups, and the scores are independently tested for the pre-test scores. Check whether there is a significant difference between the two groups of learners at the starting point of the origami problem. The analysis results are shown in Table 2.

Table 2. Independent sample t test before the two groups.

		Levene's test for equality of variances		t-test for equality of means						
		F	Sig	t	df	Sig. (2-tailed)	Mean difference	Std. Error difference	95% confidence interval of the difference	
									Lower	Upper
Test1	Equal variances assumed	1.519	.224	.934	48	.355	3.600	3.856	−4.152	11.352
	Equal variances not assumed			.934	47.158	.355	3.600	3.856	−4.156	11.356

The difference in the number of variants of Levene's Test can be found in Table 2 as follows: F = 1.519, p = 0.224 > 0.05, which did not reach significant difference. The t-values and significance results for whether the average values are equal are: t = 0.934, p = 0.355 > 0.05, and there is no significant difference. This represents no significant difference in the starting point of the two classes of learners, so it is possible to continue the experimental study of different lesson plans.

7.2   Average Score and Standard Deviation Before and After Measurement

In order to better understand the differences between the two groups of learners before and after the test scores, the researchers took the pre-test scores and post-test scores of the two groups of experimental and control groups, respectively, to calculate the average score and standard deviation of the two groups, the results are shown in Table 3. Shown. From the table, it can be found that the pre-test score of the experimental group is 3.52 points higher than the control group, and the standard deviation is 1.82 points. Comparing the post-test scores of the two groups, it is found that the score of the experimental group is 1.2 points higher than the control group, and the standard deviation is Instead, it was 1.64 points less.

Table 3. Group statistics after two groups.

		Levene's test for equality of variances		t-test for equality of means							
		F	Sig	t	df	Sig. (2-tailed)	Mean difference	Std. Error difference	95% confidence interval of the difference		
									Lower	Upper
Test1	Equal variances assumed	1.720	.196	.485	48	.630	1.200	2.477	−3.779	6.179
	Equal variances not assumed			.485	46.379	.630	1.200	2.477	−3.784	6.184

However, although there were slight differences in scores, there was no significant difference between the two groups of learners in the average score and the standard deviation. Therefore, the learning outcomes of STEAM textbooks and traditional cramming materials were not found in this study.

7.3   Conclusion

This study uses different origami teaching plans to explore the learning outcomes of adults after STEAM textbooks and traditional cramming materials. Using learning effectiveness assessments, pre-testing, comparing whether the two groups of learners have a significant impact on learning outcomes. This section presents conclusions for research purposes and analytical results for reference in subsequent studies.

In this study, the prior knowledge questionnaire was used to investigate the past cognition of the origami, and the differences were compared with the results of pre- and post-test learning. After the experiment, the results of the independent sample T test were significant. The results showed that the two groups were post-tested, and the significance P = 0.196 > .05, indicating that there was no significant difference in learning outcomes. Therefore, whether or not to use STEAM textbooks has no significant difference in learning outcomes.

Based on the above results, this study proposes the following suggestions for learning lesson plans. As a reference for the followers who also use the briefing teaching method, it can also be used as a reference for future research scholars: the research objects of this study are all related to design. College students, although the learning background and age of the tested learners are similar, it is recommended that before the teaching, the learners should first understand the learner's ability and cognition of origami (or other disciplines), so that The starting point of each learner can be the same. In addition, in order to improve the learning outcome and find out the reasons for the lack of significant differences between the two teaching plans, it is recommended that future researchers can add a qualitative feedback questionnaire to further explore whether there are other reasons that affect the learning outcome. After the study, the researchers will further try to study whether the two teaching plans have a significant impact on learning motivation and creativity.

References

Bo-Wei, Y.: Designed of STEAM-based technology learning activities in senior high school: phone passive speaker. **4**(2), 1–20 (2017) https://doi.org/10.6587/JTHRE.2017

Connor, A.M., Karmokar, S., Whittington, C.: From STEM to STEAM: strategies for enhancing engineering & technology education. Int. J. Eng. Pedagogies **5**(2), 37–47 (2015)

Honda, I.: How to Make Origami. McDowell, Obolensky, New York (1959)

Xiaotao, L., Haiyan, G., Jiaren, Z., Kun, W.: The transition from STEAM education to maker education under the background of "Internet +"-from project-based learning to the cultivation of innovative ability. Distance Educ. J. **232**, 28–36 (2016)

Yu-Hung, C., Po-Ying C., Jain: STEAM oriented maker teaching. Secondary Educ. **68**(2), 12–28 (2017)

The Effects of Green Energy Education on Students' Learning

Kelvin H.-C. Chen[1(✉)], Ying-Hsuan Wu[1], Virecia Williams[1],
Sheau-Wen Lin[1], Hua-Shu Hsu[1], Jang-Ho Son[2],
and Satoko Ishikawa[3]

[1] National Pingtung University, Pingtung, Taiwan
kelvin@mail.nptu.edu.tw
[2] Daegu National University of Education, Daegu, Korea
[3] Osaka Kyoiku University, Kashiwara, Japan

Abstract. The main purpose of this study is to investigate the effects green energy education has on a group of students by comparing their knowledge before and after the course, and to also evaluate their performance by grading the study sheets collected during the course. A total of 17 students from an elementary school in Pingtung City were chosen and they studied for a period of five weeks. After the students complete the lessons in green energy, a statistical analysis was done. Before the teacher officially started lessons, the students completed a questionnaire to determine their green energy literacy. After completing the lessons, the students did the same questionnaire again to test whether or not the students made any obvious progress in their knowledge acquisition. So, the research can be tested by study sheets and questionnaires.

P-value on knowledge, function and attitude of green energy by t-test analysis didn't reach a level of significance in this study. It was possible that the students had not yet realized the practicality of green energy and should have a will to help alleviate environmental issues in life, beginning with simple tasks such as sorting garbage or collecting used clothes and toys for others to use, rather than throwing them away. Moreover, based on study sheets, students made a progress before and after learning. So, Students learned not only by taking courses but also by improving actions in their everyday life. Through these courses, students had a better understanding of green energy.

Keywords: Effects of learning · Green energy education · Green energy literacy

1 Research Background and Motivation

With the expansion of the Earth's population and the industrialization of developing countries, human demand for energy has reached an unprecedented level. More than half of our energy comes from fossil fuels extracted from the depths of the earth's crust. However, over the past two centuries, our huge consumption of energy has caused great danger to the earth. Global scientists agree that we are heading for disasters, and that only by minimizing our dependence on fossil fuels the disaster subside. As a result, the emergence of energy crisis and environmental issues have stimulated the rise of

© Springer Nature Singapore Pte Ltd. 2020
J. Shen et al. (Eds.): IC3 2019, CCIS 1227, pp. 723–729, 2020.
https://doi.org/10.1007/978-981-15-6113-9_83

green energy. What is green energy? "Green energy refers to forms of renewable energy, specifically the ones that provide the highest environmental benefit, which usually mean that the energy is taken directly from nature, and its energy conversion process is less polluting or non-polluting to nature. These include solar energy, wind energy, geothermal energy, hydrogen energy, biomass energy, etc.

Information on energy conservation and carbon reduction is widespread in media coverage and is valued in education systems across the country. In terms of shifting energy use from fossil fuels to renewable energy sources, it is necessary for teachers to use effective teaching methods and materials in green energy education to familiarize the next generation with energy and to encourage them to actively participate in renewable energy related activities. Teaching aids made up of tangible objects help students learn abstract concepts in science because they enable students to visualize those concepts. As Orr (1992) states, "real learning is participatory and experiential, not just didactic" [1]. It is often recommended that primary school teachers provide students with opportunities for experiential learning to help them develop new and in-depth understandings in environmental topics or science.

2 Research Purpose and Question

This study investigated the learning experiences of a senior elementary school student in Pingtung City in their natural environment. An inductive, experience-based learning can lead to a more engaging, effective, and sustainable learning experience than a teacher-led strategy. The guiding inquiry questions are as follows:

(1) What is the degree of change in students' knowledge, function and attitude to green energy before and after study?
(2) Before the teacher teaches, students answered questions by brainstorming and after the teacher teaches, students will do a variety of study sheets to evaluate whether students make a good process or not?
(3) What was student performance for their knowledge of green energy after teaching by grading at a low, medium and high level?

3 Literature Review

Lin (2004) pointed out that discussion controversial science and technology issues in the science courses can promote the social nature of technical disputes, helping future citizens to demonstrate democracy literacy and social responsibility, enhancing expression ability, listening and the ability of judging thoughts, etc. [2]. And these are in line with "Science/Technology/Society" (STS) and "scientific educations must reflect relationship of contemporary science and technology and the impact of both on society" [3]. The reason why energy causes social controversy is that the application of energy also has the impact on human beings. It often has the effect of creating positive and even negative attitudes in students. Controversial energy issues are just one of many social issues, so they are incorporated in today's energy education. Teachers adopt a specific mode as an interdisciplinary teaching method combining science, technology, engineering and mathematics (STEM), aiming to combine the expertise of the four fields, to strengthen the gap between different disciplines, and combine the curriculum with real-life situations to stimulate students' curiosity and desire for knowledge of novelty and knowledge. In addition, this interdisciplinary approach can mainly train students not to think objectively, but to use different perspectives to develop more comprehensive thoughts and use "multiple" pipeline of knowledge sources to solve problems.

4   Research Method

4.1   Participants and Circumstance

The research object is a class of 17 senior students from a small township in Pingtung City, Pingtung County, Taiwan. The experimental course was taught in the natural classroom on the fourth floor of the primary school. The students were divided into five groups and one group consists of three to four students.

The total duration of each natural science teaching activity was two hours per week for five consecutive weeks. The course was divided into three stages: the first stage was the introduction of green energy; the second stage was the teacher's demonstration of the use of green energy equipment and the third stage was student practice. The teaching materials used in this study are the green energy STEM teaching curriculum designed by scholars from Taiwan, Japan and South Korea, and this curriculum has a total of ten modules, from which five modules are selected for teaching, namely: Green Energy Profile, Solar Energy, Hydropower, Hydrogen Energy and Biomass Energy (Fig. 1).

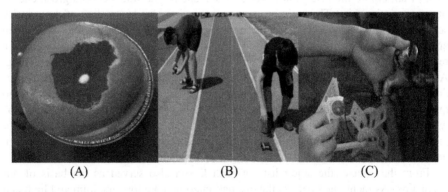

(A)   (B)   (C)

Fig. 1. Hand-made learning of renewable energy (A) biomass candles, (B) solar cars, and (C) hydropower

4.2   Data Collection and Analysis

During the course, each class has different learning sheets arranged according to the course design, for example a brainstorming study list, a "visual thinking" activity table, a power generation book, a board game, and so on. The student's completed study list is used as a source of data collection and analysis. The analysis criteria are low, medium and high. Before and after the start of lessons, the green energy questionnaire will be filled in at the beginning of the first week of the class and at the end of the last week of the course. The questionnaire included 9 knowledge-based questions, 7 function-based questions and 10 attitude-based questions. The rating scale ranged from a "strong no" which was a (1) up to a "strong yes" which was a (5) to measure what their beliefs or thoughts of each statement/question was.

Statistics were constructed to employ frequencies and proportions for categorical data and mean $\pm$ SD for continuous variables. Using two-sided t-test to compare with changes for continuous variables. $P < 0.05$ was considered significant. All statistical analysis was by IBM SPSS Statistics 19.

4.3   The Role of the Researchers

The role of the researchers in this experiment was to be "facilitators" and "analysts". Prior to the course, to assist the teacher with gathering the teaching aids required; during the course, to answer questions that confused students or to assist students with difficulties when assembling the teaching aids; and after the course, to recover data for doing analysis and statistics.

5   Research Result and Discussion

First of all, before the teacher was yet to teach, she let the students do a green energy literacy questionnaire. The main purpose was to gain an understanding of the primary school students' behavior and attitude toward green energy. When the five-week green energy course was over, the students did a questionnaire to test whether they acquired a real understanding of green energy and developed different feelings after teaching. Afterward, a joint assessment of the validity of the contents of the questionnaire was done. The questionnaire included 9 knowledge-based questions, 7 function-based questions and 10 attitude-based questions. The rating scale ranged from a "strong no" which was a (1) up to a "strong yes" which was a (5) to measure what their beliefs or thoughts of each statement/question was. Statistical significance of differences between before and after learning was tested using an independent sample t-test.

From the course, the study lists of each lesson also served as the basis of our evaluation. As mentioned before, the evaluation criteria are low, medium and high and was used to assess whether students can elaborate on the content of energy, such as principles, advantages and disadvantages or examples, or even if they needed the help of friends, in order to give a simple explanation. The study sheets were divided into group discussion (this incorporated collaborative design and personal brainstorming) in order to see students' ideas and thought directions toward green energy. After that, some table game activities were also designed to turn knowledge into games which made learn more fun and engaging. For each class, some experiments were designed to allow students to be apart of practical operations and to deepen their impressions of the green energy content. For example, orange candles can replace biomass energy, hydrogen vehicles can replace gasoline vehicles, and so on. Using the method of texture research, it was possible to discuss the interaction of students and the impact after learning.

The results of this study are listed in Table 1 and are as follows: This section analyzes the performance of students in the learning process through the "Green Energy Pre and Post Test", and the average statistic on green energy knowledge in the pre-test was 3. 74 and the standard deviation 0.56. The results show that students still have a preliminary understanding of green energy knowledge, such as geothermal and waves can be used as a source of human energy or should be used in the classroom, etc. The average value for function of green energy for the pre-test was 3.66, and the standard deviation was 0.67. The results show that most students are willing to take responsibility for environmental issues in their lives, such as sorting garbage or collecting used clothes or toys for others to use instead of throwing them away; the average value for attitude toward green energy for the pre-test was 3.90 and the standard deviation 0.72. The results also show that students' attitude towards green energy remains warm. For example, when they see vehicles emitting exhaust gas it makes them feel angry and think that the government along with citizens should invest more money and time to develop green energy. The average post-test value for knowledge was 4.05 and the standard deviation is 0.63; the average post-test value of green energy function was 3.73, the standard deviation was 0.82; the average post-test value for attitude toward green energy was 4.12, and the standard deviation was 0.51. After the teacher's teaching, the students' understanding of green energy knowledge and their attitude has obviously improved. The teacher explained and demonstrated principles, functions and how to use different energy sources, through the use of film, experimental operation and/or drawing, which has deepened the students' impression of green energy.

Table 1. Results of overall green energy knowledge, function, and attitude.

Item		n	Mean	Std. Deviation	P-value
Knowledge	Before	17	3.74	0.56	0.140
	After		4.05	0.63	
Function	Before	17	3.66	0.67	0.771
	After		3.73	0.82	
Attitude	Before	17	3.90	0.72	0.303
	After		4.12	0.51	

Using T-test analysis, knowledge of green energy had a P-value of 0.140, which didn't reach a significant value. The P-value for function of green energy using T-test analysis was 0.771, which also did not reach a significant value. It is possible that the students had not yet realized the practicality of green energy and should therefore be allowed to participate in some public activities or energy-related issues that would potentially present the seriousness of energy-related issues, so as to help them understand green energy more. T-test analysis of attitude toward green energy had a P-value of 0.303, which also did not reach a significant level. This aspect may take a longer time to adjust. Students will learn not only by taking courses but also by improving actions in their everyday life, such as saving water or electricity and helping their parents consider purchasing more energy efficient household appliances, just to name a few. This suggests that the increased knowledge gained through experiential learning through teaching aids is limited. It is assumed that primary school students are very aware about energy conservation and carbon reduction at the outset, but there is little room for further improvement from actual classroom learning [4].

6 Conclusion

Although the experiment was not very effective in changing the "energy saving and carbon reduction" behavior of primary school students, this teaching of renewable energy helps to form a positive attitude towards it and adds more knowledge in this area. The positive attitudes that have been found to be significantly influenced by instruction-assisted experiential learning involve awareness of the seriousness of the problem and recognition of the need for certain mitigation measures. The increase in knowledge is reflected in students being able to make the distinction between renewable and non-renewable energy and the reasons for fossil fuels as a global warming. In addition, students who worked with teaching aids have a stronger connection between knowledge, function and attitude, which means that teaching aids can help these children connect the three areas through experience and more manipulative techniques of learning. Wilson and Chalmers-Neubauer (1990) also pointed out that the scientific activity is primarily based on hands-on operation, demonstration of teachers could directly affect performance of relevant skills for students [5]. In our analysis, we found that the emotional response caused by sensory stimulation in the teaching aid-assisted experience may have played an important role in the formation of attitude-related issues.

7 Recommendation

The research can find that taking action to solve problems, testing the concepts learned or participating in activities, could emphasize how learners practice their understanding the topic. For example, students are allowed to set up a hydro generator and use it to generate electricity. Since teaching aids and products are tangible objects, they can stimulate sensory responses and are used to influence people's learning attitudes, making it easier for them to accept or acquire certain things [6].

In the analysis, it was found that the emotional response caused by sensory stimulation may be in the form of aids. It plays an important role in attitudes toward preferences. It is suggested that future teaching can use methods such as models to use the interaction between the emotional response, attitude and sensory stimulation of the teaching aid.

References

1. Orr, D.W.: Ecological Literacy: Education and the Transition to a Postmodern World. State University of New York Press, New York (1992)
2. Lin, S.-S.: Interpretative research on the roles of the science teacher in instruction of a controversial issue in science and technology-a case study. Chin. J. Sci. Educ. **14**(3), 237–255 (2006)
3. Hurd, P.D.: A rationale for a science, technology, and society theme in science education. In: Bybee, R.W. (ed.) Science/Technology/Society, 1985 Yearbook of the National Science Teachers Association, pp. 94–101. National Science Teachers Association, Washington, DC (1985)
4. Lee, L.S., Lin, K.Y., Guu, Y.H., Chang, L.T., Lai, C.C.: The effect of hands-on 'energy saving house' learning activities on elementary school students' knowledge, attitudes, and behavior regarding energy saving and carbon-emissions reduction. Environ. Educ. Res. (2012). https://doi.org/10.1080/13504622.2012.727781
5. Wilson, J.T., Chalmers-Neubauer, I.: A comparison of teacher roles in three exemplary hands-on elementary science programs. Sci. Educ. **74**(1), 69–85 (1990)
6. Chou, Y.C., Yen, H.Y., Yen, H.W., Chao, Y.L., Huang, Y.H.: The effectiveness of teaching aids for elementary students' renewable energy learning and an analysis of their energy attitude formation. Environ. Sci. Educ. **10**(2), 219–233 (2015)

Author Index

Printed in the United States
By Bookmasters